INVESTMENTS

SECOND EDITION

WILLIAM F. SHARPE

Timken Professor of Finance
Graduate School of Business
Stanford University

PRENTICE-HALL, INC., Englewood Cliffs, New Jersey 07632

Library of Congress Cataloging in Publication Data

SHARPE, WILLIAM F
  Investments.

  Includes bibliographical references and index.
  1. Investments.   2. Investment analysis.   I. Title.
HG4521.S48 1981   332.6   80-21974
ISBN   0-13-504613-0

Editorial production/supervision by Sonia Meyer
Interior and cover design by Suzanne Behnke
Manufacturing buyer: Gordon Osbourne

Printed in the United States of America
10   9   8   7   6   5   4   3   2   1

PRENTICE-HALL INTERNATIONAL, INC., *London*
PRENTICE-HALL OF AUSTRALIA PTY. LIMITED, *Sydney*
PRENTICE-HALL OF CANADA, LTD., *Toronto*
PRENTICE-HALL OF INDIA PRIVATE LIMITED, *New Delhi*
PRENTICE-HALL OF JAPAN, INC., *Tokyo*
PRENTICE-HALL OF SOUTHEAST ASIA PTE. LTD., *Singapore*
WHITEHALL BOOKS LIMITED, *Wellington, New Zealand*

To Robbie, Debbie, and Jon

Contents

3 Investment Value and Market Price

4 The Valuation of Riskless Securities

5 The Valuation of Risky Securities

6 Portfolio Analysis

116

7 Risk and Return: The Capital-Asset Pricing Model

141

8 Risk and Return: Modern Portfolio Theory 171

9 Taxes 186

10 Inflation   223

11 Fixed-Income Securities 251

12 Bond Prices, Yields, and Returns   288

13 Common Stocks 326

14 The Valuation of Common Stocks 365

15 Earnings 388

16 Warrants, Options, and Convertible Securities 412

17 Futures Contracts 455

18 Investment Companies   498

19 Financial Analysis   532

20 Investment Management — 575

21 Performance Measurement and Attribution — 610

22 Extended Diversification

Preface

In recent years the field of finance has truly undergone a revolution. Not too many years ago, investments textbooks were primarily devoted to discussions of the art of security analysis. Readers were introduced to the mysteries of accounting, some of the details of the operations of major industries, and various rules of thumb for selecting "good" or "bad" securities. Institutional details of securities markets, types of investment instruments, transactions costs, and the like were presented, along with historical data, but the reader was provided no framework for understanding such phenomena. A theory of the formation of prices in capital markets was lacking.

While it would be misleading to assert that a complete and completely agreed-upon theory of finance now exists, great progress has been made toward understanding how capital markets function, how prices of investment instruments are determined, and how a balance is struck between risk and return.

This book takes full advantage of the progress made in finance since Harry Markowitz published his seminal paper on portfolio theory in 1952. The overall framework is provided at the outset in sufficient detail to provide a needed base for the material to follow. Following a discussion of taxes and inflation, particular types of instruments are described and analyzed. The remaining chapters cover financial analysis, investment management, performance measurement, and extended diversification. Throughout, factual and institutional details are discussed in the context of an overall marketplace that provides investors efficient means for participating, in whole or in part, in future prospects for the economy.

The book is intended to be encyclopedic without excessive or insignificant detail, rigorous without the use of needless analytic apparatus (only high-school algebra is utilized in the chapters), internally consistent, and as integrated as possible.

Many readers will choose to cover only a portion of the material. To facilitate this approach, the chapters have been written in a modular manner.

No one can undertake a project of this magnitude without a great deal of help. I am indebted to many colleagues, both academic and professional, and to countless students. It would be impossible to list them all. My debt to some of them is, however, so great that I must express it explicitly. A number of friends were kind enough to read all or part of the manuscripts of the first or second edition, and to prepare detailed reviews, criticisms, and suggestions for change. I am particularly grateful for the help of Leo Bailey, William Beaver, Fischer Black, Richard Brealey, Walter Bunczak, Paul Cootner, Edwin Elton, James Farrell, Russell Fuller, Pearl Graham, Ronald Greenberg, James Hoag, Stewart Hodges, George Kaufman, Martin Liebowitz, John McDonald, Richard McEnally, Ronald W. Melicher, Patrick J. Regan, Hans Stoll, and Jack Treynor.

The process of preparing a book of this size is an arduous one; many people are involved before it appears in final form. Kay Lewandowski, Maxine Forgione, Jean Roberts, and Yuri Sasaki turned countless manuscripts and revisions into readable material with accuracy, rapidity, and unceasing good cheer. Encouragement and helpful suggestions were provided by Susan Anderson and David Hildebrand. Final editing was done by Robert Lentz. Sonia Meyer, the production editor, brought it all together with patience and skill. Suzanne Behnke was the designer. Some of the end-of-chapter questions and problems were prepared by Professor Don B. Panton of the University of Kansas.

To all these people, and to those unlisted, who have been my teachers, formal and informal, over the years, my thanks. Finally, I would like to express my appreciation to my wife, to my son and daughter, and to my parents, for providing the environment and encouragement necessary to support the kind of work represented in this book.

Introduction

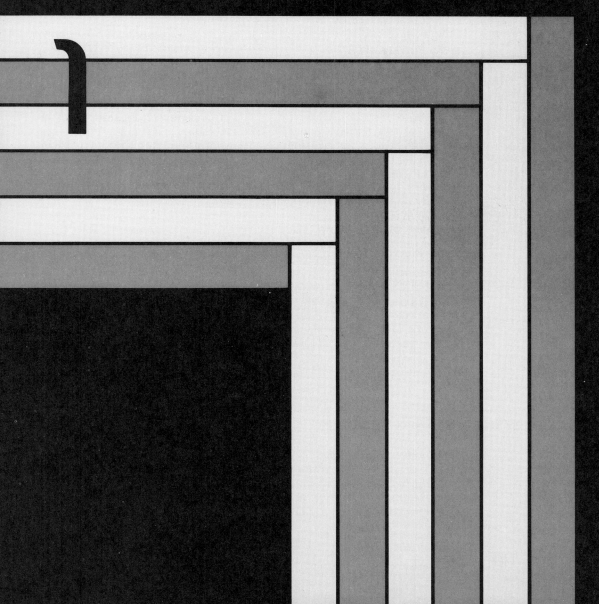

INVESTMENT

General Motors invests millions of dollars in a new model car. A wealthy doctor invests over a hundred thousand dollars in a new apartment house. A successful professor invests thousands of dollars by purchasing shares of General Motors stock from someone else. His secretary invests her savings by taking them to a federally insured savings and loan association, which in turn invests the money by purchasing a mortgage on the doctor's apartment house. Nearby a young business woman is investing money in commodity futures, based on her belief that others have misestimated the price of corn some months hence. A lawyer is studying the racing form, considering the investment of some money in a promising three-year-old in the second race at a local track. Meanwhile, a pawnbroker is investing by loaning money to a man who has fallen on hard times, but only after carefully appraising the gold watch to be held as security.

Do all these actions qualify as *investment?* By some people's definitions, yes. By others', no. Each case involves the sacrifice of something *now* for the prospect of something *later*. And this, in the broadest sense, is investment. Two different attributes may be involved: *time* and *risk*. The sacrifice takes place in the present and is certain. The reward comes later, if at all, and the magnitude may be uncertain. In some cases the element of time predominates (e.g., government bonds). In others, risk is the dominant attribute (e.g., parimutuel tickets). In yet others, both are important (e.g., shares of General Motors stock).

In this book we will use the term *investment* in its broadest sense:

> Investment is the sacrifice of certain present value for (possibly uncertain) future value.

INVESTMENT VERSUS SAVINGS

A distinction is often made between investment and savings. The latter is defined as foregone consumption, with the former restricted to "real" investment of the sort that increases national output in the future. While this definition may prove useful in other contexts, it is not especially helpful for analyzing the specifics of particular investments or even large classes of investment media. A deposit in a "savings" account at a bank is investment in the eyes of the depositor. Even cash stored in the proverbial mattress can be viewed as an investment: one yielding a dollar for every dollar invested (or less in the event of fire or theft). For our purposes, investment can be viewed broadly, as the sacrifice of certain present consumption for (possibly uncertain) future consumption.

REAL VERSUS FINANCIAL INVESTMENT

Semantics aside, there is still a difference between an "investment" in a ticket on a horse and the construction of a new plant; between the pawning of a watch and the planting of a field of corn. Some investments are simply transactions among people; others involve nature. The latter are "real" investment; the former are not.

While this distinction may be too harsh, it is nonetheless useful. Every investment can be conceived as an asset held by someone: the prospect of future returns. Some investments involve liabilities as well: someone else may have to provide the returns. A loan is a classic example. It is an asset to the lender, who will receive the required payments when and if they are made. But it is a liability to the borrower, who must make the payments. The lender has invested money, but the investment is strictly financial in nature.

At the other extreme lies the harried executive's agrarian dream. An investor buys a plot of land, some seeds, fertilizer, etc. and becomes a farmer. The newly sown land is an asset to the investor, but there is no corresponding liability (unless it be nature's). No other person must pay corn, wheat, grapes, or whatever. This is real investment.

In a complex modern economy, much investment is of the financial rather than the real variety. But highly developed institutions for financial investment greatly facilitate real investment. By and large, the forms are complementary, not competitive.

The financing of an apartment house provides a good example. Apartments are sufficiently tangible ("bricks and mortar") to be considered real investment. But where do the resources come from? Some may come from direct investment—for example, the wealthy doctor mentioned earlier. But the majority of the required money is usually provided through a mortgage. In essence, someone loans money for construction, with repayment promised in fixed amounts on a specified schedule over many years. In the typical case, the "someone" is not a person at all, but an institution, acting as a financial intermediary. In the earlier example, it was a savings and loan association, using money obtained from many of its investors, none of whom might be willing and/or able to invest in the apartment directly.

The "secondary" market for securities provides another example. At some time General Motors finds itself in need of resources for, say, plant construction. This real investment may be financed by the sale of new common stock in the "primary" market for securities (this is not a physical location, only a convenient fiction). Subsequently, people buy and sell these shares of stock, trading among themselves in the "secondary" market (for example, on the New York Stock Exchange). These transactions generate no money for General Motors. But the fact that a secondary market exists makes the original purchase more attractive and thus facilitates real investment. People would pay less for a new share of stock if there were no way to sell it quickly and inexpensively later on, if and when the initial owners' circumstances or expectations warrant it.

SECURITIES

When a nearly destitute man borrows money from a pawnbroker, he must leave some item or items of value as *security*. If he fails to repay the loan, plus interest, the lender can then sell the pawned item(s) to recover his or her costs, plus perhaps a profit or loss. The terms of the agreement are recorded via "pawn tickets." When a college student borrows money to buy a car, the lender usually holds the formal title to the car until the loan is repaid. In the event of default, the lender can repossess the car and attempt to sell it to recover his or her costs. In this case, the official certificate of title, issued by the state, serves as the tangible *security* for the loan. When someone borrows money for a vacation, he or she may simply sign a piece of paper promising repayment with interest. The loan is *unsecured* in the sense that no specific asset or *collateral* is promised the lender in the event of default. In such a situation, the lender would have to take the borrower to court and share the borrower's assets with other lenders in a similar position. Only a piece of paper, or *promissory note*, stands as tangible evidence of such a loan.

When a corporation borrows money, it may or may not offer collateral. For example, some firms back certain loans with specific pieces of property (buildings, etc.). Such loans are represented by *mortgage bonds*, which indicate the terms of repayment and the particular assets pledged to the holder of the certificate in the event of default. However, it is much more common for a corporation to simply pledge its overall assets, perhaps with some provision for the manner in which the division will take place in the event of default. Such a promise is represented by a *debenture bond*.

Finally, a corporation may promise a "piece of the action" in return for an investor's funds. Nothing is pledged, and no irrevocable promises are made. The corporation simply pays whatever its directors deem reasonable from time to time. However, to protect against serious malfeasance, the original investor is given the right to help determine the members of the board of directors. His or her property right is represented by a share of *common stock*, which can be sold to someone else, who will then be able to exercise the right. The holder of common stock is said to be an *owner* of the corporation and can, in theory, exercise control over its operation through periodic votes.

In all these cases but the first, only a piece of paper represents the original investor's rights to certain prospects and/or property and the conditions under which he or she may exercise those rights. In general, the piece of paper may be transferred to another, and with it all the associated property rights. Although the word is often clearly inappropriate in its strictest sense, the evidence of any property right is generally termed a *security*. Thus everything from a pawn ticket to a share of IBM stock is a security. We will use the term in this broad sense: *a legal representation of the right to receive prospective future benefits under stated conditions.* The task of *security analysis* is *to determine these prospective future benefits, the conditions under which they will be received, and the likelihood of such conditions.*

By and large, we will focus on securities that may be easily and efficiently transferred from one owner to another. Thus we will be more concerned with common stocks than with pawn tickets, although much of the material in this book applies to both types of instruments.

INVESTMENT, SPECULATION, AND GAMBLING

Webster's New Collegiate Dictionary contains the following definitions:

> "Invest: To commit (money) in order to earn a financial return.
>
> Speculate: To assume a business risk in hope of gain; especially: to buy or sell in expectation of profiting from market fluctuations.
>
> Gamble: To bet on an uncertain outcome."[1]

All three definitions fall within the scope of *investment* as we have defined it. And as the dictionary definitions show, distinctions among the three kinds of activity are subtle at best.

The term "speculate" is sometimes used to identify the horizon of the investor. Thus someone who buys a piece of land on which to build a house to live in might be termed an investor, while a real estate agent who buys the land and builds a house for almost immediate resale might be termed a speculator. The former is concerned primarily with the direct benefits provided by the asset over the long run, the latter with others' evaluations of those benefits (i.e., the price of the asset) in the relatively near future. Similarly, the widow who buys a stock for its dividends may be termed an investor, while a young businesswoman who buys in anticipation that good news about the company will shortly drive the price up, enabling her to sell at a gain, may be termed a speculator. While this sort of distinction is sometimes useful, the dividing line is seldom obvious. Few investors are oblivious to price movement. And since price is at base a reflection of future benefits, anyone wishing to speculate on price movements must analyze the prospects for future benefits.

A better approach concentrates on motivation: a speculator trades on the basis of information that he or she believes is not yet known to or properly evaluated by other investors; an investor makes no such assumption.

Some use the term "speculative" to refer to high-risk investments, possibly without commensurately high return. Thus a new stock issue may be denoted a "speculative investment."

[1] By permission. From *Webster's New Collegiate Dictionary* © 1980 by G. & C. Merriam Co., publishers of the Merriam-Webster dictionaries.

A final use of the term "speculative" is simply to denote activities of which the speaker disapproves. One's friends are investors, one's enemies speculators.

Turning to the term *gamble*, we encounter similar difficulties. The word is often used in a derogatory sense, perhaps even more than "speculate." Certainly the dictionary definition would apply it to any investment other than the very safest possible.

Perhaps the most useful distinction has to do with the relationship between risk and return. A person might be considered a gambler if he or she takes on risk that is greater than commensurate with expected return. Thus playing roulette at Las Vegas could be termed gambling: the risk is great, yet on average the players' return is negative, to allow for the house "take." Investment in the stock market also entails risk, but the return is positive on average.

Here, too, the dividing line is sometimes difficult to draw. Is the knowledgeable horse player a gambler if he or she has sufficient inside knowledge to expect a positive return commensurate with the associated risk? Is the knowledgeable "investor" in commodity futures a gambler? Although many would term people who "play" in the commodity futures market speculators, common usage and legal status refrain from identifying them as gamblers. Gambling is, *de facto*, whatever the law says it is. One of the differences between betting on the future price of corn and betting on the point spread in a football game is that the former is legal in all states, while the latter is legal only in some.

RISK AND RETURN

Figures 1-1(a), (b), and (c) show the year-by-year results obtained from three different types of investments over the 53-year period from 1926 through 1978. In each case, the percentage change in an investor's wealth from the beginning to the end of the year is shown. This amount, the annual *return*, reflects both payments received in cash and any change in the value of the investment.

The first type of investment involves loaning money on a short-term basis to the U.S. Treasury Department. Such a loan carries little if any risk that payment will not be made as promised. Moreover, while the rate of return varies from period to period, at the beginning of any given period it is known with certainty. The return on such investments ranged from a high of 8.0% per year to a low of virtually zero with an average value of 2.54% during the period. While this type of investment has little if any risk, it provides a rather modest return.

The second type of investment involves the purchase of a group of corporate bonds, each of which represents a fairly long-term commitment on the part of the issuer to make cash payments each year (the "coupon" amount) up to some point ("maturity"), at which point a single, final cash payment (the "principal") will be made. The amount for which such a bond can be bought or sold varies from time to time, so the overall return over a year's time is difficult to predict in advance. While coupon payments are easily determined, changes in value are not. The figure

FIGURE 1-1 Annual Returns, 1926–1978

Source: Roger G. Ibbotson and Rex A. Sinquefield, *Stocks, Bonds, Bills and Inflation:* (1926–1978, (Charlottesville, Va.: Financial Analysts Research Foundation, 1979).

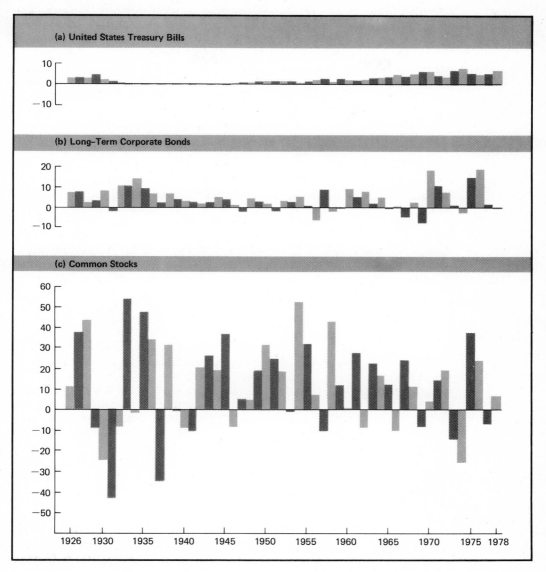

shows the overall return on a (changing) group of bonds selected by the firm of Salomon Brothers[2] to represent long-term corporate bonds. Return varied from a high of 18.65% per year to a low of − 8.09% averaging 4.10% during the period. While this type of investment has considerable risk, on average it provides considerably more return than short-term loans.

The final type of investment involves the purchase of a group of common stocks, each of which represents a commitment on the part of a corporation to periodically pay whatever seems appropriate to its board of directors as a cash dividend. While the amount of cash dividends to be paid in a year is subject to some uncertainty, it is relatively predictable. However, the amount for which a stock can be bought or sold varies considerably from time to time, making overall return highly unpredictable. The figure shows the return from a portfolio of stocks (currently 500 different issues) selected by Standard and Poor's Corporation to represent the performance of the typical dollar invested in common stocks. Returns ranged from an exhilarating + 53.99% in 1933 to a depressing − 43.34% in 1931, and averaged 11.18% per year during the period. Such investments provide substantial returns on average, but with substantial risk.

Table 1-1 provides more detail. Year-by-year returns are shown for the three types of investments plotted in Figure 1-1. The table also includes returns on long-term U.S. government bonds and the percentage change in the Consumer Price Index as an indicator of variations in the "cost of living." Average yearly values are shown at the bottom of the table, along with the standard deviation—a measure of year-to-year variability that will be described in Chapter 6. Additional information can be found in Appendix 1A.

The record illustrates a general principle: *when sensible investment strategies are compared with one another, risk and expected return tend to go together*.

It is important to note that *variability* is not necessarily an indication of *risk*. The former deals with the record over some past period; the latter has to do with uncertainty about the future. The pattern of returns on short-term loans provides one example. Although the values vary from period to period, in any given period the amount to be earned is known in advance. On the other hand, the annual return on a common stock is very difficult to predict. For such an investment, variability in the past may provide a fairly good measure of the uncertainty surrounding future return.

To see how difficult it is to predict common stock returns, cover the portion of Table 1-1 from 1941 on, then try to guess the return in 1941. Having done this, uncover the value for 1941, and try to guess the return in 1942. Proceed in this manner a year at a time, keeping track of your overall predictive accuracy. Unless you are very clever or very lucky, you will conclude that the past pattern of stock returns provides little help in predicting next year's return. We will see that this is a characteristic of an *efficient market*. At this stage, it is enough to indicate that past variability of stock returns can be taken as a rough approximation of future risk.

[2] Values produced by Standard and Poor's Corporation were used to derive the returns for the period before 1946.

TABLE 1-1 Annual Returns: Stocks, Bonds, and Treasury Bills and Change in the Consumer Price Index

YEAR	TOTAL RETURNS				CHANGE IN THE CONSUMER PRICE INDEX
	Stocks	Long-term Govt. Bonds	Long-term Corp. Bonds	T. Bills	
1926	11.62	7.77	7.37	3.27	−1.49
1927	37.49	8.93	7.44	3.12	−2.08
1928	43.61	.10	2.84	3.24	−.97
1929	−8.42	3.42	3.27	4.75	.19
1930	−24.90	4.66	7.98	2.41	−6.03
1931	−43.34	−5.31	−1.85	1.07	−9.52
1932	−8.19	16.84	10.82	.96	−10.30
1933	53.99	−.08	10.38	.30	.51
1934	−1.44	10.02	13.84	.16	−2.03
1935	47.67	4.98	9.61	.17	2.99
1936	33.92	7.51	6.74	.18	1.21
1937	−35.03	.23	2.75	.31	3.10
1938	31.12	5.53	6.13	−.02	−2.78
1939	−.41	5.94	3.97	.02	−.48
1940	−9.78	6.09	3.39	.00	.96
1941	−11.59	.93	2.73	.06	9.72
1942	20.34	3.22	2.60	.27	9.29
1943	25.90	2.08	2.83	.35	3.16
1944	19.75	2.81	4.73	.33	2.11
1945	36.44	10.73	4.08	.33	2.25
1946	−8.07	−.10	1.72	.35	18.17
1947	5.71	−2.63	−2.34	.50	9.01
1948	5.50	3.40	4.14	.81	2.71
1949	18.79	6.45	3.31	1.10	−1.80
1950	31.71	.06	2.12	1.20	5.79
1951	24.02	−3.94	−2.69	1.49	5.87
1952	18.37	1.16	3.52	1.66	.88
1953	−.99	3.63	3.41	1.82	.62
1954	52.62	7.19	5.39	.86	−.50
1955	31.56	−1.30	.48	1.57	.37
1956	6.56	−5.59	−6.81	2.46	2.86
1957	−10.78	7.45	8.71	3.14	3.02
1958	43.36	−6.10	−2.22	1.54	1.76
1959	11.95	−2.26	−.97	2.95	1.50
1960	.47	13.78	9.07	2.66	1.48
1961	26.89	.97	4.82	2.13	.67
1962	−8.73	6.89	7.95	2.73	1.22
1963	22.80	1.21	2.19	3.12	1.65
1964	16.48	3.51	4.77	3.54	1.19
1965	12.45	.71	−.46	3.93	1.92
1966	−10.06	3.65	.20	4.76	3.35
1967	23.98	−9.19	−4.95	4.21	3.04
1968	11.06	−.26	2.57	5.21	4.72
1969	−8.50	−5.08	−8.09	6.58	6.11
1970	4.01	12.10	18.37	6.53	5.49
1971	14.31	13.23	11.01	4.39	3.36
1972	18.98	5.68	7.26	3.84	3.41
1973	−14.66	−1.11	1.14	6.93	8.80

(continued on next page)

TABLE 1-1 (Continued)

YEAR	TOTAL RETURNS				CHANGE IN THE CONSUMER PRICE INDEX
	Stocks	Long-term Govt. Bonds	Long-term Corp. Bonds	T. Bills	
1974	−26.48	4.35	−3.06	8.00	12.20
1975	37.20	9.19	14.64	5.80	7.01
1976	23.84	16.75	18.65	5.08	4.81
1977	−7.18	−.67	1.71	5.12	6.77
1978	6.56	−1.16	−.07	7.18	9.03
Average	11.18	3.37	4.10	2.54	2.65
Std. dev.	22.16	5.71	5.55	2.22	4.78

Source: Roger G. Ibbotson and Rex A. Sinquefield, *Stocks, Bonds, Bills, and Inflation (1926–1978)* (Charlottesville, Va.: Financial Analysts Research Foundation, 1979).

Is one of these major types of investment the best? To oversimplify: the right investment or combination of investments depends on the ultimate beneficiary's preference for return relative to his or her distaste for risk. There may be "right" or "wrong" investments for a particular person or purpose. But it would be surprising indeed to find an investment that is clearly wrong for everyone and every purpose. Such situations are simply not present in an efficient market.

ASSET OWNERSHIP

Who owns securities in the United States? According to the most recent New York Stock Exchange survey, approximately 25 million U.S. residents directly owned shares of common stock in 1975; but many more had an interest in securities via indirect holdings. Table 1-2 shows the changes

TABLE 1-2 Shareholders of Public Corporations, 1952–1975

Year	Shareowners as Percent of U.S. Adult Population
1952	6
1956	8
1959	13
1962	17
1965	17
1970	25
1975	17

Source: The New York Stock Exchange, *1976 Fact Book*, p. 50.

TABLE 1-3 Shareholders of Public Corporations, 1975

Age	Percent of Total
Under 21 years	7.2
21 to 34 years	11.3
35 to 44 years	15.8
45 to 54 years	22.5
55 to 64 years	20.2
65 years and older	23.0
Household Income	
Under $5,000	3.3
$5,000–$9,999	11.3
$10,000–$14,999	19.5
$15,000–$24,999	37.5
$25,000 and over	28.4
Education	
Three years high school or less	6.9
Four years high school	28.1
One to three years college	22.7
Four years college or more	42.3
Occupation	
Professional and technical	18.3
Managers and proprietors	15.9
Clerical and sales	14.5
Craftsmen and foremen	5.0
Operatives and laborers	3.2
Service workers	1.9
Farmers and farm laborers	1.0
Housewives, retired persons, and nonemployed adults	40.2

Source: The New York Stock Exchange, *1976 Fact Book*, p. 52.

in direct ownership from 1952 through 1975, while Table 1-3 provides some breakdowns of the total in 1975. The typical stockholder is middle-aged, has a higher-than-average income, some college education, and is or was in a skilled profession.

As Table 1-2 shows, fewer people held stock in 1975 than in 1970. Figure 1-2 shows the other side; during the first half of the 1970s the percentage of stock held by institutions increased, reaching almost 38% in 1974. Since then the percentage has decreased somewhat. Nonetheless, indirect ownership of common stock through financial intermediaries is substantial. Table 1-4 provides a breakdown of the total, which was over $350 billion in 1977. While this is large, the total amount under professional management is even greater, since many individuals receive professional advice concerning their own investment decisions.

As might be expected, there is substantial concentration in common stock ownership, both direct and indirect. For example, in 1972 the richest .5% of the population was estimated to own 49.34% and the

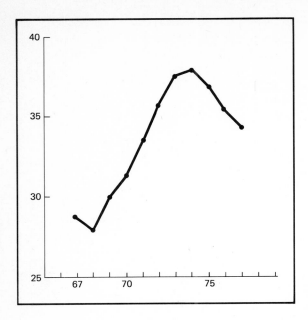

FIGURE 1-2 Percentage of Outstanding Stock Held by Institutions

Source: Securities and Exchange Commission, *Statistical Bulletin,* May 1975 and June 1978.

TABLE 1-4 Estimated Holdings of Stocks by Financial Institutions, 1977 (all figures in $ billions)

Institutions	Holdings
Insurance companies:	
Life	32.9
Nonlife	17.1
Investment companies	39.3
Noninsured pension funds:	
Private	101.9
State and local government	30.0
Nonprofit institutions:	
Educational endowments	9.8
Foundations	26.1
Trust funds	90.1
Mutual savings banks	4.8

Source: Securities and Exchange Commission. *Statistical Bulletin,* June 1978.

richest 1% to own 56.3% of the stock held by individuals.[3] Figure 1-3 uses Lorenz curves to show the distributions in each of four years for which careful estimates have been made. The horizontal axis plots the percentage of total families, arrayed from the poorest (on the left end of the axis) to the richest (on the right end); the vertical axis plots the percentage of the total value of stock owned by these families. Although the equality of distribution has increased over time, even the most recent curve is far from the 45-degree line, which represents complete equality. The extent of "people's capitalism" in the United States is still rather limited.

[3] *Statistical Abstract of the United States,* 1978, U.S. Department of Commerce, Bureau of the Census, p. 476.

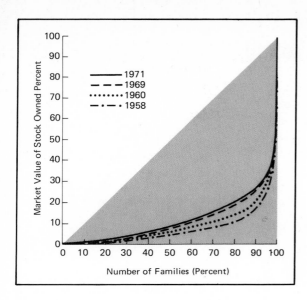

FIGURE 1-3 Trends in the Distribution of Stock Ownership 1958–1971

Source: Marshall E. Blume, Jean Crockett, and Irwin Friend, "Stock Ownership in the United States: Characteristics and Trends," *Survey of Current Business,* November 1974.

The existence of complex financial institutions makes the link between "real" assets and the ownership of securities very difficult to trace. Tables 1-5 and 1-6 provide two extreme views of assets owned by individuals.

Table 1-5 shows estimates of overall national wealth, all of which is ultimately owned by individuals. Note that each individual "owns" substantial assets in his or her role as a citizen. Particularly important classes are private residential housing and land. Investment in consumer durables (refrigerators, television sets, and so on but, most importantly, automobiles) is also substantial: in 1975 it was almost as large as that in producer durables (turret lathes, riveting machines, computers, and the like) and publicly owned equipment. Moreover, even these figures include only a portion of the total national wealth. By far the most important item is omitted entirely: human capital representing the value of the population as producers of future income.

Table 1-6 looks at wealth from the viewpoint of individual households, but only financial assets and liabilities are included. The assets require little comment, but the liabilities merit some discussion. The large value of home mortgages outstanding is not surprising, given the considerably larger value of homes owned. Although some mortgages are held as assets by individuals (as shown in the table), most are held by banks and savings and loan companies, who obtain them by lending money provided by individuals (reflected in the table by the values of the first two assets listed). Consumer credit is also large, but not overly so given the value of consumer durables owned. Other sources of credit include banks, security brokers, and life insurance companies.

The difference between assets and liabilities in Table 1-6 is large, but it is nonetheless considerably less than the true net worth of all households, since nonfinancial assets have been omitted. As shown in Table

TABLE 1-5 National Wealth, 1975 ($ billions)

CATEGORY	VALUE
Structures	
Nonfarm structures:	
Public nonresidential	745.4
Institutional	125.6
Other private nonresidential	710.5
Residential	952.9
Farm structures	20.9
Equipment	
Private business and public equipment	543.7
Consumer durables	496.6
Inventories	
Private, farm	43.9
Private, nonfarm	555.8
Public	107.5
Land	
Private, farm	336.2
Private, nonfarm	705.6
Public	243.0
	5,587.6

Source: *Statistical Abstract of the United States*, 1978, p. 478.

TABLE 1-6 Financial Assets and Liabilities of Households, 1977 ($ billions)

CATEGORY	VALUE
Assets	
Demand deposits (checking accounts) and currency	192.0
Savings accounts (at banks and savings institutions)	992.4
Value of life insurance policies	180.8
Value of pension funds	477.7
Investment company shares	42.8
Other corporation shares	591.9
U.S. government securities	146.8
State and local government obligations	77.2
Corporate and foreign bonds	65.3
Mortgages	91.4
Miscellaneous financial assets	62.3
Total financial assets	2,920.6
Liabilities	
Home mortgages	653.9
Consumer credit	259.9
Other loans	112.3
Total liabilities	1,026.1
Financial assets less liabilities	1,894.5

Source: *Statistical Abstract of the United States*, 1978, p. 531.

1-5, total national wealth is considerably larger than the difference between household financial assets and liabilities. Although much of value is represented by such instruments, much is not, even in the highly complex U.S. economy.

THE INVESTMENT INDUSTRY

Government statisticians group a number of related occupations into a sector called "Finance, Insurance, and Real Estate." Table 1-7 shows the number of people employed in such occupations in recent years. Approximately one out of every twenty workers is employed in this sector. All deal with investment, broadly construed. Some are in sales, some arrange transfers of property and/or securities from one investor to another, others manage investors' funds, and still others handle the recordkeeping involved in this, the most abstract and paper-oriented of all industries.

While of relatively modest importance in the employment figures, this sector of the economy has a profound impact on virtually everyone's life. A clear understanding of investments is obviously valuable for the one in twenty who will work in the field, but it is also worthwhile for the nineteen in twenty who will not. While most people obtain the majority of their income in the form of salary and wages, income from investments is also important. This book is intended to provide an understanding of investment for both those whose interest is professional and those whose interest is strictly personal.

TABLE 1-7 Number of Employees: Finance, Insurance, and Real Estate

EMPLOYER	NUMBER OF EMPLOYEES				
	1960	**1965**	**1970**	**1975**	**1977**
Banking	673,000	792,000	1,044,000	1,275,000	1,342,000
Credit agencies, other than banks	261,000	327,000	361,000	438,000	499,000
Security and commodity brokerages and services	114,000	129,000	205,000	170,000	181,000
Insurance carriers	832,000	893,000	1,031,000	1,105,000	1,148,000
Insurance agents, brokers, and services	196,000	233,000	274,000	331,000	365,000
Real estate	517,000	569,000	680,000	791,000	858,000
Other finance, insurance, and real estate	76,000	80,000	91,000	114,000	116,000
Total	2,669,000	3,023,000	3,687,000	4,223,000	4,508,000
Employees in this sector as a percent of total employees in nonagricultural industries	4.92%	4.97%	5.20%	5.48%	5.49%

Source: *Statistical Abstract of the United States*, 1978, p. 416.

Problems

1. In how many years since 1926 did investors lose money in stocks? What does this imply about the probability that those who invest in stocks may lose money next year?

2. In how many years since 1926 did those who invested in long-term government bonds lose money? How does this compare with the record for long-term corporate bonds? Does this imply that government bonds are riskier than corporate bonds?

3. Using the tables in Appendix 1A, determine the number of ten-year periods in which holders of common stocks would have ended up with less purchasing power than they invested, even though no cash had been withdrawn during the period. How does this compare with corporate bonds? Does this suggest that anyone with an investment horizon of ten years or so should avoid corporate bonds?

4. In terms of total return, what was the worst single calendar year for stock investors? What was the worst year in the 1970s? Compare the two years in terms of return in "constant dollars." Does this show that the stock market "slump" in the 1970s was not at all as serious as the "crash" associated with the Great Depression?

5. List two phenomena for which past variability is not entirely relevant for estimating uncertainty about next period's value.

6. In the Second World War, some Allied cargo ships adopted courses based on a chart of the level of the British stock market in the period from 1910 onward. Why was this thought to be a good strategy against German submarines? What were the possible dangers?

7. List your assets and liabilities and estimate the value of each. Which assets are real? Which are financial?

APPENDIX 1-A

The four tables in this appendix provide data on the results that would have been obtained from four different investment strategies over various holding periods. Each table assumes investment in a particular type of security: common stocks, long-term government bonds, long-term corporate bonds, or Treasury bills.

In every case it is assumed that no cash was withdrawn between the beginning and the end of the holding period: in the interim all dividends, bond interest payments, and so on are assumed to have been reinvested in the type of security indicated.

In each case the initial investment is assumed to have been $1. The table shows the ending value, expressed in terms of dollars of the same purchasing power. For example, the top left-hand number in Table 1A-1 indicates that a dollar invested in stocks at the beginning of 1926 would have grown to an amount worth $1.13 in terms of the purchasing power of a dollar at the end of 1926. The number below it indicates that an investor who put $1 in stocks at the beginning of 1926 would have had $1.59 in "constant dollars" in two years.

All values in the tables were computed from the data in Table 1-1. Two examples will show the general procedure.

Table 1-1 indicates that in 1926 stocks returned 11.62%. Thus $1 invested at the beginning of 1926 would have grown to $1.1162 by the end of the year. However, Table 1-1 also shows that prices declined by 1.49% during the year. Thus $.9851 at the end of the year would have bought as much as $1 at the beginning. An ending value of $1.1162 would thus be worth 1.1162/.9851, or $1.1331 in terms of the value of a dollar at the time of initial investment. The "real return" was thus somewhat over 13% and the rounded ending value was $1.13 in constant dollars, as shown in Table 1A-1. Similar computations gave the values at the tops of all the columns, which reflect real returns for one-year holding periods.

Note in Table 1A-1 that the real returns on stocks were approximately 13% in 1926 and 40% in 1927 (the actual values were 13.31 and 40.41). Thus $1 at the beginning of 1926 could have grown to $1.331 in purchasing power by the end of the year. But this could have grown to $1.331 × 1.4041, or $1.5910 in purchasing power, by the end of 1927. The rounded value ($1.59) is shown in Table 1A-1.

In general the ending value for any holding period was computed by multiplying all the one-year values for the years within the holding period.

In studying the tables, it is useful to note that all holding periods of a given length lie along a diagonal. Thus in Table 1A-1 ending values for two-year holding periods are $1.59, $2.04, $1.33, and so on. Ending values for three-year holding periods are $2.31, $1.86, $1.06, and so on.

TABLE 1A-1 Common Stocks

TO THE END OF	FROM THE BEGINNING OF																	
	1926	1927	1928	1929	1930	1931	1932	1933	1934	1935	1936	1937	1938	1939	1940	1941	1942	1943
1926	1.13																	
1927	1.59	1.40																
1928	2.31	2.04	1.45															
1929	2.11	1.86	1.33	.91														
1930	1.69	1.49	1.06	.73	.80													
1931	1.06	.93	.66	.46	.50	.63												
1932	1.08	.95	.68	.47	.51	.64	1.02											
1933	1.66	1.46	1.04	.72	.78	.98	1.57	1.53										
1934	1.60	1.41	1.00	.69	.76	.95	1.51	1.48	.97									
1935	2.29	2.02	1.44	.99	1.09	1.36	2.17	2.12	1.39	1.43								
1936	3.03	2.68	1.91	1.31	1.44	1.80	2.87	2.81	1.83	1.90	1.32							
1937	1.91	1.69	1.20	.83	.91	1.13	1.81	1.77	1.15	1.20	.83	.63						
1938	2.58	2.28	1.62	1.12	1.22	1.53	2.44	2.39	1.56	1.61	1.12	.85	1.35					
1939	2.58	2.28	1.62	1.12	1.22	1.53	2.44	2.39	1.56	1.61	1.13	.85	1.35	1.00				
1940	2.31	2.03	1.45	1.00	1.09	1.37	2.18	2.13	1.39	1.44	1.01	.76	1.21	.89	.89			
1941	1.86	1.64	1.17	.81	.88	1.10	1.76	1.72	1.12	1.16	.81	.61	.97	.72	.72	.81		
1942	2.05	1.81	1.29	.89	.97	1.21	1.94	1.89	1.24	1.28	.89	.67	1.07	.79	.79	.89	1.10	
1943	2.50	2.20	1.57	1.08	1.18	1.48	2.37	2.31	1.51	1.56	1.09	.82	1.31	.97	.97	1.08	1.34	1.22
1944	2.93	2.58	1.84	1.27	1.39	1.74	2.77	2.71	1.77	1.83	1.28	.97	1.53	1.14	1.13	1.27	1.58	1.43
1945	3.91	3.45	2.46	1.69	1.85	2.32	3.70	3.62	2.36	2.44	1.70	1.29	2.04	1.52	1.51	1.69	2.10	1.91
1946	3.04	2.68	1.91	1.32	1.44	1.80	2.88	2.81	1.84	1.90	1.33	1.00	1.59	1.18	1.18	1.32	1.64	1.49
1947	2.95	2.60	1.85	1.28	1.40	1.75	2.79	2.73	1.78	1.84	1.29	.97	1.54	1.14	1.14	1.28	1.59	1.44
1948	3.03	2.67	1.90	1.31	1.44	1.80	2.87	2.80	1.83	1.89	1.32	1.00	1.58	1.17	1.17	1.31	1.63	1.48
1949	3.66	3.23	2.30	1.59	1.74	2.17	3.47	3.39	2.21	2.29	1.60	1.21	1.92	1.42	1.42	1.59	1.97	1.79
1950	4.56	4.02	2.87	1.98	2.16	2.70	4.32	4.22	2.75	2.85	1.99	1.50	2.39	1.77	1.77	1.98	2.45	2.23
1951	5.34	4.71	3.36	2.31	2.53	3.17	5.06	4.94	3.23	3.34	2.33	1.76	2.79	2.07	2.07	2.32	2.87	2.61
1952	6.27	5.53	3.94	2.72	2.97	3.72	5.94	5.80	3.79	3.92	2.73	2.07	3.28	2.43	2.43	2.72	3.37	3.06
1953	6.17	5.44	3.88	2.67	2.92	3.66	5.84	5.71	3.73	3.86	2.69	2.03	3.23	2.39	2.39	2.67	3.32	3.01
1954	9.46	8.35	5.94	4.10	4.48	5.61	8.96	8.76	5.71	5.92	4.13	3.12	4.95	3.67	3.67	4.10	5.09	4.62
1955	12.40	10.94	7.79	5.37	5.88	7.36	11.75	11.48	7.49	7.75	5.41	4.09	6.49	4.81	4.81	5.38	6.67	6.06
1956	12.84	11.33	8.07	5.57	6.09	7.62	12.17	11.89	7.76	8.03	5.60	4.23	6.72	4.98	4.98	5.57	6.91	6.28
1957	11.12	9.82	6.99	4.82	5.27	6.60	10.54	10.30	6.72	6.96	4.85	3.67	5.82	4.31	4.31	4.82	5.99	5.44
1958	15.67	13.83	9.85	6.79	7.43	9.30	14.85	14.51	9.47	9.80	6.84	5.17	8.20	6.08	6.07	6.80	8.44	7.66
1959	17.28	15.25	10.86	7.49	8.20	10.25	16.38	16.00	10.44	10.81	7.54	5.70	9.04	6.70	6.70	7.50	9.30	8.45
1960	17.11	15.10	10.75	7.42	8.11	10.15	16.21	15.84	10.34	10.70	7.46	5.64	8.95	6.64	6.63	7.42	9.21	8.37
1961	21.57	19.03	13.56	9.35	10.23	12.80	20.43	19.96	13.03	13.49	9.41	7.11	11.28	8.37	8.36	9.36	11.61	10.54
1962	19.45	17.16	12.22	8.43	9.22	11.54	18.43	18.00	11.75	12.16	8.48	6.41	10.17	7.54	7.54	8.44	10.47	9.51
1963	23.49	20.73	14.77	10.18	11.14	13.94	22.26	21.75	14.20	14.69	10.25	7.75	12.29	9.11	9.11	10.19	12.65	11.49
1964	27.04	23.87	17.00	11.72	12.82	16.05	25.62	25.03	16.34	16.92	11.80	8.92	14.15	10.49	10.48	11.73	14.56	13.22
1965	29.84	26.33	18.75	12.93	14.15	17.70	28.27	27.62	18.03	18.66	13.02	9.84	15.61	11.57	11.57	12.94	16.06	14.59
1966	25.97	22.92	16.32	11.25	12.31	15.41	24.60	24.04	15.69	16.24	11.33	8.56	13.58	10.07	10.07	11.26	13.98	12.69

TABLE 1A-1 (Continued)

TO THE END OF	FROM THE BEGINNING OF																	
	1926	1927	1928	1929	1930	1931	1932	1933	1934	1935	1936	1937	1938	1939	1940	1941	1942	1943
1967	31.24	27.57	19.64	13.54	14.81	18.54	29.60	28.92	18.88	19.54	13.63	10.30	16.35	12.12	12.11	13.55	16.82	15.27
1968	33.13	29.24	20.83	14.36	15.71	19.66	31.39	30.67	20.02	20.73	14.45	10.92	17.33	12.85	12.84	14.37	17.84	16.20
1969	28.57	25.22	17.96	12.38	13.55	16.95	27.07	26.45	17.26	17.87	12.46	9.42	14.95	11.08	11.08	12.39	15.38	13.97
1970	28.17	24.86	17.71	12.21	13.36	16.71	26.69	26.08	17.02	17.62	12.29	9.29	14.74	10.93	10.92	12.22	15.17	13.77
1971	31.16	27.50	19.58	13.50	14.77	18.49	29.52	28.84	18.82	19.49	13.59	10.27	16.30	12.09	12.08	13.51	16.77	15.23
1972	35.85	31.64	22.53	15.54	17.00	21.27	33.96	33.18	21.66	22.42	15.64	11.82	18.75	13.91	13.90	15.55	19.30	17.53
1973	28.12	24.81	17.67	12.19	13.33	16.68	26.64	26.03	16.99	17.59	12.27	9.27	14.71	10.91	10.90	12.20	15.14	13.75
1974	18.42	16.26	11.58	7.99	8.74	10.93	17.46	17.06	11.13	11.52	8.04	6.07	9.64	7.15	7.14	7.99	9.92	9.01
1975	23.62	20.85	14.85	10.24	11.20	14.02	22.38	21.87	14.27	14.78	10.30	7.79	12.36	9.16	9.16	10.25	12.72	11.55
1976	27.91	24.63	17.54	12.10	13.23	16.56	26.45	25.84	16.86	17.46	12.18	9.20	14.60	10.83	10.82	12.11	15.03	13.65
1977	24.26	21.41	15.25	10.52	11.51	14.40	22.99	22.46	14.66	15.18	10.58	8.00	12.69	9.41	9.41	10.53	13.06	11.86
1978	23.71	20.93	14.91	10.28	11.24	14.07	22.47	21.95	14.33	14.83	10.35	7.82	12.41	9.20	9.19	10.29	12.77	11.59

	1944	1945	1946	1947	1948	1949	1950	1951	1952	1953	1954	1955	1956	1957	1958	1959	1960	1961
1944	1.17																	
1945	1.56	1.33																
1946	1.22	1.04	.78															
1947	1.18	1.01	.75	.97														
1948	1.21	1.03	.77	1.00	1.03													
1949	1.47	1.25	.94	1.20	1.24	1.21												
1950	1.83	1.56	1.17	1.50	1.55	1.51	1.25											
1951	2.14	1.82	1.37	1.76	1.81	1.76	1.46	1.17										
1952	2.51	2.14	1.60	2.06	2.13	2.07	1.71	1.37	1.17									
1953	2.47	2.11	1.58	2.03	2.09	2.04	1.68	1.35	1.15	.98								
1954	3.79	3.23	2.42	3.11	3.21	3.12	2.58	2.07	1.77	1.51	1.53							
1955	4.97	4.23	3.17	4.08	4.21	4.10	3.39	2.72	2.32	1.98	2.01	1.31						
1956	5.14	4.39	3.29	4.23	4.36	4.24	3.51	2.82	2.40	2.05	2.08	1.36	1.04					
1957	4.46	3.80	2.85	3.66	3.77	3.67	3.04	2.44	2.08	1.77	1.80	1.18	.90	.87				
1958	6.28	5.35	4.01	5.16	5.32	5.18	4.28	3.44	2.93	2.50	2.54	1.66	1.26	1.22	1.41			
1959	6.92	5.90	4.42	5.69	5.86	5.71	4.72	3.79	3.24	2.76	2.80	1.83	1.39	1.35	1.55	1.10		
1960	6.85	5.84	4.38	5.63	5.81	5.65	4.67	3.75	3.20	2.73	2.77	1.81	1.38	1.33	1.54	1.09	.99	
1961	8.64	7.37	5.52	7.10	7.32	7.12	5.89	4.73	4.04	3.44	3.50	2.28	1.74	1.68	1.94	1.38	1.25	1.26
1962	7.79	6.64	4.98	6.40	6.60	6.42	5.31	4.27	3.64	3.10	3.15	2.06	1.57	1.51	1.75	1.24	1.13	1.14
1963	9.41	8.03	6.01	7.73	7.97	7.76	6.42	5.15	4.40	3.75	3.81	2.48	1.90	1.83	2.11	1.50	1.36	1.37
1964	10.83	9.24	6.92	8.90	9.18	8.93	7.39	5.93	5.06	4.32	4.39	2.86	2.18	2.11	2.43	1.73	1.56	1.58
1965	11.95	10.19	7.64	9.82	10.12	9.86	8.15	6.54	5.59	4.76	4.84	3.15	2.41	2.32	2.68	1.90	1.73	1.74
1966	10.40	8.87	6.65	8.54	8.81	8.58	7.09	5.70	4.86	4.14	4.21	2.75	2.09	2.02	2.33	1.66	1.50	1.52
1967	12.52	10.67	8.00	10.28	10.60	10.32	8.53	6.85	5.85	4.99	5.07	3.30	2.52	2.43	2.81	1.99	1.81	1.83
1968	13.27	11.32	8.48	10.90	11.24	10.95	9.05	7.27	6.20	5.29	5.37	3.50	2.67	2.58	2.98	2.11	1.94	1.94

Table 1 (rows 1969–1978):

	1978	1977	1976	1975	1974	1973	1972	1971	1970	1969	1968	1967	1966	1965	1964	1963	1962
1969	1.67	1.65	1.82	2.57	2.22	2.30	3.02	4.63	4.56	5.35	6.27	7.80	9.44	9.70	9.40	7.31	9.76	11.45
1970	1.65	1.63	1.80	2.53	2.19	2.27	2.98	4.57	4.50	5.28	6.18	7.69	9.31	9.56	9.27	7.21	9.62	11.29
1971	1.82	1.80	1.99	2.80	2.43	2.51	3.29	5.05	4.97	5.83	6.83	8.51	10.29	10.57	10.25	7.98	10.64	12.48
1972	2.09	2.07	2.29	3.22	2.79	2.89	3.79	5.81	5.72	6.71	7.86	9.79	11.84	12.16	11.80	9.18	12.24	14.36
1973	1.64	1.63	1.79	2.53	2.19	2.27	2.97	4.56	4.49	5.27	6.17	7.68	9.29	9.54	9.25	7.20	9.60	11.26
1974	1.08	1.07	1.18	1.66	1.43	1.49	1.95	2.99	2.94	3.45	4.04	5.03	6.09	6.25	6.06	4.72	6.29	7.38
1975	1.38	1.37	1.51	2.12	1.84	1.91	2.50	3.83	3.77	4.42	5.18	6.45	7.80	8.02	7.77	6.05	8.07	9.46
1976	1.63	1.61	1.78	2.51	2.17	2.25	2.95	4.53	4.45	5.23	6.12	7.62	9.22	9.47	9.18	7.14	9.53	11.18
1977	1.42	1.40	1.55	2.18	1.89	1.96	2.57	3.94	3.87	4.54	5.32	6.63	8.02	8.23	7.98	6.21	8.29	9.72
1978	1.39	1.37	1.51	2.13	1.85	1.91	2.51	3.85	3.78	4.44	5.20	6.48	7.83	8.05	7.80	6.07	8.10	9.50

Table 2 (rows 1962–1978):

	1962	1963	1964	1965	1966	1967	1968	1969	1970	1971	1972	1973	1974	1975	1976	1977	1978
1962	.90																
1963	1.09	1.21															
1964	1.25	1.39	1.15														
1965	1.38	1.53	1.27	1.10													
1966	1.20	1.34	1.11	.96	.87												
1967	1.45	1.61	1.33	1.16	1.05	1.20											
1968	1.54	1.70	1.41	1.23	1.11	1.28	1.06										
1969	1.32	1.47	1.22	1.06	.96	1.10	.91	.86									
1970	1.31	1.45	1.20	1.04	.94	1.08	.90	.85	.99								
1971	1.44	1.60	1.33	1.15	1.04	1.20	1.00	.94	1.09	1.11							
1972	1.66	1.84	1.53	1.33	1.20	1.38	1.15	1.08	1.25	1.27	1.15						
1973	1.30	1.45	1.20	1.04	.94	1.08	.90	.85	.98	1.00	.90	.78					
1974	.85	.95	.78	.68	.62	.71	.59	.56	.64	.65	.59	.51	.66				
1975	1.10	1.21	1.01	.87	.79	.91	.76	.71	.83	.84	.76	.66	.84	1.28			
1976	1.29	1.44	1.19	1.03	.94	1.07	.89	.84	.98	.99	.90	.78	.99	1.51	1.18		
1977	1.13	1.25	1.03	.90	.81	.93	.78	.73	.85	.86	.78	.68	.86	1.32	1.03	.87	
1978	1.10	1.22	1.01	.88	.79	.91	.76	.72	.83	.84	.76	.66	.84	1.29	1.00	.85	.98

TABLE 1A-2 Long-Term Government Bonds

TO THE END OF	FROM THE BEGINNING OF																	
	1926	1927	1928	1929	1930	1931	1932	1933	1934	1935	1936	1937	1938	1939	1940	1941	1942	1943
1926	1.09																	
1927	1.22	1.11																
1928	1.23	1.12	1.01															
1929	1.27	1.16	1.04	1.03														
1930	1.41	1.29	1.16	1.15	1.11													
1931	1.48	1.35	1.22	1.20	1.17	1.05												
1932	1.93	1.76	1.58	1.57	1.52	1.36	1.30											
1933	1.92	1.75	1.57	1.56	1.51	1.36	1.29	.99										
1934	2.07	1.89	1.70	1.68	1.63	1.46	1.40	1.07	1.08									
1935	2.11	1.93	1.73	1.71	1.66	1.49	1.42	1.09	1.10	1.02								
1936	2.24	2.05	1.84	1.82	1.76	1.58	1.51	1.16	1.17	1.08	1.06							
1937	2.18	1.99	1.79	1.77	1.71	1.54	1.47	1.13	1.14	1.05	1.03	.97						
1938	2.36	2.16	1.94	1.92	1.86	1.67	1.60	1.22	1.23	1.14	1.12	1.06	1.09					
1939	2.51	2.30	2.07	2.04	1.98	1.78	1.70	1.30	1.31	1.22	1.19	1.12	1.16	1.06				
1940	2.64	2.41	2.17	2.15	2.08	1.87	1.78	1.37	1.38	1.28	1.25	1.18	1.21	1.12	1.05			
1941	2.43	2.22	2.00	1.98	1.91	1.72	1.64	1.26	1.27	1.18	1.15	1.09	1.12	1.03	.97	.92		
1942	2.29	2.10	1.89	1.87	1.81	1.62	1.55	1.19	1.20	1.11	1.09	1.03	1.05	.97	.91	.87	.94	
1943	2.27	2.08	1.87	1.85	1.79	1.61	1.53	1.18	1.18	1.10	1.08	1.01	1.04	.96	.90	.86	.93	.99
1944	2.29	2.09	1.88	1.86	1.80	1.62	1.54	1.19	1.19	1.11	1.09	1.02	1.05	.97	.91	.87	.94	1.00
1945	2.48	2.26	2.03	2.01	1.95	1.75	1.67	1.28	1.29	1.20	1.18	1.11	1.14	1.05	.99	.94	1.02	1.08
1946	2.09	1.91	1.72	1.70	1.65	1.48	1.41	1.09	1.09	1.01	.99	.94	.96	.89	.83	.79	.86	.91
1947	1.87	1.71	1.54	1.52	1.47	1.32	1.26	.97	.98	.90	.89	.84	.86	.79	.74	.71	.77	.81
1948	1.88	1.72	1.55	1.53	1.48	1.33	1.27	.98	.98	.91	.89	.84	.87	.80	.75	.71	.77	.82
1949	2.04	1.87	1.68	1.66	1.61	1.44	1.38	1.06	1.06	.99	.97	.91	.94	.86	.81	.77	.84	.89
1950	1.93	1.76	1.59	1.57	1.52	1.36	1.30	1.00	1.01	.93	.92	.86	.89	.82	.77	.73	.79	.84
1951	1.75	1.60	1.44	1.42	1.38	1.24	1.18	.91	.91	.85	.83	.78	.80	.74	.70	.66	.72	.76
1952	1.76	1.61	1.44	1.43	1.38	1.24	1.19	.91	.92	.85	.83	.78	.81	.74	.70	.66	.72	.77
1953	1.81	1.65	1.49	1.47	1.42	1.28	1.22	.94	.94	.88	.86	.81	.83	.77	.72	.68	.75	.79
1954	1.95	1.78	1.60	1.58	1.53	1.38	1.32	1.01	1.02	.94	.92	.87	.90	.83	.78	.74	.80	.85
1955	1.92	1.75	1.57	1.56	1.51	1.35	1.29	.99	1.00	.93	.91	.86	.88	.81	.76	.73	.79	.83
1956	1.76	1.61	1.44	1.43	1.38	1.24	1.19	.91	.92	.85	.83	.79	.81	.74	.70	.66	.72	.76
1957	1.83	1.68	1.51	1.49	1.44	1.30	1.24	.95	.96	.89	.87	.82	.84	.78	.73	.69	.75	.80
1958	1.69	1.55	1.39	1.38	1.33	1.20	1.14	.88	.88	.82	.80	.76	.78	.72	.67	.64	.70	.74
1959	1.63	1.49	1.34	1.32	1.28	1.15	1.10	.85	.85	.79	.77	.73	.75	.69	.65	.62	.67	.71
1960	1.83	1.67	1.50	1.49	1.44	1.29	1.23	.95	.95	.88	.87	.82	.84	.77	.73	.69	.75	.80
1961	1.83	1.68	1.51	1.49	1.44	1.30	1.24	.95	.96	.89	.87	.82	.84	.78	.73	.69	.75	.80
1962	1.94	1.77	1.59	1.57	1.52	1.37	1.31	1.00	1.01	.94	.92	.86	.89	.82	.77	.73	.80	.84
1963	1.93	1.76	1.58	1.57	1.52	1.36	1.30	1.00	1.01	.93	.91	.86	.89	.82	.77	.73	.79	.84
1964	1.97	1.80	1.62	1.60	1.55	1.39	1.33	1.02	1.03	.95	.94	.88	.91	.83	.78	.75	.81	.86
1965	1.95	1.78	1.60	1.58	1.53	1.38	1.32	1.01	1.02	.94	.92	.87	.90	.82	.77	.74	.80	.85
1966	1.95	1.79	1.61	1.59	1.54	1.38	1.32	1.01	1.02	.95	.93	.87	.90	.83	.78	.74	.80	.85

Table 1

Year	1944	1945	1946	1947	1948	1949	1950	1951	1952	1953	1954	1955	1956	1957	1958	1959	1960	1961
1967	1.72	1.57	1.41	1.40	1.36	1.22	1.16	.89	.90	.83	.82	.77	.79	.73	.68	.65	.71	.75
1968	1.64	1.50	1.35	1.33	1.29	1.16	1.11	.85	.86	.79	.78	.73	.75	.69	.65	.62	.67	.71
1969	1.47	1.34	1.21	1.19	1.16	1.04	.99	.76	.77	.71	.70	.66	.67	.62	.58	.56	.60	.64
1970	1.56	1.42	1.28	1.27	1.23	1.10	1.05	.81	.81	.75	.74	.70	.72	.66	.62	.59	.64	.68
1971	1.71	1.56	1.40	1.39	1.34	1.21	1.15	.89	.89	.83	.81	.76	.78	.72	.68	.65	.70	.74
1972	1.74	1.60	1.43	1.42	1.37	1.23	1.18	.91	.91	.84	.83	.78	.80	.74	.69	.66	.72	.76
1973	1.59	1.45	1.30	1.29	1.25	1.12	1.07	.82	.83	.77	.75	.71	.73	.67	.63	.60	.65	.69
1974	1.48	1.35	1.21	1.20	1.16	1.04	1.00	.77	.77	.71	.70	.66	.68	.62	.59	.56	.61	.64
1975	1.51	1.38	1.24	1.22	1.19	1.06	1.02	.78	.79	.73	.71	.67	.69	.64	.60	.57	.62	.66
1976	1.68	1.53	1.38	1.36	1.32	1.19	1.13	.87	.87	.81	.80	.75	.77	.71	.67	.63	.69	.73
1977	1.56	1.43	1.28	1.27	1.23	1.10	1.05	.81	.81	.75	.74	.70	.72	.66	.62	.59	.64	.68
1978	1.41	1.29	1.16	1.15	1.11	1.00	.96	.73	.74	.68	.67	.63	.65	.60	.56	.54	.58	.62

Table 2

Year	1944	1945	1946	1947	1948	1949	1950	1951	1952	1953	1954	1955	1956	1957	1958	1959	1960	1961
1944	1.01																	
1945	1.09	1.08																
1946	.92	.92	.85															
1947	.82	.82	.76	.89														
1948	.83	.82	.76	.90	1.01													
1949	.90	.89	.82	.97	1.09	1.08												
1950	.85	.84	.78	.92	1.03	1.03	.95											
1951	.77	.77	.71	.84	.94	.93	.86	.91										
1952	.77	.77	.71	.84	.94	.93	.86	.91	1.00									
1953	.80	.79	.73	.86	.97	.96	.89	.94	1.03	1.03								
1954	.86	.85	.79	.93	1.04	1.04	.95	1.01	1.11	1.11	1.08							
1955	.84	.84	.77	.92	1.02	1.02	.94	.99	1.09	1.09	1.06	.98						
1956	.77	.77	.71	.84	.94	.93	.86	.91	1.00	1.00	.97	.90	.92					
1957	.81	.80	.74	.88	.98	.97	.90	.95	1.05	1.04	1.01	.94	.96	1.04				
1958	.75	.74	.68	.81	.91	.90	.83	.88	.97	.96	.94	.87	.88	.96	.92			
1959	.72	.71	.66	.78	.87	.87	.80	.84	.93	.93	.90	.84	.85	.93	.89	.96		
1960	.80	.80	.74	.87	.98	.97	.90	.95	1.04	1.04	1.01	.94	.95	1.04	1.00	1.08	1.12	
1961	.81	.80	.74	.88	.98	.97	.90	.95	1.05	1.04	1.01	.94	.96	1.04	1.00	1.08	1.12	1.00
1962	.85	.85	.78	.92	1.04	1.03	.95	1.00	1.11	1.10	1.07	.99	1.01	1.10	1.06	1.14	1.19	1.06
1963	.85	.84	.78	.92	1.03	1.02	.94	1.00	1.10	1.10	1.07	.99	1.01	1.10	1.05	1.14	1.18	1.05
1964	.87	.86	.80	.94	1.05	1.05	.97	1.02	1.13	1.12	1.09	1.01	1.03	1.12	1.07	1.16	1.21	1.08
1965	.86	.85	.79	.93	1.04	1.03	.95	1.01	1.11	1.11	1.08	1.00	1.02	1.11	1.06	1.15	1.20	1.07
1966	.86	.85	.79	.93	1.04	1.04	.96	1.01	1.12	1.11	1.08	1.00	1.02	1.11	1.07	1.15	1.20	1.07
1967	.76	.75	.70	.82	.92	.91	.84	.89	.98	.98	.95	.88	.90	.98	.94	1.02	1.06	.94
1968	.72	.72	.66	.78	.88	.87	.80	.85	.94	.93	.91	.84	.86	.93	.89	.97	1.01	.90
1969	.65	.64	.59	.70	.78	.78	.72	.76	.84	.84	.81	.75	.77	.83	.80	.87	.90	.80
1970	.69	.68	.63	.74	.83	.83	.76	.81	.89	.89	.86	.80	.81	.89	.85	.92	.96	.85
1971	.75	.75	.69	.82	.91	.91	.84	.88	.98	.97	.94	.88	.89	.97	.93	1.01	1.05	.93
1972	.77	.76	.70	.83	.93	.93	.86	.90	1.00	.99	.96	.90	.91	.99	.95	1.03	1.07	.95
1973	.70	.69	.64	.76	.85	.84	.78	.82	.91	.90	.88	.81	.83	.90	.86	.94	.97	.87
1974	.65	.65	.60	.70	.79	.78	.72	.76	.84	.84	.82	.76	.77	.84	.80	.87	.91	.81
1975	.66	.66	.61	.72	.80	.80	.74	.78	.86	.86	.83	.77	.79	.86	.82	.89	.92	.82
1976	.74	.73	.68	.80	.90	.89	.82	.87	.96	.95	.93	.86	.88	.95	.91	.99	1.03	.92
1977	.69	.68	.63	.75	.83	.83	.76	.81	.89	.89	.86	.80	.81	.89	.85	.92	.96	.85
1978	.62	.62	.57	.68	.76	.75	.69	.73	.81	.81	.78	.73	.74	.80	.77	.84	.87	.77

TABLE 1A-2 (Continued)

TO THE END OF	FROM THE BEGINNING OF																
	1962	1963	1964	1965	1966	1967	1968	1969	1970	1971	1972	1973	1974	1975	1976	1977	1978
1962	1.06																
1963	1.05	1.00															
1964	1.08	1.02	1.02														
1965	1.06	1.01	1.01	.99													
1966	1.07	1.01	1.01	.99	1.00												
1967	.94	.89	.89	.87	.88	.88											
1968	.89	.85	.85	.83	.84	.84	.95										
1969	.80	.76	.76	.74	.75	.75	.85	.89									
1970	.85	.81	.81	.79	.80	.80	.91	.95	1.06								
1971	.93	.88	.89	.87	.88	.87	.99	1.04	1.16	1.10							
1972	.95	.90	.91	.89	.90	.89	1.01	1.06	1.19	1.12	1.02						
1973	.87	.82	.82	.80	.81	.81	.92	.97	1.08	1.02	.93	.91					
1974	.80	.76	.77	.75	.76	.76	.86	.90	1.01	.95	.86	.85	.93				
1975	.82	.78	.78	.76	.77	.77	.87	.92	1.03	.97	.88	.86	.95	1.02			
1976	.91	.87	.87	.85	.86	.86	.97	1.02	1.14	1.08	.98	.96	1.06	1.14	1.11		
1977	.85	.81	.81	.79	.80	.80	.91	.95	1.06	1.00	.91	.89	.98	1.06	1.04	.93	
1978	.77	.73	.73	.72	.73	.72	.82	.86	.96	.91	.83	.81	.89	.96	.94	.84	.91

TABLE 1A-3 Long-Term Corporate Bonds

TO THE END OF	FROM THE BEGINNING OF																	
	1926	1927	1928	1929	1930	1931	1932	1933	1934	1935	1936	1937	1938	1939	1940	1941	1942	1943
1926	1.09																	
1927	1.20	1.10																
1928	1.24	1.14	1.04															
1929	1.28	1.17	1.07	1.03														
1930	1.47	1.35	1.23	1.18	1.15													
1931	1.60	1.46	1.33	1.28	1.25	1.08												
1932	1.97	1.81	1.65	1.59	1.54	1.34	1.24											
1933	2.16	1.99	1.81	1.74	1.69	1.47	1.36	1.10										
1934	2.42	2.22	2.02	1.94	1.89	1.64	1.51	1.23	1.12									
1935	2.57	2.36	2.15	2.07	2.01	1.75	1.61	1.30	1.19	1.06								
1936	2.71	2.49	2.27	2.18	2.12	1.84	1.70	1.38	1.25	1.12	1.05							
1937	2.70	2.48	2.26	2.18	2.11	1.84	1.69	1.37	1.25	1.12	1.05	1.00						
1938	2.95	2.71	2.47	2.38	2.30	2.01	1.85	1.50	1.36	1.22	1.15	1.09	1.09					
1939	3.08	2.83	2.58	2.48	2.41	2.09	1.93	1.56	1.42	1.28	1.20	1.14	1.14	1.04				
1940	3.16	2.90	2.64	2.54	2.47	2.15	1.98	1.60	1.46	1.31	1.23	1.16	1.17	1.07	1.02			
1941	2.95	2.71	2.47	2.38	2.31	2.01	1.85	1.50	1.36	1.22	1.15	1.09	1.09	1.00	.96	.94		
1942	2.77	2.54	2.32	2.23	2.17	1.89	1.74	1.41	1.28	1.15	1.08	1.02	1.03	.94	.90	.88	.94	
1943	2.76	2.54	2.31	2.23	2.16	1.88	1.73	1.40	1.28	1.14	1.08	1.02	1.02	.94	.90	.88	.94	1.00
1944	2.84	2.60	2.37	2.28	2.22	1.93	1.78	1.44	1.31	1.17	1.10	1.05	1.05	.96	.92	.90	.96	1.02
1945	2.89	2.65	2.41	2.32	2.26	1.96	1.81	1.46	1.33	1.20	1.12	1.06	1.07	.98	.94	.91	.98	1.04
1946	2.48	2.28	2.08	2.00	1.94	1.69	1.56	1.26	1.15	1.03	.97	.92	.92	.84	.81	.79	.84	.80
1947	2.23	2.04	1.86	1.79	1.74	1.51	1.40	1.13	1.03	.92	.87	.82	.82	.75	.72	.71	.75	.81
1948	2.26	2.07	1.89	1.82	1.76	1.53	1.41	1.14	1.04	.93	.88	.83	.84	.77	.73	.72	.76	.86
1949	2.37	2.18	1.99	1.91	1.85	1.61	1.49	1.20	1.10	.98	.92	.88	.88	.81	.77	.75	.80	.83
1950	2.29	2.10	1.92	1.85	1.79	1.56	1.44	1.16	1.06	.95	.89	.85	.85	.78	.74	.73	.78	.86
1951	2.11	1.93	1.76	1.70	1.65	1.43	1.32	1.07	.97	.87	.82	.78	.78	.71	.68	.67	.71	.76
1952	2.16	1.98	1.81	1.74	1.69	1.47	1.35	1.10	1.00	.90	.84	.80	.80	.73	.70	.69	.73	.78
1953	2.22	2.04	1.86	1.79	1.74	1.51	1.39	1.13	1.03	.92	.86	.82	.82	.75	.72	.70	.75	.80
1954	2.35	2.16	1.97	1.90	1.84	1.60	1.47	1.19	1.09	.97	.92	.87	.87	.80	.76	.75	.80	.85
1955	2.36	2.16	1.97	1.90	1.84	1.60	1.48	1.20	1.09	.98	.92	.87	.87	.80	.76	.75	.80	.85
1956	2.13	1.96	1.78	1.72	1.67	1.45	1.34	1.08	.99	.88	.83	.79	.79	.72	.69	.68	.72	.77
1957	2.25	2.07	1.88	1.81	1.76	1.53	1.41	1.14	1.04	.93	.88	.83	.83	.76	.73	.71	.76	.81
1958	2.16	1.99	1.81	1.74	1.69	1.47	1.36	1.10	1.00	.90	.84	.80	.80	.73	.70	.69	.73	.78
1959	2.11	1.94	1.77	1.70	1.65	1.44	1.32	1.07	.98	.87	.82	.78	.78	.72	.69	.67	.71	.76
1960	2.27	2.08	1.90	1.83	1.77	1.54	1.42	1.15	1.05	.94	.88	.84	.84	.77	.74	.72	.77	.82
1961	2.36	2.17	1.98	1.90	1.85	1.61	1.48	1.20	1.09	.98	.92	.87	.87	.80	.77	.75	.80	.85
1962	2.52	2.31	2.11	2.03	1.97	1.71	1.58	1.28	1.16	1.04	.98	.93	.93	.85	.82	.80	.85	.91
1963	2.53	2.32	2.12	2.04	1.98	1.72	1.59	1.29	1.17	1.05	.99	.93	.94	.86	.82	.80	.86	.91
1964	2.62	2.41	2.19	2.11	2.05	1.78	1.64	1.33	1.21	1.09	1.02	.97	.97	.89	.85	.83	.89	.95
1965	2.56	2.35	2.14	2.06	2.00	1.74	1.61	1.30	1.18	1.06	1.00	.94	.95	.87	.83	.81	.87	.92
1966	2.48	2.28	2.08	2.00	1.94	1.69	1.56	1.26	1.15	1.03	.97	.92	.92	.84	.81	.79	.84	.90

TABLE 1A-3 (Continued)

TO THE END OF — FROM THE BEGINNING OF

TO THE END OF	1926	1927	1928	1929	1930	1931	1932	1933	1934	1935	1936	1937	1938	1939	1940	1941	1942	1943
1967	2.29	2.10	1.92	1.85	1.79	1.56	1.44	1.16	1.06	.95	.89	.85	.85	.78	.74	.73	.78	.83
1968	2.24	2.06	1.88	1.81	1.75	1.53	1.41	1.14	1.04	.93	.87	.83	.83	.76	.73	.71	.76	.81
1969	1.94	1.78	1.63	1.57	1.52	1.32	1.22	.99	.90	.80	.76	.72	.72	.66	.63	.62	.66	.70
1970	2.18	2.00	1.82	1.76	1.70	1.48	1.37	1.11	1.01	.90	.85	.80	.81	.74	.71	.69	.74	.79
1971	2.34	2.15	1.96	1.89	1.83	1.59	1.47	1.19	1.08	.97	.91	.86	.87	.79	.76	.74	.79	.84
1972	2.43	2.23	2.03	1.96	1.90	1.65	1.52	1.23	1.12	1.01	.95	.90	.90	.82	.79	.77	.82	.88
1973	2.26	2.07	1.89	1.82	1.76	1.54	1.42	1.15	1.04	.94	.88	.83	.84	.77	.73	.72	.76	.81
1974	1.95	1.79	1.63	1.57	1.52	1.33	1.22	.99	.90	.81	.76	.72	.72	.66	.63	.62	.66	.70
1975	2.09	1.92	1.75	1.68	1.63	1.42	1.31	1.06	.97	.87	.81	.77	.77	.71	.68	.66	.71	.75
1976	2.37	2.17	1.98	1.91	1.85	1.61	1.48	1.20	1.09	.98	.92	.87	.88	.80	.77	.75	.80	.85
1977	2.25	2.07	1.89	1.82	1.76	1.53	1.41	1.14	1.04	.93	.88	.83	.83	.76	.73	.71	.76	.81
1978	2.07	1.90	1.73	1.66	1.61	1.40	1.30	1.05	.95	.86	.80	.76	.76	.70	.67	.65	.70	.75

TO THE END OF	1944	1945	1946	1947	1948	1949	1950	1951	1952	1953	1954	1955	1956	1957	1958	1959	1960	1961
1944	1.03																	
1945	1.04	1.02																
1946	.90	.88	.86															
1947	.81	.78	.77	.90														
1948	.82	.78	.77	.91	1.01													
1949	.86	.80	.78	.96	1.07	1.05												
1950	.83	.84	.82	.92	1.03	1.02	.97											
1951	.76	.81	.79	.85	.95	.93	.89	.92										
1952	.78	.74	.73	.87	.97	.96	.91	.94	1.03									
1953	.80	.76	.75	.89	1.00	.98	.94	.97	1.05	1.03								
1954	.85	.78	.77	.95	1.06	1.04	.99	1.03	1.12	1.09	1.06							
1955	.85	.83	.82	.95	1.06	1.04	.99	1.03	1.12	1.09	1.06	1.00						
1956	.77	.75	.74	.86	.96	.95	.90	.93	1.01	.99	.96	.91	.91					
1957	.81	.79	.78	.91	1.01	1.00	.95	.98	1.07	1.04	1.01	.96	.96	1.06				
1958	.78	.76	.75	.87	.97	.96	.91	.94	1.03	1.00	.97	.92	.92	1.01	.96			
1959	.76	.74	.73	.85	.95	.94	.89	.92	1.00	.98	.95	.90	.90	.99	.94	.98		
1960	.82	.80	.79	.91	1.02	1.01	.96	.99	1.08	1.05	1.02	.96	.96	1.06	1.01	1.05	1.07	
1961	.85	.80	.79	.95	1.06	1.05	1.00	1.03	1.12	1.09	1.06	1.00	1.00	1.11	1.05	1.09	1.12	1.04
1962	.91	.87	.87	1.01	1.13	1.12	1.06	1.10	1.20	1.17	1.13	1.07	1.07	1.18	1.12	1.16	1.19	1.11
1963	.92	.89	.88	1.02	1.14	1.12	1.07	1.11	1.20	1.17	1.14	1.08	1.08	1.19	1.16	1.17	1.20	1.12
1964	.95	.93	.91	1.06	1.18	1.16	1.10	1.14	1.25	1.21	1.18	1.11	1.11	1.23	1.14	1.21	1.24	1.16
1965	.93	.90	.89	1.03	1.15	1.14	1.08	1.12	1.22	1.19	1.15	1.09	1.09	1.20	1.12	1.18	1.21	1.13
1966	.90	.88	.86	1.00	1.12	1.10	1.05	1.08	1.18	1.15	1.12	1.06	1.05	1.16	1.10	1.15	1.18	1.09
1967	.83	.81	.79	.92	1.03	1.02	.96	1.00	1.09	1.06	1.03	.97	.97	1.07	1.02	1.06	1.09	1.01
1968	.81	.79	.78	.90	1.01	.99	.95	.98	1.07	1.04	1.01	.95	.95	1.05	1.00	1.04	1.06	.99

26

Upper table (rows 1969–1978):

	1962	1963	1964	1965	1966	1967	1968	1969	1970	1971	1972	1973	1974	1975	1976	1977	1978	
1969	.70	.69	.67	.78	.87	.86	.82	.85	.92	.90	.87	.83	.83	.91	.86	.90	.92	.86
1970	.79	.77	.76	.88	.98	.97	.92	.95	1.04	1.01	.98	.93	.93	1.02	.97	1.01	1.03	.96
1971	.85	.83	.81	.94	1.05	1.04	.99	1.02	1.11	1.08	1.05	1.00	.99	1.10	1.04	1.08	1.11	1.03
1972	.88	.86	.84	.98	1.09	1.08	1.02	1.06	1.15	1.12	1.09	1.03	1.03	1.14	1.08	1.12	1.15	1.07
1973	.82	.80	.78	.91	1.01	1.00	.95	.99	1.07	1.04	1.02	.96	.96	1.06	1.00	1.04	1.07	1.00
1974	.71	.69	.68	.79	.88	.86	.82	.85	.93	.90	.88	.83	.83	.91	.87	.90	.92	.86
1975	.76	.74	.72	.84	.94	.93	.88	.91	.99	.97	.94	.89	.89	.98	.93	.97	.99	.92
1976	.86	.83	.82	.95	1.06	1.05	1.00	1.03	1.12	1.09	1.07	1.01	1.00	1.11	1.05	1.09	1.12	1.04
1977	.82	.80	.78	.91	1.01	1.00	.95	.98	1.07	1.04	1.01	.96	.96	1.06	1.00	1.04	1.07	.99
1978	.75	.73	.72	.83	.93	.92	.87	.90	.98	.96	.93	.88	.88	.97	.92	.95	.98	.91

Lower table (rows 1962–1978):

	1962	1963	1964	1965	1966	1967	1968	1969	1970	1971	1972	1973	1974	1975	1976	1977	1978
1962	1.07																
1963	1.07	1.01															
1964	1.11	1.04	1.04														
1965	1.08	1.02	1.01	.98													
1966	1.05	.99	.98	.95	.97												
1967	.97	.91	.90	.87	.89	.92											
1968	.95	.89	.89	.86	.88	.90	.98										
1969	.82	.77	.77	.74	.76	.78	.85	.87									
1970	.92	.87	.86	.83	.85	.88	.95	.97	1.12								
1971	.99	.93	.92	.89	.91	.94	1.02	1.04	1.21	1.07							
1972	1.03	.96	.96	.93	.95	.98	1.06	1.08	1.25	1.11	1.04						
1973	.96	.90	.89	.86	.88	.91	.99	1.01	1.16	1.04	.96	.93					
1974	.83	.77	.77	.74	.76	.79	.85	.87	1.00	.89	.83	.80	.86				
1975	.88	.83	.83	.80	.82	.84	.91	.93	1.08	.96	.89	.86	.93	1.07			
1976	1.00	.94	.93	.90	.92	.95	1.03	1.05	1.22	1.09	1.01	.97	1.05	1.21	1.13		
1977	.95	.89	.89	.86	.88	.91	.98	1.00	1.16	1.03	.96	.93	1.00	1.16	1.08	.95	
1978	.87	.82	.82	.79	.81	.83	.90	.92	1.06	.95	.88	.85	.91	1.06	.99	.87	.92

TABLE 1A-4 U.S. Treasury Bills

TO THE END OF	FROM THE BEGINNING OF 1926	1927	1928	1929	1930	1931	1932	1933	1934	1935	1936	1937	1938	1939	1940	1941	1942	1943
1926	1.05																	
1927	1.10	1.05																
1928	1.15	1.10	1.04															
1929	1.20	1.15	1.09	1.05														
1930	1.31	1.25	1.19	1.14	1.09													
1931	1.46	1.40	1.33	1.27	1.22	1.12												
1932	1.65	1.57	1.49	1.43	1.37	1.26	1.13											
1933	1.65	1.57	1.49	1.43	1.37	1.25	1.12	1.00										
1934	1.62	1.54	1.46	1.40	1.34	1.23	1.10	.98	.98									
1935	1.57	1.50	1.42	1.36	1.31	1.20	1.07	.95	.95	.97								
1936	1.55	1.48	1.41	1.35	1.29	1.19	1.06	.94	.95	.96	.99							
1937	1.51	1.44	1.37	1.31	1.26	1.15	1.03	.92	.92	.94	.96	.97						
1938	1.56	1.48	1.41	1.35	1.29	1.19	1.06	.94	.95	.96	.99	1.00	1.03					
1939	1.56	1.49	1.42	1.36	1.30	1.19	1.07	.95	.95	.97	1.00	1.01	1.03	1.01				
1940	1.55	1.48	1.40	1.35	1.29	1.18	1.06	.94	.94	.96	.99	1.00	1.02	1.00	.99			
1941	1.41	1.35	1.28	1.23	1.17	1.08	.96	.86	.86	.87	.90	.91	.93	.91	.90	.91		
1942	1.30	1.24	1.17	1.13	1.08	.99	.88	.79	.79	.80	.82	.83	.86	.83	.83	.84	.92	
1943	1.26	1.20	1.14	1.10	1.05	.96	.86	.76	.77	.78	.80	.81	.83	.81	.81	.81	.89	.97
1944	1.24	1.18	1.12	1.08	1.03	.94	.85	.75	.75	.77	.79	.80	.82	.80	.79	.80	.88	.96
1945	1.22	1.16	1.10	1.06	1.01	.93	.83	.74	.74	.75	.77	.78	.80	.78	.78	.78	.86	.94
1946	1.03	.98	.93	.90	.86	.79	.70	.63	.63	.64	.66	.66	.68	.66	.66	.67	.73	.80
1947	.95	.91	.86	.83	.79	.73	.65	.58	.58	.59	.61	.61	.63	.61	.61	.61	.67	.73
1948	.93	.89	.85	.81	.78	.71	.64	.57	.57	.58	.59	.60	.62	.60	.60	.60	.66	.72
1949	.96	.92	.87	.84	.80	.73	.66	.58	.58	.60	.61	.62	.64	.62	.61	.62	.68	.74
1950	.92	.88	.83	.80	.76	.70	.63	.56	.56	.57	.59	.59	.61	.59	.59	.59	.65	.71
1951	.88	.84	.80	.77	.73	.67	.60	.53	.54	.55	.56	.57	.58	.57	.56	.57	.62	.68
1952	.89	.85	.80	.77	.74	.68	.61	.54	.54	.55	.57	.57	.59	.57	.57	.57	.63	.69
1953	.90	.86	.81	.78	.75	.69	.61	.55	.55	.56	.57	.58	.59	.58	.58	.57	.64	.69
1954	.91	.87	.83	.79	.76	.69	.62	.55	.55	.56	.58	.59	.60	.59	.58	.58	.65	.70
1955	.92	.88	.84	.80	.77	.70	.63	.56	.56	.57	.59	.59	.61	.59	.59	.60	.65	.71
1956	.92	.88	.83	.80	.76	.70	.63	.56	.56	.57	.58	.59	.61	.59	.59	.59	.65	.71
1957	.92	.88	.83	.80	.76	.70	.63	.56	.56	.57	.59	.59	.61	.59	.59	.59	.65	.71
1958	.92	.88	.83	.80	.76	.70	.63	.56	.56	.57	.58	.59	.61	.59	.59	.59	.65	.71
1959	.93	.89	.84	.81	.77	.71	.64	.56	.57	.58	.59	.60	.62	.60	.60	.60	.66	.72
1960	.94	.90	.85	.82	.78	.72	.64	.57	.57	.58	.60	.61	.62	.61	.60	.61	.67	.73
1961	.96	.91	.87	.83	.79	.73	.65	.58	.58	.59	.61	.61	.63	.62	.61	.62	.68	.74
1962	.97	.92	.88	.84	.81	.74	.66	.59	.59	.60	.62	.62	.64	.63	.62	.63	.69	.75
1963	.98	.94	.89	.85	.82	.75	.67	.60	.60	.61	.63	.63	.65	.65	.63	.64	.70	.76
1964	1.01	.96	.91	.87	.84	.77	.69	.61	.61	.62	.64	.65	.67	.66	.64	.65	.71	.78
1965	1.03	.98	.93	.89	.85	.78	.70	.62	.62	.64	.65	.66	.68	.67	.66	.66	.73	.79
1966	1.04	.99	.94	.90	.86	.79	.71	.63	.63	.64	.66	.67	.69		.67	.67	.74	.80

	1944	1945	1946	1947	1948	1949	1950	1951	1952	1953	1954	1955	1956	1957	1958	1959	1960	1961
1967	1.05	1.00	.95	.91	.87	.80	.72	.64	.64	.65	.67	.68	.70	.68	.67	.68	.74	.81
1968	1.06	1.01	.96	.92	.88	.81	.72	.64	.64	.65	.67	.68	.70	.68	.68	.68	.75	.82
1969	1.06	1.01	.96	.92	.88	.81	.72	.64	.65	.66	.68	.68	.70	.68	.68	.69	.75	.82
1970	1.07	1.02	.97	.93	.89	.82	.73	.65	.65	.66	.68	.69	.71	.69	.69	.69	.76	.83
1971	1.08	1.03	.98	.94	.90	.83	.74	.66	.66	.67	.69	.70	.72	.70	.70	.70	.76	.84
1972	1.09	1.04	.98	.94	.90	.83	.74	.66	.66	.67	.69	.70	.72	.70	.70	.70	.77	.84
1973	1.07	1.02	.97	.93	.89	.81	.73	.65	.65	.66	.68	.69	.71	.69	.68	.69	.76	.82
1974	1.03	.98	.93	.89	.85	.78	.70	.62	.63	.64	.65	.66	.68	.66	.66	.66	.73	.79
1975	1.02	.97	.92	.88	.85	.78	.69	.62	.62	.63	.65	.66	.67	.66	.65	.66	.72	.78
1976	1.02	.97	.92	.89	.85	.78	.70	.62	.62	.63	.65	.66	.67	.66	.65	.66	.72	.79
1977	1.00	.96	.91	.87	.83	.77	.69	.61	.61	.62	.64	.65	.66	.65	.64	.65	.71	.77
1978	.99	.94	.89	.86	.82	.75	.67	.60	.60	.61	.63	.63	.65	.63	.63	.64	.70	.76

	1944	1945	1946	1947	1948	1949	1950	1951	1952	1953	1954	1955	1956	1957	1958	1959	1960	1961
1944	.98																	
1945	.96	.98																
1946	.82	.83	.85															
1947	.75	.77	.78	.92														
1948	.74	.75	.77	.90	.98													
1949	.76	.78	.79	.93	1.01	1.03												
1950	.73	.74	.76	.89	.97	.98	.96											
1951	.70	.71	.73	.85	.93	.94	.92	.96										
1952	.70	.72	.73	.86	.93	.95	.92	.97	1.01									
1953	.71	.73	.75	.87	.94	.96	.94	.98	1.02	1.01								
1954	.72	.74	.76	.88	.96	.98	.95	.99	1.03	1.03	1.01							
1955	.73	.74	.76	.89	.97	.99	.96	1.00	1.05	1.04	1.03	1.01						
1956	.73	.74	.76	.89	.97	.98	.96	1.00	1.04	1.03	1.02	1.01	1.00					
1957	.73	.74	.76	.89	.97	.98	.96	1.00	1.04	1.04	1.02	1.01	1.00	1.00				
1958	.73	.74	.76	.89	.96	.98	.95	1.00	1.04	1.03	1.02	1.01	1.00	1.00	1.00			
1959	.74	.75	.77	.90	.98	.98	.97	1.00	1.04	1.03	1.02	1.01	1.00	1.00	1.00	1.01		
1960	.75	.76	.77	.91	.99	1.00	.98	1.01	1.06	1.05	1.04	1.02	1.01	1.01	1.01	1.03	1.01	
1961	.76	.77	.79	.93	1.00	1.01	.99	1.02	1.07	1.06	1.05	1.03	1.02	1.03	1.02	1.04	1.03	1.01
1962	.77	.78	.80	.94	1.02	1.02	1.01	1.04	1.08	1.08	1.06	1.05	1.05	1.04	1.04	1.06	1.04	1.03
1963	.78	.79	.81	.95	1.03	1.04	1.02	1.05	1.10	1.09	1.08	1.06	1.07	1.06	1.05	1.07	1.06	1.04
1964	.80	.81	.83	.98	1.06	1.05	1.05	1.07	1.12	1.11	1.09	1.08	1.09	1.07	1.07	1.10	1.08	1.07
1965	.81	.83	.84	.99	1.08	1.08	1.07	1.09	1.14	1.13	1.12	1.10	1.11	1.10	1.09	1.12	1.10	1.09
1966	.83	.84	.86	1.01	1.09	1.10	1.08	1.12	1.16	1.16	1.14	1.13	1.13	1.12	1.12	1.13	1.12	1.10
1967	.83	.85	.87	1.02	1.11	1.11	1.09	1.13	1.18	1.17	1.17	1.14	1.14	1.13	1.13	1.15	1.13	1.12
1968	.84	.85	.87	1.02	1.11	1.13	1.10	1.14	1.19	1.18	1.18	1.15	1.15	1.14	1.14	1.15	1.14	1.12
1969	.84	.86	.87	1.03	1.13	1.13	1.10	1.15	1.20	1.19	1.18	1.16	1.15	1.15	1.15	1.16	1.14	1.13
1970	.85	.87	.88	1.04	1.13	1.14	1.12	1.15	1.20	1.20	1.19	1.16	1.17	1.15	1.16	1.17	1.15	1.14
1971	.86	.87	.89	1.05	1.14	1.15	1.13	1.17	1.22	1.21	1.20	1.18	1.18	1.17	1.17	1.18	1.16	1.15
1972	.86	.88	.89	1.05	1.14	1.16	1.13	1.18	1.23	1.22	1.21	1.19	1.18	1.18	1.18	1.18	1.17	1.15
1973	.85	.86	.88	1.04	1.12	1.16	1.11	1.18	1.23	1.22	1.19	1.19	1.16	1.18	1.16	1.16	1.15	1.13
1974	.82	.83	.85	1.00	1.08	1.14	1.07	1.16	1.21	1.20	1.14	1.17	1.12	1.16	1.12	1.11	1.13	1.09
1975	.81	.82	.84	.99	1.07	1.09	1.06	1.12	1.15	1.14	1.13	1.12	1.10	1.12	1.11	1.11	1.12	1.08
1976	.81	.82	.84	.99	1.07	1.09	1.06	1.11	1.16	1.15	1.13	1.12	1.11	1.12	1.12	1.09	1.10	1.08
1977	.80	.81	.83	.97	1.06	1.08	1.04	1.09	1.14	1.13	1.12	1.10	1.09	1.11	1.11	1.11	1.08	1.07
1978	.78	.80	.81	.96	1.04	1.06	1.03	1.07	1.12	1.11	1.10	1.08	1.07	1.07	1.09	1.08	1.06	1.05

TABLE 1A-4 (Continued)

TO THE END OF	FROM THE BEGINNING OF																
	1962	1963	1964	1965	1966	1967	1968	1969	1970	1971	1972	1973	1974	1975	1976	1977	1978
1962	1.01																
1963	1.03	1.01															
1964	1.05	1.04	1.02														
1965	1.07	1.06	1.04	1.02													
1966	1.09	1.07	1.06	1.03	1.01												
1967	1.10	1.09	1.07	1.05	1.03	1.01											
1968	1.11	1.09	1.07	1.05	1.03	1.02	1.00										
1969	1.11	1.10	1.08	1.05	1.03	1.02	1.01	1.00									
1970	1.12	1.11	1.09	1.07	1.04	1.03	1.02	1.01	1.01								
1971	1.13	1.12	1.10	1.08	1.06	1.04	1.03	1.02	1.02	1.01							
1972	1.14	1.12	1.11	1.08	1.06	1.05	1.03	1.03	1.02	1.01	1.00						
1973	1.12	1.10	1.09	1.06	1.04	1.03	1.02	1.01	1.01	1.00	.99	.98					
1974	1.08	1.06	1.05	1.02	1.00	.99	.98	.97	.97	.96	.95	.95	.96				
1975	1.06	1.05	1.03	1.01	.99	.98	.97	.96	.96	.95	.94	.94	.95	.99			
1976	1.07	1.05	1.04	1.01	.99	.98	.97	.96	.96	.95	.94	.94	.95	.99	1.00		
1977	1.05	1.04	1.02	1.00	.98	.97	.95	.95	.95	.94	.93	.92	.94	.98	.99	.98	
1978	1.03	1.02	1.00	.98	.96	.95	.94	.93	.93	.92	.91	.91	.92	.96	.97	.97	.98

Securities Markets

2

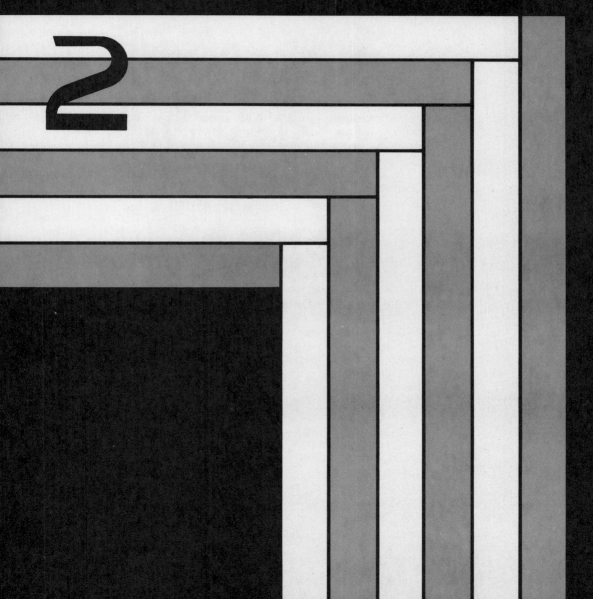

BROKERS AND DEALERS

When a security is sold, many people are likely to be involved. Although it is possible for two investors to trade with each other directly, the usual transaction employs the services provided by brokers, dealers, and/or markets.

A *broker* acts as an agent and is compensated via a commission. Like a marriage broker or real estate broker, an investment broker tries to bring two parties together and to obtain the best possible terms for his or her customer. Most individual investors deal with brokers in large *retail* or "*wire*" *houses*—firms with many offices connected by private wires with their own headquarters and, through the headquarters, with major markets. The people in brokerage firms with prime responsibility for individual accounts are termed *account executives*, *registered representatives*, or (in the vernacular) *customer's men and women*.

Institutional investors deal with both large firms offering retail brokerage service and smaller firms that maintain only one or two offices and specialize in institutional business. There are also *regional* brokerage firms and *discount* brokers. The former concentrate on transactions in a geographic area; the latter provide "bare-bones" service at low cost.

An account executive's compensation is typically determined partly by the amount of commissions paid by his or her customers—an amount that is usually greater, the greater the *turnover* in an account. This provides some temptation to recommend changes in investors' holdings and, since the commission rates on various types of investments differ, to recommend particular types of changes. In the long run, account executives who encourage excessive churning should lose customers. Nonetheless, such behavior may be advantageous for them in the short run.

It is a simple matter to open an account with a brokerage firm: simply appear at (or call) the local office. An account executive will be assigned to you and will take care of the formalities. Transactions will be posted to your account as they would to a bank account. You may deposit money, purchase securities using money from the account, add the proceeds from security sales to the account, borrow money, and so on. After the initial forms have been signed, everything can be done by mail and/or telephone. Brokers exist (and charge fees) to make securities transactions as simple as possible.

A broker acts as an agent for investors, but a *dealer* (or *market-maker*) buys and sells securities for his or her own account, taking at least temporary positions and maintaining at least small and transitory inventories of securities. Like a used-car dealer, a security dealer runs risks and ties up capital in order to make it easy for individuals to buy or sell on a moment's notice. Dealers are usually compensated by the *spread* between the *bid* price at which they buy a security and the *ask* price at which they sell it. The percentage spread is typically larger, the smaller the amount of trading activity and the greater the volatility in a security's price.

To facilitate the coming together of traders (be they investors, brokers or dealers), physical locations and/or communications facilities are required. *Security exchanges* are physical locations where trading is done on a person-to-person basis (usually by brokers and/or dealers) under specified rules. Communications networks, formal or informal, are often termed *markets*. Some have clearly defined boundaries; others do not.

Often a firm or even an individual will play more than one role in this process. Most retail brokerage firms hold some inventories of securities and may thus act as dealers (but the law requires that they inform their customers if they do so). Some exchanges have *specialists*, who serve as brokers for some trades and as dealers for others. Brokers may employ other brokers, dealers may deal with other dealers, and so on.

TYPES OF ORDERS

Brokers will accept instructions of various types concerning the conditions under which a security is to be purchased or sold. Some of the procedures are institutionalized; others are simply agreements between the investor and his or her account executive.

By far the most common procedure is that used for a *market order*. The broker is instructed to buy or sell a stated number of securities at the best available price or prices (as low as possible for a purchase, as high as possible for a sale). It is incumbent on the broker in such a situation to act on a "best efforts" basis to get the best possible deal at the time.

In most cases there is fairly good information concerning the likely price at which a market order might be executed. If this is unacceptable, a *limit order* may be placed instead. Both a quantity and an acceptable price are specified. The broker is to purchase or sell the stated number of shares only at the indicated price or better (higher for a sale, lower for a purchase). If a limit order cannot be executed immediately, it is usually kept by the broker or placed by the broker on the books of another broker (e.g., an exchange specialist) to be executed as soon as the requisite price can be obtained.

Some limit orders are *day orders*—canceled if not executed by the end of the day they are placed. However, an investor may specify that an order be considered *good-till-canceled* (GTC) or that it be canceled immediately if not executed (this is termed a *fill-or-kill* [FOK] order).

A limit order "on the books" is executed only when a security's price becomes more favorable. A *stop-loss* order operates in the opposite direction. For example, a stop-loss order at $30 per share might be placed to *sell* 100 shares of a stock currently trading at $40 per share. As long as the price remains above $30, nothing happens. But as soon as the price reaches (or drops below) $30, the order is converted to a market order, to be executed on the best possible terms. A stop-loss order to *purchase* shares becomes a market order when the price reaches or rises above the level indicated.

A *dollar-value order* is a market order to purchase as many shares as possible for a given dollar amount even though fractional holdings may result. Accounts are consolidated internally, and the brokerage firm takes positions in securities as needed. Sales of fractional shares are also allowed (of course only whole shares can be delivered to customers; fractional holdings are simply records in a computer).

The standard unit in which a stock is traded is termed a *round lot* (usually 100 shares). Any smaller quantity is an *odd lot*. An investor who wishes to purchase or sell an odd lot generally does business with a dealer instead of another investor. For example, certain brokerage firms will usually purchase an odd lot of a stock listed on the New York Stock Exchange at the price currently quoted on the exchange for a purchase (i.e., the official bid price) and sell an odd lot for the price currently quoted on the exchange for a sale (e.g., the official asked price). Specialists on most exchanges also handle odd lots, using similar procedures.

MARGIN ACCOUNTS

A *cash account* with a brokerage firm is like a regular checking account: deposits (cash and the proceeds from security sales) must cover withdrawals (cash and the costs of security purchases). A *margin account* is like a bank account with overdraft privileges: within limits, if more money is needed, a loan is automatically made by the broker.

All securities purchased on margin must be left with the brokerage firm and registered in its name (i.e., "street name"). Moreover, the account holder must sign a *hypothecation* agreement, which grants the broker the right to pledge margined securities as collateral for bank loans. Most firms also expect customers to allow them to lend securities to others who wish to sell them short (a procedure described in the next section). Such lending is done by the broker; the account holder is generally not even notified when it takes place.

The interest charged on loans advanced by a broker for a margin account is usually calculated by adding a service charge (e.g., 1%) to the broker's current *call money* rate. The latter is the rate paid by the broker to one or more banks for money used to finance margin purchases. Securities in margin accounts serve as collateral for the bank loans. The call money rate changes from time to time, and with it the interest charged for margin loans.

The Securities and Exchange Act of 1934 prohibits any broker (or bank) from making an initial loan for the purchase of a security in excess of the *loan value* of the collateral (e.g., the security to be purchased). This *initial margin* requirement differs for different types of investments—

e.g., it is usually higher for stocks than for bonds—and is changed from time to time by the Board of Governors of the Federal Reserve System as an instrument of economic policy. Since 1934 the initial margin required for exchange-listed stocks has ranged from 40% to 100%.

The *percentage margin* in an account can be calculated as follows:

$$\text{percentage margin} = \frac{\text{equity in the account}}{\text{market value of all positions}} \qquad (2\text{-}1)$$

For example, assume an investor wishes to buy 100 shares of ABC stock at $40 per share but has only $3,000. If a broker loans the remaining $1,000 for the purchase, the account's balance sheet will be:

100 shares of ABC at $40 per share = $4,000	Loan from broker = $1,000 Equity = $3,000

The percentage margin will be $3,000/$4,000, or 75%. If this exceeds the current initial margin requirement, the purchase can be made.

After the purchase, if ABC slips to $30 per share, the account's balance sheet will be:

100 shares of ABC at $30 per share = $3,000	Loan from broker = $1,000 Equity = $2,000

The percentage margin has fallen to $2,000/$3,000, or $66\frac{2}{3}$%. If the price of the stock falls farther, and the margin with it, the broker may become nervous, since an additional sudden price decline could bring the value of the collateral below the amount of the loan. To protect against such an occurrence, a broker will require that margin be kept above a *maintenance margin* level. The New York Stock Exchange requires its member firms to insist on at least 25%, but many require a larger amount.

If an account falls below the maintenance margin requirement, the broker will issue a *margin call*, requesting the account holder to add cash or securities to the account or to sell some securities currently in the account; this will raise the numerator or lower the denominator of (2-1), thus increasing the margin. If a customer does not act (or cannot be reached), in accordance with the terms of the original agreement the broker will sell securities from the account to restore the margin to the required maintenance level.

If ABC rises to $50 per share, the picture will be brighter:

100 shares of ABC at $50 per share = $5,000	Loan from broker = $1,000 Equity = $4,000

Here the percentage margin is $4,000/$5,000, or 80%. If the initial margin requirement is 75%, the account's current equity can support positions worth $5,333 (= $4,000/.75); if desired, securities worth up to $333 could be purchased and financed entirely with an additional loan from the broker. Alternatively, since only $3,750 (= .75 × $5,000) of equity is required to support positions worth $5,000, an additional $250 could be borrowed from the broker, taken as cash, and removed from the account.

When the percentage margin of an account falls below the initial margin requirement, no action need be taken. However, the account will be *restricted*. When an account is in this status, transactions will generally not be allowed if their net effect is to decrease the actual percentage margin; however, transactions occurring within a single trading day may be combined for this calculation.[1]

SHORT SALES

Most investors purchase securities first and sell them later. However, the process can be reversed: one can sell a security now and buy it back later. This is accomplished by borrowing certificates for use in the initial trade, then repaying the loan with certificates obtained in the later trade.

Any order for a *short sale* must be identified as such. The Securities and Exchange Commission has ruled that short sales may not be made when the market for the security is falling, on the assumption that the short-seller could exacerbate the situation, cause a panic, and profit therefrom—an assumption inappropriate for an efficient market with astute, alert traders. The precise rule is that a short sale must be made on an *up-tick* (for a price higher than that of the previous trade on the exchange involved) or on a *zero-plus tick* (for a price equal to that of the previous trade on that exchange but higher than that of the last trade at a different price).

At the end of the day on which a short sale is made, the seller's broker must borrow securities for delivery to the purchaser, unless the short-seller has already purchased them. Borrowed securities may come from the brokerage firm's own inventory or from that of another firm, but they are more likely to be securities held in street name for an investor with a margin account. Both the borrower and the lender have the option to terminate the agreement at any time—i.e., the lender may call for securities or the borrower may return them.

To protect the security lender against default, the borrower (short-seller) must deposit cash equal to the value of the securities involved. Initially, the proceeds from the short sale must be deposited with the security lender. When the market value rises, more cash must be deposited; when it falls, some of the deposit may be removed—i.e., the deposit is *marked to market*. When the securities are returned, the deposit is refunded.

The possible loss from a normal (*long*) position in a security is limited: only the original investment can be lost. But the potential loss from a short sale is unlimited, since a security's price can rise to several times its initial amount. Moreover, an increase in price can jeopardize the position of the lender of the security, since it may make it impossible for the borrower (short-seller) to buy the certificates required to pay back the loan.

---

[1] To meet legal requirements, more than one type of account may have to be maintained and funds transferred between accounts from time to time to allow the maximum possible amount of margin loans.

For this reason short-sellers are required to maintain a certain amount of equity in their accounts to serve as an additional cushion against adverse price changes.

Judicious use of accounts makes it possible to apply formula (2-1) to both long and short positions. For example, consider the following account:

Securities held long:
   market value = $100,000
Cash deposited with
   security lenders = $40,000
	Short positions: market
	   value = $40,000
	Loan from broker = $30,000
	Equity = $70,000

The current percentage margin is $70,000/($100,000 + $40,000), or 50%. Adverse moves greater than this amount in the positions (i.e., price declines for long positions, price increases for short positions) would wipe out the equity and place the loan from the broker and/or the loaned securities in jeopardy. For this reason all the rules concerning initial and maintenance margins, restricted accounts, and so on apply when short positions are maintained; the current market value of such positions is simply added to that of the long positions when computing the account's current margin.

A short sale neither generates cash (since the proceeds must be deposited with the security lender) nor requires it. Subsequent price increases do require cash, while declines generate cash. Although margin is required for a short sale, this means only that assets must be kept in the account to guard against default on the loan of the borrowed securities.

At times securities may be lent only on the payment of a premium; at other times lenders may pay interest on the money deposited with them. Usually, however, securities are loaned "flat"—the lending broker keeps the deposits and enjoys the use of the money and neither the short-seller nor the investor who owns the securities (in principle, but not in fact) receives any direct compensation.

During the period in which a security is "on loan," the borrower must pay to the lender amounts equal to the values of all the dividends and/or interest payments that would otherwise have been received. Such payments are not returned when the short position is *covered* (i.e., when securities are purchased and the loan repaid).

CONTINUOUS VERSUS CALL MARKETS

No market is ever truly continuous, for trades occur at discrete times. However, some markets are explicitly organized to group trades at specific times. In such *call markets*, when a security is called, all who wish to buy and sell are brought together. Enough time is allowed to elapse between calls (e.g., an hour or more) to accumulate a substantial number of offers to buy and sell. In some call markets there is an explicit *auction* in which prices are called out until the quantity demanded is as close as possible to the quantity supplied (this procedure is used by the Paris Bourse for major stocks). In other call markets, orders are left with a clerk between calls and "crossed" at a price that allows the maximum number to be executed (this procedure is used for some stocks by the Paris Bourse and the Tokyo Stock Exchange).

In a *continuous market* trades may occur at any time. While such a market could function with only investors and brokers, it would not be very effective, for an individual who wished to consummate a sale or purchase very quickly would either have to spend a great deal of money searching for a good offer or run the risk of accepting a poor one. Since orders from investors arrive more or less randomly, prices in such a market would vary considerably, depending on transitory relationships between desired purchases and sales. Such a situation could be exploited by anyone willing to take temporary positions in securities, ironing out transitory variations in demand and supply and making a profit thereby. This is the role of a dealer or market-maker, whether officially identified as such or not. Only greed and avarice are required to attract such people, but in the pursuit of personal gain they generally reduce fluctuations in price unrelated to changes in value, thereby providing liquidity for investors.

In some markets dealers compete with each other in order to offer the best possible terms for a given security. The London Stock Exchange is, in essence, a physical location where dealers ("jobbers") take orders from brokers. In the over-the-counter market in the United States, dealers' bid and ask prices are communicated to brokers via a computer network. On the floor of the Chicago Board of Trade dealers in commodities mingle with brokers in the "pits."

The New York Stock Exchange, to facilitate a continuous market, assigns *specialists* to stocks. The specialist is allowed to deal for his or her own account, but only if no better offer is forthcoming from "the floor"—i.e., from brokers acting for their customers or themselves. The specialist is allowed to make a profit but is also charged with maintaining a "fair and orderly market"—a requirement both ill-defined and difficult, if not impossible, to enforce. In return, specialists are allowed to maintain books of unexecuted limit (and stop-loss) orders. Whenever possible, a specialist executes orders from the book, crossing them with orders from the floor, or simply trading directly, using his or her own account, receiving in return a commission for serving as a "broker's broker."

INFORMATION-MOTIVATED AND LIQUIDITY-MOTIVATED TRANSACTIONS

There are two major reasons for security transactions. An investor may believe that a security has become mispriced—i.e., that its value is outside the current range between (1) the total *proceeds* from a sale and (2) the total *cost* of a purchase. One who feels this way believes that he or she has information not known to (or understood by) the market in general and may be termed an *information-motivated trader*. On the other hand, an investor may simply want to sell securities to buy a new car, buy some securities with recently inherited money, alter a portfolio to better conform to a recent change in job, or the like. Such a person may be termed *liquidity-motivated*: although feeling that value is also outside the proceeds/cost range, he or she does not presume that others in the market have evaluated the prospects for the security incorrectly.

Dealers can make money by trading with liquidity-motivated traders or with stupid information-motivated traders. But, on average, they can only lose money by trading with clever information-motivated traders. The larger a dealer's bid-ask spread, the less business he or she will do; but whatever the spread, when a clever information-motivated investor makes a trade, the dealer may expect to lose. In the absence of foolish investors, the very existence of a dealer market depends on investors' desires for liquidity. A dealer must select a bid-ask spread wide enough to limit the number of trades with customers possessing superior information, but narrow enough to attract an adequate number of liquidity-motivated transactions.

A dealer can take either a passive or an active role. For example, a bid-ask spread can be established and a tentative price set. As orders come in and are filled, the dealer's inventory (position) will vary and may even become negative when promises to deliver securities exceed promises to accept delivery. But any clear trend suggests that the price should be altered. In effect, a *passive dealer* lets the market indicate the appropriate price.

An *active dealer* tries to get as much information as possible and to alter bid and ask prices in advance to keep the flow of orders more in balance. The better a dealer's information, the smaller the bid-ask spread required to make a profit.

When there is competition among dealers, those who are not well informed either price themselves out of the market by requiring too high a bid-ask spread or go out of business after incurring heavy losses. In general, the interests of investors are best served by a market in which dealers with unlimited access to all sources of information compete with one another.

PRICES AS INFORMATION SOURCES

The usual description of a market assumes that every trader wishes to purchase or sell a known quantity at each possible price. All the traders come together, and in one way or another a price is found that clears the market—i.e., makes the quantity demanded as close as possible to the quantity supplied.

This may or may not be an adequate description of the markets for consumer goods, but it is clearly inadequate when describing security markets. The value of any capital asset depends on future prospects that are almost always uncertain. Any information that bears on such prospects may lead to a revised estimate of value. The fact that a knowledgeable trader is willing to buy or sell some quantity of a security at a particular price is likely to be information of just this sort. Offers to trade may thus affect other offers. Prices may both clear markets and convey information.

The dual role of prices has a number of implications. For example, it behooves the liquidity-motivated trader to publicize his or her motives and thereby avoid an adverse effect on the market. Thus an institution purchasing securities for a fund intended to simply hold a representative cross section of securities should make it clear that it does not consider the securities underpriced. On the other hand, any firm trying to buy or sell a large number of shares that it considers mispriced should try to conceal either its motives, its identity, or both (and many do try). Such attempts may be ineffective, however, as those asked to take the other side of such trades try to find out exactly what is going on (and many succeed).

Since offers may affect other offers, the way in which a market functions can affect the prices at which trades are made. And different markets function in different ways. For example, the New York Stock Exchange specialist's books contain information on both the prices and the quantities specified in standing orders, but only the lowest ask price and the highest bid price in the book and the quantities associated with each are revealed by the specialist to the general market. In the over-the-counter market, dealers publicly announce bid and ask prices that are firm for small quantities, but they negotiate prices for larger quantities. Orders for some stocks on the Paris Bourse are placed in a book with both prices and quantities specified, while for other stocks the book contains only the prices of orders.

The extent to which standing orders are made public may thus affect the prices at which such orders are executed, the extent to which investors will place them with brokers, and the extent to which brokers will place them in a central "book" where they can be seen by others.

Some investors depend almost entirely on price for information about value. This raises the possibility that a clever trader could make money by placing orders to trigger foolish responses from such investors. While this may occur in isolated instances, it is limited by the presence of informed traders who use external information sources to assess value. Given a large enough number of people who study fundamental aspects, it is possible for most investors to assume that market price reflects value.

MAJOR MARKETS IN THE UNITED STATES

The New York Stock Exchange

Most individual investors maintain an account with a retail brokerage firm that is a member of the New York Stock Exchange, by far the most important stock exchange.

At the end of 1977, 1,550 stocks with a market value of $830 billion were listed for trading on the New York Stock Exchange. In the course of that year 5.6 billion shares (worth $164.5 billion) changed hands on the Exchange. This compares with 1.4 billion shares traded on all other exchanges, and 1.7 billion shares traded over-the-counter using the NASDAQ system.[2] For the individual investor the New York Stock Exchange is the major market place for actively traded stocks.

The decision to list a company's stock on the Exchange is based on

[2] U.S. Securities and Exchange Commission, *Annual Report*, 1977.

"(1) the degree of national interest in the company, (2) its relative position and stability in the industry, and (3) whether it is engaged in an expanding industry, with prospects of at least maintaining its relative position." The company must apply for listing and agree to provide certain information to the public. After listing, if trading interest in a security declines substantially, it may be *delisted* by the Exchange. Companies may apply for listing on more than one exchange, and under certain conditions an exchange may set up "unlisted trading privileges" for transactions in a stock already listed on another exchange.

The operation of the New York Stock Exchange is best described by example. Mr. A asks his broker for the current price of General Motors shares. The broker punches a few buttons on a televisionlike quotation machine and finds that the current bid and ask prices on the New York Stock Exchange are 61 and $61\frac{1}{4}$ and that the specialist in GM will buy at least 100 shares at 61 and sell at least 500 shares at $61\frac{1}{4}$ (either as dealer, for his own account, or a broker, for an investor whose order is in the book). Mr. A instructs his broker to "buy 100 at market." The broker transmits the order to his firm's New York headquarters, which communicates it to a representative on the floor of the Exchange. The representative goes to the "post" where General Motors is traded, checks with the specialist who handles the stock to make certain that the quote has not changed, then calls out "100 at $1\frac{1}{8}$" (60 is taken for granted). Why this price? Because the existence of a standing order to buy at 61 means that no one else is prepared to sell at that price; and the existence of a standing order to sell at $61\frac{1}{4}$ means that no higher price need be paid. This leaves only the gap between the two prices for possible negotiation. If Mr. A is lucky, another broker (for example, one with a market order to sell 100 shares for Ms. B) will respond "take it." Information will be exchanged between the two brokers and the sale consummated.

If the gap between quoted bid and ask prices is wide enough, a little auction may even occur among selling brokers and buying brokers, with trades consummated at one or more prices between the specialist's quoted values.

What if no response had been forthcoming from the floor when Mr. A's broker's representative offered to sell at $61\frac{1}{8}$? He or she would then have tried for $61\frac{1}{4}$. Another representative on the floor might have said "take it," or the specialist might have responded. In the latter event the actual seller might be the specialist or another investor, whose limit order is being executed by the specialist.

If the bid-ask spread on a stock is no larger than the standard unit in which prices are quoted (typically $\frac{1}{8}$ of a point, or 12.5 cents), market orders are generally taken directly to the specialist.

If Mr. A places a limit order with his broker, the latter's representative will not even try to execute it if the stated price is outside the current bid-ask spreads on the available markets. Instead, the order will likely be passed on to the specialist who handles the stock at the NYSE, who will enter it in the book for subsequent execution when possible. If there are several limit orders in the book at the same price, they are executed in order of arrival (i.e., first-in, first-out).

It may not be possible to fill an entire order at a single price. Thus a broker with an order to buy 500 shares at market might obtain 300 shares at $61\frac{1}{8}$ and have to pay $61\frac{1}{4}$ for the remaining 200. A limit order to buy 500 shares at $61\frac{1}{8}$ or better might result in the purchase of 300 shares at $61\frac{1}{8}$ and the entry of a limit order in the specialist's book for the other 200 shares. And so on.

Other Exchanges

Table 2-1 shows the total dollar volume of stocks, options, rights and warrants traded on each of the active exchanges in the United States in 1976. Not surprisingly, the New York Stock Exchange dominates the list. Second in importance is the American Stock Exchange (AMEX), which lists shares of somewhat smaller companies of national interest (a few of which are also listed on the New York Stock Exchange). Other exchanges with significant volume are the Midwest, Pacific Coast, Philadelphia, and Boston. All are termed *regional exchanges*, since historically each served as the sole location for trading securities primarily of interest to investors in its region. However, the major regional exchanges now depend to a substantial extent on transactions in securities that are also listed on a national exchange.

A relative newcomer to the list is The Chicago Board of Options Exchange, which lists only stock options and dominates this portion of the market (accounting for 77% of the volume in 1976).[3]

Other stock exchanges use procedures similar to those of the New York Stock Exchange. The roles of specialists and the ways in which paperwork is handled may differ, but the basic approach is the same.

Options exchanges and commodities exchanges utilize some procedures that differ significantly from those employed by stock exchanges. Commodities exchanges substitute daily price limits for the presence of a specialist with orders to maintain a "fair and orderly market." The Chicago Board Options Exchange separates the two functions of the specialist; a "board broker" is charged with the maintenance of the book of limit orders, with one or more registered "market makers" assigned the role of dealer.

[3] U.S. Securities and Exchange Commission, *Annual Report*, 1977.

TABLE 2-1 Total Dollar Value of Stocks, Options, Rights, and Warrants Traded on Active U.S. Exchanges, 1976

Exchange	Volume ($ billions)
New York	164.7
American	9.8
Midwest	9.3
Chicago Board Options	9.0
Pacific Coast	7.6
Philadelphia	3.6
Boston	1.8
All others	.5

Source: U.S. Securities and Exchange Commission, *Annual Report,* 1977.

The Over-the-Counter Market

In the early days of the United States, banks acted as the primary dealers for bonds and stocks, and investors literally bought and sold securities "over the counter" there. Transactions are more impersonal now, but the designation remains in use for transactions that are not consummated on an organized exchange. Most bonds are sold over-the-counter, as are mutual funds, many bank and finance stocks, and the securities of small (and some not-so-small) companies.

The over-the-counter market for stocks is the most modern market-place in the United States. In 1971 the National Association of Securities Dealers (NASD), which serves as a "self-regulating" agency for its members, put into operation the NASD Automated Quotations System (NASDAQ). This nationwide communications network allows brokers to know virtually instantly the terms currently offered by all major dealers in securities covered by the system.

Dealers who subscribe to Level III of NASDAQ are given terminals with which to enter firm bid and ask prices for any stock for which they make a market. Such dealers must be prepared to execute trades for at least one "normal unit of trading" (usually 100 shares) at the prices quoted. As soon as a bid or ask price is entered for a security, it is placed in a central computer file and may be seen by other subscribers (including other dealers) on their own terminals. When new quotations are entered, they replace the dealer's former prices.

Most brokerage firms subscribe to Level II of NASDAQ for their trading rooms, obtaining terminals that can display the current quotations on any security in the system. Bid quotations are displayed in descending order, and ask quotations in ascending order. The dealer offering each quotation is also identified.

Level I of NASDAQ is used by individual account executives to get a feel for the market. It shows "representative" bid and ask prices for each security. The former is the median of the current bid prices in the system; the latter is obtained by adding to the representative bid the median bid-ask spread for the stock's current quotations.

As its name indicates, NASDAQ is primarily a quotation system. Actual transactions are made via direct negotiation between broker and dealer. However, the system is already used to report completed transactions, and it could easily be adapted to cross orders and thus provide "automatic execution."

To be included in NASDAQ, a security must have at least two registered market-makers and a minimum number of publicly held shares; moreover, the issuing firm must meet stated capital and asset requirements. At the end of 1976, 2,627 issues were included in the system.[4]

The NASDAQ system covers only a portion of the outstanding OTC stocks, and no bonds. Brokers with orders to buy or sell noncovered securities rely on quotation sheets and less formal communications networks to obtain "best execution" for their clients.

---

[4] U.S. Securities and Exchange Commission, *Annual Report*, 1977.

The Third and Fourth Markets

Until the 1970s the New York Stock Exchange required its member firms to trade all NYSE-listed stocks at the Exchange and to charge fixed commissions. For large institutions this was both cumbersome and expensive. Typically, a brokerage firm with a large transaction to complete would serve as a *block positioner*, seeking out institutions willing to take at least part of the other side of the trade but also prepared to take at least part for its own account. After both sides had been lined up, the block would be brought to the floor of the Exchange for formal execution, any public orders at the previously negotiated price would be taken, and the broker's buy and sell orders then crossed.

The requirement that NYSE member firms bring such blocks to the Exchange floor was at most a nuisance. But the required minimum commission rate was a serious problem, since it exceeded the marginal cost of arranging trades of such size. Brokerage firms that were not members of the Exchange faced no such restrictions and could thus compete effectively for trades in NYSE-listed stocks. Such transactions are said to take place in the *third market*. In its heyday (1971 and 1972) third-market volume reached 8.5% of that on the Exchange.[5]

Many institutions dispense with brokers and exchanges entirely for transactions in New York Stock Exchange-listed stocks and other securities. Trades of this type are sometimes said to take place in the *fourth market*. In the United States some of these transactions are facilitated by an automated computer/communications system called *Instinet*, which provides quotations and execution automatically.[6] A subscriber can enter a limit order in the computerized "book," where it can be seen by other subscribers who can, in turn, signal their desire to take it. Whenever two orders are crossed, the system automatically records the transaction and sets up the paperwork for its completion. Subscribers can also use the system to find likely partners for a trade, then conduct negotiations by telephone. A similar system, called *Ariel*, is used in the United Kingdom.

Some New York Stock Exchange-listed stocks are traded on other exchanges and/or through the NASDAQ system. However, most of the trades in such securities are at least formally made on the NYSE (over 88% in early 1979).[7] Partly this is due to the Exchange's *Rule 390*, which states that member firms must make all trades in NYSE-listed stocks there unless given specific permission to do otherwise. While the rule has been under attack by the Securities and Exchange Commission for some while, it remained in full effect in 1979, and prospects for its complete demise in the near future seem dim.

The Central Market

The *Securities Acts Amendments of 1975* mandated that the U.S. Securities and Exchange Commission should move as rapidly as possible

---

[5] Securities and Exchange Commission, *Annual Report*, 1974.

[6] The use of an intermediary system makes it difficult to categorize such trades (perhaps they occur in a 3.5 market).

[7] U.S. Securities and Exchange Commission, *Statistical Bulletin*, May 1979.

toward the implementation of a truly nationwide competitive central securities market:

> The linking of all markets for qualified securities through communication and data processing facilities will foster efficiency, enhance competition, increase the information available to brokers, dealers, and investors, facilitate the offsetting of investors' orders, and contribute to best execution of such orders.[8]

Implementation of these objectives has proceeded in three steps. In 1975 a *consolidated stock ticker* began to report trades in New York and American Stock Exchange-listed stocks that took place on the two exchanges, on major regional exchanges, over-the-counter using the NASDAQ system, and in the fourth market using the Instinet system. Since 1976 this information has been used to produce the *composite stock price tables* published in the daily press.

The second step involves quotations. To obtain the best possible terms for a client, a broker must know the prices currently available on all major markets. To facilitate this, the Securities and Exchange Commission instructed stock exchanges to make their quotations available for use in a *composite quotation system* (CQS). With the implementation of this system in 1978 exchange specialists' bid and ask prices were made more accessible to those subscribing to quotation services. Increasingly, a broker is able to rely on electronics to determine the best available terms for a trade, thus avoiding the need for extensive "shopping around."

The final step in the process is the establishment of a single centralized book of limit orders (CLOB), with associated procedures for linking markets electronically and the setting of rules concerning its use and disclosure. Other issues must be settled as well: should there be specialists, and if so, how should they operate? What requirements (if any) should be imposed on market-makers? Who should operate the central market system? And so on.

It is easy to envision a truly modern approach. For example, the centralized computer system might operate with a completely open book of orders. However, subscribers' computers could communicate with the central computer, interrogate it for information on recent trades in a stock and the current book, and automatically place, remove, or change orders based on such information. A subscribing firm could program its computer system to maintain a private book, fill various types of orders (e.g., stop-loss) automatically, follow certain technical rules, alter its own limit orders based on changes in the market, and so on. Competition among brokerage firms would eventually weed out the bad ideas and institutionalize the good ones, but the central market's role would be limited to facilitating procedures of all types.

There are many long-entrenched and powerful institutions in the securities industry. The eventual nature of the central market will undoubtedly depend in part on the relative political power of the various vested interests. But the goals seem relatively clear, and on net, the changes are likely to benefit investors.

[8] *Securities Acts Amendments of 1975*, section 11A.

CLEARING PROCEDURES

Most securities are sold the "regular way," which requires delivery of certificates within five business days. On rare occasions a sale may be made as a "cash" transaction, requiring delivery the same day, or as a "seller's option," giving the seller the choice of any delivery day within a specified period (typically, no more than 60 days).

It would be extremely inefficient if every security transaction had to end with the physical transfer of certificates from the seller to the buyer. On a given day, a brokerage firm might sell 500 shares of American Telephone and Telegraph stock for Mr. A and buy 300 shares for Ms. B. Mr. A's 500 shares could be delivered to the buyer's broker, and Ms. B's 300 shares obtained by accepting delivery from the seller's broker. But it would be much easier to transfer 300 of Mr. A's shares to Ms. B, send the other 200 to the first broker, and instruct the second broker to deliver the 300 shares directly to the first broker. This would be especially helpful if the firm's clients maintained their securities in street name, for the 300 shares kept within the firm would not have to be moved or have their ownership transferred on the books of the issuing corporation.

The process can be facilitated even more by a *clearing house*, the members of which are security brokerage firms, banks, and the like. Records of transactions made by members during a day are sent there. At the end of the day both sides of the trades are verified for consistency, then all transactions are netted out. Each member receives a list of the net amounts of securities to be delivered or received along with the net amount of money to be paid or collected. Every day each member settles once with the clearing house instead of many times with various other firms.

A centralized clearing house, operated by the National Securities Clearing Corporation, handles trades made on the New York and American stock exchanges and in the over-the-counter market. Some regional exchanges also maintain clearing houses. Not all exchange members join such organizations; some choose to use the services of other members. Some banks belong, in order to facilitate delivery of securities which serve as collateral for call loans and so on.

By holding securities in street name and using clearing houses, brokers can reduce the cost of transfer operations. But even more can be done: certificates can be *immobilized* almost completely. The *Depository Trust Company* (DTC) accomplishes this by maintaining computerized records of the securities "owned" by its member firms (brokers, banks, etc.). Members deposit certificates, which are credited to their accounts. The certificates are transferred to the DTC on the books of the issuing corporation and remain registered in its name unless a member subsequently withdraws them. Whenever possible, one member will "deliver" securities to another by initiating a simple bookkeeping entry in which one account is credited and the other debited for the shares involved. Dividends paid on securities held by DTC are simply credited to members' accounts based on their holdings and may be withdrawn in cash.

The Securities Acts Amendments of 1975 instruct the Securities and Exchange Commission to develop a central system of this sort to eliminate the movement of stock certificates and possibly eliminate stock certificates entirely. Eventually, at dividend time, corporations' computers may deal directly with other computers that are in touch with still other computers in banks, brokerage firms, and so on. Moreover, the central market system may be integrated with the central clearing system, so that agreement of two parties to the terms of a transaction will automatically bring about the transfer of ownership required to complete the trade.

INSURANCE

In the late 1960s many brokerage firms were confronted with an unexpectedly large volume of transactions and a lack of proven computerized systems able to handle the workload. This gave rise to back-office problems and resulted in a rash of "fails to deliver"—situations in which a seller's broker did not deliver certificates to a buyer's broker on or before the required settlement date.

Worse yet, several brokerage firms subsequently failed, and some of their clients discovered for the first time that certificates "in their accounts" were not necessarily physically available. Such events led to serious concern about the desirability of any procedure that kept certificates out of the hands of the investor. To avoid erosion of investor confidence, member firms of the New York Stock Exchange spent substantial sums to cover the losses of failed firms and/or to merge them into successful firms. But such remedies were only temporary; insurance provided a more permanent solution.

The Securities Investor Protection Act of 1970 established the *Securities Investor Protection Corporation* (SIPC), a quasi-governmental agency that insures the accounts of clients of all broker-dealers and members of exchanges registered with the Securities and Exchange Commission against loss due to the firms' failure. Each account is insured up to a stated amount. The cost of the insurance is supposed to be borne by the covered brokers and dealers through premiums, but up to $1 billion may be borrowed from the U.S. Treasury.

A number of brokerage firms have gone farther, arranging for additional coverage from private insurance companies. Many have policies that, together with SIPC coverage, insure accounts up to $500,000.

COMMISSIONS

In the 1700s people interested in buying and selling stocks and bonds met under a buttonwood tree at 68 Wall Street in New York City. In May, 1792, a group of brokers pledged "not to buy or sell from this day for any person whatsoever, any kind of public stock at a less rate than one quarter per cent commission on the specie value, and that we will give preference to each other in our negotiations."[9] A visitor to the New York Stock Exchange in the early 1970s could see this "buttonwood agreement" publicly displayed. This was not surprising, since the Exchange is a lineal descendant of the group that met under the buttonwood tree. And until 1968 the Exchange required its member brokers to charge fixed minimum commissions for stocks, with no "rebates, returns, discounts or allowances in 'any shape or manner,' direct or indirect."[10] The terms had changed, but the principle established 180 years earlier remained in effect.

In the United States most cartels designed to limit competition by fixing prices are illegal. But this one was exempted from prosecution under the antitrust laws. Before, 1934 the Exchange was, in essence, considered a private club for its members. This changed with passage of the *Securities and Exchange Act of 1934*, which required most exchanges to be registered with and controlled by the Securities and Exchange Commission (SEC). The Commission, in turn, encouraged "self-regulation" by the exchanges of most of their activities, including the setting of minimum commissions.

After repeated challenges, the system of fixed commissions was finally terminated by the Securities Acts Amendments of 1975. Since May 1, 1975 (known in the trade as "May day"), brokers have been free to *set* commissions at any desired rate or to *negotiate* with customers concerning the fees charged for particular trades. The former procedure is more commonly employed in "retail" trades executed for small investors, while the latter is frequently used by institutional investors and others who engage in large trades.

In the era of fixed commissions only competition in terms of prices was completely restricted. Brokerage firms that belonged to the New York Stock Exchange competed with one another by offering a panoply of services to customers. Large institutions were provided with security analysis, performance measurement services, and the like in return for "soft dollars"—brokerage commissions designated as payment for services rendered. Some brokers would accept as little as $3 in commissions in lieu of $2 in cash; apparently, up to two-thirds of the fixed commission rate ($2 out of $3) on such large orders was pure (marginal) profit.

Experience after May day provided confirmation. Rates for large trades fell substantially. So did those charged for small trades by firms offering only "bare-bones" brokerage services. On the other hand, broad-line firms that provided extensive services to small investors for no additional fee continued to charge commissions similar to those specified in the earlier fixed schedules. In succeeding years, as costs have risen, charges for smaller transactions have increased, while those for large trades have not.

During the 1960s and 1970s a number of procedures were used to subvert the fixed commission rates: the third market prospered, regional exchanges invented ways to serve as conduits to return a portion of the fixed commissions to institutional investors, and so on.

[9] Wilford J. Eiteman, Charles A. Dice, and David K. Eiteman, *The Stock Market* (New York: McGraw-Hill Book Company, 1969), p. 19.
[10] Eiteman, Dice, and Eiteman, *The Stock Market*, p. 138.

No legal restriction gave the New York Stock Exchange its monopoly power in the first instance. Instead, the situation has been attributed to the natural monopoly arising from economies of scale in bringing many people together (either physically or via modern communication technology) to trade with each other. The potential profits from such a monopoly are, of course, limited by the advantages it confers. The increasing institutionalization of security holdings and progress in communications and computer technology have diminished the advantages associated with a centralized physical exchange. The removal of legal protection for this particular type of price-fixing may thus have only accelerated a trend already under way.

Increased competition among brokerage houses has resulted in a wide range of alternatives for investors. Following May day, some firms "unbundled"—pricing execution and other services separately; others "went discount"—dropping almost all ancillary services and cutting commissions accordingly. Still others "bundled" new services into comprehensive packages. Some of these approaches have not stood the test of time, but just as mail-order firms, discount houses, department stores, and expensive boutiques coexist in retail trade, many different combinations are viable in the brokerage industry.

Figure 2-1 shows typical commission rates charged by retail brokerage firms in 1979. These rates are representative of those charged by full-line retail brokers that provide offices with quotation boards, research reports, account executives available for advice and information, and the like. They also apply to trades made by customers whose volume of business is small. Discount firms with little but execution capability typically charge 30% to 70% less.

As in any other competitive industry, it behooves the customer to decide what is worth paying for and then shop around to obtain the best possible price.

FIGURE 2-1 Typical Commission Rates for Selected Transactions; dollar commission as a percentage of the value of the order

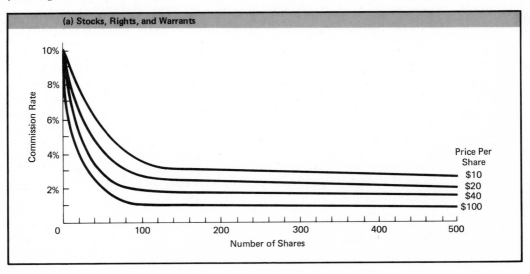

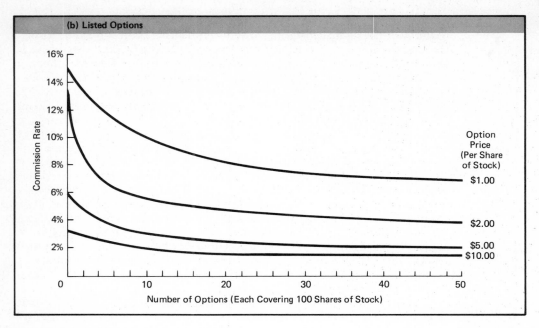

(b) Listed Options

Option
Price
(Per Share
of Stock)

$1.00

$2.00

$5.00
$10.00

Number of Options (Each Covering 100 Shares of Stock)

Commission Rate

FIGURE 2-1 (Continued)

INVESTMENT BANKING

New securities are said to be sold in the *primary market*. A few issuers—most notably, the U.S. government—deal directly with purchasers, but the majority rely on *investment bankers*, who serve as intermediaries between issuers and the ultimate purchasers of their securities.

Investment banking services are performed by brokers and dealers and, for tax-exempt general obligation bond issues, by banks. In some instances only a few large institutional investors are solicited, and the entire issue is sold to one or more of them. Such *private placements* are frequently used for bond issues. As long as relatively few potential buyers are contacted (e.g., less than 25), requirements for detailed disclosure, public notice, and so on may be waived, considerably reducing the cost of floating an issue. Such placements are often announced after the fact, via advertisements in the financial press.

When public sale is contemplated, much more must be done. Many firms may serve as intermediaries in the process. One, acting as the "lead" investment banker, will put together a *purchase group* or *syndicate* and a *selling group*. The former includes firms that purchase the securities from the issuing corporation and *underwrite* the offering; the latter includes firms that contact potential buyers and do the actual selling, usually on a commission basis.

The process begins with discussions between the issuing corporation and one or more investment bankers. Some issuers utilize *competitive bidding*, then select the investment banker offering the best overall terms.[11] This procedure is used for many government bond issues and is required by law for securities issued by firms in certain regulated industries. However, most corporations maintain a continuing relationship with a single investment banker and *negotiate* the terms of each new offering with that firm. The investment banker is likely to be heavily involved in the planning of an offering, the terms involved, the amount to be offered, and so on and serves, in effect, as a financial consultant to the corporation.

Once the basic characteristics of an offering have been established, a *registration statement* is filed with the Securities and Exchange Commission, and a preliminary prospectus disclosing material relevant to the prospective buyer is issued. The actual price of the security is not included in the preliminary prospectus, and no final sales may be made until the registration becomes *effective* and a *final prospectus* issued indicating the "offer" price at which the stock will be sold. The final prospectus may be issued as soon as, in the opinion of the Securities and Exchange Commission, there has been adequate disclosure and a reasonable waiting period has passed (usually, 20 days). The Commission, however, does not take a position regarding the investment merits of an offering or the reasonableness of the price.

A security issue may be completely underwritten by an investment banker and the other members of the purchasing group. If it is, the issuing corporation receives the public offering price less a stated percentage spread (although underwriters will occasionally be compensated with shares, warrants, etc.). The underwriters, in turn, sell the securities at the public offering price or less and may take some of the securities themselves. Underwriters who provide this sort of *firm commitment* bear all the risk once the price and underwriting spread have been determined.

Not all agreements are of this type. In the case of a rights offering an underwriter may agree to purchase at a fixed price all securities not taken by current stockholders; this is termed a *standby agreement*. In the case of a nonrights offering, members of an investment banking group may serve as agents instead of dealers, agreeing only to handle an offering on a *best-efforts* basis.

During the period when new securities remain unsold, the investment banker is allowed to attempt to "stabilize" the price of the security in the secondary market by standing ready to make purchases at or above the offering price. Such *pegging* may continue for up to ten days after the official offering date. There is a limit to the amount that can be purchased in this manner, usually stated in the agreement under which the underwriting syndicate is formed, since the members typically share the cost of such transactions. If there is to be any pegging, a statement to the effect must be included in the prospectus.

In any security transaction there may be explicit and implicit costs. In a primary distribution the explicit cost is the underwriting spread, and

---

[11] Many state and local governments determine the "best terms" for a bond issue by computing a figure called the "net interest cost" (NIC) that ignores the time value of money. For a discussion of this problem and the savings obtained by using the true interest cost (TIC), see Michael C. Hopewell and George G. Kaufman, "Costs to Municipalities of Selling Bonds by NIC," *National Tax Journal*, XXVII, no. 4 (December 1974), 531–42.

the implicit cost is any difference between the public offering price and the price that might have been obtained otherwise. The spread provides compensation for both marketing services and risk-bearing. The lower the public offering price, the smaller the risk that the issue will not be sold quickly at that price. If an issue is substantially underpriced, the investment banking syndicate can be assured that the securities will sell rapidly, requiring little or no support in the secondary market. Since many corporations deal with only one investment banker, and since the larger investment banking firms rely on each other for inclusion in syndicates, it has been alleged that issuers pay too much in spreads, given the prices at which their securities are offered. In other words, the returns to underwriting are asserted to be overly large relative to the risks involved, owing to ignorance on the part of issuers and/or the existence of an informal cartel among investment bankers.

Whether or not this is the case, on average new issues do appear to be underpriced. Figure 2-2 shows the *abnormal returns* for a group of common stock new issues underwritten from 1960 to 1969. For each of the first 60 months after the initial offering (horizontal axis) the return over and above that of stocks of equal risk is shown (vertical axis). The leftmost point indicates the abnormal return obtained by an investor who purchased such stock at its offering price and sold it for the bid price at the end of the month during which it was offered. The amount was substantial: 11.4% in a month or less (and significantly different from zero in a statistical sense). The remaining points show the returns that could have been obtained by an investor who was able to purchase the security at the bid price at the end of one month and sell it at the bid price at the end of the next month. Some of these were positive, but only one was sig-

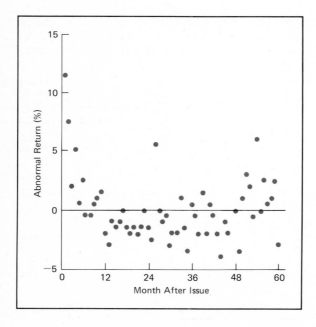

FIGURE 2-2 Abnormal Returns: 112 Common Stock New Issues, 1960–1969

Source: Roger G. Ibbotson, "Price Performance of Common Stock New Issues," *Journal of Financial Economics, 2,* no. 3 (September 1975), 252. By permission of North-Holland Publishing Co., Amsterdam.

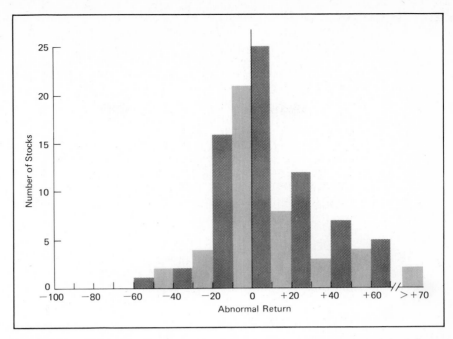

FIGURE 2-3 Abnormal Return from Offering Price to Bid Price at the End of the Offering Month, 112 Common Stock New Issues, 1960–1969

Source: Roger G. Ibbotson, "Price Performance of Common Stock New Issues," *Journal of Financial Economics, 2*, no. 3 (September 1975), 235–72. By permission of North-Holland Publishing Co., Amsterdam.

nificantly different from zero. Moreover, none was large enough to overcome the transactions costs associated with in-and-out trades on the secondary market—i.e., the fact that the ask prices, at which sales would be made, were 6% to 7% greater than the bid prices.

On average, new issues of "unseasoned" securities appear to be underpriced. Investors able to purchase a cross section of such shares at their offering prices can expect better performance than those holding other securities of equal risk. Thus it is not surprising that such offerings are often rationed by the members of the selling group to "favored" customers. It is "not uncommon for underwriters to receive, prior to the effective date, public 'indication of interest' for five times the number of shares available."[12] Unfavored customers are presumably allowed to buy only the new issues that are not substantially underpriced. And since costs may be incurred in becoming a "favored" customer, it is not clear that even such an investor obtains abnormally large returns overall.

While the return obtained by the purchaser of a new issue is substantial on average, the amount may be very good or very bad in any particular instance, as Figure 2-3 shows. While the odds are in the purchaser's favor, a single investment of this type is far from a sure bet.

[12] Securities and Exchange Commission, *Report of Special Study on Security Markets*, 1973.

BLOCK SALES

An individual or institution wishing to sell a large block of stock can do so in either of two ways. A brokerage firm may be asked to find one or more buyers and perhaps to take some of the position itself, or the stock may be sold through a *secondary distribution*. An investment banking group buys the block from the seller and then offers the shares publicly at a stated price; in a typical case the shares are first offered after normal trading hours at the day's closing price. The buyer of shares in a secondary distribution pays no commission, and the original seller receives the total proceeds less an underwriting spread (often, 4% to 5%).[13]

The Securities and Exchange Commission requires that a secondary distribution be registered, with public announcement and disclosure and a 20-day waiting period, if the seller has a "control relationship" with the firm that issued the securities. Otherwise the distribution may be unregistered.

The impact of the sale of a large block on a stock's price provides information on the resiliency of the capital market. The information that someone is selling may be expected to lower price. But even a large portion of a company's stock is a small amount compared with all outstanding securities, and one would not expect a block sale to depress price so much that it later bounces back significantly, as the market "absorbs" the shares.

Figure 2-4 provides confirmation for this hypothesis. It shows the average price adjusted for market changes for 345 secondary distributions, with the price 25 days prior to the distribution taken as 1.0. On average, a secondary distribution leads to 2% to 3% once-and-for-all reduction in price. This is undoubtedly due to the information content of the fact that someone has decided to sell. Additional analysis of these results supports the assertion. The magnitude of the decline was not related to the size of the distribution, measured by the dollar amount or the percentage of the outstanding shares of the corporation. But the decline was related to the

[13] Alan Kraus and Hans Stoll, "Price Impacts of Block Trading on the New York Stock Exchange," *The Journal of Finance*, XXVII, no. 3 (June 1972), 569–88.

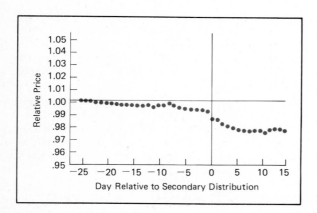

FIGURE 2-4 Prices for 345 Secondary Distributions, 1961–1965

Source: Myron S. Scholes, "The Market for Securities: Substitution versus Price Pressure and the Effects of Information on Share Prices." *The Journal of Business*, 45, no. 2 (April 1972). 179–211. © 1972 by the University of Chicago. All Rights Reserved.

TABLE 2-2 Average Price Decline versus Type of Seller: 345 Secondary Distributions, 1961–1965

Type of Seller	Percentage Change in Adjusted Price from Ten Days before the Distribution to Ten Days after the Distribution
Corporations and officers	2.9
Investment companies and mutual funds	2.5
Individuals	1.1
Estates	.7
Banks and insurance companies	.3

Source: Myron S. Scholes, "The Market for Securities: Substitution versus Price Pressure and the Effects of Information on Share Prices," *The Journal of Business*, 45, no. 2 (April 1972), 179–211. © 1972 by the University of Chicago. All Rights Reserved.

identity of the seller—being the greatest for sellers likely to be information-motivated and smallest for sellers likely to be liquidity-motivated, as shown in Table 2-2.

A similar picture was obtained when blocks of stock traded on the New York Stock Exchange were examined. To select transactions likely to have been initiated by a seller, blocks sold on a "minus tick"—at a price below that of the previous trade—were used. Figure 2-5 shows the results. The vertical axis plots the average price, adjusted for market moves, relative to that 20 days before the block trade. There appears to be a once-and-for-all decline of about 2% due to the information content of the knowledge that someone wishes to sell a large block.

FIGURE 2-5 Prices for 1,121 Large-Block Trades on Minus Ticks, Traded on the New York Stock Exchange, 1968–1969

Source: Alan Kraus and Hans Stoll, "Price Impacts of Block Trading on the New York Stock Exchange," *The Journal of Finance,* XXVII, no. 3 (June 1972), 580.

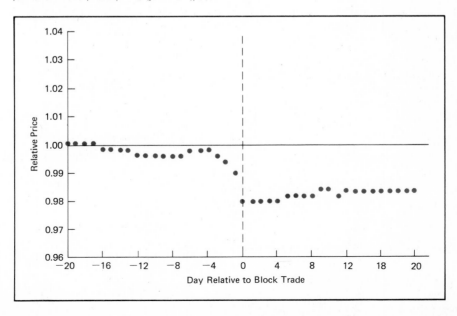

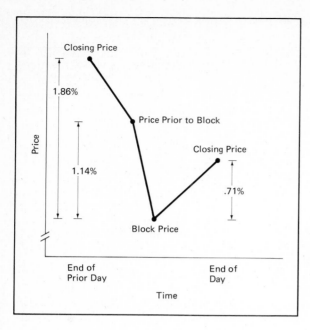

FIGURE 2-6 Within-Day Prices for 1,121 Large Block Trades on Minus Ticks, Traded on the New York Stock Exchange, 1968–1969

Source: Alan Kraus and Hans Stoll, "Price Impacts of Block Trading on the New York Stock Exchange," *The Journal of Finance,* XXVII, no. 3 (June 1972), 575.

Examination of the price behavior during the day on which a block is sold does reveal a small price-pressure effect, however. As Figure 2-6 shows, a block sale appears to depress price temporarily by an average amount of about .7%.

REGULATION OF SECURITY MARKETS

Directly or indirectly, security markets in the United States are regulated under both federal and state laws.

The *Securities Act of 1933* was the first major legislation at the federal level. Sometimes called the "truth in securities" law, it requires registration of new issues and disclosure of relevant information by the issuer and prohibits misrepresentation and fraud in security sales.

The *Securities Exchange Act of 1934* extended the principles of the earlier Act to cover secondary markets and required national exchanges and brokers and dealers to be registered.

Since 1934, both Acts (and subsequent amendments to them) have been administered by the *Securities and Exchange Commission* (SEC), a quasi-judicial agency of the U.S. government. It is run by five Commissioners appointed by the President and confirmed by the Senate; each Commissioner serves for a five-year term. The Commission is aided by a large permanent staff of lawyers, accountants, economists, and others.

The SEC is the prime administrative agency for a number of other pieces of federal legislation. The *Public Utility Holding Company Act of 1935* brought such corporations under the Commission's jurisdiction. The

Bankruptcy Act of 1938 specified that the Commission should advise the court in any reorganization of a firm under Chapter X whenever there is substantial public interest in the firm's securities. The *Trust Indenture Act of 1939* gave the Commission power to insure that bond indenture trustees were free from conflict of interest. The *Investment Company Act of 1940* extended disclosure and registration requirements to investment companies. The *Investment Advisers Act of 1940* required the registration of most advisers and the disclosure of any potential conflicts of interest. The *Securities Investor Protection Act of 1970* provided for the coverage of losses in the event of failure of a brokerage firm.

Federal securities legislation relies heavily on the principle of *self-regulation*. The SEC has delegated to exchanges its power to control trading practices for listed securities, while retaining, however, the power to alter or supplement any resulting rules or regulations. The Commission's power to control trading in over-the-counter securities has been delegated similarly to the *National Association of Securities Dealers* (NASD), a private association of brokers and dealers in OTC securities. In practice the SEC staff usually discusses proposed changes with both the NASD and the exchanges in advance, and few rules are formally altered or rejected by the Commission.

An important piece of legislation that makes security markets in the United States different from those in many other countries is the (Glass-Steagall) *Banking Act of 1933*, which separates commercial banking from investment banking. While exceptions are granted, and affiliated firms owned by bank holding companies are subject to fewer restrictions, because of this act banks have not played as prominent a role in security markets in the United States as elsewhere.

Initially, security regulation in the United States was the province of state governments. Beginning in 1911, state *blue sky laws* were passed to prevent "speculative schemes which have no more basis than so many feet of blue sky."[14] While such statutes vary substantially from state to state, most outlaw fraud in security sales, require registration of brokers and dealers (and, in some cases, investment advisers) and the registration of nonexempt securities. Some order has been brought by the passage in many states of all or part of the *Uniform Securities Acts* proposed by the National Conference of Commissions on Uniform State Laws in 1956.

Securities traded in interstate commerce, and brokers, dealers, and exchanges trading in interstate commerce, fall under the provisions of federal legislation (although some have been explicitly exempted under its terms). A considerable domain still comes under the exclusive jurisdiction of the states. Moreover, federal legislation only supplements state legislation, it does not supplant it. Some argue that the investor is overprotected as a result, while others suggest that regulatory agencies in general, and especially those that rely on "self-regulation" by powerful industry organizations, in fact protect the members of the regulated industry against competition, thereby damaging the interests of their customers rather than promoting them. Both positions undoubtedly contain elements of truth.

---

[14] *Hall v. Geiger-Jones Co.*, 242 U.S. 539 (1917).

Problems

1. New York Stock Exchange specialists are expected to make trades to maintain a "fair and orderly market." This is sometimes taken to mean that they should trade for their own accounts as required to avoid sudden and substantial price changes. Under what conditions would this be desirable? Under what conditions would it be profitable for the specialist?

2. What dangers are associated with placing a market order? A limit order?

3. Ted Turner wants to buy 100 shares of Silicon Valley Products, which is currently selling for $31 per share. Assume that initial margin requirements permit him to borrow 40% of the current stock price, and maintenance margin regulations require him to have a 25% equity position in the account at all times. If he borrows initially as much as possible in buying the 100 shares, at what price would he be subject to a margin call?

4. Some time after Ted Turner bought Silicon Valley Products, Sally Stanford sold 100 shares short at $31 per share. Initial margin on short sales was then 50%, and maintenance margin regulations required that she have an equity position equal to 30% of the value of the shorted stock. If she put up as little cash as possible at the time she sold SVP short, at what price would she be subject to a margin call?

5. What is the justification for the rule that short sales should not be made in falling markets? What is the counterargument? What problems might be involved in implementing this with competing, but not centralized, markets?

6. As a practical matter, who gets the proceeds from a short sale? What are the costs of such a sale to the short-seller?

7. Commissions on large trades are typically a smaller percentage of the value of the trade than are commissions on small trades. Is this discriminatory?

Investment Value and Market Price

3

INVESTMENT VALUE: AN OVERVIEW

Payments provided by securities may differ in both timing and riskiness. Thus a security analyst must estimate *when* and *under what conditions* payments will be received (and, of course, the magnitude of such payments). This typically requires detailed analysis of the company involved, the industry or industries in which the company operates, and the economy as a whole. Once such estimates have been made, the overall value of the security must be determined. This generally requires conversion of *uncertain future* values to equivalent *certain present* values. The current prices of other securities can usually be utilized in this process. If it is possible to obtain a similar set of prospects in some other way, the going market price of doing so provides a benchmark for the investment value of the security being analyzed, since one would not want to pay more than this for the security nor sell it for less. In some cases, however, equivalent alternatives may not exist and/or the mere act of buying or selling the security in question in the quantities being considered might substantially affect the price. Under these conditions the preferences of the investor may have to be utilized explicitly in the process of estimating the security's investment value.

The next few chapters discuss in detail the manner in which estimated future prospects can be used to determine investment value. Methods for estimating prospects and finding equivalent alternatives will be discussed in later chapters, after the characteristics of relevant investment media have been introduced. We thus deal first with the general principles of investment value, leaving procedures designed for specific types of securities for later.

SECURITY PRICE DETERMINATION

Although there are over 500 million shares of American Telephone and Telegraph common stock outstanding, on an average day only between 100 and 200 thousand shares are traded. What determines the prices at which such trades take place? A simple (and correct) answer is: demand and supply. A more fundamental (and also correct) answer is: investors' estimates of A.T.&T.'s future prospects, for such estimates greatly influence demand and supply. Before dealing with such influences, it is useful to examine the role of demand and supply in price determination.

As we have seen, securities are traded by many people in many different ways. While the forces that determine price are similar in all markets, they are slightly more obvious in markets using periodic "calls"; one such is the Paris Bourse (stock exchange).

At a designated time, all brokers holding orders to buy or sell a given stock for customers gather at a specified location on the floor of the exchange. Some of the orders are "market" orders. For example, Mr. Ricard may have instructed his broker to buy 100 shares of Michelin at the lowest possible price, whatever it might be. His demand to buy shares at the time is shown by the solid line in Figure 3-1(a): he wishes to buy 100 shares no matter what the price. While this captures the contractual nature of a market buy order, Mr. Ricard undoubtedly has a good idea that the price of Michelin will be near its previous day's value, say 950 francs per share. His true demand curve might be more like the dashed line in the figure, indicating his desire to buy more shares, the lower the price. But to simplify his and his broker's tasks, he has guessed that the price will be in the range in which he would choose to buy 100 shares.

FIGURE 3-1 Individuals' Demand-to-Buy and Supply-to-Sell Curves

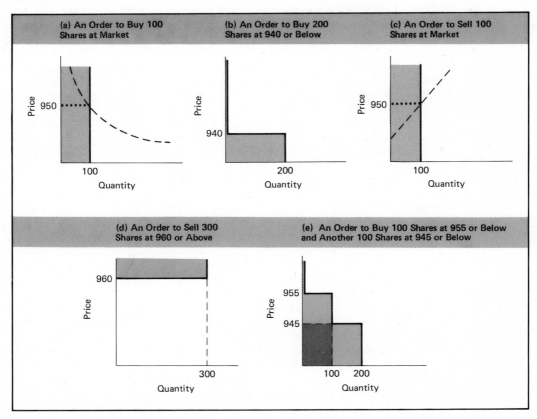

Other customers may place limit orders. Thus Mr. Dufour may have instructed his broker to buy 200 shares at the lowest possible price if and only if that price is below 940 francs per share. His demand to buy shares is plotted in Figure 3-1(b).

Brokers will also hold market and limit orders to sell shares of Michelin. The solid vertical line in Figure 3-1(c) plots the supply curve for a customer who has placed a market order for 100 shares—i.e., asked his broker to sell 100 of his shares at the highest possible price. As with market buy orders, customers generally place such orders on the supposition that the actual price will be in the range in which their true desire is to sell the stated number of shares. Thus the customer's actual supply curve might appear more like the dashed line in Figure 3-1(c), indicating his willingness to sell more shares, the higher the price. Figure 3-1(d) plots the supply curve for a customer who has placed a limit order to sell 300 shares at the highest possible price, but only if the price exceeds 960 francs per share.

Some customers may give their broker two or more orders for the same security. Thus Madame Point may wish to buy 100 shares at a price of 955 and 200 shares if the price falls below 945. To do this, she places a limit order for 100 shares at 955 and a second limit order for 100 shares at 945. Her total demand to buy shares is plotted in Figure 3-1(e).

If one could look at all the brokers' books and summarize all the orders to buy (both market and limit orders), it would be possible to determine how many shares would be bought at every possible price. The resulting *demand-to-buy* curve would have an appearance like that of Figure 3-2(a): at lower prices, more shares would be demanded. Similarly, all the orders to sell (both market and limit) could be used to determine how many shares would be sold at every possible price. The resulting *supply-to-sell* curve would have an appearance like that of Figure 3-2(b): at higher prices, more shares would be supplied.

The demand and supply curves are both shown in Figure 3-2(c). Generally, no one will have enough information to draw the actual curves. But this in no way diminishes their usefulness as representations of the underlying forces acting to determine price.

What actually happens when all the brokers gather together with their order books in hand? A clerk of the exchange "calls out" a price—for example, 940 francs per share. Brokers proceed to try to complete transactions with one another. Those with orders to buy at that price signify the number of shares they wish to buy. Those with orders to sell do likewise. Some deals will be made, but as Figure 3-2(c) shows, more shares will be demanded at 940 than will be supplied. When trading dies down, a number of brokers will be calling "buy" and none will stand ready to sell to them. The price was too low.

The clerk, seeing this, will cry out a different price, say 960. The brokers then consult their order books and signify the extent to which they are willing to buy or sell shares at this price. In this case, as the figure shows, when trading dies down, there will be a number of brokers calling "sell" and none will stand ready to buy from them. The price was too high.

Undaunted, the clerk will try again. And again, if necessary. Only

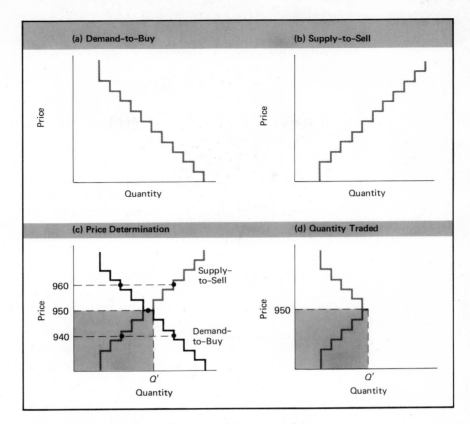

FIGURE 3-2 Aggregate Demand-to-Buy and Supply-to-Sell Curves

when there are relatively few unsatisfied brokers will the price be declared final. As Figure 3-2(c) shows, 950 is such a price. At 950, customers collectively wish to sell Q' shares. Quantity demanded equals quantity supplied. The price was "just right."

Another way to view this process focuses on the quantity actually traded. This will be the *smaller* of (1) the quantity people are willing to buy and (2) the quantity others are willing to sell. This is shown in Figure 3-2(d). At a price of 950 the quantity traded is maximized. The procedure used to determine the price thus maximizes trading as well as equating the quantity demanded with the quantity supplied.

Trading procedures employed in security markets vary, from auction markets to dealer markets and from periodic to almost continuous trading. But the similarities are more important than the differences. For example, in the United States, specialists at the New York Stock Exchange and dealers in the over-the-counter market provide some of the functions of the clerk at the Paris Bourse, and trades can take place at any time. But the basic principles of price determination still operate. In general, market price equates quantity demanded with quantity supplied.

THE DEMAND TO HOLD SECURITIES

While brokers' order books reflect some customers' attitudes at a particular time, not all relevant information is contained there. For example, many holders of a security who would be delighted to sell it at prices substantially higher than those obtained in recent trades simply do not bother placing corresponding limit orders with their brokers, since they think it unlikely that such orders would be executed under current conditions. Thus order books may indicate a supply to sell shares such as that shown by the solid curve in Figure 3-3(a), while the full situation is that shown by the dashed curve. At prices substantially higher than the current range (around P in the figure), more sell orders would be placed. And, as indicated earlier, if sellers thought price might fall substantially below P, some of the current market orders might be withdrawn.

A similar argument applies to the demand to buy shares. Many who would be willing to buy shares under current conditions at substantially lower prices than experienced in recent trades do not bother to place corresponding limit orders. And if substantially higher prices were likely, some customers would withdraw their market orders. Thus the full demand-to-buy curve would appear more like the dashed curve in Figure 3-3(b) than the solid curve, which reflects only the current orders on the books.

Demand and supply curves based on unexecuted orders on the books have another characteristic: they change frequently, as orders are executed. This is of major importance for understanding the forces determining the *volume* of trading. However, there need be no direct relationship between such volume and price. For example, if a new tax law redistributes income from one group to another, the former may sell shares to the latter, causing great volume but little or no overall impact on price. Similarly, a piece of information may be regarded by some as bad news and by others as good news; members of the former group may sell shares

FIGURE 3-3 Actual versus Potential Orders

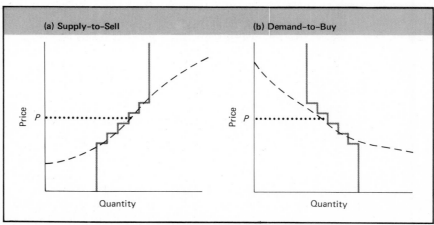

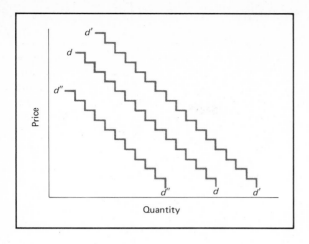

FIGURE 3-4 An Individual's Demand-to-Hold Curve

to members of the latter group, enriching brokers but affecting price little if at all. On the other hand, if a piece of good news about a company is released, people may raise their estimates of the value of the company's stock by similar amounts, generating little trading. These are, however, extreme examples. Usually a change in price will be accompanied by larger-than-normal volume. For instance, some investors will value good news more highly than others, leading to a situation in which substantial trading can and will take place. Major price changes (in either direction) are usually accompanied by abnormally large trading volume.

For some purposes it is useful to abstract entirely from moment-to-moment changes in customers' orders and focus instead on the fundamental forces at work. Instead of asking how many shares an investor wishes to *buy* at a given price, we seek to determine the number of shares he or she wishes to *hold* at that price. There is, of course, a close relationship between the two quantities. If an investor wishes to hold more shares than he or she currently has, the difference is his or her demand to buy. Conversely, if he or she wishes to hold fewer shares than currently owned, the difference is his or her supply to sell.

In Figure 3-4 one investor's *demand-to-hold* curve for a security is shown by curve *dd*. This simply plots the number of shares he or she wishes to hold at each possible price. The lower the price, in general, the larger the number of shares. Of course, the entire curve is predicated on the investor's current feelings about the security's future prospects. If something makes one more optimistic, he or she will generally wish to hold more shares at any given price—the entire curve may shift to the right, as shown by curve *d'd'*. On the other hand, if something makes one more pessimistic, the entire curve may shift to the left, as shown by curve *d"d"*.

A factor that complicates analysis of this type is the tendency for some investors to regard sudden and substantial price changes as indicators of changes in a company's future prospects. In the absence of further information, an investor may well interpret such a change as an indication that "someone knows something." While exploring the situation,

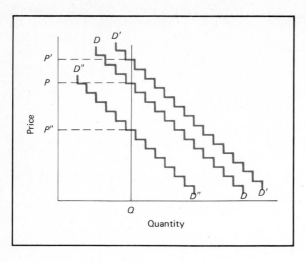

FIGURE 3-5 Aggregate Demand-to-Hold and Available Quantity

he or she may at least temporarily revise his or her own assessment of the company's prospects and *demand-to-hold* curve in the same direction. For this reason, few investors place limit orders at prices substantially different from the current trading range, for fear that such orders would be executed only if prospects changed significantly, giving recognition to the idea that a careful reevaluation would be in order before buying or selling shares under such conditions.

Despite this complication, it is possible to construct an aggregate curve indicating the total number of shares that investors will wish to hold at any given price, assuming no change in their current views of the relevant prospects. This overall demand-to-hold curve would have an appearance like that of curve DD in Figure 3-5. In the short run, at least, the available stock of any security to be held is fixed, for example, at Q in the figure. Only one free-market price will equate the demand-to-hold with the available number of shares. In Figure 3-5 it is P. At any higher price, current holders will collectively wish to hold fewer shares than are outstanding. In their attempts to sell such shares, they will drive price down until they or others are willing to hold the stock. Conversely, if price is below P, investors will collectively wish to hold more shares than are outstanding. In their attempts to buy such shares, they will drive price up until they no longer want additional shares and/or others are willing to provide them.

How flat will be the demand-to-hold curve for a security? The answer depends in part on the extent to which it is regarded as unique. The closer the available substitutes, the more elastic (flat) will be the demand curve: at lower-than-competitive prices the security will be in great demand. The poorer the substitutes, the less elastic will be the demand curve: given future prospects, a fall in price will make the security more attractive and investors will want to increase their holdings, but doing so will typically make their portfolios more risky, since the new shares cannot simply be substituted for others with similar prospects and higher prices. The dangers associated with putting all one's eggs into the same basket limit the magnitude of an investor's response to changes in a security's price. The response to a given price change will thus be smaller, the more unique the security.

If one investor becomes more optimistic about the prospects for a security while another becomes more pessimistic, they may very likely trade with one another with no effect on the overall demand-to-hold and thus on the price. On the other hand, if some investors become more optimistic and no one becomes more pessimistic, the curve may shift to the right, for example to $D'D'$, causing an increase in price, to P'. An increase in pessimism, not offset by concurrent increases in optimism, would be likely to shift the curve to the left, for example to $D''D''$, causing a decrease in price, to P''.

THE EFFECTS OF PROCEDURES FOR SHORT SALES

Thus far we have drawn the individual's demand-to-hold curve only in the region of positive quantities. But there is more to it: the higher the price, the smaller the quantity an investor will wish to hold. At some point the desired amount is zero. And if the price is very high, a short sale will be considered.

If short-sellers received the proceeds from such sales, an individual's demand-to-hold a security would look like the curve in Figure 3-6(a), which can be read in either of two ways: as a *demand curve* (i.e., at price A the person wishes to hold quantity B) or as a *marginal-value curve* (i.e., if quantity B is held, the marginal value of one share more or less will be A).

FIGURE 3-6(a) Demand-to-Hold and Marginal Value with Proceeds Received from Short Sales

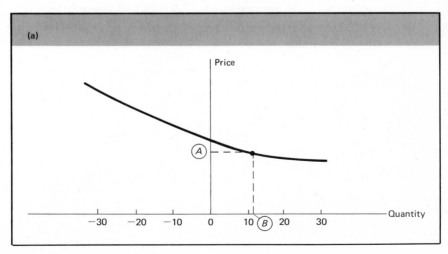

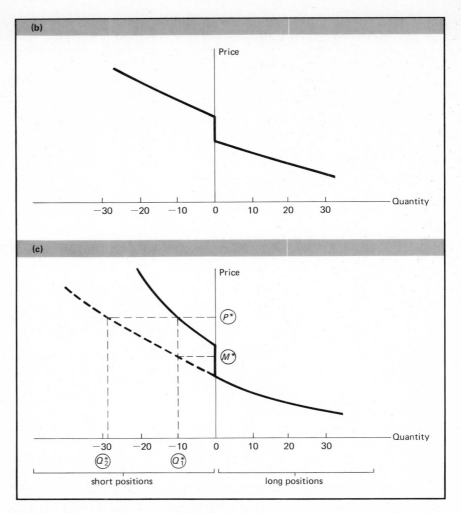

FIGURE 3-6(b) Demand-to-Hold with Typical Short Sales Procedures; **(c)** Demand-to-Hold and Marginal Value with Typical Short Sales Procedures

In fact, short-sellers do not receive the proceeds of such sales—they are escrowed to protect the lender of the security. And in most instances no interest is paid on that money. This changes the situation. Selling a security one owns generates cash that can be used for other purposes (e.g., it could earn interest). But selling a security one doesn't own generates no cash. Thus the decision to go short requires a higher price than it would otherwise. The effective demand-to-hold curve looks like the curve in Figure 3-6(b). To the right of the vertical axis it is the same as the original marginal-value curve, but to the left it is above it.

Two effects of this are shown in Figure 3-6(c). The solid curve is the effective demand-to-hold curve. The dashed curve is the original demand and marginal-value curve. If the current price of the security is P^*, this person will go short only Q_1^* shares, instead of Q_2^*. His or her pessimism about the security will thus not have as much impact on the market as it would otherwise. In a sense the person chooses a holding (Q_1^*) at which he or she considers the marginal value (M^*) to be less than the current market price (P^*).

PRICE AS A CONSENSUS

However one chooses to analyze price determination, it is important to remember that a free-market price for a security reflects a kind of consensus. This can be seen in Figures 3-7. The current price is P^*. Some individuals hold the security. For each of them the situation is like that shown in Figure 3-7(a); they will have adjusted their portfolios so that the marginal value of a share equals its market price. A few individuals will be short the security. Their situation is like that shown in Figure 3-7(b). Because of the short-sales rules each will have taken a position at which the marginal value of a share is in a sense less than the price. Many investors will choose to hold no shares. Their situation is shown in Figure 3-7(c). For each of them marginal value is equal to or (in the case shown) somewhat below the price.

Were it not for the short-selling rules, every investor would adjust portfolio holdings until the marginal value of a security to him or her equaled its price. Since the going price is the same for everyone, so would be the marginal value for all investors (at least all who paid attention to the market). Price would clearly represent a consensus of investor opinion about value.

The short-selling rules change the situation, but only slightly. Since some investors (primarily pessimists) might choose holdings at which marginal value is below the market price, the price could be slightly higher than an average of investors' marginal values.

The impact of the rules for short sales is, however, likely to be small in practice. Even for the short-seller, the disparity between price and marginal value may be small. For those who hold no shares it will be smaller yet (or zero). And for those who hold shares it will be zero. Moreover, short positions are typically a small fraction of long positions. For practical purposes price can reasonably be considered equal to a consensus opinion of investors concerning marginal investment value. For it to be seriously in error as an estimate of that value, many investors must be poorly informed and/or poor analysts. Moreover, there must be either (1) a preponderance of such investors with overly optimistic forecasts or (2) a preponderance of such investors with overly pessimistic forecasts. Otherwise, the actions of the poorly informed and foolish will cancel each other, making the consensus opinion—price—a good estimate of the value of the future prospects of the security (certain or uncertain).

FIGURE 3-7(a) An Investor with a Long Position; **(b)** An Investor with a Short Position; **(c)** An Investor with a Zero Holding

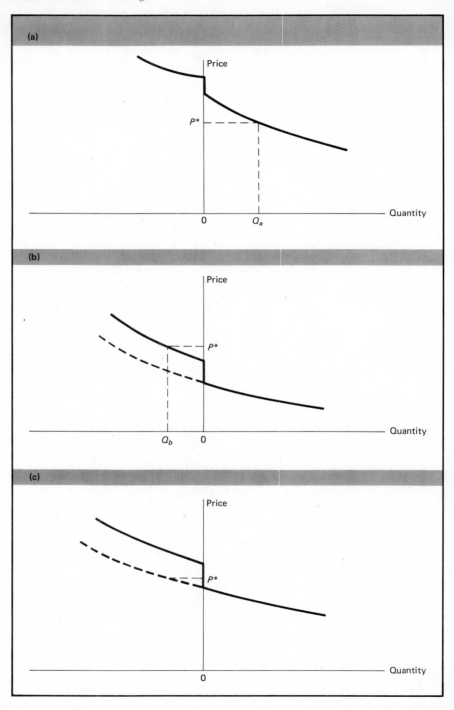

MARKET EFFICIENCY

Imagine a world in which (1) all investors have access to currently available information about the future, (2) all are good analysts, and (3) all pay close attention to market prices and adjust their holdings appropriately. The prices that would lead to an equilibrium in such a market can be termed the *investment values* of the securities.

We can now define an *efficient market:*

A (perfectly) efficient market is one in which every security's price equals its investment value at all times.

In an efficient market a set of information is fully and immediately reflected in prices. But what information? A popular taxonomy is the following.[1]

Form of Efficiency	Information fully reflected in Security Prices
Strong	All currently known
Semistrong	All publicly available
Weak	Previous prices of securities

As we will see, major securities markets appear to conform well to the model of weak-form efficiency and quite well to the model of semistrong efficiency (although lack of a precise meaning for "publicly available" makes this definition slightly ambiguous). The strong form is, as the term suggests, strong, and we will see that markets are not generally efficient in this sense.

In an efficient market any *new* information would be immediately and fully reflected in prices. New information is just that: *new*—a *surprise* (anything that is not a surprise is predictable and should have been predicted before the fact). Since happy surprises are about as likely as unhappy ones, *price changes* in an efficient market are about as likely to be positive as negative. While one might *expect* a security's price to move enough to give (in conjunction with dividend or interest payments) a reasonable return on capital, anything above or below this would, in such a market, be *unpredictable*. In a perfectly efficient market, price changes would be more or less *random*.

Now consider a crazy market, in which prices never bear any particular relationship to investment value. In such a world, price changes would also be random!

Major securities markets are certainly not crazy. They may not attain perfect efficiency, but they are certainly much closer to it than to craziness. As we will see, there is ample evidence that such markets are at least *nearly efficient*. To understand real markets, it is important to understand perfectly efficient markets.

[1] Eugene Fama, "Efficient Capital Markets: A Review of Theory and Empirical Work," *Journal of Finance*, May 1970.

In an *efficient market*, a security's price will be a good estimate of its investment value, i.e., the present value of its future prospects as estimated by well-informed and clever analysts. Any substantial disparity between price and value would reflect market in efficiency. In a well-developed and free market, such inefficiencies are rare. The reason is not hard to find. Major disparities between price and investment value will be quickly noted by alert analysts who will seek to take advantage of their discoveries. Securities priced below value will be purchased, creating pressure for price increases due to increased demand-to-buy. Securities priced above value will be sold, creating pressure for price decreases due to increased supply-to-sell. As investors seek to exploit opportunities created by temporary inefficiencies they will cause the inefficiencies to disappear, denying the less alert and/or less informed any chance to obtain abnormal profits.

In the United States there are thousands of professional security analysts and more amateurs. Not surprisingly, the major U.S. securities markets appear to be quite efficient, as do those of other major countries.

Problems

1. On the day that Congress passed by a small margin a bill increasing the tax on oil companies, the prices of the stocks of such companies actually went up, even though most stocks fell on that day. Does this suggest that the market is inefficient?

2. Is bad news always bad for stocks in the sense that it will cause their prices to fall?

3. If short-sale rules make price larger than the average marginal value as assessed by investors, then one might assume that the disparity would be greater for stocks about which there is the greatest diversity of opinion. If so, might such stocks continually be overpriced relative to others?

4. When a firm reports its earnings for a period, the volume of transactions in its stock typically increases, but often there is no significant change in price. How can this be explained?

5. Major officers and directors of corporations often make abnormally large profits from trades in the stocks of their own companies. Is this inconsistent with market efficiency?

The Valuation of
Riskless Securities

4

TIME AND RISK

In this world, it seems, nothing is riskless. Philosophically this may well be an appropriate position. However, some securities are clearly less risky than others, and as a useful first step in understanding valuation it is worthwhile to consider investments that are totally riskless, whether or not such extreme examples really exist.

In terms of *dollar* returns, the obvious candidates for this classification are the instruments representing the debt of the U.S. government. Since the government can print money whenever it chooses, the promised payments are virtually certain to be made on schedule. However, the ability and perhaps too frequent willingness of the government to create money raises the possibility of only partially predictable increases in the overall level of prices, with attendant uncertainty as to the purchasing power of the promised payments. While U.S. government bonds may be riskless in terms of dollar returns, they may be quite risky in terms of *real* returns—i.e., purchasing power.

This source of risk can be dealt with. For example, a number of governments have issued bonds whose payments are adjusted to compensate for changes in an index of their country's overall price level.

Of course, not all government debt is riskless with respect to nominal payments, let alone purchasing power, as holders of the bonds of Czarist Russia will testify.

Despite these important questions, in this chapter we will assume that there are securities whose returns are certain, and we will consider the factors that determine their values. To the extent that inflation is relevant, we will assume that its magnitude can be predicted. Such abstractions make it possible to focus on the impact of *time* on security valuation. Having accomplished this, we will then be in a position to expand our view to include *risk* as well.

INVESTMENT

To begin with the simplest possible case, let us analyze the plight of Robinson Crusoe. Poor Mr. Crusoe has been shipwrecked on an uninhabited island with little but a store of 20 bushels of corn. His knowl-

TABLE 4-1 Productivity of Crusoe's Land

Plot Number	Bushels of Corn Planted This Year on Plot	Yield in Bushels of Corn Harvested Next Year on Plot	Return on Investment on Plot (%)	Cumulative Yield from This Plus All Previous Plots
1	1	1.36	36	1.36
2	1	1.34	34	2.70
3	1	1.32	32	4.02
4	1	1.30	30	5.32
5	1	1.28	28	6.60
6	1	1.26	26	7.86
7	1	1.24	24	9.10
8	1	1.22	22	10.32
9	1	1.20	20	11.52
10	1	1.18	18	12.70
11	1	1.16	16	13.86
12	1	1.14	14	15.00
13	1	1.12	12	16.12
14	1	1.10	10	17.22
15	1	1.08	8	18.30
16	1	1.06	6	19.36
17	1	1.04	4	20.40
18	1	1.02	2	21.42
19	1	1.00	0	22.42
20	1	.98	−2	23.40

edge of shipping leads him to expect to be saved in two years. In the meantime he must decide how much corn to eat this year and how much to plant (i.e., invest) to obtain corn to eat next year. In keeping with the goals of this chapter, we assume the island is not subject to the vagaries of nature that plague most farmers; Crusoe can be certain of the results of whatever planting he undertakes.

After carefully surveying the island, Crusoe decides that there are 20 plots of arable land, each capable of taking one bushel of corn. The plots differ in exposure, soil quality, and so on. This is shown in Table 4-1, in which the plots are listed in decreasing order of yield. The best plot offers a return of 36% on an investment of one bushel of corn; the worst plot offers a negative return of −2%.

The shaded region in Figure 4-1 shows Mr. Crusoe's alternatives. He could, of course, eat all 20 bushels of corn this year, leaving him nothing to eat next year; this strategy plots at point A in the figure. If Crusoe chooses instead to plant one of his bushels of corn, reducing the amount eaten to 19 bushels, he can look forward to eating next year: the amount will be 1.36 bushels if he uses the best plot of land, keeps the birds from eating the corn, and so on.

If Crusoe chooses to invest two of his bushels of corn he will, unhappily, get less than twice as great a return. The incremental investment of one additional bushel of corn today yields only 1.34 bushels of corn next year. Why? Because poorer land must be used. This is simply a special case of the more general principle of diminishing returns. The more invested in an economy, the smaller is likely to be the return on each addi-

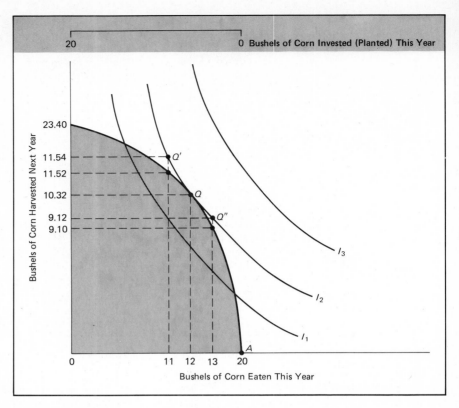

FIGURE 4-1 Consumption and Investment Selection

tional unit of investment. Since Crusoe is the entire economy of his island, the situation is quite typical.

    The shaded region in the figure portrays all the productive opportu-
nities shown in Table 4-1 for this simple economy. Which point will
Crusoe choose? The answer clearly depends on his feelings about present
versus future consumption. These feelings can be shown graphically by a
series of *indifference curves*, each one of which connects combinations
among which Crusoe is indifferent. For example, he considers any combination on curve I_1 as good as any other on that curve. Similarly, he considers any combination on curve I_2 as good as any other on that curve. Of
course, he would prefer a combination on I_2 over one on I_1, and a combination on I_3 over one on either I_2 or I_1. To keep from cluttering up the figure, only three of Crusoe's indifference curves have been drawn; many
more could, of course, be added.

    What will Crusoe do? From his available opportunities he will pick
the one he prefers. Graphically, this is the opportunity on the highest
(best) indifference curve, and it lies at a point where the curve touches but
does not cut (i.e., is tangent to) the opportunity region. In the figure,
this is shown by point Q: Crusoe chooses to eat 12 bushels of corn this

year, invest (plant) 8 (20 − 12) bushels of his initial stock and look forward to harvesting 10.32 bushels, all of which he will eat next year while waiting for his ship to come in.

What is the return on Crusoe's investment? He plants eight bushels of corn and harvests 10.32 bushels a year later. The rate of return is thus:

$$\frac{10.32 - 8}{8} = .29$$

or 29% per year.

This is the *overall* or *average* return on investment in the economy as a whole. But it is not the *incremental* or *marginal* rate of return. And the latter corresponds to the interest rate in a complex economy, as we will see.

Look closely at the area around point Q in Figure 4-1. What would happen if Crusoe decided to eat one more or one less bushel of corn this year? If he decided to eat one less bushel, the return on the extra bushel planted (invested) would be 20%—he could plan to eat 1.20 (11.52 − 10.32) bushels more next year. However, it would take 1.22 (11.54 − 10.32) bushels to keep him as happy as he is with combination Q, as shown by point Q'; for this reason he will not make the change. Looking the other way, the figure shows that if one more bushel were eaten this year, next year's consumption would be reduced by 1.22 (10.32 − 9.10) bushels, while Crusoe would be willing to reduce it by only 1.20 (10.32 − 9.12) bushels, as shown by point Q''; thus he will not make this change either.

While the effect of a change depends on both the type of change (up or down) and its magnitude, in the region of the chosen point the marginal effects are fairly similar. In this case Crusoe chooses a situation in which the marginal rate of return on investment is about 21% per year. Moreover, after he chooses the best available combination, the rate at which he is willing to trade present for future consumption is also about 21%.

INVESTMENT AND INTEREST

Let us move a step closer to reality by assuming that Crusoe is not alone. He has been preceded by Mr. Friday, who owns all the land on the island outright. However, Crusoe owns all the corn. If no one else were to intrude, the final outcome could depend on bargaining, cheating, skulduggery, or even war. To avoid such unpleasantries, let us assume that one of the clerks from the Paris Bourse is scheduled to drop by and "call out" a rate at which Crusoe and Friday can trade present corn for corn one year hence. Moreover, let us assume that both Crusoe and Friday take this rate as given, and they engage in no form of ruse trying to obtain a better rate by concealing their true desires. While this is hardly likely to be the case with two traders in a very small market, it is quite representative of most people's situation in a developed economy: for example, the interest rate at the local savings and loan is not likely to be affected by the magnitude of any single person's transactions. Since we are using Crusoe and Friday only to illustrate more complex economies, it makes sense to avoid diversion into matters of gamesmanship and potential violence.

Given a rate at which Friday can get corn, how much will he take? Assume that Crusoe will provide corn at a (corn) interest rate of 31%. In other words, for every bushel Friday takes, he must pay back 1.31 bushels next year. Referring to Table 4-1, one bushel clearly makes sense: Friday can clear a profit of .05 bushels (1.36 − 1.31) using his best plot of land. A second bushel will add .03 bushels (1.34 − 1.31) to his profit, if he plants it on his second-best plot. A third bushel will add another .01 bushels (1.32 − 1.31) to his profit. But any more would clearly be unprofitable. At an interest rate of 31%, Friday will take three bushels of corn. Figure 4-2 shows this, as well as the amount he will take at other interest rates. Not surprisingly, this is simply the information from Table 4-1, plotted in a different form. It shows the *marginal efficiency of (corn) capital* and is also the *demand for (corn) capital*. The lower the interest rate, the more investment will be profitable for producers such as Friday and the greater will be the quantity of capital demanded.

How much (corn) capital will Crusoe offer at various interest rates? The answer depends on his initial stock and his attitudes toward present versus future consumption. However, the situation shown in Figure 4-2 is typical: the higher the interest rate, the greater the amount of present consumption people are willing to forego in favor of future consumption. The *supply of capital* curve is upward-sloping.

FIGURE 4-2 Demand and Supply of Capital

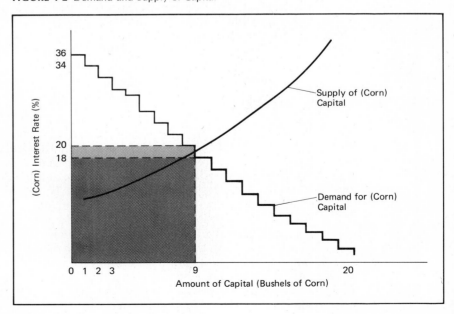

As in Paris, our visiting clerk wants to maximize the amount invested. Since this will be the smaller of (1) the amount Friday will take and (2) the amount Crusoe will provide, the appropriate interest rate, as shown in Figure 4-2, is about 19%. At this rate Crusoe will wish to supply nine bushels of corn in return for 10.71 (9 plus 19% of 9 = 1.19 × 9) bushels next year. Moreover, at this rate Friday will wish to take just nine bushels, knowing he will obtain a total yield of 11.52 bushels, leaving .81 bushels (11.52 − 10.71) in profit for his undertaking. (Not much, but a welcome supplement to his usual diet of fish.) Having arranged such a compatible situation, the clerk can steal silently away and return home.

THE INTEREST RATE

In the real world, there can be a little Friday and a little Crusoe in each of us. We all own some assets (if nothing else, ourselves) that can be invested or consumed. Further, most of us engage to some extent in production. However, this does not alter the key conclusions reached in the previous section. *In a free economy, interest rates will adjust until the total amount of capital demanded by producers equals the amount that owners of wealth are willing to supply.* Demand depends, at base, on productive opportunities, supply on preferences for present versus future consumption and on the ownership of wealth. Both affect the outcome and together determine the interest rate.

This is often difficult to see, since the day-to-day forces affecting interest rates appear to relate more to government policy, flotations of new securities by corporations, and so on. While such activities may have some impact with respect to real interest rates, they provide only ripples on the surface; the underlying forces of productive opportunities and preferences for present versus future consumption are the major determinants.

Two extreme cases illustrate the influence of demand and supply conditions. At one end of the spectrum are the interest rates paid to depositors (investors) by savings and loan associations. These change fairly frequently, but no single association is likely to adjust its rate as the demand and supply for its funds varies from day to day. As in any other competitive industry, rates are fairly consistent from firm (association) to firm (association). Only when overall demand changes relative to supply will firms find it desirable to change interest rates. And this does happen from time to time. Within the limits allowed by government regulation, demand and supply determine the rates paid by savings and loans.

At the other end of the spectrum lie the 90-day Treasury bills sold by the U.S. government every week. Each bill entitles the holder to receive $1,000 ninety days from the date of issue. The quantity to be issued (supplied) each week depends primarily on the government's financing needs. Individuals and businesses can bid for (demand) the bills. The effective interest rate thus depends directly on the bid prices (demand) relative to the quantity available (supply). Not surprisingly, the resulting values vary from week to week.

MONETARY VERSUS REAL INTEREST RATES

In real economies there is, of course, more to life than corn. One can trade present corn for future corn, present wheat for future wheat, present gin for future Volkswagens, etc.

Modern economies gain much of their efficiency through the use of money—a generally agreed-upon medium of exchange. Instead of trading present corn for a future Volkswagen, as in a barter economy, the citizen of a modern economy can trade his corn for money (i.e., "sell" it), trade the money for future money (i.e., "invest" it), then trade the future proceeds for a Volkswagen (i.e., "buy" it). The rate at which he or she can trade present money for future money is the *monetary* interest rate— usually called simply *the* interest rate.

In periods of changing prices the monetary interest rate may prove a poor guide to the real return obtained by the investor. While there is no completely satisfactory way to summarize the myriad of price changes that take place in such periods, most governments attempt to do so by measuring the cost of a specified mix of major items. The "overall" price level computed for this representative combination of items is usually termed a *cost-of-living index* or *consumer price index*. Whether or not it is relevant for a given individual depends to a major extent on the similarity of his or her purchases to the mix of goods and services used to construct the index. Moreover, such indices tend to overstate increases in the cost of living and understate decreases for people who do begin by purchasing the chosen mix of products. There are two reasons for this. First, improvements in quality are seldom taken adequately into account. Perhaps more important, little or no adjustment is made in the mix as relative prices change. The rational consumer can reduce the cost of attaining a given standard of living as prices change by substituting relatively less expensive goods for those that have become relatively more expensive.

Despite these drawbacks, cost-of-living indices provide at least rough estimates of changes in prices. And such indices can be used to determine an overall *real* rate of interest. For example, assume that during a year in which the monetary rate of interest is 8%, the cost-of-living index increases from 121 to 124. This means that the combination of goods and services that cost $100 in some base year cost $121 at the beginning of the year and $124 at the end of the year. The owner of such a bundle could have sold it for $121 at the start of the year, invested the proceeds at 8% to obtain $1.08 \times 121 = \$130.68$ at the end, then purchased $130.68/124 = 1.05387$ bundles. The real interest rate was thus 5.387%.

These calculations can be summarized in the following formula:

$$\frac{C_0 \times (1 + i_m)}{C_1} = 1 + i_r$$

where:

C_0 = cost-of-living index at the beginning of the year
C_1 = cost-of-living index at the end of the year

i_m = the monetary interest rate, expressed as a decimal number (e.g., .08)

i_r = the real interest rate, expressed as a decimal number (e.g., .05387)

An alternative version is:

$$\frac{1 + i_m}{1 + c} = 1 + i_r$$

where:

$1 + c = C_1/C_0$

   c = the change in the cost of living, expressed as a decimal number

In this case, C_1/C_0 = 124/121 = 1.02479, so prices increased by about 2.5% (c = .02479).

For quick calculation, the real interest rate can be estimated by simply subtracting the rate of change in the cost of living from the interest rate:

$$i_r \approx i_m - c$$

where $\approx$ means "is approximately equal to." In this case, the quick calculation results in an estimate of .08 − .02479 = .05521 or 5.521%, reasonably close to the true value of 5.387%.

Sad to say, in this world the fact of inflation seems to be fairly predictable, but its precise magnitude is extremely hard to estimate in advance. For this reason we defer further discussion of real versus monetary interest rates until Chapter 10. Suffice it to say here that it may be best to view the expected real interest rate as determined by the underlying forces described in earlier sections, with the monetary interest rate equal to this amount plus the likely change in prices.

FORWARD RATES

Unlike Robinson Crusoe, most of us must make plans extending well beyond the coming year: no ship is likely to come in and solve all our economic problems. People thus consider investments that will pay off next year, those that will pay off in the following year, and so on. Since interest rates are associated with investments, and investments differ in longevity, there are thus many interest rates, not just one.

To take a simple case, assume that two U.S. government bonds can be purchased at present. The first matures in a year, at which time the holder will receive $1,000. The second matures in two years, at which time the holder will receive $1,000. Although U.S. bonds of such duration entitle the holder to periodic interest payments, we will ignore this for now to keep the calculations simple. The prices asked by dealers for the two bonds are:

   One-year bond: $934.58
   Two-year bond: $865.35

It is a simple matter to determine the effective interest rate on the one-year bond. An investment of $934.58 will pay $1,000 one year hence. The return is thus:

$$\frac{1,000 - 934.58}{934.58} = .07$$

—that is, an interest rate of 7% per year.

But what is the interest rate on the two-year bond? Or should one even think of an interest rate in this case? Three approaches merit discussion.

The first is the simplest of all. One simply expresses the rate in terms of the actual life of the bond:

$$\frac{1,000 - 865.35}{865.35} = .1556$$

or 15.56% for two years. The obvious disadvantage of this measure is its inability to provide comparisons among bonds of different maturities. Moreover, it cannot be used for even a single bond with intermediate interest payments. It is little used, and with good reason.

A second method calculates the so-called "yield-to-maturity." This is the single interest rate (with interest compounded at some specified intervals) that, if paid by a bank on the amount invested, could enable the investor to obtain all the payments made by the bond in question. For example, assuming annual compounding at a rate r (expressed as a decimal), an account with $865.35 invested initially would grow to $(1 + r) \times$ $865.35 in one year. Leaving this total intact, the account would grow to $(1 + r)[(1 + r) \times \$865.35]$ by the end of the second year. The interest rate we seek must bring the account to $1,000 at the end of the second year. In other words, r must be selected so that:

$$(1 + r)^2 \times 865.35 = 1,000$$

or

$$1 + r = \sqrt{\frac{1,000}{865.35}}$$

The required value of r is .07499, so the yield-to-maturity of this bond is 7.499% per year.

Yield-to-maturity is the most commonly used measure of a bond's return. It can be computed for any investment, and it facilitates comparisons among investments of different lives and other characteristics. However, it has some serious drawbacks. In the attempt to express a complex instrument's return in a single number, it raises the possibility of serious oversimplification. It is thus desirable to look behind the yield-to-maturity to examine the fundamental determinants of value. The third method does just this.

The payment on a two-year bond can be considered the result of investment for two years at two potentially quite different rates. Thus the initial investment of $865.35 could have grown to $(1 + r_1) \times$ $865.35 at the end of the first year, and this total could then have grown to $(1 +$

$r_2) \times [(1 + r_1) \times 865.35]$ at the end of the second year. We could thus describe the bond with any of the many pairs of one-year rates r_1 and r_2 that would let the account grow to $1,000 at the end of the second year. We need only select a pair of values that satisfies the equation:

$$(1 + r_1)(1 + r_2)865.35 = 1,000$$

The yield-to-maturity is simply a special case of this in which a further requirement is imposed: that the rates be the same.

But there is no reason for the rates to be the same. In fact, they seldom are. This case is no exception. We know from the price of the one-year bond that the interest rate for money loaned now and paid back a year from now is 7%. The appropriate value for r_1 is thus .07. But what is the value of r_2? The answer can be determined readily. We seek the value that will make:

$$1.07(1 + r_2)865.35 = 1,000$$

It is .08 or 8%. This is the implied *forward rate* for year two: the interest rate for money loaned a year from now and paid back two years from now, *with the contract made now*. It is important to distinguish this from the rate for one-year loans that will prevail for deals made a year from now (the *spot* rate at that time). A forward rate applies to contracts made for a period "forward" in time. By the nature of the contract, the terms are certain now, even though the actual transaction will occur later. If, instead, one were to wait until next year to borrow money, the terms might prove better or worse than today's forward rate; in any event the terms are generally not perfectly predictable.

Forward contracts are sometimes made explicitly. For example, a contractor might obtain a commitment from a bank for a one-year construction loan a year hence at a fixed rate of interest. *Financial futures markets* (discussed in Chapter 17) provide standardized forward contracts of this type. For example, in September 1979 one could contract to pay $911.60 in September 1980 to purchase a one-year U.S. Treasury bill that would pay $1,000 in September 1981. In this case:

$$1 + r_2 = \frac{1000}{911.60} = 1.09697$$

and the forward rate (r_2) was 9.697%.

PRESENT VALUE

Given the interest rates determined in the market at any given time, it is fairly straightforward to find the present value of any investment offering future payments with certainty. As before, let us use r_1 to represent the interest rate on a one-year loan maturing in a year, and r_2 to represent the forward interest rate on a one-year loan maturing in two years. Similarly, $r_3, r_4, \ldots$ will respresent one-year loans maturing 3, 4, $\ldots$ years from now. In every case, the terms are assumed to be contracted now. Thus r_1 is today's spot rate and $r_2, r_3, \ldots$ are forward rates. As before, all values are expressed as decimals.

By proper use of existing instruments it is possible to arrange for P dollars today to grow to F_2 dollars in two years, where P and F_2 satisfy the equation:

$$[(1 + r_1)(1 + r_2)]P = F_2$$

By extension, if we let t represent any year, P dollars today can be made to grow to F_t dollars t years from now, where P and F_t satisfy the equation:

$$[(1 + r_1)(1 + r_2) \cdots (1 + r_t)]P = F_t$$

[The term in the brackets is simply a shorthand representation of the product of all the terms from $(1 + r_1)$ to $(1 + r_t)$, inclusive.]

This equation can be used to find the *present* value, P, that is equivalent to a future value of F_t, received t years in the future. Simple rearrangement provides the answer:

$$P = \left[\frac{1}{(1 + r_1)(1 + r_2) \cdots (1 + r_t)} \right] F_t$$

or:

$$P = d_t F_t \qquad \qquad \text{(4-1)}$$

The term in brackets (d_t) is the *discount factor* for year t. The multiplication of F_t by d_t is termed *discounting*: converting the given future value into an equivalent present value. The latter is equivalent in the sense that P present dollars can be converted into F_t dollars in year t via available investment instruments, given the currently prevailing interest rates. An investment promising F_t dollars in year t with certainty should sell for P dollars today. If it sells for more, it is overvalued; if it sells for less, it is undervalued. These statements rest solely on comparisons with equivalent opportunities in the marketplace. Valuation of riskless investments thus requires no assessment of individual preferences, only careful analysis of available opportunities in the market.

The simplest and, in a sense, most fundamental characterization of the structure of the market for default-free bonds is given by the current set of discount factors, known as the *discount function*. With this set of values it is a simple matter to value a riskless bond that provides more than one payment, for it is, in effect, a package of bonds, each of which provides only one payment. Each amount is simply discounted using formula (4-1), and the resultant present values summed. For example, take a bond paying a coupon of $100 at the end of the current year and $1,000 at maturity, two years hence. Assume the values from our previous example hold. Thus:

$$d_1 = \frac{1}{1 + r_1} = .9346 = \frac{1}{1.07}$$

and:

$$d_2 = \frac{1}{(1 + r_1)(1 + r_2)} = .8654 = \frac{1}{1.07 \times 1.08}$$

TABLE 4-2 Present Value of a Bond

Time	Payment ($)	Discount Factor	Present Value ($)
One year hence	100	.9346	93.46
Two years hence	1,000	.8654	865.40
		Total present value:	$958.86

The present value of the bond is thus $958.86, as shown in Table 4-2.

No matter how complex the pattern of payments, this procedure can be used to determine the value of a riskless bond of this type. The general formula is:

$$PV = \sum_t d_t F_t$$

where:

PV = present value
F_t = the (certain) payment to be made at time t
d_t = the present value of a dollar paid (with certainty) at time t
$\sum_t$ = the sum of all relevant values (e.g., $d_1F_1 + d_2F_2 + d_3F_3 + \cdots$)

YIELD-TO-MATURITY

As we have seen, if P dollars grows to F_t dollars in year t:

$$[(1 + r_1)(1 + r_2) \cdots (1 + r_t)]P = F_t$$

or

$$[(1 + r_1)(1 + r_2) \cdots (1 + r_t) = \frac{F_t}{P}$$

The yield-to-maturity, also called the internal rate of return, is the constant rate of interest that would have the same effect. In this case, we must find a value r for which:

$$[(1 + r)(1 + r) \cdots (1 + r)]P = F_t$$

where there are t values of $(1 + r)$ in the brackets. Simplifying:

$$(1 + r)^t = \frac{F_t}{P}$$

Since we know that F_t/P will also equal the product of the true interest rates, we can simply find the value of r that satisfies:

$$(1 + r)^t = (1 + r_1)(1 + r_2) \cdots (1 + r_t)$$

Taking the tth root of each side:

$$(1 + r) = \sqrt[t]{(1 + r_1)(1 + r_2) \cdots (1 + r_t)}$$

This shows that $(1 + r)$ is a kind of average of the values $(1 + r_1)$, $(1 + r_2)$, etc. It is called the *geometric mean*, as contrasted with the more common *arithmetic mean*, or simple average. The two values will usually differ; recall that in our earlier example the yield-to-maturity was 7.499%, while a simple average of the two rates would be 7.5%. In more realistic examples the two rates can differ by a substantial amount.

For more complex (and common) cases in which payments are made at different times, it is more difficult to calculate the yield-to-maturity. Generally a trial-and-error procedure must be followed. The goal is to find a value of r that will discount all future payments to present values that sum to the present price. The discount factors are, for payments one year hence:

$$\frac{1}{1 + r}$$

for payments two years hence:

$$\frac{1}{(1 + r)(1 + r)}$$

for payments t years hence:

$$\frac{1}{(1 + r)^t}$$

An example will show how the process works. In this case we wish to analyze a bond that will pay $100 one year hence and $1,000 two years hence. Imagine that it sells for $930. What is its yield-to-maturity?

To get started, let us guess 10% and calculate the implied present value. The results are shown in Table 4-3. The present value is too small. We have discounted the payments by too much. Clearly a lower interest rate is in order. Let us guess 5%. The results are shown in Table 4-4. Now the present value is too large. We have not discounted the future payments enough. We need to try some rate between 5% and 10%.

And so it would go, until the calculated present value came sufficiently close to the actual price of the bond. Here, this will happen when the discount factors are computed at a rate of about 9.21%; this is the bond's yield-to-maturity.

Happily, computers are good at trial-and-error. One can describe a very complex series of payments to a computer and get an answer concerning yield-to-maturity in short order. But even this is not necessary when valuing the normal kind of bond that promises coupon payments periodically, then pays off at maturity. Extensive bond tables are available, reducing the task to one of performing a calculation or two and looking up a number in a table. Even easier, one can use a hand-held calculator preprogrammed to find a bond's yield-to-maturity (and do present-value and compound-interest calculations). To calculate yield-to-maturity one simply enters the number of days to maturity, the annual payment, and the present price, then presses the key or keys that indicate yield-to-maturity is desired. The lights blink as the calculator engages in its trial-and-error procedure, then in a few seconds the answer appears.

TABLE 4-3 Present Value of a Bond at 10%

Time	Payment ($)	Discount Factor at 10%	Present Value ($) Using a Discount Factor of 10%
One year hence	100	.9091	90.91
Two years hence	1,000	.8264	826.40
		Total present value:	$917.31

TABLE 4-4 Present Value of a Bond at 5%

Time	Payment ($)	Discount Factor at 5%	Present Value ($) Using a Discount Factor of 5%
One year hence	100	.9524	95.24
Two years hence	1,000	.9070	907.00
		Total present value:	$1,002.24

TABLE 4-5 Calculating the Duration of a Bond

(1) Time (Years from Now)	(2) Present Value of Payment ($)	(3) Present Value of Payment as Proportion of Present Value of Bond	(4) Column 1 Times Column 3
1	93.46	.0975	.0975
2	865.40	.9025	1.8050
	$958.86	1.0000	1.9025

DURATION

Most bonds provide "coupon" (interest) payments in addition to a final ("par") payment at maturity. Depending on the relative magnitudes of these payments, a bond may be more or less like others with the same maturity date. A measure of the average time prior to the receipt of payment is obtained by calculating the bond's *duration*. This is simply a weighted average of the lengths of time prior to the payments, using the relative present values of the payments as weights.[1]

The bond analyzed earlier provides an illustration. Recall from Table 4-2 that the payment of $100 one year hence had a present value of $93.46, while the final payment of $1,000 two years hence had a present value of $865.40, making the total present value of the bond $958.86. As shown in Table 4-5 this bond has a duration of 1.9025 years.

[1] Some analysts use a bond's yield-to-maturity to estimate the present values of the payments, while others simply sum the payments and express each one as a percentage of the total.

Bonds of similar duration are more likely to react in similar ways to changes in interest rates than are bonds of similar maturity but different durations. This should not be surprising. Maturity measures only the time over which a bond provides payments; it takes no account of the pattern of those payments over time. Duration takes both factors into account and thus measures a bond's characteristics more accurately.[2]

COMPOUNDING

Thus far we have concentrated on annual interest rates and assumed that funds are compounded annually. This is often appropriate, but for more precise calculations a shorter period may be more desirable. Moreover, some lenders explicitly compound funds more often than once each year.

Compounding is, of course, the payment of "interest on interest." At the end of each compounding interval, interest is computed and added to principal. This sum becomes the principal on which interest is computed at the end of the next interval. The process continues until the final compounding interval is reached.

No problem is involved in adapting our formulas to compounding intervals other than a year. The simplest procedure is to count in units of the chosen interval. Thus, if quarterly compounding is to be used, r_t can represent the rate of interest per quarter for a three-month loan due t quarters from now, with terms contracted now.

The yield-to-maturity can also be calculated using any chosen compounding interval. If payment of P dollars now will result in a receipt of F dollars ten years from now, the yield-to-maturity can be calculated using annual compounding by finding a value r_a that satisfies the equation:

$$(1 + r_a)^{10}P = F$$

since F will be received ten annual periods from now. The result, r_a, will of course be expressed as an interest rate per year.

Alternatively, yield-to-maturity can be calculated using semiannual compounding, by finding a value r_s that satisfies the equation:

$$(1 + r_s)^{20}P = F$$

since F will be received twenty semiannual periods from now. The result, r_s, will be expressed as an interest rate per semiannual period. It can be doubled to give an annualized figure; better yet, an annualized value can be computed on the assumption of semiannual compounding, i.e.:

$$1 + r_a = (1 + r_s)^2$$

To reduce the massive confusion caused by the many different methods that can be used to express interest rates, the Federal Truth-in-Lending Act requires every lender to compute and disclose the *annual percentage rate* (APR) implied by the terms of a loan. This is simply the yield-to-maturity, computed using the most frequent time between payments on the loan as the compounding interval. While some complica-

---

[2] As we will see in Chapter 12, even more accurate measures can be obtained.

tions arise when payments are required at irregular intervals, the use of APR's has clearly simplified the task of comparing lenders' terms.

Semiannual compounding is commonly used to determine the yield-to-maturity for bonds, since interest payments are usually made twice each year. Most preprogrammed calculators use this approach, as do the publishers of most books of bond tables.

THE BANK DISCOUNT METHOD

Despite the truth-in-lending law, other methods are still used to summarize interest rates. One time-honored procedure is the "bank discount" method. If someone "borrows" $100 from a bank, to be repaid a year hence, the bank will discount the interest of, say, $8 and pay the borrower $92. According to the bank discount calculation, this is an interest rate of 8%. Not so. The borrower only receives $92, for which he or she must pay $8 in interest. The true interest rate (APR) must be based on the money the borrower actually gets to use. In this case the rate is 8.7%, since:

$$\frac{8}{92} = .087$$

It is a simple matter to convert an interest rate quoted on a bank discount basis to a true interest rate. If the discount rate is r_d, the true rate is simply:

$$\frac{r_d}{1 - r_d}$$

where both values are expressed as decimal numbers. The previous example provides an illustration.

$$\frac{.08}{1 - .08} = .087$$

CONTINUOUS COMPOUNDING

When we compute an investment's return, the compounding interval can make a difference. This becomes quite evident at times when demand and supply conditions make the appropriate rate on investments in savings and loan companies higher than allowed by Federal regulations but no restrictions are placed on compounding intervals. For example, in early 1975 the legal limit on interest paid by savings and loans on deposits committed from six to ten years was 7.75% per year. As competitive pressure grew, some companies began offering free pens, free travelers' checks, and other prizes to depositors. Soon an enterprising company announced it would pay 7.75% per year, compounded semiannually. This meant that $1 deposited at the beginning of the year would grow to $1.03875 at the end of six months, and the total would then grow to 1.03875 × 1.03875, or 1.079 by the end of the year: an increase of 7.9%.

This procedure was considered within the letter, if not the spirit, of the law.

Before long, a competitor offered 7.75% per year compounded quarterly (i.e., 1.938% per quarter), giving an effective increase of 7.978% by the end of one year. Then another offered to compound monthly (at .646% per month), for an effective increase of 8.031%. The denouement was reached when one company offered *continuous compounding* at an annual rate of 7.75%. This rather abstract procedure represents the limit approached as interest is compounded more and more frequently. If r represents the annual rate of interest (in this case, .0775) and n the number of times compounding takes place per year, the effective rate of increase, r_e, is given by:

$$\left(1 + \frac{r}{n}\right)^n = 1 + r_e$$

Thus with semiannual compounding:

$$(1.03875)^2 = 1.079$$

With quarterly compounding:

$$(1.01938)^4 = 1.07978$$

and so on. As the compounding interval grows shorter, the number of times compounding takes place (n) grows larger, as does the effective rate, r_e.

Mathematicians can prove that as n grows larger, $[1 + (r/n)]^n$ becomes increasingly close to e^r, where e stands for the number 2.71828 (to five-place accuracy). In this case, $e^{.0775} = 1.0806$ or an effective rate of 8.06% per year.[3]

A more general formula for continuous compounding can also be derived. At an annual rate of r, P dollars will grow to F_t dollars t years from now, with continuous compounding, if the values satisfy the equation:

$$e^{rt}P = F_t$$

Similarly, the present value of F_t dollars received t years hence at an annual rate of r, continuously compounded, will be:

$$P = \frac{F_t}{e^{rt}}$$

The discount factor (d_t) is thus $1/e^{rt}$ or e^{-rt}. These formulas can be used for any value of t, including fractional amounts (e.g., $t = 2.5$ for two years, six months).

Continuous compounding is often used for the analysis of interest-rate formation and change because the formulas lend themselves to algebraic treatment more readily than do those describing periodic compounding. The use of continuous compounding in practice is, how-

---

[3] Tables of natural logarithms may be used for such calculations. The natural logarithm of 1.0806 is .0775, and the antilogarithm of .0775 is 1.0806.

ever, relatively rare; the phenomenon is due more to government regulation than to a desire on the part of lenders and investors to abandon more traditional methods.

THE YIELD CURVE

At any time riskless securities will be priced more or less in accord with a set of discount factors and the associated implied forward interest rates. There is no necessary relationship among these rates. At some times rates are higher, the farther in the future the period to which they apply; at other times they are lower; at still other times, the same. It obviously behooves the security analyst to know which case prevails at present.

This is, unhappily, easier said than done. Only the bonds of the U.S. government are clearly riskless in dollar terms, and even they are not usually considered riskless in real terms. Moreover, such bonds differ in tax advantages, the ability of the government to select the effective date of maturity, and other features. Despite these problems, the U.S. Treasury Department summarizes the approximate relationship between short- and long-term yields with a *yield curve* in each issue of the monthly *Treasury Bulletin*. This provides an estimate of the current *term structure* of interest rates. Figure 4-3 shows an example.

FIGURE 4-3 Yields of Treasury Securities, August 31, 1979, (based on closing bid quotations)

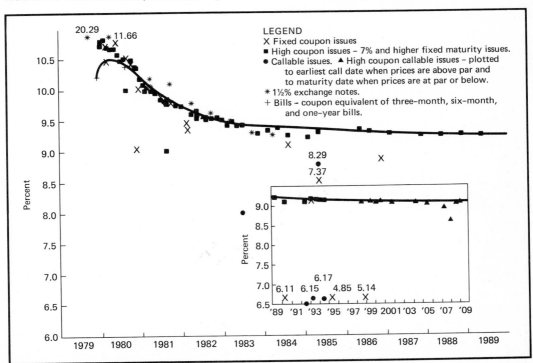

Note: The curve is fitted by eye and based only on the most actively traded issues.
Market yields on coupon issues due in less than three months are excluded.

Unfortunately, the yield curve does not relate forward interest rates to the applicable time periods. Instead it plots the yield-to-maturity for actual bonds versus their maturity.[4] As the figure shows, the relationship is less than perfect. Part of this is due to differences in taxability and the like. Part is due to the fact that yield-to-maturity figures represent averages of actual forward rates and thus obscure the underlying determinants of bond prices.

Historically, a "rising yield curve" is the most common: long-term yields exceed short-term, implying that forward rates are higher, the farther in the future is the period for which a contract is drawn. Rising yield curves tend to be associated with periods of normal or low short-term interest rates.

When short-term interest rates are fairly high, the yield curve may be "flat," implying that all forward rates are roughly the same.

In periods of very high short-term rates the yield curve may be "falling" throughout or even "humped" as in Figure 4-3. A downward-sloping curve implies that forward rates are generally smaller, the farther in the future is the period for which the contract is drawn.

The determinants of the yield curve are many and complex. Moreover, risk may play a role. For this reason, we will defer further discussion until Chapter 12.

The current yield curve provides some information on the manner in which bonds are priced in the market. More fundamental values are the discount factors and associated forward rates, for they can be used to evaluate any investment. If the investment is truly riskless, its value can be determined directly. If it is risky, additional aspects must be taken into account. But that is the subject of the next three chapters.

[4] Or, in some cases, the earliest date at which they can be "called" by the government.

Problems

1. Explain why the indifference curves in Figure 4-1 cannot cross.
2. a. In August 1979 one could buy a U.S. Treasury bill that would pay $1,000 in six months for a price of $954.10. What was the effective interest rate on the bill, expressed as a rate per six months?
   b. At the same time one could buy a U.S. Treasury bill paying $1,000 in twelve months for $910.10. What was the effective interest rate on this bill, expressed as a rate per twelve months?
   c. Assume that you wanted to express the return on the twelve-month bill in terms of an interest rate per six months, compounded every six months. What would be the resulting yield-to-maturity expressed as a rate per six months?

    d. Given the prices of these bills, can you determine the implicit forward rate for the second six-month period? If so, what is it (expressed as a rate per six months)?

3. A savings account that yields 8% per year compounded monthly has a higher effective annual yield than an account that offers 8% per year compounded quarterly. An account that offers 8% per year compounded daily has an even higher effective yield. What would be the effective yearly yield (the yield equivalent to a one-time yearly compounding) for an account offering 8% per year with continuous compounding?

4. The Beneficent Loan Company has agreed to lend you funds to complete the last year of an M.B.A. program. The company will give you $10,000 today if you agree to repay the loan four years from now with a lump-sum payment of $20,164. What annual rate of interest is Beneficent charging you?

5. Assume default-free bonds are currently priced in accordance with the following set of discount factors:

Year (t)	Discount factor (dt)
1	.9259
2	.8534
3	.7829
4	.7150

    a. What are the implicit forward rates of interest?

    b. What is the present value of a 10% coupon four-year bond that pays $100 in each year up to and including year 4 plus an additional $1,000 in year 4?

    c. What is the present value of a 5% coupon four-year bond that pays $50 in each year up to and including year 4 plus an additional $1,000 in year 4?

    d. What are the durations of the two bonds in (b) and (c)? What accounts for the nature of the difference in the two values?

The Valuation of
Risky Securities

5

INTRODUCTION

Payments received from riskless securities can be accurately predicted: neither their amounts nor their timing is uncertain. But many securities do not meet such high standards. Some or all of their payments are *contingent* on events with respect to amount, timing, or both. A bankrupt corporation may not make its promised bond payments in full. A worker who is laid off may pay his bills late (or not at all). A corporation may reduce or eliminate its dividend if its business becomes unprofitable. And so on.

The security analyst must try to evaluate these circumstances affecting a risky investment's payments and enumerate the key events upon which such payments are contingent. For example, an aircraft manufacturer's fortunes may depend on whether or not the firm is awarded a major contract by the government, whether or not its recently introduced commercial aircraft is accepted by the airlines, whether or not there is an upturn in the economy with a concomitant increase in demand for airline travel, and so on. To properly value the stock of such a company the analyst must consider each of these contingencies and estimate the corresponding effect on the firm and its stock.

The identification of important influences and the evaluation of the impact of each one is exceedingly difficult. Among other things, the appropriate level of detail must be determined. The number of potentially relevant events is almost always very large, and the analyst must attempt to focus on the relatively few that appear to be most important. In some cases it may be best to differentiate only a few alternatives (for example, whether the economy will turn up, turn down, or stay the same). In other cases, finer distinctions may be needed (for example, whether the gross national product will be up 1%, 2%, 3%, etc.).

The process of identifying and evaluating key influences is central to security analysis. Here we will concentrate on the *use* of such estimates. After the contingencies have been identified and the corresponding payments estimated, how can the value of the security be determined?

MARKET VERSUS PERSONAL VALUATION

One approach to the valuation of risky securities focuses on the investor's personal attitudes and circumstances. Given his or her assessment of the likelihood of various contingencies, and feelings about the corresponding risks involved in an investment, an investor might determine the amount he or she would be willing to pay, by some sort of introspection. This would be a "personal" valuation of the security.

Such an approach would be appropriate if there were only one investment in the world. But such is not the case. A security need not and should not be valued without considering available alternatives. Current market values of other securities provide important information, since a security is seldom so unique that nothing else is even comparable. Security valuation should not be done in a vacuum; it should instead be performed in a market context.

Key to this approach is the comparison of one investment or combination of investments with another having comparable characteristics. For example, assume that A and B in Figure 5-1(a) are similar in this respect; then the two should be equal in value.

Now imagine that alternative B includes a security we wish to value—call it X. Moreover, assume that all other securities included in A and B are regularly traded and that their market values (prices) are widely reported and easily determined. Combination B can be thought to have two components: security X and the rest, which we will represent by C, as in Figure 5-1(b). Combination C might include many securities, only one, or, as a very special case, none at all.

If people are willing to purchase combination A for a present value of PV_A, they should be willing to purchase combination B for the same amount, since the two provide comparable prospects. Thus:

$$PV_A = PV_B$$

The present value of B will, however, be simply the sum of the present values of its components:

$$PV_B = PV_X + PV_C$$

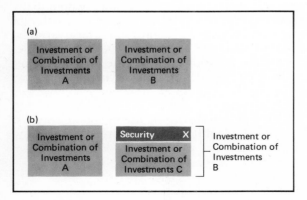

FIGURE 5-1 Comparing Combinations of Investments

This implies that the present value of security X can be determined solely by reference to market values placed on the securities comprising combinations A and C. Since:

$$PV_A = PV_X + PV_C$$

then

$$PV_X = PV_A - PV_C$$

APPROACHES TO SECURITY VALUATION

It is reasonable enough to say that market prices of "comparable investments" should be used to determine the value of a security. But when are two investments truly comparable?

An obvious case arises when investments provide identical payments in every possible contingency. If an investment's outcome is affected by relatively few events, it may be possible to purchase a set of other investments, each of which pays off in only one of the relevant contingencies. A properly selected mix of such investments may thus be completely comparable to the one to be valued. The next section illustrates this approach with an example drawn from the field of insurance.

A much more common approach to valuation is less detailed but more useful. Two alternatives are considered comparable if they offer similar expected returns and contribute equally to portfolio risk. Central to this view is the need to assess the probabilities of various contingencies. The remainder of this chapter and the next two chapters are devoted to this more widely used *risk-return approach*.

EXPLICIT VALUATION OF CONTINGENT PAYMENTS

Insurance

Insurance policies are highly explicit examples of contingent payments. One can buy a $100,000 one-year "term" life insurance policy on a reasonably healthy 60-year-old male for about $2,300. This, of course, can be viewed as an investment (albeit a morbid one): the sum of $100,000 will be paid by the insurance company if the insured dies within a year; otherwise nothing at all will be paid. Involved is the sacrifice of a present certain value ($2,300) for a future uncertain value. The only relevant event is the possible death of the insured, and the relationship between that event and the amount to be paid is crystal clear.

Now imagine that a reasonably healthy 60-year-old male executive asks you to loan him some money for a year. He would like as much as possible now; in return he promises to pay you $100,000 at the end of the year. Your problem is to determine the present value of that promise: i.e., how much to advance now. Put somewhat differently, you must determine an appropriate interest rate for the loan.

TABLE 5-1 Costs and Payments for a Loan and an Insurance Policy

| | EVENT | | |
Item	Executive Dies	Executive Lives	Cost
Loan	0	$100,000	$90,292.59
Insurance policy	$100,000	0	2,300.00
Total	$100,000	$100,000	$92,592.59

To keep the example simple, assume that the only source of uncertainty is the borrower's ability to remain in his position and thus earn the requisite money, and that this depends only on his continued presence among the living. In other words, if he lives he can and will repay the $100,000 in full; otherwise neither he nor his heirs will pay you anything.

The piece of paper representing the executive's promise to pay $100,000 is our security X. What is it worth? The answer clearly depends in an important way on the available alternatives. And a crucial factor is the current rate of interest.

Assume that the going rate for riskless one-year loans is 8%. If there were no doubt whatever that the executive would repay the loan, it would be reasonable to advance $92,592.59 (since $100,000 ÷ $92,592.59 = 1.08). However, the uncertainty connected with the loan makes this inadvisable. The appropriate amount is obviously less. But how much less?

In this case an answer can easily be determined. It would be entirely reasonable to advance at least $90,292.59, making the *promised* interest rate on the loan approximately 10.75% (since 100,000 ÷ 90,292.59 = 1.1075). The basis for this calculation is quite simple. It relies on the fact that an investor can insure against the relevant risk, obtaining an overall position that is completely riskless.

Table 5-1 provides the details. The relevant event is whether or not the executive survives the year. The loan is thus a risky investment, paying $100,000 only if he lives. The life insurance policy is also a risky investment, paying $100,000 only if he dies. But a *portfolio* that includes both investments is totally riskless: its owner will receive $100,000, no matter what happens! By paying $90,292.59 for the loan and $2,300 for the insurance policy, an investor could give up $92,592.59 now for a certain payment of $100,000 a year hence—obtaining a riskless return of 8%, which is the going rate on other riskless ventures.

FIGURE 5-2 Comparing Two Riskless Investments

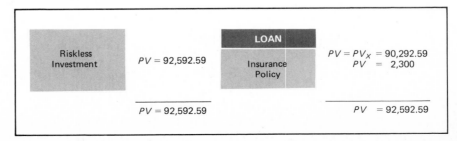

This is, of course, an application of the general procedure described in the previous section. Figure 5-2 summarizes the details in the format used earlier, for purposes of comparison.

Valuation in a Complete Market

Assume, for the present, that market values can be used to estimate the present value of any contingent payment. A market in which such detailed quotations are available is termed *complete*. While no real market conforms to this specification, it is useful to see how valuation would be done in such circumstances.

First, we need a way to represent the present value of a guaranteed commitment to pay $1 at a specified time if (and only if) a specified event or "state of the world" occurs. The following will suffice:

$$PV(\$1, \, t, \, e)$$

where:

t = the time at which the dollar is to be paid
e = the event that must occur if the dollar is to be paid

Armed with this notation, we can show how one might analyze any risky investment. Every possible contingency could, in theory, be considered separately, giving a (probably very lengthy) list of contingent payments of the following form:

Time of Payment	Event on Which Payment Is Contingent	Amount of Payment
t_1	e_1	D_1
t_2	e_2	D_2
.	.	.
.	.	.
.	.	.

Of course, some of the events might be the same, as might some of the times and/or some of the amounts.

To find the present value of the investment, we need to find the present value of each of its contingent payments, then add them up. In tabular form:

(1) Time of Payment	(2) Event on Which Payment Is Contingent	(3) Amount of Payment	(4) Discount Factor	(5) = (3) × (4) Present Value
t_1	e_1	D_1	$PV(\$1, t_1, e_1)$	$D_1 \times PV(\$1, t_1, e_1)$
t_2	e_2	D_2	$PV(\$1, t_2, e_2)$	$D_2 \times PV(\$1, t_2, e_2)$
.	.	.	.	.
.	.	.	.	.
.	.	.	.	.

Total value = _____

This method of valuation is commonly termed the *state-preference* approach, since it begins with the assumption that peoples' preferences are for *state-contingent claims* and concludes that securities will be valued on the basis of their payoffs in different "states of the world."

THE LIMITATIONS OF INSURANCE

Some believe that Lloyd's of London will insure almost anything. Perhaps so. This could ease the security analyst's task considerably. He or she would only (!) have to determine the payments $(D_1, D_2, \ldots)$ associated with an investment, the times at which they could be made $(t_1, t_2, \ldots)$ and the events on which they were contingent $(e_1, e_2, \ldots)$. The analyst could then use the premiums specified for the relevant insurance policies as estimates of appropriate discount factors [$PV(\$1, t_1, e_1)$, $PV(\$1, t_2, e_2)$, $\ldots$], and perform the required calculations.

But even if Lloyd's will insure anything, the premiums charged for many policies might attract no takers. There are a number of interrelated reasons for this. As a case in point, imagine an aerospace company, the future profits of which depend heavily on whether or not the firm will be awarded a major government contract. Why not buy an appropriate insurance policy from Lloyd's, guaranteed to pay off if the firm loses the contract? Then only Lloyd's and the other firms in the industry would care about the outcome.

The idea is obviously whimsical. If Lloyd's were even willing to issue such a policy, the cost would be more than anyone would be likely to pay. But why?

First, because of differences in *information*. Those familiar with the company and/or the government have better information about the likely outcome and can better assess the likelihood of various alternatives. Lloyd's operates at least partly in the dark. To protect itself, it will charge more than otherwise.

Second, there is the likelihood of *adverse selection*. If a policy of this sort is offered at a price low enough to attract anyone at all, the insurer can expect the firms that are least likely to win the contract to buy insurance, while those most likely to get the contract take their chances. This occurs frequently with life insurance. The less healthy an individual, the more likely he or she is to buy a policy; for this reason, the insured is usually required to pass a medical examination as a condition of sale. An examination of the health of a company's bid to win a government award might be much more difficult and/or expensive, so an insurance company must set its fees for such a policy on the assumption that it would end up insuring the riskiest client or clients.

Another factor is the thoroughly modern phenomenon described by the old-fashioned term "*moral hazard*." The purchase of insurance may affect the likelihood of the event in question. If the manager of a firm is insured against the loss of the contract, he or she may well put less effort into the attempt to win it, increasing the likelihood of its loss and the insurance company's obligation to pay off. This explains the reluctance of an insurance company to insure a house or car for more than its replacement value, and the desire of many stockholders to have a corporation's officers own some of the firm's stock and none of its competitors' issues. Here again, the insurance company will account for this effect when setting prices.

Finally, there is the simple matter of *overhead*. Insurance people like to eat, as do investors who provide the capital that insurance companies need. The costs of doing business will, over the long pull, be reflected in the prices charged for that business. No financial service is free, and insurance is no exception.

For all these reasons securities markets do not conform to the specifications of the complete-market state-preference model. While the approach is helpful for addressing certain theoretical issues, it is less useful for investment purposes than the risk-return (or "mean-variance") approach, to which we now turn.

PROBABILISTIC FORECASTING

Assessing Probabilities

Lacking a plethora of widely available and low-cost insurance policies, it is not possible to value an investment without explicitly considering the likelihood of various outcomes. Instead, the analyst must attempt to assess directly the likelihood of each major event that can affect an investment. In short, he or she must engage in *probabilistic forecasting*.

The idea is simple enough, although its implementation is exceedingly difficult. The analyst expresses his or her assessment of the likelihood of every relevant event as a *probability*. If he or she feels that the chances of an event's taking place are 50-50, a probability of .50 is attached to the event. If the chances seem to be 3 out of 4, the probability is $\frac{3}{4}$, or .75 (another way of expressing this is to say that the *odds* are 3-to-1 that the event will take place). If the analyst considers an event to be absolutely *certain*, a probability of 1.0 should be assigned. If he or she feels an event is completely impossible, its probability of occurrence is zero.

It is important, of course, to be consistent in one's estimates. For example, if the events on a list are *mutually exclusive* and *exhaustive* (i.e., one of them, but only one, will take place), the probabilities should sum to one.

Probability is, at base, a *subjective* concept. Even simple cases fall under this heading. For example, a gambler may assess the probability of a coin's coming up heads at .5, based on knowledge of coins and observations of the coin in question over the past. But the estimate is still subjective, involving the implicit assumption that the coin really is "fair" and that the past is an appropriate guide to the future. Similar cases arise frequently in security analysis. Relative *frequencies* of various returns in the past are sometimes used as estimates of the *probabilities* of such returns in the future. Clearly this procedure relies on assumptions that require subjective judgment and may in some circumstances be totally inappropriate. Forecasts based on the extrapolation of past relationships are neither wholly objective nor necessarily to be preferred over predictions obtained in more subtle ways.

Probabilistic forecasting entails a decision to confront uncertainty head-on, acknowledge its existence, and try to measure its extent. Instead of attempting to answer a question such as "What will General Motors earn next year?" the analyst explicitly considers some of the more likely alternatives and the likelihood of each one. This brings the analysis out in the open, allowing both the estimator and the user or users of such estimates to assess the reasonableness of the values. Insistence on a single number for each estimate, with no measure of associated uncertainty, would suggest naiveté or insecurity on the part of the producer and/or the consumer of such predictions.

In some organizations analysts engage in explicit probabilistic forecasting, passing on all their detailed assessments to others charged with bringing together the estimates made within the group. In other organizations the analysts make explicit probabilistic forecasts but summarize their evaluations in a relatively few key estimates, sending only the latter to others. In still other organizations analysts do not engage in explicit probabilistic forecasting; instead, they produce estimates that summarize their implicit beliefs about the probabilities of various events. As always, it is not the form but the substance that matters.

PROBABILITY DISTRIBUTIONS

It is often convenient to portray probabilistic forecasts graphically. The possible outcomes are represented on the horizontal axis and the associated probabilities on the vertical axis. Figure 5-3 provides an example.

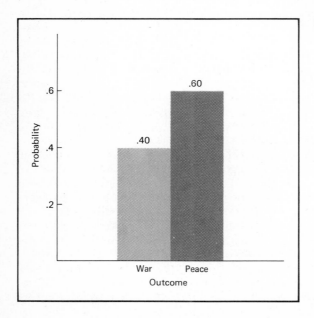

FIGURE 5-3 Probabilities of War and Peace

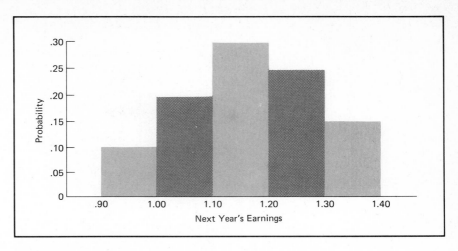

FIGURE 5-4 Probabilities of Next Year's Earnings (using wide ranges)

In this case the outcomes are qualitatively different in nature and can only be listed on the horizontal axis: the ordering and spacing are arbitrary.

Figure 5-4 shows a somewhat different case. Here the alternative outcomes differ quantitatively, and with regard to only one variable: earnings next year. In this instance the analyst has chosen to group together all possibilities from $.90 to $.99, assess the probability that the actual amount will fall within that range, then repeat the process for the range from $1.00 to $1.09, the range from $1.10 to $1.19, and so on.

The analysis could, of course, have been conducted at a more detailed level, with probabilities estimated for outcomes in the ranges from $.90 to $.94, $.95 to $.99, and so on. An even more detailed analysis would assign a probability to every possible outcome. In this case the bars would be numerous, and each would be very thin, as shown in Figure 5-5.

The ultimate in a detailed prediction is represented by a continuous curve, or *probability distribution*. Such a curve represents, in effect, the tops of many very thin bars, such as those shown in Figure 5-5. Three examples of curves of this type are shown in Figures 5-6(a), (b), and (c).

If probability distributions are to be used, the analyst can forego explicitly assessing particular outcomes, simply drawing a curve that seems to best represent the situation as he or she sees it. The relative likelihood of any outcome is indicated by the height of the curve at the appropriate point. If the outcomes portrayed are the only ones possible, the probabilities must, of course, sum to one. In practice the analyst can draw the curve without regard to the probability scale, as only *relative* probabilities are important. The height of the curve at each major point on the horizontal axis (measured in grid squares) can be read and the sum then used to determine the appropriate probability scale for the vertical axis. For example, if the sum of the heights is 50 grid units, each unit represents a probability of .02 ($\frac{1}{50}$).

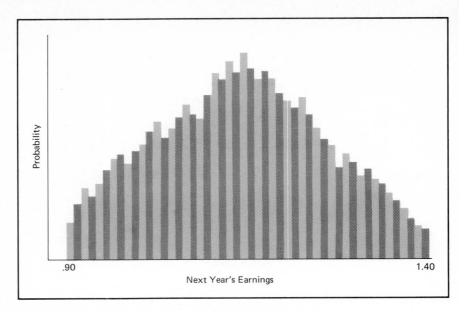

FIGURE 5-5 Probabilities of Next Year's Earnings (using narrow ranges)

FIGURE 5-6 Continuous Probability Distributions

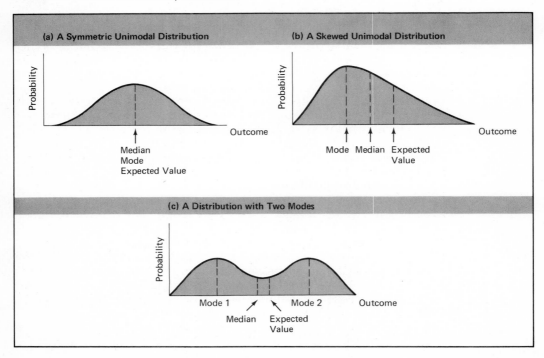

Event Trees

When events follow one another over time, or are in any sense dependent on one another, it is often useful to describe the alternative sequences with a "tree" diagram. Figure 5-7 provides an example.

A borrower has promised to pay $15 one year hence and $8 two years hence, if possible. The analyst feels the odds are only 40-60 that the first payment will in fact be made in full. Otherwise, the analyst feels the borrower will be able to pay only $10 one year hence.

As far as the second year is concerned, the likely situation depends, in this analyst's judgment, on the outcome in the first year. If the borrower manages to pay the full $15 in the first year, the analyst feels the odds are only 1 in 10 that he will be able to meet his commitment to pay $8 at the end of two years. Otherwise, he will pay less: $6. On the other hand, if the borrower pays out $10 in the first year, although there appears to be no chance of recovering the $5 shortfall, the analyst feels the odds are about even that the promised $8 will be paid in the second year. If this does not happen, he feels that $4 will be paid instead.

Figure 5-7 also shows the probability of each of the four possible sequences, or paths, through the tree. For example, the probability that both payments will be made in full is only .04, since there are only 40 chances out of 100 that the first payment will be made, and of those, only 1 out of 10 is expected to be followed by payment in full of the final obligation. This gives 4 out of 100 chances for the sequence: a probability of .04.

FIGURE 5-7 An Event Tree

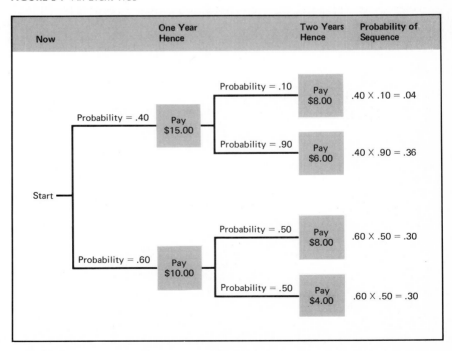

EXPECTED VALUE

Often an analyst is uncertain about an outcome but wishes, or is required, to summarize the situation with one or two numbers: one indicating the *central tendency* of the distribution of outcomes, and one measuring *relevant risk*. Both risk and return are discussed in subsequent chapters; the remainder of this chapter concentrates on the latter.

How might a single number intended to summarize a set of possible outcomes be obtained? Obviously no satisfactory way can be found if the alternative outcomes differ qualitatively (for example, war versus peace). But if the outcomes differ quantitatively, and especially if they differ in only one dimension, a number of possibilities present themselves.

Perhaps the most common procedure is to adopt the *most likely* value. This is known as the *mode* of the probability distribution. Figure 5-6 shows the mode of each of the distributions. Note that in Figure 5-6(c) there are two modes: in this case, no single number can be used to answer the question in this manner.

Another alternative is to provide a "50-50" number—a value that is as likely to be too low as to be too high. This is called the *median* of the probability distribution. As shown in Figure 5-6, it may differ significantly from the mode(s).

A third alternative is to use an *expected value*, a *weighted average of all the possible outcomes, using the associated probabilities as weights*. It takes into account all the information expressed in the distribution, both the *magnitude* and the *probability* of occurrence of each possible outcome. Almost any change in an investment's prospects or probabilities will affect the expected value of its outcomes (as it should).

In many instances there are no differences among these three measures. If the distribution is symmetric (i.e., each half is a mirror image of the other) and unimodal (i.e., there is one most likely value), then the median, mode, and expected value coincide, as in the case shown in Figure 5-6(a). Thus an analyst may choose to think in terms of, say, a 50-50 (median) value, even though the number wanted is the expected value. Only if the underlying probability distribution is highly skewed might this procedure lead to difficulties.

In those cases in which the values do differ, there are good reasons to prefer the expected value. As stated earlier, it takes all of the estimates into account. But it has another advantage. Estimates about the prospects for securities serve as inputs for the process of portfolio construction and/or revision. The expected value for a portfolio is related in a straightforward way to the expected values for its securities, but neither the median nor the mode for a portfolio can, in general, be determined from comparable values for its securities.

Table 5-2 provides an example of the computation of expected values. An analyst is trying to predict the impact on the prices of two securities of a surprise television address scheduled by the President. He has delineated a number of possible announcements, ranging from changes in the situation in the Mideast through a decision concerning domestic price controls. The alternatives represented in the table have been defined to be mutually exclusive and exhaustive (i.e., every possible combi-

TABLE 5-2 Analysis of Effects of Announcements on Two Securities and a Portfolio of Both Securities

Announcement	Probability	Predicted Price ($) of Security A	Predicted Price ($) of Security B	Predicted Value ($) of a Portfolio of A and B
a	.10	40.00	62.00	102.00
b	.20	42.00	65.00	107.00
c	.10	40.50	60.00	100.50
d	.25	41.00	61.00	102.00
e	.15	38.00	65.00	103.00
f	.10	40.50	59.00	99.50
g	.05	45.00	58.00	103.00
h	.05	40.50	58.00	98.50
	Expected Values:	$40.73	$61.90	$102.63

nation is shown in a different row). After much thought and with some trepidation, the analyst has also estimated the probability of each announcement and the resultant effect on the prices of the two securities. Finally, he has computed the associated values of a portfolio containing one share of each stock.

The expected values are shown at the bottom of the table. Each is obtained by multiplying the probability of every announcement by the associated price, then summing. For example, the expected price of security A is determined by computing $[(.10 \times 40,00) + (.20 \times 42.00) + \cdots]$; that of security B by computing $[(.10 \times 62.00) + (.20 \times 65.00) + \cdots]$; and that of the portfolio by computing $[(.10 \times 102.00) + (.20 \times 107.00) + \cdots]$. Not surprisingly, the expected value of the portfolio equals the sum of the expected values of its component securities. When the expected values for the securities are added together, one is, in effect, adding $(.10 \times 40.00 + \cdots)$ to $(.10 \times 62.00 + \cdots)$. Clearly, this will give the expected value of the portfolio, which is $.10 \times (40.00 + 62.00) + \cdots$.

EXPECTED VERSUS PROMISED YIELD-TO-MATURITY

If payments from a bond are certain, there is no difference between the expected yield-to-maturity and the promised amount. However, many bonds fail to meet these standards. Two types of risk may be involved. First, the issuer may defer some payments. A dollar received farther in the future is, of course, worth less in present value than a dollar received on schedule; thus the present value of a bond will be smaller, the greater the likelihood that this might happen. The second type of risk is potentially more serious. The borrower may default, in whole or in part, on some of the interest payments or on the principal at maturity. A firm becomes bankrupt when it is clearly unable to meet such obligations; the courts then divide the remaining assets among the various creditors, in accordance with provisions agreed upon when the debts were issued.

TABLE 5-3 Promised versus Expected Yield-to-Maturity

Payment One Year Hence ($)	Payment Two Years Hence ($)	Probability	Yield-to-Maturity (%)
15	8	.04	38.51
15	6	.36	30.62
10	8	.30	13.61
10	4	.30	−5.20
		Expected Yield-to-Maturity:	15.09%

To estimate the expected yield-to-maturity for a risky debt instrument, one should in principle consider all possible outcomes and the probability of each one. The simple example shown in Figure 5-7 can be used to illustrate the procedure. Assume the security in question costs $15; i.e., the borrower wants $15 now in return for a commitment to pay $15 one year hence and $8 two years hence. The promised yield-to-maturity is the interest rate that makes the present value of these payments equal $15. In this case it is 38.51% per year, a substantial figure indeed.

But the analyst feels that the probability of actually receiving this yield-to-maturity is only .04. Table 5-3 shows the possible sequences (paths in the event tree), as well as the probability and the yield-to-maturity for each one. The expected yield-to-maturity is simply the weighted average of these values, using the probabilities as weights (e.g., [(.04 × 38.51%) + (.36 × 30.62%) + · · ·].

The expected yield-to-maturity is considerably less than the promised amount: 15.09% as opposed to 38.51%. And the former is clearly the more relevant figure for investment analysis.

This is an important point. The yield-to-maturity, as normally calculated, is based on promised payments, made at the promised times. If there is any risk that the borrower's commitments will not be fully met, the expected yield-to-maturity is less than this figure; and the greater the risk, the greater the disparity. This is illustrated in Table 5-4, which shows the (promised) yield-to-maturity values for four groups of bonds classified by Standard and Poor's, a major rating service, as having different degrees of risk. While the *levels* of all four yields reflect general interest rates at the time, the *differences* among them are primarily due to differences in risk. If promised yields of all bonds were the same, the expected yields of high-risk bonds would be less than those of low-risk ones—an unlikely

TABLE 5-4 Standard and Poor's Composite Bond Yields, July 25, 1979

Rating	Yield-to-Maturity (%)
AAA	9.20
AA	9.42
A	9.59
BBB	10.08

Source: Standard and Poor's *Bond Guide*, August 1979.

situation indeed. Instead, riskier bonds promise higher yields so that their expected yields can be at least as large as those of less risky ones.

The nature of most debt obligations would be more obvious if contracts were written somewhat differently. At present, a standard bond with no extra features "guarantees" that the borrower will pay the lender, say, $90 per year for twenty years, then $1,000 twenty years hence. A more appropriate statement would indicate that the borrower guarantees to pay *no more than* $90 per year for twenty years, and $1,000 twenty years hence.

EXPECTED HOLDING-PERIOD RETURN

Calculating Holding-Period Return

Yield-to-maturity calculations do not take into account any changes in the market value of a security prior to maturity. This might be interpreted as implying that the owner has no interest in selling the instrument prior to maturity, no matter what happens to its price or his or her situation. The calculation also fails to treat intermediate payments in a fully satisfactory way. If the owner does not wish to spend interest payments, he or she might choose to buy more of these securities. But the number that can be bought at any time depends on the price at that time, and yield-to-maturity calculations fail to take this into account.

While few dispute the value of yield-to-maturity as at least an indicator of a bond's overall return, it should be recognized as no more than this. For some purposes other measures may prove more useful. Moreover, for other types of securities there is no maturity: common stocks provide the most important example.

A measure that can be used for any investment is *holding-period return*. The idea is to specify a holding period of major interest, then assume that any payments received during the period are reinvested. While assumptions may differ from case to case, the usual procedure assumes that any payment received from a security (e.g., a dividend from a stock, a coupon payment from a bond) is used to purchase more units of that security at the then current market price. Using this procedure, the performance of a security can be measured by comparing the value obtained in this manner at the end of the holding period with the value at the beginning. This *value-relative* can be converted to a holding-period return simply enough. The latter is just the value that satisfies the relationship:

$$1 + r_{hp} = \frac{\text{value at the end of the holding period}}{\text{value at the beginning of the holding period}}$$

Put another way: the *holding-period return is the holding-period value-relative minus one*.

Holding-period return can, of course, be converted to an equivalent return per period. Allowing for the effect of compounding, the appropriate procedure would be to find the value that satisfies the relationship:

$$(1 + r_g)^N = 1 + r_{hp}$$

or

$$r_g = (\sqrt[N]{1 + r_{hp}}) - 1$$

where:

    N = the number of periods in the holding period
    r_{hp} = the holding-period return
    r_g = the equivalent return per period, compounded every period

    Suppose that a stock sold for $46 per share at the beginning of one year, paid dividends of $1.50 during that year, sold for $50 at the end of the year, paid dividends of $2 during the next year, and sold for $56 at the end of that year. What was the return over the two-year holding period?

    To simplify the calculations, assume that all dividend payments are received at year-end. Then the $1.50 received during the first year could have bought $1.50/$50 or .03 shares of the stock at the end of the first year. In practice, of course, this would be feasible only if the money were pooled with other funds similarly invested—e.g., in a mutual fund, or simply in an investor's own portfolio (for example, the dividends from 100 shares could have been used to buy three additional shares). In any event, for each share originally held, the investor would have obtained 1.03 × $2, or $2.06 in dividends in the second year, and have had stock with value of 1.03 × $56, or $57.68 at the end of the second year. The ending value would thus have been $57.68 + $2.06, giving a value-relative of:

$$\frac{\$59.74}{\$46.00} = 1.2987$$

The holding-period return was thus 29.87% per two years. This is equivalent to $\sqrt{1.2987} - 1$ (= .1396), or 13.96% per year.

    An alternative method of computation treats the overall value-relative as the product of value-relatives for the individual periods. For example, if V_0 is the value at the beginning, V_1 the value at the end of the first year, and V_2 the value at the end of the second year:

$$\frac{V_2}{V_0} = \frac{V_2}{V_1} \times \frac{V_1}{V_0}$$

Moreover, there is no need to carry the expansion in number of shares from period to period, since the factor (1.03 in our example) will simply cancel out in the subsequent periods' value-relatives. Each period can be analyzed in isolation, an appropriate value-relative calculated, and the set of such value-relatives multiplied together.

    In our example, during the first year, ownership of a stock with an initial value of $46 led to stock and cash with a value of $50 + $1.50 at the end of the year. Thus:

$$\frac{V_1}{V_0} = \frac{\$51.50}{\$46.00} = 1.1196$$

During the second year, ownership of stock with an initial value of $50 led to stock and cash with a value of $56 + $2 at year-end. Thus:

$$\frac{V_2}{V_1} = \frac{\$58}{\$50} = 1.16$$

The two-year holding-period value-relative was therefore:

$$1.1196 \times 1.16 = 1.2987$$

which is, of course, exactly equal to the value obtained earlier.

The value-relative for each period can be viewed as 1 plus the return for that period. Thus the return on the stock being analyzed was 11.96% in the first year and 16% in the second. The holding-period value-relative is the product of 1 plus each return. If N periods are involved:

$$\frac{V_N}{V_0} = (1 + r_1)(1 + r_2) \cdots (1 + r_N)$$

To convert the result to a holding-period return stated as an amount per period, with compounding, one can take the *geometric mean* of the periodic returns:

$$1 + r_g = \sqrt[N]{(1 + r_1)(1 + r_2) \cdots (1 + r_N)}$$

More sophisticated calculations may be employed within this overall framework. Each dividend payment can be used to purchase shares immediately upon receipt, or, alternatively, allowed to earn interest in a savings account until year-end. Brokerage and other costs associated with reinvestment of dividends can also be taken into account, although the magnitude of such costs will undoubtedly depend on the overall size of the holdings in question. The appropriate degree of complexity will, as always, be a function of the use for which the values are obtained.

Unhappily, the most appropriate holding period is often at least as uncertain as the return over any given holding period. Neither an investor's situation nor his or her preferences can usually be predicted with certainty. Moreover, from a strategic view, an investment manager would like to hold a given security only as long as it outperforms available alternatives. Attempts to identify such periods in advance are seldom completely successful, but managers quite naturally continue to try to discover them.

Holding-period return, like yield-to-maturity, provides a useful device for simplifying the complex reality of investment analysis. While no panacea, it allows an analyst to focus on the most relevant horizon in a given instance and offers a good measure of performance over such a period.

Some of the discussion of "return" in this book applies strictly only to return per holding period [i.e., $(V_N/V_0) - 1$]. Although the relationships may not apply exactly to other measures of return, the differences will, in most cases, be slight. *Quantitative* conclusions may sometimes apply strictly only to holding-period returns, but the *qualitative* conclusions will usually apply quite generally.

Estimating Expected Holding-Period Return

It is a relatively straightforward matter to calculate holding-period return after the fact. It is quite another thing to estimate it in advance. Any uncertainty surrounding payments by the issuer of a security during the period must be taken into account, but this is usually much simpler than the task of estimating the market values, which often constitute a large portion of overall return. For example, it might seem a simple matter to estimate the return over the next year for a share of Xerox stock. Dividends to be paid are relatively easy to predict. But the price at year-end will depend on investors' attitudes toward the company and its stock at that time. To predict even a one-year holding-period return one must consider a much longer period and assess not only the company's future but also investors' future attitudes about that future—a formidable task indeed.

Quite clearly, estimation of holding-period return must account in some way for uncertainty. If a single estimate is required, it should conform to the principles stated earlier. Explicitly or implicitly, an *expected value* should be provided. The various possibilities should be considered along with their probabilities.

> Expected holding-period return is a weighted average of possible holding-period returns, using probabilities as weights.[1]

Estimating a Bond's Expected Holding-Period Return

Once the importance of market values is recognized, the presence of a new kind of risk becomes obvious. And the idea of a truly riskless investment becomes a relative matter.

Assume that an investor is interested in a holding period of five years. What sort of investment would be riskless for these purposes? Obviously, one with no default risk, which promises a payment at the end of five years and at no other time. Any other investment will involve some risk. The five-year holding-period return from a bond that provides semi-annual coupon payments will depend on the prices at which such payments can be used to purchase additional units of the bond (or some other instrument). The return on a bond with a maturity in excess of five years will depend on the price at which it can be sold at the end of the fifth year. The return on a shorter-maturity bond will depend on the instruments that are available when the proceeds must be reinvested, and their prices at those times.

Since bond prices depend in large part on interest rates, this source of uncertainty is sometimes termed *interest-rate risk*. In many cases it is far more important than default risk. Moreover, it makes even U.S. government debt risky, unless there is a perfect correspondence between the investor's desire for cash and the payments promised by the bond in question.

Interest-rate risk should be incorporated in any analysis of expected holding-period return. For U.S. government securities this requires esti-

---

[1] Expected return is also the *mean* of the probability distribution of holding-period returns; hence the "mean" in the term "mean-variance approach."

mates of possible future interest rates and their associated probabilities. For other securities the likely future differentials for various levels of risk must also be taken into account.

EXPECTED RETURN AND SECURITY VALUATION

There is a very simple relationship between expected holding-period return, expected end-of-period value, and current value:

$$\text{expected holding-period return} = \frac{\text{expected end-of-period value}}{\text{current value}} - 1$$

Thus:

$$\text{current value} = \frac{\text{expected end-of period value}}{1 + \text{expected holding-period return}}$$

In words: to value a security, one need only (!) estimate the expected value at the end of a holding period and the expected return for the holding period that is appropriate for such a security.

The final phrase is crucial. What is the "appropriate" expected return, and on what does it depend? Therein lies the remainder of the theory of valuation.

One possible answer is that the appropriate expected return is that available from an investment that provides a riskless return over the period in question. However desirable such a relatively simple answer might be, it is simply inconsistent with the general behavior of investors.

By and large, investors are *risk averse*. Other things equal, they prefer less risk to more. However, other things equal, they also prefer more expected return to less. Not surprisingly, this implies that in the process of valuation one should require a higher expected return on a security, the greater the relevant risk involved.

Risk is not a simple concept; it thus requires extended discussion. The next two chapters provide it.

Problems

1. The arithmetic average annual return on Standard and Poor's index of common stocks from 1926 through 1978 was 11.18%. If, on January 1, 1979, you had been required to provide an estimate of the expected return on the S&P 500 over the coming year, would you have chosen 11.18%? Why or why not?

2. The probability distribution in Figure 5-6(b) is "skewed to the right." If a distribution is skewed to the left, which will be larger—the expected value or the median?

3. Calculate the expected return, mode, and median for a stock having the following probability distribution:

Return (%)	Probability of Occurrence
−40	.03
−10	.07
0	.30
15	.10
30	.05
40	.20
50	.25

4. At the beginning of the year the market price of Tulipmania stock was $45. At the end of the year the stock was selling for $40. During the year the company paid a cash dividend of $1. What was the stock's holding-period return for the year?

5. Charles Ponzi purchased 100 shares of Postal Reply Coupons, Incorporated (PRC) and held the securities for a total of four years. Ponzi's holding-period returns in these four years were as follows:

Year	Return (%)
1	+20
2	+30
3	+50
4	−90

    a. What was the value-relative for the four-year period?

    b. What was the geometric mean return for the four-year period?

6. In August of 1979 Harrah's Casino in Reno, Nevada, accepted bets on the teams that would eventually go to the Superbowl to play for the National Football League championship. For example, one could pay $10 at that time to bet that the Oakland Raiders would represent the American Football Conference in the Superbowl. The payoff on such a bet was set at $60 if the Raiders did go to the Superbowl, and zero otherwise. Payoffs for bets on all the teams in the Western Division of the American Football Conference were:

Team	Payoff per $1 Bet
Seattle Seahawks	$ 13
Oakland Raiders	6
San Diego Chargers	5
Denver Broncos	11
Kansas City Chiefs	101

a. What was the present value of $1 contingent on the event (state of the world) "The Raiders go to the Superbowl"?

b. What was the present value of $1 contingent on the event "The Seahawks go to the Superbowl"?

c. Why did the answers for (a) and (b) differ?

d. If someone had offered to pay you $1 if *any* team in the Western Division of the American Football Conference went to the Superbowl, how much would you have paid for this bet ("security")? If you had been virtually certain that one of these teams would go to the Superbowl, would your answer differ? Why or why not?

Portfolio Analysis

6

PORTFOLIO AND SECURITY RETURNS

A major thesis of investment management is the need to consider individual investments as components of an overall investment plan. Without limiting the range of instruments covered, it is convenient to call individual investments *securities* and the totality the *portfolio*. Since it is rarely desirable to invest the entire funds of an individual or an institution in a single security, it is essential that every security be viewed in a portfolio context. This implies, for example, that a security's *total* risk is not of prime importance, only its *contribution* to the total risk of a portfolio. This distinction will be treated at length later. First, we consider the simpler case of return.

For expected return, the two measures coincide. A security's expected return *is* its contribution to portfolio expected return.

The example of a portfolio with three securities shown in Table 6-1 (a) illustrates the point. The expected holding-period value-relative for the portfolio is clearly:

$$\frac{\$19,200}{17,200} = 1.1163$$

giving an expected holding-period return of 11.63%.

TABLE 6-1(a) Security and Portfolio Values

(1) Security	(2) No. of Shares	(3) Current Price per Share	(4) Current Value = (2) × (3)	(5) Expected End-of-Period Value per Share	(6) Expected End-of-Period Value = (2) × (5)
ABC	100	$40	$4,000	$42	$4,200
DEF	200	35	7,000	40	8,000
XYZ	100	62	6,200	70	7,000
			$17,200		$19,200

TABLE 6-1(b) Security and Portfolio Value-Relatives

(1) Security	(2) Current Value	(3) Proportion of Current Value of Portfolio = (2)/\$17,200	(4) Current Price per Share	(5) Expected End-of- Period Value per Share	(6) Expected Holding- Period Value- Relative = (5)/(4)	(7) Contribution to Portfolio Expected Holding-Period Value-Relative = (3) × (6)
ABC	\$4,000	.2325	\$40	\$42	1.0500	.2441
DEF	7,000	.4070	35	40	1.1429	.4652
XYZ	6,200	.3605	62	70	1.1290	.4070
	\$17,200	1.0000				1.1163

Table 6-1(b) combines the information in a somewhat different manner. As shown, the portfolio's expected holding-period value-relative is simply a *weighted average* of the expected value-relatives of its component securities, using *current market values* as weights.

This is not too surprising. Let us represent the current market value of security 1 by v_1^c, that of security 2 by v_2^c, and that of security 3 by v_3^c. Expected end-of-period values can be represented by v_1^e, v_2^e, and v_3^e. The current market value of the portfolio is, of course, $v_1^c + v_2^c + v_3^c$, while its expected end-of-period value is $v_1^e + v_2^e + v_3^e$. The expected value-relatives for the securities are just: v_1^e/v_1^c, v_2^e/v_2^c, and v_3^e/v_3^c; while the relative market proportions are $v_1^c/(v_1^c + v_2^c + v_3^c)$, $v_2^c/(v_1^c + v_2^c + v_3^c)$, and $v_3^c/(v_1^c + v_2^c + v_3^c)$. The portfolio's expected value-relative is:

$$\frac{v_1^e + v_2^e + v_3^e}{v_1^c + v_2^c + v_3^c} \qquad (6\text{-}1)$$

This value is computed directly in Table 6-1(a).

In Table 6-1(b) each security's expected value-relative is multiplied by its relative market value and these products summed. Using the current notation:

$$\left(\frac{v_1^c}{v_1^c + v_2^c + v_3^c} \cdot \frac{v_1^e}{v_1^c}\right) + \left(\frac{v_2^c}{v_1^c + v_2^c + v_3^c} \cdot \frac{v_2^e}{v_2^c}\right) + \left(\frac{v_3^c}{v_1^c + v_2^c + v_3^c} \cdot \frac{v_3^e}{v_3^c}\right) \quad (6\text{-}2)$$

After canceling and simplifying, this reduces to formula (6-1).

The relationship is perfectly general. A portfolio's expected holding-period value-relative will be a weighted average of its component securities' expected holding-period value-relatives, using current market values as weights.

The procedure can be used as easily with holding-period returns. Table 6-1(c) provides an illustration. Holding-period return is simply 100 times the value obtained by subtracting 1 from the holding-period value-relative. Thus a weighted average of the former will have the same characteristics as a weighted average of the latter:

> The expected return of a portfolio is a weighted average of the expected returns of its component securities, using relative market values as weights.

TABLE 6-1(c) Security and Portfolio Holding-Period Returns

(1) Security	(2) Proportion of Current Value of Portfolio	(3) Expected Holding- Period Return (%)	(4) Contribution to Portfolio Expected Holding-Period Return (%)
ABC	.2325	5.00	1.16
DEF	.4070	14.29	5.82
XYZ	.3605	12.90	4.65
	1.0000		11.63

In symbols:

$$E_p = \sum_{i=1}^{N} X_i E_i$$

where:

E_p = the expected return of the portfolio
X_i = the proportion of the portfolio's value invested in security i
E_i = the expected return of security i
N = the number of securities

The summation sign means that every security must be included in the total (i.e., $E_p = X_1 E_1 + X_2 E_2 + \cdots + X_N E_N$).

Since portfolio expected return is a weighted average of the expected returns of its securities, the contribution of each security to portfolio expected return depends on its expected return and its proportionate share of the current portfolio's market value. Nothing else is relevant.

An investor who simply wants the greatest possible expected return should hold one security: the one he or she considers to have the greatest expected return. In case of ties, a coin could be flipped to decide which of the group of top candidates to hold. Very few investors do this, and very few investment advisers would counsel such an extreme policy. Instead, investors should, and do, *diversify*: their portfolios include more than one security. Why? Because diversification can reduce *risk*.

RISK

The *Webster's New Collegiate Dictionary* definition of risk includes the following meanings: ". . . possibility of loss or injury . . . the degree or probability of such loss."[1] This conforms to the connotation put on the term by most investors. Professionals often speak "downside risk" and "upside potential" on the grounds that risk has to do with bad outcomes; potential with good ones.

[1] By permission. From *Webster's New Collegiate Dictionary* © 1980 by G. & C. Merriam Co., Publishers of the Merriam-Webster dictionaries.

As formal measures of risk, such notions can be criticized on two grounds: vagueness and excessive simplicity. One might measure risk by the probability that return will fall below the expected value. But this could characterize many different investments as equally risky. (For example, the probability in question is .50 for all symmetric distributions.) A more common procedure would focus on the probability of any *negative* return. But even this is an extremely blunt measure. Which is riskier: an investment with a .30 probability of a slight loss or one with a .29 probability of a very large loss? Most investors would specify the latter.

A more useful measure of risk takes into account both the probability of an outcome and its magnitude. Instead of measuring the probability of a range of outcomes, one estimates the extent to which the actual outcome is likely to *diverge* from the expected value.

Two measures are used for this purpose: the average (or mean) absolute deviation and the standard deviation.

Table 6-2(a) shows how the average absolute deviation can be calculated. First the expected return is determined in the usual way.[2] In this case it is 6.50%. Next, each possible outcome is analyzed to determine the amount by which its value deviates from the expected amount. These figures, shown in column (5) of the table, include both positive and negative values. As shown in column (6), a weighted average, using probabilities as weights, will equal zero. This is a mathematical necessity, given the way the expected value is calculated. To assess risk, the signs of the deviations can simply be ignored. As shown in column (7), the weighted average of the absolute values of the deviations, using the probabilities as weights, is 7.65%. This constitutes the first measure of "likely" deviation.

The second measure is slightly more complex but preferable analytically. As shown in Table 6-2(b), the deviations are squared (making the values all positive); then a weighted average of these amounts is taken, using the probabilities as weights. The result is termed the *variance*. We convert it to the original units by taking the square root. The result (in Table 6-2(b), 9.3675%) is termed the *standard deviation*.

In the examples shown in Tables 6-2(a) and (b) any single measure of likely deviation would provide at best a very crude idea of the possibilities. But in the more common case in which a portfolio's prospects are being assessed, either of the measures described earlier may prove to be a very good guide to the analysts' degree of uncertainty. The clearest example arises when the situation can be reasonably well represented by the familiar bell-shaped curve: that is, the analyst is willing to use a *normal probability distribution*. This is often considered a plausible assumption for analyzing returns on diversified portfolios when the holding period being studied is relatively short (say a quarter or less). For longer holding periods, a more appropriate procedure assumes that the portfolio's *continuously compounded rate of return* is distributed in this manner (equivalently: that the return itself follows a "log-normal" distribution). Such an approach may be applied for any holding period; but for short holding periods, since actual return differs little from the continuously compounded return, either procedure may be used.

---

[2] A more consistent approach uses the median return instead of the expected return when calculating the mean absolute deviation.

TABLE 6-2(a) Calculating the Mean Absolute Deviation

(1) Event	(2) Probability	(3) Return (%)	(4) = (2) × (3) Probability × Return
a	.20	−10	−2.00
b	.35	5	1.75
c	.45	15	6.75
			Expected return = 6.50

(5) = (3) − 6.50 Deviation	(6) = (2) × (5) Probability × Deviation	(7) Probability × Absolute Deviation
−16.50	−3.300	3.300
−1.50	−.525	.525
8.50	3.825	3.825
	0	

Average absolute deviation = 7.65

TABLE 6-2(b) Calculating the Standard Deviation

(1) Event	(2) Probability	(3) Deviation	(4) = (3)² Deviation Squared	(5) = (2) × (4) Probability × Deviation Squared
a	.20	−16.50	272.25	54.45
b	.35	−1.50	2.25	.7875
c	.45	8.50	72.25	32.5125

Variance = probability weighted average squared deviation = 87.75
Standard deviation = square root of variance = 9.3675

For a normal distribution the standard deviation is about 125% of the average absolute deviation. Either value may thus be determined, once the other is known. In general, a list of portfolios ordered from highest to lowest on the basis of the standard deviation of return would differ little if at all from a list ordered on the basis of average absolute deviation.

But why count happy surprises (those above the expected value) at all in a measure of risk? Why not just consider the deviations *below* the expected return? Measures that do so have much to recommend them. But if a distribution is symmetric, the results will be the same, since the left side is a mirror image of the right! And in general, a list of portfolios ordered on the basis of "downside risk" will differ little if at all from one ordered on the basis of standard deviation. A similar statement can be made about many other reasonable measures of risk.

Although different measures of risk are often virtually interchangeable, the standard deviation is generally preferred for investment analysis. The reason is simple: the standard deviation of a portfolio's return can be determined from (among other things) the standard deviations of the returns of its component securities, no matter what the distri-

TABLE 6-3 Probabilities of Divergence for a Normal Distribution

Divergence, in Terms of Standard Deviation Units	Probability that Divergence Will Be Less than This Amount
0	0
.10	.08
.20	.16
.30	.24
.40	.31
.50	.38
.60	.45
.70	.52
.80	.58
.90	.63
1.00	.68
1.10	.73
1.20	.77
1.30	.81
1.40	.84
1.50	.87
1.60	.89
1.70	.91
1.80	.93
1.90	.94
2.00	.95
2.10	.96
2.20	.97
2.30	.98
2.40	.98
2.50	.99

butions. No relationship of comparable simplicity exists for most other measures.

Let us emphasize the meaning of this measure of risk:

> The standard deviation is an estimate of the likely divergence of an *actual* amount from an *expected* amount.

For working purposes, the returns are often assumed to follow a normal distribution, giving the relationships shown in Table 6-3. Thus the odds are thought to be about 2 out of 3 that the actual outcome will lie within one standard deviation of the expectation and about 95 out of 100 that the actual outcome will lie within two standard deviations of the expectation.

When an analyst predicts that a stock will return 12% next year, he or she is presumably stating something comparable to an expected value. If asked to express the *uncertainty* about the outcome, the analyst might reply that the odds are about 2 out of 3 that the actual return will be within 8% of the estimate (i.e., between 4% and 20%). The standard deviation is a formal measure of uncertainty, or risk, expressed in this manner, just as the expected value is a formal measure of a "best guess" estimate. Most analysts make such predictions directly, without explicitly assessing probabilities and making the requisite computations. No matter. The point is to consider uncertainty or risk and to measure its extent as best one can.

PORTFOLIO RISK

What is the relationship between the risk of a portfolio and the risks of its component securities? An answer that covers all possible cases is both complex and of limited practical importance. We will develop the general relationship briefly, then turn to some special cases that are both relatively simple and extremely important for investment analysis.

Table 6-4(a) shows the returns on two securities and on a portfolio that includes both of them. Each row in the table indicates an analyst's assessment of the likely outcomes if a particular event takes place; the probability of the event is also shown.

In Table 6-4(a), security A constitutes 60% of the market value of the portfolio and security B the other 40%. The predicted return on the portfolio in each row is simply a weighted average of the predicted returns on the securities, using the proportionate values as weights.

TABLE 6-4 Portfolio and Security Risks

(a) RETURNS

(1) Event	(2) Probability	(3) Return on Security A	(4) Return on Security B	(5) = .6 × (3) + .4 × (4) Return on Portfolio
a	.10	5.0%	−1.0%	2.6%
b	.40	7.0	6.0	6.6
c	.30	−4.0	2.0	−1.6
d	.20	15.0	20.0	17.0

(b) SUMMARY MEASURES

	Security A	Security B	Portfolio
Expected return	5.10%	6.90%	5.82%
Variance of return	45.89	48.09	42.7956
Standard deviation of return	6.7742	6.9347	6.5418

(c) COVARIANCE AND CORRELATION

(1) Event	(2) Probability	(3) Deviation of Return for Sec. A	(4) Deviation of Return for Sec. B	(5) = (3) × (4) Product of Deviations	(6) = (2) × (5) Probability Times Product of Deviations
a	.10	−.1%	−7.90%	.79	.079
b	.40	1.90	−.9	−1.71	−.684
c	.30	−9.10	−4.9	44.59	13.377
d	.20	9.90	13.1	129.69	25.938

Covariance = 38.71

$$\text{Correlation coefficient} = \frac{38.71}{6.7742 \times 6.9347} = .824$$

Table 6-4(b) shows values computed from the estimates in Table 6-4(a), using the procedures described in previous sections. As always, the expected return for the portfolio is simply the weighted average of the expected returns on its securities, using the proportionate values as weights (5.82% = .6 × 5.10% + .4 × 6.90%). However, this is not true for either the variance or the standard deviation of returns. The risk of a portfolio is not typically equal to the weighted average of the risks of its component securities. In this case, both the variance and the standard deviation of return for the portfolio are smaller than the corresponding values for either of the component securities!

This rather surprising result has a simple explanation. The risk of a portfolio depends not only on the risks of its securities, considered in isolation, but also on the extent to which they are affected similarly by underlying events. To illustrate this, two extreme cases are shown in Table 6-5.

In the first case both the variance and the standard deviation of the portfolio are the same as the corresponding values for the securities. Here diversification has no effect at all on risk.

In the second case the situation is very different. Here the security's returns offset one another in such a manner that the particular combination that makes up this portfolio has no risk at all! Diversification has completely eliminated risk.

TABLE 6-5 Risk and Return for a Two-Security Portfolio

(a) TWO SECURITIES WITH EQUAL RETURNS

(1) Event	(2) Probability	(3) Return on Security A (%)	(4) Return on Security B (%)	(5) = .6 × (3) + .4 × (4) Return on Portfolio (%)
a	.10	5.0	5.0	5.0
b	.40	7.0	7.0	7.0
c	.30	6.0	6.0	6.0
d	.20	−2.0	−2.0	−2.0
Expected return (%)		4.70	4.70	4.70
Variance of return		11.61	11.61	11.61
Standard deviation of return		3.4073	3.4073	3.4073

(b) TWO SECURITIES WITH OFFSETTING RETURNS

(1) Event	(2) Probability	(3) Return on Security A (%)	(4) Return on Security B (%)	(5) = .6 × (3) + .4 × (4) Return on Portfolio (%)
a	.10	5.0	2.5	4.0
b	.40	7.0	−.5	4.0
c	.30	6.0	1.0	4.0
d	.20	−2.0	13.0	4.0
Expected return (%)		4.70	2.95	4.0
Variance of return		11.61	26.1225	0
Standard deviation of return		3.4073	5.1110	0

The difference between these cases concerns the extent to which the security's returns are *correlated*—i.e., tend to "go together." Either of two measures can be used to state the degree of such a relationship: the *covariance* or the *correlation coefficient*.

Table 6-4(c) shows the computations required to obtain the covariance for the two securities considered earlier. The deviation of each security's return from its expected value is determined and the product of the two obtained [column (5)]:

> The *covariance* of two securities' returns is a weighted average of the products of the deviations of the returns from their expected values, using the probabilities of the deviations as weights.

A positive value for covariance indicates that the securities' returns tend to go together—for example, a better-than-expected return for one is likely to occur along with a better-than-expected return for the other. A negative covariance indicates a tendency for the returns to offset one another—for example, a better-than-expected return for one is likely to occur along with a worse-than-expected return for the other. A small or zero value for the covariance indicates that there is little or no relationship between the two returns.

A related measure is the *correlation coefficient*:

> The *correlation* of two securities' returns equals their covariance divided by the product of their standard deviations.

As shown in Table 6-4(c), in this case the value is .824. The procedure used to obtain the correlation coefficient rescales the covariance to facilitate comparison with corresponding values for other pairs of variables. *Correlation coefficients always lie between −1.0 and +1.0, inclusive*. The former value represents perfect *negative* correlation, of the type shown in the example in Table 6-5(b). The latter value represents perfect positive correlation, of the type shown in the example in Table 6-5(a). Most cases lie between, as does the example shown in Table 6-4.

The relationship between covariance and correlation can be represented as follows:

$$C_{AB} = r_{AB} S_A S_B \qquad (6\text{-}3)$$

or

$$r_{AB} = \frac{C_{AB}}{S_A S_B} \qquad (6\text{-}4)$$

where:

C_{AB} = covariance between return on A and return on B
r_{AB} = coefficient of correlation between return on A and return on B.
S_A = standard deviation of return for A
S_B = standard deviation of return for B

Armed with measures of correlation between two returns, we can now show the relationship between the risk of a portfolio of two securities and the relevant variables. The formula is:

$$V_p = X_A^2 V_A + 2X_A X_B C_{AB} + X_B^2 V_B \qquad (6\text{-}5)$$

where:

V_p = the variance of return for the portfolio
V_A = the variance of return for security A
V_B = the variance of return for security B
C_{AB} = the covariance between the return on security A and the return on security B
X_A = the proportion of the portfolio's value invested in security A
X_B = the proportion of the portfolio's value invested in security B

For the case shown in Table 6-4:

$$X_A = .6$$
$$X_B = .4$$
$$V_A = 45.89$$
$$V_B = 48.09$$
$$C_{AB} = 38.71$$

Inserting these values in formula (6-5) gives 42.7956, which is the variance for the portfolio as a whole.

The relationship that gives the variance for a portfolio with more than two securities is similar in nature but more extensive. Both the risks of the securities and all their correlations have to be taken into account. The formula is:

$$V_p = \sum_{i=1}^{N} \sum_{j=1}^{N} X_i X_j C_{ij} \qquad (6\text{-}6)$$

where:

V_p = the variance of return for the portfolio
X_i = the proportion of the portfolio's value invested in security i
X_j = the proportion of the portfolio's value invested in security j
C_{ij} = the covariance between the return on security i and the return on security j
N = the number of securities

The two summation signs mean that every possible combination must be included in the total, with a value between 1 and N substituted where i appears and a value between 1 and N substituted where j appears. In those cases in which the values are the same, the relevant covariance is that between a security's return and itself. This is the variance of the security's return, as reexamination of the procedure described before will show.

Formula (6-6) is rarely used in all its detail; it is included here primarily for completeness. The key ideas about portfolio risk can be obtained from an examination of important special cases, to which we now turn.

WHEN DIVERSIFICATION DOESN'T HELP: PERFECTLY POSITIVELY CORRELATED RETURNS

The returns from two securities are perfectly positively correlated when a cross-plot gives points lying precisely on an upward-sloping straight line, as shown in Figure 6-1(a). Each point indicates the return on security A (horizontal axis) and the return on security B (vertical axis) corresponding to one event. The example shown in Table 6-5(a) conforms to this pattern.

What is the effect on risk when two securities of this type are combined? The general formula (6-5) is:

$$V_p = X_A^2 V_A + 2X_A X_B C_{AB} + X_B^2 V_B$$

The covariance term can, of course, be replaced, using formula (6-3):

$$C_{AB} = r_{AB} S_A S_B$$

However, in this case there is perfect positive correlation, so $r_{AB} = +1$ and $C_{AB} = S_A S_B$. As always, $V_A = S_A^2$, $V_B = S_B^2$, and $V_p = S_p^2$. Substituting all these values in the general formula gives:

$$S_p^2 = X_A^2 S_A^2 + 2X_A X_B S_A S_B + X_B^2 S_B^2$$

The right-hand side can be factored into a single term squared:

$$S_p^2 = (X_A S_A + X_B S_B)^2$$

FIGURE 6-1 Returns on Two Securities

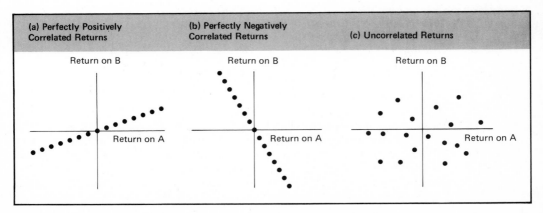

As long as the value in parentheses is not negative:

$$S_p = X_A S_A + X_B S_B \quad \text{when} \quad r_{AB} = +1 \quad\quad (6\text{-}7)$$

This is an important result. *When two securities' returns are perfectly positively correlated, the risk of a combination, measured by the standard deviation of return, is just a weighted average of the risks of the component securities, using market values as weights.* The principle holds as well if more than two securities are included in a portfolio. In such cases, diversification does not provide risk *reduction*, only risk *averaging*.

WHEN DIVERSIFICATION CAN ELIMINATE RISK: PERFECTLY NEGATIVELY CORRELATED RETURNS

The returns from two securities will be perfectly negatively correlated when a cross-plot gives points lying precisely on a downward-sloping straight line, as shown in Figure 6-1(b). The example shown in Table 6-5(b) conforms to this pattern.

Since $r_{AB} = -1$ in such a situation, the general formula becomes:

$$S_p^2 = X_A^2 S_A^2 - 2 X_A X_B S_A S_B + X_B^2 S_B^2$$

This can be factored to obtain:

$$S_p^2 = (X_A S_A - X_B S_B)^2 \quad \text{when} \quad r_{AB} = -1 \quad\quad (6\text{-}8)$$

Now, imagine a portfolio in which the proportionate holdings are inversely related to the relative risks of the two securities. That is:

$$\frac{X_A}{X_B} = \frac{S_B}{S_A}$$

Rearranging:

$$X_A = \frac{S_B X_B}{S_A}$$

For this combination the parenthesized term in formula (6-8) will be:

$$X_A S_A - X_B S_B = \frac{S_B X_B}{S_A} S_A - X_B S_B = 0$$

If this term is zero, of course, the portfolio's standard deviation of return must be zero as well.

When two securities' returns are perfectly negatively correlated, it is possible to combine them in a manner that will eliminate all risk. This principle motivates all *hedging* strategies. The object is to take positions that will offset each other with regard to certain kinds of risk, reducing or completely eliminating such sources of uncertainty.

Hedging strategies, used extensively in the commodity futures market, by certain bond managers, and in the market for options on common stock, will be discussed at length in later chapters.

THE INSURANCE PRINCIPLE: UNCORRELATED RETURNS

A special case of extreme importance arises when a cross-plot of security returns shows no pattern that can be represented even approximately by an upward-sloping or downward-sloping line. In such an instance, the returns are uncorrelated. The correlation coefficient, r_{AB}, is zero, as is the covariance. Figure 6-1(c) provides an example.

In this situation, the general formula (6-5) becomes:

$$S_p^2 = X_A^2 S_A^2 + X_B^2 S_B^2 \qquad \text{when} \quad r_{AB} = 0 \qquad (6\text{-}9)$$

At first glance it might appear that diversification has no effect here. But this is not at all the case. To see this, consider a portfolio divided equally between two securities of equal risk, say 10.0%. That is:

$$X_A = .5, \quad X_B = .5, \quad S_A = 10, \quad S_B = 10$$

Substituting these values in formula (6-9) gives:

$$(.5)^2(10)^2 + (.5)^2(10)^2 = (.25 \times 100) + (.25 \times 100)$$

Thus:

$$S_p^2 = 50 \quad \text{and} \quad S_p = 7.07$$

The risk of the portfolio is less than the risk of either of its component securities. Diversification has indeed helped. If more than two securities with uncorrelated returns are included in a portfolio, the result is similar. In such a case the complete formula (6-6) becomes:

$$S_p^2 = X_1^2 S_1^2 + X_2^2 S_2^2 + \cdots + X_N^2 S_N^2 \qquad (6\text{-}10)$$

when all returns are uncorrelated. In this formula:

S_p = the standard deviation of the return on the portfolio

$X_1, X_2, \ldots$ = the proportions invested in securities 1, 2, etc.

$S_1, S_2, \ldots$ = the standard deviations of the returns for securities 1, 2, etc.

N = the number of securities included.

This is an extremely important relationship for investment analysis. It also provides the basis for insurance, or *risk-pooling*.

This can be seen by extending the previous example. Imagine a portfolio of equal parts of a number of securities, each with a risk (standard deviation of return) of 10%. If two securities are included:

$$S_p^2 = (\tfrac{1}{2})^2 10^2 + (\tfrac{1}{2})^2 10^2$$
$$= 2(\tfrac{1}{2})^2 10^2$$

If three securities are included:

$$S_p^2 = (\tfrac{1}{3})^2 10^2 + (\tfrac{1}{3})^2 10^2 + (\tfrac{1}{3})^2 10^2$$
$$= 3(\tfrac{1}{3})^2 10^2$$

To generalize, represent the number of securities by N. Then:

$$S_p^2 = \left(\frac{1}{N}\right)^2 10^2 + \left(\frac{1}{N}\right)^2 10^2 + \cdots$$

$$= N \left(\frac{1}{N}\right)^2 10^2$$

Simplifying:

$$S_p^2 = \frac{N}{N^2} 10^2 = \frac{10^2}{N}$$

$$S_p = \frac{10}{\sqrt{N}}$$

Table 6-6 shows the relationship between the number of securities included and the risk of the corresponding portfolio, while Figure 6-2 provides a graphical representation.

TABLE 6-6 Risk of Portfolios with Different Numbers of Securities when Returns Are Uncorrelated and all $S_i = 10\%$

Number of Securities	Standard Deviation of Return
1	10.00
2	7.07
3	5.77
4	5.00
5	4.47
10	3.16
20	2.24
50	1.41
100	1.00
1,000	.32
5,000	.14
10,000	.10
100,000	.03

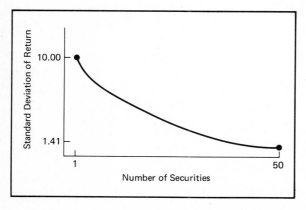

FIGURE 6-2 Risk versus Number of Securities, When Returns Are Uncorrelated and all $S_i = 10\%$

Diversification provides substantial risk reduction if the components of a portfolio are uncorrelated. In fact, *if enough are included, the overall risk of the portfolio will be almost (but not quite) zero!* This is why insurance companies attempt to write many individual policies and spread their coverage so as to minimize overall risk. Death from natural causes can be insured at low cost, since payments on various policies are virtually uncorrelated. On the other hand, death arising from a major war cannot be insured at low cost, since payments are likely to be correlated, at least to some extent.

Some risks can be substantially reduced by pooling, and others cannot. This has crucial implications for investment management. Most importantly, it provides the basis for understanding the relationship between risk and return, as will be shown in the next chapter.

BORROWING AND LENDING: COMBINING RISKY AND RISKLESS SECURITIES

What happens to risk when a risky security (or portfolio) is combined with a riskless one? Once again we can find the answer by adapting the general formula (6-5) in the appropriate manner. If security A's return is certain, while that of security B is uncertain, $S_A = 0$, as does C_{AB}, and the relationship becomes:

$$S_p^2 = X_A^2 0 + 2X_A X_B 0 + X_B^2 S_B^2$$
$$= X_B^2 S_B^2$$

Thus:

$$S_p = X_B S_B \qquad \text{when} \quad S_A = 0 \qquad (6\text{-}11)$$

When a risky security or portfolio is combined with a riskless one, the risk of the combination is proportional to the amount invested in the risky component.

An obvious case of this sort arises when an investor splits his funds between a common stock portfolio and a savings account. Table 6-7 shows some representative values. Cases C and D involve splitting funds between the risky alternative (B) and the riskless one (A). *Investing* in a riskless security is equivalent to *lending* money. For example, by in-

TABLE 6-7 Combining a Risky and a Riskless Investment

	Security A (Savings Account)	Security B (Common Stock Portfolio)	Combination C	Combination D	Combination E
Proportion in A (X_A)	1.0	0	.6	.4	−.2
Proportion in B (X_B)	0	1.0	.4	.6	1.2
Expected return	5.0%	10.0%	7.0%	8.0%	11.0%
Standard deviation of return	0%	20.0%	8.0%	12.0%	24.0%

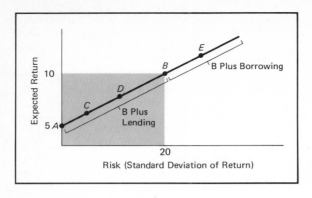

FIGURE 6-3 Risk and Return for Combinations of a Risky and Riskless Investment

vesting in U.S. Treasury bills, one is in effect lending money to the U.S. government.

Combinations C and D are plotted in Figure 6-3, along with the original alternatives, A and B. Each point shows the expected return and risk (standard deviation) of an alternative combination. Since both risk and return will be proportional to the investment proportions in a case of this sort, both point C and point D lie on the straight line connecting points A and B. This relationship is quite general: by combining riskless lending (A) with investment in any risky situation (B), an investor can obtain any risk-return combination plotting along the straight line (AB) connecting the two points in a risk-return diagram such as that shown in Figure 6-3.

When formulas involving investment proportions are used, the proportions must, of course, sum to 1, since the whole must equal the sum of its parts. Moreover, thus far we have focused on cases in which the individual proportions are all positive. But this need not be the case. For example, X_A could equal $-.20$ and X_B could equal $+1.20$, as shown by combination E in Table 6-7 and point E in Figure 6-3.

What does this mean? Imagine a person with $10,000 to invest. If willing to take the risk involved, such an investor might invest all his or her own money and also borrow additional money to take advantage of some (hopefully profitable) opportunity. For example, $2,000 might be borrowed, with a promise to repay the loan plus interest at 5%. A total of $12,000 could then be invested in the project. Everything left over after repaying the loan would belong to the investor.

Table 6-8(a) shows the effect of this sort of leverage under favorable circumstances. Here the investment returns 10%, leaving the investor with a profit on his or her own investment and a net contribution from the investment of the borrowed funds. The result is a total return of 11.0% on the investor's own capital.

The final column of Table 6-7 shows a similar set of computations for combination E. If borrowed funds are invested in a risky alternative with an expected return in excess of the interest rate to be paid, the result is an increase in the expected return on the investor's capital. This is the good news about *leverage*: point E lies above point B in Figure 6-3.

However, leverage can also bring bad news. This is shown in Table 6-8(b), which indicates the outcome when the investment in question returns less than the rate paid on borrowed funds. The investor must make up the difference, reducing the return on his or her own capital to an amount below that on the investment itself. Clearly, he or she would have been better off without borrowing. This sort of outcome constitutes the *risk* associated with leverage.

The effect of leverage on risk is shown in the fourth line of Table 6-7. Borrowing increases risk. This is also shown in Figure 6-3: point E is to the right of point B.

Investors can and do borrow from a number of sources. Banks will loan money, using cars, houses, or securities as collateral. Credit unions often loan money with no explicit collateral at all. Security brokers loan money, on margin accounts, using securities as collateral.

Interest rates charged for loans differ from time to time. Moreover, at any time the amount charged may depend on the borrower, the lender, the collateral, the purpose for which the loan is made, the length of time involved, and the amount of money borrowed. If there is a chance that the loan will not be repaid in full and on time, the rate charged will, of course, be higher, and the loan will not be riskless, making the use of formula (6-11) inappropriate.

In those cases in which leverage is used within the limits required to keep the loan riskless, the relationship will be that shown in Figure 6-3. Margined or leveraged purchases of any risky investment (e.g., B) can be used to obtain a combination of risk and return plotting above and to the right of point B on the straight line connecting the points representing the two components (A and B). The prospect obtained in this manner will depend on the amount of leverage: the greater the leverage, the farther to the right of the risky investment's point will be the point representing the new combination.

TABLE 6-8 The Effects of Leverage

(a) With a Favorable Outcome:	
Investment return	10%
Dollar return on total investment	.10 × \$12,000 = \$1,200
Interest rate on loan	5%
Dollar amount of interest	.05 × \$2,000 = 100
	Net proceeds = \$1,100
Return on investor's capital $= \dfrac{1{,}100}{10{,}000} = .110 = 11.0\%$	
(b) With an Unfavorable Outcome:	
Investment return	2%
Dollar return on total investment	.02 × \$12,000 = \$240
Interest rate on loan	5%
Dollar amount of interest	.05 × \$2,000 = 100
	Net proceeds = \$140
Return on investor's capital $= \dfrac{140}{10{,}000} = .014 = 1.4\%$	

Leverage is commonly used by corporations. For example, point *B* in Figure 6-3 might represent the risk and return obtained by a firm on its total assets. If, however, the corporation has issued debt, both the risk and return of its common stock should be greater than this. For example, if the firm had obtained an initial capital of $12,000 by issuing $2,000 worth of debt and $10,000 worth of equity, the results would conform to the example shown in Table 6-7 and Figure 6-3.

Many corporations issue sufficient debt to make at least some of it risky. Thus the relationship is more complex than this. But the point remains: *leverage generally increases both risk and expected return*. It is thus neither obviously desirable nor obviously undesirable.

WHEN LEVERAGE MAY NOT MATTER: MARKET ALTERNATIVES

One of the great debates in the field of corporate finance concerns the appropriate amount of debt in a firm's capital structure. In essence, the question is whether or not to lever the firm's assets and, if so, to what extent. Putting it slightly differently, the issue concerns the appropriate "packaging" of the firm's overall prospects.

One answer to this question was provided in 1938 by John Burr Williams.[3] His *law of the conservation of investment value* asserts that it simply doesn't matter. As long as investors can make deals among themselves, the initial packaging may be irrelevant. For example, if an investor would like a leveraged version of a firm's prospects, and the firm has chosen to issue no debt, the investor can accomplish his or her goal by margined purchase of the firm's stock. On the other hand, if he or she would like an unleveraged version and the firm has issued debt, the investor can simply hold proportionate shares of the firm's debt and equity, thus "putting the firm back together."

An extended analysis of this relationship, provided by Modigliani and Miller in 1958, is now generally known as the *M-M hypothesis*.[4] Subsequent discussion has centered on tax effects, bankruptcy costs, and other factors that may make it more efficient for firms to provide certain combinations than for investors to do so.

Many investment institutions exist solely to allow low-cost packaging, unpackaging, or repackaging of various investment projects. Their very existence is evidence that such a function is not costless. However, these institutions make such activity possible and relatively inexpensive. If a firm packages its prospects inappropriately, some other procedure may be used to repackage the outcomes. A firm's choice of leverage may matter, but much less than it would in a less well-developed capital market.

[3] John Burr Williams, *The Theory of Investment Value* (Cambridge: Harvard University Press, 1938).

[4] Franco Modigliani and Merton Miller, "The Cost of Capital, Corporation Finance, and the Theory of Investment," *American Economic Review*, 48, no. 3 (June 1958), 261–97.

WHEN LEVERAGE DOES MATTER:
PERSONAL INVESTMENT POLICY

Eventually everyone must select an overall investment policy. In doing so, one should consider all sources of future income: salary, savings, insurance, social security, pension, stocks and bonds, etc. The sum total can be viewed as a total portfolio. Alternatively, all the risky elements can be considered one portfolio and the riskless elements another. Figure 6-4 shows the latter view, highlighting the decision concerning the appropriate amount of borrowing or lending. This particular investor's attitudes toward risk and return are summarized in a family of indifference curves. He or she is indifferent among combinations lying on curve I_1. He or she is also indifferent among combinations lying on curve I_2 but would prefer any of them to any combination lying on I_1. The curves are upward-sloping, indicating the common preference for higher expected return and aversion to risk. Thus, if a person considers two combinations equally good, the one with the greater expected return must also be more risky.

The particular shape of the indifference curves reflecting an investor's preferences depends on his or her unique attitudes, circumstances, and general psychology. While all risk-averse investors will be characterized by upward-sloping curves, the precise shapes will generally differ. The investor shown in Figure 6-4(a) prefers to split funds between the risky combination shown by point R and the riskless alternative shown by point P. The preferred combination is C_1—it lies on his or her highest (best) attainable indifference curve, which says nothing more than that he or she prefers it over all the available alternatives on line PRZ.

The investor shown in Figure 6-4(b), presented with the same alternatives, chooses to borrow funds. His or her preferred combination is C_2—which lies on the highest (best) attainable indifference curve. Such a person may be richer, younger, or simply more adventuresome. But no one can say that he or she is right and the other investor is wrong. The ultimate choice between risk and return is up to the person who will bear

FIGURE 6-4 Selecting a Personal Investment Policy

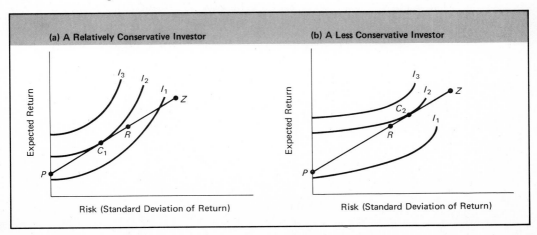

the consequences of that choice. Investment advisers can help a client obtain the best possible alternatives, understand the prospects for those alternatives, and think carefully about his or her feelings about those prospects. But the final decision must depend on the client's preferences.

INVESTMENT SELECTION: AN OVERVIEW

Figure 6-5 provides a graphical summary of the conceptual steps involved in investment selection.

The first step requires analysis of the prospects of potential investment media. This is traditionally known as *security analysis*. Both the expected return and the risk of each alternative must be assessed. This information is portrayed graphically in Figure 6-5(a). In addition, some assessment must be made of the correlations among the various returns. As discussed in the next chapter, this process can be simplified considerably, but it cannot be ignored.

The second step is *portfolio analysis*. In essence, the predictions obtained in the first step must be combined to determine the prospects of alternative portfolios (combinations). From these a set of *efficient* alternatives can be identified:

An *efficient portfolio* has less risk than any other with comparable expected return and more return than any other with comparable risk.

In Figure 6-5(b1) no riskless alternatives are available. Every point in the shaded area, or opportunity set, represents an attainable portfolio, and the *efficient portfolios* plot along the upper left-hand border of this area. This is the *efficient risk-return trade-off*. To find it, relatively sophisticated computer analysis may have to be performed. For present purposes it suffices to state that, given the estimates of security analysts, determination of the efficient set of portfolios is a strictly mechanical procedure.

Figure 6-5(b2) shows the results of portfolio analysis when it is possible to both lend and borrow (within reason) at some riskless interest rate P. The procedure can be broken into two parts. First, the set of efficient risky portfolios is determined, as before. Then one of these is chosen to be combined with borrowing or lending; in Figure 6-5(b2) it is the portfolio represented by point R. By combining this portfolio with borrowing or lending, an investor can obtain any desired risk-return combination lying on the relevant portion of line PRZ. Such combinations are clearly better than any shown in the original shaded area and any obtained by combining borrowing or lending with any other risky portfolio. Graphically, the preferred combination of risky securities is obtained by swinging a line from point P until it just touches the upper border of the shaded area. Combining P with any other portfolio would clearly give a risk-return combination lying on a lower, and thus less desirable, line. The portfolio plotting at point R is thus the *optimum combination of risky securities*.

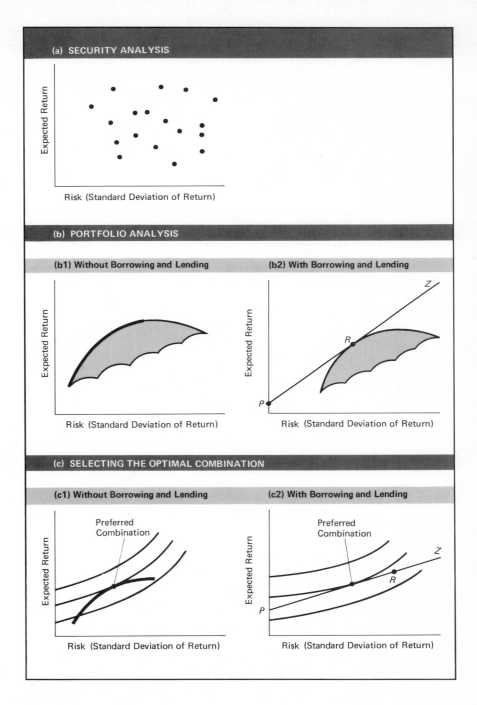

FIGURE 6-5 Investment Selection

The final step in the overall process is the selection of the preferred investment strategy for the investor in question. If borrowing and lending are available, this simply requires a decision regarding the amount to be borrowed or lent to purchase the optimal risky portfolio identified in the previous stage, as shown in Figure 6-5(c2). If this is not the case, the combination must be chosen from a more complex set of efficient portfolios, as shown in Figure 6-5(c1).

This overall procedure is at least implicit in investment selection, whether the client is a person or an institution. In many cases, constraints and/or alterations must be included to reflect the circumstances surrounding the ultimate beneficiary. Some institutional investors are more concerned with long-run returns than many private investors. Tax status differs considerably. Some investors may require a minimum level of current income from their portfolios, and so on.

Other differences occur in the final step. In some cases a professional adviser will present a client with at least a rough idea of his or her assessment of the risk-return trade-off, then ask the client to choose a preferred portfolio. In other cases the adviser will attempt in advance to assess the client's circumstances and attitudes, then make the complete choice. In yet other cases a money management organization may describe a set of attitudes that it plans to assume in its portfolio management, then invite those with similar attitudes to provide funds for investment. Mutual funds provide a good example of the latter procedure.

The three stages of investment selection are often performed by different people. One or more *security analysts* may be responsible for stage 1, a *portfolio manager* for stage 2, and an *investment counselor* (or *adviser*), plus the client, for stage 3. Some investors fill some or all the roles themselves, and some professionals take on two or even all three roles. Even in organizations with large staffs, there is often some overlap in functions.

Whatever procedure is followed, it is important to recognize that conceptually different functions are involved, and that rather different skills may be required for successful performance. Properly accounting for this provides a challenge and an opportunity for both investors and money managers.

Problems

1. If portfolio expected return is always equal to the weighted average of the expected returns of the component securities, why is not portfolio risk always equal to the weighted average of security risks?
2. What assumptions lie behind the notion that only efficient portfolios are worthy of consideration?

3. An investment has the following possible returns and associated probabilities:

Return	Probability
−10%	.24
0	.16
+10%	.36
+25%	.24

Compute the expected return and standard deviation of return for this investment.

4. Two investments (A and B) have the following returns for the specified events:

		EVENT		
		1	2	3
Returns	Security A	10	5	−20
	Security B	0	2	−10
	Event Probability	.5	.4	.1

Calculate the variances (V_A and V_B), standard deviations (S_A and S_B), the covariance (C_{AB}), and the correlation (r_{AB}).

5. Three securities have the following expected returns, variances and covariances:

EXPECTED RETURNS (%)	
Security	Expected Return
1	6
2	8
3	12

VARIANCES AND COVARIANCES			
		Security	
	1	2	3
Security 1	500	100	100
2	100	700	200
3	100	200	900

Find the expected return, variance of return, and standard deviation of return for a portfolio having proportions $X_1 = .5$, $X_2 = .3$, and $X_3 = .2$.

6. Why might an insurance company limit the number of homes it would insure against loss by fire or flood in a given area while remaining willing to write such policies in many different areas?

7. Mr. Hartford estimates the risk of security A to be 20% (return per year) and the risk of security B to be the same. He also believes their returns

will be determined by completely unrelated events (i.e. that their returns are uncorrelated).

a. Assuming he is right, what will be the risk of a portfolio divided equally between the two securities?

b. What about a portfolio with 60% invested in security A and 40% in B?

c. What combination of the two securities is likely to have the smallest risk?

d. Is the combination in (c) the one that Mr. Hartford should choose?

8. A successful investment consultant has decided that he prefers sailing in the Caribbean to any other possible type of vacation. He can charter (rent) a boat when he wishes to go there or he can purchase a boat, lease it to the chartering company, and use it when he goes. Why might he choose the latter alternative?

9. A professor purchased a house for $100,000, using $20,000 of her own money and $80,000 borrowed at an interest rate of 12%. A year later she sold the house for $120,000 and paid off the mortgage.

a. What was the return on the total investment?

b. What was the return on her investment?

c. How would you have answered (a) and (b) if the sales price had been $110,000?

d. *Before the fact*, would you have advised the professor to obtain a larger or smaller mortgage? Why?

Risk and Return: The Capital-Asset Pricing Model

7

THE IMPORTANCE OF RISK *AND* RETURN

Risk and return are the two key features of investment media and investment strategy. It is thus important to know their sources. The major factors contributing to each must be identified and evaluated. This is the primary task of security analysis, and the results are crucial ingredients for portfolio construction, revision, and evaluation, as well as for setting long-range investment policy.

The analysis of risk and return should not be undertaken without careful consideration of the impact of other investors' actions on security prices. In an efficient capital market there will be likely relationships between risk and return; investment analysis should begin by considering such relationships, then proceed to assess the possible extent of deviations in particular cases.

To repeat: ways must be found to think about the sources of risk and return and the likely relationships among them. These two tasks are almost inextricably intertwined and can rarely be completely separated. One issue lies in the realm of *descriptive* analysis: how are risk and return likely to be related? The other issue lies in the realm of *decision-making*: how should risk and return be taken into account in investment management? This chapter deals with the former question; the next chapter is concerned with both aspects.

THE NEED FOR SIMPLIFICATION

The discussion of risk and return in previous chapters provides the conceptual basis for investment analysis. However, it is far from usable at the practical level. No analyst can be expected to delineate every possible contingency of relevance, then estimate its probability of occurrence and the effect it will have on every possible investment alternative. This can be avoided to some extent if expected returns are estimated directly, along with the likely divergence of each security's return from its expected value.

But a problem still remains. To estimate the risk of a portfolio, one must estimate the likely degrees of correlation for all possible pairs of securities. This is too much. *Simplification* is required. The analyst must *abstract* from the full complexity of the situation, focusing instead on the most important elements.

A mathematician would describe this process as building a *model* of the world, the market, and the security or securities in question. This is a useful view and one that well describes a number of valuation methods developed and used by members of the investment community. In each case the assumptions are necessarily simplistic, in order to provide a sufficient degree of abstraction to allow some success in the analytic process. The "reasonableness" of the assumptions (or lack thereof) is, in the final analysis, of little direct relevance. Just as the test of a cake is in the eating, so the test of a model is its ability to help one understand (and perhaps predict) the process being modeled. At the very least, it is useful to know how analysts simplify the valuation process simply because their actions influence prices.

We proceed then with the process of abstraction: moving from some very simple views (or "models") to somewhat more complex alternatives. Models intended to apply to most or all types of investment media will be described in this chapter and the next, while those designed primarily for the valuation of specific types of securities will be described in later chapters.

THE CAPITAL-ASSET PRICING MODEL

Security prices are the result of different analyses of somewhat different sets of information, along with different conditions and preferences relevant for various investors. One analyst's estimates of risk and return for a security are likely to differ from those of other analysts. Since both risk and return are subjective estimates dealing with the future, there is ample room for disagreement. People differ in their predictions of the future, be it the future of the economy or of the return from a single security. Moreover, a single analyst's predictions will change over time, as he or she receives news of relevance for the situation being predicted. These differences make the security markets exciting, unpredictable, and profitable for brokers and others. They also make it impossible to categorically measure risk and return and the relationship between them.

However, it is useful to consider the *consensus* opinion of analysts regarding these matters. Votes in the marketplace are not taken democratically: those managing the most money have the most influence on prices. The majority of dollar votes is under the control of a rather well-informed and careful group of analysts and money managers. To the extent that they share similar information and use similar types of analysis, their consensus opinion is likely to reflect as good a set of estimates of risk and return as one can find.

But will this opinion be reflected in prices? What about the ill-informed and the incompetent? Might they artificially inflate prices of "fad" stocks or depress those of securities currently "out of favor"? They can, and upon occasion they may. But the net effect may be fairly small. First, lack of information and/or poor analysis will lead some to overly optimistic assessments of future prospects, and others to overly pessimistic assessments. Such people will tend to cancel each other out, in terms of impact on the market. Second, any substantial divergence of price from the value estimated by the professional investment community will set in motion powerful forces. If a price seems unreasonably low to those in the know, purchase orders will flood in, driving the price back up. If the price seems unreasonably high, many orders to sell will appear, driving the price back down.

In short, prices may not diverge much or for long from those consistent with a consensus professional view of risk and return. This makes it both possible and necessary to analyze the manner in which such a view is likely to affect security prices.

A simple, yet powerful description of the relationship between risk and return in an efficient market is provided by the *capital-asset pricing model* (CAPM). This approach, developed in the mid-1960s, provides the intellectual basis for much of the current practice in the investment industry. Since the introduction of the model a number of extensions and modifications have been proposed. We will describe some of these in later chapters. Here we concentrate on the original version.

To focus on risk and return, the capital-asset pricing model reduces the situation to an extreme case. Every investor is assumed to have the same information and to analyze and process it in the same way. Everyone thus agrees about the future prospects for securities. Moreover, investors are assumed to be concerned *only* with risk and return. Since risk and return relate present price to future prospects, every investor in such a never-never land agrees with every other regarding all the ingredients required for portfolio analysis. And, since everyone knows all the relevant aspects of portfolio analysis, all will process the available information in the same way.

To complete the scenario, transactions costs are ignored (brokers are assumed to work for nothing) and every investor is able to borrow or lend money at the Treasury bill rate. Moreover, taxes are assumed to have no noticeable effect on investment policy. This constitutes the world of the (original) capital-asset pricing model.

What would happen in such a world? First, everyone would analyze the situation and determine a set of efficient risky portfolios, but *everyone would obtain the same set*. Since borrowing and lending at the same rate of interest are possible, no adviser need stop at this point, since he or she can proceed to select one of the efficient portfolios as the preferred combination of risky securities, regardless of a client's preferences. Moreover, *each adviser would recommend the same combination of risky securities*. Each investor would thus be advised to spread his or her funds "at risk" among securities in the same indicated proportions, adding borrowing or lending to taste to achieve a personally preferred combination of risk and return.

But what if it won't work? In this world every adviser will recommend the same proportionate holdings of risky securities. What if shares of the Little Gem Mining Company are not included on the list? No one will want to hold them, and orders to sell will be received in substantial quantities. Prices will fall, as brokers try to find someone who will buy. But now all the analysts must go back to their drawing boards. If Little

Gem's future prospects are unchanged, but the current price is lower, expected return will be greater than before. This alone makes a new analysis necessary. Eventually, of course, when the price has fallen far enough, analysts will recommend the stock to their clients after all.

The converse situation could also arise. What if all analysts conclude that 20% of every investor's funds at risk should be invested in Ford Motors stock, but at current prices Ford shares constitute considerably less than 20% of total market value? Orders to buy will flood in, and brokers will raise the price in search of sellers. This will alleviate the problem in two ways. First, Ford will represent an increasing share of market value. Second, it will be less and less attractive as its price rises, causing analysts to recommend smaller proportionate holdings.

How can everything balance out? When will all the adjustment stop, bringing the market into *equilibrium?* First, *when there is consistency between the total amount one group of investors wishes to borrow and the amount another group wishes to lend. Second, when the preferred combination of risky securities contains every such security, each in proportion to its market value outstanding.*

THE MARKET PORTFOLIO

A combination of all securities, each in proportion to market value outstanding, is called the *market portfolio.* Included may be stocks, bonds, real estate, and so on. Such a portfolio plays a central role:

Under the assumptions of the original capital-asset pricing model, efficient investment strategies include *only* the market portfolio, borrowing, and/or lending.

While no counterpart for the overall market portfolio is described in the daily press, indices intended to measure the performance of major components are available. One of the most widely known is Standard and Poor's 500-stock index, a value-weighted average of 500 important stocks. Since each stock is weighted by the market value of outstanding shares, and since primarily stocks with large values outstanding are included, this index represents the results obtained in the stock market segment of the overall capital market reasonably well.

Complete coverage of the stocks listed on the New York Stock Exchange is provided by the Exchange's composite index, which also weights stocks in proportion to total value outstanding. The American Stock Exchange computes a similar index for the stocks it lists, and the National Association of Security Dealers provides a value-weighted index of over-the-counter stocks traded via the NASDAQ system. The Wilshire 5000 index, covering 5,000 stocks, is the most comprehensive index of this type published regularly and should thus be closer than others to a representation of the true market portfolio.

Without question the most widely quoted market index is the Dow Jones Industrial Average. Although based on the performance of only 30 stocks, and utilizing a less satisfactory averaging procedure, the "DJIA" provides at least a fair idea of what is happening to stock values.

TABLE 7-1 The Top 50 Securities in Standard and Poor's 500-Stock Index (based on total market value outstanding, June 29, 1979)

Company	Percent of Total Value	Cumulative Percent of Total Value
International Business Machines	6.34	6.34
American Telephone and Telegraph Co.	5.78	12.12
Exxon Corp.	3.53	15.65
General Motors Corp.	2.53	18.18
General Electric Co.	1.68	19.86
Royal Dutch Petroleum Co.	1.55	21.41
Standard Oil Co. of Indiana	1.42	22.83
Schlumberger Ltd.	1.39	24.22
Eastman Kodak Co.	1.36	25.58
Mobil Oil Corp.	1.23	26.81
Standard Oil Co. of California	1.23	28.04
Atlantic Richfield Co.	1.13	29.17
Texaco Inc.	1.11	30.28
Minnesota Mining and Manufacturing Co.	.98	31.26
Procter and Gamble Co.	.94	32.20
Sears Roebuck and Co.	.92	33.12
Shell Oil Co.	.92	34.04
Du Pont E.I. de Nemours and Co.	.88	34.92
Phillips Petroleum Co.	.87	35.79
Gulf Oil Corp.	.79	36.58
Ford Motor Co.	.76	37.34
Merck and Co. Inc.	.75	38.09
Xerox Corp.	.72	38.81
Caterpillar Tractor	.71	39.52
Coca-Cola Co.	.70	40.22
Dow Chemical Co.	.70	40.92
Johnson and Johnson	.65	41.57
American Home Products Corp.	.63	42.20
Philip Morris Inc.	.63	42.83
Continental Oil Co.	.61	43.44
Getty Oil Co.	.61	44.05
Bankamerica Corp.	.58	44.63
Halliburton Co.	.58	45.21
Lilly, Eli and Co.	.58	45.79
General Telephone and Electronics Corp.	.57	46.36
Weyerhaeuser Co.	.55	46.91
Tenneco Inc.	.52	47.43
Union Oil Co. of California	.49	47.92
International Telephone and Telegraph Co.	.48	48.40
K-Mart	.48	48.88
Union Pacific	.48	49.36
Citicorp	.46	49.82
Burroughs Corp.	.43	50.25
Sun Co. Inc.	.43	50.68
Avon Products Inc.	.42	51.10
Hewlett Packard	.42	51.52
Reynolds (R. J.) Industries	.41	51.93
Smithklein Corp.	.41	52.34
Aetna Life and Casualty	.39	52.73
Georgia Pacific Corp.	.39	53.12

Source: Canavest House Limited.

Table 7-1 shows the top 50 stocks in Standard and Poor's 500-stock index, based on total market values in mid-1979. Although relative rankings change from time to time, these securities, representing ownership of large, widely known firms, continue to make up a large portion of this index of the overall market portfolio.

Table 7-2 provides another view of the composition of Standard and Poor's 500-stock index. Each security is classified by Standard and Poor's as belonging to a given industry; in the table, the relative values in mid-1979 have been summed by industry. While any such classification involves elements of arbitrariness, the figures do suggest the relative importance of major industrial sectors in the economy.

TABLE 7-2 Industrial Groups in Standard and Poor's 500-Stock Index (based on total market value outstanding, June 29, 1979)

Industrial Group	Percent of Total Value
Aerospace	1.44
Air Transport	.42
Aluminum	.68
Automobiles	3.40
Auto Parts (after market)	.20
Auto Parts (original equipment)	.66
Auto, Trucks, and Parts	.11
Banks (New York City)	1.24
Banks (outside New York City)	1.44
Beverages (brewers)	.29
Beverages (distillers)	.45
Beverages (soft drinks)	1.13
Building Materials (air conditioning)	.17
Building Materials (cement)	.11
Building Materials (heating and plumbing)	.15
Building Materials (roofing and wallboard)	.36
Chemicals	2.66
Coal (bituminous)	.26
Conglomerates	1.86
Containers (metal and glass)	.42
Containers (paper)	.15
Copper	.34
Cosmetics	.88
Drugs	3.80
Electric Companies	4.13
Electrical Equipment	.77
Electrical—Household Appliances	.25
Electronic—Major Companies	2.21
Electronics (instrumentation)	.71
Electronics (semiconductors/components)	.96
Entertainment	.58
Fertilizers	.24
Finance Companies	.18
Financial—Miscellaneous	.53
Foods	2.76
Forest Products	1.46
Gold	.18

TABLE 7-2 (Continued)

Industrial Group	Percent of Total Value
Home Furnishings	.02
Homebuilding	.08
Hospital Management Companies	.19
Hospital Supplies	1.45
Hotel-Motel	.24
Insurance (life)	.79
Insurance (multiline)	.79
Insurance (property–casualty)	.83
Leisure Time	.20
Machine Tools	.10
Machinery (agricultural)	.62
Machinery (construction and materials handling)	.91
Machinery (industrial/specialty)	.64
Metal Fabricating	.05
Metals (miscellaneous)	1.09
Miscellaneous	4.08
Mobile Homes	.04
Natural Gas Distributors	.76
Natural Gas Pipelines	.79
Office and Business Equipment	8.46
Offshore Drilling	.16
Oil (crude producers)	.82
Oil (integrated domestic)	6.78
Oil (integrated international)	9.44
Oil Well Equipment and Services	2.61
Paper	1.19
Personal Loans	.23
Pollution Control	.12
Publishing	.32
Publishing (newspapers)	.50
Radio–TV Broadcasters	.58
Railroad Equipment	.27
Railroads	1.40
Restaurants	.48
Retail Stores (department)	.69
Retail Stores (drug)	.18
Retail Stores (food chains)	.56
Retail Stores (general merchandise chains)	1.81
Savings and Loan Companies	.26
Shoes	.23
Soaps	1.49
Steel	.86
Sugar Refiners	.03
Telephone	6.73
Textile (apparel manufacturers)	.26
Textile (textile products)	.18
Textile (synthetic fibers)	.12
Tire and Rubber Goods	.35
Tobacco	1.32
Toys	.03
Transportation—Miscellaneous	.05
Truckers	.18
Vending and Food Service	.07
	100.00

Source: Canavest House Limited.

THE CAPITAL MARKET LINE

In the fictional world of the capital-asset pricing model it is a simple matter to determine the relationship between portfolio risk and return. Figure 7-1 portrays it graphically. Point M represents the market portfolio and point P the riskless rate of interest. Preferred investment strategies plot along line PMZ, representing alternative combinations of risk and return obtainable by combining the market portfolio with borrowing or lending. This is known as the *capital market line*.

All investment strategies other than those employing the market portfolio and borrowing or lending would lie below the capital market line, although some might plot very close to it. In such a world, any investor could devise an appropriate strategy alone; no security analyst, portfolio manager, or investment adviser would be needed. This may seem paradoxical, but it is not. The activities of professional analysts help make the market efficient. Their *total* value to investors and to the economy as a whole is thus very great indeed. However, the major results of their analysis are reflected in current security prices. The investor need pay only a small amount for a newspaper to obtain these results of millions of dollars of analysis. The *marginal* value of additional analysis may thus be rather small: in the world of the original capital-asset pricing model it would be zero. In the real world, where analysts do not work for nothing, the marginal value of additional analysis should be positive but, given adequate competition in the investment industry, should just equal the cost of doing such analysis in the most efficient manner.

The slope of the capital market line can be regarded as the *reward per unit of risk borne*. As Figure 7-1 shows, this equals the difference between the expected return on the market portfolio and that of the riskless security $(E_m - p)$ divided by the difference in their risks $(S_m - 0)$.

Equilibrium in the capital market can be characterized by two key numbers. The first is the *reward for waiting* or riskless interest rate, shown by the vertical intercept of the capital market line (point P in Figure 7-1).

FIGURE 7-1 The Capital Market Line

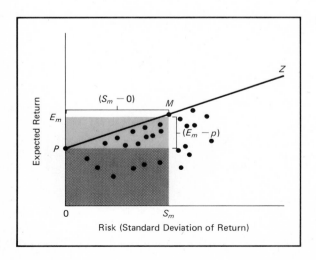

Risk (Standard Deviation of Return)

The second is the reward per unit of risk borne, shown by the slope of the line. In essence, the capital market provides a place where time and risk can be traded and their prices determined by the forces of demand and supply. The interest rate can be thought of as the *price of time*, and the slope of the capital market line as the *price of risk*.

CHARACTERISTIC LINES

An old and rather quaint Wall Street aphorism asserts that "when they raid the brothel they take all the girls."[1] The reference is to a so-called "bear raid," in which bears (pessimists) raid the market, driving prices down. Completing the translation: the statement asserts that when the market falls dramatically, all stocks go down together.

This sort of view is subject to criticism on several grounds besides taste. The market is rarely divided into bears (pessimists) and bulls (optimists). A decline is more likely to come about when the consensus opinion about the future simply becomes more pessimistic or less optimistic. Moreover, such changes in opinion seldom apply equally to all securities. Pessimism about the prospects for automobiles may accompany optimism about the prospects for rapid-transit stocks.

Nonetheless, there is an element of truth in the assertion. In major market moves, most securities move in the same direction, although at different rates. Moreover, the sensitivity of a security's price to changes in the overall market is of crucial importance, for it constitutes the major component of the security's contribution to portfolio risk.

[1] Cited in Albert Haas, Jr., and Don D. Jackson, M.D., *Bulls, Bears and Dr. Freud* (Cleveland: William Collins Publishers, Inc., 1967), p. 19.

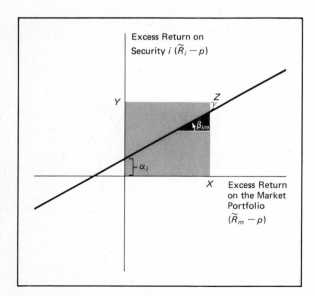

FIGURE 7-2 A Security Characteristic Line

These concepts can be made more precise. An analyst's view of the relationship between a security's prospects and those of the market portfolio can be summarized by means of a *characteristic line*. Figure 7-2 shows an example. The vertical axis plots the *excess return* on the security in question. This is the difference between the holding-period return on the security and the riskless rate of interest for that period. In symbols:

$$\text{excess return on security } i = \tilde{R}_i - p$$

where:

$$\tilde{R}_i = \text{holding-period return on security } i$$
$$p = \text{riskless rate of interest}$$

For clarity, variables whose actual value is uncertain before the fact (ex ante) are indicated by tildes (i.e., squiggly lines such as ˜).

The horizontal axis in Figure 7-2 plots the excess return on the market portfolio; in symbols:

$$\text{excess return on the market portfolio} = \tilde{R}_m - p$$

where:

$$\tilde{R}_m = \text{holding-period return on the market portfolio}$$
$$p = \text{riskless rate of interest}$$

The market portfolio is, formally, that described earlier: it includes all securities, each in proportion to market value outstanding.

The characteristic line, summarizing the relationship between the two excess returns, can be written as follows:

$$\tilde{R}_i - p = \alpha_i + \beta_{im}(\tilde{R}_m - p) + \tilde{r}_i \tag{7-1}$$

The values of *alpha* (α_i) and *beta* (β_{im}) indicate the vertical intercept and slope, respectively, of the line, as shown in Figure 7-2. The vertical intercept is one important attribute:

> A security's *alpha value* (α_i) is the excess return that would be expected on the security if the excess return on the market portfolio were zero.

Intuitively, one would think that a positive value of alpha would be desirable and a negative value undesirable. As we shall see, this is indeed the case.

The value of β_{im} measures the *sensitivity* or *responsiveness* of the security's excess return to that of the market portfolio. (It is common practice to simply refer to "beta" whenever one means "beta relative to the market portfolio.") A beta of 1 indicates that if the market portfolio's excess return is 1% larger than expected, then the best guess is that the security's excess return is also likely to be 1% larger than expected. A beta of .5 indicates that if the market portfolio's return is 1% larger than expected, the best guess is that the security's excess return is likely to be ½ of 1% larger than expected. A beta of 2.0 indicates that if the market portfolio's excess return is 1% larger than expected, the best guess is that the security's excess return is likely to be 2% larger than expected.

In general:

A security's *beta value* (β_{im}) measures the expected change in its excess return per 1% change in the excess return on the market portfolio.

Securities with beta values less than 1 (e.g., most utility stocks) are termed *defensive*: in up markets their prices tend to rise at a slower rate than the average security. On the other hand, they tend to fall at a slower rate in down markets. Securities with beta values greater than 1 (e.g., most airline stocks) are termed *aggressive*: in up markets their prices tend to rise at a faster rate than the average security. On the other hand, they tend to fall at a faster rate in down markets.

The final value in formula (7-1), $\tilde{r}_i$, represents the uncertain portion of the *nonmarket* component of the excess return on security i. This can be seen more clearly by dividing the total into two parts, as follows:

$$\tilde{R}_i - p = \underset{\substack{\text{market component of} \\ \text{excess return}}}{[\beta_{im}(\tilde{R}_m - p)]} + \underset{\substack{\text{nonmarket component} \\ \text{of excess return}}}{[\alpha_i + \tilde{r}_i]} \qquad (7\text{-}2)$$

The term in the first set of brackets is the market-related portion of excess return; the term in the second set is the nonmarket portion. By convention, α_i represents the *expected* nonmarket excess return, while $\tilde{r}_i$ represents the deviation from this expectation. Before the fact, the best guess is that $\tilde{r}_i$ will be zero. After the fact, it almost certainly will not be. Unexpected good news will cause $\tilde{r}_i$ to be positive, while unexpected bad news will cause it to be negative.

How far might the nonmarket component of a security's excess return diverge from its expected value? As with other estimates, it is convenient to express the answer in standard deviation terms. Thus the *nonmarket risk* is measured by the likely divergence of nonmarket excess return from its expected value. Formally, the estimated standard deviation of $\tilde{r}_i$ is used:

A security's nonmarket risk $[S(\tilde{r}_i)]$ is the standard deviation of its excess return for a *given* return on the market portfolio.

$$S(\tilde{r}_i) = \text{the nonmarket risk of security } i$$

Graphically, nonmarket risk measures the likely distance, measured vertically, between the point representing the actual outcome and the characteristic line. Thus in Figure 7-2, if the excess return on the market portfolio turns out to be X, while that on the security is Y, the actual nonmarket excess return is Z. Nonmarket risk is an estimate of the likely amount of this difference. Some analysts estimate this directly, thinking in terms of a divergence likely to be exceeded only one time out of three (i.e., the chances are two out of three that the actual difference will be less).

Three key measures summarize a security's prospects in this type of analysis: α_i, β_{im}, and $S(\tilde{r}_i)$. Estimation of these variables is, in principle, the responsibility of the security analyst. He or she may utilize statistical analysis of historical data in the process, but fundamental knowledge of the company and industry in question may also be employed.

Different means may be utilized to obtain such estimates from analysts. Some organizations simply request the three values directly. Others ask for an estimate of dividends and end-of-period security price for two assumed end-of-period market levels. This fixes two points on the characteristic line, and thus the values of α_i and β_{im}. The analyst may then be asked for a measure of the likely divergence from the estimates, to obtain $S(\tilde{r}_i)$. Another procedure, used by several organizations, asks for three estimates for each of two or more assumed market conditions. In each case the estimates are thought of as "pessimistic," "likely," and "optimistic." Depending on the interpretations given these terms, the values are then used to estimate α_i, β_{im}, and $S(\tilde{r}_i)$.

Whatever the method used, two features are central in this type of analysis. First, the security analyst is asked to make *conditional* estimates: all forecasts are conditional on market levels. This leaves the task of estimating the expected excess return on the market portfolio, and the attendant uncertainty about it, to others with (hopefully) more appropriate skills. It also facilitates consistency in the estimates obtained for different securities. If analysts are asked to make *unconditional* estimates, they must make their own implicit forecasts of market moves, and each one is likely to make a different forecast, leading to unsatisfactory results when such estimates are combined and compared by a portfolio manager.

The other hallmark of this approach is the explicit recognition of *uncertainty*. In a sense, the analyst is not expected to draw a clear characteristic line, but a fuzzy one. Putting it differently, the line drawn is simply a "best guess," and the estimate of nonmarket risk indicates the likely precision of that guess. The greater the nonmarket risk, the wider is the band around the characteristic line within which the analyst feels the actual result might fall.

Not every organization uses such procedures to estimate security returns. People continue to ask for, and get, single estimates, ignoring the influence of overall market moves and the presence of uncertainty. Such procedures are, however, too simplistic: most returns *are* uncertain, and they *do* depend on market moves. These two factors are too important to be ignored.

PROBABILISTIC CHARACTERISTIC LINES

Analysts asked to provide information on characteristic lines usually do so explicitly, or nearly so. However, such relationships rest, at base, on estimates of the outcomes associated with events and the probabilities of such events. While few people actually make these detailed estimates, it is useful to see how the key attributes of a characteristic line can be derived from them, for this provides the conceptual foundation for the entire procedure.

Table 7-3 shows an analyst's estimates of the excess returns for a security (column 3) and the market portfolio (column 4) associated with each of several events, as well as estimates of the probabilities of the

TABLE 7-3 Estimating Beta from Probabilistic Predictions

(1) Event	(2) Probability	(3) Excess Return on Security i (%)	(4) Excess Return on the Market Portfolio (%)	(5) = (2) × (3)
a	.10	18.0	13.0	1.8
b	.20	13.0	.0	2.6
c	.10	8.0	11.0	.8
d	.30	−8.0	−6.0	−2.4
e	.30	25.0	18.0	7.5
				10.3
				Expected excess return on security i

(6) = (2) × (4)	(7) Deviation of Excess Return on Security i = (3) − 10.3	(8) Deviation of Excess Return on the Market Portfolio = (4) − 6.0	(9) Weighted Deviations for Market Portfolio Squared = (2) × (8)²	(10) Weighted Products of Deviations = (2) × (7) × (8)
1.3	7.7	7.0	4.9	5.39
.0	2.7	−6.0	7.2	−3.24
1.1	−2.3	5.0	2.5	−1.15
−1.8	−18.3	−12.0	43.2	65.88
5.4	14.7	12.0	43.2	52.92
6.0			101.0	119.80
Expected excess return on the market portfolio			Variance of excess return on the market portfolio	Covariance between the excess return on security i and the excess return on the market portfolio

$$\beta_{im} = \frac{119.80}{101.0} = 1.186$$

events (column 2). In columns 5 and 6 the expected values are computed in the usual way; each outcome is multiplied by its probability, then summed. The variance of the excess return on the market portfolio is computed in column 9. Finally, in column 10 the covariance between the two excess returns is computed by taking a weighted average of the products of the deviations from the expectations, using probabilities as weights.

Given these figures, the value of β_{im} for the security can be easily found. The formula is:

$$\beta_{im} = \frac{\text{Cov } (\tilde{R}_i - p, \tilde{R}_m - p)}{\text{Var } (\tilde{R}_m - p)} \tag{7-3}$$

where:

$\text{Cov } (\tilde{R}_i - p, \tilde{R}_m - p) =$ the covariance between the excess return on security i and the excess return on the market portfolio

$$\text{Var } (\tilde{R}_m - p) = \text{the variance of the excess return on the market portfolio}$$

Formula (7-3) is the rigorous definition of a security's beta relative to the market portfolio. In this case it is 119.80/101.0, or 1.186. The security is thus aggressive: its excess return is 18.6% more sensitive to market swings than is that of the average security.

The value of α_i is the expected value of the nonmarket component of a security's excess return. The expected value of the market component will equal the security's beta times the expected excess return on the market portfolio. The value of alpha is thus the difference between the security's total expected excess return and this amount. In symbols:

$$\alpha_i = E(\tilde{R}_i - p) - \beta_{im} E(\tilde{R}_m - p) \qquad (7\text{-}4)$$

where:

$E(\tilde{R}_i - p)$ = the expected excess return on security i

$E(\tilde{R}_m - p)$ = the expected excess return on the market portfolio

In this case $\alpha_i = 10.30 - (1.186 \times 6.00)$, or 3.184. The analyst thus considers the security underpriced, since the value of alpha is positive.

We come finally to the estimation of nonmarket risk. This is shown in Table 7-4. Columns 1 through 4 repeat the initial estimates from the previous table. Column 5 shows the excess return on the security accompanying each level of the excess return on the market, using the charac-

TABLE 7-4 Estimating Nonmarket Risk from Probabilistic Predictions

(1) Event	(2) Probability	(3) Excess Return on Security i (%)	(4) Excess Return on the Market Portfolio (%)
a	.10	18.0	13.0
b	.20	13.0	.0
c	.10	8.0	11.0
d	.30	−8.0	−6.0
e	.30	25.0	18.0

(5) Characteristic Line Value of Excess Return on Security i = 3.184 + 1.186 × (4)	(6) Deviation of Nonmarket Return = (3) − (5)	(7) Probability Times Nonmarket Deviation Squared = (2) × (6)^2
18.602	−.602	.036
3.184	9.816	19.271
16.230	−8.230	6.773
−3.932	−4.068	4.965
24.532	.468	.066

Var $(\tilde{r}_i)$ = Variance of $\tilde{r}_i$ = 31.111

$S(\tilde{r}_i)$ = Standard deviation of $\tilde{r}_i = \sqrt{31.111} = 5.578$

teristic line obtained earlier for the estimates. The next column shows the difference between this estimate and the actual one: if the event in question takes place, this will be the actual deviation (r_i). To calculate the nonmarket risk we must find the standard deviation of these values. This is accomplished in the usual manner, as shown in the final column in Table 7-4.

PORTFOLIO CHARACTERISTIC LINES

A characteristic line for a portfolio can be constructed in the manner used for a security. The result can be represented as follows:

$$\underbrace{(\tilde{R}_P - p)}_{\substack{\text{Excess return on} \\ \text{portfolio } P}} = \underbrace{[\beta_{Pm}(\tilde{R}_m - p)]}_{\substack{\text{Market component of} \\ \text{portfolio } P\text{'s excess} \\ \text{return}}} + \underbrace{[\alpha_P + \tilde{r}_P]}_{\substack{\text{Nonmarket component} \\ \text{of portfolio } P\text{'s} \\ \text{excess return}}} \quad \text{(7-5)}$$

where:

$\tilde{R}_P$ = return on portfolio P

α_P = expected value of the nonmarket component of portfolio P's excess return

$\tilde{r}_P$ = deviation of the actual nonmarket component of portfolio P's excess return from its expected value

β_{Pm} = the sensitivity of portfolio P's excess return to the excess return of the market portfolio

While a portfolio's characteristic line may be estimated directly, it is much more common to do this indirectly, using estimates obtained for the securities in the portfolio. This is simpler and also avoids potential inconsistencies. By and large, the relationships are straightforward:

A portfolio's alpha value is a weighted average of the alpha values for its component securities, using the relative market values in the portfolio as weights.

$$\alpha_P = \sum_{i=1}^{N} X_i \alpha_i \quad \text{(7-6)}$$

where:

α_P = value of alpha for portfolio P

X_i = proportion of the market value of portfolio P invested in security i

α_i = value of alpha for security i

N = the number of securities in the portfolio

Similarly:

A portfolio's beta value is a weighted average of the beta values for its component securities, using the relative market values in the portfolio as weights.

$$\beta_{Pm} = \sum_{i=1}^{N} X_i \beta_{im} \qquad (7\text{-}7)$$

where:

β_{Pm} = value of beta for portfolio P

X_1 = proportion of the market value of portfolio P invested in security i

β_{im} = value of beta for security i

N = the number of securities in the portfolio

The nonmarket risk of the portfolio is not as easy to estimate, since its magnitude depends on the correlations among the values of $\tilde{r}_i$ for the component securities. If all the securities in a portfolio come from the same industry, nonmarket risk is likely to be higher than if each security comes from a different industry. At the other extreme, it may be possible to reduce nonmarket risk considerably by hedging, that is, constructing a portfolio of positions with negatively correlated nonmarket returns.

In general:

The nonmarket risk of a portfolio depends on (1) the nonmarket risks of its component securities, (2) any correlations among their nonmarket returns, and (3) the relative market values of the securities in the portfolio.

$$[S(\tilde{r}_p)]^2 = \sum_{i=1}^{N} \sum_{j=1}^{N} [X_i X_j \rho(\tilde{r}_i, \tilde{r}_j) S(\tilde{r}_i) S(\tilde{r}_j)] \qquad (7\text{-}8)$$

where:

$S(\tilde{r}_p)$ = the nonmarket risk of the portfolio

X_i = the proportion of the market value of the portfolio invested in security i

X_j = the proportion of the market value of the portfolio invested in security j

N = the number of securities in the portfolio

$\rho(\tilde{r}_i, \tilde{r}_j)$ = the correlation between $\tilde{r}_i$, the nonmarket return of security i, and $\tilde{r}_j$, the nonmarket return of security j [note: $\rho(\tilde{r}_i, \tilde{r}_i) = 1$]

$S(\tilde{r}_i)$ = the nonmarket risk of security i

$S(\tilde{r}_j)$ = the nonmarket risk of security j

One procedure, termed the *single index model*, often used to estimate nonmarket risk assumes that all the values of $\tilde{r}_i$ are uncorrelated. Under this assumption:

$$[S(\tilde{r}_P)]^2 = \sum_{i=1}^{N} X_i^2 [S(\tilde{r}_i)]^2 \qquad \text{when all values of } \tilde{r}_i \text{ are uncorrelated} \qquad (7\text{-}9)$$

This works well for highly diversified portfolios (i.e., those with many securities and no concentration of holdings in any one industry, economic sector, geographic area, etc.). For portfolios not meeting these conditions it may seriously under- or overestimate nonmarket risk, and the more complete procedure in formula (7-8) should be used.

MARKET AND NONMARKET RISK AND RETURN

The characteristic line procedure dichotomizes return into two components, one market-related and one not. Since the expected value of the latter is α_i, it is a simple matter to relate an expected excess return to the expected values of the two parts. In symbols:

$$E(\tilde{R}_i - p) = \alpha_i + [\beta_{im}E(\tilde{R}_m - p)] \qquad (7\text{-}10)$$

Expected value of security or portfolio i's excess return	Expected value of the nonmarket component of security or portfolio i's excess return	Expected value of the market component of security or portfolio i's excess return

or, equivalently:

$$E_i = p + \alpha_i + \beta_{im}(E_m - p) \qquad (7\text{-}11)$$

where:

$$E_i = \text{the expected return on security or portfolio } i$$

$$E_m = \text{the expected return on the market portfolio}$$

What about risk? By definition, the nonmarket component of excess return is uncorrelated with the market component (and the formal procedures described in the previous section insure that this will indeed be the case). The variance of the sum will thus equal the sum of the variances of the parts:

$$\text{Var}(\tilde{R}_i - p) = \text{Var}(\tilde{r}_i) + \text{Var}[\beta_{im}(\tilde{R}_m - p)] \qquad (7\text{-}12)$$

Variance of security or portfolio i's excess return	Variance of the nonmarket component of security or portfolio i's excess return	Variance of the market component of security or portfolio i's excess return

Since the variance of a constant times a variable equals the constant squared times the variance of the variable, this can be rewritten as follows:

$$\text{Var}(\tilde{R}_i - p) = \text{Var}(r_i) + \beta_{im}^2 \, \text{Var}(\tilde{R}_m - p) \qquad (7\text{-}13)$$

Both formulas (7-12) and (7-13) show that risk, measured by variance, can also be broken into two parts: one that is not related to market risk and one that is. Moreover, the latter will be larger, the more sensitive the security or portfolio's return is to market moves (i.e., the greater is β_{im}). A commonly used measure indicates the importance of market risk:

The value of R-*squared* for a security or portfolio indicates the proportion of total risk (measured by variance) attributable to market factors.

$$R\text{-squared} = \frac{\beta_{im}^2 \, \text{Var}(\tilde{R}_m - p)}{\text{Var}(\tilde{R}_i - p)}$$

A typical value of R-squared for a single stock is about .30. Uncertainty about the overall market thus accounts for only 30% of the uncertainty about the prospects for a typical stock over holding periods from one to a few months. However, the proportion is much higher when highly diversified holdings are considered. The value of R-squared for a large institutional portfolio such as a pension fund is more likely to be well above .90. At the portfolio level, the market component of risk is likely to dominate the nonmarket component by a substantial margin.

THE EFFECTIVENESS OF DIVERSIFICATION

Formula (7-9) can be used to gauge the potential effectiveness of diversification. Consider a portfolio of common stocks, chosen randomly, with investment spread evenly over the securities. Generally, the greater the number of stocks included in the portfolio, the smaller will be its risk.

For simplicity, assume that all stocks have a beta of 1. Then the market component of risk will be the same, no matter how many securities are included (since β_{Pm} will always equal 1.0). But the nonmarket component of risk will generally decline as more and more securities are included. If holdings are equal, each value of X_i will equal $1/N$, and formula (7-9) can be written:

$$S(\tilde{r}_P)^2 = \sum_{i=1}^{N} \left(\frac{1}{N}\right)^2 S(\tilde{r}_i)^2$$

$$= \frac{1}{N} \left[\frac{1}{N} \{ S(\tilde{r}_1)^2 + S(\tilde{r}_2)^2 + \cdot \cdot \cdot + S(\tilde{r}_N)^2 \} \right]$$

The value in the square brackets is simply the average nonmarket risk, measured by variance, for the component securities. But the nonmarket risk (measured by variance) for the portfolio is only one-Nth as large as this.

For a well-diversified portfolio of equal holdings of N securities, then:

$$S(\tilde{r}_p)^2 \approx \frac{\overline{S(\tilde{r}_i)^2}}{N} \tag{7-14}$$

where $\overline{S(\tilde{r}_i)^2}$ is the average value of $S(\tilde{r}_i)^2$ for the N securities.

Table 7-5 shows values for a case in which the standard deviation of the annual excess return on the market portfolio is 20% and where 30% of the risk of a security can be attributed to market risk (e.g., each security has an R-squared of .30). Figure 7-3 plots the relationship between total risk and the number of securities.

Figure 7-4 shows that this is more than an ivory-tower exercise. In Figure 7-4(a) the relationship between the standard deviation of the actual return over time and the number of securities in a portfolio is shown for portfolios of securities chosen randomly from the New York Stock Exchange. In Figure 7-4(b) such values are shown for portfolios chosen from exchanges located in the United States, the United Kingdom, France, Germany, Italy, Belgium, the Netherlands, and Switzerland. In each figure the vertical axis plots the ratio of the standard deviation of portfolio return to that of a typical stock from the group analyzed.

TABLE 7-5 The Potential Effect of Diversification on Risk

(1) Number of Securities in the Portfolio	(2) Standard Deviation of Nonmarket Component of Portfolio Excess Return	(3) Standard Deviation of Portfolio Excess Return	(4) R^2: Proportion of Total Risk Due to the Market
1	30.55	36.51	.300
2	21.60	29.44	.462
3	17.64	26.67	.563
4	15.28	25.17	.632
5	13.66	24.22	.682
10	9.66	22.21	.811
20	6.83	21.13	.896
30	5.58	20.76	.928
40	4.83	20.58	.945
50	4.32	20.46	.955
60	3.94	20.39	.963
70	3.65	20.33	.968
80	3.42	20.29	.972
90	3.22	20.26	.975
100	3.06	20.23	.977
200	2.16	20.12	.988
300	1.76	20.08	.992
400	1.53	20.06	.994
500	1.37	20.05	.995

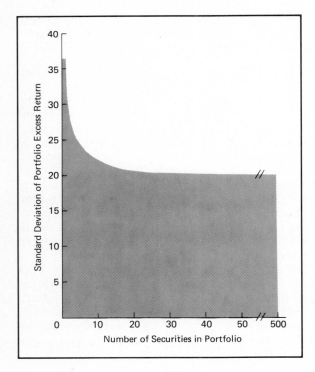

FIGURE 7-3 The Potential Effect of Diversification on Risk

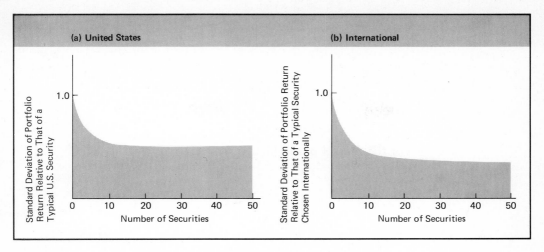

FIGURE 7-4 The Effect of Domestic and International Diversification on Risk

Source: Bruno Solnik, "Why Not Diversify Internationally Rather than Domestically? *Financial Analysts Journal*, 30, no. 4 (July/August 1974), 48–54.

While *ex post* variations in actual return over time are not necessarily the same as risk perceived *ex ante*, it is interesting to note that the historical record is highly consistent with the approach described here. Diversification does reduce risk, and the reduction can be greater, the wider the range of possible investments. But there is a limit: nonmarket risk can be lowered by diversification, but market risk generally remains.

The figures shown in Table 7-5 are fairly representative of results that might be obtained by investing in stocks listed on the New York Stock Exchange. Recall, however, that the values assume diversification in two senses: equal holdings, and no industry or other concentration. Actual portfolios usually have more risk, as managers explicitly or implicitly concentrate their holdings in one way or another, to be in a position to take advantage of "corrections" they anticipate will occur as the market realizes that certain securities are mispriced.

Finally, note that even if all the assumed conditions are met, a highly diversified portfolio's annual return can still diverge from that of the overall market portfolio by a considerable amount. Even with a portfolio of 100 securities, the chances are 1 in 3 that the difference can be as great as 3.06% (for example, the excess return on the market portfolio might be 10.0% and that on the portfolio 6.94%).

CHARACTERISTIC LINES FOR EFFICIENT INVESTMENT STRATEGIES

One of the major implications of the original capital-asset pricing model concerns sensible investment strategies: only combinations involving the market portfolio plus borrowing or lending are efficient. This makes the characteristic lines for such strategies especially important.

The characteristic line for a portfolio that is the market portfolio itself is simple:

$$\tilde{R}_p - p = \tilde{R}_m - p$$

Casting this in terms of formula (7-1):

$$\tilde{R}_p - p = 0 + 1(\tilde{R}_m - p) + 0$$

For the market portfolio, then:

$$\text{alpha} = 0$$

$$\text{beta} = 1$$

$$\text{nonmarket return} = 0$$

The market portfolio clearly has no nonmarket risk. Its characteristic line, denoted (m), is shown in Figure 7-5.

The characteristic line for a portfolio invested solely in Treasury bills is also simple:

$$R_p - p = 0$$

In terms of formula (7-1):

$$R_p - p = 0 + 0(\tilde{R}_m - p) + 0$$

For Treasury bills, then:

$$\text{alpha} = 0$$

$$\text{beta} = 0$$

$$\text{nonmarket return} = 0$$

A Treasury bill thus has neither market nor nonmarket risk. Its characteristic line, denoted p, is also shown in Figure 7-5.

What about a combination of Treasury bills and the market port-

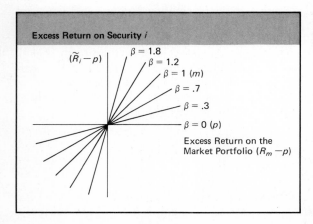

FIGURE 7-5 Characteristic Lines of Correctly Priced Securities and Portfolios

folio? Recall formulas (7-6), (7-7), and (7-8), and let X_m represent the proportion of the investor's funds placed in the market portfolio; then, for such a combination:

$$alpha = 0$$

$$beta = X_m \cdot 1$$

$$nonmarket\ risk = 0$$

Figure 7-5 shows characteristic lines for several strategies of this type; each is described by its beta value, with investment solely in the market portfolio ($\beta_{im} = 1$) and investment solely in Treasury bills ($\beta_{im} = 0$) as special cases.

RISK AND RETURN IN A PORTFOLIO CONTEXT

What will be the relationship between the return on a security and its risk? And what aspect of a security's risk will be relevant for establishing its return?

To answer these questions in the context of the capital-asset pricing model one must adopt a *portfolio view*. In this model the relevant aspects of a security are:

> its *contribution* to the *return* of an *efficient* portfolio,
> its *contribution* to the *risk* of an *efficient* portfolio.

Expected return is the contribution of a security to the expected return of *any* portfolio. But the contribution of a security to the risk of a portfolio depends on the portfolio chosen. The capital-asset pricing model implies that only portfolios highly correlated with the market portfolio (plus, perhaps, borrowing or lending) are efficient. Thus the relevant measure of a security's risk is its contribution to the risk of such a portfolio. But this is exactly what *beta* measures: for a highly diversified portfolio market risk constitutes by far the largest part of total risk. And market risk is directly proportional to the beta value of the portfolio. Thus:

> A security's beta value measures its contribution to the risk of a highly diversified portfolio. Under the assumptions of the capital-asset pricing model only such a portfolio is efficient, and a security's beta value is a measure of its *contribution to the risk of an efficient portfolio*.

As indicated earlier, many large institutional portfolios are highly diversified, with over 90% of their risk due to uncertainty about market moves. The composition of a portfolio of this type is in general accord with the implication of the capital-asset pricing model that the market portfolio is efficient; it also follows that the beta value of a security provides a good measure of its contribution to the risk of such a portfolio.

A more detailed description of beta as a measure of contribution to portfolio risk is provided in the Appendix to this chapter.

THE SECURITY MARKET LINE

Now that we have identified the two relevant aspects of a security in the context of the original capital-asset pricing model, it is a short step to the major implication of the theory portrayed by the *security market line* shown in Figure 7-6. The vertical axis plots the expected return of a security or portfolio; the horizontal axis plots its beta value. As shown:

Under the assumptions of the original capital-asset pricing model, all securities and portfolios plot on a *security market line* going through a point representing the market portfolio and a point representing the riskless rate of interest.

Why? We can see the answer best by first considering a counterexample. Imagine a situation in which two securities had the same beta value but different expected returns. Clearly the one with the higher expected return would dominate. Investors would flock to buy the former and sell the latter. But this would drive up the price of the first security, lowering its expected return, and drive down the price of the second security, increasing its expected return. For equilibrium to prevail, then, *securities with the same beta values should be priced to give the same expected returns*.

In Figure 7-6 point p represents the riskless security (e.g., a Treasury bill). The argument just given implies that *every security with a beta value of zero should provide an expected return equal to the riskless rate of interest*.

Point m in Figure 7-6 represents the market portfolio: it has a beta value of 1.0 and an expected return denoted E_m. But it could be employed as a "security" in some other portfolio. Therefore, *every security with a beta value of 1.0 should be priced to give an expected return of E_m*.

Point x represents a combination with 50% invested in the market

FIGURE 7-6 The Security Market Line

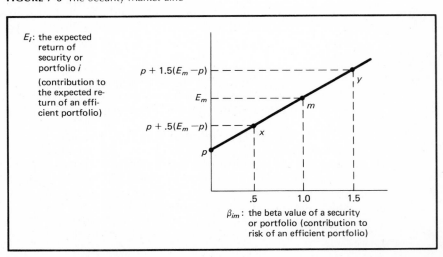

E_i: the expected return of security or portfolio i

(contribution to the expected return of an efficient portfolio)

$p + 1.5(E_m - p)$

E_m

$p + .5(E_m - p)$

p

y

m

x

.5   1.0   1.5

β_{im}: the beta value of a security or portfolio (contribution to risk of an efficient portfolio)

portfolio and 50% invested in Treasury bills. Its beta value is .5 and its expected return is midway between p and E_m [i.e., $p + .5(E_m - p)$]. But, since this is competitive with every other investment with a beta value of .5, *every security with $\beta_{im} = .5$ should be priced to give an expected return of $p + .5 (E_m - p)$.*

Point y represents an investment in which all of the investor's own funds, plus 50% more borrowed at the Treasury bill rate, are invested in the market portfolio. Its beta value is 1.5 and its expected return is $p + 1.5(E_m - p)$. Thus *every security with $\beta_{im} = 1.5$ should be priced to give an expected return of $p + 1.5(E_m - p)$.*

Many more examples could be given, but the general point should now be clear:

Under the assumptions of the original capital-asset pricing model:

$$E_i = p + \beta_{im}(E_m - p) \tag{7-15}$$

This is the equation of the security market line.

Thus far we have confined most of the discussion to securities. But if all securities plot on the security market line, so must all portfolios, since a portfolio's expected return and beta value are simply weighted averages of security expected returns and beta values, respectively. The argument is thus complete.

CHARACTERISTIC LINES FOR EFFICIENCY PRICED SECURITIES

In the context of the original capital-asset pricing model an efficiently priced security is one that plots on the security market line. Using formula (7-15):

$$E_i = p + \beta_{im}(E_m - p)$$

This can be compared with formula (7-11) derived from the equation for a characteristic line:

$$E_i = p + \alpha_i + \beta_{im}(E_m - p)$$

How can the two be reconciled? Easily:

Under the assumption of the original capital-asset pricing model an efficiently priced security will have an alpha value of zero.

Or, putting it slightly differently:

Under the assumptions of the original capital-asset pricing model the characteristic lines of all efficiently priced securities will go through the origin.

If all security characteristic lines go through the origin, so will the characteristic lines of all portfolios. Thus Figure 7-5 can serve as a representation of characteristic lines for all efficiency priced securities and portfolios.

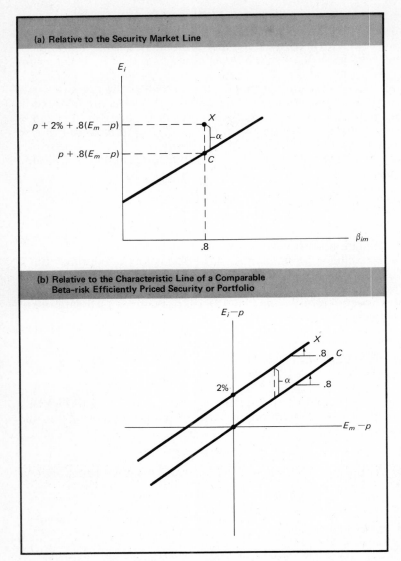

(a) Relative to the Security Market Line

E_i

$p + 2\% + .8(E_m - p)$

$p + .8(E_m - p)$

X

α

C

.8

β_{im}

(b) Relative to the Characteristic Line of a Comparable Beta-risk Efficiently Priced Security or Portfolio

$E_i - p$

X

.8   C

2%

α

.8

$E_m - p$

FIGURE 7-7
Alpha Values

This gives substance to the intuitive interpretation of alpha given earlier. A security with a nonzero alpha value is mispriced. If alpha is positive, the security is expected to return more than it should; if alpha is negative, the security is expected to return less than it should.

Figures 7-7(a) and (b) show such a situation. Security X has a beta of .8 and an expected return of $[p + 2\% + .8(E_m - p)]$. Its alpha value is thus $+2\%$ and it is underpriced. In Figure 7-7(a) the security's alpha value is represented by the *distance it plots above the security market line*. As shown, it is expected to return 2% more than a typical security or portfolio of comparable beta risk (i.e., one plotting at point C).

Figure 7-7(b) shows the characteristic lines for security X and comparison security or portfolio C. They are parallel (since both have beta values of .8) and 2% apart (since their alpha values differ by 2%). Thus, *no matter what the market return, security X is expected to return 2% more than security or portfolio C*—a situation not likely to last long, once enough investors recognize its existence.[2]

---

[2] The characteristic-lines interpretation of alpha [Figure 7-7(b)] applies strictly only to securities for which a line best represents the relationship between security excess return and that of the market portfolio. However, the interpretation of alpha in the context of the security market line [Figure 7-7(a)] applies in all cases, using the formal definition of beta.

Problems

1. Why shouldn't a security having a very return variance, but very low beta, be expected to provide a large excess return?
2. Is the investor who owns any portfolio of risky assets other than the market portfolio exposed to some nonmarket risk?
3. A security analyst forecasts that there exists equal probability for the occurrence of: (1) a boom, (2) controlled growth, and (3) a severe recession during the next year. Under these three states of the world he or she projects returns on a specific security, the market portfolio, and Treasury bills as shown in the table below.

STATE OF THE WORLD			
	Optimistic (Boom)	Likely (Controlled Growth)	Pessimistic (Recession)
Probability of state	$\frac{1}{3}$	$\frac{1}{3}$	$\frac{1}{3}$
Return on market portfolio	20%	15%	−5%
Return on security A	25%	20%	−10%
Return on Treasury bills	7%	7%	7%

a. What is the equation for the capital market line?
b. What would be the expected return and variance for a portfolio of which 50% is invested in Treasury bills and 50% in the market portfolio?
c. What is the equation for the security market line?
d. Is the beta for security A such that you would consider the security aggressive or defensive?

e. What is the expected return on security A? What expected return would be appropriate (based on the security market line) for a security with the beta value of security A?

4. Assume that the risk-free rate is 9% and the market portfolio has an expected return of 17%. What expected return would be consistent with the capital-asset pricing model for a security with a beta value of 0? 0.5? 1.0? 1.5?

5. Assume that the risk-free rate is 9% and the market portfolio has an expected return of 17% and a standard deviation of return of 20%. Under equilibrium conditions as described by the capital-asset pricing model, what would be the expected return for a portfolio having no nonmarket risk and a standard deviation of return of 15%?

6. A neighbor purchased a lottery ticket yesterday but now, owing to an unpredicted crisis, is in desperate need of cash. He offers to sell the ticket to you. You know the payoff and the probability of winning. All of your considerable fortune is invested in a highly diversified portfolio. How would you determine an appropriate price for the ticket?

7. You are trying to choose between two investment strategies. The first involves putting 80% of your funds in a highly diversified portfolio of common stocks and 20% in Treasury bills. The second involves putting all your money in a group of utility stocks, based on the recommendation of your broker, who believes that utilities are currently "out of favor" and represent a "great play." What aspects should you consider before making a decision?

8. If you buy a group of stocks designed to represent the market portfolio, will you have to buy and sell shares every time the relative prices of the stocks you hold change? Why? If not, when would you have to buy and sell?

9. A friend tells you about a gold mining company stock that typically goes down when the stock market rises and goes up when the stock market falls (she estimates its beta value to be −.2). Treasury bills currently return 9%, and the consensus opinion is that the stock market is expected to return 16%. If the stock of the mining company is priced efficiently, what return should you expect from it? How would you explain this to someone not familiar with investment theory?

APPENDIX 7-A

Beta as a Measure of Relative Contribution to Efficient Portfolio Risk

This chapter gives an intuitive argument for the assertion that beta provides a measure of relative contribution to the risk of an efficient portfolio. This appendix offers a more rigorous proof.

Consider a portfolio p with risk (stated as variance) of V_p. Let the variance of security i be V_i and the covariance between security i's return and that of the portfolio be C_{ip}. Now imagine a new portfolio with X_p invested in the original portfolio and X_i invested in security i. Using formula (6-5), the risk of the new portfolio will be:

$$V = X_p^2 V_p + 2X_i X_p C_{ip} + X_i^2 V_i$$

What will be the impact on V of a small change in X_i? If X_i is changed from X_i to $X_i + \Delta X_i$, the variance will become:

$$V' = X_p^2 V_p + 2(X_i + \Delta X_i) X_p C_{ip} + (X_i + \Delta X_i)^2 V_i$$
$$= V + 2 \Delta X_i X_p C_{ip} + 2X_i \Delta X_i V_i + (\Delta X_i)^2 V_i$$

and the change in variance will be:

$$\Delta V = V' - V = 2 \Delta X_i X_p C_{ip} + 2X_i \Delta X_i V_i + (\Delta X_i)^2 V_i$$

while the change in variance per unit change in X_i will be:

$$\frac{\Delta V}{\Delta X_i} = 2X_p C_{ip} + 2X_i V_i + \Delta X_i V_i$$

If the change in X_i is very small, the last term will be insignificant and:

$$\frac{\Delta V}{\Delta X_i} \approx 2X_p C_{ip} + 2X_i V_i$$

where $\approx$ means "is approximately equal to." The value of $\Delta V / \Delta X_i$ when ΔX_i is very small is termed the *first derivative of* V *with respect to* X_i, and written dV/dX_i. It represents the *marginal contribution of security i to the risk of portfolio p.*

Now assume that in the initial mix, $X_i = 0$ and $X_p = 1$ (i.e., that the only holding of security i was that included in portfolio p). Then:

$$\frac{dV}{dX_i} = 2C_{ip}$$

If the original portfolio was the market portfolio:

$$\frac{dV}{dX_i} = 2C_{im}$$

But recall that the rigorous definition of β_{im} is C_{im}/V_m, where V_m is the variance of return on the market portfolio. Thus:

$$\frac{dV}{dX_i} = \beta_{im}[2V_m]$$

and the *relative* risk of any two securities will be proportional to their beta values, since $[2V_m]$ is the same for every security.

Risk and Return: Modern Portfolio Theory

8

INTRODUCTION

If security markets were perfectly efficient and conformed to the specifications of the original capital-asset pricing model, sensible investment management would be a relatively simple task. Funds "at risk" should be invested in broadly diversified, highly passive portfolios, in which holdings would be changed little if at all. And each client's attitude toward risk should be accommodated by appropriately allocating his or her funds between risky and riskless assets.

Not surprisingly, many investment managers believe that there is more to be done. Explicitly or implicitly they reject one or both of these premises. Some believe that the market is efficient but more complex than suggested by the original capital-asset pricing model. Others believe that there are occasions when securities are mispriced—i.e., that the market·is not perfectly efficient. And some believe that the market is both complex and inefficient.

The term *modern portfolio theory* is used within the investment industry to describe techniques used by those who adopt one or both of these ideas but still manage investments in a disciplined and logically consistent manner. This chapter describes some key ingredients of approaches using such techniques; subsequent chapters cover further aspects.

EFFICIENT INVESTMENT POLICIES WHEN BORROWING IS RESTRICTED OR EXPENSIVE

The original capital-asset pricing model assumes that investors can borrow without limit at the riskless rate of interest at which funds can be invested in, say, Treasury bills. In fact, of course, such borrowing is likely to be either unavailable or restricted in amount. What impact might this have on investment policy and security prices if the market were (otherwise) efficient?

A useful way to answer the question makes the following working assumptions: (1) investors can purchase assets with a riskless return of p or (2) borrow without limit at a higher rate of interest b. These values are shown on the vertical axis of Figure 8-1; the shaded area represents

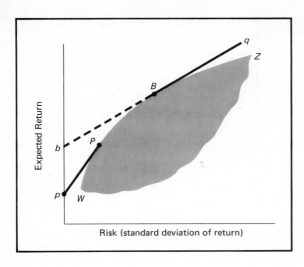

FIGURE 8-1 Efficient Investment Strategies when Borrowing Costs More than Investing in Riskless Securities

risk-return combinations available from investment solely in risky assets.

Were there *no* opportunities to borrow or "lend" (invest in the riskless asset), the efficient frontier would be the curve *WPBZ* and many combinations of securities would be efficient. However, the availability of a riskless asset returning *p* makes risky portfolios between W and P uninteresting—combinations of the riskless asset and the portfolio plotting at P provide more return for the same risk. Portfolio P is thus the optimal mix of risky securities for anyone whose attitude toward risk dictates holding any of the riskless asset. Graphically, point P is found by swinging a line out of point *p* until it just touches the original frontier of efficient combinations.

The ability to borrow money at rate *b* makes another portfolio—B—of interest. Formerly efficient portfolios between B and Z are now uninteresting: levered holdings of B dominate them, providing more return for the same risk. Portfolio B is the optimal mix of risky securities for anyone whose attitude toward risk dictates any borrowing (e.g., margined purchase of stocks). Graphically, point B is found by swinging a line out of point *b* until it just touches the original frontier of efficient combinations.

Investors with attitudes toward risk that dictate neither borrowing nor lending should hold combinations of risky securities plotting along curve PB. Their holdings should thus be *tailored* to be consistent with differences in their degrees of aversion to risk.

The capital market line is now two lines and a curve: in Figure 8-1, *pPBq*.

THE "ZERO-BETA" VERSION OF THE SECURITY MARKET LINE

What becomes of the security market line when borrowing rates exceed the riskless rate of interest? The answer depends on whether or not the market portfolio is in fact one of the efficient combinations of risky se-

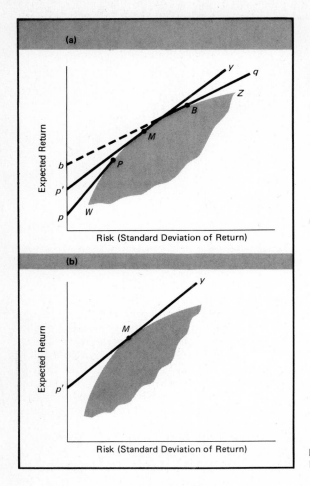

(a)

Expected Return

Risk (Standard Deviation of Return)

(b)

Expected Return

Risk (Standard Deviation of Return)

FIGURE 8-2 Risk and Return when the Market Portfolio is Efficient

curities along the frontier between *P* and *B* in Figure 8-1.[1] If it is not, little more can be said. If it is, a great deal can be said.

Figures 8-2(a) and (b) show a case in which the market portfolio (shown by point *M*) is efficient. The line $p'Mq$, drawn tangent to the efficient frontier at point *M*, intercepts the vertical axis at a return of p'. In Figure 8-2(a) the portions shown in Figure 8-1 have been repeated; in Figure 8-2(b) only the new ingredients are shown.

The striking characteristic of Figure 8-2(b) is this: *it is precisely the same picture that would be produced in a market in which investors could borrow and lend without limit at the riskless rate p'.* Of course, only point *M* along line $p'My$ would be attainable, but security prices would be the same as they would be in a market with borrowing and lending at p', and *all securities and portfolios would be priced to plot along a security market line going through point p',* as shown in Figure 8-3.

---

[1] If investors could obtain the proceeds from short sales and there were no restrictions on such sales, the market portfolio would definitely plot on the efficient frontier between points *P* and *B*.

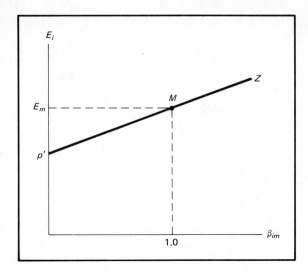

FIGURE 8-3 The "Zero-Beta" Security Market Line

The vertical intercept of a security market line of this sort is often termed the return on a "zero-beta" portfolio (or security), since it indicates the expected return on any efficiently priced security or portfolio with a zero beta value. The overall approach is termed the *zero-beta* or, sometimes, the *two-parameter* version of the capital-asset pricing model.

This extension of the original capital-asset pricing model implies that the security market line will be flatter than implied by the earlier theory, since p' will be above p. As a practical matter, it means that the intercept (p') must be inferred from the prices of risky securities — it cannot simply be found in the quotations of current returns on Treasury bills. As described in later chapters, many organizations do estimate such a security market line; and they generally find that it conforms more to the "zero-beta" extension than to the original model.

Cases in which borrowing either is impossible or costs more as one borrows larger amounts lead to only minor modifications in the conclusions. As long as the market portfolio is efficient, all securities will plot along a security market line, but the "zero-beta" return will exceed the riskless rate at which funds can be invested.

OTHER FACTORS:
THE SECURITY MARKET HYPERPLANE

The original capital-asset pricing model assumes that investors are concerned only with risk and return. But other factors may matter. Owing to differences in tax status, some investors may prefer return in the form of capital gains to an equal amount in the form of dividends; Chapter 9 considers this aspect. For most investors, real return is what counts: other things equal, securities that provide better hedges against inflation would be preferred over those that do not; Chapter 10 considers this. The prices of certain securities may be affected because they are associated with activities considered immoral by some investors. Potentially, then, a great many factors could be reflected in security prices.

To illustrate this general principle, we will focus on *liquidity*: the cost of selling or buying a security "in a hurry" (roughly, its typical bid/ask spread). It is reasonable to assume that in the opinion of most investors, other things equal, the more liquid a portfolio the better. However, investors undoubtedly differ in their attitudes toward liquidity. For some it is very important; for others, fairly important, and for yet others, of little importance.

Under these conditions security prices would adjust until, overall, investors would be content to hold the outstanding securities. Each security can be characterized by three important attributes:

1. Its marginal contribution to the *expected return* of an efficient portfolio.
2. Its marginal contribution to the *risk* of an efficient portfolio.
3. Its marginal contribution to the *liquidity* of an efficient portfolio.

The first two attributes are familiar (E_i and β_{im}, respectively[2]). The third can be denoted L_i.

Note that, other things equal, large values of E_i and L_i are good and large values of β_{im} are bad. But in an efficient market, other things will not be equal. For example, one would not expect to find two stocks with the same expected returns and beta values but different liquidities, since the stock with the greater liquidity would dominate the other. In an efficient market, dominance does not occur—there are no "free lunches."

Figure 8-4 shows the relationship one might expect among E_i, β_{im}, and L_i in an efficient market. For a given level of contribution to risk (β_{im}), more liquid securities have lower expected returns (the former is the "good news," the latter is the "bad news," and, in an efficient market, they always go together). For a given level of liquidity, more risky securities (bad news) have higher expected returns (good news) as in the original capital-asset pricing model. And for a given level of expected re-

[2] As before, we assume that the market portfolio is an efficient combination of securities.

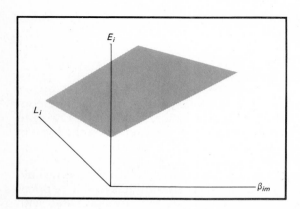

FIGURE 8-4 A Possible Relationship between Expected Return, Beta, and Liquidity

turn, higher beta securities (bad news) have higher levels of liquidity (good news).

The security market line has now become a *security market plane*.[3] More aspects could be added, requiring a "diagram" in four or more dimensions. Such a diagram cannot be plotted (an equation has to suffice) but the relationship can be given a name: by analogy to the three-dimensional *plane*, it is termed a *hyperplane:*

> In an efficient market, all securities will plot on a *security market hyperplane*, the axes of which plot contributions to all attributes of efficient portfolios that matter (on average) to investors.

The relationship of expected return to contributions to the attributes of efficient portfolios depends on the attitudes of investors to the attributes:

If, on average, an attribute is *liked* by investors, securities that contribute more to that attribute will, other things equal, offer *lower* expected returns.

while:

If, on average, an attribute is *disliked* by investors, securities that contribute more to that attribute will, other things equal, offer *higher* expected returns.

In an efficient market with many relevant attributes, the task of tailoring a portfolio for a specific investor is more complicated:

In a complex efficient market, only an investor with average attitudes and circumstances should hold market proportions of all securities.

In general:

If an investor likes an attribute more (or dislikes it less) than the average investor, he or she should generally hold a portfolio with relatively more of that attribute than is provided by holding securities in proportion to their market values. If an investor likes an attribute less (or dislikes it more) than the average investor, he or she should generally hold a portfolio with relatively less of that attribute than is provided by holding securities in proportion to their market values.

Of course, the right combination of "tilt" away from market proportions will depend on the extent of the difference between the investor's attitudes and those of the average investor and on the nonmarket risk involved in such a strategy.

A complex market, even if it is perfectly efficient, requires all the tools of portfolio analysis for managing the money of any investor who is significantly different from the "average investor." On the other hand, in such a world, investment management should be relatively *passive:* after the selection of an initial portfolio, there should be minor and infrequent changes.

---

[3] The term "security market plane" is a trademark of Wells Fargo Bank. Chapter 9 describes the manner in which the concept is employed by Wells Fargo.

ACTIVE INVESTMENT MANAGEMENT

Portfolios should be constructed and periodically revised to accommodate any special circumstances of the ultimate beneficiary or beneficiaries of the investments. However, most investment advisers (and investors) choose to do more than this. Besides establishing an appropriate *strategic* mix of holdings they also engage in *tactical* maneuvers, attempting to take advantage of perceived deviations of market prices from "intrinsic values." Since perceptions of such deviations tend to be short-lived, such managers are *active*, buying and selling securities relatively often.

It is useful to think of the process of portfolio construction as being performed in two steps. First the *optimal passive strategy*, tailored to the investor(s) in question, is devised. Then *deviations* are made, with relatively more invested in securities thought to be underpriced and relatively less invested in securities thought to be overpriced.

The key to active investment management is *alpha:* the difference between the expected return on a security and what it "should be"—i.e., what it would be if the security were correctly priced. In the original and zero-beta versions of the capital-asset pricing model, this is the distance the security plots above (positive alpha) or below (negative alpha) the security market line. In expanded versions of the model, it is the distance above (positive alpha) or below (negative alpha) the security market hyperplane.

One should exceed normal passive portfolio proportions for a security with a positive value of alpha, since its expected return exceeds that obtainable by investment in typical securities with comparable attributes. Conversely, one should take a smaller-than-normal position in a security with a negative value of alpha, since its expected return is less than that obtainable from comparable securities. Other things equal, the greater the divergence of alpha from zero, the greater should be the departure of a holding from its normal position.

Analysts may choose to depart from passive portfolio proportions security by security, industry by industry, and/or by broad classes of investment. An example of the latter is provided by managers who attempt to "time the market," moving portfolios to smaller or larger proportions of fixed-income instruments (e.g., bonds) relative to equities (stocks), depending on whether or not they think the former are temporarily over- or underpriced relative to the latter. Such a strategy involves risks, as well as transactions costs. Unless the "timer" is right more often than he or she is wrong, the investor is likely to be worse off with such an active strategy than with an appropriate passive strategy. The record shows that it is extremely difficult for managers to successfully time the market. However, the potential rewards are very high, encouraging many to keep trying.

It is important to remember that in any period, before added costs, active management is a *zero-sum game:* total winnings must equal total losses; and after added costs, it is a *negative-sum game:* net winnings will fall short of net losses. To see this, imagine a world in which one group (passive managers) holds precisely market proportions of all securities while others (active managers) hold concentrated portfolios. In this case, although no single active manager holds a market portfolio, the sum of all their holdings must include all securities in precisely market proportions. Thus in any given period the overall performance of active managers must precisely equal that of the market and of passive managers.

But active management involves two kinds of explicit cost (transactions costs and added management fees) and one kind of implicit cost (increased risk due to lack of diversification). Thus the client of the average active manager will be worse off than if he or she had adopted an appropriate passive strategy. To benefit from active management one must select a manager who is considerably *better* than other money managers, not merely one who is *good*.

MARKET VERSUS ECONOMIC RISK

It is important to remember that although the value of beta is usually described in terms of dividends and market price changes over a fairly short period, it really reflects relationships among expectations about the values of fundamental economic variables over a much longer period.

This is most easily seen in the case of a firm financed entirely with equity (stock). The present value of the outstanding stock of such a firm at any time will depend on investors' expectations about the firm's revenues and costs (broadly construed) from that time forward—in concept, forever. The present value a year later will depend on investors' expectations at that time about the firm's then remaining revenues and costs. The rate of return on the stock between the two dates will equal the difference between these two present values plus the cash paid out in dividends during the period. One source of uncertainty about this return concerns the failure or success of its activities during the period; but in the usual case the more important source is uncertainty concerning investors' expectations at the end of the year about the firm's prospects from that time forward.

The market portfolio is, in essence, the sum of all claims on all capital assets. Its present value at any time will depend on investors' assessments of the prospects from that time forward for all such assets. Since the benefits obtained from capital assets are almost synonymous in many people's minds with the state of "the economy," the relationship can be stated more simply. The current level of the market reflects investors' current feelings about the prospects for the economy. The greater their expectations for the economy, other things equal, the higher will be the level of the market. On the other hand, the greater their uncertainty about the economy, the lower will be the level.

One source of uncertainty regarding the return on the market portfolio over a period will be the uncertainty about what will happen to the economy during the period. More important yet will be uncertainty about investors' feelings at the end of the period about the economy's prospects from that time forward.

What has this to do with beta? A great deal. Beta measures the sensitivity of a security's market return over a fairly short period to changes in the market return on all assets. More fundamentally:

The beta of a *firm* measures the sensitivity of the underlying assets' prospects (and investors' assessments thereof) to those of the economy as a whole.

For a firm financed wholly by stock, the beta of the *firm* and the beta of its *stock* will be the same. This will, in turn, depend on the basic economics of the firm's activities. Most airlines have high "firm betas," since many of their costs are fixed and their revenues depend heavily on the state of the economy. On the other hand, most utilities have low firm betas, since regulatory authorities control rates in a manner that makes the spread between revenue and cost affected less by swings in economic activity.

Most firms are financed with both debt and equity. Thus the firm's prospects are divided up among various groups of claimants. Both the overall risk and the overall return of such a firm have been apportioned so that debt-holders bear proportionately less risk and expect proportionately less return than do equity holders. The "stock beta" of a firm financed in this way will exceed the "firm beta," with the difference depending on the amounts and types of debt.

COMPONENTS OF RISK AND RETURN

Security analysts can and should provide estimates of risk and return, taking into account the fundamental economic aspects of a firm's operations and financing. This can be done by thinking solely in terms of a monolithic "market" or "economy." However, a more careful analysis will go behind such notions to examine the key components of both risk and return.

The "market" goes up when investors reassess the future in a way that causes a net increase in their valuation of securities. The securities that go up the most will be those for which prospects are most sensitive (positively) to the news that causes the change. If the market rise is due to news of a peace treaty in the Middle East, the prices of securities of firms most likely to benefit thereby will rise the most. If the change results from news of an improved outlook for the domestic economy, prices of the securities of firms doing most of their business at home will rise the most. Announcement of an unanticipated lifting of price controls will affect the prices of securities of firms constrained by such controls; etc.

Investment analysts attempt to take such considerations into account in a number of ways. Figure 8-5(a) shows one approach. Each security is classified as belonging to a single market *sector*—in this approach, often an industry—and its excess return is related to the excess return on a portfolio of securities in its sector via a characteristic line, as shown in Figure 8-5(b). The excess return on each sector's portfolio is, in turn, related to that of the overall market portfolio via another characteristic line, as shown in Figure 8-5(c).

Figure 8-6(a) shows a somewhat different approach. The market is again broken into two or more sectors (e.g., industries, small versus large firms, bonds versus stocks, etc.). As before, each security is assigned to a sector and its excess return related to that of its sector via a characteristic

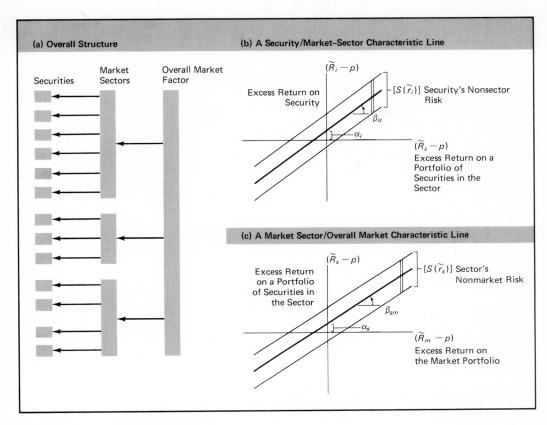

FIGURE 8-5 One Type of Market-Sector Model

FIGURE 8-6 A More Complex Market-Sector Model

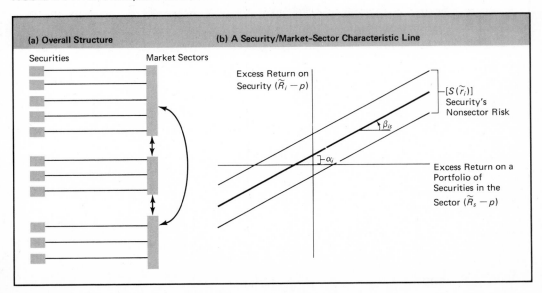

line, as shown in Figure 8-6(b). Here, however, interrelationships among the excess returns of the sectors are taken into account directly by estimating the relevant degrees of correlation, rather than via relationships to some common overall market factor. In this case, the "market" is not an explicit part of the model. Instead, it is included implicitly: the market is simply the sum of all the securities; it is also the sum of all the market sectors.

Figure 8-7 shows a more complex, but more realistic approach. Here the excess return on each security is related to one or more interrelated underlying economic factors. Examples are: long-term interest rates, predicted inflation, prospects for peace, the likelihood of devaluation, and the predicted future price of crude oil. A change in any such factor will generally affect many securities, some more than others. This model accounts for such effects by estimating the sensitivity of each security's excess return to each relevant factor.

Analysts can use multifactor models to consider the impact of key economic variables on the risk and return of individual securities. For example, the return on American Telephone and Telegraph stock is quite sensitive to changes in interest rates: the greater the uncertainty about future rates, other things equal, the greater will be the risk of this stock (and, if the market is efficient, its expected return). Another example: at a time when there is great uncertainty about the position of the dollar in international exchange, securities of companies with substantial sales abroad are more likely to be in the higher end of the risk-return spectrum than at other times. And so on.

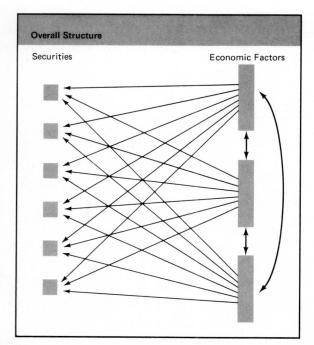

FIGURE 8-7 A Model Utilizing Economic Factors

Overall Structure

Securities

Economic Factors

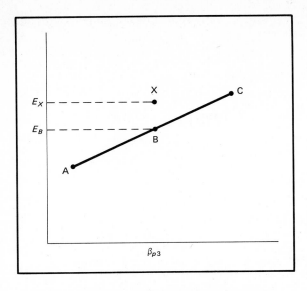

FIGURE 8-8 The Arbitrage Pricing Theory

THE ARBITRAGE PRICING THEORY

Figure 8-7 portrays a situation in which expected return should be related in a straightforward way to *components* of risk. As indicated, each security is assumed to be sensitive to a limited number of common economic factors; all other sources of risk are assumed to be uncorrelated and thus avoidable via diversification.

To be specific, assume that there are three factors and that security i's sensitivities to these factors are β_{i1}, β_{i2}, and β_{i3}, respectively. A portfolio's sensitivities can be denoted β_{p1}, β_{p2}, and β_{p3}, with each beta an average of the corresponding beta values of the component securities, using market values as weights. Assume there are enough securities so that it is possible to form a portfolio with any desired set of sensitivities $(\beta_{p1}, \beta_{p2}, \beta_{p3})$ and (effectively) no other sources of risk due to the effects of diversification.

Under these conditions there must be a direct relationship between expected return and each of the sensitivities. To see why, consider the four portfolios (A, B, C, and X) in Figure 8-8. Assume that each one has $\beta_{p1} = 1$ and $\beta_{p2} = 1$ and is highly diversified. Thus they differ only with regard to sensitivity to factor 3, and *this is their only source of risk*.

Could the portfolios be priced to plot as shown if the market were efficient? Clearly not. For example, portfolio X would dominate portfolio B: since sensitivity to factor 3 is their only source of risk, an investor could buy portfolio X and sell portfolio B short, completely hedging all risk via *arbitrage*, and locking in the return differential $E_X - E_B$.

Even if portfolio B had not been included in the diagram, the argument against the existence of a portfolio plotting at point X would have held, for a portfolio like B could be created by dividing one's funds between portfolios A and C. Thus *all portfolios would have to lie on a line in Figure 8-8.*

Of course Figure 8-8 shows sensitivity to only one factor. A complete picture would include sensitivities to all common factors. The result would be a hyperplane. And, if all portfolios are to plot on such a hyperplane, so must all securities. This is the essence of the *arbitrage pricing theory*:

In an efficient market, arbitrage will lead to a situation in which the expected return of a security or portfolio will be a linear function of its sensitivities to all important common sources of risk.

In symbols:

$$E_i = a + b\beta_{i1} + c\beta_{i2} + \cdots$$

where:

E_i = the expected return on a security or portfolio

β_{i1} = the sensitivity of the return of security or portfolio i to common factor 1

β_{i2} = the sensitivity of the return of security or portfolio i to common factor 2

. . . , and a, b, c, . . . are constants.

In a sense the arbitrage pricing theory breaks market risk into its components. As a practical matter, it may never be possible to precisely estimate β_{im}, since the all-inclusive "market portfolio" is probably impossible to measure adequately. On the other hand, it should be possible to measure sensitivities to important common factors that account for much of the risk of the market portfolio. The arbitrage pricing theory provides a basis for believing that such an approach should be fruitful for investment management, even though it falls short of the more ambitious goals associated with the capital-asset pricing model and its extensions.

Much more can be said about risk and return, and about investment value in general. But the basic principles have been described, and it is now time to fill in the details of the complex "real world" of investment and apply these and other principles to that world.

Problems

1. If there were no riskless asset and borrowing were impossible, would there be any relationship between risk and return for individual securities? If so, what would it be? On what assumption or assumptions does your answer depend?

2. It has been said that investors care about expected return and risk in real (purchasing-power) terms, not in monetary terms. But in most countries

no asset is riskless in real terms. What might this imply about the relationship between risk and return for securities? What changes might be required in the definition and measurement of expected return and beta in this instance?

3. According to some, the zero-beta version of the capital-asset pricing model is not as "strong" a theory as the original version (i.e., it makes fewer predictions and is consistent with more possible situations). In what sense is this true? Are the implications of the original version inconsistent with those of the zero-beta version?

4. Assume that many investors are revulsed by the antisocial behavior of a certain company. Would you expect its stock to return more than other stocks with similar attributes in all other dimensions? If so, what would be your advice to someone with an average revulsion to the company's behavior? To someone who did not consider the company's actions antisocial at all? To someone who was extremely disturbed by the company's behavior?

5. Should an investor hold only stocks with positive alphas? Should stocks with negative alphas be sold short?

6. What dangers are associated with holding only stocks of "small emerging growth companies"?

7. Assume that a major source of uncertainty in the economy concerns the future price of oil. Your investment adviser provides you with a list of stocks. At the top are companies whose profits are most sensitive to oil prices; in the middle are those whose profits are affected less by oil prices; at the bottom are those unaffected by oil prices. Based on this factor alone, what could you say about the expected returns on the companies' stocks? Why? Might other factors make a list based on expected returns look different? Why?

8. Other things equal, what is the likely relationship between the beta value of a stock and:
   a. The sensitivity of the company's sales to overall national income?
   b. The ratio of fixed costs to variable costs in the company's operations?
   c. The ratio of debt to equity in the company's financial structure? Why?

9. Assume that over the last twelve months returns on stocks averaged 18% and the riskless interest rate was 8%. An investment advisory service categorized a list of 1,000 stocks on the basis of "predicted beta" at the beginning of the year. Three groups were identified. Their returns over the subsequent year were:

Low-beta group	20%
Average-beta group	18%
High-beta group	16%

Is this experience consistent with likely expectations, given the overall performance of the market? Does it refute the capital-asset pricing model? Why or why not?

Taxes

9

INTRODUCTION

A well-worn saying holds that nothing is certain but death and taxes. Unhappily, governments are often responsible for the former, and they are virtually always the source of the latter. Moreover, governmental activities normally play a central role in determining changes in the overall price level of an economy. Upon occasion such changes are in the downward direction—i.e., there is deflation. The more common experience, however, is that of rising prices, or inflation.

Neither taxation nor inflation should be regarded as an unmitigated evil. Each benefits some at the expense of others. If government policy is responsive to some type of consensus opinion regarding socially desirable actions, the benefits may well outweigh the costs. Whatever the case, both taxes and inflation impact investment results, investment decisions, and the pricing of securities. And they are sufficiently important in present-day societies to warrant considerable discussion. This chapter deals with taxes; the next with inflation.

TAXES IN THE UNITED STATES

Since the United States is the world's largest capital market, we will focus on taxes levied on U.S. citizens and corporations. Many other countries, however, impose taxes similar in kind to those of the United States, so much of the discussion is at least partly relevant for non-U.S. citizens.

Most of the specific tax rates and provisions in this chapter applied in the latter 1970s. Changes do occur from year to year, and current regulations should, of course, be consulted when preparing tax returns or considering major investment decisions. However, the material given here can be considered broadly representative of current taxation (primarily federal) in the United States.

By far the most important taxes for investment decision-making are the personal and corporate income taxes, but gift and estate taxes often prove relevant as well. We will describe the essential elements of each, then consider their major influences on the investment market.

THE CORPORATE INCOME TAX

In the United States and most other countries, the corporate form of organization is the most important in terms of the dollar value of assets owned, although many more firms are organized as partnerships or as single proprietorships. Legally, a corporation is regarded as a separate entity, while a proprietorship or partnership is considered an extension of its owner or owners. Income earned by proprietorships and partnerships is taxed primarily through the personal income tax levied on their owners. Income earned by a corporation may be taxed twice—once when it is earned, via the corporate income tax, and again when it is received as dividends by holders of the firm's securities, via the personal income tax.[1]

Double taxation may at first seem inefficient, if not immoral. It also raises questions about the efficiency of the corporate form of organization. Suffice it to say that limited liability, the ability to subdivide ownership and to easily transfer shares of that ownership, appear to be of sufficient value to more than offset the disadvantages arising from tax law for the firms that do most of the business in the United States. Moreover, without the corporate income tax, personal tax rates would have to be increased if the level of government expenditures were to remain constant without increasing the national debt. If the burden is properly distributed at present, the overall impact of such a change might be smaller than one might first expect.

CORPORATE TAX RATES

The corporate income tax is relatively simple in one respect. There are usually only a few basic rates. For example, in 1979 there was a tax rate of 17% applicable to the first $25,000 of taxable income each year, a rate of 20% applicable to the next $25,000, a rate of 30% applicable to the next $25,000, and a rate of 40% applicable to the next $25,000, and a rate of 46% applicable to all income over $100,000. The result is shown in Figure 9-1. The top line shows the *marginal* rate—i.e., the rate applied to an additional dollar. The bottom line shows the *average* tax rate—i.e., the total amount of taxes paid, divided by the total income subject to tax. This ratio is equal to the marginal rate for incomes below $25,000, but it is below the marginal rate for higher incomes. This is generally the case when marginal rates increase with income. For example, a corporation earning $65,000 would pay:

$$.17 \times \$25,000 = \$4,250$$
$$.20 \times \$25,000 = \$5,000$$
$$.30 \times \$15,000 = \underline{\$4,500}$$
$$\$13,750$$

or 21.15% = 100 × 13,750/65,000) of its total income in taxes.

---

[1] Certain corporations with fifteen or fewer shareholders may elect to be treated as partnerships for tax purposes. Such firms, often called "Subchapter S corporations" (after the enabling provision of the Internal Revenue Code), constitute an exception to the general rule.

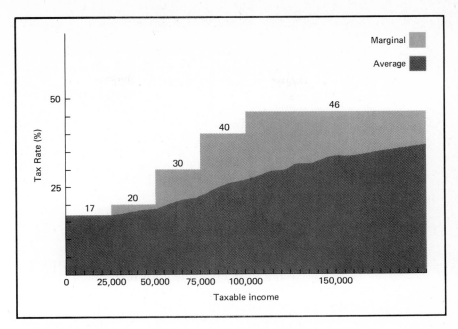

FIGURE 9-1 Marginal and Average Corporate Tax Rates, 1979

The average rate measures the overall impact of taxes, but the marginal rate is more relevant for most decisions. For example, if a corporation were considering an investment that would increase its income from $65,000 to $70,000 each year, the increase in income after tax would be $(1 - .46) \times \$5,000$, or $2,700, not $(1 - .2115) \times (\$5,000)$.

As shown in Figure 9-1, the larger a corporation's taxable income, the closer its average tax rate comes to the higher marginal rate. Most corporations with publicly traded shares have sufficiently large incomes to make the distinction between marginal and average rates minor at best. Overall, such corporations pay taxes equal to virtually the largest marginal rate (e.g., 46%) of the income reported for tax purposes.

DEFINING INCOME

Corporate income is partly a philosophic concept, partly an artifact of legal requirements, partly a result of accounting conventions, partly an indication of the hopes of the firm's management, and sometimes only incidentally related to underlying economic factors. We will deal with this issue in more detail in later chapters; only the elements related to taxation will be discussed here.

Corporate income is defined as revenue minus expenses. The problems arise in measuring these two elements. Simply put, the problem is to match cash flows with relevant time periods. If an airplane is sold this year, but payment is to be made in installments over the next five years, when is the sales price to be considered taxable revenue? If a new plant is to be built and paid for this year, but is to be used to produce goods for the next twenty years, when is the outlay to be considered expense? Accountants have a menu of procedures, known as Generally Accepted Accounting Principles, that can be utilized to handle these and many more subtle cases. However, there is extremely wide latitude within these principles.

The government has thus prescribed certain limits on the methods used to calculate income when determining a corporation's income tax liability. In some cases the firm is required to use the same procedures when reporting to its stockholders; in other cases it can (and often does) use a different set of assumptions, sometimes coming up with a very different estimate of income (although differences of this sort are usually described in the firm's annual report).

DEPRECIATION

The most dramatic instance of the latter sort concerns depreciation of assets used in a business or held for investment. If a corporation buys a computer for $1 million, it is entitled to eventually charge off this cost as a deductible expense when computing taxable income. Each dollar deducted will reduce such income by a dollar, and hence taxes paid by $.46, assuming the corporate income remains in the 46% range. The $1 million outlay thus represents eventual tax savings of $460,000. The *present* value of these tax reductions depends, of course, on the years in which they are obtained. The sooner the cost can be "written off," the greater the benefit to the firm. The best of all possible worlds for the corporation and its owners would be to *expense* the computer—i.e., charge the entire cost as a current expense in the year in which it is incurred. Barring this, the firm would like to allocate the cost against income as soon as possible.

Congress, in making tax laws, and the Internal Revenue Service, in administering them, looks at the situation in a different way. The taxpayer would like to minimize the present value of tax liabilities; other things equal, the tax collector would like to maximize them. Thus the Internal Revenue Service prescribes limits on the manner in which outlays for fixed assets may be charged as costs. For example, the cost of land *per se* may not be deducted at all, since it is not normally considered to be a depreciating asset, although the cost of improvements to land (e.g., buildings) can generally be deducted as depreciation expense over the life of the improvement. For fixed assets that are regarded as having a limited useful life, cost may be charged subject to two important constraints: (1) the estimated life must be allowable and (2) the pattern used to allocate the cost over this period must also be acceptable.

ESTIMATED USEFUL LIFE

For purposes of reporting corporate income to stockholders, a manager might want to allocate the cost of a fixed asset over the period during which it is expected to contribute to revenue. This is usually termed the asset's estimated useful life. For tax purposes it is clearly advantageous to underestimate this in order to write the cost off as rapidly as possible. To control this urge, the Internal Revenue Service publishes tables of "class lives," giving acceptable ranges for a large number of different types of assets. For each class a "guideline" depreciation period is given, along with lower and upper limits ranging 20% on either side, with all values rounded to the nearest half-year. When possible, corporations generally use the lower limit, for obvious reasons.

DEPRECIATION METHODS

Once a period has been chosen over which to allocate the cost of an asset (or the cost less some assumed salvage value at the end of its useful life), a decision must be made concerning the pattern of the allocation. The amount deducted in a year is termed the *depreciation expense*, the figure obtained by deducting all such charges to date from the original cost is the *undepreciated value* of the asset, and the procedure used is the *depreciation method*.

The simplest method is *straight-line* depreciation, in which an equal amount is charged in each year. The procedure takes its name from the pattern over time of the remaining book value (called "adjusted basis" in tax parlance). This is shown in Figure 9-2(a); the annual charges are plotted in Figure 9-2(b). Straight-line depreciation is used by many firms for purposes of evaluating income to be reported to stockholders.

The Internal Revenue Service accepts the straight-line method for virtually all depreciable assets, but in many cases it allows various *accelerated* methods. These accelerated methods permit a taxpayer to write off relatively more of the cost in early years and are thus advantageous from the viewpoint of the corporation. Most firms, acting in their owner's interests, use the most accelerated method allowed for each class of assets.

FIGURE 9-2

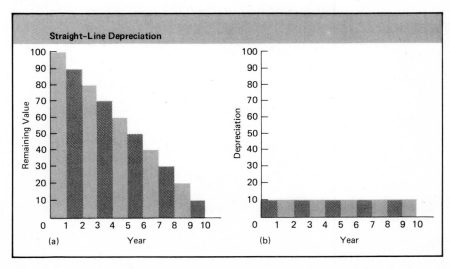

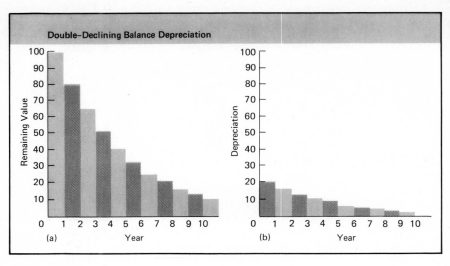

FIGURE 9-3

Two major accelerated methods are used. The first is the *declining balance method*. This involves the write-off of a given percent of the remaining (undepreciated) value of the asset in question each year. The percentage is computed by multiplying (1) the percentage that would be written off in the first year with straight-line depreciation by (2) a given factor. For example, if 200% declining balance depreciation (often called double-declining balance) is to be used, the percentage is twice that for the first year with straight-line depreciation. For an asset with a useful life of ten years, 20% of the remaining value would thus be written off each year. Figure 9-3(a) shows the pattern of undepreciated value and Figure 9-3(b) the annual charges for this procedure. Since formally it fails to allocate the entire cost within the assumed life of the asset, a switch to straight-line depreciation may be made toward the end of the period to bring the undepreciated value to the desired figure.

The *sum-of-the-years'-digits* method provides another type of accelerated depreciation. It is best illustrated with an example. If the useful life is ten years, a sum is calculated as follows:

$$1 + 2 + 3 + 4 + 5 + 6 + 7 + 8 + 9 + 10 = 55$$

In the first year, 10/55, or 18.18% of the outlay is charged to expense; in the second year, 9/55, or 16.36%, and so on. Figure 9-4(a) shows the resulting pattern of undepreciated value and 9-4(b) the annual charges.

There are many reasons why corporate income reported to stockholders may differ from that used for tax purposes, but different depreciation assumptions are often the major factor. If the tax paid by a large corporation diverges significantly from 46% of the apparent taxable income, as reported to stockholders, examination of the depreciation procedures may prove illuminating.

Table 9-1 shows the most rapid depreciation methods authorized for newly acquired assets in 1979.

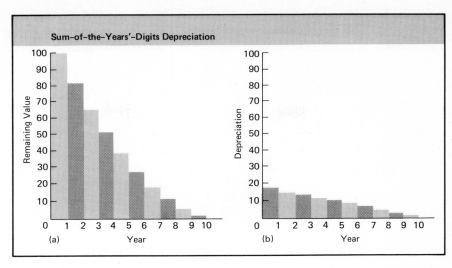

FIGURE 9-4

TABLE 9-1 Most Rapid Depreciation Method Allowed for Newly Acquired Assets in 1979

Certain intangible property (e.g., patents, copy-rights, leases)	Straight-line
Tangible assets with a useful life of less than three years	Straight-line
Tangible assets with a useful life of at least three years (except real property)	
New	Double-declining balance or sum-of-the-years' digits
Used	150% declining balance
Depreciable Real Property	
New residential rental property	Double-declining balance or sum-of-the-years' digits
Used residential rental property with a remaining useful life of at least 20 years	125% declining balance
New nonresidential construction	150% declining balance
Other depreciable real property	Straight-line

INVENTORY VALUATION

Another vexing problem associated with the measurement of corporate income concerns the cost of inventory sold during the year. This arises when prices are changing fairly rapidly and a firm holds inventory for long periods. To take a fairly simple case, imagine a retailer of sailboats. At the start of the year he has 100 in stock, all purchased for $10,000 each. During the year he takes delivery on 100 more, but must pay $11,000 each for them. He sells 110 boats during the year at a price of $15,000 each, ending with 90 in stock. What was his income?

The question, of course, concerns the relevant cost of the 110 boats that were sold, and of the 90 that remain. The firm may have sold all the

TABLE 9-2 The Impact of Different Inventory Valuation Methods

REVENUE: 110 BOATS AT $15,000 = $1,650,000		
Cost by FIFO Method	**Cost by LIFO Method**	**Cost by Average-Cost Method**
100 at $10,000 = $1,000,000	100 at $11,000 = $1,110,000	55 at $10,000 = $ 550,000
10 at 11,000 = 110,000	10 at 10,000 = 100,000	55 at 11,000 = 605,000
$1,110,000	$1,210,000	$1,155,000
Income $ 540,000	$ 440,000	$ 495,000
Tax (at 46%) −248,400	−202,400	−227,700
Income after tax $ 291,600	$ 237,600	$ 267,300
Cost of remaining inventory:		45 at $10,000
90 at $11,000 = $ 990,000	90 at $10,000 = $ 900,000	+ 45 at $11,000 = $ 945,000

"old" boats first, or all the "new" boats, or a mixture of the two. However, this is rarely taken into account in the calculations. An accountant may assume any of the above combinations, without regard for the actual facts of the situation.

The impact of different assumptions is shown in Table 9-2. In the first column all the old boats are assumed to have been sold first—this is the *first-in-first-out* (FIFO) method. In the second column all the new boats are assumed to have been sold first—this is the *last-in-first-out* (LIFO) method. In the third column equal numbers of both old and new boats are assumed to have been sold—this is an *average-cost* method.

When prices have been rising, the LIFO method will permit a corporation to charge more to cost in the present and less in the future. This will lower taxes in the present and raise them in the future. The net result is a fall in the present value of taxes paid—clearly beneficial to the owners of the firm. Since rising prices are so much a phenomenon of modern society, one would expect firms to adopt LIFO inventory valuation for tax purposes, just as they choose accelerated depreciation in most cases in which it is allowed. However, there is a difference between the two situations. The Internal Revenue Code requires a firm to use the same inventory valuation method for computing taxable income and income reported to shareholders. The firm can thus either report a high income or pay a small tax. This can be seen in Table 9-2. FIFO accounting gives the largest current income, both before and after tax, but it also requires the payment of the largest tax. Before 1970, many firms used FIFO accounting, suggesting that in times of moderate inflation many managers were willing to sacrifice some real benefits to improve the appearance of their firm's financial statements. However, as the pace of inflation increased, LIFO accounting became much more common.

AMORTIZATION AND DEPLETION

Allocation of the cost of an asset over its estimated useful life is termed depreciation; a comparable procedure applied to a natural resource (e.g., an oil reserve) is called *depletion*, while it is called *amortization* if applied to certain intangible assets (e.g., research and development costs). Amortization is often handled via procedures akin to those used for the depreciation of tangible assets. But depletion is another matter.

Depletion is utilized to allocate the cost of finding and/or purchasing a so-called "wasting asset" to the units of the asset removed and sold. For example, the cost of bringing in an oil well may be divided by the estimated number of barrels of oil that can be pumped out, and the resulting amount written off as an expense for each barrel sold. If the initial estimate proves to have been in error, adjustments can be made so that the entire cost, but no more, is deducted. This is the *cost method* of depletion; it differs only in detail from the procedure used for the depreciation of fixed assets.

More controversial is the *percentage depletion* method. Here the amount charged as cost need bear no relationship to the actual cost. Instead, a stated percentage of the *gross* income from the property (before any costs) may be deducted as expense. If this falls below the amount obtained via the cost method, the latter may be used, so the result is generally to increase deductions, lower taxes paid, and thus increase profits after tax. An upper limit is generally placed on the amount deducted in this manner—in 1979 it was 50% of the *net* taxable income (after nondepletion deductions) from the property.

The depletion allowance is used to encourage exploitation (and depletion!) of certain natural resources and, some skeptics argue, to provide political support for certain elected officials. In 1979 the largest percentage (22%) was allowed for oil and gas wells owned by "small" independent producers, with rates beween 5% and 22% allowed for various other minerals.

DEDUCTIBILITY OF INTEREST PAYMENTS

One of the major attributes of both corporate and personal income taxes in the United States is the deductibility of interest payments. Interest is regarded as an expense and can thus be deducted from revenue when calculating taxable income. For example, consider two firms, each with revenues of $25,000 and noninterest expenses of $15,000. Firm A was financed by both debt and equity and pays $5,000 in interest to its creditors. Its net income after taxes is thus $4,150, which is available to be paid as dividends, if desired. Thus a total amount of $9,150 can be paid to

TABLE 9-3 The Effect of Deducting Interest Payments

	Firm A	Firm B
Revenue	$25,000	$25,000
Cost of goods sold	15,000	15,000
Revenue minus expense	10,000	10,000
Interest paid	5,000	0
Taxable income	5,000	10,000
Tax (at 17%)	850	1,700
Available for dividends	$ 4,150	$ 8,300

those who provided the firm's capital. The calculations are shown in Table 9-3.

The other part of the table shows the results for firm B, which differs only with respect to financing. All its capital was provided by shareholders. Thus the entire $10,000 of income is subject to tax, leaving only $8,300 for distribution.

The deductibility of interest payments provides an apparent tax advantage for the use of debt over equity funds. For this reason it may seem surprising that firms do not choose to obtain more of their capital via bond issues. Indeed, the dramatic difference in tax treatment raises substantial questions about the definition of debt and interest, on the one hand, and stocks and dividend payments, on the other. The Internal Revenue Service pays considerable attention to exotic arrangements designed to provide the tax characteristics of debt with the financial characteristics of equity. To qualify as debt, there must be a definite obligor, a definite obligee, a definite ascertainable obligation, and a time of maturity. Moreover, corporate debt that greatly exceeds stock may be treated as stock for tax purposes. In general, debt should be represented by an instrument that contains an unconditional promise to pay a certain sum either on demand or on a specific date, with fixed interest.[2] Payments made under any other arrangement are not likely to be deductible for purpose of income taxation.

Obligations of the type required to make payments eligible for deduction are not trivial. Failure to make interest payments, so defined, may have serious consequences for the firm and its management. In many cases bankruptcy results, with mandatory and costly corporate reorganization. The greater the magnitude of nondiscretionary interest payments vis-à-vis discretionary dividend payments, other things equal, the greater the probability of this type of unfortunate event. This provides a brake on excessive use of debt financing, despite its obvious tax advantage.

There is another reason why equity financing may be more competitive with debt financing from the viewpoint of a corporation. As discussed in later sections, the *personal* income tax provides preferential treatment for returns taken in the form of capital gains over those taken as interest or dividends. Since some or all of the return on a stock may take the form of capital gains, equity funds may be cheaper on a *before*-corporate-tax basis, and this may offset some or all of their disadvantages in terms of corporate income taxation.

CORPORATE INCOME FROM DIVIDENDS, INTEREST, AND CAPITAL GAINS

To avoid the possibility of taxing dividends time and time again, Congress provided that 85% of most dividends received by a corporation from non-affiliated domestic corporations can be deducted from income before calculating the firm's income tax liability. The effective tax rate on an addi-

---

[2] Prentice-Hall, *Federal Tax Handbook* 1980 (Englewood Cliffs, N.J.: Prentice-Hall, Inc.), p. 249.

tional dollar of dividends received by a corporation with an income in the 46% range is thus $(1 - .85) \times .46 = .069$, or 6.9%.

No deduction is allowed for interest received by a corporation; it is simply added to income and taxed at the regular rates.

Special treatment may, however, be accorded gains from the sale or exchange of certain assets. Such gains must usually be made on assets used in or held for investment by the business (e.g., equipment and securities, respectively) as contrasted with assets held primarily for sale to customers in the ordinary course of the business (e.g., inventory). Moreover, the assets must have been held at least one year. The excess of such gains over certain short-term capital losses may be taxed at a lower rate than that applied to ordinary income.

THE INVESTMENT TAX CREDIT

To stimulate investment, the tax code allows a portion of the amount spent on certain qualified business property during a year to be credited against taxes due. For example, if a new machine costing $100,000 is purchased, the buyer may be allowed to reduce the total taxes paid at year-end by 10% of this amount, or $10,000. In addition, the total cost may be deducted from revenues during the asset's useful life, in accordance with an accepted depreciation method, to determine taxable income.

In 1979 an investment tax credit of 10% was allowed for all eligible property.

TAX-EXEMPT ORGANIZATIONS

Many organizations are wholly or partly exempt from federal income taxes. Nonprofit religious, charitable, or educational foundations generally qualify. A small tax (2% in 1979) is levied on the net investment income of such a foundation. In addition, the foundation should pay out all income received by the end of the year following receipt or a minimum percent of its assets (5% in 1979), whichever is higher, since failure to do so can result in a confiscatory tax on the difference.

Investment companies, often called *mutual funds*, may elect to be treated as *regulated investment companies* for tax purposes. This privilege is granted if various conditions are met. For example, funds must be invested primarily in securities, without undue concentration in any one. A regulated investment company pays income tax only on income and capital gains not distributed to shareholders. Such companies thus distribute substantially all income and gains, although the "distribution" is often coincident with an automatic reinvestment in new shares of the fund.

Employee pension, profit-sharing, and stock-bonus plans may also qualify for tax-exempt status. Such plans may entrust their assets to a "fiduciary" (e.g., a bank), which accepts new contributions, makes required payments, and provides investment management. A fiduciary under a "qualified plan," which meets all the requirements of applicable legislation, pays no tax on income or capital gains.

In many cases a fiduciary will serve as a trustee of funds provided for the benefit of one or more individuals by another individual or individuals. Some trusts are created by wills, others by a contract among living persons. Whatever the origin, such a trust, if either long-term or irrevocable, pays tax only on income not distributed to the designated beneficiary or beneficiaries.

Income and capital gains earned by investment companies, pension funds, and personal trusts do not go untaxed forever. Payments made to investment company shareholders (whether automatically reinvested or not), pension fund beneficiaries, and the beneficiaries of personal trust funds are subject to applicable personal income taxation. The exemptions apply only to taxes that might otherwise be levied at the previous stage.

THE PERSONAL INCOME TAX

While the corporate income tax is an important feature of the investment scene, its impact on most individuals is indirect. Not so the personal income tax. Few investors avoid dealing with it in detail, at both an economic and an emotional level. Its provisions have major and direct impacts on behavior in general, and investment behavior in particular.

Personal Tax Rates

Tax must be paid on an individual's income, defined as "all wealth which flows in to the taxpayer other than as a mere return of capital. It includes gains and profits from any source, including gains from the sale or other disposition of capital assets."[3] Certain items are *excluded* from the definition of income; others are *deducted* from it before computing the tax due. Moreover, capital gains and losses are subject to special procedures. The latter are described in a later section. Deductions and exclusions of special importance for investment purposes are described in this and later sections.

Two figures are relevant for tax purposes. The *adjusted gross income* is obtained by subtracting certain allowed deductions (mainly business expenses) from gross income. This amount less a number of personal expense deductions equals *taxable income*, the figure on which tax liability is based. The amount of tax calculated on this basis must be paid unless the taxpayer is able to claim *tax credits*, which may be subtracted directly from the tax liability to obtain a final amount due the government.

Nothing about the personal income tax in the United States is simple. Four different schedules of tax rates are in effect, the appropriate one depending on the status of the taxable entity. The two most commonly used are those for an unmarried taxpayer and married taxpayers filing a joint return. Under some circumstances an unmarried taxpayer may use the more advantageous "head of household" rates; and married taxpayers may find it worthwhile to file separate returns, for which yet another set of rates applies.

[3] Prentice-Hall, *Federal Tax Handbook* 1980 (Englewood Cliffs, N.J.: Prentice-Hall, Inc.), p. 120.

TABLE 9-4 Personal Income Tax Rates, 1979

TAXABLE INCOME		UNMARRIED INDIVIDUAL RETURNS			MARRIED JOINT RETURNS		
(1) From ($)	(2) To ($)	Tax ($) on Amount in Column (1)	Marginal Rate (%) on Excess over Amount in Column (1)	Average Rate (%) on Amount in Column (1)	Tax ($) on Amount in Column (1)	Marginal Rate (%) on Excess over Amount in Column (1)	Average Rate (%) on Amount in Column (1)
0	2,300	—no tax—		0	—no tax—		0
2,300	3,400	0	14	0	—no tax—		0
3,400	4,400	154	16	4.53	0	14	0
4,400	5,500	314	18	7.14	140	14	3.18
5,500	6,500	512	18	9.31	294	16	5.35
6,500	7,600	692	19	10.65	454	16	6.98
7,600	8,500	901	19	11.86	630	18	8.29
8,500	10,800	1,072	21	12.61	792	18	9.32
10,800	11,900	1,555	24	14.40	1,206	18	11.17
11,900	12,900	1,819	24	15.29	1,404	21	11.80
12,900	15,000	2,059	26	15.96	1,614	21	12.51
15,000	16,000	2,605	30	17.37	2,055	21	13.70
16,000	18,200	2,905	30	18.16	2,265	24	14.16
18,200	20,200	3,565	34	19.59	2,793	24	15.35
20,200	23,500	4,245	34	21.01	3,273	28	16.20
23,500	24,600	5,367	39	22.84	4,197	28	17.86
24,600	28,800	5,796	39	23.56	4,505	32	18.31
28,800	29,900	7,434	44	25.81	5,849	32	20.31
29,900	34,100	7,918	44	26.48	6,201	37	20.74
34,100	35,200	9,766	49	28.64	7,755	37	22.74
35,200	41,500	10,305	49	29.28	8,162	43	23.19
41,500	45,800	13,392	55	32.27	10,871	43	26.20
45,800	55,300	15,757	55	34.40	12,720	49	27.77
55,300	60,000	20,982	63	37.94	17,375	49	31.42
60,000	81,800	23,943	63	39.91	19,678	54	32.80
81,800	85,600	37,677	68	46.06	31,450	54	38.45
85,600	108,300	40,261	68	47.03	33,502	59	39.14
108,300	109,400	55,697	70	51.43	46,895	59	43.30
109,400	162,400	56,467	70	51.62	47,544	64	43.46
162,400	215,400	93,567	70	57.62	81,464	68	50.16
215,400	—	130,667	70	60.78	117,504	70	54.65

Table 9-4 shows the rates in effect in 1979 for (1) unmarried and (2) married taxpayers filing a joint return. The values are plotted in Figures 9-5(a) and 9-5(b). The top line in each figure shows the marginal tax rate—i.e., the proportion of an additional dollar of income that will be taxed away. This is constant over various ranges of income, but it increases as the taxpayer moves to higher "brackets."

It is important to remember that the total amount of tax paid is generally a smaller proportion of taxable income than indicated by the marginal tax rate. When one's income increases, and with it the marginal rate, only the additional dollars are affected. Thus the often-heard com-

FIGURE 9-5 Marginal and Average Tax Rates: (a) Unmarried Individual Taxpayer; (b) Married Couple Filing a Joint Return

Source: Table 9-4.

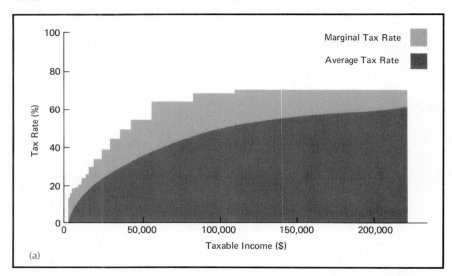

(a)

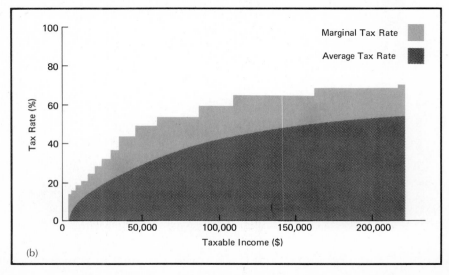

(b)

plaint that "by earning more (before tax), I will actually have less (after tax)" is simply incorrect. The lower curves in Figures 9-5a and b show the *average* tax rate—i.e., the ratio of total tax paid to total taxable income. Values for selected taxable incomes are also shown in Table 9-4.

As the figures and Table 9-4 show, a married couple pay less tax than an unmarried person with comparable taxable income. This is often attacked as discriminatory. On the other hand, such a couple may pay more tax than two single persons, each with half the couple's taxable income. Owing to the progressive nature of the tax, it is usually profitable for tax purposes for two people to marry if their incomes differ substantially. Differences may not be trivial. The value of a nonincome-producing spouse in terms of taxes saved may be estimated by comparing the figures in the relevant columns of Table 9-4. The total difference is in fact even larger, since income is reduced by $1,000 per person included (this is the "personal exemption") when computing taxable income. If someone with a taxable income of $50,000 marries someone earning nothing, their total tax liability may be reduced by almost $3,800. On the other hand, if two people, each with a taxable income of $25,000, marry, their liability may be increased by almost $2,900. From the viewpoint of taxes alone, marriage is a serious step.

EVALUATING THE TAX IMPACT OF A DECISION

It is almost a truism that most decisions are made at the margin. Thus the marginal tax rate is likely to be more relevant than the average. For example, consider a married couple with taxable income of $35,200 considering an opportunity to increase their income by $3,000. Using the figures in Table 9-4, the impact on taxes will be as follows:

	Before	After	Difference
Taxable income ($)	35,200	38,200	3,000
Tax ($)	8,162	8,162 + (.43 × 3000) = 8,162 + 1,290	1,290

An increase of $3,000 in income before taxes thus results in an increase of $1,290 in taxes, leaving a net increase in spendable income of $3,000 − 1,290, or $1,710. The calculations are simple because the change left the taxpayer in the same bracket. Thus 43% of the income was taxed away, leaving 57% to be spent. The fact that the average tax rate was well below these figures is virtually irrelevant.

When a decision will move income across brackets, the computations are more complex. For example, assume the opportunity in question would increase income by $20,000. The impact on taxes would then be:

	Before	After	Difference
Taxable income ($)	35,200	55,200	20,000
Tax ($)	8,162	12,720 + (.49 × 9,400) = 17,326	9,164

This result can also be determined by breaking the change into the portions in each bracket, then calculating a weighted average of the marginal rates, using the proportions as weights:

(1) Bracket ($)	(2) Amount ($)	(3) = (2)/20,000 Proportion	(4) Marginal Rate (%)	(5) = (3) × (4) Proportion Times Marginal Rate
35,200 to 45,800	10,600	.53	43	22.79
45,800 to 55,200	9,400	.47	49	23.03
			Effective incremental rate:	45.82

Both calculations show that the incremental tax liability, 45.82% of the increment to taxable income, is a function of the marginal rates for the brackets over which additional income will be earned.

TAX-EXEMPT BONDS

A major consideration for investors with large taxable incomes is the possibility of obtaining tax-free income. The simplest way to accomplish this exists because the notion of federalism has been interpreted to imply that the federal government should not tax states and municipalities, nor the income produced from their bonds. While the legal basis is complex, the facts are simple. Interest income from most bonds of states, municipalities, and their agencies need not be included in taxable income for federal taxes (and in some cases, for state taxes). The benefits for high-bracket taxpayers are obvious. For example, consider the couple in the

FIGURE 9-6 Ratio of Prime Long-Term Municipal Bond Yields to Long-Term Aa Public Utility Bond Yields, 1950–1978

Source: Salomon Brothers, *An Analytical Record of Yields.*

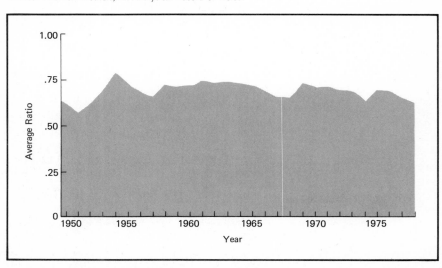

previous example. Assume that they can obtain an increment of $20,000 in taxable income each year by investing in corporate bonds or $12,000 per year by purchasing tax-free bonds. As shown earlier, their effective tax rate on an increment of $20,000 in taxable income would be 45.82%, leaving 54.18% or $10,836 to be spent. But $12,000 in tax-free income could all be spent—clearly a preferable situation.

This relationship is no secret. Not surprisingly, tax-exempt bonds offer lower rates of interest than others. Thus they are not attractive for investors with low marginal tax rates.

Figure 9-6 provides evidence on this point. It shows the ratio, over time, of the yield-to-maturity for a group of tax-exempt municipal bonds to that of a group of bonds of public utilities not subject to favorable tax treatment. There is, of course, more to be considered in such a comparison than (promised) yield-to-maturity. On this basis, however, municipal bonds appear to be competitive for those with taxable income subject to marginal tax rates of 30% (when the ratio of before-tax yields is 70%) to 40% (when the ratio is 60%). As shown in Table 9-4, in 1979 marginal rates in excess of 40% applied when a single person's taxable income passed $28,800 and a married couple's taxable income passed $35,200. For those fortunate enough to be considering investments that provide income in higher ranges than this, municipal bonds are well worth investigation. Less fortunate investors are likely to find them unattractive.

MAXIMUM TAX RATE ON EARNED INCOME

As shown in Table 9-4, marginal income tax rates can be as high as 70%. Fortunately, an important restriction softens the blow for many taxpayers. The marginal rate on *personal service* income may not exceed 50%. The distinction is subject to legal subtleties, and certain adjustments but

FIGURE 9-7 Marginal Tax Rates for a Married Taxpayer with $100,000 Earned Income and $50,000 Income from Capital

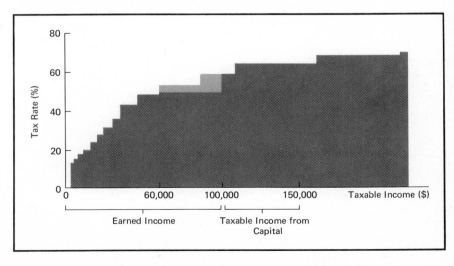

by and large such income is limited to that resulting from personal services (e.g., wages and pension payments). Income from capital is not given this preferential treatment. The effect is shown in Figure 9-7 for a married taxpayer with a salary of $100,000 and taxable income from capital of $50,000. The lightly shaded area represents the net reduction in taxes due to this feature of the tax laws.

THE DIVIDEND EXCLUSION

Most dividend income is subject to tax at full rate. However, up to $100 of such income may be excluded from taxable income each year by an unmarried taxpayer and up to $200 by a married couple filing either a joint return or separate returns. Thus an investment of $5,000 in stocks with a dividend yield of 4% would result in tax-free income for a married couple, in addition to the prospect of favorable tax rates on capital gains. As intended by Congress, this provides a considerable incentive to hold at least modest amounts of stock.

Payments from some institutions (e.g., credit unions, savings and loan associations), though termed dividends, are more akin to interest payments, and are not entitled to be excluded from income. Details are contained in the applicable regulations.

DEDUCTIBLE EXPENSES

As with the corporate income tax, interest payments may be deducted from an individual's income to determine taxable income (although the total amount deducted in any year for interest on funds borrowed to finance investments may generally not exceed net investment income plus $10,000). This deduction significantly lowers the effective cost of financing an investment by borrowing. Since property taxes are also deductible, the after-tax cost of home ownership is likely to be considerably lower than the before-tax cost, the magnitude of the difference depending on the relevant marginal tax rates for the taxpayer involved. Since the "income" associated with home ownership is taken in kind, by living in the home, and any capital gains are subject to preferential treatment, such an investment is likely to prove attractive for many taxpayers. This is the intent of Congress, and the high degree of ownership of homes (including condominiums) in the United States is at least partly due to such incentives to own rather than rent.

Many expenses associated with investment may be deducted from income. The test is that they be ordinary and necessary and in line with reasonable expectations of profitable return. Thus, the fees of investment advisers and subscriptions to financial publications may be deducted. Investments that habitually produce financial losses but nonfinancial pleasure may be considered hobbies and some or all of the associated deductions denied by the Internal Revenue Service. This possibility should concern the gentleman racehorse owner, but not the serious investor.

CAPITAL GAINS AND LOSSES

Without question the provisions of the personal income tax laws that have had the greatest impact on investor behavior deal with the treatment of capital gains and losses. Only the basic elements can be described here. Complete understanding of the details requires sufficient effort to keep thousands of lawyers, tax accountants, and investment advisers employed.

Realization

A change in the value of a capital asset is not relevant for tax purposes until it is *realized* by sale or exchange. If a security purchased for $50 appreciates to a value of $100 in a year, no tax is due. But if it is sold for $120 two years after purchase, the difference of $70 must be declared as capital gains realized at the time of sale, and applicable tax paid.

This rule makes the end of the year an interesting time for stock brokers. Depending on their situations, taxpayers may either be anxious to realize capital gains or losses before a new tax year begins, or reluctant to do so. Investment brokers aid the former by publishing lists pairing similar stocks for those who wish to sell one for tax purposes and buy another with similar characteristics to maintain the essence of their investment position. Such *tax exchanges* are used to accomplish this, because the tax laws preclude a deduction associated with a loss on a *wash sale* in which a security is sold and a "substantially identical" one bought within 30 days.

End-of-year sales and purchases motivated by tax considerations are fairly common. Volume in securities that experienced substantial price changes during the year tends to be high as holders sell to realize gains or losses. However, no major fall in prices appears to result from this pressure. Buyers apparently recognize that the sellers are motivated by knowledge of the tax laws, and not some previously unrecognized news of disastrous developments affecting the companies in question.

Capital gains and losses are, of course, those realized on capital assets, but the regulations define the latter rather narrowly. Capital assets include all kinds of property except that held in conjunction with the taxpayer's trade or business (e.g., inventories, business property); gains or losses on property that is an integral part of a taxpayer's business are considered regular income. Gains on the sale of one's personal residence are capital gains, but, owing to special provisions in the tax law, some gains on property held only to rent to others may be considered income. *Pro rata* appreciation of a fixed-income security issued at a significant discount (e.g., a 90-day Treasury bill) may also be considered income, as it is more like interest than capital gains.

The capital gain or loss realized when an asset is sold or exchanged is the difference between the value received and the asset's *adjusted basis*. The latter is the asset's *original cost* (if purchased outright, the actual outlay; if inherited or received as a gift, the basis of the donor).[4] While an

---

[4] With the exception that if the asset was purchased by the donor before 1977, the adjusted basis is the estimated value on Dec. 31, 1976.

asset is held, improvements may be made and their cost added to the basis. On the other hand, any return of capital must be deducted from the basis. The required accounting can become rather complicated. For example, if an investor buys 100 shares of a stock at $40 each, then buys another 100 at $50, and later sells 100 shares at $60, what is the realized capital gain? If the lots had been kept separate and only shares priced at the higher amount sold, the gain is $10 per share. This would be the preferred alternative, since it minimizes current tax outlays. If, however, adequate identification of the lots is not possible, regulations require first-in-first-out accounting, which would place the basis at $40 and the gain at $20 per share.

The ability to control the realization of capital gains and losses has a number of obvious advantages. Most important, tax can be paid at the most opportune time. The clearest case involves investment during years of high income (and marginal tax rates) with capital gains realized after retirement, when income and marginal tax rates may be considerably lower.

Short- and Long-Term Gains

The treatment of a capital gain or loss depends critically on the period the asset is held. For most assets, if the period is equal to or less than one year, the gain or loss is *short-term*; if more than one year, it is *long-term*. The only exception concerns future contracts for which the relevant period is six months. When making the calculation, the day the asset was acquired is excluded and the day it was sold or exchanged is included. Taxwise investors keep these distinctions in mind and watch the calendar with care.

When determining the impact of capital gains and losses on overall tax liability, short- and long-term changes must be considered separately at first. All short-term capital gains and losses must be brought together to obtain the *net short-term capital gain or loss*. Similarly, all long-term gains or losses must be brought together to determine the *net long-term capital gain or loss*. Finally, all gains and losses can be brought together to obtain the *net gain or loss from capital-asset transactions*.

Taxation of Capital Gains and Losses

The treatment of capital gains and losses for tax purposes is a logician's nightmare. By and large, if after the above nettings, there are net short-term gains, they are treated as ordinary income; if there are net short-term losses, they are treated as deductions from income. *Net long-term gains* are generally not taxed at full rates. Although such gains are added to taxable income, a deduction equal to 60% of the excess of long-term gains over short-term gains (if any) is allowed. This means that the effective marginal rate on a net long-term gain can be as low as .4 times that on a short-term gain or on ordinary income. *Net long-term losses* also require special treatment. They may be used to offset net short-term capital gains (if any) dollar-for-dollar. However, only *half* of any excess of net long-term losses over net short-term gains (or half of the long-term losses if there are no net short-term gains) may be deducted from income.

No more than $3,000 in losses may be deducted from income in any single year, although any excess may be carried forward for use in subsequent tax years. Moreover, losses on personal-use property (except those due to various casualties and theft) are not deductible at all, although gains will be taxed.

Special provisions apply to capital gains realized from the sale of an individual's principal residence. If a new residence is purchased within eighteen months, no tax need be paid if the price of the new home exceeds the proceeds realized from the old one. The untaxed gain on the old home will be added to any gain from the new one if it is sold later, but the upward-mobile individual who would never think of buying a less expensive home can look forward to a life free from the payment of capital gains taxes on increases in property values.

An additional provision softens the blow if cheaper (or rental) housing is desired later in life. A person 55 or older can elect to make a once-in-a-lifetime exclusion of the first $100,000 of realized gain on the sale of a residence if he or she has lived there for three of the preceding five years.

STATE INCOME TAXES

Most states levy personal income taxes, following a format similar to that of the federal government. Although lower, such taxes are also likely to be progressive. Table 9-5 (page 208) provides a summary collated in 1977.

The impact of these taxes is not quite as large as might first appear, for all taxes paid to state governments may be deducted from income before computing federal income tax. For example, consider an investor whose marginal rates for state and federal income taxes are 10% and 50%, respectively. An additional $100 of income will result in $10 of state tax. This leaves $90 subject to federal income tax, which will thus add $45 to total federal income taxes. Overall, then, $55 will be taxed away, giving an effective combined marginal rate of 55%.

As indicated earlier, income from bonds issued by municipalities within a state may be exempt from that state's income tax. Some states extend this exemption to include dividends from certain corporations domiciled within the state or to income taxes paid to the federal government. State income taxes may thus affect one's investment decisions.

THE FEDERAL ESTATE TAX

A person may escape taxes by dying, but his or her estate may not. State governments usually impose "death taxes," and the federal government requires payment of an estate tax. Double taxation is, however, reduced or avoided, as some or all state tax paid may be credited against the federal tax liability.

TABLE 9-5

No. 492. State Government Individual Income Taxes: 1977

[As of **January 1**. Only basic rates, brackets, and exemptions are shown. Taxable income rates and brackets apply to single individuals only; other schedules are used for married taxpayers filing separately or jointly or for heads of households in Alaska, California, Georgia, Hawaii, New Mexico, Oklahoma, Utah, and West Virginia. No income tax is levied in Florida, Nevada, South Dakota, Texas, Washington, and Wyoming]

STATE	Taxable income rates (range in percent)	TAXABLE INCOME BRACKETS		PERSONAL EXEMPTIONS [1]			SIZE OF STANDARD DEDUCTIONS			Federal income tax deductible
		Lowest: amount under—	Highest: amount over—	Single	Married— joint return	Dependents	Percent	Single	Married— joint return	
Ala	1.5–5.0	$1,000	$5,000	$1,500	$3,000	$300	10	$1,000	$1,000	Yes
Alaska	3.0–14.5	2,000	200,000	750	1,500	750	(X)	2,200	3,200	No
Ariz	2.0–8.0	1,000	6,000	1,000	2,000	600	10	500	1,000	Yes
Ark	1.0–7.0	3,000	25,000	[2]17.50	[2]35	[2]6	10	1,000	1,000	No
Calif	1.0–11.0	2,000	15,500	[2]25	[2]50	[2]8	(X)	1,000	2,000	No
Colo	[3]3.0–8.0	1,000	10,000	750	1,500	750	10	1,000	1,000	Yes
Conn	[4]1.0–9.0	(5)	100,000	100	200	(X)	(X)	(X)	(X)	No
D.C.	2.0–11.0	1,000	25,000	750	1,500	750	10	1,000	1,000	No
Del	1.6–19.8	1,000	100,000	600	1,200	600	10	1,000	1,000	[6]Yes
Ga	1.0–6.0	750	7,000	1,500	3,000	700	15	2,000	2,000	No
Hawaii	2.25–11.0	500	30,000	750	1,500	750	10	1,000	1,000	No
Idaho	2.0–7.5	1,000	5,000	750	1,500	750	(X)	2,200	3,200	No
Ill	2.5	Flat rate		1,000	2,000	1,000	(X)	(X)	(X)	No
Ind	2.0	Flat rate		1,000	(7)	500	(X)	(X)	(X)	No
Iowa	.5–13.0	1,000	75,000	[2]15	[2]30	[2]10	10	1,000	1,000	Yes
Kans	2.0–9.0	2,000	25,000	750	1,500	750	16	2,400	2,800	[6]Yes
Ky	2.0–6.0	3,000	8,000	[2]20	[2]40	[2]20	(X)	650	650	[6]Yes
La	2.0–6.0	10,000	50,000	[8]2,500	[8]5,000	[8]400	([8])	([8])	([8])	Yes
Maine	1.0–10.0	2,000	25,000	1,000	2,000	1,000	16	2,400	2,800	No
Md	2.0–5.0	1,000	3,000	800	1,600	800	10	500	[9]1,000	No
Mass	[10]5.0	Flat rate		2,000	2,600	600	(X)	(X)	(X)	No
Mich	4.6	Flat rate		1,500	3,000	1,500	(X)	(X)	(X)	No
Minn	[11]1.6–15.0	500	20,000	[2]21	[2]42	[2]21	10	1,000	1,000	Yes
Miss	3.0–4.0	5,000	5,000	4,500	6,500	750	15	750	[12]1,500	No
Mo	1.5–6.0	1,000	9,000	1,200	2,400	400	(X)	2,200	3,200	Yes
Mont	[13]2.0–11.0	1,000	35,000	650	1,300	650	10	500	1,000	Yes
Nebr	(14)	Flat rate		(14)	(14)	(14)	(14)	(14)	(14)	No
N.H.	[15]5.0	Flat rate		600	(16)	(X)	(X)	(X)	(X)	No
N.J.[17]	2.0–2.5	20,000	20,000	1,000	2,000	1,000	(X)	(X)	(X)	No
N. Mex	.9–9.0	500	100,000	750	1,500	750	(X)	2,200	3,200	No
N.Y.	[18]2.0–15.0	1,000	25,000	650	1,300	650	15	2,000	2,000	No
N.C.	3.0–7.0	2,000	10,000	1,000	(19)	600	10	500	(19)	No
N. Dak	[20]1.0–10.0	1,000	8,000	750	1,800	750	16	2,400	2,800	Yes
Ohio	.5–3.5	5,000	40,000	650	1,300	650	(X)	(X)	(X)	No
Okla	.5–6.0	1,000	7,500	750	1,500	750	15	2,000	2,000	[6]Yes
Oreg	4.0–10.0	500	5,000	750	1,500	750	13	1,500	1,500	[6]Yes
Pa	[21]2.0	Flat rate		(X)	(X)	(X)	(X)	(X)	(X)	No
R.I.	(14)	Flat rate		(14)	(14)	(14)	(14)	(14)	(14)	No
S.C.	2.0–7.0	2,000	10,000	800	1,600	800	10	500	1,000	[6]Yes
Tenn	[15]6.0	Flat rate		(X)	(X)	(X)	(X)	(X)	(X)	No
Utah	2.25–7.75	750	4,500	750	1,500	750	15	2,000	2,000	Yes
Vt	(14)	Flat rate		(14)	(14)	(14)	(14)	(14)	(14)	No
Va	2.0–5.75	3,000	12,000	600	1,200	600	15	2,000	2,000	No
W. Va	2.1–9.6	2,000	200,000	600	1,200	600	10	1,000	1,000	No
Wis	3.1–11.4	2,000	14,000	[2]20	[2]40	[2]20	15	2,000	2,000	No

X Not applicable.   [1] Many States also commonly allow other types of exemptions, such as physical or mental disability exemptions, and tax credits for items such as specified contributions or taxes paid to other jurisdictions.   [2] Tax credit.   [3] Effective minimum rate is 2.5% due to application of a tax reduction credit.   [4] Tax on capital gains and dividends applicable to taxpayers (individual or joint) with a Federal adjusted gross income in excess of $20,000.   [5] $20,000 to $21,999.   [6] Subject to specified limitations.   [7] Minimum exemption is $1,000; maximum exemption is $2,000.   [8] All exemptions and deductions are incorporated into tax tables which must be used when filing State tax returns.   [9] Incomes of husbands and wives filing joint returns are treated separately for purposes of taking the standard deduction; therefore, minimum deduction is $500 and maximum deduction is $1,000.   [10] Data apply to tax on earned income and annuities; 10% (flat rate) imposed on net capital gains, interest, and dividends. Only income in excess of $3,000 for single taxpayers and $5,000 for married taxpayers filing jointly is taxable. A 7.5% surtax on tax liability is additional.   [11] No tax is due at specified minimum levels of income because an allowance is made for a tax credit equal to   tax liability.   [12] Incomes of husbands and wives filing joint returns are treated separately for purposes of taking the standard deduction; therefore, minimum deduction is $750 and maximum deduction is $1,500.   [13] 10% surtax on tax liability is additional.   [14] Based on Federal income tax liability as follows: Nebraska, 18%; Rhode Island, 17%; Vermont, 25% plus 9% surtax. Since State tax is computed as a percentage of the Federal tax liability, in effect the Federal standard deduction and exemptions are adopted. As of January 1, 1977, the Federal standards comparable to the ones presented in this table were: Personal exemptions, single-$750, married filing joint return-$1,500, dependents-$750; standard deduction, percent-zero, single $2,200, married filing joint return-$3,200.   [15] Tax on interest and dividends.   [16] Each spouse having taxable income is eligible for $600 deduction; maximum exemption is, therefore, $1,200.   [17] Data apply to recently adopted personal income tax applicable July 1, 1976. Provisions vary for New York, Pennsylvania, and Delaware commuter taxes.   [18] No tax is due if adjusted gross income is below $2,500 for single taxpayers and $5,000 for married taxpayers filing jointly.   [19] Joint returns are inapplicable; however, a husband and wife may elect to file separate returns on a combined form.   [20] Plus a 1% tax on net income in excess of $2,000 of taxpayers who derive income from the operation of a business, trade, or profession other than as an employee. A 2% surtax on tax liability is additional.   [21] Refunds or forgiveness of tax due are based on specified poverty income levels.

Source: U.S. Bureau of the Census, *State Government Tax Collections in 1977*, series GF77, No. 1.

TABLE 9-6 Estate Tax Rates, 1979

(A) Taxable Estate More than ($)	(B) Taxable Estate Less than or Equal to ($)	(C) Tax on Amount in Column (A) ($)	(D) Rate of Tax on Excess over Amount in Column (A) (%)
0	10,000	0	18
10,000	20,000	1,800	20
20,000	40,000	3,800	22
40,000	60,000	8,200	24
60,000	80,000	13,000	26
80,000	100,000	18,200	28
100,000	150,000	23,800	30
150,000	250,000	38,800	32
250,000	500,000	70,800	34
500,000	750,000	155,800	37
750,000	1,000,000	248,300	39
1,000,000	1,250,000	345,800	41
1,250,000	1,500,000	448,300	43
1,500,000	2,000,000	555,800	45
2,000,000	2,500,000	780,800	49
2,500,000	3,000,000	1,025,800	53
3,000,000	3,500,000	1,290,800	57
3,500,000	4,000,000	1,575,800	61
4,000,000	4,500,000	1,880,800	65
4,500,000	5,000,000	2,205,800	69
5,000,000	· · ·	2,550,800	70

The estate tax is quite progressive, reflecting the idea that egalitarian principles may be met with less adverse impact on incentives via such a tax than perhaps any other, although the effect of the tax appears to have been rather small. Rates in effect in 1979 are shown in Table 9-6.

Not all of an estate is subject to tax. Half a married person's estate or $250,000 (whichever is larger) may be deducted for property passed to a surviving spouse. Property transferred to nonprofit organizations that qualify for an income tax charitable deduction may also be deducted. The *taxable estate* is the amount left after all deductions.

The actual tax that must be paid on an estate will equal an amount calculated using Table 9-6 less a *tax credit* ($42,500 in 1980 and $47,000 thereafter).

THE FEDERAL GIFT TAX

Partly to foil attempts to evade or reduce estate and income taxes, the federal government levies taxes on large gifts. Any transfer of property without adequate compensation may make the *donor* subject to tax.

A number of provisions make the gift tax of little or no consequence for many people. Up to $3,000 may be given to each individual every year, tax-free. Thus one can give away hundreds of thousands of dollars each year without incurring any gift tax liability, as long as each recipient receives no more than $3,000 per year. Moreover, gifts to nonprofit organizations are exempt. Since such gifts may be made in kind, it is possible for a wealthy person to give appreciated securities to his or her alma mater, escape both capital gains and gift taxes, and deduct both the original cost and part of the appreciation from current income as a charitable contribution. Small wonder that gifts to nonprofit organizations tend to increase in bull markets.

The principle underlying the federal gift tax is relatively straightforward. Taxable gifts are cumulated over time and considered equivalent to a prepayment on a decedent's estate. No tax is paid until the tax due on the cumulative total (using Table 9-6) exceeds the standard estate tax credit; afterward, taxes are levied as required to bring the total tax paid up to that required for the cumulative total of taxable gifts. Upon death, taxable gifts are added to the donor's estate and the tax liability on the total amount computed. Gift taxes paid are subtracted from this liability to determine the tax actually due. While exceptions and special provisions complicate the calculations, the gift and estate taxes are essentially *unified*.

TAX SHELTERS

In 1971 the press revealed that Ronald Reagan, then Governor of California, had paid no state income tax in 1970. This caused some surprise, but there was nothing improper about the Governor's calculations. Although a millionaire with a substantial salary, true to his image as a former star of western movies, he had invested in, among other things, some cattle, on which he had apparently sustained a business loss during the year in question.

At the time, many high-tax-bracket investors put their money in cattle, as well as oil drilling, certain kinds of real estate, and other investments with purportedly attractive tax characteristics. Such "tax shelters" are devised to take advantage of tax provisions allowing large deductions to create a "tax loss" in the present, followed by a later profit, preferably in the form of a capital gain. To make the loss deductible from current income and still retain the advantages of limited liability, such enterprises are generally formed as limited partnerships. A promoter, or general partner, puts together the operation, with individual investors as limited partners. The hoped-for results are tidy profits for the promoter and the investors, at the expense of the tax collector.

A little thought should call into question the likely permanence of such a situation. The key provisions of the tax law may, of course, be changed (and many have been changed dramatically since 1976[5]). But even if loopholes remain unplugged, economic forces may diminish any opportunities for abnormally high profit.

If large gains can be made, why should the promoter share them to any major extent with the investors? Instead, such investments might be priced to prove only advantageous enough on the basis of risk and return

[5] For example, the tax loss writeoff is now generally limited to the amount the individual has "at risk" in the investment.

to attract needed capital. Moreover, since the attractiveness is greater, the higher one's marginal tax rate, presumably only those in the highest brackets should find such investments interesting.

But one can go even farther. If large profits remain for promoters, why won't more promoters enter the business? The answer is that they will, potentially until the risk and return available from promoting tax shelters is competitive with that in other occupations. These anomalies in the tax laws are more likely to bring abnormally large amounts of investment into cattle feeding programs, oil drilling, and so on than to provide well-lighted roads to untold riches for high-bracket investors.

This is not to deny that advantages can be gained from the early discovery of some scheme for tax-sheltered investment. But often investors in such deals reduce their taxes, as advertised, but only by taking real and permanent losses. Upon occasion the arrangements appear more like "con games" in which the professional swindler profits at the expense of the amateur swindler, leaving the latter's intended victim (the Internal Revenue Service) unscathed.

DIVIDENDS VERSUS CAPITAL GAINS

Over any holding period, there are two fundamental ways to make money on an investment: (1) by receiving interest or dividend payments and (2) via sale or exchange at an increase in value, i.e., capital gains. As the previous sections of this chapter have shown, taxation of returns from these sources differs considerably. Corporations are taxed more heavily on capital gains than on dividends received. Tax-exempt organizations are taxed on neither but may have a preference for one or the other, depending on the nature of their fiduciary relationships with beneficiaries, legal constraints on spending out of capital, and so on. Individuals need pay no tax at all on small amounts of dividend income but are generally taxed at full rates on the remainder and on all interest received. Realization of capital gains may be deferred until a propitious time for tax purposes and will, if realized at least a year after purchase, be taxed at lower rates than would dividend and interest income received in the same year. And so on.

Given all these complications, it is very difficult to predict, *ex cathedra*, the overall impact of taxes on likely returns from alternative sources and thus to determine preferred investment policies for those with different tax situations. Instead, one must look at the data to see what sorts of relationships appear to obtain among returns from these major sources.

Unfortunately, risk, which is such a key attribute of the investment environment, makes it difficult to obtain precise answers on this score. In the absence of any tax effects, expected returns on securities would differ primarily on the basis of differences in relevant risks. But these very risks make it hard to assess before-the-fact expected returns with any precision, since after-the-fact average returns may diverge considerably from prior expectations.

The entire return from a U.S. Treasury bill is treated as interest for tax purposes. At the other extreme, some stocks are certain to pay no dividends at all in the near future, by explicit policy of the Board of Directors. Any return on such a stock over, say, the next year, must thus come from capital appreciation. Since this type of security is considerably more risky than a government bond, its total expected return should be greater, at least after taxes. But for whom? An individual investor in a high tax bracket, a tax-exempt institution, or a corporate investor?

If two investments have comparable risk, but one has a higher dividend yield, the other must offer a larger expected capital gain. But what will be the ratio at which the two types of return will trade? Will "the market" give up a dollar of expected dividends only in exchange for an additional dollar of expected capital appreciation? Or will, say, $.75 of the latter be accepted for a dollar of the former?

To even begin to answer this question, we should examine investments with roughly comparable degrees of relevant risk. This suggests the desirability of focusing on common stocks with different dividend yields, rather than comparing, say, bonds and stocks.

Yield can be measured by dividing the dividends paid by the price of the stock. In general, low-yield stocks are expected to increase in value. The market is willing to sacrifice some dividend yield in return for the prospect of capital gains. Potential increases in value are not obtained by magic, of course. Securities expected to increase substantially in value are generally those of companies that retain a large proportion of earnings to "plow back" into the firm.

Table 9-7 shows this relationship. Overall, high-yield stocks tend to be those with high payout ratios and relatively poor prospects for large increases in value per share. At the other extreme, low-yield stocks tend to be those with relatively small payout ratios and relatively good prospects for future growth in value. Of course, reinvesting earnings in a business does not guarantee an increase in value. The result depends on both the amount invested and the return on the investment. But on average, the expected relationship holds.

By and large, stocks with low dividend yields in one year tend to have low yields in the next year. Thus it is not too difficult to create a portfolio likely to have a small yield, another to have a larger yield, another likely to have yet a larger yield, and so on. If each portfolio is also constructed to have an estimated beta of approximately 1.0, differences in before-tax return may be attributed to differences in yield. Figure 9-8 shows the results obtained when this approach was applied to data cover-

TABLE 9-7 Dividend Yield Versus Payout: 1,000 Stocks Grouped by Yield, 1950–1970

Yield Group	Average Annual Dividend Yield (%)	Average Payout Ratio: Dividends/Earnings
I	5.9	.78
II	5.2	.63
III	4.5	.59
IV	3.8	.55
V	2.4	.43

Source: Fischer Black and Myron Scholes, "The Effects of Dividend Yield and Dividend Policy on Common Stock Prices and Returns," *Journal of Financial Economics*, 1, no. 1 (May 1974), 1–22.

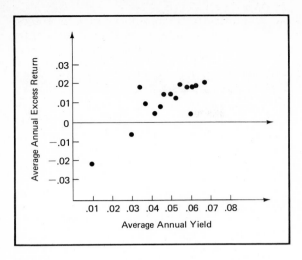

FIGURE 9-8 Average Annual Excess Return and Dividend Yield: Seventeen Portfolios with Estimated Beta = 1.0, 1947–1970

Source: Bernell K. Stone and Brit J. Bartter, "The Effect of Dividend Yield on Stock Returns: Empirical Evidence on the Relevance of Dividends," Working Paper No. E-76-8, Georgia Institute of Technology, 1979.

ing the period from 1947 through 1970. Each point plots one portfolio's average annual excess return (roughly, its return minus the return on the market as a whole) and dividend yield. In general, the greater the yield, the greater the before-tax return, although the relationship is far from perfect.

An example shows what this implies. Assume that two stocks—A and B—are similar in risk (beta) but have different dividend yields. Stock A will pay dividends equal to 5% of its current value, while B will pay dividends equal to 6% of its current value. Assume that A is expected to increase 7% in value, for a total return of 12%. The relationship in Figure 9-8 suggests that the total return on B should be greater than 12%, since its yield is greater than that of A. For example:

	Stock A	Stock B	Difference (B − A)
Yield	5.0%	6.0%	+1.0%
Expected capital gain	7.0	6.4	−.6
Total expected return	12.0	12.4	+.4

Stock B offers .4% more expected return than does stock A to compensate for the fact that it provides more of its return in the form of yield. As the last column shows, by pricing the two stocks to give these returns, the market allows an investor, by switching between A and B, to "trade" 1% of yield for .6% of gain or, more generally, to trade $1 of yield for $.60 of expected capital gain.

Stock B offers a higher total expected return *before tax.* But what about expected returns *after tax?* The answer depends, of course, on the investor's tax status.

For a tax-exempt investor, expected return before tax *is* expected return after tax. For such a person, stock B would be more attractive than stock A.

For an investor who pays an effective marginal tax rate of 50% on dividends and 20% on gains,[6] the two investments would be fairly similar on an after-tax basis:

	STOCK A		STOCK B	
	Before Tax	After Tax	Before Tax	After Tax
Yield	5.0%	2.5%	6.0%	3.0%
Expected capital gain	7.0	5.6	6.4	5.12
Total expected return	12.0	8.1	12.4	8.12

For an investor who pays an effective marginal tax rate of 70% on dividends and 28% on gains,[7] stock A would be more desirable on an after-tax basis:

	STOCK A		STOCK B	
	Before Tax	After Tax	Before Tax	After Tax
Yield	5.0%	1.50%	6.0%	1.8%
Expected capital gain	7.0	5.04	6.4	4.608
Total expected return	12.0	6.54	12.4	6.408

For the investor in the 50% bracket, the two securities are equally desirable; diversification considerations suggest that both be held. If securities are generally priced in this manner—i.e., so that $1 in dividends can be traded for $.60 in capital gains—such an investor should consider holding market proportions of all securities.

Those, such as tax-exempt investors, with less preference for gains vis-à-vis dividends should invest relatively more in security B and relatively less in A. That is, they should *tilt* their portfolios toward higher yields, with the extent of the tilt determined by diversification considerations.

Investors with more preference for gains vis-à-vis dividends should tilt in the direction of lower yields. Thus the investor in the 70% bracket should hold relatively more of security A and relatively less of B.

In general:

The market portfolio will be most appropriate for those whose *willingness* to trade expected capital gains for dividends is equal to the rate at which they *can* trade gains for dividends in the market. Investors with greater preferences for gains vis-à-vis dividends should tilt their holdings toward lower yields. Those with smaller (or no) preferences for gains vis-à-vis dividends should tilt their holdings toward higher yields.

[6] For example, if an investor realizes all gains after a year and pays tax on 40% of the gain at a 50% marginal rate, the effective rate on gains is .4 × 50%, or 20%.

[7] That is, .4 × 70%.

How much should one tilt a portfolio? And in what way should a given level of tilt be achieved? A full answer requires assessment of risks and the weighing of risk versus tax-induced changes in after-tax expected return. To do this effectively, one should use all the techniques of portfolio analysis.

FIGURE 9-9 Average Annual Excess Return and Dividend Yield, Seventeen Portfolios with Estimated Beta = 1.0

Source: Bernell K. Stone and Brit J. Bartter, "The Effect of Dividend Yield on Stock Returns: Empirical Evidence on the Relevance of Dividends," Working Paper No. E-76-8, Georgia Institute of Technology, 1979.

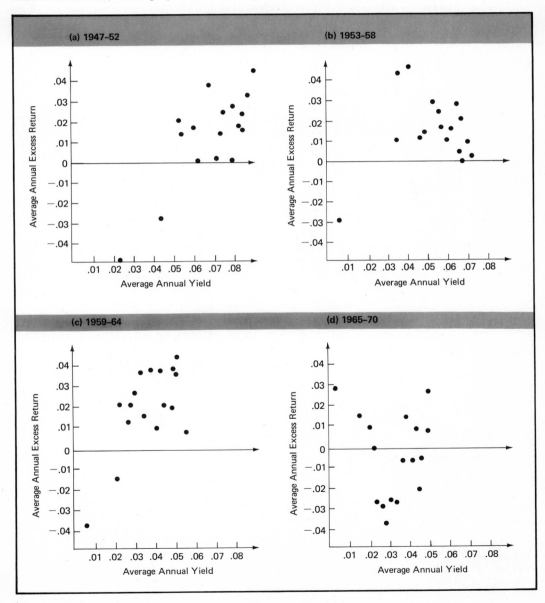

A particularly important consideration is the fact that the relationship between yield and before-tax return is by no means always the same. Figures 9-9(a) through (d) show that even when periods of several years are considered, the relationship can differ substantially from expectations. Each portion shows one of the six-year subperiods from 1947 through 1970. While the overall results (shown in Figure 9-8) indicated higher before-tax returns for higher-yield portfolios, the results in intermediate periods varied considerably from this relationship. Thus a "yield tilt" may increase expected after-tax return, but it will also increase risk—a fact that must be taken into account when deciding how far to go in such a direction.

EXPECTED RETURN, YIELD, AND BETA

To assess the impact of yield on expected return, one needs to separate effects that are due to other factors, most notably to differences in beta values. Figures 9-8 and 9-9 accomplish this by examining *portfolios*, all of which have estimated beta values of 1.0. An alternative is to use individual *securities*, plotting their attributes in a three-dimensional diagram with expected return, beta, and yield on the axes, and then fit a plane to portray the overall relationship.

Such a procedure has been adopted by a number of investment organizations. The first to implement it was the Wells Fargo Bank, which has given it the trademarked name of the *security market plane*. Figure 9-10 provides an example. For ease of interpretation, two "cuts" can be used to show its location. Figure 9-11 shows one such cut—the *security risk line*. This is a plot of expected return versus beta for securities with yield equal to that of Standard and Poor's 500-stock index. The second such cut—the *security yield line*—is shown in Figure 9-12. This is a plot

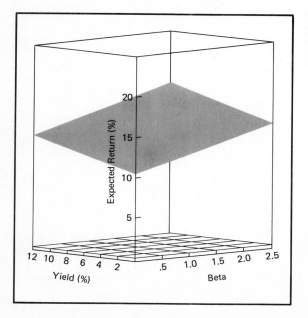

FIGURE 9-10 The Wells Fargo Security Market Plane

Source: Wells Fargo Investment Advisors, *Security Market Plane Report*, October 1979.

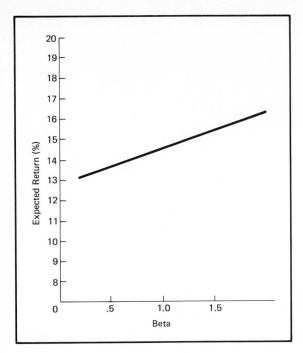

FIGURE 9-11 As Estimated Security Risk Line, August 31, 1979

Source: Wells Fargo Investment Advisors, *Security Market Plane Report*, October 1979.

of expected return versus yield for securities with beta equal to that of Standard and Poor's 500-stock index (i.e., beta = 1.0). Note that in this diagram yield increases as one goes from right to left.

As Figures 9-10, 9-11, and 9-12 show, given Wells Fargo's assessments of future prospects at the time, securities were priced so that higher-beta securities offered higher expected returns, other things equal (i.e., the security market plane sloped upward from left to right along the beta axis and the security risk line sloped upward to the right). Moreover, higher-yield securities offered higher expected returns, other things equal (i.e., the security market plane sloped upward going to the left along the yield axis and the security yield line sloped upward to the left). The "market" thus appeared to dislike both return received in the form of dividend yield instead of capital gains and risk.

Figures 9-10, 9-11, and 9-12 are based on *forward-looking expectations*, which are, of course, the relevant values for investment decisions. However, the same procedure can be applied to past data to see what relationship held between (1) average *actual* returns and (2) beta values and yields. A detailed study covering all the stocks on the New York Stock Exchange from 1936 through 1977[8] showed that, overall, higher-yield stocks did, in fact, return more, after adjustment for differences in beta values.

[8] Robert H. Litzenberger and Krishna Ramaswamy, "The Effect of Personal Taxes and Dividends on Capital Asset Prices: Theory and Empirical Evidence," *Journal of Financial Economics*, June 1979, pp. 163–196. By permission of North-Holland Publishing Co., Amsterdam.

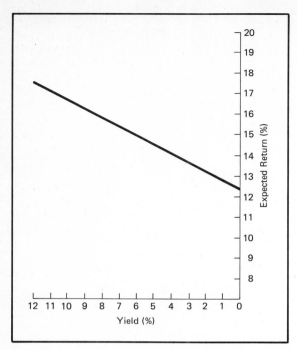

FIGURE 9-12 An Estimated Security Yield Line, August 31, 1979

Source: Wells Fargo Investment Advisors, *Security Market Plane Report,* October 1979.

On average, for each 1% increase in yield, other things equal, average return increased .236%. On average, the market allowed one to trade $1 of dividends for .764 of expected capital gains.

EX-DIVIDEND PRICE DECLINES

Another manifestation of the impact of taxes on investors' attitudes towards dividends and capital gains focuses on the behavior of a security's price after it goes "ex-dividend." A security may sell for $50 per share at the close of trading on the last day on which buyers are entitled to receive a dollar of dividends from the stock. Those who purchase the stock the next day will not get the dividend, and it is then said to sell *ex*-dividend. Other things equal, the stock's price should be less.

We can see this most easily by considering an investor who has decided to buy the stock at about the time it is scheduled to go ex-dividend. Assume that he or she expects to sell it in some later year at, say, $60, and can either buy it for $50 "cum (with) dividend" or for $49.25 ex-dividend. The alternatives are thus:

	(1) Buy with Dividend	(2) Buy Ex-dividend	(2) − (1) Difference
Capital gain ($)	60 − 50 = 10	60 − 49.25 = 10.75	+.75
Dividend income ($)	1	0	−1.00

By purchasing the stock ex-dividend, the investor can thus give up $1 in dividends in exchange for an additional $.75 in capital gains.

A study of the magnitude of this phenomenon[9] in 1966 and 1967 showed that by the end of the day when a stock goes ex-dividend, on average the price fell by about this amount. The exact figure was .78— almost precisely the magnitude of the average trade-off between 1937 and 1977.

THE CLIENTELE EFFECT

Since taxpayers with different marginal tax rates have different attitudes toward dividends vis-à-vis capital gains, high-bracket investors tend to hold relatively more low-yield stocks, and low-bracket and tax-exempt investors tend to hold relatively more high-yield stocks. Different securities thus have somewhat different clienteles. This is reflected in ex-dividend price behavior as well. Figure 9-13 shows the average one-day price fall relative to the dividend involved for each of ten groupings of stocks based on dividend yield. The results are generally consistent with the "clientele hypothesis." Investors attracted to stocks in the highest-yield group appear to be unwilling to give up a dollar of dividends unless they receive at least a dollar in expected capital gain, while those attracted to those in the

[9] Edwin Elton and Martin Gruber, "Marginal Stockholder Tax Rates and the Clientele Effect," *Review of Economics and Statistics*, 52, no. 1 (February 1970), 68–74.

FIGURE 9-13 Ex-Dividend Price Changes versus Divided Yield

Source: Edwin Elton and Martin Gruber, "Marginal Stockholder Tax Rates and the Clientele Effect," *Review of Economics and Statistics*, 52, no. 1 (February 1970), 68–74.

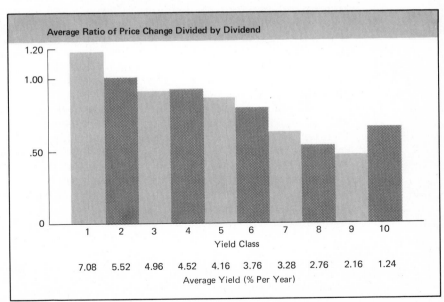

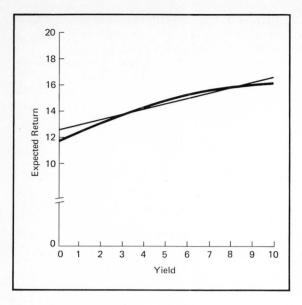

FIGURE 9-14 Estimated Relationships between Expected Return and Yield, July 1979

Source: Ralph Goldsticker, "A History of Ex-Ante Yield Effects," Wells Fargo Investment Advisors, 1979.

lowest-yield groups appear to be willing to forego a dollar of dividends in return for considerably less than a dollar in capital gain.

The existence of a clientele effect could also affect the relationship between expected return and yield. It is possible that large numbers of tax-exempt investors, preferring to concentrate their holdings in high-yield securities, will push down the expected returns at that end of the yield spectrum, while large numbers of high-tax-bracket investors, preferring to concentrate their holdings in low- or zero-yield securities, will push down expected returns at that end of the yield spectrum.[10] Figure 9-14 provides some support for this hypothesis. It shows a security yield line fitted to a set of estimates of security returns and a curve fitted to the same data. The curve is, in fact, "pushed down" at the ends. The relationship between actual average return and yield over the 1937–1977 period showed a similar relationship.[11]

As indicated earlier, it is difficult to provide definitive and precise statements of the relationship between expected return and various factors, and the magnitudes of such relationships undoubtedly change over time as well. Thus the "yield effect" on expected return may not have been as large as it appears to have been in the past and may be smaller yet in the future. Moreover, the phenomenon may be due at least in part to some other factor that tends to go with yield—i.e., high-yield stocks also have more of something else that is undesirable or less of something else that is desirable. Some have questioned the existence of the phenomenon and/or the taxation interpretation of its causation on

[10] This sort of concentration makes sense only if the short sale of securities is impossible or relatively costly. Otherwise the most effective policy for any investor can include long or short positions all along the spectrum and there would be no reason to expect the relationship between return and yield to be nonlinear.
[11] See Litzenberger and Ramaswamy, *op. cit.*

the grounds that clever tax planning may make it possible for investors to turn dividends into capital gains and that, if there were such a strong preference for gains, corporations would pay fewer or no dividends.

All these aspects merit consideration and further study. But the evidence suggests that, whatever the reason, higher-yield stocks have done better pre-tax on average in the past. It thus behooves the serious investor to consider whether or not they are likely to do better in the future and to carefully weigh the resulting expectations about return against estimates of risk, taking into account his or her particular tax status.

Problems

1. A friend reports that she has just received a raise of 10%. Will her after-tax income go up by 10%? Why? Assume that prices are expected to be 10% higher next year. Will her real (constant-purchasing-power) income after taxes be the same next year as it was this year? Why?

2. At what levels of corporate income is the marginal corporate tax rate precisely equal to the average rate? At what levels are they almost the same?

3. A corporate bond is selling for $950. It matures in a year and a day, at which time the holder will receive $1,000. In addition, the bond will pay $50 in interest during the year. What would be the after-tax return on the bond for an investor in the 70% personal income tax bracket? What if the bond had been a municipal bond?

4. Can the effective tax rate on capital gains be more than 40% of the rate on regular income? Can it be less than 40%? Why?

5. Assume that a particular bond issued by the State of New York is completely default-free, as is a similar bond issued by the State of California. Would you recommend that an investor who is a resident of California hold both bonds? Why? What about a resident of New York? A resident of the State of Washington? What if neither bond were completely riskless?

6. Assume that you are the trustee for a small fund left by a lawyer to support his widow. The provisions of the trust state that all income from dividends and interest payments will go to the widow. On her death the "corpus" of the fund will go to the lawyer's brother or his heirs. The brother is fabulously wealthy and the widow is very poor. What sorts of investments would you select? What if the trust provisions allowed you to "invade capital" for the widow—i.e., pay her out of income and/or sell investments and pay her the proceeds?

7. An investor buys 100 shares of a stock selling for $50 per share at the beginning of 1980. At the beginning of 1981 it is selling for $60 per share. At the beginning of 1982 it is selling for $70 per share. He pays an effective marginal tax rate of 28% on realized capital gains.

a. How much would he have after taxes if he held the stock until the beginning of 1982, then sold it? (Ignore transactions costs.)

b. How much would he have after taxes in 1982 if he sold all his shares at the beginning of 1981, then bought back as many shares as possible with the difference between the proceeds and the tax on gains realized in 1981? (Ignore transactions costs.)

c. What is the cost of realizing capital gains earlier (i.e., in 1981) rather than later (i.e., in 1982)?

8. You have a house worth $100,000 on today's market. You paid $50,000 for it some years ago and now own it outright. Your neighbor is in precisely the same situation. He suggests to you the following business deal. First, you sell your house to him for $100,000 and he sells his house to you for $100,000. Then you rent your (present) house from him for $200 per month and he rents his (present) house from you for $200 per month. Neither of you has to move.

a. What are the tax implications of the deal?

b. What if each of you had a mortgage with $40,000 outstanding and arranged to have the mortgages transferred with the houses?

c. What is the main tax advantage of home ownership?

Inflation

10

INTRODUCTION

The story is told of the modern-day Rip Van Winkle, who awoke in the year 2000 and immediately called his broker. (Fortunately, pay phones at the time permitted a call of up to three minutes without charge.) He first asked what had happened to the $5,000 he had instructed the broker to put in short-term Treasury bills, continually reinvesting the proceeds. Owing to high interest rates and the power of compounding, this had grown to over $1 million. Incredulous, Mr. Van Winkle inquired about his stocks, which were also worth about $5,000 when he dozed off. The broker told him that he was in for an even more pleasant surprise: they were now worth $2.5 million. "In short, Mr. Van Winkle," said the broker, "you are a millionaire 3.5 times over." At this point an operator cut in: "Your three minutes are over, please deposit one hundred dollars for an additional three minutes."

While this clearly overstates the case, there is no doubt that inflation is a major concern for investors. By and large, people have come to expect a significant amount of inflation and to fear rampant or even runaway inflation.

INFLATION IN THE UNITED STATES

Figure 10-1 provides some historical perspective. It shows the U.S. Consumer Price Index (CPI) from 1925 through 1978, adjusted so that the value in 1925 equals 100. As an aid to interpretation, the values are plotted on a *logarithmic* or *ratio* scale. This makes a given vertical distance repre-

TABLE 10-1 Growth Rates of the U.S. Consumer Price Index

From	To	Rate of Growth (% per Year)
1925	1933	−3.8
1933	1952	3.6
1952	1965	1.3
1965	1978	6.0

sent a specific percentage change, no matter where it is plotted. Such scales are often used when interest centers on percentage rates of growth or decline. In such a graph, a series of values growing at a constant percentage rate plot as a straight line. Such is not the case in Figure 10-1. Following the substantial deflation from 1925 to 1933, prices increased in almost every year, but there were three subperiods with different rates of inflation: fairly rapid from 1933 to 1952, mild from 1952 to 1965, and substantial from 1965 to 1978. Table 10-1 shows the rate of growth of prices for each of these subperiods, computed by taking the geometric mean of the ratio of the ending value to the beginning value. For example, at the end of 1978 the consumer price index was 113% higher than it had been at the end of 1965, thirteen years earlier. A similar result could have been obtained with a constant growth rate of 6.0% per year, since:

$$\sqrt[13]{2.13} = 1.06$$

FIGURE 10-1   The U.S. Consumer Price Index at Year-End, 1925–1978

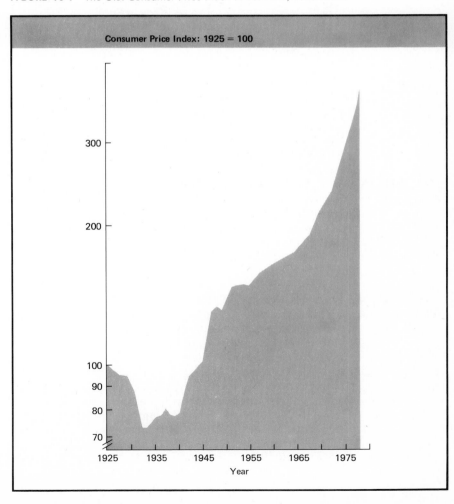

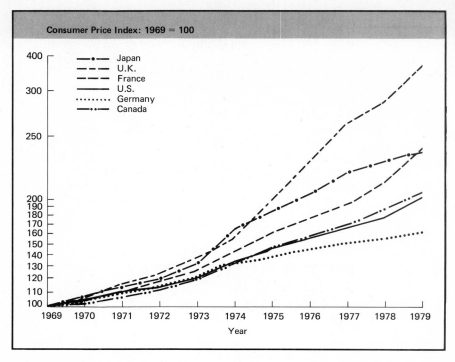

FIGURE 10-2 Inflation in Canada, France, Germany, Japan, the United Kingdom, and the United States, 1969–1979

Source: International Monetary Fund, *International Financial Statistics.*

INFLATION IN OTHER COUNTRIES

Figure 10-2 shows that inflation is by no means solely an American problem. Most industrial countries have experienced the phenomenon, and in some there is a feeling that unless fundamental changes are made, substantial inflation may become a way of life.

INFLATION, THE MONEY STOCK, AND FISCAL POLICY

Economists are hardly unanimous in their views concerning the importance of various causes of inflation, and differences of opinion on the subject are even greater among politicians. However, most agree that the stock of money in an economy plays an important role. Simply put, inflation is said to result from too much money chasing too few goods. Barring a change in the velocity with which money circulates, any difference between the rate of increase in the money stock and that of real output will be manifested in a price change.

Figures 10-3(a), (b), and (c) show the growth of money, prices, and real output in the United States since 1914. Figure 10-3(a) shows the

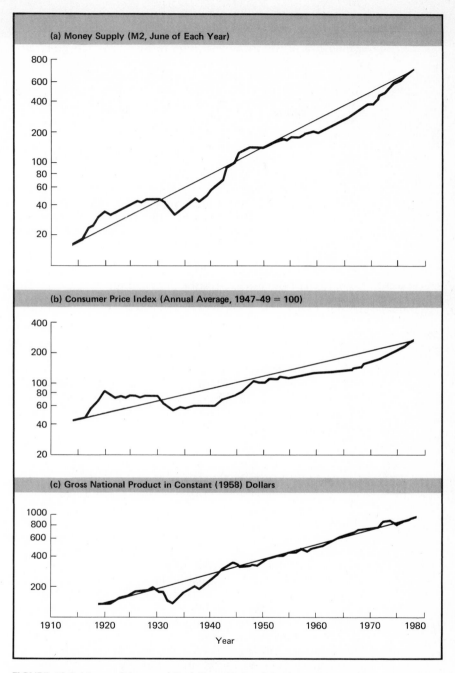

FIGURE 10-3 Money, Prices, and Real Gross National Product, 1914–1978

amount of currency, demand deposits (checking account balances), and time deposits (e.g., savings account balances) held by the public (this measure of the money supply, termed "M2," is generally considered the most useful of the published figures). Figure 10-3(b) shows the levels of the Consumer Price Index in each year, while Figure 10-3(c) shows the gross national product, expressed in constant dollars. This latter figure is obtained by dividing the dollar value of each year's total product by the level of prices in that year.

Since all the values in Figure 10-3 are plotted on ratio scales, trend lines can be used to represent constant percentage rates of growth. The ones shown in the figure, drawn to connect the values for 1914 and 1978, reflect annual growth rates.

The long-run trends are consistent with the monetarist thesis. Over this long period, the money supply grew at an annual rate of 6.2% per year while real output grew at a rate of 3.2% per year. In fact, prices rose at an annual rate of 3.0% per year, which just equaled the difference between the growth in the money supply and the growth in output (6.2 − 3.2).

While changes in the money supply usually affect prices, the strength of the linkage is subject to dispute. Moreover, there is generally a lag between a change in the money supply and the resulting change in prices.

Some believe that fiscal policy is the most important determinant of the rate of inflation. When the government spends a great deal more than it takes in from taxes, financing the deficit by borrowing, prices are likely to rise by a greater amount than if the budget had been balanced. Often both monetary and fiscal policy work in the same direction—for example, the Federal Reserve System may allow the money supply to expand rapidly in a period characterized by a large governmental deficit—making it difficult to assess the relative impacts of the two factors.

INFLATION VERSUS UNEMPLOYMENT

In setting medium- or long-term targets for price levels, there is an increasing feeling that moderate inflation may be a necessary evil. Inflation and unemployment are thought to be inversely related, given the institutions of modern society. This thesis is often summarized in a "Phillips curve," after A. W. Phillips, who suggested that attainable combinations of the rate of inflation and the rate of unemployment lie along a downward-sloping curve. However, experience in the United States in the last two decades has been quite different, with higher unemployment often accompanied by high levels of inflation. The evidence provides more support for an alternative thesis that unemployment is correlated with *changes* in the rate of inflation—decreasing when the rate of inflation increases and increasing when the rate decreases. Yet a third approach holds that unemployment is, in essence, unaffected by inflation.

Whatever the nature of the relationship may be, since many government officials hold the view that inflation and unemployment are inversely related, differences in recommended policy may be due to differences in relative aversion to the two evils, to differences in estimates of the likely trade-off between them, or to both.

PRICE INDICES

As indicated in Chapter 4, no price index can prove totally satisfactory as an indicator of the "cost of living" for all consumers, and most indices are likely to overstate the extent to which the cost of attaining a given level of satisfaction actually increases during any inflationary period, even for the people whose purchases the index was intended to reflect. Although this is fairly well understood, and most governments compute a number of alternative indices to provide a wider choice for analysis, people tend to focus on one index as an indicator of "the" price level. In the United States the Consumer Price Index, computed by the Bureau of Labor Statistics, often fills this role, despite some attempts by government officials to discourage such widespread use.[1] The composition of this index has been changed from time to time to provide a more representative basket of goods and services. The process by which data are gathered and verified has also been improved periodically.

For better or worse, most people consider a given percentage change in the consumer price index to be as good or as bad as a comparable change in the price of every good and service. While this is at best only approximately true, in the remainder of this chapter we will sidestep the issue, simply referring to changes in "the price level" or "prices."

NOMINAL AND REAL RETURNS

As shown in Chapter 4, the real interest rate on a loan will be approximately equal to the nominal or monetary rate less the percentage change in prices during the period in question. This can be generalized to cover any return, certain or uncertain:

$$\tilde{R}^r \approx \tilde{R}^n - \tilde{c} \tag{10-1}$$

where:

$$\tilde{R}^r = \text{the return in real terms}$$
$$\tilde{R}^n = \text{the return in nominal or monetary terms}$$
$$\tilde{c} = \text{the change in prices}$$

The tildes ($\tilde{\ }$) indicate that the values of the variables may not be known with certainty in advance.

The simplest view of investors' attitudes toward inflation is that described in Chapter 4: they are concerned with real, not monetary, returns, and a single price index is adequate to characterize the difference.

---

[1] A number of authorities prefer the personal-consumption expenditures deflator—an index derived from the gross national product figures, but it has not received the publicity accorded the Consumer Price Index.

This makes it imperative to account for the impact of inflation on both the expected value and the risk associated with the real return from a security or portfolio.

The impact on expected return is straightforward: the expected real return equals the expected nominal return less the expected change in prices:

$$E(\tilde{R}^r) = E(\tilde{R}^n) - E(\tilde{c}) \qquad \text{(10-2a)}$$

where:

$E(\tilde{R}^r)$ = the expected real return on a security or portfolio
$E(\tilde{R}^n)$ = the expected nominal, or monetary, return on a security or portfolio
$E(\tilde{c})$ = the expected rate of change in prices

If a security is to provide a given expected real return, the expected nominal return must be larger by the amount of inflation expected over the relevant holding period.[2] This can be seen by rearranging the equation:

$$E(\tilde{R}^n) = E(\tilde{R}^r) + E(\tilde{c}) \qquad \text{(10-2b)}$$

If investors are concerned with real returns, all securities will be priced so that expected monetary returns incorporate expected inflation. The expected return on every security should thus account for *expected* inflation (though not necessarily for unanticipated departures of actual inflation from expectations, as we will see shortly).

INTEREST RATES AND INFLATION

Before the fact, nominal interest rates for securities with no risk of default should cover both a requisite expected real return and the amount of inflation expected over the period in question. After the fact, of course, the real return will be the difference between the nominal return and the amount of inflation actually experienced. Only when actual inflation equals expected inflation will actual real return equal expected real return on such securities.

Figure 10-4(a) shows how short-term interest rates varied over the last 53 years, while Figure 10-4(b) indicates the variation of the annual changes in the consumer price index. The differences between the two, shown in Figure 10-4(c) represent actual real returns.

A number of inferences can be drawn from the data. The rate of inflation has been increasing over the last 25 years. Perhaps more important, inflation appears to have become more predictable: the typical difference between the rate of inflation in one year and that in the previous year was less after 1950 than before. More relevant: the variation in the actual real return, shown in Figure 10-4(c) was also smaller. Some of this may be due to the better estimation procedures used to construct the con-

---

[2] This discussion, entirely in terms of before-tax income, ignores the impact of taxation of interest income (described in a later section).

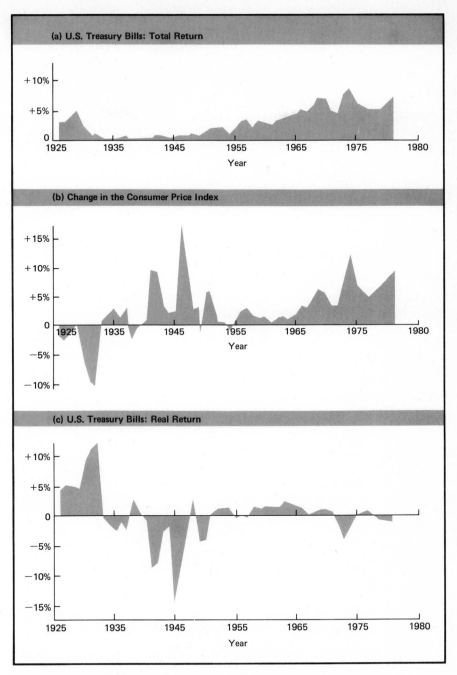

FIGURE 10-4 Nominal and Real Returns on Short-Term Default-Free Investments 1926–1978

Source: Roger G. Ibbotson and Rex A. Sinquefield, "Stocks, Bonds, Bills and Inflation: Year-by-Year Historical Returns (1926–78)." (Charlottesville, Va.: The Financial Analysts Research Foundation, 1979).

sumer price index in recent years, but there is probably more to it than this.

One cannot help be struck with the fact that those who invested in short-term securities over this period frequently ended up with less purchasing power than they started with: real return was negative in 23 of the 53 years. Perhaps even more surprising, the average real return over the period was *zero!*

While *expected* real returns may well vary from year to year, the variation may be relatively small. If so, investors may well have been willing to invest in short-term highly liquid securities even though they expected to earn nothing at all in real terms. If they are willing to do so still, such securities will be priced to give an expected real return of approximately zero.

If this assumption is made, the "market's" predicted rate of inflation over the near future can be estimated by simply looking at the current annual yield on short-term government securities. In a sense, Treasury bill yields represent a *consensus prediction* of inflation—a prediction likely to be more accurate in many cases than the predictions of any single forecaster.

REMOVING THE MONEY VEIL

The overall price level can be considered a unit of measure for expressing relative prices. If agreement were reached to call every dollar one cent, nothing of true economic importance would have to be changed, simply the manner in which accounts were kept. To some extent, money simply acts as a veil, obscuring the real underlying economic forces.

This can be seen most clearly in a prototypically simple agrarian economy in which wheat is invested (planted) this year to obtain wheat next year. In such a situation, the only uncertainty in terms of wheat is productive uncertainty: i.e., how much will come up. The real return depends solely on the relationship between the wheat harvested and that planted. In terms of the value-relative:

$$1 + \tilde{R}^r = \frac{\tilde{W}_1}{W_0}$$

where:

$$\tilde{W}_1 = \text{wheat harvested in year 1}$$
$$W_0 = \text{wheat planted in year 0}$$
$$\tilde{R}^r = \text{real return in terms of wheat}$$

What about the nominal, or monetary, return? We can represent the price of wheat at the time of planting by P_0 and the (generally uncertain) price at time of harvest by $\tilde{P}_1$. Then the "cost" of the investment would be $P_0 W_0$ and the value of the harvest would be $\tilde{P}_1 \tilde{W}_1$. The nominal return, expressed as a value-relative, would be:

$$1 + \tilde{R}^n = \frac{\tilde{P}_1 \tilde{W}_1}{P_0 W_0}$$

To convert a nominal return into a real return, one adjusts for price changes. In this case we can simply divide by $\tilde{P}_1/P_0$, which will give $\tilde{W}_1/W_0$.

The point illustrated here is simple enough. No matter what happens to prices (e.g., $\tilde{P}_1$), the real return on the wheat will be unaffected. It may be high or low, but the determining factors do not include the actual level of overall prices.

In the real world much more is uncertain than the results of physical production. But many, if not all, of these influences concern relative prices—for example, the level of the prices of a firm's outputs relative to those of its inputs. The real profits obtained from some capital assets may be affected by the overall level of prices, but when the effects are averaged across all assets, such effects may well balance out. The real return on the overall "market portfolio," which includes all capital assets, may thus be related primarily to overall real output and only secondarily to the level of overall prices.

This suggests that uncertainty about inflation per se may directly add little to the uncertainty about the real return on a widely diversified set of capital assets. However, it may contribute indirectly, through the impact of inflation on real output.

There are limits to the ability of an economy to accommodate substantial rates of inflation, especially those not perfectly anticipated. For example, if the money stock is increased rapidly, it will be very difficult for firms and individuals to merely increase all prices and wages by the appropriate percentage. Some prices and wages are fixed by long-term contracts, others are subject to government control, and so on. This can cause distortions in relative prices and an overall drop in the efficiency with which the economy functions. Resources must be used to convey and obtain information about the latest prices, revalue inventories, and the like. Inflation that differs from expectations can thus cause a decrease in both real output and the overall real return obtained by producers.

THE IMPACT OF UNEXPECTED INFLATION ON BORROWERS AND LENDERS

While deviations of actual inflation from expected inflation may have relatively little effect on investments as a whole, they may well affect specific investments. In fact, one would expect a direct impact on the real returns associated with investments whose payments are fixed in monetary terms.

A simple example will illustrate the relationship. Assume that in year zero everyone expects inflation to run at an annual rate of 5% per year forever. This is shown by the solid line in Figure 10-5. (Note that the vertical axis is a ratio scale, so that constant percentage changes plot along a straight line.) Now imagine that a lender has agreed to provide funds at a zero real expected return. Thus one can borrow $100 now and pay back $105 next year or borrow $100 now and pay back $110.25 in two years. If actual inflation equals expected inflation, a one-year loan would require a payment of $100 in constant (year-zero) dollars a year hence, while a

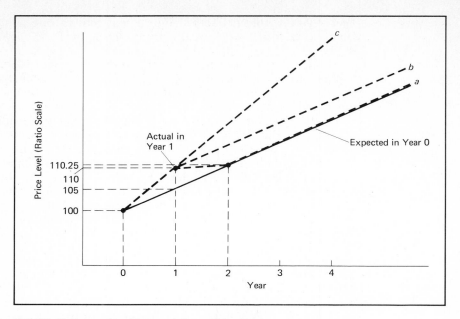

FIGURE 10-5 Actual and Expected Future Price Levels

two-year loan would require a payment of $100 in constant (year-zero) dollars two years hence. In each case, the real rate of interest would be zero, as intended.

Now imagine that two individuals take advantage of the lender's offer; one borrows short-term (one year) and the other long-term (two years). How will they be affected if actual inflation differs from expected inflation?

Say that in year 1 prices rise by 10% instead of the expected 5%. This is shown by the dashed line in Figure 10-5. Clearly the short-term borrower gains. He or she now pays back $105, but in terms of year-zero dollars, this is only $105/1.10 = $95.45, giving an actual real rate of interest of −4.55%. When actual inflation exceeds expected inflation, those with commitments to make payments fixed in nominal terms (debtors) gain in real terms at the expense of those to whom payments are to be made (creditors). Conversely, when actual inflation is less than expected inflation, monetary creditors gain and monetary debtors lose.

But what about the person who borrowed long-term? Will he or she gain or lose? If the loan is paid as scheduled, the answer will depend on the actual level of prices in year 2. If it is paid early, on terms agreeable to the lender, the answer will depend on the lender's expectations *in year 1* about prices in year 2. And if the obligation is transferred to someone else at an agreed-upon price, the answer will depend on the other party's expectations in year 1 about prices in year 2.

Figure 10-5 shows three possible patterns of expected future price levels, given the unanticipated increase in year 1. Pattern *a* assumes that investors consider unanticipated deviations to be irrelevant for predicting

TABLE 10-2 Value of Payment in Year-Zero Dollars

Pattern	Amount Paid in Year 2 ($)	Expected Price Level in Year 2 ($)	Expected Value of Amount Paid in Year-Zero Dollars
a	110.25	110.25	100.00
b	110.25	115.50	95.45
c	110.25	121.00	91.12

future price *levels*. Thus after a 10% rise an increase of slightly less than ¼ of 1% (from 110 to 110.25) is expected. Pattern *b* assumes that investors consider unanticipated deviations to be irrelevant for predicting the *rates* of increases of future prices. Increases of 5% per year will still be anticipated, but from a new, higher base. Pattern *c* assumes that the actual rate is expected to continue in the future. Thus every subsequent year is expected to bring a 10% increase in prices.

The impact of revised expectations on the long-term borrower is substantial. Table 10-2 shows the value of the payment in year-zero dollars for each of the three patterns. With pattern *a* the borrower expects to gain nothing; with pattern *b* he or she expects to pay back the same amount in real terms as the short-term borrower pays; with pattern *c* he or she expects to pay back less in real terms than does the short-term borrower.

Which pattern is most likely? The answer generally depends on the cause of the unexpected change, but a typical response would probably lie somewhere between patterns *b* and *c*. When actual inflation exceeds expectations, investors are likely to use the current level of prices as a base and also raise their estimates of the future rate of inflation, but not by the full amount of the difference. When actual inflation falls below expectations, investors are likely to lower their expectations of the rate of future inflation, but not by the full amount of the difference.

The implication is that long-term borrowers are likely to gain somewhat more than short-term borrowers when actual inflation exceeds expected inflation and lose somewhat more when actual inflation falls below expectations. Similarly, long-term lenders are likely to lose somewhat more than short-term lenders when actual inflation exceeds expectations and gain somewhat more when actual inflation falls below expectations.

THE IMPACT OF UNEXPECTED INFLATION ON THE PRICE OF A COMMON STOCK

A company's financial statements can be used to obtain a rough estimate of the impact of a divergence between actual and expected inflation on the value of the firm's common stock. Each item can be classified as either a real, short-term monetary, or long-term monetary asset or liability. In some cases the classification is fairly obvious; in others it is somewhat arbitrary. However, detailed knowledge of a company and/or careful reading of its reports can often reduce the arbitrariness of such breakdowns.

Two additional monetary assets need to be considered. Both relate to future taxes. The amount of dollar income subject to taxation will undoubtedly depend on the extent of inflation. However, taxable income is reduced by two items: depreciation charges and interest payments. For example, future federal corporate income taxes can be reduced by roughly 46% of the current amount of a firm's undepreciated plant and equipment. The present value of such tax reductions is a long-term monetary asset, since the amounts will not vary with subsequent inflation. This present value will, of course, depend on the timing of the depreciation charges and be smaller than the total (undiscounted) value.

A similar consideration applies to the interest payment on currently outstanding debt. Taxes will be reduced by approximately 46% of this amount; the present value of such reductions thus constitutes another long-term monetary asset.

To carefully estimate a stock's exposure to unanticipated inflation, market values of assets and liabilities should be used if possible. Moreover, the value of future tax reductions should be discounted. Finally, explicit account should be taken of differences in maturity and the likely effects of current surprises on future expectations. However, a crude estimate can be obtained by using book (accounting) values of assets and liabilities, estimating only the total (undiscounted) value of future tax reductions, and making a very rough adjustment for the impact of changing expectations (for example, according long-term assets and liabilities twice the weight of short-term assets and liabilities on the assumption that a dollar of a long-term commitment has twice the overall effect of a dollar of a short-term commitment). With such assumptions a firm's *net monetary position* can be estimated. If monetary assets exceed monetary liabilities, the firm is a *net monetary creditor* and its stockholders can be expected to *lose* if inflation is greater than expected and to *gain* if inflation is less than expected. On the other hand, if monetary assets are less than monetary liabilities, the firm is a *net monetary debtor* and its stockholders can be expected to *gain* if inflation is greater than expected and to *lose* if inflation is less than expected.

REPLACEMENT COST ACCOUNTING

One definition of earnings or profit holds that if a firm paid out the entire amount of profit each year, it would neither increase nor decrease in size, measured by the real value of its productive capacity. This notion is often summarized by the term "sustainable earnings." A firm that pays out more than the total amount of such earnings can be expected to decline, while one that pays out less can be expected to grow.

While there may be some objections to this definition on principle, they are overshadowed by the problems associated with its implementation. And these problems are seriously aggravated in an inflationary environment.

Consider a firm that purchases ten units of some semifinished good at the beginning of each year, hires labor to work on it, then sells the finished product at the end of the year. For simplicity assume that labor is paid from the proceeds of the sales. In the absence of inflation, the firm's operations might be summarized as follows:

At the beginning of the year:	
Buy 10 units at $100 each:	$1,000
At the end of the year:	
Sell 10 units at $200 each:	2,000
Pay labor	−800
Net cash received	$1,200

The firm thus invests $1,000 to obtain $1,200 a year later, giving a return of 20%. Viewed somewhat differently, after an initial investment of $1,000, profits of $200 can be paid out each year, assuming no inflation. The latter is the magnitude of sustainable earnings or profit.

Now assume that in the course of the year all prices and wages increase 10%. The results would then be:

At the beginning of the year:	
Buy 10 units at $100 each:	$1,000
At the end of the year:	
Sell 10 units at $220 each:	2,200
Pay labor	880
Net cash received	$1,320

An investment of $1,000 thus produces receipts of $1,320 a year later, for a return of 32% and a difference of $320. Is this the amount of sustainable earnings? Clearly not. Assuming no further inflation, $1,100 will be required to replace the inventory at the beginning of the next year. Thus only $220 can be paid out if the firm is to avoid a decline in real productive capacity. Put somewhat differently, the total "profit" of $320 resulted from an increase in the value of the firm's inventory plus normal operations.

To keep these aspects separate, a number of authorities recommend *replacement cost accounting*. In essence, this involves the use of estimated replacement costs instead of historic costs when calculating profit. In this case such a procedure would give:

Receipts from sales		$2,200
Less cost of goods sold		
Wages	$ 880	
Materials, at replacement cost	1,100	1,980
Equals net profit		$ 220

An equivalent procedure subtracts from reported profit an *inventory valuation adjustment*, representing the excess of replacement cost over the amount utilized in the standard accounts:

Reported profit		$320
Less inventory valuation adjustment		
Replacement cost	$1,100	
Reported cost	1,000	
Adjustment		100
Adjusted profit		$220

Even after the adjustment, profit is stated in current dollars. To compare the amount with that of a previous year, the value must be adjusted for price-level changes. In this case the amount in current dollars is $220, while the amount in constant, year-zero dollars is 220/1.10, or $200 (which is the amount that would have been obtained in the absence of inflation).

The magnitude of the appropriate inventory valuation adjustment depends on the length of time inventory is held, the extent of the rise in its replacement cost, and the method used to account for such costs when calculating reported profit. As discussed in Chapter 9, the LIFO method comes closest to replacement costs, while the FIFO method lies at the other end of the spectrum.

A similar situation arises with capital assets. Their historic costs are charged to operations over assumed productive lives, using various depreciation formulas. As discussed in Chapter 9, accelerated depreciation is generally used for tax purposes, but more gradual procedures may be used for reporting profits and earnings to stockholders. However, assets "used up" in the production process are generally valued at historic, not replacement costs. Other things equal, this will cause an understatement of cost and an overstatement of sustainable earnings.

At the beginning of each year a firm will have an "inventory" of capital assets. During the year the replacement costs of these assets may change, resulting in associated gains or losses, although such changes may not be realized at the time. The portion of this inventory of assets

TABLE 10-3 Profits Before and After Inventory Valuation and Capital Consumption Adjustments: U.S. Nonfinancial Corporations, 1970–1978

Year	Profits before Taxes ($ billions)	Profits before Taxes after Adjustments ($ billions)	Percentage Difference	Percentage Change in the Consumer Price Index
1970	55.1	51.6	6.4	5.5
1971	63.3	58.7	7.3	3.4
1972	75.9	72.0	5.1	3.4
1973	92.8	75.9	18.2	8.8
1974	103.8	63.2	39.1	11.5
1975	102.3	78.3	23.5	7.0
1976	130.6	101.9	22.0	4.8
1977	143.5	116.5	18.8	6.8
1978	166.1	128.3	22.8	9.0

Source: U.S. Department of Commerce, Survey of Current Business.

used up in production should be valued at replacement cost to estimate sustainable profit from operations. If historic costs are used instead, the resulting amount should be adjusted to account for the difference between replacement and historic costs.

In 1979 the Financial Accounting Standards Board issued its statement of Accounting Standards Number 33, which requires companies with total assets of more than $1 billion or inventories, property, plant, and equipment with a gross value of more than $125 million to provide supplementary inflation-adjusted financial statements. Initially two methods are to be used experimentally: a *constant-dollar* procedure that accounts for general inflation and a *current-cost* method that accounts for specific price changes. The former, requiring only adjustments for changes in the general price level, was required to be included in reports issued beginning in 1980, while the latter, requiring estimates of the costs of replacing specific types of inventory, property, plant, and equipment, had to be included in reports issued beginning in 1981. The standard also requires that assets and liabilities be classified as monetary or nonmonetary and that an estimate be made of the gain or loss on the net monetary position resulting from general inflation.

The U.S. Department of Commerce shows the estimated portion of aggregate corporate profits attributable to inventory valuation increases in its *Survey of Current Business*. The estimated difference between aggregate depreciation based on historic cost ("capital consumption") and that based on replacement cost ("economic capital consumption") is also reported. Table 10-3 shows how profits are altered in inflationary times when the *inventory valuation adjustment* (IVA) and *capital consumption adjustment* are taken into account. Not surprisingly, as a comparison of the last two columns shows, the effect is generally greater, the greater the rate of inflation.

TAXATION, INFLATION, AND THE RETURN ON CAPITAL

One of the potential beneficiaries of inflation in most countries is the government. This result derives from the nature of the tax structure and can arise in several ways.

One source of such a shift of real wealth from the private to the public sector is the taxation of dividends, interest, and capital gains. For example, consider an investment with a real return of 7% held by someone in a 30% marginal tax bracket. In the absence of inflation, the investor would retain .7 × 7% for an after-tax nominal and real return of 4.9%. Now assume that there is inflation at the low rate of 2%, and that the return on the asset rises accordingly to 9%. The investor's after-tax nominal return becomes .7 × 9 = 6.3%, but in real terms this is approximately 6.3 − 2.0, or 4.3%. The effective tax rate has increased—a larger portion of the real return is being allocated through the public sector. If inflation rises to 4%, and with it the return to 11%, the investor's after-tax return becomes .7 × 11 = 7.7%, and his or her real return approximately 7.7 − 4.0, or 3.7%.

Barring a change in the tax structure, the greater the rate of inflation, the greater will be the resulting shift of earnings on capital from the private to the public sector. Moreover, an increase in the anticipated rate of inflation will, under these conditions, lower the present value of capital assets.

For an asset's real after-tax return to be the same with a high inflation rate as with a low rate, its price must fall enough to increase the nominal before-tax return sufficiently to compensate for *both* inflation and the larger effective tax rate. In the previous example the return would have to rise to 9.86% if the rate of inflation were 2% and to 12.72% if it were 4%:

Rate of inflation	0%	2%	4%
Before-tax return	7.0	9.86	12.72
Return after tax	4.90	6.90	8.90
(= .7 × return before-tax)			
Real return after tax	4.90	4.90	4.90
(≈ return after tax − inflation rate)			

In this case a 2% increase in the rate of expected inflation would increase the expected return on the asset by 2.86%. In other words, expected return would change by 1.43 times the change in the expected rate of inflation.

This phenomenon could be avoided by levying taxes on *real* returns. Alternatively, tax rates could be changed often enough to give a similar result. If such changes were expected to be made when required, prices of capital assets might not fall when the rate of anticipated inflation increased, and expected returns would change one-for-one with changes in the expected rate of inflation.

SECURITIES AS HEDGES AGAINST INFLATION

Presumably, investors are concerned more with real returns than with nominal returns. This implies that securities that provide a hedge against inflation should be considered more attractive, other things equal, than those that do not. Of course in an efficient capital market other things would not be equal, and the former would be priced to be inferior in some other dimension—for example, expected return.

But what does it mean to say that a security is a "hedge" against inflation? And what does empirical research suggest about the abilities of various classes of assets to act as such hedges?

For a tax-exempt investor a security would provide a perfect hedge against inflation if its return moved one-for-one with changes in inflation, for then its real return would be the same no matter what the rate of inflation. For an investor paying taxes the relationship might have to be more than one-for-one. And, of course, most security returns are subject to additional uncertainty because of factors unrelated to inflation. The ability of a security to hedge against inflation could be summed up in a number (h_i) in an equation of the form:

$$\tilde{R}_i = a_i + h_i\tilde{c} + \tilde{\epsilon}_i \qquad \text{(10-3)}$$

where:

a_i = a constant

h_i = the security's sensitivity to inflation

$\tilde{c}$ = the rate of inflation

$\tilde{\epsilon}_i$ = the uncertain portion of the return of the security not related to inflation

Formula (10-3) has one drawback—it fails to differentiate between *expected* and *unexpected* inflation. For instance, all securities might serve as hedges against expected inflation, but only certain ones might hedge against unexpected changes in the rate of inflation. It is thus preferable to treat the two aspects separately:

$$\tilde{R}_i = a_i + h_i^e c_e + h_i^u\tilde{c}_u + \tilde{\epsilon}_i \qquad \text{(10-4)}$$

where:

a_i = a constant

h_i^e = the security's sensitivity to expected inflation

c_e = the expected rate of inflation

h_i^u = the security's sensitivity to unexpected inflation

$\tilde{c}_u$ = the unexpected inflation (i.e., the difference between the actual rate of inflation and the rate that was expected)

$\tilde{\epsilon}_i$ = the uncertain portion of the return of the security not related to inflation

Before the fact, both $\tilde{c}_u$ and $\tilde{\epsilon}_i$ are uncertain, and roughly as likely to be positive as negative.

As indicated earlier, a good estimate of short-term expected inflation is provided by the return on short-term Treasury bills. Thus, if investors are willing to settle for an expected real return of zero on six-month Treasury bills, the return on such a bill will indicate a consensus estimate of inflation over the forthcoming six months. The difference between the actual rate of inflation during a period and the Treasury bill rate at the beginning of the period can thus be considered the amount of unexpected inflation ($\tilde{c}_u$).

This relationship makes it possible to estimate for any short period both expected and unexpected inflation. By comparing returns on various securities with these estimates of expected and unexpected inflation over a number of periods, we can measure *ex post* sensitivities to the two aspects.[3]

Table 10-4 provides estimates derived in this manner for several types of investments. Since the values are based on after-the-fact relationships rather than before-the-fact expectations about such relationships, little attention should be paid to minor differences in magnitudes. However, the major differences warrant attention.

---

[3] The procedure involves the use of multiple regression to estimate the coefficients in formula (10-4).

TABLE 10-4 Sensitivities of Assets to Expected and Unexpected Inflation, Six-Month Holding Periods, July 1959–July 1971

Asset	Sensitivity to Expected Inflation (h_i^e)	Sensitivity to Unexpected Inflation (h_i^u)
6-month U.S. Treasury bills*	1.0	0
1–2 year U.S. government bonds	1.08	−1.15
2–3 year U.S. government bonds	1.03	−1.75
3–4 year U.S. government bonds	.88	−2.37
4–5 year U.S. government bonds	.79	−2.75
Private residential real estate	1.27	1.14
Common stocks†	−4.26	−2.09

* Values are assumed.
† Value-weighted average of all stocks listed on the New York Stock Exchange.

Source: Eugene F. Fama and G. William Schwert, "Asset Returns and Inflation," *Journal of Financial Economics*, November 1977, pp. 115–146. By permission of North-Holland Publishing Co., Amsterdam.

The evidence shows that the interest rate on a six-month Treasury bill is a relatively unbiased estimate of the rate of inflation expected over the next six months. It thus hedges one-for-one against expected inflation. This suggests that investors either are unaware of tax consequences or assume that rates will be revised as needed to avoid changes in effective rates as inflation changes.

Of course a six-month Treasury bill cannot provide a hedge against unanticipated inflation over its life. If inflation is expected to be 5% per six months, such a bill might be priced to return 5% over six months. If inflation actually turns out to be 6% over the period, the return on the bill will still be 5%. Thus the value of h_i^u is zero.

Longer-term U.S. government bonds appear to have provided hedges against expected inflation on roughly a one-for-one basis. However, all failed to serve as hedges against unexpected inflation. In fact, all had *negative* sensitivities, with the value of h_i^u more negative, the longer the term of the bond. This relationship is not especially surprising in light of the way investors revise expectations based on recent experience.

Assume that inflation is expected to run at the rate of 5% per six months throughout the year. At the beginning of the year a one-year government bond is priced to return 5% per six months. Now assume that during the first half of the year inflation runs at the rate of 6% (per six months). Investors will likely revise upward their estimate of inflation for the second half of the year—say from 5 to 5.5%. But if the bond is to return 5.5% over the second half of the year, its price at midyear must be lower than it would have been otherwise. Investors who held it during the first half of the year thus would not obtain a return of 5%, but less. Higher-than-anticipated inflation caused them to obtain a lower-than-anticipated return. There were thus two sources of *bad* news: (1) inflation was greater than expected and (2) their investments did worse than expected. Of course, had inflation been less than expected, the situation would have been reversed and there would have been two sources of *good* news.

The longer the remaining life of a bond, the longer the period over which revised expectations of inflation are relevant. Thus it is not surprising that prices of longer-term bonds are affected more by unexpected changes in inflation than are the prices of shorter-term bonds.

Residential real estate provides a bright spot in an otherwise somewhat gloomy record. Of the investments studied, it alone served as a hedge against both expected and unexpected inflation. To some extent the reason is that the Consumer Price Index includes the cost of such real estate, but there is undoubtedly more to it.

The record of common stocks is depressing, to say the least. They did not serve as hedges against either expected or unexpected inflation during this period. Quite the contrary—stock returns tended to be lower, the greater the rate of expected or unexpected inflation.

Rudimentary notions of market efficiency suggest that all assets should be priced to take expected inflation into account. The fact that stocks tended to do worse when inflation was expected to be large is thus puzzling. The fact that they did worse when inflation was greater than expected is perhaps less surprising. It could reflect the impact of larger effective corporate tax rates in periods of high inflation, the costs of accommodating to rapid inflation, and so on. While the results in Table 10-4 might simply be due to the chance arrival of news about inflation concurrent with news about the *real* aspects of the economy, they do call into question the assertion that common stocks are hedges against inflation. However, they do not imply that stocks cannot provide returns greater than inflation. There is every reason to expect stocks to provide positive *real* returns. But they may provide greater *real* returns in periods of low inflation than in periods of high inflation.

Inflation Hedging and Expected Return

The traditional capital-asset pricing model deals with nominal returns. If the rate of inflation is reasonably predictable, this causes no problem, for inflation will add little to the uncertainty concerning the return of any asset. But if there is considerable uncertainty about the rate of inflation, the situation is different. The real return of a default-free investment such as a U.S. Treasury bill will not be certain; the risk associated with the real return of the market portfolio may differ considerably from the risk associated with its nominal return; and the beta of a security relative to the market portfolio may change when both returns are expressed in real terms instead of nominal terms.

If investors think in terms of real returns, the relationship between risk and return may look like that shown in Figure 10-6. The shaded area in Figure 10-6(a) indicates the available risk-return combinations in terms of *real* returns (note that there is no riskless alternative). Point M represents the market portfolio, which is assumed to be an efficient investment. The situation is thus formally equivalent to the "zero-beta" model discussed in Chapter 8. As Figure 10-6(a) shows, securities will be priced as if it were possible to borrow or lend without limit at a riskless rate of Z^r.

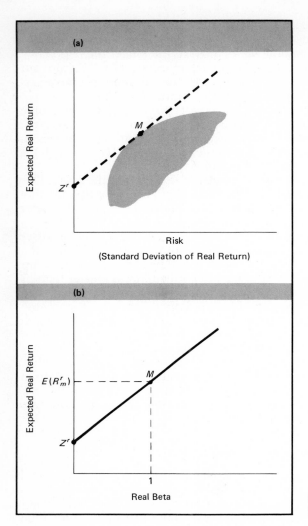

FIGURE 10-6 A Capital Asset Pricing Model in Real Terms

Thus all securities and portfolios will plot along a straight line such as that shown in Figure 10-6(b), relating expected real return to "real beta." The equation of this "real" security market line is:

$$E(R_i^r) = Z^r + \beta_i^r[E(R_m^r) - Z^r] \tag{10-5}$$

where:

$E(R_i^r)$ = the expected real return on security i

$E(R_m^r)$ = the expected real return on the market portfolio

Z^r = the expected real return of a security or portfolio with a zero real beta

β_i^r = security i's real beta [= cov (R_i^r, R_m^r)/var (R_m^r)]

Equation (10-5) provides a succinct statement of the effect of uncertain inflation on security expected returns. But what does it imply about the relationship among expected nominal returns, traditional beta values and sensitivities of nominal returns to inflation? As shown in Appendix 10A, in such a world, securities will also plot on a *security market plane* with these three attributes on the axes. The equation of such a plane is:

$$E(R_i) = Z_1 + Z_2\beta_i - Z_3 h_1^u \qquad (10\text{-}6)$$

where:

$E(R_i)$ = the expected nominal return on security i

Z_1 = the expected nominal return on a security or portfolio with both β_i and h_i^u equal to zero

β_i = security i's (traditional) beta value
$[= \text{cov }(R_i, R_m)/\text{var }(R_m)]$

h_i^u = security i's sensitivity to unexpected changes in inflation
$[= \text{cov }(R_i, c)/\text{var }(c)]$

Z_2 = a positive constant
Z_3 = a positive constant

As the third term indicates:

In a world of uncertain inflation: securities will be priced to give lower expected returns, other things equal, the greater their ability to hedge against unexpected changes in inflation.

The value of Z_3 indicates the reduction in expected return per unit increase in inflation sensitivity. Not surprisingly, the greater the uncertainty about inflation, the greater will be the magnitude of this trade-off. However, since uncertainty concerning the market portfolio's return is typically much greater than that concerning inflation, the effect of differences in β_i on $E(R_i)$—indicated by the magnitude of Z_2—will generally be considerably greater.

Stocks of firms with large net monetary debtor positions should be better hedges against unexpected inflation than those of firms with large net monetary creditor positions. However, differences in inflation sensitivities among stocks may be relatively small (and difficult to predict in advance). If so, the inclusion of inflation sensitivity in a security market plane or hyperplane may add only slightly to the explanation of differences in expected returns under normal circumstances. But when uncertainty about inflation is considerable, differences in hedging abilities—especially among different classes of assets—are likely to be accompanied by substantial differences in expected returns.

As is typical in an efficient market, bad news tends to accompany good news. For example, the good news might be that real estate is a good hedge against inflation and the bad news that its expected return is less than that of assets that entail similar risk in other regards but are poorer hedges against inflation.

INDEXATION

In a world of uncertain inflation, even default-free bonds are subject to *purchasing power risk*. Contractual interest rates can cover expected inflation, but the actual real return from any investment with payments fixed in nominal terms will depend on the actual amount of inflation. As long as the two may differ, real return will be uncertain.

While one can invest in some consumption goods directly (by storing canned goods in the basement) or indirectly (via commodity futures contracts), for other goods and services such alternatives are either costly or unavailable. For example: barber's services cannot be stored and there is no organized futures market.

If a specified price index can adequately measure purchasing power, there is no reason why a contract cannot be written with specified *real* but not nominal payments. Thus if the index stands at P_0 in year 0, and will be $\tilde{P}_1$ in year 1, $\tilde{P}_2$ in year 2, and so on, a borrower might promise to pay $\$10\tilde{P}_1$ in year 1, $\$10\tilde{P}_2$ in year 2, . . . , and $\$100\tilde{P}_{10}$ in year 10, in return for a loan of $100P_0$ dollars in year zero. To convert these amounts to constant real dollars, we simply divide each value by the price level:

Year	Amount	Price Level	Amount in Constant Dollars
0	$-100P_0$	P_0	-100
1	$10\tilde{P}_1$	$\tilde{P}_1$	10
2	$10\tilde{P}_2$	$\tilde{P}_2$	10
.			
.			
.			
10	$100\tilde{P}_{10}$	$\tilde{P}_{10}$	100

The real value of each payment will be the amount shown in the final column, no matter what happens to prices (e.g., no matter what the actual values of $\tilde{P}_1$, $\tilde{P}_2$, and so on may be). Moreover, the real rate of interest on the loan is certain as long as there is no risk of default. The loan is completely *indexed*; that is, all amounts are tied to a stated price index on a one-for-one basis.

In some countries a great many contracts are tied to standard price indices (two notable cases are Israel and Brazil). Government bonds, returns on savings accounts, wage contracts, pension plans, insurance contracts—all can be indexed and have been at various times and places. In the United States, social security payments are indexed, as are the wages and pension plans of many employees. Some of these are fully indexed: for example, the payment is increased by 10% when the price index increases by 10%. Others incorporate only partial indexation: for example, the payment might be increased by 7% when the price index increases by 10%.

The key advantage of indexation is its role in reducing or eliminating purchasing power risk. Typically, higher expected inflation is accompanied by increased uncertainty about the actual rate of inflation. Thus pressures for indexation increase when countries move into periods of seemingly unchecked inflation. If an index of general enough relevance can be computed, indexed contracts should dominate nonindexed contracts. When uncertainty about inflation is substantial, one would thus expect indexation to become widespread. However, government action is usually required to enable truly effective indexation, especially on debt instruments. Laws regulating interest rates preclude completely indexed debt, since they usually limit the nominal rate of interest, not the real rate. This leads to predictable inefficiencies when expected inflation increases: the effective limit placed on the expected real rate of interest falls, requiring rationing of the types of credit subject to such limits. A notable example occurred in the 1970s in the United States, as limits placed on interest rates paid by Savings and Loan Companies, coupled with increased inflationary expectations (and thus higher unregulated interest rates), caused a substantial diminution in funds flowing to such companies and a corresponding reduction in the money made available by them for home mortgages.

EFFECT OF UNCERTAIN INFLATION ON DEBT MATURITY

Since inflation is generally harder to predict, the longer the period over which the prediction is made, uncertainty about inflation often leads to a reduction in the length of time over which nonindexed agreements are made. Thus the average maturity of debt issued in periods of great inflationary uncertainty is usually less than in more stable times. In some cases this can be mitigated by creative financing. Key examples are "floating rate" loans, mortgages, and bonds, which provide medium- to long-term debt at short-term rates. Interest payments are allowed to vary, with each one determined by adding a fixed differential (e.g., 1%) to a specified base, such as the "prime rate" or the yield on a 90-day U.S. Treasury bill in the prior period. If short-term interest rates anticipate inflation reasonably well, such a security is at least a partial substitute for a fully indexed bond.

Inflation, if allowed to run rampant, with great uncertainty about the actual level, can threaten the entire structure of a monetary economy, and with it the whole financial sector. On the other hand, it can be controlled within limits, and financial instruments can be designed to avoid some of its serious side-effects.

Problems

1. An investor is considering purchase of a stock with risk characteristics that make an expected real rate of return of 5% appropriate. He expects the rate of inflation to continue at about 7% per year, believes that the stock will pay no dividends during the coming year, and thinks that it will sell for approximately $40 at the end of the year. How much should he be willing to pay for the stock if he intends to hold it for one year?

2. Why are the effects on borrowers and lenders likely to be different when actual inflation deviates from expected inflation?

3. Why might inflation (without indexation) lead to a shift of real wealth from the private to the public sector?

4. In 1980 a U.S. Government bond due in 1985 sold at a price that made its yield-to-maturity equal 8.5%. Does this imply that in 1980 investors were predicting that inflation over the next few years would average 8.5% per year, more, or less? Why?

5. If net monetary debtors gain when inflation exceeds expectations, why doesn't everyone become a net monetary debtor?

6. Will someone who finances a home with a conventional fixed-rate mortgage gain if inflation is less than expected? What about someone who finances with a floating (variable)-rate mortgage?

7. If the expected return on common stocks is 12% when no inflation is expected, and the figures in Table 10-4 represent sensitivities to changes in inflation in the future, what would be the expected return on stocks if inflation were expected to run at a rate of 10%? Is this consistent with market efficiency?

8. Commodity futures allow one to purchase a good such as wheat several months in advance of delivery. The values of contracts of this sort tend to rise with increases in the general level of prices. Given this, why doesn't everyone invest in commodity futures instead of common stocks, since stock prices have tended to fall with increases in the general level of prices? Should the average investor hold commodity futures, common stocks, or both?

9. Assume that the consensus expectation is that inflation over the coming year will run at a rate of 10% but you are convinced that it will be 8%. Assuming that the figures in Table 10-4 represent likely sensitivities to changes in inflation, what investments would be particularly attractive to you?

10. An investor has estimated that the current relationship among expected returns, beta values, and inflation sensitivities is:

$$E(R_i) = 6.0 + 4.0\beta_i - .2h_i^u$$

Stock A has a beta of 1.0 and provides no hedge against inflation ($h_i^u = 0$). What should its expected return be? Stock B has a beta of 1.1; how sensitive to inflation would its return have to be to make its appropriate expected return equal to that of stock A?

APPENDIX 10-A

Expected Returns, Beta Values, and Inflation Hedging

In a world of uncertain inflation where investors are concerned with real returns, security prices could adjust until all securities and portfolios plotted on the "real security market line" given in formula (10-5). To see how this relates to more traditional concepts, we make use of the approximation for converting nominal returns to real returns:

$$R_i^r \approx R_i - c \qquad \text{(10A-1)}$$

$$R_m^r \approx R_m - c \qquad \text{(10A-2)}$$

where:

R_i = the nominal return on security i
R_i^r = the real return on security i
c = the rate of inflation
R_m = the nominal return on the market portfolio
R_m^r = the real return on the market portfolio

We also use the following relationships (which come from the definition and construction of covariances and variances):

$$\text{cov}\,[(a - b), (c - d)] = \text{cov}\,(a, c) - \text{cov}\,(a, d)$$
$$- \text{cov}\,(b, c) + \text{cov}\,(b, d) \qquad \text{(10A-3)}$$
$$\text{var}\,(a - b) = \text{var}\,(a) - 2\,\text{cov}\,(a, b) + \text{var}\,(b) \quad \text{(10A-4)}$$

From (10A-1) and (10A-2):

$$E(R_i^r) = E(R_i) - E(c)$$

$$E(R_m^r) = E(R_m) - E(c)$$

Substituting in (10-5):

$$E(R_i) - E(c) = Z^r + \beta_i^r[E(R_m) - E(c) - Z^r] \qquad \text{(10A-5)}$$

By definition:

$$\beta_i^r = \frac{\text{cov}\,(R_i^r, R_m^r)}{\text{var}\,(R_m^r)}$$

Using (10A-1) and (10A-2), we can write this as:

$$\beta_i^r = \frac{\text{cov}\,[(R_i - c),\,(R_m - c)]}{\text{var}\,(R_m^r)}$$

which can be converted, using (10A-3) and (10A-4), to:

$$\beta_i^r = \frac{\text{cov}\,(R_i,\,R_m)}{\text{var}\,(R_m^r)} - \frac{\text{cov}\,(R_i,\,c)}{\text{var}\,(R_m^r)} - \frac{\text{cov}\,(R_m,\,c)}{\text{var}\,(R_m^r)} + \frac{\text{var}\,(c)}{\text{var}\,(R_m^r)}$$

or:

$$\beta_i^r = \frac{\text{cov}\,(R_i,\,R_m)}{\text{var}\,(R_m)} \cdot \frac{\text{var}\,(R_m)}{\text{var}\,(R_m^r)}$$

$$- \frac{\text{cov}\,(R_i,\,c)}{\text{var}\,(c)} \cdot \frac{\text{var}\,(c)}{\text{var}\,(R_m^r)}$$

$$+ \frac{\text{var}\,(c) - \text{cov}\,(R_m,\,c)}{\text{var}\,(R_m^r)}$$

Substituting the definitions of β_i and h_i^u:

$$\beta_i^r = \beta_i \frac{\text{var}\,(R_m)}{\text{var}\,(R_m^r)} - h_i^u \frac{\text{var}\,(c)}{\text{var}\,(R_m^r)}$$

$$+ \frac{\text{var}\,(c) - \text{cov}\,(R_m,\,c)}{\text{var}\,(R_m^r)}$$

Substituting in (10A-5) and simplifying:

$$E(R_i) = \left\{ E(c) + Z^r \right.$$

$$+ \left[E(R_m) - E(c) - Z^r \right] \left[\frac{\text{var}\,(c) - \text{cov}\,(R_m,\,c)}{\text{var}\,(R_m^r)} \right] \Bigg\}$$

$$+ \left\{ [E(R_m)] - E(c) - Z^r] \left[\frac{\text{var}\,(R_m)}{\text{var}\,(R_m^r)} \right] \right\} \beta_i$$

$$- \left\{ [E(R_m)] - E(c) - Z^r] \left[\frac{\text{var}\,(c)}{\text{var}\,(R_m^r)} \right] \right\} h_i^u$$

Or, using the notation in (10-6):

$$E(R_i) = Z_i + Z_2 \beta_i - Z_3 h_i^u$$

Note that:

$$\frac{Z_2}{Z_3} = \frac{\text{var}\,(R_m)}{\text{var}\,(c)}$$

and, since the variance of R_m is large (e.g., $400 = 20^2$) relative to that of c (e.g., $16 = 4^2$), Z_2 [the effect of β_i on $E(R_i)$] is likely to be considerably greater than Z_3 [the effect of h_i^u on $E(R_i)$].

Note also that if var $(c) = 0$, the formula simplifies to the zero-beta version of the traditional capital-asset pricing model.

Fixed-Income
Securities

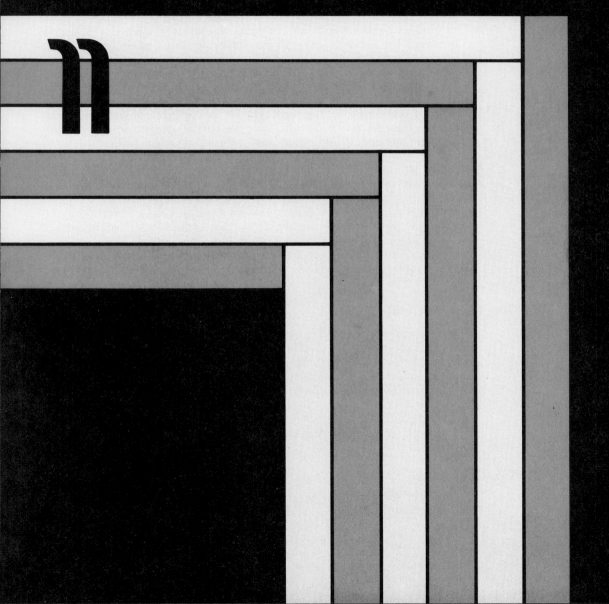

INTRODUCTION

This chapter begins the analysis of particular kinds of securities. The goal is to survey the major types, with emphasis on those currently popular in the United States. Such a survey cannot be exhaustive. A security is, after all, a representation of rights to future prospects. The prospects of organizations differ, and with them the prospects represented by their securities. A firm may divide up its prospects among two or more groups of people by issuing more than one type of security. An organization may even be created solely to acquire some securities and issue others, thus rearranging prospects into related but different packages. The number of securities that can be created is thus great indeed. Which ones will be created? The answer depends on tastes, relevant risks, and government policies (among other things). Mere classification is difficult, enumeration of every possibility virtually out of the question.

Fortunately, many seemingly novel securities can be analyzed relatively easily by analogy. For example, a "convertible" bond can be viewed as a package combining a regular bond and a "call option" and analyzed accordingly (this is done in Chapter 16). Armed with the major concepts, one can analyze both familiar and exotic securities.

FIXED-INCOME SECURITIES

The term commonly used to cover the types of securities discussed in this chapter is a bit misleading. They have in common stated amounts to be paid and times of payment. Many have specified termination dates. However, all the terms are *promised*, not necessarily *realized*, or even *expected* (in the formal sense in which each possible outcome is weighted by its probability of occurrence). In many cases there is at least some risk that a promised payment will not be made in full and on time. In such instances the income is not fixed, only its upper limit.

SAVINGS DEPOSITS

Perhaps the most familiar type of fixed-income investment is the personal savings account at a bank, savings and loan company, or credit union.

Such an account provides substantial or complete safety of principal, low probability of failure to receive interest, substantial liquidity, and (inevitably) relatively low return.

Virtually all savings accounts in the United States are insured by some agency of the federal government, and virtually all are highly regulated. Government regulation generally leads to a host of special procedures and the appearance of nonprice competition where effective price competition is constrained, and this area is no exception. Moreover, financial regulation frequently leads to situations in which certain types of investment are at least temporarily inferior to others, penalizing investors who remain unaware of such situations or are unable to take advantage of them.

Commercial Banks

Almost everyone maintains a checking account in a commercial bank. Formally, these are termed *demand deposits*, since the depositor can remove his or her money on demand. Such an account has two quite different aspects. The bookkeeping required to support check-writing, deposits, and so on is costly; other things equal, the customer would bear this cost. On the other hand, the balance in such an account is available to support interest-earning loans made by the bank; other things equal, the customer would be paid something for making funds available for this purpose. But other things are not equal. In the United States, federal and state regulations sometimes preclude the payment of interest on demand deposits. This causes a few problems when interest rates are low and the bookkeeping costs for a typical account exceed the appropriate interest payment on the balance—the bank simply charges the difference. But when interest rates are high, banks begin to compete by offering "free" checking accounts, extra services (e.g., "free" safe-deposit boxes), and the like. Most checking accounts have a hidden interest payment, and a little comparison shopping can often reveal a way to earn a substantial return in reduced service charges and/or increased service by maintaining a modest minimum balance.

To earn interest explicitly at most commercial banks one must make a *savings or time deposit* (so termed because the bank may make the depositor wait a specified amount of time before the funds may be withdrawn).

The simplest type is a standard *savings account*. Although a written request for a withdrawal may be required up to 30 days in advance, in practice requests for withdrawals are almost always honored on demand. The rate of interest paid on such accounts is well publicized and changes relatively infrequently. Almost any amount may be invested in a savings account. No security is issued; instead, the current balance plus interest earned is posted to the bank's records and (if desired) to the depositor's "passbook."

Some banks offer an *automatic transfer service*, which results in an automatic transfer of funds from a customer's savings account to his or her checking account whenever the latter reaches a zero balance. There is usually a fee for each transfer.

Better yet is the *negotiable order of withdrawal* (NOW) account, which pays interest and on which checks may be written. In 1980 only banks and savings and loan associations in the New England states and New York State were allowed to offer such accounts. In the future, expansion to other states is planned under the Depositary Institutions Deregulation and Monetary Control Act of 1980, which provides for a phased removal of many of the restrictions on such institutions. Credit unions can offer services similar to NOW accounts, via *share draft accounts*, and certain investment companies called *money market funds* (described in Chapter 18) provide at least limited check-writing services.

The standard ("passbook") savings account is only one of many types of time deposits. A *single-maturity deposit* may be withdrawn at a stated maturity date (e.g., one year after the initial deposit). A *multiple-maturity deposit* may be withdrawn at a stated date or left for one or more periods of equal length (thus a 90-day multiple-maturity deposit can be withdrawn three, six, nine, . . . months after the deposit). In practice, both single- and multiple-maturity deposits can usually be withdrawn at any time, but at the cost of recomputing the interest earned, using a lower rate, and deducting the difference plus an additional penalty from the account balance.

Some types of time deposits may be made in almost any amount, while others may be made only in units of, say, $10,000 each. The latter may be represented by *certificates of deposit*, which clearly qualify to be called securities. Large-denomination certificates of deposit may be *negotiable*—i.e., the original depositor may sell the certificate to someone else before maturity. In most cases the certificate is equivalent to a transferable discount bond, since all interest is paid, along with the principal, at maturity.

Table 11-1 shows the maximum interest rates allowed in 1980 on traditional time and savings deposits for banks that are members of the Federal Reserve System and for nonmember banks insured by the Federal Deposit Insurance Corporation. These limits, established by the Board of Governors of the Federal Reserve System under "Regulation Q," are intended to guarantee the soundness of such deposits, ration credit, and reduce competition among various types of financial institutions. Not surprisingly, rates on large amounts (in 1980, accounts with over $100,000) are not controlled, so banks may compete with unregulated borrowers who operate at this level. The situation is different for smaller amounts. Since many alternative outlets are also regulated, it is less difficult to hold rates below free-market levels (although this inevitably leads to a difference between the amount of credit demanded and the amount supplied, and hence to nonprice rationing). Of course, not all investors are oblivious to such phenomena, and an adequate number of entrepreneurs stand ready to exploit opportunities created by regulation of this sort. When interest rates climb well above the maximum amounts allowed, funds tend to flow from banks to money market funds, which borrow from investors in small amounts and then loan the money to banks in large amounts, bringing to the small investor the advantages intended by the regulators for only the large investor.

TABLE 11-1 Maximum Interest Rates Payable on Fixed Ceiling Time and Savings Deposits at Commercial Banks in 1980

Type of Deposit	Interest Rate (%)
Savings deposits	5.25
Negotiable order of withdrawal accounts	5.00
Time deposits:	
30 to 89 days	5.25
90 days to 1 year	5.75
1 to $2\frac{1}{2}$ years	6.00
$2\frac{1}{2}$ to 4 years	6.50
4 to 6 years	7.25
6 to 8 years	7.50
8 years or more	7.75
issued to governmental units (all maturities)	8.00
individual retirement accounts (3 years or more)	8.00

Source: *Federal Reserve Bulletin*, April 1980

Maximum interest rates established by regulation are usually treated as simple interest rates. Thus it is possible for a borrower to offer "5% interest, compounded daily" and still stay within the legal limit of 5%. When unregulated interest rates exceed the legal maximums, this kind of calculation becomes widespread.

Most bank accounts in the United States are insured by the *Federal Deposit Insurance Corporation*, a government agency that guarantees the payment of principal on any account up to a stated limit ($40,000 in 1979) if the bank is closed and liquidated. The FDIC, created in 1933, levies insurance premiums on its member banks and is authorized to borrow funds from the U.S. Treasury, if needed, although it has never done so. By opening certain kinds of multiple accounts, each with less than the limit, an investor can usually insure a considerable amount.

Savings and Loan Companies and Mutual Savings Banks

Savings and loan companies and mutual savings banks accept relatively short-term deposits, then use the money to make relatively long-term loans, primarily for home mortgages. All mutual savings banks, and many savings and loan companies, are nominally owned by their members, while other savings and loan companies (like commercial banks) are owned by stockholders who may or may not deposit funds or obtain loans there.

Savings and loan companies and mutual savings banks pay "dividends" instead of "interest." The distinction is more semantic than real, however. The Internal Revenue Service treats such payments as interest for tax purposes.

TABLE 11-2 Maximum Interest Rates Payable in 1980 on Fixed-Ceiling Accounts by Savings and Loan Associations and Mutual Savings Banks

Type of Account	Interest Rate (%)
Savings deposits	5.50
Negotiable order of withdrawal accounts	5.00
Time deposits:	
1 to $2\frac{1}{2}$ years	6.50
$2\frac{1}{2}$ to 4 years	6.75
4 to 6 years	7.50
6 to 8 years	7.75
8 years or more	8.00
issued to governmental units (all maturities)	8.00
individual retirement accounts (3 years or more)	8.00

Source: *Federal Reserve Bulletin*, April 1980

In the United States most accounts in savings companies are insured by a government agency—either the Federal Deposit Insurance Corporation or the Federal Savings and Loan Insurance Corporation. The principal of each account is insured up to the limit used for bank accounts (e.g., $40,000 in 1980), but here, too, judicious use of multiple accounts makes it possible to insure even more.

The terms offered by institutions of this type are also regulated and are generally slightly more favorable than those allowed commercial banks.

Table 11-2 shows the maximum rates payable on fixed-ceiling accounts in such institutions in 1980. As with banks, no limits are placed on large accounts (those over $100,000 in 1980).

Credit Unions

A credit union accepts deposits from employees of an organization and then loans these funds to other (or the same) employees of the organization. Typically, loans are relatively small and for relatively short terms (e.g., to finance the purchase of an automobile). Excess funds are invested in highly liquid short-term assets.

Each credit union is owned by its members, who elect a board of directors. Deposits are generally similar to passbook accounts in a bank or savings and loan company and also earn "dividends" instead of interest.

Deposits in all federally chartered credit unions are insured by the National Credit Union Administration, a U.S. government agency that serves the same function as the Federal Deposit Insurance Corporation and the Federal Savings and Loan Insurance Corporation. The insurance coverage provided by all these agencies is identical in both amount and provisions.

Other Types of Personal Savings Accounts

A number of institutions similar to those described above can be found. For example, there are companies chartered to accept deposits and use the proceeds to make consumer loans. In some countries the government post office accepts savings deposits. Certain kinds of life insurance policies include a savings component, since payments often exceed the amount strictly required to cover the insurance involved. The "cash value" of such a policy may be obtained by cancellation; alternatively, some or all of it may be "borrowed" without canceling the policy. The implicit rate of return on the cash value of an insurance policy is typically quite low, reflecting the extremely low risk to the policyholder and the length of the insurance company's commitment.

MONEY MARKET INSTRUMENTS

Certain types of short-term, highly marketable loans play a major role in the investment and borrowing activities of operating corporations and financial intermediaries. Individual investors with substantial funds may invest in such instruments directly, but most do so indirectly, for example, via money market accounts at banks or savings and loans, or money market funds that issue shares in small denominations and invest in money market instruments in large denominations.

Some money market instruments are negotiable and are traded in active secondary markets; others are not. Some may be purchased by anyone with adequate funds, others only by particular types of institutions. Many are sold on a discount basis—e.g., a $100,000 90-day note might be sold for $98,000, the difference representing interest payable at maturity. Interest rates are usually reported on a bank discount basis. Such a note might be described as having a discount of 2% per quarter, or 8% per year. Of course, the true interest rate on the funds involved is higher—in this case, 2,000/98,000 or 2.04% per quarter, equivalent to 8.41% per year with quarterly compounding.

Short-term obligations of the U.S. government and its agencies are also considered money market instruments, but they will be described in the next section.

Bankers' Acceptances

Historically, bankers' acceptances were created to finance goods in transit. In such a transaction the buyer of the goods promises to pay a given sum within a short period of time (e.g., 180 days or less). A bank then "accepts" this promise, obligating itself to pay the amount of the note if requested, and obtaining in return a claim on the goods as security. The note representing the loan becomes a liability of both the bank and the buyer of the goods and is thus subject to very low risk of default.

Recently some bankers' acceptances have been created as a by-product of short-term loans by banks to corporations for working capital, with no underlying goods as security. Others have been used to create dollar exchange for international trade. All represent joint obligations of the original borrower and the accepting bank. An indication of the low risk involved is provided by the promised interest rates on such instruments: they are usually only 1% or 2% higher than those of U.S. Treasury instruments of equal duration (e.g., 9%, compared to 8%).

"Prime" bankers' acceptances have short maturities (90 days or less), are backed by goods, and qualify for acceptance by the Federal Reserve System for loans to member banks.

Negotiable Certificates of Deposit

These are certificates representing time deposits at commercial banks or savings and loan associations. Issued in denominations of $100,000 or more, with a specified maturity, such "CD's" are highly marketable and compare in risk and return with bankers' acceptances. Such certificates are insured, but only for the maximum amount ($40,000 in 1980).

Commercial Paper

This term refers to unsecured short-term promissory notes issued by corporations, finance companies, or banks. Many notes of this type are issued by large firms with open lines of bank credit, making it highly likely that the loan will be paid off when it becomes due. Interest rates reflect this: rates of "prime commercial paper" are normally close to those of CD's and bankers' acceptances.

Commercial paper is usually issued in denominations of $100,000 or more, with maturities of up to 270 days (the maximum allowed by the Securities and Exchange Commission without registration). Such paper is generally not negotiable, but the issuer may be willing to prepay the note (perhaps by issuing another) if necessary.

Federal Funds

Banks that belong to the Federal Reserve System must maintain specified reserves in Federal Reserve Banks. However, no interest is paid on any excess. As a result, much activity is devoted to overnight "loans" from banks with excess reserves to those with deficiencies. The interest rate on such loans is termed the *Federal Funds rate*. While it cannot diverge substantially or for long from rates available to the general public, the fact that it applies to very short-term loans within a limited community leads to a certain amount of seemingly erratic behavior.

Brokers' Call Loans

When an individual buys securities "on margin," he or she borrows money from a broker to finance part of the purchase. The broker, in turn, borrows money from a bank, using the securities as collateral and promising to repay the loan "on call" at any time the bank requests it (although such an occurrence is rare). The rate charged on such loans is about 1% greater than short-term rates on U.S. Treasury bills; the broker adds a small amount to determine the interest charged the customer for the margin loan.

Eurodollars

In the rarefied atmosphere of international finance, large short-term loans or deposits are often made in dollars to or through banks outside the United States. The demand and supply conditions for such loans may differ from those for other U.S. money market instruments, owing to restrictions imposed (or likely to be imposed) by the United States and other governments. However, enough commonality exists to keep interest rates from diverging too much from those available on domestic alternatives.

Analysts refer to transactions of this sort in a number of ways. Popular terms include the "Eurodollar," "Asian Dollar," and "Petrodollar" markets, although none is very well defined.

MONEY MARKET AND VARIABLE CEILING ACCOUNTS

To stem the flow of savings from highly regulated commercial banks and savings and loan associations to less regulated money market funds in periods of high interest rates, regulatory authorities have authorized banks and savings and loan companies to offer *money market* and *variable ceiling accounts*.

The first type of account involves a 26-week time deposit with a minimum amount of $10,000. In 1980 the interest rate offered by a commercial bank on such an account could not exceed the *discount rate* on the six-month Treasury bill issued in the prior week. Note, however, that this made the rate on the account less than the effective rate on a Treasury bill. Thus if a $10,000 bill sold for $9,500, the effective interest rate would be 500/9,500 or 5.263% per six months. However, this would be considered a rate of 500/10,000 or 5.0% per six months stated on a discount basis. An investor who put $10,000 in a commercial bank would thus receive $10,500, giving an effective rate of 5%. Putting it another way, the person investing in a Treasury bill got the same amount of interest ($500) with a smaller investment ($9,500 instead of $10,000).

In 1980 savings and loan associations were allowed to pay .25% more than commercial banks on six-month time deposits if the Treasury bill rate was less than 8.75%; above 9%, the two types of institution were subject to the same maximum rates.[1]

The second type of account involves a variable ceiling account with a maturity of two and one-half years or more. In 1980 no minimum amount

[1] If the rate on bills was between 8.75% and 9.00%, banks had to offer the bill rate, while savings and loan associations could offer 9.00%.

was required and the interest-rate maximum was pegged to the average yield on two and one-half-year U.S. Treasury securities. Commercial banks were required to pay interest rates that were no more than .25% less than Treasury security yields, while savings and loan associations were allowed to pay rates equal to the Treasury security yields. Such accounts were inferior to direct investment in Treasury securities for certain investors but did offer some advantages to others (especially those with small amounts to invest).

U.S. GOVERNMENT SECURITIES

It should come as no surprise that the U.S. government relies heavily on debt financing. Revenues seldom cover expenses, and the difference is financed primarily by issuing debt instruments. Moreover, old debt issues come due and new ones must be sold to obtain needed funds. Some refunding is done in kind, with holders of maturing or other issues exchanging them directly for new issues, and often receiving beneficial treatment for tax purposes for doing so. One way or another, the U.S. Treasury is omnipresent in the capital market.

Some idea of the magnitude and the ownership of this debt can be gained from Table 11-3. The largest holder is the government itself, with the Federal Reserve System not far behind. However, a large amount is held by nongovernment organizations and individuals. These securities are a major factor in the portfolios of commercial banks and other financial institutions. Operating corporations also use them, primarily as outlets for relatively short-term excess working capital. The amount held by individuals is also substantial, with well over half the total invested in Series E and H savings bonds.

Over half the public debt is marketable—i.e., represented by securities that can be sold by the original purchaser. The major nonmarketable issues are held by government agencies, foreign governments, and

TABLE 11-3 Ownership of Outstanding U.S. Public Debt, June 1979

Held By	Amount ($ Billions)	
U.S. government accounts		179.1
Federal Reserve Banks		109.2
Private investors:		
Commercial banks	94.0	
Mutual savings banks	4.7	
Insurance companies	14.4	
Corporations	22.8	
State and local governments	70.5	
Individuals	112.5	
Foreign and international investors	119.5	
Other investors (including savings and loan		
associations, corporate pension funds, etc.)	78.1	
		516.6
		804.9

TABLE 11-4 Interest-Bearing Public Debt, June 1979

CATEGORY	AMOUNT ($ BILLIONS)	
Nonmarketable		
Government account series	166.3	
U.S. Savings Bonds	80.5	
Foreign series	26.8	
Other	26.9	
		300.5
Marketable		
Bills	159.9	
Notes	272.1	
Bonds	67.4	
		499.3
		799.9

Source: Tables 11-3, 11-4 from *U.S. Treasury Bulletin*, November 1979.

individuals (the latter in the form of U.S. Savings Bonds). Marketable issues include Treasury bills, notes, and bonds. Table 11-4 shows the amounts in each category in 1979.

The maturity structure of the debt is influenced by a number of factors. As time passes, of course, the time to maturity of an outstanding issue will decrease. Moreover, the Treasury has considerable latitude in selecting maturities for new issues and can also engage in refunding operations. From time to time, legislative limits on amounts issued or interest paid on certain types of instruments may force reliance on other types. Debt operations are also employed as a conscious instrument of policy in an attempt to influence the term structure of interest rates.

Table 11-5 shows the maturity structure of marketable, interest-bearing debt in June 1979. The average maturity was $3\frac{1}{2}$ years at the time.

A great many types of debt have been issued by the federal government and by government agencies and organizations sponsored by the federal government. Figure 11-1 shows a typical list of price quotations for such securities. Each type will be discussed in the sections that follow.

TABLE 11-5 Maturity Distribution of Marketable Interest-Bearing U.S. Public Debt Held by Private Investors, June 1979

Maturity	Amount ($ Millions)
Within 1 year	184.1
1–5 years	124.4
5–10 years	33.4
10–20 years	17.3
20 years and over	18.5

Source: *U.S. Treasury Bulletin*, September 1979.

Treasury Issues * *Bonds, Notes & Bills*

Friday, December 21, 1979

Over-the-Counter quotations; sources on request.

Decimals in bid-and-asked and bid changes represent 32nds; 101.1 means 101 1/32. a-Plus 1/64. b-Yield to call date. d-Minus 1/64. n-Treasury notes.

U.S. TREASURY BONDS

Rate	Mat.	Date	Bid	Asked	Bid Chg.	Yld.
7 1/8s,	1979	Dec n	99.26	99.30	+ .1	11.34
7 1/2s,	1979	Dec n	99.26	99.30	+ .1	11.68
7 1/2s,	1980	Jan n	99.14	99.18	....	11.67
4s,	1980	Feb	98.13	98.21	....	13.68
6 1/2s,	1980	Feb n	99.1	99.5	+ .1	12.40
7 5/8s,	1980	Feb n	99	99.4	− .2	12.33
7 1/2s,	1980	Mar n	98.17	98.21	+ .1	12.57
7 3/4s,	1980	Apr n	98.4	98.8	− .2	12.88
6 7/8s,	1980	May n	97.22	97.26	....	12.70
8s,	1980	May n	97.28	98	− .1	12.85
7 5/8s,	1980	Jun n	97.16	97.24	− .1	12.28
8 1/4s,	1980	Jun n	97.26	97.30	+ .1	12.52
8 1/2s,	1980	Jul n	97.18	97.22	+ .1	12.62
6 3/4s,	1980	Aug n	96.10	96.18	+ .1	12.49
9s,	1980	Aug n	98.9	98.17	....	11.44
8 3/8s,	1980	Aug n	97.9	97.13	+ .2	12.46
6 7/8s,	1980	Sep n	95.27	96.3	+ .1	12.38
8 5/8s,	1980	Sep n	97.6	97.10	....	12.41
8 7/8s,	1980	Oct n	97.7	97.15	− .2	12.10
3 1/2s,	1980	Nov	93.20	93.28	+ .2	10.91
7 1/8s,	1980	Nov n	95.21	95.29	+ .1	12.12
9 1/4s,	1980	Nov n	97.16	97.24	+ .2	11.87
5 7/8s,	1980	Dec n	94.18	94.26	....	11.44
9 7/8s,	1980	Dec n	98.2	98.10	....	11.68
9 3/4s,	1981	Jan n	98	98.8	+ .2	11.49
7s,	1981	Feb n	95.3	95.11	+ .1	11.47
7 3/8s,	1981	Feb n	95.16	95.24	....	11.45
9 3/4s,	1981	Feb n	98	98.8	....	11.37
6 7/8s,	1981	Mar n	94.19	94.27	− .1	11.36
9 5/8s,	1981	Mar n	97.26	98.2	....	11.31
9 3/4s,	1981	Apr n	97.28	98.4	....	11.29
7 3/8s,	1981	May n	94.24	95	− .2	11.37
7 1/2s,	1981	May n	94.24	95	− .2	11.49
9 3/4s,	1981	May n	97.28	98.4	....	11.20
6 3/4s,	1981	Jun n	93.19	93.27	− .1	11.29
9 1/8s,	1981	Jun n	96.26	97.2	− .5	11.29
9 3/8s,	1981	Jul n	97.2	97.10	....	11.26
7s,	1981	Aug	93.10	94.10	....	10.88
7 5/8s,	1981	Aug n	94.10	94.18	− .2	11.35
8 3/8s,	1981	Aug n	95.16	95.24	− .2	11.28
9 5/8s,	1981	Aug n	97.8	97.16	− .1	11.30
6 3/4s,	1981	Sep n	92.18	92.26	− .1	11.36
10 1/8s,	1981	Sep n	98	98.8	− .2	11.25
12 5/8s,	1981	Oct n	101.24	101.28	− .3	11.29
7s,	1981	Nov n	92.20	92.28	− .2	11.29
7 3/4s,	1981	Nov n	93.30	94.6	....	11.25
12 1/8s,	1981	Nov n	101.4	101.8	....	11.39
7 1/4s,	1981	Dec n	92.28	93.4	− .1	11.16
11 3/8s,	1981	Dec n	99.30	100	....	11.37
6 1/8s,	1982	Feb n	91	91.8	− .1	10.81
6 3/8s,	1982	Feb	91.4	91.20	− .14	10.86
7 7/8s,	1982	Mar n	93.24	94	− .4	10.94
7s,	1982	May n	91.29	92.5	− .5	10.81
8s,	1982	May n	93.31	94.7	− .5	10.81
9 1/4s,	1982	May n	96.24	97	− .2	10.71
8 1/4s,	1982	Jun n	94.10	94.18	− .1	10.78
8 1/8s,	1982	Aug n	93.30	94.6	− .2	10.71
9s,	1982	Aug n	96	96.8	− .3	10.67
8 3/8s,	1982	Sep n	94.10	94.18	− .2	10.70
7 1/8s,	1982	Nov n	91.6	91.14	− .2	10.61
7 7/8s,	1982	Nov n	92.30	93.6	− .5	10.68
9 3/8s,	1982	Dec n	96.27	97.3	− .3	10.53
8s,	1983	Feb n	92.29	93.5	− .5	10.62
9 1/4s,	1983	Mar n	96.6	96.14	− .4	10.57
7 7/8s,	1983	May n	92.5	92.13	− .7	10.60
11 5/8s,	1983	May n	102.28	103.4	− .8	10.51
3 1/4s,	1978-83	Jun	81.30	82.30	− .4	9.21
8 7/8s,	1983	Jun n	95.5	95.13	− .4	10.47
9 3/4s,	1983	Sep n	97.24	98	− .4	10.41
7s,	1983	Nov n	89.10	89.18	− .4	10.33
7 1/4s,	1984	Feb n	89.22	89.30	− .7	10.30
9 1/4s,	1984	May n	96.5	96.9	− .5	10.32
6 3/8s,	1984	Aug	85.17	86.17	− .2	10.08
7 1/4s,	1984	Aug n	89.6	89.14	− .5	10.16
8s,	1985	Feb n	90.12	90.20	− .4	10.40
3 1/4s,	1985	May	76.20	77.20	− .4	8.51
4 1/4s,	1975-85	May	77.27	78.27	− .3	9.33
10 3/8s,	1985	May n	99.13	99.17	− .10	10.49
8 1/4s,	1985	Aug n	90.26	91.2	− .5	10.38
7 7/8s,	1986	May n	88	88.8	− .7	10.44
8s,	1986	Aug n	88.14	88.22	− .8	10.40
6 1/8s,	1986	Nov	83	84	− .6	9.32
9s,	1987	Feb n	92.24	93	− .11	10.41
7 5/8s,	1987	Nov n	86.6	86.10	− .2	10.19
8 1/4s,	1988	May n	88.4	88.12	− .13	10.36
8 3/4s,	1988	Nov n	90.21	90.29	− .23	10.34
9 1/4s,	1989	May n	93.12	93.20	− .12	10.33
10 3/4s,	1989	Nov n	102.4	102.8	− .4	10.38
3 1/2s,	1990	Feb	76.16	77.16	− .4	6.58
8 1/4s,	1990	May	87.26	88.10	− .4	10.09
4 1/4s,	1987-92	Aug	77.6	78.6	....	6.86
7 1/4s,	1992	Aug	78.27	79.11	− .3	10.14
4s,	1988-93	Feb	76.18	77.18	− .6	6.58
6 3/4s,	1993	Feb	75.15	76.15	+ .1	10.01
7 7/8s,	1993	Feb	82.2	82.18	− .6	10.33
7 1/2s,	1988-93	Aug	78.26	79.26	− .8	10.29
8 5/8s,	1993	Aug	87.5	87.21	− .8	10.33
8 5/8s,	1993	Nov	87.6	87.22	− .8	10.31
9s,	1994	Feb	89.26	90.10	− .6	10.32
4 1/8s,	1989-94	May	76.23	77.23	− .1	6.54
8 3/4s,	1994	Aug	87.23	88.23	− .9	10.25
10 1/8s,	1994	Nov	98.8	98.24	− .10	10.16
3s,	1995	Feb	76.15	77.15	− .4	5.16
7s,	1993-98	May	76.23	77.23	− .3	9.60
3 1/2s,	1998	Nov	76.25	77.25	− .11	5.39
8 1/2s,	1994-99	May	85.22	86.6	− .10	10.14
7 7/8s,	1995-00	Feb	80.4	80.12	− .11	10.19
8 3/8s,	1995-00	Aug	84.6	84.14	− .9	10.20
8s,	1996-01	Aug	81.4	81.20	− .9	10.11
8 1/4s,	2000-05	May	83.3	83.11	− .7	10.08
7 5/8s,	2002-07	Feb	78.2	78.10	− .13	9.95
7 7/8s,	2002-07	Nov	84.10	84.26	− .10	9.43
8 3/8s,	2003-08	Aug	84.6	84.14	− .12	10.04
8 3/4s,	2003-08	Nov	87.21	87.29	− .13	10.04
9 1/8s,	2004-09	May	90.28	91.4	− .12	10.07
10 3/8s,	2004-09	Nov	101.30	102	− .12	10.16

U.S. Treas. Bills

Mat. date	Bid Discount	Asked Discount	Yield
-1979-			
12-27	10.06	9.66	10.10
-1980-			
1- 3	10.45	9.93	10.00
1- 8	10.36	9.90	10.17
1-10	10.36	9.82	10.07
1-17	10.50	10.02	10.22
1-24	10.64	10.16	10.38
1-31	10.86	10.44	10.70
2- 5	11.68	11.38	11.69
2- 7	11.63	11.37	11.69
2-14	11.63	11.35	11.69
2-21	11.45	11.39	11.76
2-28	11.87	11.65	12.06
3- 4	12.00	11.76	12.23
3- 6	12.04	11.86	12.35
3-13	11.99	11.85	12.37
3-20	12.08	12.02	12.58
3-27	12.02	11.86	12.44
4- 1	11.99	11.81	12.40
4- 3	11.98	11.82	12.42

Mat. date	Bid Discount	Asked Discount	Yield
-1980-			
4-10	11.98	11.82	12.45
4-17	12.04	11.88	12.55
4-24	12.12	12.00	12.71
4-29	12.09	11.89	12.61
5- 1	12.05	11.89	12.62
5- 8	12.05	11.89	12.65
5-15	12.06	11.94	12.74
5-22	12.03	11.87	12.69
5-27	12.02	11.82	12.65
5-29	11.99	11.83	12.67
6- 5	11.89	11.79	12.66
6-12	11.82	11.72	12.61
6-19	11.84	11.78	12.71
6-24	11.74	11.58	12.50
7-22	11.63	11.49	12.42
8-19	11.56	11.40	12.36
9-16	11.28	11.12	12.09
10-14	11.16	11.00	12.01
11- 6	11.00	10.84	11.88
12- 4	10.90	10.84	11.96

FIGURE 11-1 Price Quotations for U.S. Treasury Securities

Source: Reprinted with permission of the *Wall Street Journal,* © Dow Jones & Co. (December 24, 1979).

U.S. Treasury Bills

Treasury bills are issued on a discount basis, with maturities of up to one year. Offerings of three-month and six-month bills are usually made every Monday with nine-month and twelve-month bills usually offered at the end of each month. All are sold by auction. Bids may be entered on either a *competitive* or *noncompetitive* basis. For example, a buyer might enter a bid for a stated number of three-month bills at a price of 98.512. If the bid is accepted, he or she will pay $985.12 for each $1,000 of par value—i.e., an investment of $985.12 will generate a receipt of $1,000 if held to maturity three months later.

The Treasury accepts a number of competitive bids at every auction, filling each one in whole or in part at the price entered on the bid. A quantity-weighted average is also computed, and all noncompetitive bids are filled in whole or in part at this price. The yield obtained by the purchaser is, of course, a function of the price paid. Reported yields on Treasury bills are usually stated on a bank discount basis.

Treasury bills are generally issued in denominations of $10,000 or more, although at times denominations as small as $1,000 have been offered. All are in *bearer* form (i.e., the possession of the bill itself constitutes proof of ownership).

Individuals may purchase new issues of Treasury bills directly from one of the Federal Reserve Banks or indirectly via a bank or broker. Government security dealers maintain an active secondary market in bills, and it is a simple matter to buy or sell one prior to maturity. Terms offered by such dealers are reported daily in the financial press, stated on a discount basis. For example, a bill with 120 days left to maturity might be listed as "7.48% bid, 7.19% ask." To determine the relevant prices, one need only "undo" the bank discount computation. For example, the bid discount of 7.48% was obtained by dividing the actual discount by 120/360 (the portion of a 360-day year involved). To find the actual discount, merely multiply:

$$7.48 \times (120/360) = 2.493$$

The dealer is bidding $100 - 2.493 = \$97.507$ per $100 of par value; this is the price he or she will pay to buy such a bill. On the other hand, the dealer is offering to sell such a bill at $97.603 per $100 of par value, as can be seen by repeating the calculation using 7.19%. The difference between the prices—the dealer's spread—is compensation for carrying inventories of bills, taking associated risks, and bearing the clerical and other costs associated with market-making.

Although Treasury bills are sold at discount, their yield is treated as interest for tax purposes.

A special type of Treasury bill is the *tax anticipation bill* ("tab"). These are offered in the usual way but are designed to mature about a week after income taxes must be paid. Moreover, they may be turned in on a tax day to cover taxes due, *at par*. This provides an outlet for corporate funds set aside for payment of federal income taxes. Moreover, the effective yield to an investor planning to use them for this purpose exceeds that obtained by one who waits until the maturity date to obtain cash: each pays the same price and receives the same amount in the end, and thus the same increase in value, but the former does it in one week less time, obtaining a correspondingly greater increase in value per week, and thus a higher yield.

U.S. Treasury Notes

Treasury notes are issued with maturities from one to seven years and generally pay interest semiannually. Some are in *bearer* form, with interest coupons attached; the owner simply submits each coupon on its specified date to receive the interest due. Others are in *registered* form; the current owner is registered with the Treasury, which sends him or her each interest payment when due and the principal value at maturity. When a registered note is sold, the new owner's name and address are substituted for that of the old owner on the Treasury's books.

Treasury notes are issued in denominations of $1,000 or more. A new issue is offered approximately every three months. Coupon rates are set so the notes will initially sell close to par value. In some cases the price may be fixed and resulting orders filled in whole or in part. In other cases an auction may be held, with both competitive and noncompetitive bids. The bids may be submitted in terms of yield-to-maturity; if so, the Treasury fixes the coupon rates after the auction, setting the actual price for each bidder to give the appropriate yield-to-maturity.

Treasury notes are traded in an active secondary market made by dealers in U.S. government securities. For example, as shown in Figure 11-1, the *Wall Street Journal* carried the following quotation in December, 1979:

			Bid	Asked	Bid. Chg.	Yld.
8's	1983	Feb.	92.29	93.5	−.5	10.62

This indicated that a note maturing in February, 1983, could be sold to a dealer for $92\frac{29}{32}$ (i.e., $92.91) per $100 of par value; alternatively, such a note could be purchased from a dealer for $93\frac{5}{32}$ (i.e., $93.16) per $100 of par value. (The custom of expressing the fractional part in term of $\frac{1}{32}$'s has outlived its usefulness but lingers on nonetheless.) On the day in question the bid price was $\frac{5}{32}$ less than it had been in the previous trading day. The note in question entitles its owner to receive $8 per $100 of par value each year, in semiannual payments of $4 each. The effective yield-to-maturity at the time was, of course, greater. Based on the asked price, it came to approximately 10.62% per year.

In practice, the situation is a little more complicated. The buyer is generally expected to pay the seller not only the stated price, but also any *accrued interest*. For example, if four months have elapsed since the last interest payment, an amount equal to four-sixths of the semiannual payment is added to the stated purchase price to determine the total amount required. This procedure is commonly followed with both government and corporate bonds.

U.S. Treasury Bonds

Treasury bonds may be issued with any maturity, but they are generally used for long-term financing (more than five years). Both registered and bearer forms are available, in denominations as small as $500. Some are callable during a specified period (usually five to ten years prior to maturity); during this period the Treasury has the right to force redemption at par value at any scheduled interest payment date. Callable issues are identified by stating the range of years during which the call can be exercised instead of a single maturity date. Thus the $7\frac{1}{2}$'s of 1988–93 mature in 1993 but may be called beginning in 1988.

Dealers' bid and asked quotations for Treasury bonds in the secondary market are stated in the same form used for Treasury notes.

A select group of bonds, initially issued in times of low interest rates, have been designated as acceptable *at par* for payment of federal estate taxes under certain conditions. Since they would otherwise sell at considerable discounts in times of high interest rates, such bonds represent attractive investments for wealthy individuals in danger of an early demise. Known in the trade as *flower bonds*, such issues are priced to reflect their unique advantage, and they constitute a relatively unattractive investment for one who enjoys good health and/or lacks a substantial estate.

U.S. Savings Bonds

These nonmarketable bonds are offered only to individuals and selected organizations. No more than a specified amount (e.g., $15,000) may be purchased by any person in a single year. Two types are available. Series EE bonds are essentially discount bonds; no interest is paid prior to maturity. The time to maturity is changed from time to time; for bonds issued in 1980 it was 11 years. Series HH bonds mature in ten years and pay interest semiannually. Both types are registered. Series EE bonds are available in small denominations (beginning at $50 par value) and may be purchased from commercial banks and many other institutions or obtained via payroll savings plans. Series HH bonds are available in denominations from $500 upward and may be purchased at banks or from the Treasury Department.

If held to maturity, both types yielded approximately 7% per year, compounded semiannually, in 1980. Either may be redeemed prior to maturity at stated prices that produce a lower yield, the earlier the redemption date. Neither is callable.

The terms on which Savings Bonds are offered have been revised from time to time. In some cases improved terms were offered to holders of outstanding bonds. Terms have often been inferior to those available on less well-known and/or less accessible instruments with similar characteristics. At such times the Treasury Department sold Savings Bonds by appealing more to patriotism than to the desire for high return.

Government, Agency and Miscellaneous Securities

Friday, December 21, 1979
Over-the-Counter quotations; sources on request.
Decimals in bid-and-asked and bid changes represent 32nds; 101.1 means 101 1/32. a-Plus 1/64. b-Yield to call date. d-Minus 1/64. n-Treasury notes.

FNMA Issues

Rate	Mat	Bid	Asked	Yld
6.88	3-80	98.19	98.23	13.01
7.25	3-80	98.21	98.25	13.06
7.38	4-80	98.7	98.11	13.12
8.55	4-80	98.18	98.22	13.03
6.70	6-80	97.1	97.9	12.98
8.50	6-80	97.31	98.3	12.88
6.88	7-80	96.22	96.30	12.92
7.50	9-80	96.15	96.23	12.46
8.75	9-80	97.8	97.16	12.51
8.70	10-80	96.31	97.7	12.47
6.60	12-80	94.20	95.4	12.15
8.00	12-80	96.9	96.17	11.94
7.05	3-81	94.13	94.29	11.68
7.35	3-81	94.23	95.7	11.69
6.85	4-81	93.25	94.9	11.74
10.00	4-81	98.1	98.13	11.33
7.25	6-81	93.13	94.13	11.53
7.95	6-81	94.25	95.9	11.56
8.85	7-81	96.1	96.13	11.46
7.25	9-81	92.23	93.23	11.39
9.38	9-81	96.19	96.31	11.36
9.70	9-81	96.25	97.25	11.14
7.88	10-81	93.31	94.15	11.35
6.45	12-81	91.4	91.20	11.34
7.30	12-81	92.8	93.8	11.24
7.15	3-82	91.30	92.14	11.17
8.88	3-82	94.28	95.28	11.02
7.38	4-82	92.6	92.22	11.06
6.65	6-82	90.6	91.6	10.83
7.10	6-82	91.20	92.4	10.83
9.45	7-82	96.28	97.8	10.70
6.80	9-82	89.30	90.30	10.74
8.40	9-82	94	94.16	10.74
8.60	10-82	94.16	95	10.71
9.00	10-82	95.16	95.28	10.69
7.35	12-82	90.22	91.22	10.70
7.75	3-83	91.12	91.28	10.81
9.50	3-83	96	96.16	10.81
9.25	4-83	93.28	94.12	10.82
6.75	6-83	87.14	88.14	10.85
7.30	6-83	89	90	10.85
8.10	6-83	91.24	92.8	10.85
10.85	7-83	99.28	100	10.88
6.75	9-83	87	88	10.75
8.50	9-83	92.16	93	10.83
9.25	10-83	94.20	95.4	10.84
8.00	12-83	90.4	91.4	10.81
8.40	12-83	91.16	92.16	10.68
9.50	3-84	95.16	96	10.70
7.35	4-84	88.8	88.24	10.68
8.20	4-84	90.28	91.16	10.72
6.25	6-84	84.16	85.16	10.39
9.25	6-84	94.20	95.4	10.65
8.20	7-84	90.4	91.4	10.72
9.05	7-84	93.20	94.4	10.72
7.95	9-84	88.26	89.26	10.76
9.75	9-84	96.16	97	10.56
11.70	10-84	103.4	103.12	10.77
6.90	12-84	84.14	85.14	10.77
7.55	12-84	87.12	87.28	10.77
7.65	3-85	86.24	87.24	10.78
8.60	6-85	90.28	91.12	10.73
7.25	7-85	85	85.16	10.79

Federal Land Bank

Rate	Mat	Bid	Asked	Yld
6.70	1-80	99.11	99.15	14.02
7.75	1-80	99.14	99.18	13.65
7.35	4-80	97.31	98.3	13.39
8.60	4-80	98.13	98.17	13.19
7.50	7-80	96.26	97.2	12.99
8.85	7-80	97.19	97.27	12.87
8.70	10-80	96.18	96.30	12.72
7.10	1-81	95	95.16	11.70
6.20	4-81	93.2	93.18	11.60
6.70	4-81	93.21	94.5	11.59
9.10	7-81	95.30	96.30	11.28
7.45	10-81	92.30	93.14	11.54
6.65	1-82	91.4	91.20	11.30
7.80	1-82	93.7	93.23	11.29
6.90	4-82	90.28	91.28	10.96
8.15	4-82	93.19	94.3	11.10
8.70	7-82	94.24	95.8	10.86
7.30	10-82	90.20	91.20	10.82
8.00	10-82	92.30	93.14	10.75
7.20	1-83	90.11	90.27	10.78
8.20	1-83	93	93.16	10.74
8.65	7-83	93.12	93.28	10.76
7.30	10-83	88.10	89.10	10.78
7.35	10-83	89	89.16	10.77
8.10	7-85	88.24	89.8	10.71
7.95	10-85	87.24	88.8	10.71
8.80	10-85	91.16	92	10.67
7.60	4-87	84.4	84.20	10.68
7.25	7-87	82	82.16	10.68
8.20	1-90	84.16	85	10.67
7.95	4-91	82.8	83	10.55
7.95	10-96	80.8	81.8	10.32
7.35	1-97	75.28	76.24	10.24

Fed. Home Loan Bank

Rate	Mat	Bid	Asked	Yld
7.05	2-80	98.25	98.29	13.55
7.75	2-80	98.29	99.1	13.44
8.10	2-80	98.31	99.3	13.39
6.65	5-80	97.7	97.11	13.26
8.40	8-80	97.31	98.3	13.11
7.30	8-80	96.9	96.13	13.09
9.75	8-80	98.1	98.5	12.68
7.80	10-80	96.4	96.12	12.65
6.70	11-80	94.27	95.3	12.53
7.75	11-80	95.28	96.8	12.19
9.30	11-80	97.10	97.18	12.18
7.60	2-81	95.10	95.26	11.52
10.00	2-81	98	98.12	11.50
9.55	5-81	97	97.16	11.50
9.65	5-81	97.4	97.20	11.50
7.05	8-81	92.28	93.12	11.52
12.30	8-81	101.4	101.8	11.44
8.65	11-81	94.30	95.14	11.36
6.60	11-81	91.3	92.3	11.29
7.95	2-82	93.14	93.30	11.17
8.63	2-82	92.4	92.20	11.00
7.46	5-82	92.4	92.20	11.00
9.15	5-82	96	96.16	10.83
11.25	8-82	100.26	101.6	10.71
8.25	11-82	93.16	94	10.69
9.00	2-83	95.8	95.24	10.61
7.30	5-83	89.14	90.14	10.69

7.45	9-85	85.16	86	10.79
7.90	10-85	87.8	87.24	10.79
8.80	10-85	91.8	91.24	10.74
8.20	3-86	88.4	88.20	10.75
9.50	3-86	94	94.16	10.73
9.20	4-86	92.12	92.28	10.78
7.95	7-86	86.16	87	10.77
7.90	9-86	86	86.16	10.77
7.30	12-86	82.28	83.12	10.75
7.75	3-87	84.22	85.6	10.75
7.65	6-87	84.2	84.18	10.71
9.10	7-87	91.16	92	10.67
7.50	10-87	82.24	83.8	10.72
9.55	9-88	87.24	88.8	10.65
8.20	6-89	91.20	92.4	10.64
7.80	10-91	80.8	81.8	10.62
7.00	3-92	75.2	76.2	10.53
7.05	6-92	75.6	76.6	10.52
7.10	12-97	72.16	73.16	10.38

World Bank Bonds

Rate	Mat	Bid	Asked	Yld
8.00	1-80	99.24	100	8.00
7.75	3-80	98.16	99	12.16
8.30	7-80	97	97.16	13.11
8.35	9-80	96.12	96.28	12.99
4.75	11-80	94.8	94.24	11.41
8.35	12-80	96.4	96.20	12.14
9.85	3-81	97.4	97.20	11.97
8.00	7-81	94.4	94.20	11.98
9.40	9-81	95.20	96.4	11.94
3.25	10-81	95	97	5.05
4.50	2-82	88.24	89.24	10.04
7.00	5-82	90.16	91	11.43
7.13	8-82	90	90.16	11.45
8.15	1-85	88.12	89.12	10.96
5.00	2-85	77.24	78.8	10.60
8.60	7-85	89.28	90.12	10.96
8.85	12-85	90.12	90.28	10.97
8.38	7-86	87.20	88.4	10.97
7.80	12-86	84.12	84.28	10.97
7.65	5-87	83.4	83.20	10.95
7.75	8-87	83.12	83.28	10.93
4.50	2-90	63.4	63.20	10.40
5.38	7-91	65.28	66.12	10.47
5.38	4-92	64.24	65.8	10.47
5.88	9-93	66	66.16	10.56
6.50	3-94	69.28	70.12	10.57
6.38	10-94	68	68.16	10.65
8.63	8-95	81.28	82.12	11.01
8.13	8-96	77.24	78.8	11.00
9.35	12-00	86.8	86.12	10.98
8.85	7-01	82.8	82.24	10.95
8.38	12-01	78.8	78.24	10.95
8.25	5-02	77	77.16	10.96
8.35	8-02	77.28	78.12	10.95

Inter-Amer. Devel. Bk.

Rate	Mat	Bid	Asked	Yld
4.25	12-82	84.12	84.28	10.29
4.50	4-84	78.24	79.8	10.68
4.50	11-84	77.4	77.20	10.51
8.25	1-85	89.12	89.28	10.91
8.00	3-85	88.4	88.20	10.93
8.38	2-86	88.4	88.20	10.93
5.20	1-92	65.24	66.24	10.01
6.50	11-92	72	72.16	10.43
6.63	11-93	72	72.16	10.42
8.63	10-95	82	82.16	10.98
9.00	2-01	83.20	84.4	10.94
8.75	7-01	81.16	82	10.94
8.38	6-02	78.8	78.21	10.93
9.63	1-04	88	88.16	10.99

Asian Development Bank

Rate	Mat	Bid	Asked	Yld
8.50	4-80	98.12	98.28	12.15
8.50	1-81	95.16	96	12.66
8.63	8-86	88	88.16	11.12
7.75	4-96	73.28	74.20	11.16

11.60	5-83	101.30	102.6	10.81
9.30	8-83	95.16	96	10.64
9.50	11-83	96.4	96.20	10.57
7.38	11-83	89.10	89.26	10.62
9.05	2-84	94.16	95	10.56
7.75	5-84	90.28	91.12	10.22
8.75	5-84	93.16	94.16	10.33
11.00	5-84	101.16	101.24	10.47
7.85	8-84	90	90.16	10.47
7.38	11-84	87.8	87.24	10.64
7.38	2-85	86.20	87.4	10.68
8.13	5-85	89.12	89.28	10.62
9.35	8-85	95.4	96.4	10.26
8.10	11-85	89	89.16	10.53
9.55	2-86	94.28	95.12	10.58
11.30	11-86	102.16	102.24	10.72
7.65	5-87	84.20	85.4	10.59
7.60	8-87	84.4	84.20	10.57
7.38	11-93	77.2	78.2	10.39
7.88	2-97	80.12	81.12	10.19

Bank for Co-ops

Rate	Mat	Bid	Asked	Yld
6.85	4-81	94.6	94.22	11.46
7.75	1-86	86.12	86.28	10.77

Federal Farm Credit

Rate	Mat	Bid	Asked	Yld
9.60	1-80	99.28	99.31	10.97
10.25	1-80	99.30	100.1	7.79
10.10	2-80	99.19	99.22	12.29
10.30	2-80	99.20	99.23	12.48
10.20	3-80	99.9	99.12	12.90
10.65	3-80	99.13	99.16	12.97
9.60	4-80	98.27	98.30	13.16
10.20	5-80	98.26	98.29	12.96
11.40	4-80	99.14	99.17	12.89
11.40	5-80	100.9	100.12	12.99
10.60	6-80	98.23	98.26	13.06
12.30	6-80	99.21	99.24	12.81
11.30	7-80	99.4	99.7	12.58
13.15	7-80	100.3	100.2	13.02
14.35	8-80	100.20	100.23	12.79
12.80	9-80	99.21	99.24	12.55
9.90	10-80	97.26	98.2	12.42
12.80	10-80	100	100.2	12.71
10.00	7-81	98	98.16	11.06
9.90	1-82	95.10	95.26	11.22
8.45	4-82	94.18	95.2	10.96
9.65	9-82	97	97.16	10.74
7.20	9-82	91.8	91.24	10.82
8.05	3-83	92.4	92.20	10.84
10.90	4-83	100.8	100.16	10.70
9.50	1-84	94.4	94.20	10.66
9.45	1-84	96.8	96.24	10.50
9.70	6-84	96.12	96.28	10.57
10.65	12-84	99.30	100.2	10.63
10.75	10-86	99.28	100.4	10.72
10.60	10-89	99.24	100	10.58
9.10	7-91	89.28	90.12	10.56

FIC Bank Debs.

Rate	Mat	Bid	Asked	Yld
7.40	1-80	99.24	100	7.14
7.30	7-80	96.31	97.11	12.80
7.90	1-81	96.2	96.18	11.55
7.00	4-82	91.12	91.28	11.15
7.95	4-86	87	87.16	10.74
6.95	1-87	81.4	81.20	10.74

GNMA Issues

Rate	Mat	Bid	Asked	Yld
8.00		81.22	82.6	10.72
8.25		83.10	83.26	10.73
8.50		84	84.16	10.86
9.00		85.22	86.6	11.11
9.50		88	88.16	11.25
10.00		90.10	90.26	11.39
11.00		96.2	96.10	11.51

FIGURE 11-2 Price Quotations for U.S. Government, Agency and Miscellaneous Securities

SECURITIES OF U.S. GOVERNMENT AGENCIES
AND GOVERNMENT-SPONSORED INSTITUTIONS

There is nothing simple about the government of the United States. While much of its activity is supported directly, via taxes and debt issued by the Treasury Department, much is financed in other ways. Some government departments issue securities to support their own activities. Others provide explicit or implicit support for the securities of quasi-governmental agencies. Some of these arrangements are so convoluted that cynics suggest that the original legislative intent was to obscure the nature and extent of governmental support. In any event, a wide range of bonds with different degrees of government backing has been created in this manner, many considered second in safety only to the debt obligations of the U.S. government itself.

Table 11-6 lists several major securities of this type and the amounts outstanding in 1979. A typical list of price quotations is shown in Figure 11-2.

Bonds of Government Agencies

Bonds issued by government agencies provide funds for support of housing (either through direct loans or the purchase of existing mortgages),

TABLE 11-6 Interest-Bearing Securities and Participation Certificates Issued by Government Agencies and Government-Sponsored Institutions Outstanding in June 1979

Interest-Bearing Securities of Government Agencies	Amount Outstanding ($ Millions)
Defense Department: Family Housing and Homeowner's Assistance	796
Federal Housing Administration	562
Government National Mortgage Association	3,039
Export-Import Bank of the U.S.	960
Postal Service	250
Tennessee Valley Authority	1,725
Other	2
	7,334
Interest-Bearing Securities of Nongovernment Agencies	
Banks for Cooperatives	785
Federal Home Loan Banks	43,159
Federal Intermediate Credit Banks	5,122
Federal Land Banks	18,389
Federal National Mortgage Association	45,775
Other	20
	113,250
Participation Certificates	
Export-Import Bank	252
Government National Mortgage Association	3,039
	3,291

Source: *U.S. Treasury Bulletin*, September 1979.

export and import activities (via loans, credit guarantees, and insurance), the postal service, and the activities of the Tennessee Valley Authority. Many issues are guaranteed by the full faith and credit of the U.S. government, but some (e.g., those of the Tennessee Valley Authority) are not.

Bonds of Government-Sponsored Agencies

Government-sponsored agencies that issue securities have been established to support the granting of credit to farmers, homeowners, and the like. A common procedure involves the creation of a series of banks to buy securities representing loans of this type from private organizations that grant them in the first instance. Some or all the initial capital for these banks may be provided by the government, but subsequent amounts typically come from bond issues and contributions from those who utilize their services.

While the debts of agencies of this type are usually not guaranteed by the federal government, governmental control is designed to insure that each issue is backed by extremely safe assets (e.g., mortgages insured by another quasi-governmental agency). Moreover, it is generally presumed that governmental assistance of one sort or another would be provided, were there any danger of default on such a bond.

Banks for Cooperatives support loans made to farmers' cooperative associations. *Federal Home Loan Banks* make loans to thrift institutions (primarily savings and loan associations). *Federal Intermediate Credit Banks* support loans made to agricultural credit corporations and similar organizations. *Federal Land Banks* provide funds for first mortgages on rural real estate. The *Federal National Mortgage Association* (known in the trade as "Fannie Mae") purchases and sells real estate mortgages—primarily those insured by the Federal Housing Administration or guaranteed by the Veterans Administration.

Participation Certificates

To support credit for export and import operations and encourage the use of home mortgages, the government has authorized the issuance of *participation certificates*. A group of assets (e.g., mortgages) is placed in a pool, and certificates representing interests in those assets issued to pay for them. The holders of certificates receive the interest and principal payments, minus a small service charge. The most important certificates of this type are those issued by the *Government National Mortgage Association*. Such "Ginnie Mae passthroughs" are guaranteed by the Association and backed by the full faith and credit of the U.S. government. Unlike regular bonds, they are self-extinguishing, like the mortgages they represent. The holder receives monthly payments until maturity, each of which includes interest and a return of principal. A similar instrument, issued in denominations of $100,000 or more, is the "guaranteed mortgage certificate" sold by the *Federal Home Loan Mortgage Corporation*. A number of banks have offered similar pass-through mortgage certificates backed by private insurance companies.

BONDS OF INTERNATIONAL AGENCIES

Certain international organizations also receive support from the U.S. government. The *International Bank for Reconstruction and Development* (the "World Bank") raises funds via the issuance of bonds in various currencies, and it finances development loans in a number of countries. The *Inter-American Development Bank* and Asian Development Bank perform similar functions for the countries of North and South America and Asia.

GOVERNMENT-GUARANTEED BONDS

To encourage urban development, the U.S. merchant marine, and other activities deemed worthy of support, the full faith and credit of the United States has been pledged to guarantee both principal and interest on bonds issued by private organizations. Thus some bonds issued by, e.g., property developers and shipping companies are comparable in risk and return to similar instruments issued by the government itself.

STATE AND MUNICIPAL GOVERNMENT SECURITIES

The 1977 Census of Governments showed that there were 79,912 governmental units in the United States, in addition to the federal government itself:[2]

    50 states
  3,042 counties
18,862 municipalities
16,822 townships and towns
25,962 special districts
15,174 school districts

A great many of these units borrow money and, as discussed in Chapter 9, the interest (but not any capital gain) is exempt from federal income taxes. For this reason, securities of this type are often called *tax-exempts*. More often they are all termed *municipals* ("muni's" for short), with only the securities of the U.S. government referred to as "governments."

Whatever they are called, municipal securities are important. Table 11-7 provides estimates of the amounts of various types of fixed-income securities outstanding at the end of 1978. Representing over $300 billion in value, municipals clearly warrant attention.

Issuing Agencies

Table 11-8 shows the dollar values of municipal bonds issued in 1978 by various issuing agencies.

[2] *Statistical Abstract of the United States*, 1978.

Type of Security	Amount ($ Billions)
Privately held Treasury debt	504.9
Privately held federal agency debt	177.0
Corporate bonds	399.7
State and local securities	301.4

Source: Salomon Brothers, *Prospects for the American Financial Markets in 1979.*

States issue debt to finance capital expenditures (primarily for highways and education); in principle, the revenue generated by the resulting facilities can be used to make the required debt payments. In some cases the link is direct (e.g., tolls may be used to pay for a bridge), in other cases somewhat indirect (e.g., gasoline taxes may be used to pay for highway construction) or very indirect (e.g., state sales or income taxes may be used to pay for the construction of new government buildings). In some cases no capital expenditure is involved (e.g., for the payment of a veterans' bonus).

States may not be sued without their consent. Thus the bondholder may have no legal recourse in the event of default. However, bonds backed by the full faith and credit of a state government are considered quite safe. In this century only one state has defaulted (Arkansas in 1932), and the bonds in question were subsequently paid off after some adjustments. Bonds issued by states but dependent on particular revenues may, of course, involve considerable risk.

Local governments may be sued against their will, making it possible for bondholders to force officials to collect whatever revenues may be available to meet required debt payments. In many cases only revenues from specific projects may be used (e.g., the tolls collected on a particular throughway). In other cases collections from a particular tax may be used, although possibly only up to some statutory limit.

Some local governments have defaulted on their debts. In the 1930s

TABLE 11-8 Municipal Bonds Issued, 1978, Classified by Issuer

Issuer	Amount ($ Billions)
States	6.6
Counties, municipalities, townships, and school districts	17.7
Special districts and statutory authorities	24.2
	48.6

Source: *Federal Reserve Bulletin*, October 1979.

many did (although most of the debts were eventually paid, at least in part). Since World War II defaults have been rare, although some have occurred, as the holders of bonds issued by Benavides, Texas (population approximately 2,000) and Medly, Florida (population about 350) know. In 1975 New York City "restructured" its debt, giving holders new certificates offering lower or deferred interest and longer maturities in exchange for old holdings. Lawyers and semanticists may understand why this was not termed a default, but investors may be forgiven for failing to make the distinction. In 1978 and 1979 the city of Cleveland, Ohio, defaulted on some of its debt held by large banks.

Counties and municipalities are familiar to most people, but other local governments exist, most notably school and other districts and authorities created by statute to finance and operate ports, airports, and the like. All are created by state charter and may be granted monopoly powers as well as rights to collect certain types of taxes. Often limits are placed on the amount of taxes collected, the tax rate charged, and the amount or type of debt issued. The primary source of tax revenue for such agencies is the property tax. Since a given property may be liable to taxes levied by several agencies (e.g., a city, a county, a school district, a port authority, a sewer district), the risk of the bonds of an issuer may depend on both the value of property subject to its taxes and the amount of other debt dependent on the same property.

Purposes for Which Debt Is Issued

Much of the debt issued each year by state and local governments is short-term, designed to cover outlays prior to the receipt of taxes. Such obligations are often called *tax-anticipation notes* or (misleadingly) *warrants:* the taxes due but not yet paid serve as security.

Table 11-9 shows the purposes for which municipal bonds were issued in 1978.

TABLE 11-9 Municipal Bonds Issued, 1978, Classified by Purpose

Purpose of Bonds	Amount ($ Billions)
Education	5.0
Transportation	3.5
Utilities and conservation	9.0
Social welfare	10.5
Industrial aid	3.5
Refunding previous issues	11.0
Other purposes	6.1
	48.6

Source: *Federal Reserve Bulletin,* October 1978.

Types of Municipal Bonds

In 1978 new municipal bonds with a par value of $48.6 billion were issued: $17.9 billion of *general obligation bonds* ("G.O.'s") and $30.7 billion of *revenue bonds*.

General obligation bonds ("G.O.'s") are backed by the full faith and credit (and thus the taxing power) of the issuing agency. Most are issued by agencies with unlimited taxing power, although in a minority of cases the issuer is subject to limits on the amount of taxes and/or the tax rate.

Revenue bonds are backed by revenues from a designated project, authority, or agency, or by the proceeds from a specific tax. In many cases such bonds are issued by agencies that hope to sell their services, pay the required expenses, and have enough left over to at least meet required payments on outstanding debt. Except for the possible grant of monopoly powers, the authorizing state or local government may provide no further assistance. In such a case the bonds are as good as the enterprise in question, but no better. Issuers of revenue bonds of this type can default, as the holders of bonds issued by the Calumet Skyway (Chicago), the Bellevue Bridge (Nebraska), and the West Virginia Turnpike, among others, discovered.

Many revenue bonds are issued to finance capital expenditures for publicly owned utilities (e.g., water, sewer, electricity, and/or gas). Others are issued to finance quasi-utility operations (e.g., public transportation). Some are financed by *special assessments* levied on properties benefiting from the original expenditure (e.g., those connected to a new sewer system). *Industrial development bonds* are used to finance the purchase and/or construction of industrial facilities to be rented or leased to firms on a favorable basis. Such bonds in effect provide tax-exempt interest loans to businesses choosing to locate in the area in question.

Other Tax-Exempt Issues

The avoidance of federal income tax on interest earned on a bond makes such a security attractive to wealthy individual investors and corporate investors as well. Accordingly, such issues can be sold to yield a considerably lower rate of interest than that required from taxable securities. This lowers the cost of financing to the issuer and provides a federal subsidy to any agency allowed to issue bonds of this type.

Over the years this subsidy has been used to support activities deemed worthy of encouragement (albeit somewhat hidden encouragement). Private universities may issue tax-exempt bonds to finance certain types of improvements, and private firms may do so to finance certain pollution-reducing activities. Such instruments are generally backed only by the resources of the issuer, with government involvement limited to the granting of favorable tax treatment.

Ownership of State and Local Government Securities

Since interest on municipal securities is exempt from both personal and corporate income taxes, and since the rate on the latter is substantial,

TABLE 11-10 Ownership of State and Local Securities, Year-end 1978

	Amount ($ Billions)	Percent
Mutual savings banks	3.2	1.1
Savings and loan associations	1.2	0.4
Life insurance companies	5.8	1.9
Property liability companies	61.2	10.4
State and local retirement funds	3.5	1.2
Municipal bond funds	16.7	5.5
Security brokers and dealers	0.9	0.3
Commercial Banks	120.6	40.0
Business corporations	3.4	1.1
Individuals and miscellaneous investors	84.9	28.2
	301.4	100.0

Source: Salomon Brothers, *Prospects for the American Financial Markets in 1979.*

such securities are particularly attractive to corporate investors and especially to financial institutions. This is shown in Table 11-10, which provides estimates of the ownership of state and local securities at the end of 1978.

The Market for Municipal Bonds

Municipal bonds are usually issued in *serial* form. One group matures a year after issue, another two years after issue, another three years after, and so on. The overall package is generally offered by the issuer on a competitive basis to various *underwriters*. The winning bidder then *reoffers* the individual bonds, either publicly or via a *private placement*. An offering may include both serial and *term bonds* (i.e., bonds that mature on a given date in the fairly distant future). Some issues consist entirely of term (i.e., normal) bonds.

Municipal bonds may be callable at specified dates and prices. Occasionally the issuing authority is obligated to make designated payments into a *sinking fund*, which is used to buy either its own or similar bonds.

A secondary market in municipal bonds is made by various dealers. However, the relatively small amounts of particular issues and maturities outstanding limit the size of the market. Many individuals who invest in municipals simply buy new issues and hold them to maturity.

Municipal Bond Insurance

An investor concerned about possible default of a municipal bond can purchase an insurance policy to cover losses incurred if interest or principal is not paid in full and on time.

Some issues are insured at the time of offering. Alternatively, an investor can contract with a company to have a specific portfolio insured. Premiums depend on the bonds included and their ratings.

FOREIGN BONDS

A number of foreign governments, agencies, and corporations have issued "dollar bonds": the security is initially sold for dollars, and both principal and interest are paid in dollars. At the end of 1978 about $43 billion of such bonds were held in the United States.[3] Canadian issues led the list, but substantial amounts from European, Latin American, and Asian countries were outstanding as well. The issuers of such bonds can default on required payments, as the holders of bonds of Czarist Russia found out. An assessment of the risk involved requires both economic and political analysis.

EUROBONDS

Owing in part to governmental restrictions on investment in foreign securities, a number of borrowers have found it advantageous to sell securities in other countries. The term *Eurobond* is loosely applied to bonds that are offered outside the country of the borrower and usually outside the country in whose currency the securities are denominated.

Interest rates on Eurobonds move more or less in concert with those on domestic bonds denominated in the same currency. However, since movement of capital between domestic and foreign markets may be difficult or costly for some issuers and/or some purchasers, occasional disparities do arise at times.

CORPORATE BONDS

In some respects corporate bonds are similar to those issued by state and local governments. They promise to make specified payments at specified times, legal remedies being provided in the event of default. Restrictions are often placed on the activities of the issuing corporation to provide additional protection for bondholders. Interest received by the owner of such a bond is not tax-exempt, of course, and typically only the issuing corporation is obligated to make the required payments. A great many variations on the general theme exist, but the essential idea is both simple and familiar.

Debt Versus Equity Financing

From the viewpoint of the issuing corporation, debt differs from equity in two crucial respects. First, principal and interest payments are obligatory. Failure to make any payment in full and on time can expose the firm to expensive, time-consuming, and potentially disruptive legal actions. In return for this drawback, debt financing provides a major tax advantage. Interest payments are considered expenses and hence can be deducted

---

[3] Salomon Brothers, *Prospects for the American Financial Markets in 1979.*

from profit before calculating the corporation's income tax liability. A dollar paid in interest reduces profit before tax by a dollar. As a result, taxes are also reduced (by 46 cents for a firm in the 46% marginal tax bracket), leading to less than a dollar decline in profit after tax (for example, of 54 cents). A dollar paid in dividends reduces profit after tax by a dollar. Other things equal, debt financing is cheaper.

Of course, other things are not equal. In particular, extensive use of debt in a firm's capital structure increases the likelihood of bankruptcy, with its associated costs. Thus, in the United States, the highest leverage (i.e., the ratio of the amount of debt to the total value of the firm) is found in the utility industry, where stability of earnings reduces the dangers associated with substantial interest payments.

The Indenture

An issue of bonds is generally covered by a *trust indenture*, in which the issuing corporation promises a specified *trustee* that it will comply with a number of stated provisions. Chief among these is, of course, the payment of required interest and principal on the issue. But terms are often included to control the sale of pledged property, the issue of other bonds, and the like.

The trustee for a bond issue, usually a bank or trust company, acts for the bondholders either automatically as required by the indenture, voluntarily, or in response to a request from the holders of some specified portion of the issue.

If the corporation defaults on an interest payment, after a relatively short period of grace (e.g., one to six months) the entire principal (par value) typically becomes due and payable—a procedure designed to enhance the holders' status in bankruptcy or related legal proceedings.

Types of Bonds

An exhaustive list of the names used to describe bonds would be intolerably long. Different names are often used for the same type of bond, and occasionally the same name will be used for two quite different bonds. A few major types do predominate, however, with relatively standard nomenclature.

Mortgage Bonds
Bonds of this type represent debt that is secured by the pledge of specific property. In the event of default, the bondholders are entitled to obtain the property in question and sell it to satisfy their claims on the firm. In addition to the property itself, the holders of mortgage bonds have an unsecured claim on the corporation.

Mortgage bondholders are usually protected by a number of terms included in the bond indenture. The corporation may be constrained from pledging property for other bonds (or such bonds, if issued, must be "junior" or "second" mortgages, with a claim on the property only after the first mortgage is satisfied). Certain property acquired after the issue may also be pledged to support the bonds.

Collateral Trust Bonds	These bonds are backed by other securities, usually held by a trustee. A common situation of this sort arises when the securities of a subsidiary firm are pledged as collateral by the parent firm.
Equipment Obligations	Known also as *equipment trust certificates*, these securities are backed by specific pieces of equipment—railroad rolling stock, commercial aircraft, and the like. The equipment is usually readily salable and can be delivered inexpensively to a new owner. The legal arrangements used to facilitate the issuance of such bonds can be very complex. The most popular procedure uses the "Philadelphia Plan," in which a trustee holds the equipment, issues obligations, and leases the equipment to the using corporation. Money received from the corporation is used to make interest and principal payments to the holders of the obligations; if all payments are made on schedule, the corporation takes title to the equipment.
Debenture Bonds	These are general obligations of the issuing corporation and thus represent *unsecured* credit. To protect the holders of such bonds, the indenture will usually limit the issuance of secured debt as well as additional unsecured debt, and possibly other operations of the firm that might be inimical to the welfare of the holders.
Subordinated Debentures	When more than one issue of debentures is outstanding, a hierarchy may be specified. For example, subordinated debentures are junior to unsubordinated) debentures; in the event of insolvency, junior claims are intended to be considered only if senior claims can be fully satisfied.
Other Types of Bonds	*Income bonds* are more like preferred stock (described in a later section) than bonds. Payment of interest in full and on schedule is not absolutely required, and failure to do so need not send the corporation to court. Interest on such bonds may or may not qualify as a deductible expense for corporate income taxes. The type is rarely used, except in reorganizations of insolvent railroads.

Guaranteed bonds are issued by one corporation but backed in some way by another (e.g., a parent firm). *Participating bonds* require stated interest payments but provide additional amounts if earnings permit. *Voting bonds*, unlike regular bonds, give the holders some voice in management. *Serial bonds*, with different portions of the issue maturing at different dates, are sometimes used by corporations, primarily for equipment financing.

Convertible bonds may, at the holder's option, be exchanged for other securities, often common stock. Such bonds, which have become very popular in recent years, are discussed in detail in Chapter 16.

Call Provisions

Corporate management would prefer to have the right to pay off any bond at par at any time prior to maturity. This provides desirable flexibility, since debt can be reduced, its maturity altered via refunding, and, most important, expensive debt issued in times of high interest rates replaced with cheaper debt if rates decline.

Not surprisingly, investors hold quite different opinions on the matter. The issuer's ability to redeem an issue at par at any time virtually precludes a rise in price over par and robs the holder of potential gains associated with declining interest rates; moreover, it introduces a new form of uncertainty. A bond with such a feature will almost certainly sell for less when issued and afterward than one without it.

Despite the cost of obtaining this sort of flexibility, many corporations include *call provisions* in their bond indentures. The corporation retains the option to "call" some or all of the bonds from their holders at stated prices during specified periods. In a sense, the firm sells a bond and simultaneously buys an option contract: the net price of the bond is thus the difference between the two values.

Investors are usually given some *call protection:* during the first few years an issue may not be callable. In addition, a *premium* may be paid when a bond is called; often this amount is smaller, the closer the date of call to the scheduled maturity of the issue.

An entire issue may be called, or only specific bonds (drawn by lot by the trustee). In either case, a *notice of redemption* will appear in advance in the financial press.

When a convertible bond can be exchanged for securities worth more than the bond's call price, the issuer may notify remaining holders of an intent to call the bond to force conversion.

Sinking Funds

Often a bond indenture will require the issuing corporation to make annual payments into a sinking fund. The idea is to pay part of the principal of the debt as well as the interest and thus to reduce the amount outstanding at maturity.

The corporation may transmit cash to the trustee for the issue, who can then purchase bonds in the open market. Alternatively, the corporation may obtain the bonds itself, by either purchase or call, and deposit them with the trustee. Call prices for sinking fund purchases may differ from those specified for optional redemptions.

Required contributions to a sinking fund may or may not be the same each year. In some cases the required amount may depend on earnings, output, and so on; in others the goal is to make the total paid for interest and principal the same each year.

Private Placements

Bonds intended for eventual public sale are usually issued in denominations of $1,000 each. Both *coupon* and *registered* forms may be utilized. Often, however, a single purchaser or a small group of purchasers will buy an entire issue. Such private placements now provide roughly half the capital borrowed by corporations in the United States. The purchasers are typically large institutional investors.

A related instrument is the *term loan.* Running for several years, it is a corporate loan made by a commercial bank. Payments on principal may or may not be required prior to maturity. Credit of this type is generally unsecured, but restrictions may be imposed on the corporation as a condition for the granting of the loan.

Bankruptcy

When a corporation fails to make a scheduled payment of either interest or principal on a bond, the firm is said to be in *default* on that obligation. If the payment is not made within a relatively short period, some sort of litigation almost inevitably follows.

A corporation unable to meet its obligatory debt payments is said to be *technically insolvent* or *insolvent in the equity sense*. If the value of the firm's assets falls below its liabilities, it is said to be *insolvent*, or *insolvent in the bankruptcy sense*.

Behind these definitions lie much legislation, many court cases, and varied legal opinions. While the details differ, the usual situation begins with a default of one or more required payments. If voluntary agreements with creditors cannot be obtained, this usually leads to a filing of bankruptcy—usually "voluntary"—by the corporation itself. Subsequent developments involve courts, court-appointed officials, representatives of the firm's creditors, and the management of the firm, among others.

A question that arises in most cases is whether the firm's assets should be *liquidated* and the proceeds divided among the creditors. Such an action is taken only if the court feels the resulting value would exceed that likely to be obtained if the firm continued in operation (perhaps after substantial reorganization).

If the firm's assets are liquidated in a "straight bankruptcy," secured creditors receive the property pledged for their loans or the proceeds from its sale. If this falls short of their claims, the difference is considered an unsecured debt of the firm; on the other hand, any excess is made available for other creditors. Next, assets are used to pay the claims of *priority* creditors to the extent possible. These include claims for such items as administrative expenses, wages (up to a stated limit per person), uninsured pension claims, taxes, and rents. Anything left over is used to pay unsecured creditors in proportion to their claims on the firm.

In one set of cases, secured creditors received 76.4% of their claims, priority creditors 34.1%, and unsecured creditors 7.8%.[4] The administrative expenses of the bankruptcy proceedings used up 23.4% of the available funds.[5]

Reorganization If the value of a firm's assets when employed as part of a "going concern" appears to exceed the value in liquidation, a reorganization of the firm and its liabilities may be ordered. Such proceedings are usually conducted under the provisions of Chapter X of the Federal Bankruptcy Act. A number of parties must concur in the proposed reorganization, including the holders of two-thirds of the value in each general class of creditor affected by the reorganization. If substantial amounts of bonds are held by the public, the Securities and Exchange Commission is also involved.

[4] Administrative Office of the U.S. Courts, *Table of Bankruptcy Statistics*, 1969.
[5] *Ibid.*, p. 13.

Typically, creditors are given new claims on the reorganized firm, intended to be at least equal in value to the amounts that would have been received in liquidation. For example, holders of debentures might receive bonds of longer maturity, holders of subordinated debentures might become stockholders, and stockholders might be left without any interest in the firm.

Among the goals of reorganization are "fair and equitable" treatment of various classes of securities, and the elimination of "burdensome" debt obligations. Neither concept is founded on a very secure base of financial theory. Presumably, a fair and equitable plan is one that investors expected to apply in the circumstances in question. A debt obligation that can be covered by assets need not be burdensome if the firm is prepared to alter its activities sufficiently, and so on.

**Arrange-
ments**
A third procedure is available to financially embarrassed corporations. Chapter XI of the Federal Bankruptcy Act authorizes certain corporations to voluntarily seek an *arrangement*, in which debts may be extended (to longer maturities) and/or *composed* (reduced). While Chapter XI proceedings are going on, the corporation is protected by the court from creditor lawsuits. Eventually, a plan for handling debts will be proposed; if a majority of creditors approve, the changes can be made and the firm returned, at least temporarily, to the ranks of the solvent.

**Some
Financial
Aspects of
Bankruptcy**
While the subject is far too complex for detailed treatment here, two aspects of bankruptcy deserve some discussion.

First, the choice between continuation of a firm and liquidation of its assets should be unrelated to considerations of bankruptcy. If an asset can be sold for more than the present value of its future earnings, it should be. Management may have to be taken to court to be forced to do this, but the issue is not really one of solvency or lack thereof.

Second, the definition of insolvency is rather vague. Assume, for the sake of argument, that assets can be adequately valued at the larger of liquidating or going-concern value. A firm is said to be insolvent if this value is less than that of the firm's liabilities. But how should the latter be valued? Their current market value will inevitably be less than the value of the assets as long as stockholders can expect to receive something under at least some circumstances.

An alternative procedure could value liabilities using the forward interest rates implicit in default-free bond prices. If assets cover liabilities calculated in this manner, the firm could meet its obligations by selling assets (perhaps to another firm) and purchasing government bonds with appropriate interest payments and maturities. Or it could simply buy its own bonds in the open market. Thus, the possibility of a technically but not "really" insolvent firm would not arise.

Neither of these procedures is very satisfactory. One might argue that the goal is to value the liabilities as if the firm had not gone bankrupt. But this involves circular reasoning.

Rightly or wrongly, par value is typically utilized to compute liabilities for this purpose, although it can lead to anomalies, such as the award of a greater value to a claimant than the present value of a government bond with equal terms.

OWNERSHIP OF CORPORATE BONDS

At the end of 1978, $399.7 billion of domestic U.S. corporate bonds was estimated to be outstanding. Such securities were held by both institutional and individual investors, as shown in Table 11-11 (which also includes holdings of $42.8 billion of foreign bonds).

Prices of Corporate Bonds

Some corporate bonds are traded on the New York Stock Exchange, and the prices at which such trades are made can be found in the financial press. Figure 11-3 provides an example. Thus, the entry:

| ATT | 7s01 | 10. | 294 | $70\frac{1}{2}$ | $70\frac{1}{8}$ | $70\frac{1}{8} + \frac{1}{2}$ |

indicates that American Telephone and Telegraph Company's bonds carrying a 7% coupon and maturing in 2001 traded at prices ranging from $70\frac{1}{4}$ to $70\frac{1}{8}$, inclusive, with the last trade of the day at $70\frac{1}{8}$. The *current yield*, based on the latter price, was 7/70.125 or 10.0%.[6] In all, 294 bonds, worth $1,000 each, traded hands on the exchange during the day, and the closing price was $\frac{1}{2}$ above that of the previous day.

    In a sense, the New York Stock Exchange is the "odd-lot" market for bonds. Major trades are negotiated elsewhere by dealers and institutional investors, either directly or through brokers. Thus, reported prices may be poor guides to values associated with large transactions.

[6] This is not shown for convertible bonds; "cv" is listed instead.

TABLE 11-11 Ownership of Corporate and Foreign Bonds, Year-end 1978

	Amount ($ Billions)	Percent
Mutual savings banks	22.1	5.0
Life insurance companies	159.9	36.1
Property liability companies	22.9	5.2
Private noninsured pension funds	54.8	12.4
State and local retirement funds	65.9	14.9
Open-end mutual funds	7.0	1.6
Closed-end corporate bond funds	.9	.2
Commercial banks	8.0	1.8
Foreigners	7.1	1.6
Foundations and endowments	13.5	3.1
Security brokers and dealers	.4	.1
Individuals and miscellaneous investors	80.0	18.1
	442.5	100.0

Source: Salomon Brothers, *Prospects for the American Financial Markets in 1979.*

New York Exchange Bonds

Friday, December 21, 1979

CORPORATION BONDS

Volume, $24,830,000

Bonds*	Cur Yld	Vol	High	Low	Close	Net Chg.
AMF 10s85	11.	26	90⅜	90¼	90¼	−1¼
AMInt 9⅜95	13.	30	70¼	70	70	.....
APL 10¾97	14.	25	78⅜	76⅞	78⅜	− ⅛
ARA 4⅝s96	cv	10	56½	56½	56½	−1½
AetnLf 8⅛07	10.	5	78	76½	78	+1⅜
AlaBn 10.55s99	11.	5	98½	98½	98½	....
AlaBnc 9½84	10.	25	92½	92	92	.....
AlaP 9s2000	13.	41	72½	71⅛	71⅛	−2⅝
AlaP 8½s01	12.	5	70¼	69⅞	70¼	+ ⅜
AlaP 7¾s02	12.	15	64½	64½	64½	−1½
AlaP 8⅞s03	13.	45	71	70½	71	+ ¾
AlaP 9¾s04	13.	16	78⅛	76⅞	78	.....
AlaP 10⅞05	13.	5	86¼	86¼	86¼	−3¾
AlaP 10½05	12.	20	87½	87⅛	87⅛	− ⅞
AlaP 8⅞06	13.	36	71½	69⅛	69⅛	−1
AlaP 8⅝87	10.	20	83	82½	83	− ½
AlaP 9¼07	13.	10	74	74	74	.....
AlaP 9⅝08	13.	15	75⅛	75	75	− ¼
Alskln 6s96	cv	6	153½	152	153½	+1
Alexn 5½96	cv	15	51	50½	50½	−1⅝
AllgL 4s81	cv	1	91⅝	91⅝	91⅝	− ⅜
Allen 11½94	cv	1	131	131	131	+3
AlldC 8⅜83	9.3	45	90¾	90⅜	90⅜	− ⅛
Alcoa 5¼s91	cv	9	96½	96½	96½	.....
Alcoa 6s92	8.7	10	68⅞	68⅞	68⅞	− ⅛
Alcoa 9s95	11.	10	83½	82½	82½	− ¾
Alcoa 9.45s00	11.	3	87	87	87	− ¼
AluCa 4½80	4.6	1	98	98	98	+1⅞
AMAX 8s86	9.4	25	85⅛	85⅛	85⅛	− ⅜
AMAX 8½96	11.	5	79	79	79	−4
AMAX 9⅜00	11.	5	85	85	85	+1
Amerce 5s92	cv	14	77	77	77	.....
AHes 6¾96	9.9	15	68	68	68	.....
AFoP 4.8s87	7.7	15	62¼	62	62	− ¼
AAirl 4¼s92	cv	20	45⅛	45	45	.....
AAirl 10s89	11.	6	88	88	88	.....
ABrnd 4⅝90	7.0	1	65¾	65¾	65¾	−1⅜
ABrnd 8⅛85	9.2	35	88	86⅛	88	+2⅛
ABdt 9.35s00	11.	3	87	87	87	−1
ACeM 6¾91	cv	11	59½	58½	59½	−2½
ACyan 7⅜01	9.6	2	76½	76½	76½	+1½
AExC 8½s85	10.	1	85⅛	85⅛	85⅛	−1
AGnIn 6½94	5.9	11	110	110	110	+1
AHoist 4¾92	cv	3	138⅛	138⅛	138⅛	−1⅞
AHoist 5½93	cv	5	108½	108½	108½	−3½
AInvt 8¾s89	11.	20	77¼	77¼	77¼	−1¾
AMF 4¼s81	cv	1	91	91	91	+1
AmMot 6s88	cv	9	81¾	81¾	81¾	+ ¾
ASmel 4⅝88	7.6	5	61¼	61	61	+1
AmStr 9⅞90	11.	39	89⅛	89⅛	89⅛	.....
ATT 2¾s80	2.9	1	94¾	94¾	94¾	.....
ATT 2¾s82	3.2	17	85½	85½	85½	.....
ATT 3¼s84	4.3	16	75¼	75¼	75¼	− ⅝
ATT 4⅜s85	5.7	44	76¾	76⅛	76⅛	− ⅝
ATT 2⅞s87	4.5	17	64	63⅝	64	+ ⅛
ATT 3⅞s90	6.4	37	61⅞	60½	60½	−1
ATT 8¾00	11.	252	83	82⅜	82⅞	− ⅛
ATT 7s01	10.	294	70½	70⅛	70⅛	+ ½
ATT 7⅛s03	10.	153	71¼	70⅞	70⅞	− ⅛
ATT 8.80s05	11.	411	83½	82¾	83⅜	+ ⅝
ATT 7¾s82	8.4	109	92¾	92½	92¾	.....
ATT 8⅝s07	11.	242	82⅝	81¾	81¾	− ¾
Amfac 5¼94	cv	23	67¾	67½	67½	+1⅛
Ampx 5½94	cv	29	69	68½	69	+ ⅜
Anhr 9.9s86	10.	20	98	98	98	+2
AppP 10½84	11.	5	95¼	95¼	95¼	− ¾
AppP 11s87	12.	15	93⅝	93⅝	93⅝	.....
Arco 8.70s81	9.4	30	92⅛	92⅛	92⅛	−1
Arco 8s82	8.7	25	92⅛	92⅛	92⅛	− ¾
Arco 8s84	8.9	10	89½	89½	89½	+ ⅞
Arco 7½82	8.3	45	90	89⅛	90	+ ¾
Arco 7¾86	9.3	1	83¾	83¾	83¾	+ ⅛
ArizP 7.45s02	11.	11	67	66	66	−1
ArizP 9½s82	10.	29	94⅞	93½	93½	+ ¼
ArizP 9.8s80	10.	17	97 25-32	97 25-32	97 25-32	−7-32
ArlnRlt 5s86	cv	20	44	44	44	.....
Armr 5s84	5.6	32	88½	88½	88½	.....
Armr 5s84r	5.6	1	88½	88½	88½	.....
ADGC 8⅞83	9.9	5	89⅜	89⅜	89⅜	.....
AsCp 8⅝81	9.1	3	95	95	95	.....
AsCp 8.2s87	10.	1	81	81	81	−2
Atchn 4s95st	8.0	6	52	50	50	−2½
Atchn 4s95r	8.2	5	49	49	49	.....
Atchsn 4s95	7.8	15	51¾	51½	51½	− ⅛
Atchn 4s95r	7.9	68	50½	50½	50½	.....
ARich 8⅝00	11.	1	80	80	80	+1
AvcoC 5½93	cv	26	66	66	66	.....
AvcoC 7½93	12.	6	65	64⅞	65	.....
AvcoF 6⅛87	8.3	10	73½	73½	73½	−5¾
AvcoF 9¼89	11.	30	84⅝	84½	84½	.....
AvcoF 11s90	11.	6	97¾	97¾	97¾	.....
AvcoF 9¾83	10.	25	92⅞	92⅞	92⅞	− ⅛
AvcoF 8.2s86	10.	5	81	81	81	.....
AvcoF 8⅞91	11.	2	78	78	78	+3
Avery 9⅛81	9.7	5	94	94	94	.....
Bally 6s98	cv	74	124½	123	124	.....

EXPLANATORY NOTES
(For New York and American Bonds)

Yield is current yield. cv-Convertible bond.

ct-Certificates. f-Dealt in flat. m-Matured bonds, negotiability impaired by maturity. r-Registered. st-Stamped. wd-When distributed. ww-With Warrants. x-Ex-interest. xw-Without warrants.

vi-In bankruptcy or receivership or being reorganized under the Bankruptcy Act, or securities assumed by such companies.

FIGURE 11-3 Price Quotations for Bonds Traded on the New York Stock Exchange

Source: Reprinted with permission of the *Wall Street Journal,* © Dow Jones & Co. (December 24, 1979). All Rights Reserved.

REAL ESTATE MORTGAGES

While many people purchase fixed-income securities, even more issue them. Almost any loan can be regarded as such a security, and anyone who borrows money can be considered to have issued one.

The most important type of personal loan in the United States is the home mortgage. As the name implies, this is secured debt, similar to the mortgage bonds issued by corporations. The loan represents a general obligation of the borrower, with the home in question pledged as security. In the event of default, the lender can sell the property; any excess received over the debt outstanding is returned to the borrower, while any deficiency constitutes a remaining debt.

The traditional home mortgage in the United States is written for a *long term*, with *fixed interest*, and is *fully amortized*. This differs from traditional corporate mortgage bonds, which only require the issuer to make interest payments prior to maturity, with the entire principal due at maturity. A fully amortized loan requires the issuer to make payments for both principal and interest during the life of the loan, so the debt is completely repaid via the periodic payments by maturity.

In the usual case equal monthly payments are required. For example, a 30-year mortgage of $40,000 at 9% per year (more precisely, $\frac{9}{12}$ of 1% per month) would involve 360 monthly payments of $321.85 each. Not surprisingly, the present value of $321.85 per month for 360 months at $\frac{9}{12}$ of 1% per month is $40,000. In fact, the monthly payment is determined by finding the amount that will have the required present value. This can be done with a business calculator, a book of tables, or a standard formula.

The present value (*PV*) of a payment of $*P* per period for *N* periods at a discount rate of *r* (stated as a decimal) per period is:

$$PV = P \left[\frac{1 - \dfrac{1}{(1 + r)^N}}{r} \right] \tag{11-1}$$

In this case:

$$40,000 = 321.85 \left[\frac{1 - \dfrac{1}{(1 + .0075)^{360}}}{.0075} \right]$$

To find the periodic payment $*P* with a specified present value, one can rearrange formula (11-1) to give:

$$P = \frac{PV}{\left[\dfrac{1 - \dfrac{1}{(1 + r)^N}}{r} \right]}$$

In this case:

$$321.85 = \frac{40,000}{\left[\dfrac{1 - \dfrac{1}{(1 + .0075)^{360}}}{.0075} \right]}$$

A fully amortized loan is similar to an issue of serial bonds or a regular bond issue with a sinking fund. In each case the amount owed decreases during the life of the loan. Since the value of the property pledged as security may also decrease over time, amortization (or an equivalent procedure) reduces the probability that the value of the property will fall below the amount of debt outstanding prior to maturity.

Most home mortgages in the United States include a *prepayment option*, which is, in effect, a call option. Typically the borrower may repay the principal amount at any time, although a "prepayment penalty" (call premium) is often assessed if the option is exercised during the first few years after the loan is written.

Some mortgage loans are only partially amortized: each payment exceeds the amount of interest due at the time, but unpaid principal remains at maturity. Second mortgages, often written by the seller of a home, are usually of this type. For example, a ten-year $10,000 mortgage at 12% per year (more precisely, 1% per month) might require monthly payments of $130 and a "balloon" payment of $3,098.83 at maturity. This is equivalent to two loans, one fully amortized and one with no payments prior to maturity. Formula (11-1) shows that the present value of the 120 monthly payments is:

$$130 \left[\frac{1 - \frac{1}{(1.01)^{120}}}{.01} \right] = 9,061.07$$

The remaining amount borrowed, $938.93 (= 10,000 − 9,061.07), must be paid with interest at maturity. The future value 120 months hence is thus:

$$938.93 \times (1.01)^{120} = 3,098.83$$

Partially amortized mortgages at fixed interest rates for fairly short terms (e.g., five years) are used in a number of countries to avoid long-term commitments at fixed interest rates. The borrower need not pay the remaining principal in full at maturity; instead, the amount may be refinanced in whole or in part via another mortgage at the then-prevailing rate of interest.

An alternative mechanism for avoiding a long-term commitment at a fixed interest rate is the long-term *variable-rate* mortgage. A borrower may agree to pay a stated amount each month until his or her loan is repaid, with each month's interest rate dependent on, for example, the average cost of capital for savings and loan companies in a particular area. The interest required on the current principal would be deducted from the payment each month and the balance applied to reduce the principal. The number of payments required to pay off the loan would then depend on the interest charged. Alternative procedures involve variation in the amount paid each period as interest rates fluctuate.

Mortgages are written on many types of real estate, including commercial property and farms. Table 11-12 shows the estimated amounts outstanding in various categories at the end of 1978. The total amount is substantial—for example, almost three times the amount of corporate bonds outstanding.

TABLE 11-12 Real Estate Mortgages Outstanding, Year-End 1978

Type	Amount ($ Billions)	Percent
One- to four-family nonfarm home mortgages	756.7	64.8
Multifamily mortgages	122.3	10.5
Commercial mortgages	214.5	18.4
Farm mortgages	74.2	6.4
	1,167.7	100.0

Source: Salomon Brothers, *Prospects for the American Financial Markets in 1979.*

The most important sources of mortgage loans are savings companies, life insurance companies, and commercial banks, as Table 11-13 shows. Mortgages may be sold by the initial issuer to another firm or individual. In addition, federal agencies purchase mortgages from lending institutions to help support the market, explaining the relatively large amount shown under this heading in Table 11-13.

CONSUMER LOANS

Secured consumer loans are usually of the fixed-interest, fully amortized type, with relatively short maturities. For example, a loan for which an automobile is pledged as security might be written for four years. Other types of *installment loans*, such as those for which appliances and home improvements are pledged, can run up to ten years. The length of the term is usually keyed to the rate at which the value of the pledged asset is likely to decline.

Some consumer loans are unsecured. A major type is the "revolving charge account." Purchases are added to the current balance of the account; if the customer pays this amount in full when billed, no interest is charged. Otherwise, interest is added (often at the rate of $1\frac{1}{2}\%$ per

TABLE 11-13 Ownership of Real Estate Mortgages Outstanding, Year-End 1978

Owner	Amount ($ Billions)	Percent
Federal agencies	167.8	14.4
Mutual savings banks	95.4	8.2
Savings and loan associations	433.5	37.1
Credit unions	3.4	.3
Life insurance companies	105.2	9.0
Private noninsured pension funds	3.1	.3
State and local retirement funds	11.2	1.0
Foundations and endowments	1.1	.1
Real estate investment trusts	5.5	.5
Commercial banks	211.8	18.1
Finance companies	10.5	.9
Individuals and miscellaneous investors	119.2	10.2
	1167.7	100.0

Source: Salomon Brothers, *Prospects for the American Financial Markets in 1979.*

TABLE 11-14 Ownership of Consumer Loans Outstanding, Year-End 1978

Owner	Amount ($ Billions)	Percent
Mutual savings banks	3.0	1.0
Savings and loan associations	9.6	3.2
Credit unions	46.0	15.2
Commercial banks	140.5	46.5
Finance companies	63.2	20.9
Business corporations	40.0	13.2
Total	302.3	100.0

Source: Salomon Brothers, *Prospects for the American Financial Markets in 1979.*

month). In most cases a stated minimum payment exceeding the interest due must be made each month.

At the end of 1978, $302.3 billion of consumer loans was estimated to be outstanding in the United States. Of the total, $256.0 billion was of the installment (i.e., fixed-payment) type, and $46.3 billion of the noninstallment (i.e., charge-account) type.[7]

Table 11-14 shows the ownership of consumer loans outstanding at the end of 1978. Relatively few of these loans are sold by the original lender to another firm. Thus, department stores, finance companies, credit unions, and commercial banks provide the bulk of such financing, as anyone who has charged a purchase or signed an automobile loan might suspect.

PREFERRED STOCK

In some respects preferred stock is like a perpetual bond. A given amount is to be paid each year. This may be stated as a percent of the stock's par value (e.g., 8% of $100, or $8 per year) or directly as a dollar figure. Since the security is a stock, such payments are *dividends* instead of interest and hence do not qualify as an expense for purposes of computing the issuing corporation's income tax. On the other hand, failure to make such a payment does not constitute grounds for bankruptcy proceedings.

Preferred stock is generally *preferred as to dividends*. Specified payments must be made on the preferred stock before any dividends may be paid to holders of the firm's common stock. Failure to pay a preferred dividend in full does not constitute default, but unpaid dividends are usually *cumulative*: all must be paid (but seldom with interest) before a dividend may be declared on the common stock.

No indenture is provided with a preferred stock issue, but protective provisions against potentially harmful actions (e.g., issue of new senior securities) may be written into the corporation's charter. Preferred stockholders may or may not be given voting rights (in some cases such rights are granted only when dividends are in arrears).

Many issues of preferred stock are *callable*, often at a premium; such stock is sometimes said to be *redeemable* at a stated *redemption price*. *Par-*

[7] Salomon Brothers, *Prospects for the American Financial Markets in 1979.*

ticipating preferred stock entitles the holder to receive extra dividends when earnings permit. *Convertible* preferred stock may, at the option of the holder, be converted into another security (usually the firm's common stock) on stated terms. Some firms issue more than one class of preferred stock, with preference accorded the various classes in a specified order.

In the event of a dissolution of the firm, preferred stock is often *preferred as to assets*. For example, holders might be entitled to receive the stock's par value before any payment is made to common stock holders.

Since preferred stock has many features of a bond without the substantial tax advantage the latter gives to the issuer, its use has diminished in the United States in recent years. For example, in 1977 only $2.4 billion of such stock was issued, compared with $22.0 billion of corporate bonds.[8] Utilities, whose rates are tied to their cost of capital, often find it advantageous to issue preferred stock; it is held primarily by corporations.

As indicated in Chapter 9, interest income from bonds held by a corporation is subject to the corporate income tax, but 85% of any dividend income received may be deducted before the tax liability is determined. This makes the effective tax rate on dividends from preferred stock held by a corporation approximately 6.9% ($.46 \times .15$), compared to a full 46% for interest received from other fixed-income securities. For this reason, preferred stocks tend to sell at prices that give lower before-tax yields than long-term bonds, even though the latter may be considerably lower in risk. Thus, preferred stocks are generally unattractive holdings for noncorporate investors.

Many preferred stocks are traded on major exchanges. Prices at which trades are completed are reported in the financial press in the same format used for common stocks.

[8] *Statistical Abstract of the United States, 1978.*

Problems

1. Explain the differences in interpreting quotations for U.S. Treasury bills and U.S. Treasury notes.
2. Many bond indentures include call provisions. What are the potential effects of such provisions on the corporation and its bondholders?
3. What are the differences in the following three yield figures: current yield, yield-to-maturity, and coupon yield?
4. When is a bond's current yield greater than its coupon rate?
5. Figure 11-1 shows the following bid and asked prices for $7\frac{1}{4}$% U.S. Treasury bonds maturing August 1992:

	Bid	Asked
	78.27	79.11

What is the dollar spread between bid and asked prices for this bond?

6. Consider a 7.5% 25-year Treasury bond having a 15-year deferred call provision that has just been sold for $1,002. If the current yield-to-maturity on fully callable Treasury bonds is 8%, what dollar value are investors placing on the deferred call provision? Assume interest payments are made annually.

7. Suppose that on January 1, 1980, you purchased a U.S. Treasury bill that matures in 360 days. Your purchase price was $9,300.
   a. What was the interest rate reported in the *Wall Street Journal* for the bill you purchased?
   b. Is it possible that you could receive a realized yield greater than that calculated in (a) if you were to sell the bill before its maturity? Explain fully.

8. An investor has $20,000 in cash. She will need the cash in six months, but not before. Compare the relative advantages to her of investing her money in (a) a six-month U.S. Treasury bill, (b) a bank passbook savings account, and (c) a savings and loan six-month money market account.

9. In 1979 some lenders began to offer mortgages with monthly payments that increased from year to year. How could you be sure that the scheduled set of payments was correct, given the stated rate of interest? How would the decline of principal on such a mortgage compare with that on a conventional mortgage with equal payments every month?

Bond Prices, Yields, and Returns

12

INTRODUCTION

Five attributes of a bond greatly influence its price: (1) maturity, (2) coupon rate, (3) call provisions, (4) tax status, and (5) "agency rating" (an estimate of the likelihood of default). At any time the structure of prices for bonds differing in these dimensions can be examined and used to estimate the prices of other bonds (whether already issued or not). The underlying relationships are usually described in terms of equivalent yields, with the overall pattern called the *yield structure*. Often attention is confined to differences along a single dimension, holding the other attributes constant. Thus the set of yields of bonds of different maturities constitutes the *term structure*, the set of yields of bonds of different risk the *risk structure*, and so on.

The return on a bond over any given holding period depends to a major extent on its price at the beginning of the period and its price at the end of the period. Thus the return on a bond over, say, a one-year period will depend on the yield structure at the beginning of the year and the structure at the end of the year. To analyze possible bond returns one must thus analyze possible changes in the yield structure. Indeed, this is the essential element in bond analysis. While the characteristics of the issuer are relevant for estimating default risk, well-known agencies regularly analyze such factors for major issues and assign standard ratings. Though many may disagree with a bond's rating, its market price will tend to follow the prices of bonds with similar terms and ratings.

FORWARD AND SPOT INTEREST RATES

Chapter 4 introduced the idea of a forward interest rate. The *forward interest rate* for a commitment made today to loan money in year t_1, to be repaid (with interest) in year t_2, can be described by:

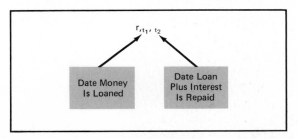

The only risk associated with a forward contract arises when there is some possibility that one of the parties might fail to meet the terms of the contract. Although the commitments are made now, no money need change hands until time t_1.

A *spot interest rate* is one in which money is borrowed now, to be repaid at some later date. At any time there can be a one-year spot rate, a two-year spot rate, and so on. There can also be a forward rate for a one-year loan beginning in one year, another beginning in two years, and so forth, as well as a forward rate for a two-year loan beginning in one year, another for one beginning in two years, and so on.

Some structure of spot and forward rates will apply to default-free commitments. The promised terms in such cases will equal the actual results, and there will be no divergence between actual and expected values. However, in cases in which there is some possibility of default, promised terms will be higher, to compensate for the potential shortfall. Expected results will, in such cases, be below the promised amounts.

Most analysts consider the interest rates for default-free bonds to form "the" structure of yields; "risk differentials" are then added to obtain the relevant yields for bonds of lower quality. While subject to some criticism, this procedure makes it possible to think about a complicated set of relationships sequentially.

Differentials between yields of related instruments are usually termed *yield spreads* and measured in *basis points*. One basis point equals .01%. If the yield-to-maturity for one bond is 7.50% and that of another is 7.90%, the spread is 40 basis points.

ESTIMATING DISCOUNT FACTORS AND FORWARD INTEREST RATES

Arbitrage is the act of buying something at one price and selling it or something equivalent at a higher price, virtually concurrently. The advantages associated with this sort of activity make arbitrage situations well worth discovering and exploiting. This insures that any disparity will be quickly discovered; as arbitrageurs exploit such a disparity, prices will tend to move back into line as buying pressure drives up the price of one investment and selling pressure drives down the price of the other. Arbitrageurs can make money, but not much and not for long from any one situation. With small and temporary exceptions, equivalent things will not sell at two different prices.

This means that the entire structure of prices for default-free bonds could (in the absence of taxes) be described by a set of discount factors:

d_1 = the present value of $1 received with certainty one period hence

d_2 = the present value of $1 received with certainty two periods hence

and so on. The set of such factors constitutes the current *market discount function*.

If the U.S. government were thoughtful enough to issue many zero-coupon bonds, with maturities covering a wide range, the task of estimating the current discount factors would be rather easy. For example, if a $1,000 par three-year zero-coupon bond sells at $830:

$$d_3 = .83$$

The structure of prices for such bonds would be the discount function.

Unfortunately, the U.S. government does not issue zero-coupon bonds, only Treasury bills, with maturities of up to one year. Moreover, although many maturities of coupon bonds and notes are outstanding, they do not cover as wide a range as a bond analyst would wish.

The price of a coupon bond depends on discount factors in a much more complicated way than does that of a zero-coupon bond. For example, a three-year bond paying $80 at the end of each year and $1,000 at maturity would be worth:

$$(d_1 \times \$80) + (d_2 \times \$80) + (d_3 \times \$1,080)$$

Many combinations of the three discount factors could be consistent with the bond's actual price. To determine which combination actually holds, we would have to analyze other bonds.

A number of procedures have been employed to determine market discount factors. Some employ statistical methods, others mathematical programming techniques, and still others relatively simple calculations. All suffer from the lack of a large enough set of bonds with different patterns of cash flows and maturities, and most resort to some type of smoothing and/or interpolation to reduce the impact of errors and temporary fluctuations in prices.

Some idea of the current discount factors can be obtained by a fairly simple analysis of the prices of Treasury issues with similar tax status. For example, at the end of 1979 one could purchase the following U.S. Treasury securities:

A six-month Treasury bill for $941.60
A 12-month Treasury bill for $891.50
A 9⅛% Treasury note maturing 18 months hence for $969.69

If we let a *period* be six months, the cash flows associated with the three investments were:

Period	Six-month Bill	Twelve-month Bill	Note
1	$1,000	$0	$ 45.625
2	0	$1,000	45.625
3	0	$0	$1,045.625

The discount factors in the market at the time can be denoted d_1, d_2, and d_3. The price of each security should equal its present value, given the factors at the time. For the six-month bill:

Period	Cash Flow	Discount Factor	Present Value
1	$1,000	d_1	$1,000 d_1$
2	$0	d_2	0
3	$0	d_3	0
			$1,000 d_1$

The value was thus $1,000 d_1$; the price was \$941.60; for price to equal value:

$$1,000 d_1 = 941.60$$

Thus $d_1 = .9416$—a dollar six months hence was worth \$.9416 at the time.

Similarly, the price of the twelve-month bill gives $d_2 = .8915$—a dollar twelve months hence was worth \$.8915 at the time.

To find the discount factor for payments eighteen months hence we can use the information obtained from the shorter maturity security prices and "work up." Thus:

Period	Cash Flow	Discount Factor	Present Value
1	$ 45.625	.9416	$ 42.96
2	45.625	.8915	40.67
3	1,045.625	d_3	$1,045.625 d_3$
			$83.63 + 1,045.625 d_3$

For value to equal price:

$$83.63 + 1045.625 d_3 = \$969.69$$

Thus:

$$d_3 = .8474$$

and the price of the eighteen-month note implied that \$1 in eighteen months was worth \$.8474 at the time.

Once the discount factors have been determined, it is a simple matter to calculate the implied forward rates. As shown in Chapter 4:

$$d_1 = \frac{1}{1 + r_{01}} \tag{12-1a}$$

$$d_2 = \frac{1}{(1 + r_{01})(1 + r_{12})} \tag{12-1b}$$

$$d_3 = \frac{1}{(1 + r_{01})(1 + r_{12})(1 + r_{23})} \tag{12-1c}$$

and so on. Here, too, one can work from shorter to longer maturities. In the previous example:

$$.9416 = \frac{1}{1 + r_{01}}$$

so:

$$r_{01} = .0620, \text{ or } 6.20\% \text{ per six months}$$

Thus the six-month spot rate of interest at the time was 6.20% (per six months).

Since the present value of $1 twelve months hence was $.8915:

$$.8915 = \frac{1}{(1 + r_{01})(1 + r_{12})} = \frac{1}{(1.0620)(1 + r_{12})}$$

and:

$$r_{12} = .0562, \text{ or } 5.62\% \text{ per six months}$$

So the forward rate for a six-month loan to begin six months hence was 5.62% at the time.

Similarly:

$$.8474 = \frac{1}{(1.0620)(1.0562)(1 + r_{23})}$$

and:

$$r_{23} = .0521, \text{ or } 5.21\% \text{ per six months}$$

For some purposes relatively simple procedures such as this may suffice, but often a more complex approach is called for. Figure 12-1 shows

FIGURE 12-1 Estimated Yield Curves, February 1966

Source: J. Huston McCulloch, "Measuring the Term Structure of Interest Rates," *The Journal of Business*, 44, no. 1 (January 1971), 19–31. © by the University of Chicago. All Rights Reserved.

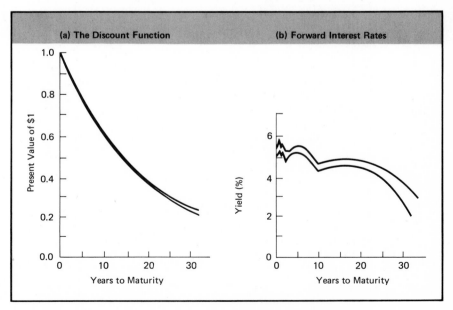

the results obtained applying one such procedure to the prices of taxable U.S. government bills, notes, and bonds in February 1966. Since other factors affected the prices used in the analysis, the values did not fit a single set of discount factors perfectly; to reflect the likely degree of error in the estimation process, each diagram thus shows a "high" and "low" estimate for the actual curve. Figure 12-1(a) plots the estimated discount function. Figure 12-1(b) shows the associated set of forward interest rates.

THE TERM STRUCTURE OF INTEREST RATES

To determine appropriate prices for default-free bonds one needs to know the relevant discount factors—i.e., the current market prices of $1 one period hence, two periods hence, and so on. Alternatively, one needs to know the current set of forward interest rates, for from them the discount factors can be computed. A set of interest rates for different time periods is called a *term structure*.

What factors influence the term structure? To address the question, it is useful to consider two aspects: (1) the determination of spot interest rates and (2) the relationship between forward rates and expected future spot rates.

The first aspect was discussed at some length in earlier chapters. Supply and demand for credit are the direct determinants of spot interest rates. But the fundamental forces are productive opportunities, preferences for present versus future consumption, and expected inflation. The first two factors determine the expected real rate of interest; when expected inflation is added, the result approximates the nominal rate of interest.

The second aspect is more difficult. Several theories have been advanced to explain the term structure. One, the *expectations theory*, holds that every forward rate represents a consensus opinion of the expected spot rate for the period in question. This leads to the notion of a fairly stable long-run rate of interest involving a "normal" real rate and "normal" inflation. When current conditions make short-term rates abnormally high (owing, say, to excessive rates of inflation), the term structure will be downward-sloping. When current conditions make short-term rates abnormally low (owing, say, to temporary recession and deflation), the term structure will be upward-sloping.

This approach is reasonably consistent with experience. But it suggests that the term structure is likely to be downward-sloping as often as it is upward-sloping. However, upward-sloping structures tend to be more common.

To explain this, the notion of *liquidity preference* has been advanced. If investors are concerned with relatively short holding periods, short-term instruments will be considered less risky than long-term ones (since any subsequent change in interest rates will affect the year-end value of a long-term instrument, and hence its one-year return). To hold a long-term instrument, investors may thus require a risk premium in the form of greater expected return. Moreover, governments and corporations may be willing to pay such a premium. There are two possible

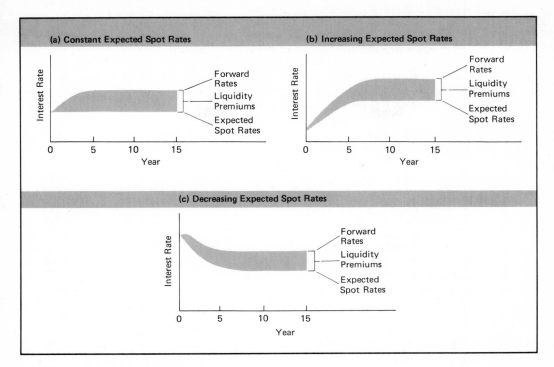

FIGURE 12-2 Effects of Liquidity Premiums on Forward Interest Rates

reasons why issuers might prefer long-term borrowing, even at higher interest rates. First, frequent refinancing may be costly in terms of registration, advertising, paperwork, and so on. Second, issuers may be concerned with longer holding periods. If so, long-term bonds will be less risky than short-term bonds in their view, and they will be willing to pay (via higher expected interest costs) to reduce risk.

This theory implies that each forward rate will equal the expected spot rate for the period in question plus a liquidity premium, and that the latter will be larger, the farther in the future is the period.

Figure 12-2 shows possible effects of such premiums on forward rates. In Figure 12-2(a) spot rates are expected to remain constant. Liquidity premiums are presumed to increase, but at a decreasing rate, leading to an upward-sloping forward rate curve. In Figure 12-2(b) liquidity premiums are similar, but spot rates are expected to increase from presently low levels to more normal values. Both elements contribute to make the term structure upward-sloping. In Figure 12-2(c) current spot rates are considered abnormally high. A combination of decreasing expected spot rates and increasing liquidity premiums may lead to forward rates that either decrease or else increase and then decrease, giving a "humped" pattern such as that shown in the figure.

A third explanation for the determination of the term structure rests on the assumption that there is *market segmentation:* various holders and issuers are asserted to be restricted by law, preference, or custom to *preferred habitats* in terms of maturity. This implies that only major disparities in rates for securities of different maturities may lead to substantial changes in the buying, selling, and issuance of bonds.

Empirical evidence provides some insight into the determinants of the term structure, but it is difficult to assess the relative importance of these three factors with any precision.

The market-segmentation hypothesis receives relatively slight empirical validation. While there is some lack of flexibility on the part of bond buyers, sellers, and issuers, it apparently does not cause substantial and persistent anomalies in the term structure.

The liquidity-premium hypothesis is supported to a somewhat greater extent by empirical evidence. In the majority of years over the last four decades long-term bond yields have exceeded short-term interest rates. Moreover, on average, the one-year holding-period return from a long-term bond has been higher than that from a short-term investment. For example, from 1926 to 1978 the average annual holding-period return from long-term government bonds was 3.4%, while that from Treasury bills and similar short-term instruments was 2.5%.[1] A cautious conclusion might hold that liquidity premiums range from zero for one-year commitments to 1% at most for long-term ones.

THE EFFECT OF COUPON RATE ON YIELD-TO-MATURITY

As indicated earlier, one of the attributes of a bond considered relevant for price determination is its coupon rate. In part, this is due to the differential tax treatment of interest income and capital gains. But there is another factor: the influence of the coupon rate on the effective maturity of a bond.

To illustrate the point, consider two default-free noncallable bonds, each with ten years remaining until maturity; one has a 3% coupon rate, the other a 10% rate. Assume further that taxes need not be considered. Table 12-1 shows the forward rates for each year, the associated present-value (discount) factors, the payments for each of the bonds, and the present values of the payments.

The price of each bond is simply the sum of the present values of its payments. Thus the low-coupon bond will sell at a discount ($71.39), while the high-coupon bond will sell at a premium ($121.98). Although priced appropriately, the bonds do not provide the same yield-to-maturity: that of the low-coupon bond exceeds that of the high-coupon bond by 20 basis points.

The reason is not hard to see. Relatively more of the low-coupon bond's value is provided at maturity. Thus the payment at maturity represents 72% of the value of the low-coupon bond (51.20/71.39 ≈ .72). But

---

[1] Roger G. Ibbotson and Rex A. Sinquefield, "Stocks, Bonds, Bills and Inflation: Historical Returns (1926–1978)" (Charlottesville, Va.: Financial Analysts Research Foundation, 1979).

TABLE 12-1 Prices and Yields of Low- and High-coupon Bonds

			LOW-COUPON BOND		HIGH-COUPON BOND	
Year (t)	Forward Rate (%)	Present Value of $1 ($d_t$)	Payment ($)	Present Value of Payment ($)	Payment ($)	Present Value of Payment ($)
1	5.0	.9524	3.00	2.8572	10.00	9.524
2	5.5	.9027	3.00	2.7081	10.00	9.027
3	6.0	.8516	3.00	2.5548	10.00	8.516
4	6.5	.7997	3.00	2.3991	10.00	7.997
5	7.0	.7473	3.00	2.2419	10.00	7.473
6	7.5	.6952	3.00	2.0856	10.00	6.952
7	8.0	.6437	3.00	1.9311	10.00	6.437
8	8.5	.5933	3.00	1.7799	10.00	5.933
9	9.0	.5443	3.00	1.6329	10.00	5.443
10	9.5	.4971	103.00	51.2013	110.00	54.681
				71.3919		121.983
			Yield-to-maturity:	7.09%		6.89%

it represents only 45% of the value of the high-coupon bond ($54.68/121.98 \approx .45$). A low-coupon bond is, in effect, a "longer" bond than a high-coupon bond of similar maturity. And when the term structure is upward-sloping, longer bonds offer higher yields.

The yield spread between low- and high-coupon bonds of the same maturity clearly depends on the disparity in their coupons. It also depends on the structure of interest rates. In the absence of tax effects, with an upward-sloping term structure high-coupon bonds would offer lower yields than low-coupon bonds (as in the example in Table 12-1); with a flat term structure coupon rates would not affect yields; and with a downward-sloping term structure high-coupon bonds would offer higher yields than low-coupon bonds. This is illustrated in Figures 12-3(a), (b), and (c), which show curves for forward rates, the yields-to-maturity for zero-coupon bonds, and the yields-to-maturity for regular (positive) coupon bonds.

The yield-to-maturity on a zero-coupon bond is, in effect, an average of all the forward rates up to the maturity date.[2] Thus when forward rates increase (decrease) with maturity, the yield-to-maturity on a zero-coupon bond will be less (more) than the forward rate for the bond's maturity date. The yield-to-maturity on a positive-coupon bond is a more complicated kind of average that places even more weight on earlier years' forward rates; thus it will be smaller (larger) than the yield-to-maturity on a zero-coupon bond when forward rates increase (decrease) with maturity.

[2] If y_T represents the yield-to-maturity on a zero-coupon bond maturing in year T:
$$1 + y_T = \sqrt[T]{(1 + r_{01})(1 + r_{12}) \cdots (1 + r_{T-1,T})}$$
and $(1 + y_T)$ is the geometric mean of $(1 + r_{01})$ through $(1 + r_{T-1,T})$.

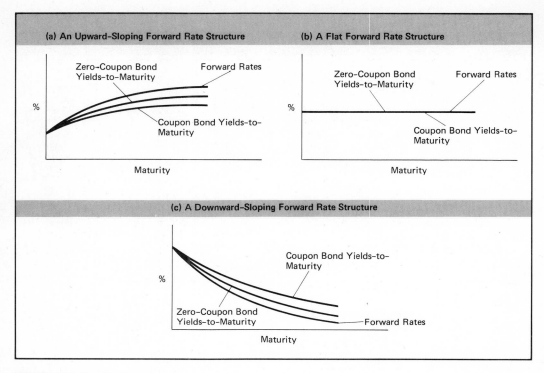

FIGURE 12-3 Possible Term Structures

CHANGES IN THE TERM STRUCTURE

When interest rates change, most bond prices also change, but some react more than others. To predict the magnitude of the effect of a shift in interest rates on a given bond's price, more must be known about the shift. We will consider, first, a situation in which every yield changes in the same way, then realistic cases in which shorter-term yields change more than longer ones.

Let y_t represent the yield-to-maturity on a t-year zero-coupon bond, expressed as a decimal. For example, if the yield on a three-year bond of this type is 7%, $y_3 = .07$ and $(1 + y_3) = 1.07$. Now assume that each value of $(1 + y_t)$ changes by the same percentage; then the change in a bond's present value can be estimated by:

$$\% \text{ change in PV} \approx - \left[\sum_{t=1}^{T} \left(\frac{t \cdot PV(P_t)}{PV} \right) \right] \times \% \text{ change in each } (1 + y_t) \quad \textbf{(12-2)}$$

where:

$$T = \text{the period in which the bond matures}$$
$$PV(P_t) = \text{the present value of } P_t, \text{ the payment in period } t$$
$$PV = \text{the current present value of the bond}$$

The bracketed expression is the bond's *duration*. As discussed earlier, this is a weighted average of the times when payments are made, with each weighted by the proportion of present value contributed by the payment made at the time.

In Chapter 4 we said that bonds of similar duration tend to react similarly to changes in interest rates. Formula (12-2) shows that when all yields change in the manner assumed here, prices of bonds of equal duration change by approximately equal percentages. However, rarely do yields on long-term bonds move as much as those on short-term ones. For example, a common cause of a shift in the yields on default-free bonds is a change in expectations regarding inflation. If the likely degree of near-term inflation increases, short-term yields will rise. So will long-term yields, but unless expectations for long-term inflation are revised upward to the same extent, long-term yields will rise by a smaller amount. Figure 12-4 shows the mean change in yield-to-maturity for bonds of various maturities from month to month, from 1953 through 1973. On average, one-year bond yields changed (up or down) by slightly over two-tenths of one percent (.212) each month, while those of 30-year bonds changed by less than one-tenth of one percent (.089), with intermediate maturities falling between these values.

If long-term rates did change as much as short-term rates when the term structure shifted, duration would provide a good estimate of the sensitivity of a bond's price to changes in interest rates. But, since long-term rates tend to move less than short-term rates, duration will generally *overstate* the magnitude of the reaction of a bond's price to changes in short-term rates and *understate* the magnitude of the reaction to changes in long-term rates. However, it can still serve as a useful mea-

FIGURE 12-4 Mean Monthly Changes in Yield-to-Maturity for Bonds of Various Maturities 1953–1973

Source: Jess B. Yawitz, George H. Hempel, and William J. Marshall, "The Use of Average Maturity as a Risk Proxy in Investment Portfolios," *The Journal of Finance*, XXX, no. 2 (May 1975), 325–33.

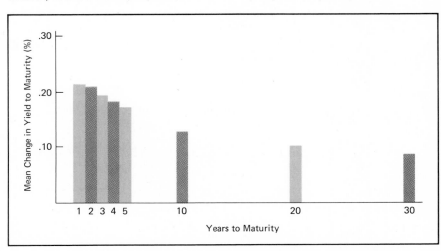

sure, since bonds with similar durations will still react in relatively similar ways to typical shifts in the term structure.

If more precision is needed, we can obtain it by considering the nature of changes in the term structure directly. The change in any default-free bond's price can be related to the changes in the relevant discount factors:

$$\% \text{ change in } PV \approx \frac{P_1}{PV} \times \Delta d_1$$

$$+ \frac{P_2}{PV} \times \Delta d_2 \qquad \text{(12-3a)}$$

$$+ \cdots ;$$

where:

Δd_1 = change in the discount factor for money one period hence

Δd_2 = change in the discount factor for money two periods hence, and so on

Empirical evidence indicates that if one knows the changes in any two interest rates, it is possible to make good estimates of the changes in all the discount factors. Let Δ_s be the change in a short-term rate (e.g., the six-month Treasury bill rate) and Δ_l the change in a long-term rate (e.g., the yield-to-maturity on a very long-term Treasury bill). Then, using historical data, one can estimate relationships such as:

$$\Delta d_1 \approx b_{1s} \Delta_s + b_{1l} \Delta_l$$
$$\Delta d_2 \approx b_{2s} \Delta_s + b_{2l} \Delta_l$$
$$\begin{matrix} \cdot \\ \cdot \\ \cdot \end{matrix} \qquad \text{(12-3b)}$$

where:

b_{ts} = the sensitivity of the discount factor for period t to a change in the short-term rate

b_{tl} = the sensitivity of the discount factor for period t to a change in the long-term rate

Substituting (12-3b) in (12-3a):

$$\% \text{ change in } PV \approx \frac{P_1}{PV} (b_{1s} \Delta_s + b_{1l} \Delta_l)$$

$$+ \frac{P_2}{PV} (b_{2s} \Delta_s + b_{2l} \Delta_l)$$

$$+ \cdots$$

or:

$$\% \text{ change in } PV \approx B_s \Delta_s + B_l \Delta_l \qquad \text{(12-4)}$$

where:

$$B_s = \frac{P_1}{PV} b_{1s} + \frac{P_2}{PV} b_{2s} + \cdots$$

$$B_l = \frac{P_1}{PV} b_{1l} + \frac{P_2}{PV} b_{2l} + \cdots$$

and:

B_s = the sensitivity of the bond's present value to changes in the short-term rate

B_l = the sensitivity of the bond's value to changes in the long-term rate

Given estimates of typical term structure changes [e.g., formulas (12-3b)], one can estimate the sensitivity of different bonds to changes in short- and long-term rates [e.g., formula (12-4)]. This can be used, in conjunction with estimates of expected changes in rates, to estimate the implied *expected* changes in the prices of various bonds. It can also be used, in conjunction with estimates of the *risks* associated with interest-rate changes, to estimate the *risks* of various bonds.

BOND PRICES OVER TIME

If the yield structure changes, so will bond prices. The previous section dealt with the effects of a change in yields without taking into account any effects due to the mere passage of time. Usually, however, both aspects are relevant. For example, the holding period return on a bond over one year depends on the yield structures at the beginning and at the end of the year. But at year-end, every bond has one year less left before maturity and is thus in a sense a different bond than it was at the beginning of the year. Its price may have changed because the yield structure changed, because its years-to-maturity changed, or both.

For purposes of analysis it is useful to separate these two influences. We have already dealt with the effects of a change in the yield structure. It remains to discuss the effect on bond prices of the passage of time when the yield structure stays the same.

But what does it mean to say that the yield structure "stays the same"? Table 12-2 provides an illustration. The first section shows a hypothetical structure of rates prevailing on January 1, 1985. The forward rate for each year is composed of two elements. The first is the expected spot rate for the *calendar* year in question. The second is the liquidity premium, which is a function of the number of years *between* the present and the future year. To simplify the computations, the premium is expressed as a ratio. For example, in 1985 the expected spot rate for 1987 is 7%, and the liquidity premium ratio is 1.004; $1.07 \times 1.004 = 1.07428$, giving the forward rate of 7.428% shown in the table.

The second portion of Table 12-2 shows the rates that would prevail in 1986 if the situation "stayed the same." The actual spot rate in 1986

TABLE 12-2 Hypothetical Present and Future Yield Curves

INTEREST RATES, JANUARY 1, 1985			
Year	Expected Spot Rate (%)	Liquidity Premium Ratio	Forward Interest Rate (%)
1985	5*	1.00	5*
1986	6	1.002	6.212
1987	7	1.004	7.428
1988	8	1.006	8.648

INTEREST RATES, JANUARY 1, 1986			
Year	Expected Spot Rate (%)	Liquidity Premium Ratio	Forward Interest Rate (%)
1986	6*	1.00	6*
1987	7	1.002	7.214
1988	8	1.004	8.432

* Actual spot rate.

equals the rate expected in 1985, and expected spot rates for 1987 and 1988 are the same as they were a year earlier. Finally, liquidity premium ratios are the same (but of course each calendar year is one year closer to the present than in 1985).

What will happen to the price of a long-term bond between January 1, 1985, and January 1, 1986, if the situation shown prevails? The simplest case is that of a zero-coupon bond; consider, for example, one maturing at the end of 1988. Its value at the beginning of 1985 will be:

$$V_{1985} = \frac{100}{(1.05 \times 1.00) \times (1.06 \times 1.002) \times (1.07 \times 1.004) \times (1.08 \times 1.006)}$$

If the rates shown in the table prevail in 1986, the value of the bond then will be:

$$V_{1986} = \frac{100}{(1.06 \times 1.00) \times (1.07 \times 1.002) \times (1.08 \times 1.004)}$$

Note that two items have disappeared from the denominator: 1.05 (the spot rate in 1980) and 1.006 (the liquidity premium ratio for a four-year bond). Thus:

$$V_{1986} = V_{1985} \times 1.05 \times 1.006$$
$$= V_{1985} \times 1.0563$$

Since this is a zero-coupon bond, its one-year holding-period return is simply the change in its value. In this case it is 5.63%, greater than that of a one-year bond (5%), with the difference determined by the liquidity premium appropriate for the number of years prior to its maturity date.

Under the conditions shown in this example, longer-term zero-coupon bonds will provide greater one-year returns than shorter-term zero-coupon bonds, with the difference due to the greater liquidity premium associated with years farther in the future. Since a medium- or long-term coupon bond is equivalent to a package of zero-coupon bonds, in this circumstance its one-year holding-period return would exceed that on a one-year bond, with the difference greater, the greater its effective maturity.

BOND RETURNS

Future yield curves are, of course, subject to uncertainty. In Table 12-2 the interest rates shown for 1986 should thus be considered *expected values*. Thus in 1985 investors expect that at the beginning of 1986 the spot rate will be 6%, the forward rate for 1987 will be 7.214%, and so on. Correspondingly, they expect to obtain a one-year holding period return of 5.63% during 1985 from a zero-coupon bond maturing at the end of 1988. However, they know full well that the *actual* yield curve in 1986 may differ considerably from that shown and thus that the *actual* one-year return on such a bond may differ considerably from 5.63%.

An upward-sloping pattern of liquidity premiums implies that expected one-year returns will be greater for long-term bonds than for short-term bonds. This is reasonable enough, as the uncertainty associated with one-year returns is also greater for long-term bonds. The prices of long-term bonds (and hence their short-term returns) are more sensitive to changes in the yield curve than are those of short-term bonds; the former thus have more "interest-rate risk." This type of risk is reduced but not eliminated when a highly diversified market portfolio, including both bonds and stocks, is held. It is not surprising that bonds with greater amounts of such risk should offer greater expected returns.

TAXES AND BOND YIELDS

We have already seen the impact of differential tax treatment on the yields of tax-free municipal bonds vis-à-vis those on otherwise similar taxable bonds. As shown in Chapter 9, the former have yields-to-maturity 30% to 40% lower than those of the latter.[3]

Taxation affects bond prices and yields in other ways. For example, any low-coupon bond selling at a discount provides return in two forms: coupon payments and capital gains. In the United States the former are taxable as ordinary income, while the latter may qualify for the more favorable treatment accorded capital gains. This suggests that low-coupon ("deep discount") bonds might be priced to give lower before-tax yields than high-coupon bonds, other things equal.

This suggests that there may be at least three separate though related sets of discount factors (and associated forward interest rates) for

---

[3] Flower bonds provide another example.

default-free bonds: one for fully taxable returns, another for price changes taxed as capital gains and losses, and a third for the return of principal and tax-exempt interest. Given a large enough set of bonds of different types, it is possible to estimate all three sets of rates concurrently. However, this is generally not done. Instead, a yield curve for taxable coupon bonds selling at or near par is estimated. Yields of tax-exempt bonds are either analyzed separately or compared with those of taxable bonds and "normal" yield spreads estimated. The latter procedure is usually applied to deep-discount bonds.

YIELDS ON CALLABLE BONDS

Callable bonds issued at times of high yields appear to offer more than they are likely to deliver. A 12% ten-year bond issued at par ($100) might be callable five years later at $100. At that time, if yields on similar five-year bonds were substantially less than 12%, the bond would probably be called. For example, if yields on similar five-year bonds were 8%, an investor who had planned to hold the original bond for ten years might end up with an 8% five-year bond with the proceeds obtained when the first bond was called. If the second bond were not subsequently called, the apparent and actual results would be as shown below. This suggests that the higher the yield-to-maturity of a callable bond, the greater is the likely divergence between actual and apparent yields.

This is borne out by experience. Figure 12-5 plots the coupon rate at time of issue (horizontal axis) and actual yield obtained up to the original maturity date by an investor (vertical axis), assuming that payments obtained in the event of a call were reinvested in noncallable bonds with appropriate maturities. The curve is based on experience for a group of callable bonds issued by utility companies from 1956 through 1964, a period of fluctuating interest rates.

The effect of a call provision on the price of a bond can best be analyzed by dividing the value into two components, since the value of a callable bond is equal to that of a noncallable bond minus the value of the option provided by the bondholder to the issuer for the latter to call the bond under stated terms and conditions.

Options are discussed at length in Chapter 16. At this point it suffices to indicate that a callable bond cannot be properly valued without an understanding of the valuation of options.

	COUPONS RECEIVED IN YEAR											
Investment		1	2	3	4	5	6	7	8	9	10	Principal Received in Year 10	Yield-to-Maturity
Apparent	$100	$12	$12	$12	$12	$12	$12	$12	$12	$12	$12	$100	12.0%
Actual	$100	12	12	12	12	12	8	8	8	8	8	100	10.5%

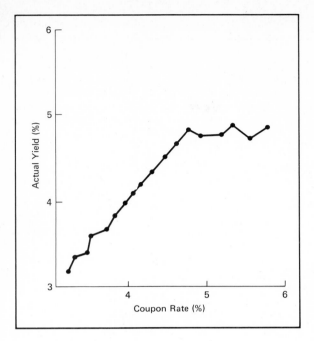

FIGURE 12-5 Promised and Actual Yields of Callable Aa Utility Bonds, 1956–1964

Source: Frank C. Jen and James E. Wert, "The Effect of Call Risk on Corporate Bond Yields," *The Journal of Finance,* XXII (December 1967), 646.

BOND RATINGS

In 1909 John Moody began to rate bonds; in 1979 Moody's Bond Record covered over 25,000 corporate and municipal issues, with ratings assigned to all those for which sufficient data were available. Standard and Poor's also provides bond ratings.

Figure 12-6 shows the ratings used by Moody's for both corporate and municipal bonds. Figure 12-7 shows the classifications used by Standard and Poor's.

Sometimes an additional symbol is used to provide gradations within a category. Standard and Poor's affixes a plus or minus to indicate a better- or worse-than-average bond in a category; and Moody's denotes the better municipal bonds in categories A and Baa as A1 and Baa1, respectively.

Regulations make it desirable and often necessary for banks to purchase "investment grade" bonds for their own accounts. A bond of this quality is considered to be a "marketable obligation in which the investment characteristics are not distinctly or predominantly speculative."[4] The Comptroller of the Currency, charged with regulating federally chartered commercial banks, generally regards any bond given a rating in one of the top four categories by Moody's or Standard and Poor's as qualifying under this provision.

[4] *Moody's Bond Record,* February 1976.

FIGURE 12-6 Moody's Bond Ratings

Aaa

Bonds which are rated **Aaa** are judged to be of the best quality. They carry the smallest degree of investment risk and are generally referred to as "gilt edge." Interest payments are protected by a large or by an exceptionally stable margin and principal is secure. While the various protective elements are likely to change, such changes as can be visualized are most unlikely to impair the fundamentally strong position of such issues.

Aa

Bonds which are rated **Aa** are judged to be of high quality by all standards. Together with the **Aaa** group they comprise what are generally known as high grade bonds. They are rated lower than the best bonds because margins of protection may not be as large as in **Aaa** securities or fluctuation of protective elements may be of greater amplitude or there may be other elements present which make the long term risks appear somewhat larger than in **Aaa** securities.

A

Bonds which are rated **A** possess many favorable investment attributes and are to be considered as upper medium grade obligations. Factors giving security to principal and interest are considered adequate but elements may be present which suggest a susceptibility to impairment sometime in the future.

Baa

Bonds which are rated **Baa** are considered as medium grade obligations, i.e., they are neither highly protected nor poorly secured. Interest payments and principal security appear adequate for the present but certain protective elements may be lacking or may be characteristically unreliable over any great length of time. Such bonds lack outstanding investment characteristics and in fact have speculative characteristics as well.

Ba

Bonds which are rated **Ba** are judged to have speculative elements; their future cannot be considered as well assured. Often the protection of interest and principal payments may be very moderate and thereby not well safeguarded during both good and bad times over the future. Uncertainty of position characterizes bonds in this class.

B

Bonds which are rated **B** generally lack characteristics of the desirable investment. Assurance of interest and principal payments or of maintenance of other terms of the contract over any long period of time may be small.

Caa

Bonds which are rated **Caa** are of poor standing. Such issues may be in default or there may be present elements of danger with respect to principal or interest.

Ca

Bonds which are rated **Ca** represent obligations which are speculative in a high degree. Such issues are often in default or have other marked shortcomings.

C

Bonds which are rated **C** are the lowest rated class of bonds and issues so rated can be regarded as having extremely poor prospects of ever attaining any real investment standing.

Source: *Moody's Industrial Manual, 1979.*

FIGURE 12-7 Standard and Poor's Bond Ratings

AAA

This is the highest rating assigned by Standard and Poor's to a debt obligation and indicates an extremely strong capacity to pay principal and interest.

AA

Bonds rated **AA** also qualify as high-quality debt obligations. Capacity to pay principal and interest is very strong, and in the majority of instances they differ from **AAA** issues only in small degree.

A

Bonds rated **A** have a strong capacity to pay principal and interest, although they are somewhat more susceptible to the adverse effects of changes in circumstances and economic conditions.

BBB

Bonds rated **BBB** are regarded as having an adequate capacity to pay principal and interest. Whereas they normally exhibit adequate protection parameters, adverse economic conditions or changing circumstances are more likely to lead to a weakened capacity to pay principal and interest for bonds in this category than for bonds in the **A** category.

BB B CCC CC

Bonds rated **BB, B, CCC** and **CC** are regarded, on balance, as predominantly speculative with respect to the issuer's capacity to pay interest and repay principal in accordance with the terms of the obligation. **BB** indicates the lowest degree of speculation and **CC** the highest degree of speculation. While such bonds will likely have some quality and protective characteristics, these are outweighed by large uncertainties or major risk exposures to adverse conditions.

C

The rating **C** is reserved for income bonds on which no interest is being paid.

D

Bonds rated **D** are in default, and payment of principal and/or interest is in arrears.

Source: *Standard and Poor's Bond Rating Definitions* (1977).

Investment grade bonds are sometimes thought to command "superpremium" prices, and hence disproportionately low yields, since an important group of buyers is encouraged or forced to purchase them. However, such a disparity in yields could attract a great many issuers who would increase the supply of such bonds, causing their prices to fall and their yields to rise. For a significant superpremium to persist, rather substantial market segmentation on both the buying and the selling side would be required. There is no clear evidence that the differences in yields between investment grade bonds and others are more than commensurate with the differences in risk.

According to Moody's, ratings are designed to provide "investors with a simple system of gradation by which the relative investment qualities of bonds may be noted."[5] Moreover:

> Since ratings involve a judgment about the future on the one hand, and since they are used by investors as a means of protection, on the other, the effort is made when assigning ratings to look at "worst" potentialities in the "visible" future rather than solely at the past record and the status of the present. Investors using the ratings should not, therefore, expect to find in them a reflection of statistical factors alone, since they are an appraisal of long-term risks including the recognition of many nonstatistical factors.[6]

Despite this disclaimer, the influence of "statistical factors" on the raters is apparently not insignificant. Several studies[7] have investigated the relationship between historical measures of a firm's performance and the ratings assigned its bonds. Many of the differences in the ratings accorded various bonds can in fact be attributed to differences in the issuer's situations, measured in traditional ways. For corporate bonds, better ratings are generally associated with: lower leverage (debt-to-total assets), smaller past variation in earnings over time, larger asset base (firm size), more profitable operations, and lack of subordination to other debt issues.

DEFAULT AND RISK PREMIUMS

Stocks make no promises; thus they are not subject to default. To assess the prospects for such securities, one might consider all possible outcomes, estimate the probability of each, and summarize the situation (among other ways) in terms of an expected holding-period-return, with each possible return weighted by its probability.

A similar procedure can be employed with bonds. Most commonly, the analysis focuses on yield-to-maturity. Formally, every possible value is considered, along with its probability, and a weighted average computed to determine an expected yield-to-maturity.[8] As long as there is any possibility of default or late payment, the expected value will fall below the promised (maximum) value. In general, the greater the risk of default and the greater the amount of loss in the event of default, the greater will be this disparity.

This is illustrated in Figure 12-8 for a hypothetical bond. Its promised yield-to-maturity is 12%, but, owing to a high default risk, the expected yield is only 9%. The difference (300 basis points) is the *default*

---

[5] *Moody's Industrial Manual*, 1979.

[6] *Ibid.*

[7] For examples, see: Thomas F. Pogue and Robert M. Soldofsky, "What's in a Bond Rating?" *Journal of Financial and Quantitative Analysis*, 4, no. 2 (June 1969), 201–28. George E. Pinches and Kent A. Mingo, "A Multivariate Analysis of Industrial Bond Ratings," *The Journal of Finance*, XXVII (March 1973), 1–18, and Robert S. Kaplan and Gabriel Urwitz, "Statistical Models of Bond Ratings: A Methodological Inquiry," *Journal of Business*, 52, no. 2 (1979).

[8] Chapter 4 showed that yield-to-maturity is subject to a number of criticisms; these hold, *a fortiori*, for values obtained by averaging many different yields-to-maturity. This discussion follows common practice in focusing on this measure despite its obvious flaws. Fortunately, the basic relationships described here apply rather generally.

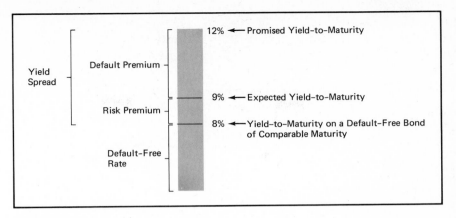

FIGURE 12-8 Yield-to-Maturity for a Risky Bond

premium: the difference between promised and expected return. Any bond that could default should offer such a premium, and it should be greater, the greater the risk of default.

As discussed in previous chapters, it is useful to compare the expected return of a security with the certain return on a default-free instrument. In an efficient market the difference will be related to the relevant risk of the security. For stocks the expected holding-period return over a period of a year or less is commonly compared with the yield of a Treasury bill of the appropriate maturity.

The traditional approach with bonds considers expected yield-to-maturity and contrasts it with that of a default-free bond of roughly comparable maturity. Any difference is the bond's *risk premium*.

In the case shown in Figure 12-8 default-free bonds of similar maturity offer a certain 8% yield-to-maturity, 1% (100 basis points) below the bond's expected 9% yield-to-maturity. The difference is the bond's risk premium.

The Default Premium

How large should a bond's promised yield-to-maturity be to allow for possible default? The answer depends, of course, on both the probability of default and the likely loss in the event of default.

Imagine a bond equally likely to default in every year (if it has not already defaulted), with the probability that it will default in any given year represented by p_d. Assume that if the bond does default, a payment equal to $(1 - \lambda)$ times its price a year earlier will be received. Pye[9] has shown that a bond of this type will be priced to promise a yield to maturity of:

$$y = \frac{r + \lambda p_d}{1 - p_d}$$

[9] Gordon Pye, "Gauging the Default Premium," *Financial Analysts Journal*, 30, no. 1 (Jan.–Feb. 1974), 49–52.

where:

y = promised yield to maturity

r = the bond's expected return each year while in a nondefault status

The difference between a bond's yield-to-maturity and its expected return can be used as a measure of its default premium:

$$d = y - r = \left(\frac{r + \lambda p_d}{1 - p_d}\right) - r$$

From 1920 to 1939, 2.3% of all outstanding medium-grade bonds defaulted per year on average, and the holder of a defaulted bond lost about half its par value.[10] If a bond with these characteristics is to have an expected return of, say, 9%, it must be priced so that:

$$d = \left(\frac{.09 + (.5 \times .023)}{1 - .023}\right) - .09 = .0139$$

Its default premium would thus be about 139 basis points.

The Risk Structure of Interest Rates

The greater a bond's risk of default, the greater its default premium. This alone will cause riskier bonds to offer higher promised yields-to-maturity. If risk premiums also increase with risk, the relationship will be even more pronounced. In any event, bonds given lower agency ratings should offer higher yields-to-maturity if such ratings really do indicate relative risk of default.

Figure 12-9 shows that this is indeed the case. Each of the curves plots the yield-to-maturity of a group of corporate bonds assigned the same rating by Moody's. Note that the scale is "upside down," so that higher yields plot at lower positions on the diagram. This procedure is often employed. For a previously issued bond, low yields correspond to high prices, and high yields to low prices. A fall in yields plots as an upward movement on the diagram, and a rise in yields as a downward movement. Since the value of a corresponding portfolio of previously purchased bonds will move in the same direction, such a diagram captures the feelings of anyone holding such bonds; falling yields are good news, and rising yields are bad news.

As Figure 12-9 shows, bonds are priced so that higher promised yields go with lower ratings. However, the spreads vary considerably over time.

This suggests that agency ratings do not indicate *absolute* levels of risk. It would be convenient if each classification were associated with a particular range of probabilities of default. As overall uncertainty about the economy increased, bonds could then be reclassified as necessary. If this were done, yield spreads among classes might change relatively little. However, rating agencies prefer to avoid wholesale changes. Instead, the

[10] *Ibid.*

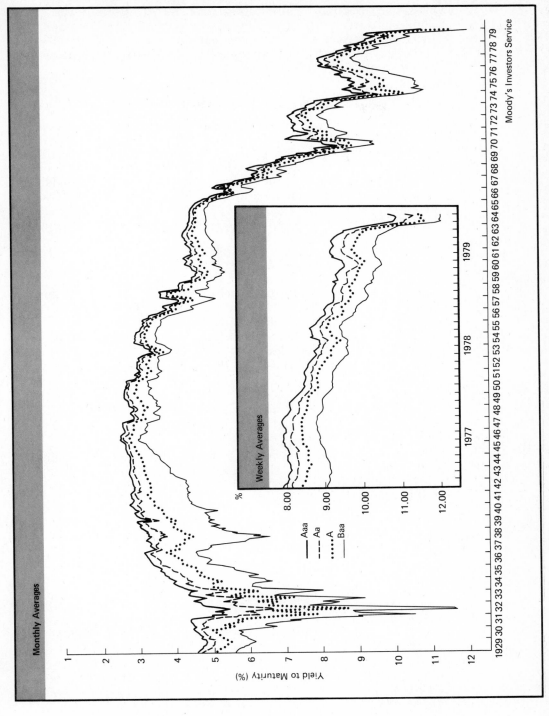

FIGURE 12-9 Corporate Bond Yields, by Ratings

Source: Moody's Bond Record, December 1979.

classes are used more to indicate *relative* risk. Overall increases in economic uncertainty result in only minor reclassifications and are manifested to a greater extent in increased yield spreads among classes of corporate bonds and an increased spread between corporate and government bond yields.

Determinants of Yield Spreads

The spread between a corporate bond's promised yield-to-maturity and that of a government bond of the same maturity and coupon rate is the sum of its default and risk premiums. The greater the risk of default, the greater should be this difference. Moreover, bonds that can be bought or sold more readily and/or more cheaply might command an additional "marketability" premium in price (and hence offer a lower yield-to-maturity). Given a large enough sample of bonds, and surrogate measures for risk and marketability, it should be possible to see if these relationships really do exist.

In a classic study of corporate bonds prices, Fisher[11] did just this. Three measures were used to assess the probability of default:

1. the extent to which the firm's net income had varied over the preceding nine years (measured by the coefficient of variation—the ratio of standard deviation of earnings to the average value)
2. the length of time that the firm had operated without forcing any of its creditors to take a loss
3. the ratio of the market value of the firm's equity to the par value of its debt.

The fourth measure provided an indication of marketability.[12]

4. the market value of the firm's outstanding debt

For each of 366 bond values, Fisher computed the yield spread and each of the four measures. He then took the logarithm of every value and used statistical analysis (multiple regression) to obtain the relationship that best fit all the data. It was:

$$\log (\text{yield spread}) = .987$$
$$+ .307 \log (\text{earnings variability})$$
$$- .253 \log (\text{time without default})$$
$$- .537 \log (\text{equity/debt ratio})$$
$$- .275 \log (\text{market value of debt})$$

This relationship accounted for roughly 75% of the variation in the bonds' yield spreads.

[11] Lawrence Fisher, "Determinants of Risk Premiums on Corporate Bonds," *Journal of Political Economy*, 67, no. 3 (June 1959), 217–37. © 1959 by the University of Chicago. All Rights Reserved.
[12] Although it may also have served as a proxy for other relevant variables.

The advantage of an equation such as this is that the coefficients may be easily interpreted. Since all values have been converted to logarithms, the effect is similar to that of using ratio scales on all axes of a diagram. Thus a 1% increase in earnings variability can be expected to bring about an increase of about $\frac{3}{10}$ of 1% in yield spread (.307%), other things equal. A 1% increase in the time without default can be expected to cause a decrease of approximately $\frac{1}{4}$ of 1% (.253%) in yield spread, etc. Each coefficient is an *elasticity*, indicating the percentage change in yield spread likely to accompany a 1% change in the associated value. Note that every factor operates in the expected direction, providing substantial support for the hypothesized relationships.

A subsequent study[13] showed that this relationship can be used to predict agency ratings with a reasonable degree of accuracy. This is not surprising. Agencies attempt to measure risk of default, and their estimates impact yield spreads. If historical measures provide information on the likelihood of future default, all three elements will be related.

Risk Premiums

Every bond that might default should offer a default premium. But the risk premium is another matter. A security's expected return should be related only to its contribution to portfolio risk; its total risk is not directly relevant. For example, if a group of companies all faced the possibility of bankruptcy, but from totally unrelated causes, a portfolio including all their bonds would provide a yield very close to its expected value. There would be little reason for this expected yield to differ significantly from that of a default-free bond, and the bonds should be priced to offer little or no premium for risk (but substantial premiums for default).

However, the risks associated with bonds are not unrelated. Figure 12-10 shows, for each year from 1900 to 1965, the ratio of the (par) value of bonds defaulting during the year to the (par) value outstanding at the

[13] R. R. West, "An Alternate Approach to Predicting Corporate Bond Ratings," *Journal of Accounting Research*, 8, no. 1 (Spring 1970), 118–25.

FIGURE 12-10 Default Rates 1900–1965

Source: Thomas R. Atkinson and Elizabeth T. Simpson, *Trends in Corporate Bond Quality*, (Columbia University Press, 1967).

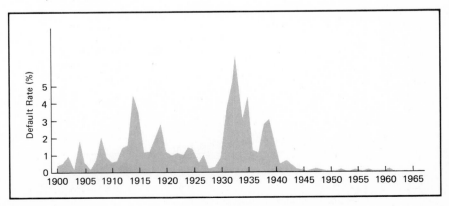

beginning of the year. Not surprisingly, the peaks coincide with periods of economic distress. When business is bad, most firms are affected. The value of a firm's equity will decline when a downturn is anticipated; if the likelihood of default on its debt also increases, the value of outstanding bonds will follow suit. Thus, the holding-period return on a bond may be correlated with the returns of other bonds and with those of stocks. Most important, a risky bond's holding-period return is likely to be correlated, to at least some extent, with the return on a widely diversified "market portfolio" (which includes both corporate bonds and stocks, in proportion to outstanding values). This part of the risk of a bond is nondiversifiable market risk and should command a risk premium in the form of greater expected return.

The riskier a bond is, the greater its likelihood of default and thus its potential sensitivity to market declines representing lowered assessments of prospects for the economy as a whole. This is illustrated in Table 12-3, which analyzes the performance of the three bond funds in the Keystone group over a ten-year period. All values are based on quarterly returns. As one might anticipate, the riskier bonds outperformed the more conservative ones on average, but quarter-to-quarter returns on the former were much more variable. To estimate sensitivity to changes in stock prices the returns were compared with those of Standard and Poor's 500-stock index. The beta values indicate the sensitivity of each fund to stock market swings; all are significantly different from zero and indicate that riskier bonds also move more with stocks and thus should have higher returns on average. The final row in the table shows the proportion of the quarter-to-quarter variation in returns associated with stock market swings; as indicated, relatively more of a risky bond portfolio's total risk is

TABLE 12-3 Risk and Return, Keystone Bond Funds 1966–1975

Item	B-1	B-2	B-4
Average quarterly return (% per quarter)	.80	.97	1.52
Standard deviation of quarterly return (% per quarter)	2.57	3.49	5.62
Beta value, relative to S&P 500-stock index	.17	.28	.50
Proportion of variance explained by S&P index	.37	.56	.67

Descriptions of funds:*

B-1 is Keystone's Investment Bond Fund. Assets are invested in 30 to 65 highly marketable issues limited to obligations of the U.S. government or its agencies and to other bond issues of high or good grade. Objective is relative price stability with liberal yield.

B-2 is Keystone's Medium-Grade Bond Fund. Primary objective is to obtain the maximum income possible without undue risk of principal. Assets are invested in bonds normally characterized by relatively liberal returns and moderate price fluctuations.

B-4 is Keystone's Discount Bond Fund and the largest of the Bond Funds under its management. The portfolio includes 50 to 150 issues selected for generous income return. The fund may invest in domestic foreign and restricted securities. Investments generally include a substantial representation of bonds selling at discounts from par value. This class of bond is subject to a relatively wide range in price fluctuations and income payments with changes in business conditions.

* Source: Wiesenberger Financial Services, *Investment Companies, 1970.*

associated with the stock market than is the case with a less risky bond. For conservative bonds, interest-rate risk is by far the more important factor, and even their relatively small correlation with stock returns may be due to the impact of interest rates on both bonds and stocks.

While the sensitivity of a bond to short-term stock market swings should have a major influence on its risk premium, it may not be the only relevant factor. A better-than-average return on a stock is typically as likely to be followed by another better-than-average return as is a worse-than-average return. Stock returns exhibit almost no *serial correlation*: the particular value of return in the last period provides little if any help in predicting the likelihood of various possible returns in the next period.

Not so with bonds. An obvious case arises when a default-free bond has two years remaining before maturity. Consider a 10% bond currently priced at 100. If its price rises to 102, it will return 12% this year. But it will then return about 8% next year $[(100 + 10 - 102)/102 = .0784]$. Conversely, a return of 8% this year, via a price decline to 98, will be followed by a return of about 12% next year $[(100 + 10 - 98)/98 = .1224]$. Bond returns thus tend to be *negatively serially correlated*: above-average returns are more likely to be followed by below-average returns, and conversely.

An investment adviser might tell a bondholder, "There is good news and bad news: the good news is that you can now get more on your money (interest rates have risen), the bad news is that your portfolio is worth less as a result." There is thus a relationship between bond returns and future investment opportunities—a relationship that may be absent for stocks. However, the relationship is concerned more with *nominal* than with *real* returns. When interest rates rise solely to offset increases in expected inflation, *real* investment opportunities are no better than before (and there is no good news after all). Real returns on bonds need not be serially correlated. Since investors are presumably more concerned with real than with nominal returns, the negative serial correlation of nominal returns may thus be of little if any relevance in their valuation.

BONDS VERSUS STOCKS

Figure 12-11(a) compares corporate bonds and stocks, based on an analysis of quarterly excess returns (i.e., holding-period return minus that of a default-free 90-day instrument) from 1938 through 1971. Both the average excess return (vertical axis) and the standard deviation of excess returns (horizontal axis) are shown. Point S plots the results obtained via stocks (represented by the Dow Jones Industrial Average) and point B those obtained with medium-grade bonds (represented by Keystone's B-2 fund). The results that could have been obtained by investing solely in Treasury bills plot at the origin, since such a strategy would always provide an excess return of zero. The line connecting a point with the origin indicates combinations of average excess return and variability (standard deviation) of excess return that could have been obtained by combining the risky investment in question with Treasury bills or via leverage at the Treasury bill rate.

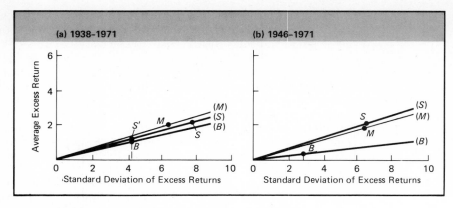

FIGURE 12-11 Reward and Variability of Bonds and Stocks

Source: William F. Sharpe, "Bonds versus Stocks: Some Lessons from Capital Market Theory," *Financial Analysts Journal*, 29, no. 6 November–December, 1973), 78.

One risky investment can be said to have been better than another if the line through its point was higher. On this basis, stocks can be said to have outperformed bonds over the 1938–1971 period. Putting it somewhat differently, the combination of stocks and default-free short-term instruments represented by point S′ would have provided more excess return on average, with the same variability as an all-bond portfolio.

But this does not rule out bonds as candidates for a diversified portfolio. In an efficient market, combining all capital assets in proportion to outstanding value should be worthwhile. Point M in Figure 12-11(a) represents such a strategy. As shown, it outperformed both bonds and stocks

FIGURE 12-12 Ten-Year Returns: Government Bonds and Corporate Stocks, 1926–1978

Source: Roger G. Ibbotson and Rex A. Singuefield, "Stocks, Bonds, Bills and Inflation: Historical Returns (1926–1978)," Financial Analysts Research Foundation, 1979.

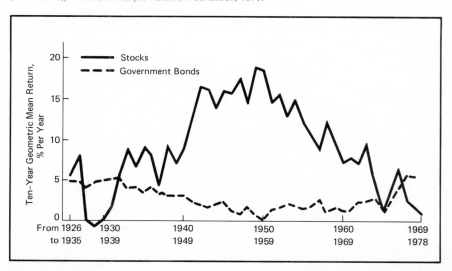

during the period. Combinations of this portfolio with short-term instruments would have plotted along line (M), which is preferable to lines (B) and (S), which show the results that would have been obtained by combining short-term instruments with bonds and stocks, respectively.

This analysis shows that bonds may well have been priced, like stocks, in accordance with their market risks. However, a closer look at the relationships in the post-World War II period raises some doubts. Figure 12-11(b) shows the results obtained using data for the 1946–1971 period only. Again stocks outperformed bonds, but they also outperformed the market combination of stocks and bonds.

Figure 12-12 shows that the dominance of stocks over bonds extended over a relatively long time. Every ten-year period from 1926 through 1978 was analyzed and the (geometric) mean return obtained for stocks (represented by Standard and Poor's 500-stock index) and long-term government bonds. The former outperformed the latter in most ten-year periods. This led some to argue in the early 1970s that no long-term investor should hold bonds. The subsequent behavior of the markets tended to quiet such critics, at least temporarily.

Are bonds bad investments? It seems unlikely. They may be priced for their long-term attributes and hence can be expected to appear inferior when short-term holding-period returns are considered. Perhaps more important, they may be priced to reflect their relative resistance to deep recessions and depressions and thus pale in comparison to stocks over any period, no matter how long, in which such events do not occur.

PROMISED VERSUS REALIZED YIELDS

What sort of experience might the long-run bond investor anticipate? And how is it likely to be related to the risk of the bonds held?

In a massive study of all large bond issues and a sample of small bond issues, Hickman attempted to answer this question. He analyzed investor experience for each bond from 1900 through 1943 to determine the actual yield to the date on which the bond matured, defaulted, or was called—whichever came first. He then compared this with the promised yield-to-maturity based on the price at time of issue. Every bond was also classified according to the ratings assigned at time of issue. Table 12-4(a) shows the major results.

As one would expect, riskier bonds promised higher yields at time of issue. Moreover, a higher percentage of such bonds defaulted, in whole or in part, before maturity.

What about actual yield-to-maturity? As the table shows, in four out of five classifications it exceeded the promised amount, on average. Why? Because during the period studied, a substantial drop in interest rates made it attractive for issuers to call old bonds at premiums.

To see what might have happened had this not been the case, Fraine and Mills reanalyzed the data for large investment-grade issues. Their results are shown in Table 12-4(b). The initial columns differ from those of Table 12-4(a) only because smaller issues are excluded. The major difference appears in the final column. It was obtained by substi-

TABLE 12-4 Actual and Realized Bond Yields-to-Maturity, 1900–1943

(a) ALL LARGE AND A SAMPLE OF SMALL ISSUES

Composite Rating	Comparable Moody's Rating	Promised Yield-to-Maturity at Issue (%)	Percent Defaulting Prior to Maturity	Actual-Yield-to-Maturity (%)
I	Aaa	4.5	5.9	5.1
II	Aa	4.6	6.0	5.0
III	A	4.9	13.4	5.0
IV	Baa	5.4	19.1	5.7
V–IX	below Baa	9.5	42.4	8.6

(b) ALL LARGE ISSUES

Composite Rating	Comparable Moody's Rating	Promised Yield-to-Maturity (%)	Actual Yield-to-Maturity (%)	Modified Actual Yield-to-Maturity (%)
I	Aaa	4.5	5.1	4.3
II	Aa	4.5	5.1	4.3
III	A	4.9	5.0	4.3
IV	Baa	5.4	5.8	4.5

Source: (a) W. Braddock Hickman, *Corporate Bond Quality and Investor Experience* (Princeton, N.J.: Princeton University Press, 1958). (b) Harold G. Fraine and Robert H. Mills, "The Effect of Defaults and Credit Deterioration on Yields of Corporate Bonds," *The Journal of Finance*, XVI, no. 3 (September 1961), 433.

tuting promised yield for realized yield whenever the latter was larger, thus removing the effects of most calls.

Both sets of results suggest that within the highest grades there was little if any difference in realized returns. Such bonds are all quite low in market risk and thus should carry similar (and small) risk premiums. Medium-grade (Baa) bonds performed somewhat better, which is consistent with a premium for their somewhat larger market risk. Low grade bonds seem to have done even better on average, which is not surprising, given their substantial sensitivity to changes in anticipations about the economic climate.

FINANCIAL RATIOS AS PREDICTORS OF DEFAULT

For years analysts have used ratios of accounting values to indicate the probability that a firm will fail to meet its financial obligations. Cash inflows and outflows are seen as variable contributions to and drains from the firm's cash balance. When the balance falls to zero, default is likely to occur. The smaller the balance, the smaller the average net cash inflow before payments to creditors and stockholders, and the more variable the cash flows, the greater the probability of default.

In an examination of various measures used to assess these factors, Beaver found that the ratio of cash flow (income before depreciation, depletion, and amortization charges) to total debt was particularly useful. Figure 12-13(a) shows the mean value of this ratio for a group of firms that defaulted on a scheduled payment and for a companion group that did not. As early as five years before default the two groups' ratios diverged, and the spread widened as the year of default approached.

This suggests that the probability of default may not be constant through time. Instead, warning signals may indicate an increase in the probability, which will in turn cause a fall in the price of the firm's bonds (and hence a rise in their promised yield-to-maturity) along with a fall in the price of its stock. Figure 12-13(b) shows that such signals are recognized by the market. The median value of stock in the firms that did not

FIGURE 12-13 Financial Ratios and Market Prices for Firms that Defaulted and Those that Did Not

* Source: William H. Beaver, "Financial Ratios as Predictors of Failure," *Empirical Research in Accounting, Selected Studies,* The Institute of Professional Accounting, Graduate School of Business, University of Chicago (1966), pp. 71–127.

†Source: Based on median values of annual returns in William H. Beaver, "Market Prices, Financial Ratios and the Prediction of Failure," *Journal of Accounting Research,* 6, no. 2 (Autumn 1968), 179–92.

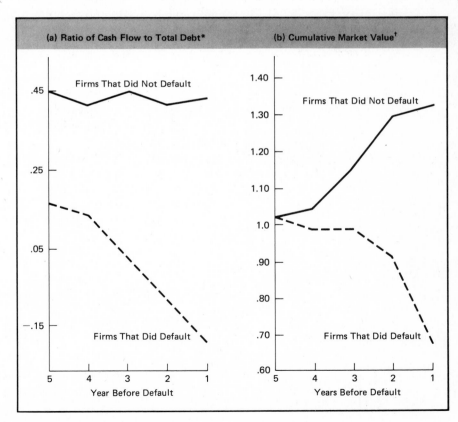

default went up, while that of the other firms went down as the date of default approached.

Does this mean that securities of firms whose cash-flow-to-total debt ratio has fallen should be avoided, since further declines in the ratio, and hence market prices, can be anticipated? Hardly. The firms represented by the dashed lines in Figures 12-13 were chosen because they did eventually default. Had all firms with declining ratios been selected, recent decreases in price would undoubtedly have been observed, reflecting the increased probability of future default. But only some of them would have continued down to disaster while the others recovered, and the gains on the latter might well have offset the losses on the former.

HORIZON ANALYSIS

It may or may not be possible to identify transitory shifts in yield structures. In any event, the analyst who believes he or she has found an anomaly of this sort will want to translate belief into action.

To fully analyze the impacts of future yields on alternative bond portfolios is an almost impossible task. First, all possible future yield structures would have to be identified and the likelihood of each combination assessed. Then the optimal initial portfolio and every appropriate revi-

FIGURE 12-14 The Effect of Time and Yield Change on a 4% Coupon Bond

Source: Martin L. Leibowitz, "Horizon Analysis for Managed Bond Portfolios," *Journal of Portfolio Management*, 1, no. 3 (Spring 1975), 26.

| Yield to Maturity (%) | YEARS TO MATURITY | | | | | | |
	10 Yrs	9 Yrs	...	5 Yrs	...	1 Yrs	0 Yrs
7.00	78.68	80.22		87.53		97.15	100.00
7.50	75.68	77.39		85.63		96.69	100.00
y_H (8.00)	72.82	74.68		(83.78) P_H		96.23	100.00
8.50	70.09	72.09		81.98		95.77	100.00
y_0 (9.00) P_0	(67.48)	69.60		(80.22) P_A		95.32	100.00
9.50	64.99	67.22		78.51		94.87	100.00
10.00	62.61	64.92	...	76.83	...	94.42	100.00
10.50	60.34	62.74		75.21		93.98	100.00
11.00	58.17	60.64		73.62		93.54	100.00

Actual Price Pattern Over Time

Yield Change Effect

Time Effect

sion to it would have to be determined. Even with an unlimited computer budget this would be a formidable task indeed. In practice, much simpler approaches are taken. *Horizon analysis*, advocated by Martin L. Leibowitz of Salomon Brothers, provides a good example. A single holding period is selected for analysis and possible yield structures at the end of the period (i.e., at the "horizon") considered. The possible returns for two bonds—one currently held and one candidate to replace it—are then analyzed. Both are assumed to be free of default risk up to the horizon date. In the process of the analysis, the sensitivities of the returns to changes in key assumptions regarding yields are estimated, allowing at least a rough assessment of some of the relevant risks.

Figure 12-14 represents a page from a standard yield book for bonds with a 4% coupon. As indicated, a 4% bond with ten years remaining to maturity priced at $67.48 has a 9% yield-to-maturity. In the future, such a bond's time-to-maturity will decrease and the relevant yield-to-maturity will also probably change. The bond might thus follow a path through the table such as that shown by the dashed line. If so, it would end up at a price of $83.78 at the *horizon* (five years hence) with an 8% yield-to-maturity.

Over any holding period a bond's return will typically be affected by both the passage of time and a change in yields. Horizon analysis breaks this into two parts: one due solely to the passage of time, with no change in yields; the other due solely to a change in yield, with no passage of time. This is illustrated in Figure 12-14. The total change from $67.48 to $83.78 is broken into a change from $67.48 to $80.22, followed by an instantaneous change from $80.22 to $83.78. The intermediate value is the price the bond would command at the horizon if its yield-to-maturity had remained unchanged at its initial level. The actual price is that which it commands at its actual yield-to-maturity.

The total price change can be broken into two parts, representing the two effects:

$$\text{price change} = \text{yield change effect} + \text{time effect}$$

Thus far no account has been taken of the coupon payments to be received before the horizon date. In principle one should consider all possible uses of such flows or at least analyze possible alternative yield patterns during the period to determine likely reinvestment opportunities. In practice, this is rarely done. Instead a single reinvestment rate is assumed and the future value of all coupon payments at the horizon date determined by compounding each one forward using this rate. This takes care of both interest (coupons) and "interest on interest"—i.e., interest received by investing coupon payments. For example, if $2 is received each six months for five years and every payment is reinvested at 4.25% per six months, the value at the end of five years will be approximately $25.32. Of this amount, $20 can be considered interest (coupon payments) and $5.32 "interest on interest."

For relatively short horizons this treatment of coupon payments may be acceptable. But for longer horizons the importance of interest on interest is likely to be greater than that of any changes in capital value, and alternative possible future reinvestment rates may have to be considered. There are thus two components: the total amount of coupons and the interest on interest, with only the former completely predictable in advance.

A bond's overall return can thus be broken into four components. In the example:

$$= \left(\frac{83.78 - 80.22}{67.48}\right) + \left(\frac{80.22 - 67.48}{67.48}\right) + \left(\frac{20.00}{67.48}\right) + \left(\frac{5.32}{67.48}\right)$$

$$= .0528 + .1888 + .2964 + .0788$$

The first term is the (uncertain) return due to yield change, the second the (assumed certain) return due to the passage of time, the third the (certain) coupon return, and the fourth the (uncertain) return due to interest on interest.

Since the first term is uncertain, it is important to analyze it further.

FIGURE 12-15 The Structure of a Bond's Yields at the Start and the End of a Workout Period

Source: Martin L. Leibowitz, "An Analytic Approach to the Bond Market," *Financial Analysts's Handbook* (Homewood, Ill.: Dow Jones-Irwin, Inc., 1975), p. 262.

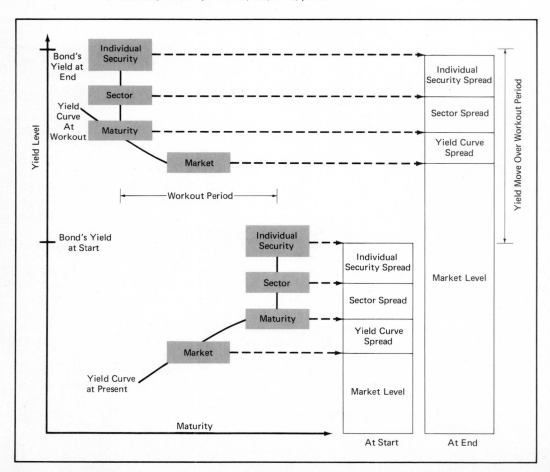

Moreover, as Leibowitz points out, it is helpful to relate the market yield movements that a bond manager *follows* to the resulting price changes that he or she *feels*.

In the example, a change in yield from 9.0% to 8.0% at the horizon will change price from $80.22 to $83.78. By substituting an expected value for the yield at the horizon, one can compute an expected holding-period return. By using different values with their probabilities, one can estimate the probabilities of different values of the holding-period return and thus the bond's risk.

Bond analysts devote a great deal of attention to predictions of future yields. This is often done by considering a *hierarchy* of yields. Figure 12-15 provides an example. A bond's yield at any time is assumed to be related to that of a *sector* of the bond market, the average yield for which is related to that of all bonds of like *maturity*, the average yields of which are related, via the term structure, to that of all bonds in the *market*. At the horizon, or "workout period," any or all of the relationships can change, and of course the bond will have moved leftward on the maturity axis. The total yield move may thus be decomposed into the changes due to the various components, each of which may be estimated separately.

BOND SWAPS

Given a set of predictions about future bond yields, one can estimate holding-period returns over one or more horizons (workout periods) for one or more bonds. The goal of *bond swapping* is to actively manage a portfolio, switching bonds to take advantage of any superior ability to predict such yields.

Bond swaps are made for many reasons. Four idealized categories have been described by Homer and Leibowitz:[14]

> The *Substitution Swap* is ideally an exchange of a bond for a perfect substitute or "twin" bond. The motivation here is a temporary price advantage, presumably resulting from a momentary imbalance in the relative supply/demand conditions in the marketplace.
>
> The *Intermarket Spread Swap* is a more general movement out of one market component and into another with the intention of exploiting a currently advantageous yield relationship. The idea here is to trade off of these changing relationships between the two market components. Short-term Workout Periods are usually anticipated. While such swaps will almost always have some sensitivity to the direction of the overall market, the idealized focus of this type of swap is the spread relationship itself.
>
> On the other hand, the *Rate Anticipation Swap* is frankly geared towards profiting from an anticipated movement in overall market rates.
>
> The *Pure Yield Pickup Swap* is oriented toward yield improvement over the long term with little heed being paid to interim price movements in either the respective market components or the market as a whole.

[14] Martin L. Leibowitz, "Horizon Analysis for Managed Bond Portfolios," *Journal of Portfolio Management* 1, no. 3 (Spring 1975), 32, 33.

More complicated approaches, using linear programming, consider the possibility of swapping one set of bonds for another set to take advantage of any tax effects or any transitory market inefficiencies.[15] Such approaches can improve the process of *bond arbitrage* and thus the overall efficiency of the bond market.

[15] See, for example, S. D. Hodges and S. M. Schaefer, "A Model for Bond Portfolio Improvement," *Journal of Financial and Quantitative Analysis* (forthcoming). Schaefer has also shown that as a by-product of such a formulation one can obtain estimates of the current term structure of forward interest rates.

Problems

1. Why may it be inappropriate to mix yields of "flower bonds" with those of other Treasury bonds when plotting yield curves?

2. Empirical evidence indicates that the cash-flow-to-total-debt ratio is, to some extent, a valid indicator of the probability that a bond issuer will default. Does this evidence, therefore, lead to the contention that a trading mechanism exists for obtaining a yield greater than that justified by the commensurate risk?

3. Would an observed, downward-sloping yield curve be inconsistent with the notion of liquidity preference?

4. Would you expect the yield-to-maturity of a fully callable bond to be higher than that of a bond with a deferred call provision?

5. Assume that the current structure of forward interest rates is upward sloping (going from left to right). Which will have a lower yield-to-maturity:

   a. A fifteen-year zero-coupon bond or a ten-year zero-coupon bond?

   b. A ten-year 5% coupon bond or a ten-year 6% coupon bond?

6. What would be your answers to Problem 5 if the forward interest-rate structure had been downward-sloping (going from left to right)?

7. Assume the currently available one-year rate is 6% per year, and the forward one-year rates for one year hence and two years hence, are, respectively:

$$r_{12} = 7\%, \qquad r_{23} = 8\%$$

What would be the current price of a $1,000, 6% coupon bond redeemable at the end of three years? The first interest payment is one year from today.

8. Assume that the spread between the yield-to-maturity on BBB bonds and that on AAA bonds has recently widened considerably. What might this indicate?

9. Assume that you are advising an investor whose tax bracket makes holding municipal bonds attractive. What would you say about a corporate bond selling at a substantial discount from par value? A corporate bond selling at a premium (i.e., at a price above par value)?

10. The government of a nearby country has issued three bonds that pay in dollars. The first, which pays $1,000 in one year, is now selling for $909.09. The second, which pays $100 at the end of this year and $1,100 at the end of next year, is selling for $991.81. The third, which pays $100 at the end of this year, $100 at the end of next year, and $1,100 at the end of the following year, is selling for $977.18.

    a. What are the current discount factors for money one, two, and three years hence?

    b. What are the forward interest rates?

    c. A friend offers to pay you $500 at the end of this year, $600 at the end of next year, and $700 at the end of the following year if you loan him some money today. How much should you loan him?

11. You estimate that a company has a probability of .10 of defaulting on its bonds each year and that, if default occurs, bondholders will receive an amount equivalent to half the value of the bonds in the prior year. You believe that the bonds, if fairly priced, should offer an expected return of 10%. What yield-to-maturity would you consider appropriate?

Common Stocks

13

CHARACTERISTICS OF COMMON STOCK

Common stocks are easier to describe than fixed-income securities, but they are harder to analyze. Fixed-income securities almost always have a limited life and an upper limit on cash payments. Common stocks have neither. Although the basic principles of valuation apply to both, the role of uncertainty is larger for common stocks, so much so that it often dominates all other elements in their valuation.

Common stock represents *equity*, or an *ownership* position in a corporation. It is a *residual* claim, in the sense that creditors and preferred stockholders must be paid as scheduled before common stockholders can receive any payments. In bankruptcy, equity holders are in principle entitled only to any value remaining after all prior claimants have been satisfied (although in practice courts sometimes violate this principle).

The great advantage of the corporate form of organization is the *limited liability* of its owners. Common stock is generally "full-paid and nonassessable." Stockholders may lose their investment, but no more. They are not further liable for any failure on the part of the corporation to meet its obligations. This limits the ability of the corporation to obtain credit at low rates of interest, of course. But it makes possible the impersonality of corporate ownership and the simple transfer of the certificates representing that ownership.

The Charter

A corporation exists only when it has been granted a *charter* or *certificate of incorporation* by a state. This document specifies the rights and obligations of stockholders. It may be amended, with the approval of some specified proportion of the stock (in some states a majority, in others two-thirds, etc.). Both the initial terms and the terms of any amendment must be approved by the state in which the corporation is chartered. Because it is particularly hospitable in this respect and in levying corporate taxes, Delaware has captured a disproportionate share of corporate charters.

Stock Certificates

In the United States an investor's holding of a firm's stock is typically represented by a single certificate, with the number of shares filled in. Such a stock certificate will be registered, with the name and the holdings of the investor included on the corporation's books. Payments, voting material, reports, etc. are mailed directly, taking into account the size of the investor's holdings.

Stock holdings may be transferred to a new owner in whole or in part via endorsement and presentation to either the issuing corporation or (more commonly) its designated *transfer agent* and/or *registrar* — usually a bank or trust company. These rather cumbersome procedures are slowly being obviated via clearing arrangements that substitute computerized records for embossed certificates.

Voting

Since the holder of common stock is an owner of the corporation, he or she is entitled to vote for its directors and to vote on matters brought before the annual meeting. Any owner may attend and vote in person, but most choose instead to vote by *proxy*. Typically, the incumbent directors solicit every stockholder. The recipient is asked to sign a "proxy statement," which is a power of attorney authorizing the designated party to cast all the investor's votes on any matter brought before the meeting. Occasionally, desired positions on specific issues may be solicited on the proxy statement. Most votes are perfunctory. The majority of votes is held by the incumbent management via proxy statements, and there is little if any controversy or excitement.

Once in a while, however, a *proxy fight* develops. Insurgents or aggressors from outside the corporation solicit proxies to vote against current management, often in order to effect a merger of some sort. Stockholders are deluged with literature and appeals. The incumbents usually win, but the possibility of a loss in such a skirmish tends to curb activities clearly not in the stockholders' interests.

In the United States the number of votes given an investor equals the number of shares held. Each director is typically elected by a simple majority of all votes cast. Thus a majority of shares voting can elect an entire board. This is the ordinary or *statutory* voting procedure.

Some corporations use *cumulative* voting, in which the number of votes given an investor equals the number of shares held times the number of directors to be elected, and directors are appointed in order of total votes received. With this procedure, votes may be allocated to candidates in any manner desired. Thus investors holding less than 50% of a corporation's shares can, by concentrating their votes, elect some members to the board.

Tender Offers

Periodically, a firm or wealthy individual, convinced that the management of a corporation is not exploiting its opportunities, will attempt a *takeover*. First, a substantial number of shares must be acquired. This is usually attempted via a *tender offer*. Advertisements are placed in the financial press and/or material mailed to the stockholders. The raiding party offers to buy, at a stated price, some or all shares tendered by present stockholders. The offer is usually contingent on the tender of a minimum number of shares by a fixed date and may include other restrictions as well. When the offer is first made, the tender price is generally set considerably above the current market price, although the offer itself usually leads to a subsequent price increase.

Attempted takeovers provide spice in a stockholder's otherwise routine relationship with a corporation. Management usually counters with advertisements, mailings, etc. Takeovers often fail, but every now and then one succeeds.

Occasionally a corporation will issue a tender offer to buy back some of its own stock. Such an offer may provide a signal that the corporation considers its shares underpriced; if so, the stock price is likely to rise. However, if the corporation has simply chosen to pay out cash in the form of capital gains rather than dividends, no increase in price may result.

Ownership versus Control

Much has been written about the effects of the separation of ownership and control of the modern corporation. While it is true that over a wide range, incumbent management can exercise its discretion with little if any effective control from its nominal owners, the potential of a proxy fight or tender offer takeover provides at least some check on excesses. Moreover, management typically owns stock in the corporation and thus has strong incentives to increase the value of the stock whenever possible.

To align the interests of management and stockholders, many corporations offer *stock options* to officers of the firm. A specified number of shares may be purchased at a stated price (often below the market price). However, as the corporation's shares become more and more important in a manager's portfolio, adding to his or her already large investment of human capital in the firm, a new problem emerges. The manager's holdings may be more concentrated than those of many of the corporation's other owners. While the latter are concerned primarily or exclusively with *nondiversifiable* risk, the manager may also worry about *diversifiable* risks, resulting in a divergence of interests when, for example, a new project is considered. The most appropriate level of ownership for a corporation's managers thus requires a balance between *incentive* and *concentration* effects.

Par Value

When a corporation is first chartered, it is *authorized* to issue up to a stated number of shares of common stock, each of which will often carry a specified *par value*. Historically, this was considered the amount of capital invested by owners for the protection of creditors. Legally, a corporation may be precluded from making payments to common stockholders if doing so would reduce the stated value of the equity below the amount represented by the par value of outstanding stock. For this reason the stated par value is typically low relative to the price for which the stock is initially sold. A par value of $1 is now used frequently. Some corporations issue *no-par* stock, but state and local taxes tend to make *low-par* issues more advantageous.

As long as stock is initially sold by the corporation for more than its par value, it is "full-paid and nonassessable." Otherwise, the stock could be considered "watered" (a reference to early fraudulent sales of Florida land, much of which was under water), and stockholders might be liable for the difference between the par value and the amount paid for the stock.

When stock is sold for more than its par value, the difference is usually carried separately on the corporation's books. For example, Hewlett-Packard's 1978 annual report showed:

	Value ($ Millions)
Shareholder's equity:	
Common stock, par value $1 a share: issued and outstanding, 29,010,000 shares	29
Capital in excess of par value	247

Book Value

As a corporation's life proceeds, it generates income, much of which is paid out to creditors (for interest and principal) and stockholders (as dividends). Any remainder is added to the amount shown as cumulative *retained earnings* on the corporation's books. For example, Hewlett-Packard's 1978 balance sheet showed:

	Value ($ Millions)
Common stock, issued and outstanding	29
Capital in excess of par value	247
Retained earnings	726
Total shareholders' equity	1,002

The sum is the *book value* of the equity. The *book value per share* is obtained by dividing this figure by the number of shares outstanding. In this case:

$$\frac{\$1,002,000,000}{29,010,000} = \$34.54 \text{ per share}$$

Reserved and Treasury Stock

Typically a corporation will issue only part of its authorized stock. Some of the remainder may be specifically *reserved* for outstanding options, convertible securities, etc. For example, Hewlett-Packard's situation in 1978 was as follows:

Authorized:	40,000,000 shares
Reserved for:	
Stock option plans	612,000
Stock purchase plans	478,000
Service award plan	92,000
Issued and outstanding	29,010,000

When a corporation buys its own stock, either in the open market or via a tender offer, the stock may be "held in the treasury." It is not entitled to vote or receive dividends and is equivalent economically (though not legally) to unissued stock.

If a corporation wishes to issue new stock in excess of its original authorization, the charter must be amended, requiring approval by both the state and a given proportion of the voting stock.

Classified Stock

Some corporations issue two or more classes of common stock. For example, Class A stock might have a preferred position vis-à-vis dividends, but no voting rights, and Class B a lower claim on dividends but full voting rights. Often this is equivalent to an issue of preferred stock with no maturity date, along with a "normal" type of common.

Letter or Restricted Stock

In the United States, securities regulation requires that most stock be *registered* before it may be sold in a public offering. Under some conditions *unregistered* stock may be sold directly to a purchaser, but its subsequent sale is *restricted*, usually by a letter from the buyer stating that the stock is to be held as an investment. Such *letter stock* must be held at least two years and cannot be sold even then unless ample information on the company is available and the amount sold is a relatively small percentage of the total amount outstanding.

Dividends

Payments to stockholders made in cash are termed *dividends*. These are typically declared quarterly and paid to *stockholders of record* at a specified date. Since transfer of ownership requires some time, major stock exchanges specify an *ex-dividend date* several days prior to the date of record. Shares purchased before an ex-dividend date are entitled to receive the dividend in question. Those purchased afterward do not receive it.

A corporation's board of directors may declare a dividend of almost any amount or none at all, subject only to restrictions contained in the charter, bond indentures, state laws, and so on. Dividends may even exceed earnings, although the reverse is more common.

Stock Dividends and Stock Splits

Occasionally a corporation's management decides to forego a cash dividend but "pay" a *stock dividend* instead. For example, if a 5% stock dividend is declared, the owner of 500 shares receives 25 additional shares, issued for the occasion. Par value is not changed, but since more shares are outstanding, the stated value of common stock on the corporation's balance sheet will increase; to keep the total book value of equity the same, the surplus account is simply decreased by a corresponding amount.

A *stock split* is similar but differs in both magnitude and accounting treatment. In this case par value is adjusted appropriately and the surplus account left unchanged. For example, if a $1-par stock is split "2-for-1," the holder of 500 old shares will receive 1,000 new $.50-par shares.

A *reverse split* reduces the number of shares and increases the par value per share. For example, in a reverse 2-for-1 split, the holder of 500 $1-par shares would exchange them for 250 $2-par shares.

Stock dividends and splits must be taken into account when following the fortunes of a company's shares. For example, a fall in price per share may be due solely to a large stock dividend. To reduce confusion, most financial services provide data *adjusted* for at least some of these changes. Thus, if a stock split 2-for-1 on January 30, 1980, prices prior to that date might be divided by two to facilitate comparison.

Why do corporations issue stock dividends and split their stocks? Nothing of importance is changed, only the size of the units in which ownership may be bought and sold. Moreover, the process involves administrative effort and cost.

It is sometimes argued that shareholders respond positively to "tangible" evidence of the growth of their corporation. Another view holds that splits and stock dividends, by decreasing the price per share, may bring a stock into a more desirable trading range and hence increase the total value of the amount outstanding.

Figure 13-1 summarizes the results of 219 stock splits (including some cases involving stock dividends of 25% or more) that occurred between 1945 and 1965. For each case the stock's "normal" performance was determined by relating monthly returns to the returns on the overall stock market and "abnormal" performance, then computed for the 54 months prior to the split and the 54 months following it. These values were averaged across the cases and then cumulated.

As the figure shows, prior to splitting, the stocks tended to increase in value relative to normal market moves by a substantial amount (about 30% in 54 months). Was this due to anticipation of the coming split? Not necessarily. The causal relationship could well be just the reverse: stocks split after unusual price increases; unexpected positive developments increased the value of these firms, then management decided to split the stock. The behavior of (adjusted) postsplit prices indicates that after the split, investors did not continue to gain. In the study shown in Figure 13-1 they actually lost some ground. Other studies, using different stocks and

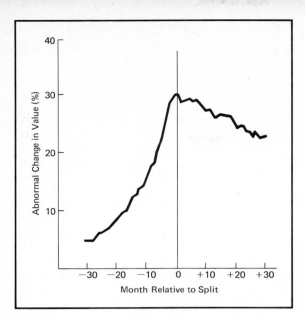

FIGURE 13-1 Abnormal Changes in Value Before and After Stock Splits.

Source: Sasson Bar-Yosef and Lawrence D. Brown, "A Re-examination of Stock Splits Using Moving Betas," *Journal of Finance* (September 1977).

time periods, found postsplit patterns that were either horizontal or slightly upward-sloping.[1]

The evidence also suggests that rather than *decreasing* transactions costs, stock splits actually *increased* them. A study[2] of pre- and postsplit behavior showed that after splits, trading volume rose less than proportionately, and both commission costs and bid-ask spreads, expressed as a percent of value, increased. Hardly the reactions claimed by proponents of stock splits.

Preemptive Rights

Under common law (and most state laws) a stockholder has an inherent right to maintain a proportionate share of the corporation. When new shares are to be sold, old stockholders may be given the right of first refusal. A certificate is issued to each person indicating the number of new shares for which subscription is authorized (this will be proportional to the number of old shares held). Usually the new shares will be priced below the current market value, making such *rights* valuable. The stockholder can *exercise* the rights by purchasing additional stock and maintaining his or her proportional ownership in the firm, but at the cost of providing additional capital. Alternatively, the rights can be sold or simply allowed to expire, causing the person's share in the corporation to decline as others are given ownership in the expanded firm in return for the provision of new capital.

---

[1] See Eugene Fama, Lawrence Fisher, Michael Jensen, and Richard Roll, "The Adjustment of Stock Prices to New Information," *International Economic Review* (February 1969), and Guy Charest, "Split Information, Stock Returns and Market Efficiency—I," *Journal of Financial Economics* (June/September 1978). By permission of North Holland Publishing Company.

[2] Thomas E. Copeland, "Liquidity Changes Following Stock Splits," *Journal of Finance*, March 1979.

STOCK PRICE AND VOLUME QUOTATIONS

Figure 13-2 provides examples of quotations summarizing a day's trading in stocks traded over-the-counter (i.e., through dealers) and those traded on the New York Stock Exchange. Active stocks traded with the aid of the National Association of Securities Dealers' Quotation System (NASDAQ) are summarized in the form shown in Figure 13-2(a). Volume traded through NASDAQ during the day is shown (in hundreds of shares) along with the highest price *bid* and lowest price *asked* by market makers (dealers) as of 4 P.M. Eastern time. Investors pay the asked price to purchase shares and receive the bid price when shares are sold. In addition, markdowns or markups and commissions may be added by the investor's retail broker.

FIGURE 13-2(a) Stock Quotations

Over-the-Counter Markets

4:00 p.m. Eastern Standard Time Prices, Friday, December 21, 1979

All over the counter prices printed on this page are representative quotations by the National Association of Securities Dealers through Nasdaq, its automated system for reporting quotes. Prices don't include retail markup, markdown or commission. Volume represents shares that changed ownership during the day. Figures include only those transactions effected by Nasdaq market makers but may include some duplication where Nasdaq market makers traded with each other.

Stock & Div.	Sales 100s	Bid	Asked	Net Chg.
--A A--				
Academy Insu	134	4⅝	4⅞	+ ⅛
Accelrtn Corp	98	5½	6½	...
Accuray Corp	120	4¾	5¼	...
Acme Elec .24	13	7	7¾	...
Acme Genl .60	12	9½	10¼	...
AdamRes .10d	300	11½	11⅞	− ¼
AddWesley .50	37	9	9¾	+ ¼
Advance Ross	40	4⅜	4¾	...
Advanced Pat	253	7⅜	7⅞	− ¼
Advent Corp	185	2	2½	...
AEL InduA 5k	157	7	7½	− ⅜
Aero Syst Inc	131	2½	2⅞	...
Aerosonic Cp	65	12	12½	...
Aerotron Inc	130	7¼	7¾	...
Affil Bksh 1.40	11	25	26	...
A E S Technlg	52	6¾	7¾	+ ¾
AgMet Incorp	167	6½	7¼	...
AgnicoEa .10b	321	8 5-16	8 9-16	− ⅛
AIC Phot .06b	39	3	3½	...
Air Florida Sy	702	5½	6	− ⅜
Airlift Intrnatl	280	9-16	¾	...
AlaBancp 1.32	1	20¼	21¼	...
AlaTnNG 2.40	2	28	29½	...
AlamoSavng 1	x4	18	21	− ¾
AlexandA 1.40	155	33¼	34	+ ¼
Alex Bald 1.30	49	25⅞	26⅜	+ ⅛
AlicoIncp .25b	16	35	36½	...
AllAm Burger	327	1⅞	2¼	+ ⅛
Allegh Bev .30	48	3⅞	4⅛	...
AlliedBncsh 1	50	42⅞	43⅜	+ ⅝
Allied Leisure	51	2½	2⅞	...
Allied Tech	270	⅝	⅞	...
Allied Tel .84g	29	14⅜	14⅞	+ ⅛
Allyn Bac .37h	37	13	14	− ¼
Alphanumric	25	7-16	11-16	...
Altex Oil Corp	705	3⅜	3⅝	− 1-16
Alton Box .30b	z33	17½	18¼	...
Amarco Resrc	335	1⅝	1¾	...

Stock & Div.	Sales 100s	Bid	Asked	Net Chg.
C H Heist .10	21	9⅛	9⅝	+ ⅛
Champ Pts .20	49	5⅞	6¼	+ ¼
Champ Prod 1	6	17½	18½	...
Chaparrl Resr	48	10¼	11	...
Charles Rv .42	x43	36	37½	+ 1⅜
Char Shops .18	138	8⅞	9⅜	+ ⅛
Chart Hse 1.04	x980	21⅜	21⅞	+ 1⅜
ChateauDe Vil	8	4	5½	...
ChathamM .80	3	9⅝	10⅛	...
Chattem .40	54	9½	10	...
Checkpnt Syst	17	12¼	13¼	...
CheezmD .10b	6	7	7½	− ¼
ChemNucl .05f	129	20	20¾	+ 1¼
Chemd Cp 1.80	3	33	34	...
ChemLea 1.20	51	36½	38½	+ ½
Chemineer .24	57	7⅝	8⅛	+ ¼
Chemlawn Cp	37	30½	32½	...
Cherry El .12	58	13¾	14½	− ¼
Ch NW Trans	22	14½	15½	− ¼
ChiChis Incrp	9	11⅜	11⅞	...
Chomerics Inc	35	24	25½	+ ½
ChubbCrp 2.40	181	38	38½	...
Chur Dwt 1.60	3	29	32	+ 1
Chyron Corpn	90	8⅜	8⅞	+ ¼
CinnFncl 1.28g	10	30½	31¼	+ ¼
Cindys Inc	61	2¼	2¾	...
CircleIS 1.30b	21	11¾	12¼	...
Citz FedSv .72	7	29	31	+ 1
CitizenFid 1.40	5	24	25	...
CitzSthnC 1.12	24	16½	17½	+ ¼
CitzSoNB Ga	188	6⅜	6¾	...
CtzUtil A 4.1k	22	34½	35¼	...
Citz UtilB 2.56	6	31½	32¼	...
CityNatl Cp 1g	67	35	36	+ 1½
Clark Mfg 1.30	6	29	30½	...
ClevTrRlt .15b	100	7⅝	8⅛	+ ¼
Clow Corp .40	66	6½	7	− ⅛
Coastland Cp	102	4¼	5	− ½
Cobe Labrator	97	22¾	23½	− ½

Stock & Div.	Sales 100s	Bid	Asked	Net Chg.
1stAlaBs 1.32g	61	19	20	...
1stAmBk 1.20	10	15¾	16½	...
FirstAmFi .50	22	22¼	23¼	...
1st Amtenn .64	55	9⅞	10⅜	...
1stArkBst .50g	40	10½	11¼	...
FirstArtist Pd	134	4⅝	5⅛	+ ⅞
FstAtlanta .88	34	11½	12¼	...
FstBancp 1.40	x28	23¼	24¼	− ¼
1stBcsFla .28b	2	9¾	10½	...
1stBcgpAla .84	5	15	15¾	...
1stBnkSys 2.04	195	39¼	40	+ ¼
1stBshrSC 1.12	25	19	20	+ 1½
FirstBost .25b	14	16½	17¼	...
1stCapitalCp 2	z60	30	31½	...
FstCaro Invst	87	6⅜	6⅞	...
1stColny Lf .76	74	32	34	+ 1½
FsConnBc 1.52	23	22	23	− ¼
1stCtlRE 1.16b	12	8⅛	8⅝	...
1stDenvr Mtg	34	2⅛	2½	...
1stEmpSt .20b	30	10⅜	10⅞	...
Fst Exec 10k	141	14⅜	14⅞	+ ⅛
FstExec pf .50	13	31¾	32½	...
1stFarwest .25	23	11⅝	12⅛	+ ⅛
1stFlaBnks .36	139	4½	5	...
1st Hawai 2.12	2	25	26	+ ¾
1stJersNtl 1.40	6	12	13	...
FstKtyNtl 1.88	10	29¼	30¼	+ ¼
1stLincoln Fcl	75	9¾	10¾	...
1stMarnBk .30	377	6⅛	6½	...
1stMdBnc 1.40	28	24¼	25	+ ¼
FstMemRlt Tr	3	4⅜	4⅞	...
1st MerCp 1.60	15	20¼	21	...
FstMtge Invst	204	1⅜	1 9-16	...
FstNtlBcp 1.08	6	15¼	16¼	...
FsNBNJ 1.60g	x7	18¾	19¾	+ ½
FstNatlCinci 2	21	28	29	...
1stNatSup .02d	25	5¾	6¾	...
FstNMBsh .84	10	16	17	...
FstNewprt Cp	170	2	2⅜	...

NYSE-Composite Transactions

Friday, December 21, 1979

Quotations include trades on the New York, Midwest, Pacific, Philadelphia, Boston and Cincinnati stock exchanges and reported by the National Association of Securities Dealers and Instinet.

52 Weeks High	Low	Stock	Div.	Yld %	P-E Ratio	Sales 100s	High	low	Close	Net Chg.
73/8	43/4	Damon	.20	3.4	73	424	61/8	57/8	57/8	− 1/8
20	115/8	DanRiv	1.12	6.2	5	278	18	163/8	18	+11/2
303/8	241/4	DanaCp	1.56	5.8	5	180	271/4	263/4	27	+ 1/4
253/4	151/8	Daniel	.26b	1.1	11	33	247/8	241/2	241/2	− 1/4
495/8	371/4	DartInd	1.80	4.5	6	368	403/4	40	40	− 1
491/4	37	Dart pf	2	5.1	..	16	40	391/2	391/2	−11/8
741/2	46	DataGen			..	11	304	545/8	533/8	533/8 + 1/4
481/8	33	DataTer	.30	.8	13	115	387/8	381/4	381/4	− 1/2
1053/8	63	Datapnt			..	16	154	1031/4	1021/4	1021/4 − 1/4
181/2	131/2	Dayco	.56b	3.8	4	97	151/4	143/8	145/8	− 5/8
46	331/4	DaytHd	1.80	4.2	6	67	431/2	421/2	421/2	−11/8
171/4	137/8	DaytPL	1.74	12.	7	129	141/8	14	141/8	.....
787/8	623/8	DPL pf	7.70	12.	..	z550	621/2	d61	621/2	−11/2
411/2	321/2	Deere	1.80	5.0	7	449	387/8	383/8	383/8	− 3/8
141/8	115/8	DeimP	1.38	11.	7	128	123/8	121/8	121/4	− 1/8
473/8	36	DeltaA	1.20	3.0	7	138	401/8	393/4	40	.....
81/4	53/8	Deltec	2.50c	..	..	14	71/4	71/4	71/4	.....
143/4	83/8	Deltona			3	14	97/8	93/4	97/8	− 1/8
213/4	161/8	DenMf s	1	5.4	7	16	185/8	181/2	181/2	−− 1/4
265/8	141/4	Dennys	.88	5.9	6	141	15	147/8	147/8	− 1/8
20	141/2	Dentsply	.88	4.9	10	71	191/8	181/8	181/8	− 7/8
13	10	DeSoto	1	8.3	8	65	12	111/2	12	+ 1/4
157/8	125/8	DetEd	1.60	13.	6	544	125/8	d123/8	123/8	− 1/4
90	711/8	DetE	pf9.32	13.	..	z220	711/4	711/8	711/4 + 1/8
763/4	59	DetE	pf7.68	13.	..	z120	601/2	591/2	591/2 + 1/2
75	561/2	DetE	pf7.36	13.	..	z1000	581/2	581/2	581/2 −11/2
263/8	21	DE	pfF 2.75	13.	..	11	213/4	215/8	215/8	.....
261/4	21	DE	pfB 2.75	13.	..	15	211/4	d207/8	207/8	− 3/8
217/8	17	DetE	pr2.28	13.	..	26	171/4	17	171/4 + 1/8
255/8	191/4	Dexter	1	4.8	8	181	211/4	21	21	+ 1/8
147/8	91/8	DiGior	.56	4.5	7	189	123/4	121/4	123/8	− 1/8
25	14	DiGior	pf.88	4.4	..	z20	20	20	20	.....
24	205/8	DiGior	pf2.25	9.8	..	15	231/2	23	23	− 1/4
261/2	165/8	DialCp	1.20	6.4	6	19	19	181/2	183/4 + 1/4
431/4	311/2	DialInt	2.20b	5.6	8	35	391/2	39	39	.....
191/2	141/2	DialInt	pf1.20	6.5	..	7	181/2	181/2	181/2 +11/2
.297/8	19	DiamS	1.60	5.5	9	641	297/8	287/8	291/4	− 3/8
263/8	201/2	GTE	pf 2.48	12.	..	35	213/4	213/8	213/8	− 1/4
143/8	111/4	GTFI	pf1.30	11.	..	z380	121/4	12	121/4 +1
911/4	70	GTFI	pf8.16	11.	..	z2010	733/8	733/8	733/8 − 33/8
27	19	GTire	1.50	7.3	5	375	207/8	201/4	201/2	− 3/8
53/4	33/8	Genesco			..	100	171	4	33/4	4 + 1/4
24	171/4	Genst g	s1.20	..	..	10	221/8	22	22	.....
267/8	21	GenuPt	s.88	3.7	11	188	241/8	235/8	237/8 + 1/4
303/8	231/2	GaPac	1.20	4.5	8	430	261/2	261/8	263/8 + 1/4
361/4	30	GaPac	pf2.24	6.8	..	13	33	323/4	323/4	− 1/4
343/4	30	GaPac	pfB	7.2	..	1	31	31	31	.....
245/8	201/8	GaPw	pf2.56	13.	..	25	201/4	201/4	201/4	− 1/4
251/4	197/8	GaPw	pf2.52	13.	..	13	201/4	20	20	− 1/4
271/4	22	GaPw	pf2.75	11.	..	8	243/8	241/8	241/2	− 1/2
771/4	593/8	GaPw	pf7.72	13.	..	z120	60	591/2	591/2	− 1/8
507/8	353/8	Geosrc	.80	1.6	14	29	501/4	50	50	.....
307/8	23	GerbPd	1.62	6.6	7	197	243/4	241/2	245/8	− 3/8
811/4	33	Getty	1.60	2.2	12	330	751/4	74	741/4	− 7/8
181/2	143/4	Getty	pf1.20	7.9	..	5	151/4	151/4	151/4	.....
117/8	61/4	GiantPC	.60j	..	9	76	61/2	61/4	63/8 + 1/8
165/8	10	GibrFn	.60	5.3	5	113	111/2	111/4	111/4	.....
291/4	123/4	GidLew	1	3.7	.	232	273/4	271/4	273/8	− 1/2
177/8	12	GiffHil	s .92	5.4	5	72	173/8	17	17	− 3/8
28	233/8	Gillette	1.72	6.6	7	280	261/4	251/2	26	− 1/4
111/2	63/4	GinosInc	.40	4.0	6	119	10	95/8	10 + 3/8
253/4	141/8	GleasW	.80	3.8	6	14	211/2	211/8	211/8 − 1/4
425/8	121/2	GlobMar	.20	..5	16	269	42	415/8	413/4 + 3/8
17	101/2	GldWFn	.54	3.5	5	18	157/8	155/8	155/8 − 1/8
24	163/4	Gdrich	1.20	..	6	943	13	121/4	121/4	.....
101/2	83/4	Gdrich	pf.97	11.	..	z1040	83/4	83/4	83/4	.....
187/8	117/8	Goodyr	1.30	10.	6	943	13	121/4	123/4 + 3/8
28	167/8	GordJw	.72	3.2	5	51	23	221/2	221/2 − 1/2
30	22	Gould	1.72	7.2	8	137	233/4	231/4	233/4	.....
411/4	253/8	Grace	2.05	5.1	9	208	403/4	401/8	401/8 − 3/8
39	311/8	Graingr	.92	2.5	11	63	37	361/4	361/4 −1
141/8	101/4	Granitvl	1	8.7	..	27	111/2	111/2	111/2	.....
161/4	95/8	GrayDr	.80	7.4	5	56	111/8	105/8	107/8 + 1/4
103/8	51/4	GtAtPc			..	..	99	71/2	73/8	71/2 + 1/8

FIGURE 13-2(b) Stock Quotations

Activity in stocks traded on major exchanges is summarized in the form shown in Figure 13-2(b). High and low prices for the preceding 52 weeks are shown, along with an annual dividend rate (in dollars) based on the latest declared amount (letters refer to footnotes providing details concerning extra or special dividends and yields). This amount is divided by the price to obtain the figure shown for yield. The ratio of the current price to the last twelve months' earnings is given next. The remaining entries summarize the day's transactions in the major markets in which the stock is traded. Sales, in hundreds of shares, are indicated, followed by the highest and lowest prices at which trades were completed during the day. The next entry is the *closing price*—the price at which the last trade of the day was made (this is also used to compute yield and the price-earnings ratio). The final entry shows the difference between the day's closing price and that of the preceding day.

INSIDER TRADING

The United States Securities and Exchange Acts of 1933 and 1934 require the officers and directors of a corporation whose securities are traded on an organized exchange and anyone who owns more than 10% of the outstanding amount of such a security to report their transactions in it within ten days following the month in which the transaction takes place. The information is subsequently published in the Securities and Exchange Commission's monthly *Official Summary of Securities Transactions and Holdings*. For example, the summary of trades made in January (and reported by early February) is published early in March. Thus up to two months may elapse before knowledge of an insider's trade is widespread.

The Securities and Exchange Acts also require corporate insiders to return all short-term profits from security transactions in their own stocks to the corporation. For this purpose, "short-term" is defined as less than six months. As one might expect, few insiders are sufficiently devoted to their firm to realize such profits; most prefer to wait until the six-month period is over.

In the United States it is illegal for anyone to make a security transaction that takes advantage of "inside" corporate information unavailable to the other person or persons involved in the trade. This proscription includes corporate insiders and also those to whom such insiders give secret information (the recipient of such a "tip" is termed the "tipee").

Legally, there are two types of nonpublic information: that which is "private" (i.e., legal) and that which is "inside" (i.e., possibly illegal). The law-abiding but dedicated security analyst must try to obtain as much of the former as possible, while completely avoiding the latter. Unfortunately, the distinction between the two types is highly ambiguous, guaranteeing continuing employment for lawyers specializing in the subject and continuing problems for security analysts.

Legal issues aside, two questions of relevance to outside investors may be posed: (1) do insiders make unusual profits on transactions in their own stocks, and (2) if they do, can others profit by following their example as soon as it becomes public knowledge?

Insiders trade their stock for many reasons. Some purchases result from the exercise of options, some sales from the need for cash, etc. Moreover, it is not unusual to find some insiders purchasing a stock during a month in which others are selling it. However, when a major piece of inside information suggests that a stock's value differs significantly from its present price, and insiders find it difficult to resist the temptation to profit from this knowledge, one would expect a preponderance of insider trades on one side of the market (i.e., either purchases or sales).

One way to search for such situations is to examine the *Official Summary* and count the number of days during a month each insider traded his or her stock (excluding the exercise of options). If the days on which purchases were made exceeds those on which sales were made, the individual can be counted as a net purchaser during that month; and if the converse holds, as a net seller. Next, the number of purchasers and sellers for the stock can be considered. If there were at least, say, three more

TABLE 13-1 Abnormal Performance Associated with Insider Trading

SAMPLE			AVERAGE ABNORMAL RETURN (%) OVER EIGHT MONTHS FOLLOWING:	
Cutoff (No. of Net Purchasers or Sellers)	No. of Cases	Period	Month of Transaction	Month Information Became Publicly Available
1	362	1960s	1.36	.70
3	861	1960s	5.07	4.94
4	293	1950s	5.14	4.12
5	157	1950s	4.48	4.08

Source: Jeffrey F. Jaffe, "Special Information and Insider Trading," *The Journal of Business*, 47, no. 3 (July 1974), 410–29. © 1974 by the University of Chicago. All Rights Reserved.

purchasers than sellers, one might infer that positive inside information motivated at least some insider trades during the month. In the opposite case, one might infer that negative insider information played a role.

Different cut-off levels could be used in this process to reflect the intensity of insider trading. A cut-off of 1 would require more trades of one type than the other, a cut-off of 5, a substantial balance on one side of the market, and so on.

Such a procedure was used in a detailed study of insider transactions during the 1950s and 1960s.[3] Table 13-1 summarizes the key results. Each figure indicates the "abnormal" return above that expected, given market moves, over an eight-month period for trades of the same type as the predominant insider transaction. For example, during the 1960s, if one purchased every stock in the sample for which there were three or more net purchasers and sold every stock for which there were three or more net sellers during a month, more or less coincident with the transactions of the insiders themselves, an average abnormal return of 5.07% could have been earned over the subsequent eight months. If the transactions had been made instead at roughly the time the information was published in the *Official Summary*, an average abnormal return of 4.94% could have been earned over the next eight months.

As the first row in the table shows, a bare majority of insider trades does not appear to isolate possible effects of insider information. But a majority of 3, 4, or 5 does seem to do so. The figures shown are gross of any transactions costs, but even so one might well conclude that insiders can and do make money from special knowledge of their companies. This is not surprising. If insiders do not know the value of their firms, who does? Profits of 4% or 5% per eight months are hardly large enough to arouse the suspicion of regulatory authorities, let alone provide adequate evidence for punitive action.

On the other hand, the abnormal returns associated with transac-

[3] Jeffrey F. Jaffe, "Special Information and Insider Trading," *The Journal of Business*, 47, no. 3 (July 1974), 410–29. © 1974 by the University of Chicago. All Rights Reserved.

tions that could have been made by outsiders, using only publicly available information on insider trading, *are* surprising. Moreover, those associated with cut-offs of 3, 4, or 5 pass statistical tests designed to see if they might be simply due to chance. After transactions costs, trades designed to capitalize on such information would not prove wildly profitable, but the argument that "if you can't beat them, join them" (even two months later) does seem to have some merit.

In the 1970s the *Value Line Investment Survey*[4] began to include an "index of insider decisions" for each stock covered in its weekly service. In essence, this is a cumulative index of the net number of purchasers including those who exercise options (counted as plus values) and sellers (counted as negative values). The increasingly public nature of such information may make it less valuable as more and more investors attempt to profit by it. It might thus be unwise to expect to obtain abnormal returns as large as those shown in Table 13-1 now.

EX ANTE AND EX POST ASSESSMENTS OF STOCK RETURNS

The capital-asset pricing model implies that in the consensus opinion of well-informed analysts, stocks with high degrees of market risk will, other things equal, have larger expected returns, while those with less market risk will have smaller expected returns. Such concepts are based on opinions held *before the fact* (in Latin: *ex ante*) about possible outcomes and their relative probabilities. After the fact (in Latin: *ex post*) only one outcome will be recorded for each stock. Analysts will then form new and possibly different opinions, another set of stock returns will subsequently be recorded, and so on.

This makes it extremely difficult to tell whether risk and return do in fact go together in the manner implied by theory. Moreover, the efficient-market model is relatively silent concerning simple ways in which a security's future risk and return might be estimated by processing historic data on its past performance.

To bridge this gap, a number of investigators have used past outcomes of security and market returns as surrogates for *ex ante* expectations. This requires an assumption that relevant predictions do not change from year to year and that sufficient information will thus eventually be available to determine what such expectations actually were. Thus actual *average* return is used as an estimate of *expected* return, slopes of regression lines based on *actual* security and market returns are used as estimates of *predicted* betas, etc. Two obvious objections may be made. First, expectations almost certainly change from time to time: nothing in valuation theory suggests otherwise. Second, even if expectations did not change over time, an extremely long historic record might be required to obtain reasonable estimates of their magnitudes.

Despite these and other problems, historic data are worth examining.

[4] Published by Arnold Bernhard and Co., Inc., New York.

HISTORIC VERSUS FUTURE BETA VALUES

For purposes of portfolio management, the relevant risk of a security concerns its impact on the risk of a reasonable portfolio. In an efficient market reasonable portfolios will be well diversified and subject primarily to market risk. This suggests the importance of a security's sensitivity to likely future market moves. As suggested in Chapter 7, to estimate this, one should in principle consider possible sources of such moves in the future, project the security's reactions to such sources, and the probabilities of each. In the process, the economics of the relevant industry and firm, the impact of both operating and financial leverage on the firm, and other fundamental factors can and should be taken into account.

But what about simply investigating the extent to which a security's price moved with the market in the past? Such an approach ignores a myriad of possible differences between past and future. However, it is simple, and it does have some merit.

As shown in Chapter 7, a security's beta value can be regarded as the slope of the characteristic line that best fits the relationship between its excess return and that of the market. If such a relationship were constant from period to period, one could estimate the value of beta for a stock by fitting a characteristic line to points representing the stock's excess return and the excess return on an index chosen to serve as a surrogate for the market portfolio. A simpler procedure would use only the period-by-period percentage changes in the price of the stock and percentage changes in the level of the index. Happily for those who must calculate such numbers, the estimates obtained using the two procedures are very similar. One study showed that well over 99% of the differences in the estimated beta values of 1572 securities obtained via the complex procedure were associated with the differences among the estimates obtained in the simpler manner.[5]

Estimates Derived from Historic Data

Figure 13-3 shows a page from a report prepared monthly by Merrill Lynch, Pierce, Fenner and Smith, Inc. Price changes for each of up to 60 months are compared with changes in Standard and Poor's 500-stock index via regression analysis. Five of the resulting values are of interest. The figure shown for *beta* indicates the slope of the best-fit line for each stock. For example, during the period covered, the stock of the Timken Company exhibited slightly aggressive behavior, moving roughly 13% more than the index in a typical market move. The value of *R-squared* shows the proportion of total variance in the security's monthly price changes accounted for by market moves. Forty percent of the variation in Timken's price could be attributed to the market over the period studied. The *residual standard deviation* is the standard deviation of the distances of the points from the line; it provides ex post evidence of nonmarket risk. In roughly two months out of three, Timken's price change equaled that

[5] William F. Sharpe and Guy M. Cooper, "Risk-Return Classes of New York Stock Exchange Common Stocks, 1931–1967," *Financial Analysts Journal*, 28, no. 2 (March/April 1972), 46–54.

FIGURE 13-3 Sample Page from: Merrill Lynch, Pierce, Fenner & Smith, Inc., Market Sensitivity Report for November 1979

TKR Symb	Security Name	10/79 Close price	Beta	Alpha	R-Sqr	Resid Std Dev-n	Std.Err. of Beta	Std.Err. of Alpha	Adjusted Beta	Number of Observ
THRS	THREASHOLD TECKNOLOG	9.750	.85	1.92	.06	12.99	.40	1.69	.90	60
FXN	THREE D DEPTS	4.375	1.71	4.54	.18	17.07	.45	2.21	1.47	60
TDMC	THREE DIMENTIONAL CI	.562	-.63	8.65	.02	41.62	1.46	5.78	-.08	52
TFTA	THRIFTIMART INC A	21.375	.80	1.21	.13	8.49	.26	1.11	.87	60
THRF	THRIFTWAY LEASING CO	.000	1.02	3.84	.02	26.06	.66	3.38	1.01	60
TFD	THRIFTY CORP	11.625	1.92	.87	.46	8.80	.27	1.15	1.61	60
TEXT	TI-CARO	20.500	.94	1.58	.23	7.17	.22	.93	.96	60
TIM	TIDEWATER INC	25.750	.86	.39	.19	7.30	.22	.95	.91	60
TDW	TIDWELL INDS INC	5.750	5.11	4.85	.17	46.73	1.42	6.10	3.73	60
FLY	TIGER INTL INC	19.750	1.63	1.55	.33	9.87	.30	1.29	1.42	60
TI	TIME INC	43.250	1.24	1.39	.36	6.87	.21	.90	1.16	60
TPLX	TIMEPLEX INC	9.125	2.38	5.23	.11	26.83	.82	3.50	1.91	60
PWII	TIMBERLAND INDUSTRIES	6.250	.78	3.18	.06	13.68	.35	1.77	.85	60
TMC	TIMES MIRROR CO	32.500	1.60	1.19	.61	5.41	.16	.71	1.39	60
TKR	TIMKEN CO	51.000	1.13	.65	.40	5.82	.18	.76	1.09	60
TNSL	TINSLEY LABS INC	6.000	.84	1.60	.03	17.49	.48	2.27	.90	60
TLK	TIPPERARY CORP	11.250	.95	2.12	.08	12.86	.39	1.68	.97	60
TIN	TITAN GROUP	1.500	1.53	-1.81	.04	24.91	.85	3.22	1.35	60
TICT	TLL INDUS	3.000	1.61	-.23	.12	17.29	.53	2.26	1.40	60
AIKZ	TOBIAS KOIZIN CO	5.000	1.18	2.44	.07	16.98	.52	2.22	1.12	60
TBN	TOBIN PACKING INC	3.625	1.10	-.41	.09	13.89	.42	1.81	1.06	60
TOCM	TOCOM INC	10.500	1.72	2.98	.19	14.69	.45	1.92	1.48	60
TOD	TODD SHIPYARDS CORP	23.750	.31	3.12	.01	16.88	.51	2.20	.54	60
TOK	TOKHEIM CORP	15.875	2.39	2.46	.39	12.72	.39	1.66	1.92	60
TKM	TOKIO MARINE INS ADR	129.500	.32	1.43	.01	7.57	.23	.99	.55	60
TED	TOLEDO EDISON CO	18.125	.79	-.28	.34	4.60	.14	.60	.86	60
NOHO	TOLEDO TRUSTCORP	27.500	.35	.91	.09	4.35	.13	.57	.57	60
TILLY	TOLLEY INTL CORP	1.000	.21	-2.34	.01	19.46	.59	2.54	.48	60
TLOC	TOMLINSON OIL INC	10.500	1.28	3.68	.07	17.49	.53	2.28	1.19	60
TKA	TONKA CORP	10.875	1.77	.47	.33	10.60	.32	1.38	1.51	60

BASED ON S&P 500 INDEX, USING STRAIGHT REGRESSION

expected, given its beta value and the behavior of the market at the time, plus or minus 5.82% (e.g., 582 basis points).

If a security's "true" beta remained the same forever, its "measured" beta, obtained in the manner illustrated in Figure 13-3, would still change from time to time because of sampling error. If a nonmarket factor caused a large price increase in a month when the market rose, beta would probably be overestimated. If the good news came when the market was falling, beta would probably be underestimated. Since nonmarket factors affect the typical stock more than does the market itself, the likelihood of such a situation is quite high.

The *standard error of beta* attempts to indicate the extent of such errors. For example, given a number of necessary assumptions (e.g., stability of beta), the chances are roughly two out of three that the true value of Timken's beta is within .18 of the estimated value.

Adjusting Beta Values

But more needs to be said. Absent *any* information at all, one would presume a stock's beta relative to a representative index of all stocks to be 1.0. Given a chance to see how the stock moved relative to the market over some period, a modification of this *prior* estimate would seem appropriate. But a sensible *posterior* estimate would undoubtedly lie between the two values.

Formal procedures for making such estimates have been adopted by most producers of beta values. The specific adjustments made typically differ from time to time and, in some cases, from stock to stock. In Figure 13-3 the *adjusted beta* values were obtained by giving approximately 66% weight to the measured beta and approximately 34% weight to the prior value of 1.0 for each stock. Thus for Timken:

$$\text{adjusted beta} = (.34 \times 1.0) + (.66 \times 1.13)$$
$$= 1.09$$

(13-1)

Table 13-2 shows the extent to which such procedures anticipate differences between past and future betas. The first column lists the unadjusted betas for eight portfolios of 100 securities each, based on monthly price changes from July 1947 through June 1954 (the portfolios were designed to have significantly different betas during this period). The second column of the table shows the values obtained when an adjustment of the type used in the Merrill Lynch service was applied. The betas in the third column are based on price changes over the subsequent seven years. For many of the portfolios, the ex post value was even closer to 1.0 than the adjusted ex ante figure. The final column shows the values obtained using the data for the following seven years. By and large, continued reversion to the mean of 1.0 is evident.

Apparently "true" betas not only vary over time but have a tendency to move back toward average levels. This is plausible enough, for extreme postures are likely to be moderated over time. A firm whose operations or financing make the risk of its equity considerably different from that of other firms is more likely to move back toward the average than away from it. Such changes in beta values are due to real economic phenom-

TABLE 13-2 Ex Ante and Ex Post Beta Values for Portfolios of 100 Securities Each

	PERIOD			
	July 1947–June 1954			
Portfolio	**Unadjusted**	**Adjusted**	**July 1954–June 1961**	**July 1961–June 1968**
1	.36	.48	.57	.72
2	.61	.68	.71	.79
3	.78	.82	.88	.88
4	.91	.93	.96	.92
5	1.01	1.01	1.03	1.04
6	1.13	1.10	1.13	1.02
7	1.26	1.21	1.24	1.08
8	1.47	1.39	1.32	1.15

Source: Marshall E. Blume, "Betas and Their Regression Tendencies," *The Journal of Finance*, XXX, no. 3 (June 1975), 785–96.

ena, not simply an artifact of overly simple statistical procedures. There is, however, no reason to expect every stock's true beta to move in the same way, to the same average, and at the same speed. In this regard, a little fundamental security analysis may prove more useful than the adoption of more sophisticated statistical methods for processing past price changes.

Changes in Stock Beta Values

Table 13-2 shows that *at the portfolio level* historic data can provide substantial information on future beta values, although the precise adjustment required to estimate the numeric magnitudes may be difficult to determine. However, as the standard errors of beta in Figure 13-3 suggest, estimates of beta for *individual securities* are subject to great error and should be treated accordingly. Nonetheless, a security's past risk characteristics provide some indication of its future prospects.

Figure 13-4 shows that the predictive ability of historic beta improves as more diversified portfolios are considered. The vertical axis plots the percent of the differences in (measured) portfolio betas (based on weekly price changes) in one year that can be attributed to differences in their (measured) betas in the prior year. The horizontal axis indicates the number of securities in each portfolio. Data from other countries give similar results.

Table 13-3 provides another view of stock risk characteristics. Every stock listed on the New York Stock Exchange was assigned to one of ten risk classes in each year from 1931 through 1967, based on its beta value over the preceding five years. The stocks in the top 10% of each January's "beta book" were assigned to class 10, the next 10% to class 9, and so on. The table shows the percent of the stocks in each class that were (a) in the same class and (b) within one class five years later. Also shown are the entries that would be expected if there were *no* relationship between past and future risk classes.

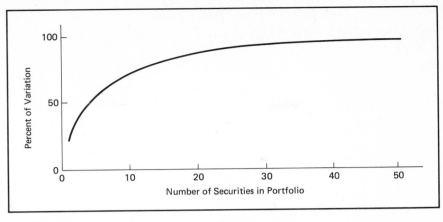

FIGURE 13-4 Percent of Differences in Beta Values Attributable to Differences in Prior Year's Betas.

Source: Robert A. Levy, "On the Short-term Stationarity of Beta Coefficients," *Financial Analysts Journal*, 27, no. 6 (November/December 1971), 55–62.

Although both true beta values and, *a fortiori*, measured beta values of individual stocks do change, a security's past sensitivity to market moves is still worth examining. This is especially so since even when a number of rather inaccurate (but unbiased) estimates of security beta values are used, quite an accurate estimate of a diversified portfolio's beta value may be obtained. And portfolio risk is, after all, more relevant than security risk.

TABLE 13-3 Movement of Stocks Among Risk Classes

RISK CLASS	PERCENT OF STOCKS IN THE SAME RISK CLASS FIVE YEARS LATER		PERCENT OF STOCKS IN THE SAME RISK CLASS OR WITHIN ONE RISK CLASS FIVE YEARS LATER	
	Actual	Expected if There Were No Relationship	Actual	Expected if There Were No Relationship
10 (highest beta values)	32.2	10	69.3	20
9	18.4	10	53.7	30
8	16.4	10	45.3	30
7	13.3	10	40.9	30
6	13.9	10	39.3	30
5	13.6	10	41.7	30
4	13.2	10	40.2	30
3	15.9	10	44.6	30
2	21.5	10	60.9	30
1 (lowest beta values)	40.5	10	62.3	20

Source: William F. Sharpe and Guy M. Cooper, "Risk-Return Classes of New York Stock Exchange Common Stocks, 1931–1967," *Financial Analysts Journal*, 28, no. 2 (March/April 1972), 46–54.

Industry Beta Values

The future beta value for a *firm* depends on the sensitivity of the demand for its products or services and of its costs to the economic factors about which there is the greatest uncertainty. The beta value of a firm's *stock* depends on the beta of the firm and its degree of financial leverage.

One might expect firms in industries characterized by highly cyclical demand and/or large fixed costs to have higher betas than those in industries with more stable demand and/or greater freedom to vary costs. Differences in financial leverage could wholly offset such factors, leaving few if any differences among the beta values of the common stocks of firms in different industries. However, this does not seem to be the case. Stocks of firms in certain industries do tend to have higher beta values than those in other industries, and by and large the classifications accord with prior expectations.

Table 13-4 shows the average values of beta for stocks in various industry classifications, based on monthly returns between 1966 and 1974. Stocks of firms whose products are termed "necessities" tend to respond less than most stocks when expectations about the future health of the economy are revised, while the stocks of firms that manufacture consumer and producer durables and products considered "luxuries" tend to respond more than most. However, there are significant exceptions.

Information of the type shown in Table 13-4 can be used to "adjust" historic beta values. For example, the knowledge that a corporation is in the air transport industry suggests that a reasonable estimate of the beta value of its stock is greater than 1.0. It thus makes more sense to adjust a historic beta value toward a value above 1.0 than to the average for all stocks.

TABLE 13-4 Average Values of Beta for Stocks in Selected Industries, 1966–1974

Industry	Beta Value	Industry	Beta Value
Air transport	1.80	Chemicals	1.22
Real property	1.70	Energy, raw materials	1.22
Travel, outdoor recreation	1.66	Tires, rubber goods	1.21
Electronics	1.60	Railroads, shipping	1.19
Miscellaneous finance	1.60	Forest products, paper	1.16
Nondurables, entertainment	1.47	Miscellaneous, conglomerate	1.14
Consumer durables	1.44	Drugs, medicine	1.14
Business machines	1.43	Domestic oil	1.12
Retail, general	1.43	Soaps, cosmetics	1.09
Media	1.39	Steel	1.02
Insurance	1.34	Containers	1.01
Trucking, freight	1.31	Nonferrous metals	.99
Producer goods	1.30	Agriculture, food	.99
Aerospace	1.30	Liquor	.89
Business services	1.28	International oil	.85
Apparel	1.27	Banks	.81
Construction	1.27	Tobacco	.80
Motor vehicles	1.27	Telephone	.75
Photographic, optical	1.24	Energy, utilities	.60
		Gold	.36

Source: Barr Rosenberg and James Guy, "Prediction of Beta from Investment Fundamentals," *Financial Analysts Journal*, 32, no. 4 (July/August 1976), 62–70.

Beta Prediction Equations

The procedure used to "adjust" historic betas involves an implicit *prediction equation* for future beta. Writing formula (13-1) in a more general way:

$$\text{future beta} = a + b \cdot \text{historic beta} \qquad (13\text{-}2)$$

But a stock's historic beta value is only one of several pieces of information that can be used to predict its future beta value. For example, firms in the airline industry tend to have higher betas than those in the utility industry. This can be incorporated by including industry effects in the equation.[6]

future beta = a

$+\ b \cdot$ historic beta

$+\ c_1 \cdot$ percent of earnings in the airline industry $\quad$ (13-3)

$+\ c_2 \cdot$ percent of earnings in the utility industry

$+\ \cdots$

Other factors can also be used. For example, stocks with high dividend yields tend to have lower betas (perhaps because more of their value is associated with near-term than with far-term dividends). The equation could thus be augmented to:

future beta = a

$+\ b \cdot$ historic beta

$+\ c_1 \cdot$ percent of earnings in industry 1

$+\ c_2 \cdot$ percent of earnings in industry 2 $\quad$ (13-4)

$+\ \cdots$

$+\ c_n \cdot$ percent of earnings in industry n

$+\ d \cdot$ yield

To determine appropriate values of the constants in such an equation (i.e., a, b, c_1, . . . , c_n, d), statistical processing of past data can be employed. For example, on January 1, 1965, one knew General Motors' historic beta, earnings by industry, and yield. Time has passed since then, and General Motors' actual beta value subsequent to January 1, 1965, can be determined. This provides one *observation* of the relationship between the *predicting* (independent) variables on the right-hand side of the equals sign in (13-4) and the *predicted* (dependent) variable on the left-hand side. Values for other stocks at the same time provide additional observations. The behavior of General Motors and other stocks after January 1, 1966, related to variables known on January 1, 1966, provides another set of observations. And so on.

---

[6] For stocks with all earnings in one industry this is equivalent to adjusting historic betas toward an industry average.

By examining different stocks at different times, many observations can be obtained and statistical analysis used to "fit" equations such as (13-4)—i.e., to determine the values of the constants that best relate ex post beta values to values of variables known beforehand.

Prediction equations that incorporate industry information, market capitalization and yield, in addition to measures of historic risk, fit the data considerably better than those that use only historic betas; improvements of up to 60% have been obtained.[7] Equations that add further information from balance sheets and income statements fit the data even better. One analysis, based on 56 predictive variables plus 38 industry variables, reported an improvement of 86%[8] over the more simple "adjusted beta" approach. Of course, such figures describe the extent to which the equations fit a given set of data. Since the true test of a prediction equation is its ability to *predict*, only extensive experience with such approaches will, in the final analysis, determine how many variables to use in predicting beta, which ones to use, and how to use them (i.e., the best procedure for estimating the constant terms in the appropriate prediction equation).

Beta Services

Services providing betas on a regular basis in book form or directly for use in computer systems are available in several countries. Many use only past price changes to form estimates, but some incorporate other information. Procedures differ. One service uses weekly data for two years; another, monthly data for five years. One estimates beta values for U.S. securities relative to Standard and Poor's 500-stock index; another, relative to the New York Stock Exchange Composite Index; etc. In each case, estimates for individual securities are subject to error. It is thus hardly surprising that measured values for a given security obtained by different services using different procedures are not the same. This does not indicate that some are useless, only that they should be used appropriately.

SOURCES OF NONMARKET RISK

Most of the risk associated with a highly diversified portfolio will be market-related. Those who choose passive investment strategies designed to mirror the market as a whole have to be concerned with nonmarket risk only to the extent needed to insure that little of it remains in their portfolios. An obvious way to do this is to hold a great many securities in market proportions. However, unless the number is quite large (i.e., in the hundreds) and the securities are chosen without excessive concentration in specific industries, sectors, etc., the portfolios may still have significant nonmarket risk.

---

[7] Source: Canavest House Limited.

[8] Barr Rosenberg and Vinay Marathe, "The Prediction of Investment Risk: Systematic and Residual Risk," *Proceedings of the Seminar on the Analysis of Security Prices, University of Chicago*, November 1975.

Those who choose active investment strategies or tailored strategies designed to differ from the market as a whole must, of course, be even more concerned with nonmarket risk. Any decision to diverge from market proportions exposes a portfolio to nonmarket factors. Such divergence should be undertaken only to the extent that one expects to be rewarded enough to offset the accompanying increase in nonmarket risk. Estimates of the effect of portfolio concentration on such risk are crucial for any investor or investment manager who plans to perform this delicate balancing act.

Two problems arise in this connection. First, the nonmarket risk of each security under consideration must be estimated. Second, any nonmarket factors that affect two or more securities must be taken into account.

As with market risk, analysis of future sources of uncertainty, taking into account all available information about the firm, its customers, suppliers, labor unions, etc., should provide the best estimates of nonmarket risk. Here, too, historic data can prove helpful.

In general, securities with large market risk tend to have large nonmarket risk. For example, in one study[9] 14 portfolios of 25 securities each were constructed from a list of 350 stocks and their performance from July 1963 through June 1973 examined. Nonmarket risk, represented by the standard deviation of the difference between actual monthly return and that expected given the portfolio's beta and the market return, averaged 2.5% per month for the 14 portfolios. The comparable figure for the three portfolios with the lowest beta values was 1.7%, while that for the three portfolios with the highest beta values was 3.6%.

As discussed in Chapter 8, for some purposes it is convenient to assume that the returns of different securities are related only through their common relationships with the market in general. This amounts to an assumption that nonmarket components of return are uncorrelated. But such an assumption is at best a useful first approximation. Prices of securities of firms in the same industry tend to move together more than those of firms in different industries; prices of stocks with similar yields tend to move together; prices of stocks of large firms tend to move together; etc. Thus there are *extra*market sources of covariance among security returns.

Homogeneous Security Groups

Interrelationships of this type can be taken into account via market-sector models in the manner discussed in Chapter 8. Some idea of the forms such an approach might take, and their potential advantages, can be gained from the results of two studies designed to identify groups of stocks whose prices move together in response to common nonmarket factors.

The first study investigated the influence of industrywide factors. A major problem in this connection involves the very concept of an industry. Classification of stocks by industries, always a difficult task, has be-

[9] Robert C. Klemkosky and John D. Martin, "The Effect of Market Risk on Portfolio Diversification," *The Journal of Finance*, XXX, no. 1 (March 1975), 147–54.

come even more arbitrary with the rise of conglomerate firms producing many diverse products and services. Nonetheless, the U.S. Securities and Exchange Commission publishes lists in which corporations are assigned two-digit *Standard Industrial Codes*,[10] Standard and Poor's Corporation classifies a number of stocks by industry,[11] and Value Line[12] assigns the stocks covered in its service to industry groups. If industry effects are pronounced, one would expect the prices of stocks classified as belonging in the same industry to display at least some resulting comovement.

To see whether this was the case, a sample of 63 stocks in six different industries (based on Standard Industrial Classification codes) was selected. Monthly prices from 1927 through 1960 were examined, and the market's average effect on each stock estimated using standard regression analysis. Price changes of each stock in each month were then broken into two components—that due to market behavior, and the remainder, due to all nonmarket factors.

The key part of the study involved a step-by-step analysis of the correlations among the nonmarket returns. A computer was told to search for the two stocks for which this was the largest. They were then grouped together to form a new "pseudo-stock." The analysis was then repeated, using the 61 stocks plus the new pseudo-stock. The highest correlation was again determined, and the two items combined, leaving 60 remaining. The process was repeated, again and again, clustering together stocks with similar price behavior. Figure 13-5 shows the results. Each column represents a stage in the analysis, while each type of bar indicates a different group of stocks.

As the figure shows, stocks in the same industry tended to group together. This happened even though the grouping procedure was based entirely on comovement of prices—i.e., the computer did not know which stocks were from which industries. There is little doubt that during the period covered, industry factors accounted for significant amounts of nonmarket risk. How much? For the typical stock, approximately 50% of total price variance from 1927 through 1960 could be attributed to market effects. Roughly an additional 10% could be attributed to industrywide factors. The first figure declined through the period, reaching approximately 30% for the typical stock in the latter part—approximately its current level in the United States—while the second figure changed little. Thus market and industry factors together might now account for about 40% (30 + 10) of the variation in the price of a typical stock.

A second study was designed to find possible comovement due to neither market nor industry effects. One hundred stocks were selected to cover many different industries in the hope of thwarting any attempt by the computer to group along industry lines. Table 13-5 shows the stocks used and their associated industries, based on both Standard and Poor's and Standard Industrial classifications. Monthly price changes from 1961 through 1969 were analyzed using procedures similar to those of the previous study.

[10] Securities and Exchange Commission, "Directory of Companies Filing Annual Reports with the Securities and Exchange Commission."

[11] Standard and Poor's Corporation, "Trade and Security Statistics."

[12] Published by Arnold Bernhard and Co., Inc., New York.

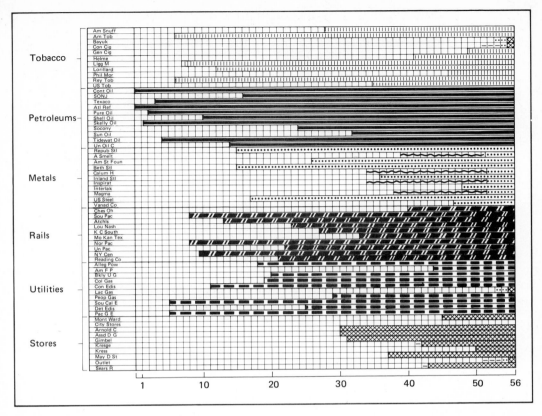

FIGURE 13-5 Grouping Stocks by Nonmarket Risk: Industry Effects.

Source: Benjamin F. King, "Market and Industry Factors in Stock Price Behavior," *The Journal of Business,*
39, no. 1 (January 1966), 139–40. © by the University of Chicago. All Rights Reserved.

TABLE 13-5 Influence of Market and Sector Factors on Security Returns

	AVERAGE PERCENT OF VARIATION IN MONTHLY RETURN FROM 1961 THROUGH 1969 DUE TO:	
Sector	The Market Factor	The Sector Factor
Growth stocks	31	15
Stable stocks	29	12
Cyclical stocks	33	9
Oil stocks	31	31

Source: James L. Farrell, Jr., "Analyzing Covariation of Returns to Determine Homogeneous Stock Groupings," *The Journal of Business* 47, no. 2 (April 1974), 186–207. © 1974 by the University of Chicago. All Rights Reserved.

TABLE 13-6 Sector Concentration and Portfolio Return

| | PERCENT INVESTED | | |
Sector	Standard and Poor's 500-Stock Index	Affiliated Fund	T. Rowe Price Fund
Growth	39.8	10.5	80.2
Cyclical	24.0	57.5	8.7
Stable	20.0	18.0	4.1
Oil	16.2	14.0	7.0
Estimated beta	1.00	1.09	1.11
Performance, Dec. 31, 1972– July 31, 1974	−29%	−16%	−42%

Source: James L. Farrell, Jr., "Homogeneous Stock Groupings: Implications for Portfolio Management," *Financial Analysts Journal*, 31, no. 3 (May/June 1975), 58.

In this case the computer was instructed to stop grouping stocks together when four major clusters remained. With relatively few exceptions, stocks in the first cluster were those considered by most analysts to be *growth stocks:* "companies expected to show an above average rate of secular expansion."[13] The second cluster contained mostly *cyclical stocks:* "those of companies that have an above average exposure to the vagaries of the economic environment."[14] The third group included predominantly *stable stocks:* "those of companies whose earning power is less affected than the average firm by the economic cycle."[15] The final group showed that at least one industry had sufficient homogeneity to stand out despite the attempt to ignore industry effects: during the period studied, the eight oil companies' prices moved together in a manner sufficiently unique to cause the computer to group them in a completely separate cluster.

How much variation in prices could be attributed to these factors? Table 13-5 shows the average values for the stocks in each of the four clusters. Also shown is the size of the market effect (roughly 30%). The results, combined with those of the earlier study, suggest that sector comovement can be as important as industry comovement.

Table 13-6 provides a dramatic indication of the possible results from concentration in market sectors. The relative proportions in the four sectors are shown for the portfolio represented by Standard and Poor's 500-stock index and for two mutual funds. The two funds had similar market exposures, as indicated by their estimated beta values. During the nineteen-month period from December 31, 1972, through July 31, 1974, the "market" fell 29%, suggesting that one might have expected the two funds to fall by roughly 32% (since $1.1 \times 29\% = 31.9\%$).

---

[13] James L. Farrell, Jr., "Homogeneous Stock Groupings: Implications for Portfolio Management," *Financial Analysts Journal*, 31, no. 3 (May/June 1975), 50.

[14] *Ibid.*

[15] *Ibid.*

In fact, one fund's shares fell much less than the market, and the other's shares fell much more. The portfolio composition figures show why. This was a period when growth stocks did especially poorly. The first fund was well positioned, concentrating more money in cyclical stocks and less in growth stocks than did the market as a whole. The second was poorly positioned, with a heavy concentration in growth stocks, to its investors' detriment. The results could be reversed in a period in which growth stocks do especially well. The point is not that one fund or investment strategy is better than another—rather, that neither fund was in fact as well diversified as a simple check of the number of stocks might suggest.

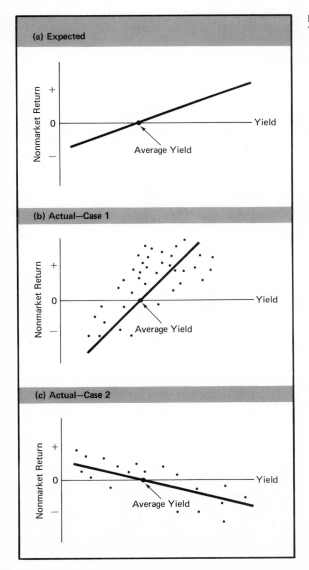

FIGURE 13-6 Non-market Return versus Dividend Yield.

The studies described in Figure 13-5 and Table 13-5 attempt to identify *homogeneous groups* of stocks that tend to move together in ways not directly related to overall market moves. Such groups typically combine the effects of industry and other *nonmarket common factors*. A more detailed approach involves the identification of surrogates for the sensitivities of stocks to such factors and the risks associated with the factors.

Common-Factor Risk

The idea is illustrated in Figure 13-6 on the previous page. The horizontal axis plots a security *attribute* (in this case, dividend yield). The vertical axis plots *nonmarket return*—return over and above (if positive) or below (if negative) the amount that would be expected, given the security's beta value and the actual return on the market as a whole. The solid line in Figure 13-6(a) shows a relationship that might be *expected* between nonmarket return and dividend yield (owing to the inferior tax status of dividends, high-yield stocks are expected to provide greater before-tax returns). But this is an ex ante relationship. In any single period (e.g., a month) the relationship will not be perfect (points representing securities will be scattered) and the average relationship might be much greater, as in Figure 13-6(b) or smaller or even reversed, as in Figure 13-6(c). Since the actual relationship is subject to uncertainty, a portfolio with yield significantly different from the average will be exposed to added nonmarket risk.

The slope of the relationship between nonmarket return and yield can be termed the *yield factor*. When it is positive, high-yield stocks outperform low-yield stocks; when it is negative, low-yield stocks outperform high-yield. While it may be *expected* to be positive ex ante, the yield factor may in fact be positive or negative in any given period. Uncertainty about the magnitude of this factor is thus a source of extramarket covariance. And the yield of a portfolio indicates the degree of its exposure to this source of risk.

Several commercial services provide estimates of extramarket covariance for computer analysis of a portfolio's overall risk. Common factors vary. One service[16] uses two (yield and capitalization), another[17] six ("market variability," "earnings variability," "unsuccess and low valuation," "immaturity and smallness," "growth orientation," and "financial risk"), with each of the six computed as a weighted average of from five to fourteen basic security attributes. As with beta prediction, the ultimate test of such procedures is their ability to predict *future* risk, and only experience will provide adequate information concerning their relative predictive abilities.

SPECIFIC RISK

Factors that affect the majority of stocks to a greater or lesser extent lead to *market risk*. Those that affect more than one stock but less than all re-

[16] Provided by Canavest House Limited.
[17] Provided by Barr Rosenberg Associates.

sult in *extramarket covariance*. Those that affect only one stock are responsible for *security-specific risk*.

Future specific risk is related to historic specific risk, and we can estimate it by adjusting experienced values for a tendency for such risk to move back toward average values. But, as with beta, other information can be used to improve predictions. Several services use prediction equations for specific risk that incorporate other information in a manner similar to that used for predictions of beta.

The Components of Risk

Figure 13-7 shows a typical breakdown of risk into its major components. For an individual security, specific risk is most important, but for the typical portfolio held by an institutional investor such as a pension fund, market risk is most important. Diversification reduces security-specific risk most rapidly, common-factor and industry risk less rapidly, and market risk not at all. For investors holding highly diversified portfolios, market risk is the most important type to estimate and to control, with extramarket covariance next in importance and security-specific risk last.

FIGURE 13-7 Components of Risk.

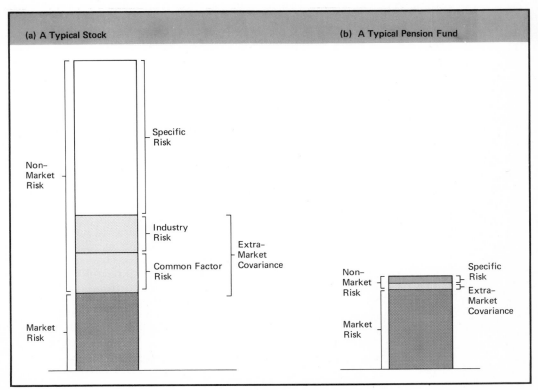

Note: Proposition represents typical amount of variance of return.

But for investors hoping to profit from concentrated positions in "undervalued" groups, industries, or individual securities, good estimates of nonmarket sources of risk are crucial.

More analysis of factors contributing to nonmarket risk is needed. However, prudence decrees that one assume that such risk will be greater, the greater the concentrations of stocks in the same industry or market sector or the more extreme a crucial attribute (e.g., yield) of the portfolio. Such concentration need not be undesirable, but the associated increase in risk should be identified and should be undertaken only when there is a reasonable prospect for a concomitant increase in return.

RISK AND RETURN FOR COMMON STOCKS

Both the original and the expanded version of the capital-asset pricing model suggest that, other things equal, securities with large ex ante beta values should have large ex ante expected returns. This does not mean that they will necessarily have large ex post actual returns. If the market goes up substantially, one expects actual returns to be higher for higher-beta stocks; on the other hand, if the market goes down, one expects high-beta stocks to go down the most. But even these are expectations. A stock's ex ante beta is based on a composite of possible sources of market moves. Ex post, only some of those sources will have contributed in the same direction to the market move, and some factors not even considered in advance will undoubtedly also have played a role. For all these reasons, actual returns over even reasonably long periods may bear little if any relationship to ex ante expectations and hence to ex ante beta values.

To compound the problem, it is difficult to know what a security's ex ante beta really was at any time. Partly this is due to the lack of widely published estimates incorporating fundamental factors and subjective judgments. Empirical studies thus usually rely either on "quality" ratings, designed partly for other purposes, or on historic beta values (under the unreasonable assumption that analysts use only past price behavior in assessing future risk).

A final problem concerns the definition of beta itself. The relevant figure measures a security's sensitivity to a widely diversified market portfolio including all types of stocks, bonds, real estate, etc. Empirical studies have instead typically used a broad-based index of widely traded stocks, since adequate data on other securities have been difficult or impossible to obtain. Clearly, a security's beta relative to, say, the New York Stock Exchange "market portfolio" could differ significantly from that measured relative to the full United States market portfolio, let alone an international market portfolio.

Despite all these problems it is instructive to see how well common stocks with different historic beta values and quality ratings have done over time. Most research has been directed to the United States market. However, there have been some analyses of experience in other countries.

FIGURE 13-8 Composition of Risk-Return Groups.

Risk-Return Group	Stocks from Beta Book Included
10 (highest)	top 10%
9	top 30%
8	top 50%
7	top 70%
6	top 90%
5	bottom 90%
4	bottom 70%
3	bottom 50%
2	bottom 30%
1 (lowest)	bottom 10%

Source: Data used for study reported in William F. Sharpe and Guy M. Cooper, "Risk-Return Classes of New York Stock Exchange Common Stocks, 1931–1967."

Risk-Return Groups

The development of a computerized file of monthly returns for all stocks listed on the New York Stock Exchange from 1926 to the present[18] facilitated extensive investigations of risk and return for such securities. Most studies used an unweighted average of the returns on all securities listed on the Exchange at any time as a surrogate for the market portfolio. The relationship between risk and return was generally examined by measuring each security's beta relative to this index over some historic period (e.g., five years), then forming portfolios designed to include many stocks but also to differ as much as possible in this respect. For example, on January 1, 1931, equal dollar amounts of the top 10% of all securities listed by historic beta might be placed in one portfolio, equal dollar amounts of the top 20% in another portfolio, etc. On January 1, 1932, the process might be repeated, rebalancing each portfolio to again contain equal dollar proportions of the stocks in the appropriate part of the then-current "beta-book."

This approach defines several *risk-return groups* of stocks with similar historic betas and thus, hopefully, similar ex ante market risk and expected return.

Figure 13-8 shows the stocks included in ten groups used in one such study, and Figure 13-9 shows some of the results. Each bar indicates the arithmetic average annual return from 1931 through 1967 for a risk-return group. Figure 13-9(b) shows the ex post beta values, and Figure 13-9(c) provides a cross-plot of the average returns and ex post beta values for all ten groups along with the best-fit regression line. Despite the potential problems with such analyses, the results are substantially consistent with the theoretical relationship between return and market risk.

Figure 13-10 shows the results from a study concerned with longer

---

[18] Performed at the Center for Research in Security Prices at the University of Chicago, and sponsored by Merrill Lynch, Pierce, Fenner and Smith, Inc.

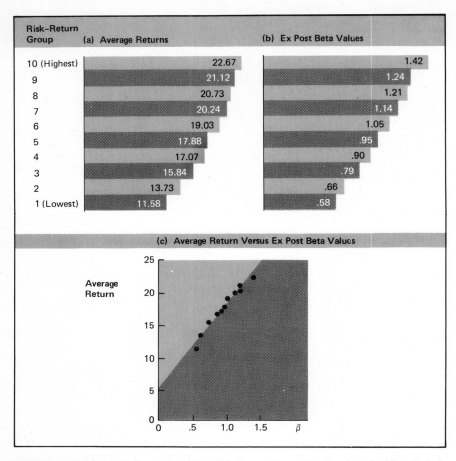

Risk–Return Group	(a) Average Returns	(b) Ex Post Beta Values
10 (Highest)	22.67	1.42
9	21.12	1.24
8	20.73	1.21
7	20.24	1.14
6	19.03	1.05
5	17.88	.95
4	17.07	.90
3	15.84	.79
2	13.73	.66
1 (Lowest)	11.58	.58

(c) Average Return Versus Ex Post Beta Values

FIGURE 13-9(a)(b)(c) Performance of Ten Risk-Return Groups for One-Year Holding Periods 1931–1967

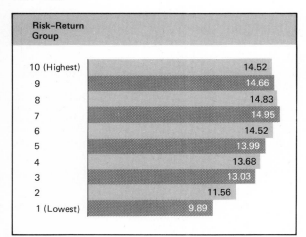

Risk–Return Group	
10 (Highest)	14.52
9	14.66
8	14.83
7	14.95
6	14.52
5	13.99
4	13.68
3	13.03
2	11.56
1 (Lowest)	9.89

FIGURE 13-9(d) Equivalent Constant Annual Returns, 1931–1967

Source: Based on data used in the study reported in William F. Sharpe and Guy M. Cooper, "Risk-Return Classes of New York Stock Exchange Common Stocks, 1931–1967," *Financial Analysts Journal*, 28, no. 2 (March/April 1972), 46–54.

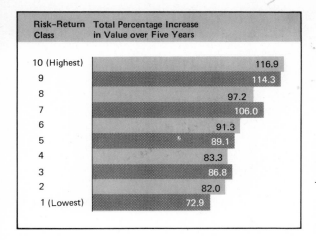

Risk–Return Class	Total Percentage Increase in Value over Five Years
10 (Highest)	116.9
9	114.3
8	97.2
7	106.0
6	91.3
5	89.1
4	83.3
3	86.8
2	82.0
1 (Lowest)	72.9

FIGURE 13-10 Average Performance of Ten Risk-Return Classes over Eight Five-Year Holding Periods, 1928–1968.

Source: Marshall E. Blume and Irwin Friend, "Risk, Investment Strategy, and the Long-run Rates of Return," *Review of Economics and Statistics*, LVI, no. 3 (August 1974), 259–69.

holding periods. In this case the eight five-year nonoverlapping periods from mid-1928 through mid-1968 were analyzed and the percentage change in value determined for an account that remained fully invested during each period (i.e., all dividends received during the five years were reinvested).[19] The results are roughly consistent with a positive relationship between market risk and medium-term return.

What about return over very long holding periods? Figure 13-9(d) shows performance for the risk-return groups used in the first study over the 37-year period from 1931 through 1967. Each bar indicates the geometric mean return for one of the ten groups. This equals the constant annual return that would have given the same terminal value as the actual strategy, assuming a fully invested position throughout the period, with no withdrawals. The picture is less clear than those obtained earlier, but overall it shows that there appears to be a positive relationship between market risk and long-run return as well.

[19] Portfolios were rebalanced monthly, and each portfolio contained the 10% of the stocks with historic betas in the same decile.

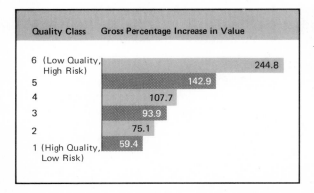

Quality Class	Gross Percentage Increase in Value
6 (Low Quality, High Risk)	244.8
5	142.9
4	107.7
3	93.9
2	75.1
1 (High Quality, Low Risk)	59.4

FIGURE 13-11 Average Performance of Fitch Quality Classes over Eight Five-Year Holding Periods 1926–1971.

Source: Marshall E. Blume and Irwin Friend, "Risk Investment Strategy, and the Long-run Rates of Return," *Review of Economics and Statistics*, LVI, no. 3 (August 1974), 259–69.

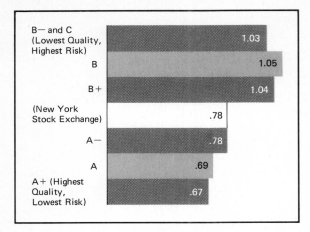

FIGURE 13-12 Performance of Standard and Poor's Quality Classes, 1960–1970.

Source: W. H. Wagner and S. C. Lau, "The Effect of Diversification on Risk," *Financial Analysts Journal,* 27, no. 6 (Nov./Dec. 1971), 48–57.

Quality Classes

A study using the *quality ratings* published by the Fitch service until 1963 as surrogates for ex ante risk showed a strong relationship between the average increase in value over eight five-year holding periods and this subjective measure of quality. Figure 13-11 on page 357 shows the results for six classes based on these ratings.

Figure 13-12 indicates the usefulness of the quality ratings assigned by Standard and Poor's[20] as surrogates for ex ante risk. In all, 236 securities were analyzed. The figure shows the mean monthly return from mid-1960 through mid-1970 for each of six quality classes, along with the value for the New York Stock Exchange Average, which was used as a surrogate for the market portfolio. Even over this relatively short period, return was related to an ex ante measure of investment quality.

Short-Term Returns

Neither quality ratings nor historic beta values can be counted on to predict returns precisely, even relative to market moves, over every period. Figures 13-13 and 13-14 illustrate the point.

Figures 13-13(a) through (d) plot the average monthly returns over four different 105-month periods for ten risk-return classes based on historic beta values. In each case the market return (indicated by a square) exceeded the riskless rate of interest. Three of the lines of best fit are upward-sloping as expected, but one is not.

Figure 13-14 shows that the relationships for individual years are even more varied. Each diagram plots the returns obtained from each of ten risk-return classes based on historic beta values, along with that of the market as a whole (indicated by the horizontal dashed line). Many of the graphs conform to expectations: in years of substantial market increases, high risk-return classes outperform lower ones; in years of substantial market declines, high risk-return classes underperform the others; and in

[20] Listed in Standard and Poor's Monthly *Stock Guide*.

years in which the market return differs little from riskless interest rates, there is little difference among the returns of the ten classes. However, several diagrams show substantial discrepancies from expectations. As indicated earlier, this is hardly surprising. In up markets one *expects* high-beta stocks to outperform low-beta stocks, but just the reverse can happen. In down markets one *expects* high-beta stocks to do worse than low-beta stocks, but just the reverse can happen. The possibility that the actual relationship between return and beta will differ from that expected, given the actual performance of the market, is another form of risk that should be taken into account in portfolio management.

FIGURE 13-13 Performance of Ten Risk-Return Classes, Four 105-Month Periods 1931–1965.

Source: Fischer Black, Michael C. Jensen, and Myron Scholes, "The Capital Asset Pricing Model: Some Empirical Tests," in Michael C. Jensen (ed.), *Studies in the Theory of Capital Markets* (New York: Praeger Publishers, Inc., 1972).

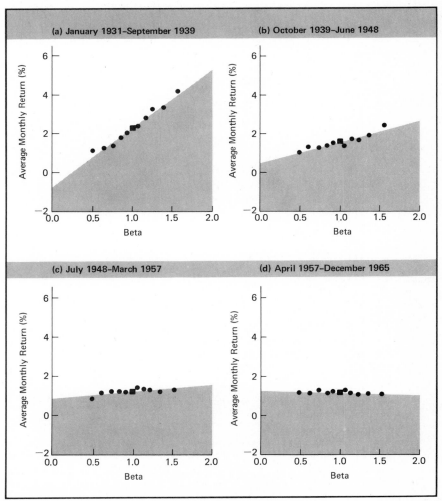

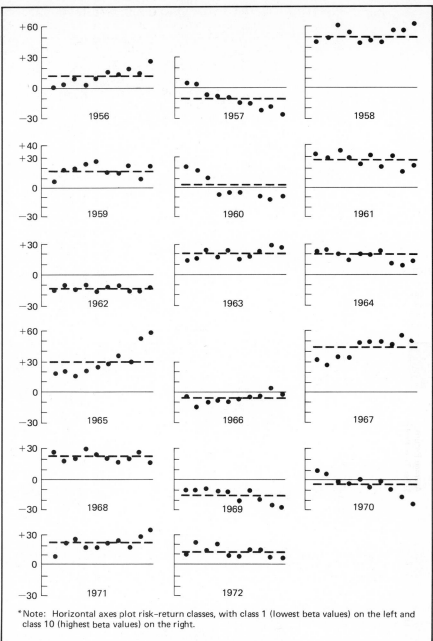

*Note: Horizontal axes plot risk–return classes, with class 1 (lowest beta values) on the left and class 10 (highest beta values) on the right.

FIGURE 13-14 Performance of the Ten Risk-Return Classes, Seventeen Years, 1956–1972.

Source: William L. Fouse, William W. Jahnke, and Barr Rosenberg, ''Is Beta Phlogiston?'' *Financial Analysts Journal*, 30, no. 1 (January/February 1974), 72.

Returns Outside the United States

Computerized files of the prices of securities over many years are not presently available for stocks traded outside the United States. Studies of other countries' securities have thus relied primarily on data from the 1960s and 1970s.

Figure 13-15 shows some of the results. In each diagram the risks (beta values relative to an index of the country's stock market) and returns for several portfolios, formed using historic beta values, are indicated (by dots), along with the (solid) line of best fit.

The relatively short periods covered and the small number of securities analyzed (except for Japan) make these results suggestive at best. In addition to the problems involved in any such study, the use of an index of the local (country) stock market as a surrogate for "the" market portfolio is even more subject to criticism here, where relatively small portions of an international market are being considered, than when the United States, a relatively large portion, is under study.

FIGURE 13-15 Performance of Portfolios Selected on the Basis of Historic Beta in Four Countries

Sources: (a), (b), (c): Franco Modigliani, Gerald Pogue, Myron Scholes, Bruno Solnik, "Efficiency of the European Capital Markets and a Comparison with the American Market," paper presented at First World Congress on the Stock Exchange (March 1972). (d): Carl M. Ramsey, Sheila C. Lau, Stuart R. Quay, "Application of Capital Asset Pricing Model to the Tokyo Stock Exchange," Wells Fargo Bank (February 1972).

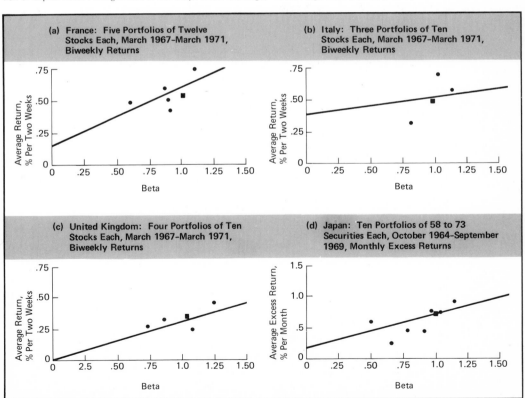

Despite these major drawbacks, the results shown in Figure 13-15 are at least not violently inconsistent with the basic ideas of the capital-asset pricing model: in each case the best-fit line is upward-sloping.

Full consideration of risk and return for *any* security that trades internationally requires a viewpoint extending beyond the borders of the country of the issuing firm. It suffices to say here that nothing shown in Figure 13-15 suggests that these four capital markets behave differently from that of the United States.

The Relationships between Risk and Return

To what extent do investors receive additional return for taking additional risk? The final results are not in yet. Investigators are using more extensive sets of data, more detailed theoretical models, and more sophisticated statistical methods to provide better answers to the many questions involved. Some tentative conclusions may be given, nonetheless.

There is every reason to believe that in most capital markets prices do adjust so that expected return and ex ante market risk go together.

On the other hand, *actual* returns may diverge substantially from *expected* returns, even over rather long periods.

While securities with high nonmarket risk often appear to outperform those with low nonmarket risk, this may well be due to the fact that the former also have higher market risks than the latter. Thus one should not reject the notion that high expected return is a reward for bearing *market* risk.

Considerable debate has centered on the magnitude of the relationship between risk and return. For example, the line of best fit in Figure 13-9(c) intercepts the return axis slightly above 5%. During the period covered, the average interest rate on default-free short-term securities was about 2%. Since this is the longest period available for study and the data come from the largest stock market in the world, many have argued that in general the actual line will be flatter than that suggested by the original capital-asset pricing model.

As suggested in Chapter 8, there are many reasons why this could be the case. More sophisticated procedures have been applied to try to sort out the possible effects of yield, liquidity, inflation hedging, and other security attributes that may affect expected return. Overall, the evidence lends more support to some of the expanded versions of the capital-asset pricing model than it does to the original version. However, the studies continue to show a positive relationship between returns and beta values, despite the fact that the measure of "the market" employed typically involves only a subset of the true market portfolio.[21]

A final issue concerns the returns on very high-risk securities. Many believe that such investments attract congenital optimists who tend to pay too much, making their expected returns less than appropriate, given the risk involved. While this may apply to the lunatic fringe of get-rich-quick

---

[21] For a detailed discussion of this point and a number of related issues, see Richard Roll, "A Critique of the Asset Pricing Theory's Tests," Cahier de Recherche, No. 45/1976, Centre d'Enseignement Superieur des Affaires (Jouy-en-Josas, France).

schemes, there is only limited evidence that it is true for widely traded stocks listed on major stock exchanges. It is true, however, that such stocks often have very high nonmarket risks, for which additional return should not be expected and will not generally be forthcoming. Concentration in such stocks is thus likely to lead to inferior performance relative to total risk, as it should.

To summarize: empirical studies of the returns from stocks with different historical beta values and/or quality ratings generally provide support for the concepts described in earlier chapters. But they also point to the need for the best possible estimates of ex ante risk and return. And they provide a sobering note for all who invest in common stock. No matter how sophisticated the analysis of available information, the future will still be very uncertain. Actual stock returns can, and usually will, differ substantially from the expectations of even the most well-informed and sophisticated analysts. This is, after all, what risk is all about.

Problems

1. Three dates are involved in most stock splits: (1) the date when the management proposes a split, (2) the date when the stockholders approve the split, and (3) the date that the split actually becomes effective. Figure 13-1 is concerned with only the third date. In an efficient market what would you expect to be the average behavior of abnormal changes in stock values before and after each of the other two dates? If the evidence were not consistent with market efficiency, how might you exploit it?

2. What might account for the differences in the bid/ask spreads in Figure 13-2(a)? Why are bid and ask values not shown in Figure 13-2(b)?

3. Some have advocated that insider trading be allowed, even if the insider involved has information not known to those outside the firm, on the grounds that this will bring the information to the marketplace in an efficient and timely manner. Yet public policy places severe limits on this action on the grounds of equity. What considerations are involved in this issue? What form of public policy would you advocate?

4. State public utility commissions are charged with the task of setting rates for telephone, electricity, and gas companies that will provide a "reasonable return on capital." Many of the hearings involve testimony as to the implications of the capital-asset pricing model and the relevant values of beta for the firms involved. What issues are important for such decisions in terms of (1) models of risk and return and (2) estimation of beta values?

5. Assume that every stock is classified so that its earnings come completely from one industry. Show that an equation such as (13-3) is equivalent to adjusting each stock's beta value back toward an "average beta" for its industry.

6. Empirical evidence shows that, other things equal, stocks with low prices per share tend to have higher beta values than those with high prices per share. Why might this be the case? Under what conditions should it definitely *not* be the case that a lower price would indicate a higher beta value?

7. Empirical evidence indicates that, other things equal, stocks with large market values of equity outstanding tend to move together, over and above market moves, while those with small amounts of equity outstanding tend to move together in the other direction. What sorts of changes in future prospects might have differential effects on large versus small stocks?

8. Stocks with above-average beta values tend to have below-average yields. If tax effects make both yield and beta relevant for expected return, why might an analysis in which average return is compared with beta values be likely to understate the true relationship between return and beta per se?

9. Give some examples of likely sources of (a) market risk, (b) common-factor risk, (c) industry risk, and (d) stock-specific risk. In what sense is this sort of taxonomy slightly arbitrary?

10. a. A friend tells you that he selects his portfolio by throwing 100 darts at a page of *The Wall Street Journal*, then purchasing the 100 "selected" stocks. Is it important that he obtain good estimates of the resulting portfolio's market risk? extramarket covariance? securityspecific risk? Why?

    b. Another friend likes to make "industry plays." She feels that she cannot identify superior and inferior stocks within industries but can determine situations in which the stocks in one industry are overvalued while those in another are undervalued. Accordingly, she concentrates her holdings by industry but holds many stocks from each of the selected industries. What types of risk estimates are particularly important for her?

    c. A third friend is a "stock picker." He likes to identify a few "undervalued" stocks and "plunge." What sorts of risk estimates are especially relevant for him?

The Valuation of Common Stocks

14

STOCK VALUATION BASED ON
EXPECTED DIVIDENDS

The value of a noncallable default-free bond can be determined in a relatively straightforward manner. Each cash flow to be received by its owner can be discounted, using current discount factors or forward interest rates, and the sum of all such values computed; this is the present value of the bond.

If there is some chance that a bond will default, two changes can be made. First, *expected* cash payments can be estimated for each period. Second, these can be discounted using interest rates appropriate for the relevant risk involved (i.e., risk in a portfolio context).

The valuation of a common stock can proceed along similar lines. One obvious modification is required: while bonds mature, stocks typically do not and can, in principle, provide cash flows forever. Taking this into account, we can write the basic formula for the valuation of a common stock as:

$$v_0 = \frac{\overline{d}_1}{1 + r_1} + \frac{\overline{d}_2}{(1 + r_1)(1 + r_2)}$$
$$+ \frac{\overline{d}_3}{(1 + r_1)(1 + r_2)(1 + r_3)} + \cdots$$

(14-1)

where:

$$\overline{d}_1, \overline{d}_2, \overline{d}_3, \ldots = \text{the expected dividends per share (plus the value of any other distributions) in years 1, 2, 3, } \ldots$$

$$r_1, r_2, r_3, \ldots = \text{the appropriate discount rates for the relevant risk involved}$$

$$v_0 = \text{the present value of the stock at time zero}$$

The dots indicate that the terms continue on—i.e., that this is an *infinite series*.

It should be emphasized that only items of value *received* by the stockholder are relevant in the valuation process. Generally these take the form of cash dividends. Other distributions (e.g., stock dividends) can be treated by adding the expected proceeds from their sale. Alternatively, the assumption can be made that the resulting shares are held, and their dividends can be included in subsequent cash flows.

It might seem that this formula could imply an infinite value. This is mathematically, but not economically, possible. The present value of a dollar will be less, the farther in the future its receipt. Unless dividend payments grow faster than the rate of discount, the present values of more and more distant dividends will eventually become smaller and smaller, and the series will converge to a finite value.

VALUATION BASED ON HOLDING-PERIOD RETURN

Formula (14-1) is relevant for an investor who plans to hold a stock forever. But what about someone who plans to sell in a year? Clearly, the relevant value in such a case will depend on the price for which the stock can be sold at year-end. The valuation formula is thus:

$$v_0 = \frac{\overline{d}_1}{1 + r_1} + \frac{\overline{P}_1}{1 + r_1} \qquad \text{(14-2a)}$$

where $\overline{P}_1$ is the expected price of the stock at the end of year 1.

It may seem easier to estimate near-term dividends and future price than to estimate dividends over the infinite future. However, the former procedure does not really obviate the latter. To estimate further price, one must predict the valuation procedure that will be used by purchasers and the ingredients that will go into it at the time.

The simplest approach assumes that the purchaser will offer a price based on the then-remaining expected dividends, and that the best estimate (at present) is that next year neither expected dividends nor the appropriate discount rates will have changed. The expected price is thus:

$$\overline{P}_1 = v_1 = \frac{\overline{d}_2}{1 + r_2} + \frac{\overline{d}_3}{(1 + r_2)(1 + r_3)} + \cdots \qquad \text{(14-2b)}$$

Substituting this into (14-2a) gives:

$$\begin{aligned} v_0 &= \frac{\overline{d}_1}{1 + r_1} + \frac{1}{1 + r_1}\left[\frac{\overline{d}_2}{1 + r_2} + \frac{\overline{d}_3}{(1 + r_2)(1 + r_3)} + \cdots\right] \\ &= \frac{\overline{d}_1}{1 + r_1} + \frac{\overline{d}_2}{(1 + r_1)(1 + r_2)} + \frac{\overline{d}_3}{(1 + r_1)(1 + r_2)(1 + r_3)} + \cdots \end{aligned}$$

which is exactly the same as formula (14-1).

A similar process can be used to show that no matter how long the desired holding period, under these conditions the present value will be the same.

Most stocks are held by a long series of investors, each of whom is interested only in the price paid, the price received when the stock is sold, and the dividends received while it is held. But every selling price is someone else's buying price. Intermediate prices thus wash out, leaving dividends as the essential elements of value.

THE RISK STRUCTURE OF DISCOUNT RATES

When bonds are analyzed, both the term structure and the risk structure of interest rates are generally considered. The relative precision with which receipts can be estimated warrants attention to such details. Practice is quite different, however, when stocks are considered. The difficulty involved in projecting dividends years into the future makes attention to a detailed structure of different interest rates seem misplaced in the eyes of most analysts. Even though dividends might be considered more risky the farther in the future their date of payment, a single discount rate is typically used for all dividends of stocks in the same risk class, and no attempt is made to identify any sort of term structure.

The resulting valuation equation is thus:

$$v_0 = \frac{\overline{d_1}}{1 + r} + \frac{\overline{d_2}}{(1 + r)^2} + \frac{\overline{d_3}}{(1 + r)^3} + \cdots \qquad (14\text{-}3)$$

where:

r = the appropriate discount rate for the stock's risk class.

As discussed in previous chapters, the appropriate method for identifying a risk class focuses on *market risk*—i.e., the sensitivity of a stock's returns to market swings (or of the company's earnings to changes in the level of the economy). Stocks with similar *beta* values should thus be considered to be in the same risk class. According to the original capital-asset

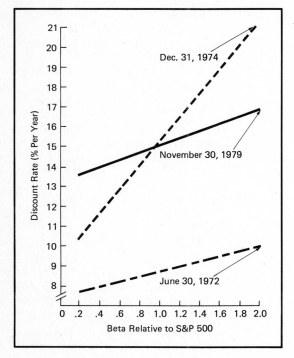

FIGURE 14-1 Stock Discount Rates versus Beta.

Source: Wells Fargo Bank *Security Market Plane Report,* December 1979.

pricing model, expected returns should be related only to beta values; according to some of the expanded versions of the model, expected returns should be related to beta values and to other factors (e.g., yield, liquidity, inflation hedging).

Figure 14-1 shows Wells Fargo bank's estimates of the security risk line[1]—relating discount rates to beta values—at various times. Beta values are plotted on the horizontal axis and discount rates on the vertical axis. As the figure shows, the risk structure of stock discount rates appears to change from time to time. Upward shifts in the line typically reflect increases in expected inflation. Increases in the slope of the line may reflect either increased aversion to risk or (more likely) increased estimates of the risk associated with equities. Decreases in the slope may, correspondingly, reflect either decreased aversion to risk or a reduction in the estimated risk of equity investment.

VALUATION BASED ON EARNINGS

A repeated but somewhat pointless controversy concerns the relevance of dividends versus earnings as a source of value. Earnings are important, but only because they can provide dividends. One cannot eat earnings. But there is a sense in which they can be considered a source of value.

In the course of a year, a firm produces revenue and incurs costs. The difference is termed "cash flow," although often both revenues and costs include estimates made by accountants of the values of noncash items. Depreciation charges, taxes, interest payments, and so on are deducted from cash flow to obtain *earnings*. Moreover, each year some amount is invested in the business. Of the total (*gross*) investment, a portion will be equal in value to the estimated depreciation of capital; the rest is *net* (new) investment.

The amount of new investment each year should be a function of investment opportunities, not of earnings, cash flow, and the like. Any investment project with an expected return in excess of that available in the market from comparable (e.g., equal beta risk) investments should be undertaken. Desirable projects may be financed via depreciation, retained earnings, and/or new capital, but this is a separate issue.

The investment decisions of a firm can and should be relatively independent of its financial decisions. The future prospects of the firm can thus be described by a series of expected total earnings $(E_1, E_2, E_3, \ldots)$ and the expected total (net) investment required to produce such earnings $(I_1, I_2, I_3, \ldots)$, all predicated on the firm's expected investment decisions.

Figure 14-2(a) shows the usual disposition of earnings. Some of the total is used to make dividend payments for the year (D_t); the remainder is *retained* by the firm and used to finance the next year's investment (I_t).

In Figure 14-2(a), total dividends are equal to earnings minus new investment $(E_t - I_t)$. This need not be the case, however. In the situation shown in Figure 14-2(b) more is paid out and new capital obtained to

[1] A "cut" from the security market plane, described in Chapter 9. The method used by Wells Fargo to estimate the location of the plane is described later in this chapter.

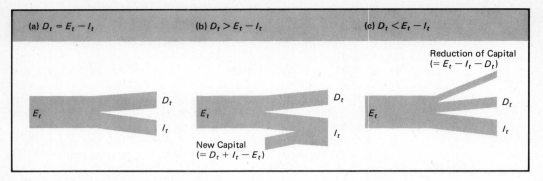

(a) $D_t = E_t - I_t$ **(b)** $D_t > E_t - I_t$ **(c)** $D_t < E_t - I_t$

Reduction of Capital
$(= E_t - I_t - D_t)$

D_t

E_t

I_t

New Capital
$(= D_t + I_t - E_t)$

FIGURE 14-2 Earnings, Dividends, and Investment.

complete the financing of planned investment. In Figure 14-2(c) the situation is reversed. Here dividends and investment do not exhaust total earnings, and the remainder is used to reduce outstanding capital—for example, by purchasing outstanding shares of common stock.

What will be the total value of a corporation if any of the strategies illustrated in Figure 14-2 can be adopted? The simplest way to answer this is to consider an investor presently holding 1% of the total stock of the firm. If markets are efficient, the value of such a holding should be the same whether the owner intends to sell some or all of it and/or buy additional shares in the future. Imagine then that our investor is determined to maintain ownership of 1% of the firm. When earnings are used as shown in Figure 14-2(a), no problem arises; his or her dividends will equal $.01D_t$, or $.01(E_t - I_t)$, and can be spent at will.

When the distribution is similar to that shown in Figure 14-2(b), however, the investor must put up additional capital to avoid a diminished proportional ownership of the firm. How much is needed? One percent of the total, or $.01(D_t + I_t - E_t)$. The net amount available to be spent is thus:

$$.01D_t - .01(D_t + I_t - E_t) = .01(E_t - I_t)$$

In a case similar to that shown in Figure 14-2(c), when the firm reduces capital by purchasing shares, our investor must sell back some of his or her holdings to maintain ownership of 1% of the firm. This will generate additional income, bringing the total to:

$$.01D_t + .01(E_t - I_t - D_t) = .01(E_t - I_t)$$

Thus no matter what the firm's financing policy, an investor choosing to maintain a constant proportional ownership will be able to spend a proportional share in the firm's earnings net of investment $(E_t - I_t)$ each year. Discounting the expected values by a (constant) interest rate, the value of 1% of the current shares outstanding will be:

$$\frac{.01(\overline{E}_1 - \overline{I}_1)}{1 + r} + \frac{.01(\overline{E}_2 - \overline{I}_2)}{(1 + r)^2} + \frac{.01(E_3 - I_3)}{(1 + r)^3} + \cdots$$

And the value of all shares outstanding—i.e., the total value of the firm's equity—will be:

$$V_0 = \frac{\overline{E}_1 - \overline{I}_1}{1 + r} + \frac{\overline{E}_2 - \overline{I}_2}{(1 + r)^2} + \frac{\overline{E}_3 - \overline{I}_3}{(1 + r)^3} + \cdots \qquad \text{(14-4a)}$$

or:

$$V_0 = \left[\frac{\overline{E}_1}{1 + r} + \frac{\overline{E}_2}{(1 + r)^2} + \frac{\overline{E}_3}{(1 + r)^3} + \cdots \right]$$
$$- \left[\frac{\overline{I}_1}{1 + r} + \frac{\overline{I}_2}{(1 + r)^2} + \frac{\overline{I}_3}{(1 + r)^3} + \cdots \right] \qquad \text{(14-4b)}$$

Formula (14-4a) shows that the value of equity is the present value of expected earnings net of required investment; the second version, formula (14-4b), shows that it equals the present value of expected earnings (the first bracketed series) less the present value of the expected investment required (the second bracketed expression).

DETERMINANTS OF DIVIDENDS

Both interviews with corporate executives and empirical analyses of financial data indicate that most firms have a *target payout ratio* that changes relatively little from year to year. Such a value represents a desired ratio of dividends to earnings over some relatively long period. Alternatively, it may be thought of as a target ratio of dividends to long-run or sustainable earnings.

Few firms attempt to maintain a constant ratio of dividends to *current* earnings, since at least some of the variation in earnings from year to year is likely to be transitory. Moreover, since many corporate executives appear to dislike cutting dividends, regular payments are often increased only when management believes it will be relatively easy to maintain the new, higher level in the future (sometimes "special" or "extra" dividends are declared, usually at year-end, to indicate that the increase may not be

TABLE 14-1 Dividend and Earnings Changes for 392 Major Industrial Firms, 1946–1964

EARNINGS CHANGES			PERCENT OF CASES IN WHICH FIRMS		
Current Year	Previous Year	Percent of Cases	Increased Dividends	Did Not Change Dividends	Decreased Dividends
+		59.3	65.8	13.9	20.3
−		40.7	42.8	17.9	39.5
+	+	33.4	74.8	11.4	13.8
−	−	16.0	31.8	19.4	48.8

Source: Eugene F. Fama and Harvey Babiak, "Dividend Policy: An Empirical Analysis," *American Statistical Association Journal*, 63, no. 324 (December 1968), 1132–61.

maintained). Nonetheless, larger earnings are likely to be accompanied by some sort of increase in dividends, as Table 14-1 shows.

Although dividend payments are increased more often than they are decreased, reductions do take place. Moreover, a decline in earnings is more likely to be accompanied by a decline in dividends than is an increase in earnings. During the period covered in Table 14-1, almost half the firms experiencing two successive years of declining earnings reduced dividends.

A formal representation of the kind of behavior implied by a constant long-run target payout ratio was suggested by Lintner.[2] Assume that the goal is to pay out k^* (e.g., .6) of long-run earnings. If this target ratio were maintained every year, total dividends paid in year t would be:

$$D_t^* = k^* E_t$$

where:

D_t^* = target for total dividends paid in year t
k^* = target payout ratio
E_t = total earnings in year t

The difference between target dividends in year t and the previous year's actual dividends would be:

$$D_t^* - D_{t-1} = k^* E_t - D_{t-1}$$

Few if any firms would adjust dividends by this amount. Instead, actual dividends change by some proportion of the difference:

$$D_t - D_{t-1} = p(D_t^* - D_{t-1}) \qquad \textbf{(14-5a)}$$

[2] John Lintner, "Distribution of Incomes of Corporations Among Dividends, Retained Earnings, and Taxes," *American Economic Review*, XLVI, no. 2 (May 1956), 97–113.

TABLE 14-2 Target Payout Ratios and Speed of Dividend Adjustment Factors for 298 Firms, 1946–1968

SPEED OF ADJUSTMENT COEFFICIENT		TARGET PAYOUT RATIO		PERCENT OF VARIANCE EXPLAINED	
Value	Percent of Firms with Smaller Value	Value	Percent of Firms with Smaller Value	Value (%)	Percent of Firms with Smaller Value
.104	10	.401	10	11	10
.182	30	.525	30	32	30
.251	50	.584	50	42	50
.339	70	.660	70	54	70
.470	90	.779	90	72	90
average .269		average .591		average 42	

Source: Eugene F. Fama, "The Empirical Relationship Between the Dividend and Investment Decisions of Firms," *American Economic Review*, LXIV, no. 3 (June 1974), 304–18.

where p is a "speed of adjustment" coefficient (less than 1.0). Rearranging formula (14-5a):

$$D_t = pk^*E_t + (1 - p)D_{t-1} \qquad \text{(14-5b)}$$

Statistical analysis can be used to estimate a firm's target payout ratio (k^*) and speed of adjustment (p). Table 14-2 summarizes some of the values obtained in one such study. The typical firm had a target payout ratio of about 60% (.591) and adjusted dividends on average about one-fourth (.269) of the way toward its target per year. However, most firms' dividends varied substantially from the pattern implied by their targets and adjustment factors. Somewhat less than half (42%) of the annual variance in the typical firm's dividends could be explained in this manner.

THE INFORMATION CONTENT OF DIVIDENDS

Given an estimate of a firm's target payout ratio and speed of dividend adjustment, it is possible to estimate "normal" dividends for a year. If a lower or higher amount is announced, it seems reasonable to interpret the action as conveying information about management's assessment of the prospects for future earnings. For example, a higher dividend than normally associated with an increase in earnings might indicate that management expects the increase to be more permanent than usual. A lower-than-normal dividend increase under such circumstances might suggest that management considers the increase more transitory than usual, and so on.

One test of this procedure yielded fairly disappointing results. Statistical analysis was used to estimate each firm's target payout ratio and speed of adjustment and then to classify dividends as unexpectedly larger or smaller than normal. Earnings were also categorized as unexpectedly larger or smaller than "normal" (i.e., relative to an average trend-line annual increase). Table 14-3 shows the results obtained when dividend changes were compared with earnings changes in the subsequent year. While unexpectedly high dividends were more likely to signal unexpect-

TABLE 14-3 Unexpected Dividend Changes versus Unexpected Earnings Changes in the Subsequent Year, 310 Firms, 1945–1968

	NUMBER OF CASES IN WHICH THE UNEXPECTED CHANGE IN EARNINGS IN THE SUBSEQUENT YEAR WAS		
Unexpected Change in Dividends	**Positive**	**Negative**	**Total Number of Cases**
Positive	1,667	1,457	3,124
Negative	1,507	1,569	3,076
	3,174	3,026	

Source: Ross Watts, "The Information Content of Dividends," *The Journal of Business*, 46, no. 2 (April 1973), 191–211. © 1973 by the University of Chicago. All Rights Reserved.

edly high earnings in the next year than were unexpectedly low dividends, the information content of dividends measured in this manner was rather low. Similar tests to see if dividends, when analyzed in this way, provide information about earnings more than one year hence reached roughly similar conclusions.

These results may indicate that even managers of corporations find it difficult to predict their future earnings. Alternatively, the results may simply reflect the fairly crude methods used to categorize dividends as un-

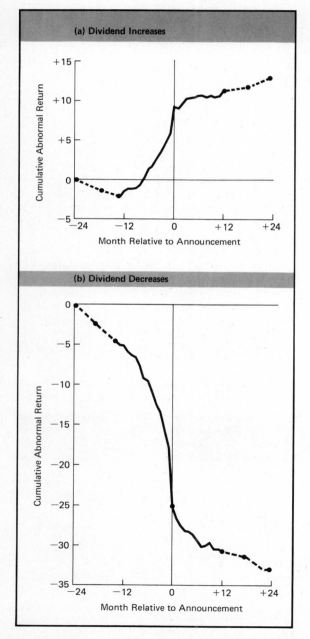

FIGURE 14-3 Abnormal Returns Before and After Substantial Dividend Changes.

Source: Guy Charest, "Dividend Information, Stock Returns and Market Efficiency—II," *Journal of Financial Economics*, June/September 1978. By permission of North-Holland Publishing Company.

expectedly large or small. An "outside" analyst familiar with a company might be able to better classify dividends and thus capture more of their information content concerning future earnings.

Another way to assess the information content of dividends is to see how the market reacts when a fairly long-standing dividend pattern is broken. One study,[3] which examined changes of 10 cents a share or more after two years of a stable dividend pattern, obtained somewhat surprising results. Figure 14-3(a) plots the cumulative "abnormal" performance of the 913 stocks that increased their dividends in this manner; the performance is shown from 24 months before the announcement of the change until 24 months afterward. Figure 14-3(b) plots the results for the 397 stocks that decreased their dividends. In each case the "normal" return was taken to be that of stocks with beta values similar to that of the stock in question, and "abnormal" return to be the difference between the stock's return and this normal value.

In both Figures 14-3(a) and (b) the behavior of stock returns *up to* the date of the dividend announcement can be easily explained. The news could have been anticipated before the actual announcement, causing abnormal changes in price. If so, the dividend changes were the *cause* and the price changes the *effect*. Alternatively, the *causes* of the price changes may have concerned the prospects of the firms, with *both* the dividend changes and the price changes representing effects of these more fundamental aspects.

Whatever the explanation for price changes *in advance* of dividend-change announcements, the evidence is not inconsistent with market efficiency. But the patterns *after* the announcements suggest the possibility of some inefficiency. In the two years after a significant increase in dividends, the stocks provided returns 4% greater than normal, on average. In the two years after a significant decrease, the stocks provided returns 8% smaller than normal, on average.

To some extent this may be due to tax effects: stocks with increased dividends are likely to provide more of their return in the form of yield and may thus be priced to give higher before-tax total returns. Conversely, stocks with decreased dividends may provide less of their return in the form of yield and be priced to give smaller before-tax returns. But there is probably more to it than this.

While the magnitudes of the "abnormal" returns are not large and there is no guarantee that any single stock will react in this manner, this evidence does create a suspicion that the market may not "fully reflect" all information virtually as soon as it is knowable. The market may thus be *highly* but not *perfectly* efficient.

PRICE-EARNINGS RATIOS

Despite the credentials of valuation approaches based explicitly on dividends, many security analysts use a much simpler procedure. First, a

[3] Guy Charest, "Dividend Information, Stock Returns and Market Efficiency—II," *Journal of Financial Economics*, June/September 1978. By permission of North-Holland Publishing Company.

stock's future *earnings per share* (eps) a year or so hence will be estimated; then the analyst (or someone else) will estimate a "normal" *price-earnings ratio* (P/E) for the stock. The product of these two numbers gives the estimated future price. Together with estimated dividends to be paid during the period (e.g., over the next year) and current price, this determines the estimated holding-period return. Some organizations expand the procedure, estimating alternative earnings and/or price-earnings ratios (e.g., optimistic, most likely, and pessimistic) to produce a rudimentary probability distribution of holding-period returns.

How can such procedures be related to the determinants of value? And what characteristics will cause a stock to sell at a high or a low price relative to earnings?

Such questions can be answered by rearranging equation (14-3) and introducing some new variables. As indicated earlier, a firm's (actual) *payout rate* is simply the ratio of dividends to earnings in a year. This can be written using per-share values:

$$k_t = \frac{d_t}{e_t}$$

Thus $d_t = k_t e_t$ and $\overline{k}_t \overline{e}_t$ can be substituted for $\overline{d}_t$ in the valuation formula:[4]

$$v_0 = \frac{\overline{k}_1 \overline{e}_1}{1 + r} + \frac{\overline{k}_2 \overline{e}_2}{(1 + r)^2} + \frac{\overline{k}_3 \overline{e}_3}{(1 + r)^3} + \cdots$$

where:

$\overline{k}_1, \overline{k}_2, \overline{k}_3, \ldots$ are the expected payout ratios in years 1, 2, 3, ...

Expected earnings in any year can be expressed as a function of expected earnings in the prior year. Thus we can define *expected earnings growth rates* ($\overline{g}_1, \overline{g}_2, \overline{g}_3, \ldots$) so that:

$$\overline{e}_1 = (1 + \overline{g}_1)e_0$$
$$\overline{e}_2 = (1 + \overline{g}_2)e_1 = (1 + \overline{g}_1)(1 + \overline{g}_2)e_0$$
$$\overline{e}_3 = (1 + \overline{g}_3)e_2 = (1 + \overline{g}_1)(1 + \overline{g}_2)(1 + \overline{g}_3)e_0$$
$$\vdots$$

where:

e_0 is earnings per share in the current year

A "normal" price-earnings ratio results when a stock sells for its "intrinsic value"—i.e., $P_0 = v_0$. Making this substitution, along with those relating expected future earnings to present earnings, the valuation formula becomes:

---

[4] The product of two expected values will not equal the expected value of the product unless the two variables are uncorrelated. This subtlety is ignored here and in the subsequent formulas.

$$P_0 = \frac{\overline{k}_1(1 + \overline{g}_1)e_0}{1 + r} + \frac{\overline{k}_2(1 + \overline{g}_1)(1 + \overline{g}_2)e_0}{(1 + r)^2}$$
$$+ \frac{\overline{k}_3(1 + \overline{g}_1)(1 + \overline{g}_2)(1 + \overline{g}_3)e_0}{(1 + r)^3} + \cdots$$

Rearranging:

$$\frac{P_0}{e_0} = \frac{\overline{k}_1(1 + \overline{g}_1)}{1 + r} + \frac{\overline{k}_2(1 + \overline{g}_1)(1 + \overline{g}_2)}{(1 + r)^2}$$
$$+ \frac{\overline{k}_3(1 + \overline{g}_1)(1 + \overline{g}_2)(1 + \overline{g}_3)}{(1 + r)^3} + \cdots \qquad (14\text{-}6)$$

This shows the determinants of a stock's normal price-earnings ratio (P_0/e_0). Other things equal, it will be *higher*:

the *greater* the expected payout ratios ($\overline{k}_1, \overline{k}_2, \ldots$)
the *greater* the expected earnings growth rates ($\overline{g}_1, \overline{g}_2, \ldots$)
the *smaller* the rate of interest on default-free securities, and hence the appropriate discount rate (r)
the *smaller* the market (beta) risk and hence the appropriate discount rate (r)

The qualifying phrase "other things equal" should not be overlooked. For example, a firm cannot increase the value of its shares by simply planning greater payouts. This will increase $\overline{k}_1, \overline{k}_2, \ldots$, but decrease expected growth in earnings per share ($\overline{g}_1, \overline{g}_2, \ldots$). As shown previously, if the firm's investment policy is not altered, the effects of the reduced growth in earnings per share will just offset the effects of the increased payouts, leaving value per share unchanged. Another example involves an increase in the rate of interest on default-free securities. If this reflects an increase in expected inflation, projected growth rates in *nominal* earnings per share should be adjusted upward as well. Unless the firm can be expected to gain or lose from inflation, the two effects should offset each other, leaving value per share unchanged.

CONSTANT-GROWTH MODELS

Little in life grows forever at a constant rate, and stocks are no exception. However, many analysts use a simplified valuation model that assumes that they do.

The key idea is to replace $\overline{g}_1, \overline{g}_2, \overline{g}_3$, etc. with a single expected rate, g, at which earnings per share are assumed to grow forever. Clearly, it must be less than the appropriate discount rate, or the value of the stock would be infinite. To further simplify the problem, a constant payout ratio is assumed, and $\overline{k}$ replaces $\overline{k}_1, \overline{k}_2, \ldots$. Formula (14-6) thus becomes:

$$\frac{P_0}{e_0} = \frac{\overline{k}(1 + \overline{g})}{1 + r} + \frac{\overline{k}(1 + \overline{g})^2}{(1 + r)^2} + \frac{\overline{k}(1 + \overline{g})^3}{(1 + r)^3} + \cdots$$

Happily there is a formula for the value of an infinite series of this type, which applies as long as g is less than r. It provides the *constant-growth valuation model*:[5]

$$\frac{P_0}{e_1} = \frac{\overline{k}}{r - \overline{g}} \qquad \text{(14-7a)}$$

or:

$$P_0 = \frac{\overline{k}e_1}{r - \overline{g}} = \frac{d_1}{r - \overline{g}} \qquad \text{(14-7b)}$$

Some insight into the model can be gained by rearranging (14-7b) to obtain:

$$r = \frac{d_1}{P_0} + \overline{g} \qquad \text{(14-7c)}$$

Thus the expected return equals yield (d_1/P_0) plus expected growth $(\overline{g})$. In the constant-growth model everything grows at the same rate. Since the payout ratio is constant, dividends will grow at the same rate as earnings. And since the price-earnings ratio is constant [as formula (14-7a) shows], price will also grow at this rate.

Formula (14-7c) holds, no matter what, if $\overline{g}$ is interpreted as the expected growth in *price* over the coming year, for expected total return *must* equal the expected value of yield plus expected capital gain. The difference here is that both price and earnings are assumed to grow at the same rate each year, and that this rate is to be the same from year to year.

A variation of the constant-growth model makes further assumptions concerning the sources of earnings growth. Assuming that no new capital is obtained and no shares repurchased, the portion of earnings not paid out will constitute the net investment each year:

$$I_t = (1 - k_t)E_t$$

If this investment produces a proportional return of ρ per year, it will add ρI_t to earnings in year $t + 1$ (and every year thereafter). If every previous investment also produces perpetual earnings at a constant rate of return, next year's earnings will equal this year's plus the new earnings resulting from this year's incremental investment:

$$E_{t+1} = E_t + \rho I_t$$
$$= E_t + \rho(1 - k_t)E_t$$
$$= E_t[1 + \rho(1 - k_t)]$$

Growth rate in earnings per share is defined by:

$$E_{t+1} = E_t(1 + g_t)$$

---

[5] Note that these formulas use e_1 and d_1 instead of e_0 and d_0. Some analysts replace e_1 and d_1 with $e_0(1 + g)$ and $d_0(1 + g)$, respectively. Others simply replace them with e_0 and d_0, on the grounds that the resulting errors will be small. The latter changes can be shown to be exactly correct under the somewhat unrealistic assumptions that earnings and dividends grow continuously at the rate g, and that dividends are paid out and discounted continuously at the interest rate r.

and thus:

$$g_t = \rho(1 - k_t)$$

If expected growth is to be constant, $\bar{\rho}$, the *expected (average) return on incremental investment*, must also be the same in every year. The constant-growth valuation formula thus becomes:

$$\frac{P_0}{e_1} = \frac{\bar{k}}{r - \bar{\rho}(1 - \bar{k})} \qquad \text{(14-8a)}$$

or:

$$P_0 = \frac{\bar{k}e_1}{r - \bar{\rho}(1 - \bar{k})} = \frac{d_1}{r - \bar{\rho}(1 - \bar{k})} \qquad \text{(14-8b)}$$

Under these assumptions, a stock's price-earnings ratio will be greater, the greater its expected return on incremental investment, other things equal. Earnings growth depends on how much is kept $(1 - \bar{k})$ and what it earns $(\bar{P})$. And the greater earnings growth (other things equal), the greater a stock's value.

Many analysts assume that after some date a firm will find that none of its available investment opportunities offers an abnormally high return. At this point the firm is usually said to have reached *maturity*. The price-earnings ratio for such a firm can be found simply. As long as management does not choose to invest in projects with inferior returns, $\bar{\rho}$—the average return on incremental investment—will equal r—the appropriate discount rate, and formula 14-8(a) can be simplified to:

$$\frac{P_0}{e_1} = \frac{\bar{k}}{r - r(1 - \bar{k})} = \frac{1}{r} \qquad \text{(14-8c)}$$

Thus *the appropriate price-earnings ratio for a mature firm is one over the discount rate*, or, equivalently, *the appropriate earnings-price ratio is the discount rate*.

ABNORMAL-GROWTH MODELS

Between the generality of formula (14-6) and the extreme simplifications incorporated in constant-growth models lie countless possibilities for simplified models of earnings growth. Many of these have been proposed and a number of them implemented. Most are characterized by the assumption that at some estimated future date, growth will become, and henceforth forever remain, "normal," with the stock in question priced accordingly. At this point (time T), the stock's price can be estimated by applying a "normal" price-earnings multiple to its earnings, or by assuming that subsequent growth will be constant, and applying the constant-growth model. In either case, given estimates of earnings growth rates and payout ratios during the "abnormal" period, and given estimates of the relevant characteristics for the (infinitely long) "normal" period, it is possible either (1) to estimate present value, for an appropriate assumed return, or (2) to calculate a holding-period return associated with the current price of the stock.

Two examples will serve to illustrate the approach. The next section describes an approach that uses the constant-growth model to determine price at time T. The remainder of this section is devoted to a model in which earnings growth and dividend yield are assumed to be constant up to time T, at which point the firm is assumed to reach maturity.

To find the present value of a stock with dividends increasing forever at a growth rate g, formula 14-7(a) can be rearranged:

$$P_0^* = \frac{ke_1}{r - \bar{g}} = \frac{d_1}{r - \bar{g}} \tag{14-9a}$$

The present value *at time* T of the infinitely many remaining dividends on such a stock would be:

$$P_T^* = \frac{d_{T+1}}{r - \bar{g}} = \frac{d_1(1 + \bar{g})^T}{r - \bar{g}} \tag{14-9b}$$

The present value *now* of the dividends received after time T can be found by discounting this amount:

$$PV(P_T^*) = \left[\frac{1}{(1 + r)^T}\right] P_T^* = \frac{d_1(1 + \bar{g})^T}{(1 + r)^T (r - \bar{g})} \tag{14-9c}$$

The present value of the dividends to be received *up to* time T is the difference between (14-9a) and (14-9c):[6]

$$PV(d_1, \ldots, d_T) = \frac{d_1}{r - g}\left[1 - \left(\frac{1 + g}{1 + r}\right)^T\right] \tag{14-9d}$$

Assume that at time T the stock is expected to sell at a "normal multiple," m_T, of the next year's earnings:

$$m_T = \frac{P_T}{e_{T+1}} \tag{14-9e}$$

With earnings growing at g, $e_{T+1} = e_1(1 + \bar{g})^T$ and:

$$P_T = m_T e_1(1 + \bar{g})^T \tag{14-9f}$$

The present value of this amount is:

$$PV(P_T) = \left[\frac{1}{(1 + r)^T}\right] P_T = m_T e_1 \left(\frac{1 + \bar{g}}{1 + r}\right)^T \tag{14-9g}$$

We now have the two components of the present value of the stock. Combining (14-9d) and (14-9g):[7]

$$P_0 = PV(d_1, \ldots, d_T) + PV(P_T)$$
$$= \frac{d_1}{r - g}\left[1 - \left(\frac{1 + g}{1 + r}\right)^T\right] + m_T e_1 \left(\frac{1 + \bar{g}}{1 + r}\right)^T \tag{14-9h}$$

[6] Although (14-9a) holds only if r is greater than $\bar{g}$, (14-9d) applies in every case but that in which $r = \bar{g}$. In this instance:

$$PV(d_1, \ldots, d_T) = Td_1$$

[7] As indicated in the previous footnote, if $r = g$, the first term becomes $T \cdot d_1$.

This can be divided by e_1 to obtain m_0—the stock's current price-earnings multiple:

$$m_0 = \frac{P_0}{e_1} = \frac{\overline{k}}{r - g} \left[1 - \left(\frac{1 + \overline{g}}{1 + r} \right)^T \right] + m_T \left(\frac{1 + \overline{g}}{1 + r} \right)^T \quad (14\text{-}9\mathrm{i})$$

If period T is considered to be *maturity*, after which the firm has no further abnormal investment opportunities, the appropriate multiple is that given by formula (14-8c):[8]

$$m_T = \frac{1}{r}$$

THE WELLS FARGO APPROACH

A somewhat different growth model is used by the Wells Fargo Bank. Security analysts are responsible for providing a number of estimates for each stock covered, including:

> the expected dividends (d_1, d_2, d_3, d_4, d_5) and earnings (e_1, e_2, e_3, e_4, e_5) year by year, for the next five years
> the expected rate of growth in earnings from the fifth to the sixth year (g_5)
> the expected payout ratio in the fifth year (k_5)
> the length of the period before "normal" growth begins (T)
> the expected (constant) rate of growth in earnings beginning in year $T(g_T)$
> and the expected (constant) payout ratio beginning in year $T(k_T)$

Between year 5 and year T the firm's payout ratio is assumed to move linearly from k_5 to k_T, as illustrated in Figure 14-4(a). The rate of growth in earnings is also assumed to follow a specified pattern from g_5 to g_T, but the analyst can select any one of the three alternatives illustrated in Figure 14-4(b): straight-line, sum-of-the-years'-digits, or reverse sum-of-the-years'-digits.

Given all these estimates, it is relatively straightforward to determine the present value of the expected dividends associated with any specified discount rate. First the constant-growth model is used to find the value in year T of all subsequent dividends. This is then discounted to the present and added to the discounted value of all dividends to be received prior to year T (of which the first five were estimated explicitly, and the remainder implicitly, from the assumed earnings growth rates and payout ratios).

Using computerized trial-and-error, it is also possible to determine the discount rate that makes the value of a stock's projected dividends equal its current price. This is the long-run internal rate of return for the security that is implied by the analyst's estimates.

[8] More generally, m_T should be the normal value for stocks of firms with similar investment opportunities.

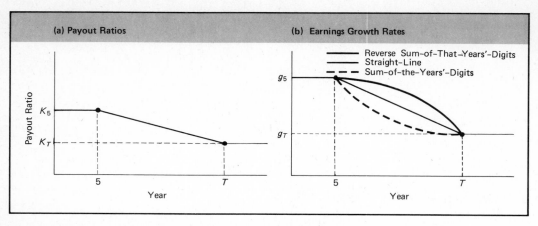

FIGURE 14-4 Payout Ratio and Earnings Growth Assumptions Used in the Wells Fargo Approach.

After an internal rate of return has been estimated for each stock, the information is plotted (in effect) on a three-dimensional diagram with rate of return on the vertical axis and beta value and dividend yield on the horizontal axes. A plane is then fitted to the points to estimate the overall relationship among return, risk (beta), and yield in the market. Figures 9-10, 9-11, and 9-12 showed some of the relationships obtained in this manner.

In the next stage, each security's estimated internal rate of return is compared with the "normal" return for stocks with the same beta and yield (i.e., the value given by the security market plane fitted in the previous stage). The greater the disparity between the two, the more the security is, in effect, considered by the analyst to be underpriced (if the return exceeds the normal amount) or overpriced (if the return is less than the normal amount).

CROSS-SECTIONAL VALUATION APPROACHES

The procedures used by Wells Fargo constitute a *cross-section* approach to security valuation. Attributes of individual stocks are utilized to estimate an *average* relationship, and differences from that relationship are taken as indications of possible deviations of price from intrinsic value, and hence potential sources of abnormal returns relative to risk.

The initial stages of the Wells Fargo system are grounded on the basic principles of valuation and the rather complex relationships involved therein. This contrasts with cross-sectional approaches that assume much simpler relationships. Typically price-earnings ratios are assumed to be linearly (and additively) related to attributes measuring payout ratios, earnings growth rates, and one or more types of risk. Whenever possible, analysts' estimates of future values are utilized, but in some instances historic values are used.

A procedure of this type was employed by the Bank of New York in the 1960s.[9] In mid-1962, for example, analysts' estimates for 135 stocks were used to compute the following "average" relationship:

$$P/E = 8.2 + 1.5 \text{ (growth rate)}$$
$$+ 6.7 \text{ (payout ratio)} - .2 \text{ (risk)} \tag{14-10}$$

where:

P/E = current price divided by *normalized* earnings (defined as the level that would be expected if the economy were experiencing mid-cyclical business conditions)

growth rate = the projected growth rate in normal earnings

payout ratio = the prospective ratio of dividends to earnings

risk = the anticipated standard deviation of earnings around the projected growth rate

All projected values were defined to apply over at least the next five years, and all were provided by analysts who had been given corresponding historic values for possible modification.

Table 14-4 provides an example of the use of formula (14-10). According to these calculations, IBM appeared to be priced at close to its intrinsic value at the time, while General Motors was somewhat overpriced (by 13%).

A preliminary test of this procedure provided promising results. Table 14-5 shows, for each of four quarters, the changes in the values of (1) a portfolio of all stocks that appeared to be more than 15% overvalued at the beginning of the quarter, (2) Standard and Poor's 500-stock index, and (3) a portfolio of all stocks that appeared to be more than 15% undervalued at the beginning of the quarter. In every quarter the changes were in the desired order.

These results are, of course, far from conclusive. In none of the four quarters did the market decline. Since the measure of risk utilized in equation (14-10) may be a poor surrogate for market sensitivity, the procedure may have tended to identify low-beta stocks as overvalued and high-beta stocks as undervalued. If so, some or all the differences in per-

[9] See Volkert S. Whitbeck and Manown Kisor, Jr., "A New Tool in Investment Decision-making," *Financial Analysts Journal*, 19, no. 3 (May/June 1963), 55–62.

TABLE 14-4 An Example of the Use of the Bank of New York Model

	IBM	General Motors
(1) Growth rate (%)	17.0	3.0
(2) Payout ratio	.25	.75
(3) Risk (standard deviation, %)	5.0	20.0
(4) *P/E* ratio implied by formula (14-10)	34.4	13.7
(5) Actual *P/E* ratio	35.3	15.4
(6) Price relative to intrinsic value = (5)/(4)	1.02	1.13

Source: Volkert S. Whitbeck and Manown Kisor, Jr., "A New Tool in Investment Decision-making," *Financial Analysts Journal*, 19, no. 3 (May/June 1963), 55–62.

TABLE 14-5 Quarterly Results Using the Bank of New York Model

		PERCENTAGE CHANGE IN VALUE		
Year	Quarter	All Stocks with Price Relative ≥ 1.15 ("Overvalued")	Standard and Poor's 500-Stock Index	All Stocks with Price Relative ≤ 85 ("Undervalued")
1960	4	5.7	6.6	11.9
1961	1	8.3	12.3	16.8
1961	2	−1.4	1.0	3.0
1961	3	2.1	2.4	3.2

Source: Volkert S. Whitbeck and Manown Kisor, Jr., "A New Tool in Investment Decision-making," *Financial Analysts Journal*, 19, no. 3 (May/June, 1963), 55–62.

formance might have been due simply to differences in risk. Moreover, the (presumably) small number of stocks selected for the comparison portfolios suggest that luck may also have accounted for a large portion of the apparent success.

A subsequent study,[10] using averages of estimates made by a number of investment firms, showed that suspicions of this type were well founded. Expectational values for earnings growth rates, payout ratios, and risk were obtained for 178 stocks at the end of each year from 1961 through 1965, along with ratios of price to normalized earnings. For each of the five years an average relationship similar to that of formula (14-10) was determined via regression analysis. For example, using year-end 1963 values the following equation was obtained:

$$P/E = 2.94 + 2.55 \text{ (growth rate)}$$
$$+ 7.62 \text{ (payout ratio)} - .27 \text{ risk)} \qquad (14\text{-}11)$$

where the terms were defined to be similar to those used in formula (14-10).

Equation (14-11) accounted for 75% of the variation in the stocks' P/E ratios at the time (compared to about 50% that could be accounted for using historical growth rates, payout ratios, and risk measures). Although the type of risk considered is of questionable importance, examination of the estimates showed that they corresponded closely to historic beta values, and replacement of the former with the latter gave comparable results. Analysis of data for the other four years led to conclusions similar to those that can be drawn from these results: to a considerable extent, stocks appear to be priced in accordance with the basic principles of valuation applied to the consensus expectations of analysts concerning the future.

But are deviations from such relationships likely to signal opportunities for abnormal profit? Apparently not. As a test, the percentage difference between actual price and that implied by the valuation equation

[10] Burton G. Malkiel and John G. Cragg, "Expectations and the Structure of Share Prices," *American Economic Review*, LX, no. 4 (September 1970), 601–17.

can be computed for each stock, along with its return over a subsequent period. The question can then be posed as follows: is there a relationship between (1) the price relative to intrinsic value and (2) return; and is the relationship of the desired type?

In fact, 1964 returns were slightly related to measured "misvaluation" at the end of 1963, and in the desired way.[11] But only 4% of the variation in actual returns could have been predicted in this manner. In the other four years the results were mixed: in one year, the procedure worked to some extent, in two years the predictions predicted nothing, and in one year they were perverse—the purportedly overvalued stocks tended to do better than the purportedly undervalued stocks. Tests using actual performance over shorter holding periods gave similar results.

PREDICTING RETURNS

The use of deviations from a cross-sectional valuation equation to identify potential opportunities for profit assumes that prices will converge fairly rapidly to the indicated intrinsic values. Unfortunately, they often fail to do so. First, deviations tend to persist, indicating that they may be due more to relevant factors ignored in the valuation equation than to temporary mispricing. For example, in the study described earlier, the deviations from each year's valuation equation were positively correlated with those from the previous year's equation.[12] Second, and perhaps more vexing, both the average valuation relationship and the relevant attributes for a security are likely to change as well, giving a new intrinsic value. The analyst must thus attempt to shoot at a moving target.

The solution for these problems is as straightforward conceptually as it is difficult to achieve. Say that one-year holding period returns are to be predicted. First, the average valuation equation *one year hence* should be estimated. Then the values of dividends and earnings for the coming year and the relevant consensus expectations to be held by analysts *one year hence* should be predicted. Applying the predicted valuation equation to these estimates, one can predict the stock's intrinsic value a year later. Estimating the likely reduction in deviations per year, the amount expected to remain after a year can be added or subtracted from this to estimate the ending price. Comparing this to the present price, and adding dividends expected to be paid during the year, one can obtain the desired prediction of return.

In the Wells Fargo system, this requires a prediction of next year's security market plane, each stock's beta value, predicted dividends, earnings, growth rates, and so on, as well as the likely amount by which deviations from the security market plane will be reduced in a year's time. In more traditional valuation approaches, the coming year's earnings and next year's estimates of future growth rates, payout ratios, and risk are required, along with the likely valuation equation and the likely degree of reduction of deviations from that equation.

---

[11] A somewhat more complex valuation model than that shown in formula (14-11) was used for this analysis.

[12] Burton G. Malkiel and John G. Cragg, "Expectations and the Structure of Share Prices," *op. cit.*

TABLE 14-6 Estimated Valuation Equations, 1961–1965

1961:	P/E = 4.73 + 3.28 (growth)	+ 2.05 (payout)	− .83 (risk)
1962:	11.06 + 1.75	+ .78	−1.61
1963:	2.94 + 2.55	+ 7.62	− .27
1964:	6.71 + 2.05	+ 5.33	− .89
1965:	.96 + 2.74	+ 5.01	− .35

Source: Burton G. Malkiel and John G. Cragg, "Expectations and the Structure of Share Prices," *American Economic Review*, LX, no. 4 (September 1970), 601–17.

Figure 14-1 showed the extent to which security risk lines appear to move from time to time. Table 14-6 shows that the problem is even more serious when a traditional equation is utilized.

In the best of all possible worlds, one would try to accurately predict future valuation relationships and all the required ingredients. However, to gain abnormal profits, only a better-than-average ability to predict *some* element is required. A capacity to foresee deviations from the market's consensus predictions of *any* aspect could prove profitable. Not surprisingly, few organizations forecast all the required ingredients.

This does not imply that cross-sectional studies are useless. Quite the contrary. They provide estimates of the manner in which the market currently values securities, and this is essential information. Even if the deviations were of no significance whatever, the relationship itself could be a good estimate of the current trade-off among return, risk, and yield, amply justifying the entire effort. And if the deviations indicate likely mispricing rather than errors in the firm's security analysis, the procedure can be even more valuable.

Problems

1. Why is the assumption that *g* is less than *r* necessary for the constant-growth valuation model?
2. Suppose that the dividend yield on IBM stock is $2\frac{1}{2}$% lower than the interest rate on U.S. government bonds. Does this mean that IBM can raise equity capital more cheaply than the U.S. government can borrow in the bond market?
3. The stock of the Mississippi Bubble Corporation currently pays a yearly dividend of $3 per share. The dividend is expected to grow at 4% per year forever. Stocks with similar characteristics are currently priced to give an expected return of 12%. What is an appropriate price for MBC?
4. Assume you are convinced that at the end of this year the security risk line will be steeper than it is at present. What does this suggest about the rela-

tive performance between now and the end of the year of high-beta stocks versus that of low-beta stocks?

5. Analysts typically classify a security as a *growth stock* if earnings per share are expected to grow rapidly. It is often said that growth stocks should have higher price-earnings multiples than other stocks to reflect the relatively greater earnings they will produce in the future. Others say that the multiple of a growth stock should depend on the source of the growth—i.e., whether it is from highly profitable investment opportunities or simply a substantial plow-back of earnings into the business. In what sense should a stock's price-earnings multiple be related to future growth? to the source of that growth?

6. In what sense should value be related to dividends? to earnings? Under what conditions is double-counting involved if all dividends and all earnings are taken into account in determining value? Are there reasonable valuation methods that take *some* dividends and *some* earnings into account?

7. According to the text, the patterns in Figures 14-3(a) and (b) before the announcement of dividend changes are not inconsistent with market efficiency while those after the announcement are inconsistent. Why might one be able to make abnormal returns after the announcement but not before?

8. Silicon Valley Electronics is expected to pay out 40% of its earnings and to earn an average return of 15% per year on its incremental reinvested earnings forever. Stocks with similar characteristics are currently priced to return 12% to investors. By what percentage can SVE's earnings per share be expected to grow each year? What is an appropriate price-earnings multiple for the stock? What portion of SVE's total return is likely to come from capital gains? from dividend yield?

9. Feathered Feast, a fast-food enterprise that sells barbequed chicken, currently pays a dividend of $1 per share. Its earnings are $3 per share. You expect the dividend to grow at a rate of 20% per year for the next ten years. At that time the firm will be mature and you assume that it will be priced accordingly. Stocks with similar characteristics return 10% per year. What price is appropriate for FF?

10. A venture-capital firm currently is paying a dividend of $2 per share on earnings of $4 per share. Its stock is selling for $200 per share. Stocks of comparable risk and yield are currently priced to return 15% per year. What kind of return on incremental investment could explain investors' willingness to pay a price equal to 50 times earnings on this stock?

Earnings

15

ACCOUNTING VERSUS ECONOMIC EARNINGS

Rightly or wrongly, the prediction of earnings plays a central role in security analysis and investment research. This makes essential a review of what is known about earnings and the relationship between earnings and prices. More fundamental is a consideration of the concept itself. Just what is meant by "earnings" to those who produce the figures, and how does this affect the valuation process?

A firm's accountant, in cooperation with management, operating under constraints and guidelines imposed by regulatory authorities and professional organizations, produces a figure each quarter for the firm's "earnings." In a broad sense, such earnings represent the difference between revenues and costs, including the costs associated with nonequity sources of funds. This difference, the *total earnings* "available for common stock," is divided by the number of shares outstanding to calculate *earnings per share*. It may also be divided by a measure of the value of the equity to calculate the *return on equity*.

Earnings are related to cash flows, which are the ultimate source of value. However, value is related to potential *future* cash flows, while reported (accounting) earnings represent a combination of past, current, and estimated future cash flows.

A basic principle of accounting makes the "book" value of a firm's equity at the end of a year equal to (1) its value at the end of the previous year plus (2) any retained earnings (assuming no change in stock outstanding, etc.):

$$B_t = B_{t-1} + E_t - D_t \qquad (15\text{-}1)$$

where:

B_t = the book value of equity at the end of year t
E_t = accounting earnings in year t
D_t = dividends paid in year t

Accounting earnings can thus be considered the change in book value plus dividends paid:

$$E_t = (B_t - B_{t-1}) + D_t \qquad (15\text{-}2)$$

Economic earnings may be defined as the amount that would be obtained if each year's book value equaled economic value:

$$E_t^e = (V_t - V_{t-1}) + D_t \qquad (15\text{-}3)$$

where:

V_t = the economic value of the firm's equity at the end of year t

E_t^e = the economic earnings in year t

The *accounting return on equity* relates accounting earnings to book value:

$$R_t = \frac{E_t}{B_{t-1}} = \frac{B_t - B_{t-1} + D_t}{B_{t-1}} \qquad (15\text{-}4)$$

where:

R_t = the accounting return on equity in year t

The *economic return on equity* relates economic earnings to economic value:

$$R_t^e = \frac{E_t^e}{V_{t-1}} = \frac{V_t - V_{t-1} + D_t}{V_{t-1}} \qquad (15\text{-}5)$$

where:

R_t^e = the economic return on equity in year t

Investors' estimates of the economic value of a firm's equity are reflected in the market value of its outstanding shares. The economic return on equity thus equals the market return on the firm's stock. No new principles are required to understand the behavior of *economic* earnings, only the application of what is known concerning the behavior of stock returns.

A firm's *expected* economic return on equity should be related primarily to its nondiversifiable risk. Its *actual* economic return on equity in any given year will often diverge from this amount, but the divergence will generally be unpredictable and unrelated to that of the previous year. In other words, a firm's annual economic returns on equity are not likely to be serially correlated (positively or negatively).

Table 15-1 provides an illustration of the way in which variations in return on equity can impact economic value (V_t) and economic earnings (E_t^e). The firm in question begins with an economic value of $1,000 and earns 10% on its equity on average, but occasionally earns more (e.g., 15% in year 3) or less (e.g., 5% in year 6). Each year 40% of economic earnings is paid out in dividends. As usual, the economic value at the end of the year equals the beginning value plus earnings, minus dividends.

As the table shows, relatively modest fluctuations in return on equity can cause substantial changes in economic earnings. Better-than-average years are likely to cause large transitory increases in earnings (e.g., a +59% change from year 2 to year 3), but such increases are likely to be followed by substantial decreases (e.g., a -27% change from year 3 to year 4). As year 6 illustrates, worse-than-average years can have the opposite effects.

TABLE 15-1 Economic Earnings for a Firm

Year (t)	Beginning Economic Value ($) (V_{t-1})	Economic Return on Equity (%) (R_t^e)	Economic Earnings ($) $(E_t^e) = R_t^e \times V_{t-1}$
1	1,000.00	10	100.00
2	1,060.00	10	106.00
3	1,123.60	15	168.54
4	1,224.72	10	122.47
5	1,298.20	10	129.82
6	1,376.09	5	68.80
7	1,417.37	10	141.74
8	1,502.41	10	150.24
9	1,592.55		

Dividends $(= .4E_t^e)$ ($) (D_t)	Ending Economic Value ($) $(V_t = V_{t-1} + E_t - D_t)$	Growth in Economic Earnings (%) $= 100 \times (E_t^e - E_{t-1}^e)/E_{t-1}^e$
40.00	1,060.00	
42.40	1,123.60	+6
67.42	1,224.72	+59
48.99	1,298.20	−27
51.93	1,376.09	+6
27.52	1,417.37	−47
56.70	1,502.41	+106
60.10	1,592.55	+6

Growth rates in a firm's total economic earnings or economic earnings per share over successive years will generally be negatively related, as these are. Following a major increase in earnings, the best estimate of next year's earnings will be *smaller* than the most recent value. Following a major decrease, the best estimate will be larger than the most recent value. Simply increasing current economic earnings by a fixed percentage to obtain an estimate of next year's economic earnings would give very poor results following a major change (such as that in year 3 or year 6).

To predict economic earnings, one should multiply the appropriate expected return on equity by the current economic value of equity. The expected return will change little if at all from year to year, but the economic value of equity will, owing to both unanticipated changes in future prospects and additional investment (including that obtained via retained earnings). Economic earnings—the product of these two factors—will thus change from year to year in partly predictable and partly unpredictable ways.

If accountants attempted to report economic earnings, annual earnings fluctuations of the sort shown in Table 15-1 would be common, and any attempt to value securities by applying a standard "multiple" to current earnings would give bizarre results. However, if economic earnings *were* reported, valuation would be simple, since the accountant would have already done the job. The economic value of a stock would be its book value, and there would be no reason to even consider earnings per se.

Little evidence is required to show that investors often consider stocks to be worth considerably more or less than reported book values. Figure 15-1 shows the ratio of (1) the average market price per share for Standard and Poor's 400 Industrial Stock index, to (2) the average book value per share. The ratio is typically greater than 1.0 and has fluctuated considerably from year to year.

Figure 15-2 plots book values (horizontal axis) and market values (vertical axis) for the 30 stocks in the Dow-Jones Industrial Average at the end of 1978. As the extensive scatter of the points indicates, investors feel that economic values differ from book values by different amounts for different stocks. Clearly, accounting earnings also differ from investors' estimates of economic earnings.

Additional evidence is provided by the behavior of accounting earnings over time. As shown in the next section, reported earnings are much less erratic than the economic earnings implicit in market values. This is due in part to the accountant's greater reliance on *realized* and *objective* figures than on *predicted* and *subjective* estimates of future events and their implications for current values.

FIGURE 15-1 Ratio of Price to Book Value, Standard and Poor's 400 Industrial Stock Price Index,* 1946–1978.

Source: Standard and Poor's *Trade and Securities Statistics*.

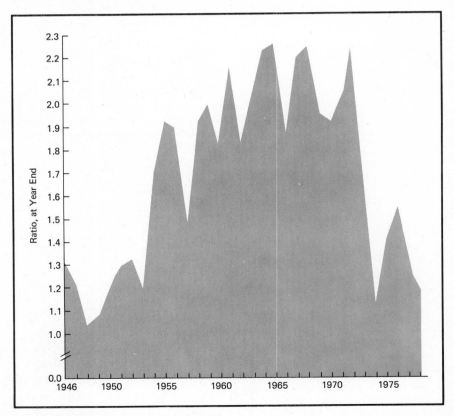

* Prior to 1974, Standard and Poor's 425-Stock Index.

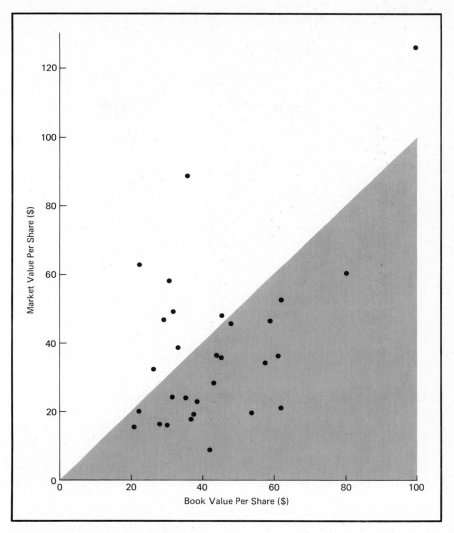

FIGURE 15-2 Market and Book Values, 30 Stocks in Dow-Jones Industrial Average, Year-End 1978.

A rather old-fashioned view holds that the accountant's task is strictly to communicate facts about *past* events, leaving the task of estimating the *future* prospects of a firm (and thus its *present* value) to the security analyst. As the editor of the *Financial Analysts Journal* put it, the accountant's function is to *measure* and *report*, while that of the security analyst is to *judge* and *value*, but this is not the case in practice.[1] Accountants estimate the present value of future prospects in many ways, although often implicitly. The manner in which a capital asset is depreciated is an implicit decision about its economic life. The manner in

[1] See Jack L. Treynor, "The Trouble with Earnings," *Financial Analysts Journal*, 28, no. 5 (September/October 1972), 41–43.

which research and development expenses are charged over time amounts to a decision about the future value of the products developed, and so on. All such decisions affect current earnings, from which analysts estimate value.

The trouble with earnings is accountants' awareness that investors consider current and recent earnings when estimating the value of a security. This leads to the temptation to try to "manage" earnings to make a firm appear more valuable than it is, thus fooling investors, at least temporarily. Management may pressure accountants to maximize the level of reported earnings, to maintain a high growth rate of reported earnings, and/or to reduce the year-to-year variability of earnings around a growth rate. Some of these activities can be continued only for a limited number of years; others can go on indefinitely.

To obtain a truly independent estimate of value, an analyst must dissect reported earnings. Anyone who estimates value by applying a formula (no matter how complex) to reported earnings is not producing a completely independent estimate.

This is not to say that such figures are irrelevant for security valuation. However, reported earnings are best viewed as a *source of information about the future prospects of a firm*. Since the present value of a firm's equity is related to its future prospects, there should be a *correlation* between reported earnings and price. But since reported earnings generally differ from economic earnings, this correlation will be less than perfect. Accounting earnings are thus an important source of information about value, but neither a perfect source nor the only relevant one.

THE TIME-SERIES BEHAVIOR OF EARNINGS

Figure 15-3 provides some evidence on the behavior of overall earnings and prices for industrial firms, represented by the Dow-Jones Industrial Average. Figure 15-3(a) shows earnings per share, plotted on a ratio scale to highlight percentage changes. Figure 15-3(b) shows the price-earnings ratio, computed by dividing year-end price per share by the year's earnings per share. Figure 15-3(c) indicates the percentage change in earnings per share from each year to the next. Since the figures have not been adjusted to obtain "normal" earnings, one might expect a larger-than-average change to tend to be followed by a smaller-than-average change, and conversely. Figure 15-3(d) shows that this is the case, but only to a small extent. Each point plots the percentage change in earnings in one year (on the horizontal axis) and that in the next (on the vertical axis). The slightly negative relationship between changes in adjacent years shown here has also been found for individual stocks' earnings.[2]

[2] For example, as reported in *An Introduction to Risk and Return from Common Stocks* (Cambridge, Mass.: MIT Press, 1969), Richard Brealey, using data from 1951 through 1964 for 700 companies, found an average correlation coefficient of $-.06$. Another study, reported in Ray Ball and Ross Watts, "Some Time Series Properties of Accounting Incomes," *The Journal of Finance*, XXVII, no. 3 (June 1972), 663–82, used data on 679 firms from 1949 through 1960. When no adjustment was made for trends in expected earnings per share over time, the best fit was obtained using a model of approximately the form:

$$\text{expected EPS}_{t+1} = \text{EPS}_t - .05(\text{EPS}_t - \text{EPS}_{t-1})$$

FIGURE 15-3 Earnings per Share, Price-Earnings Ratios, and Percentage Change in Earnings Per Share: Dow-Jones Industrial Average 1937–1975.

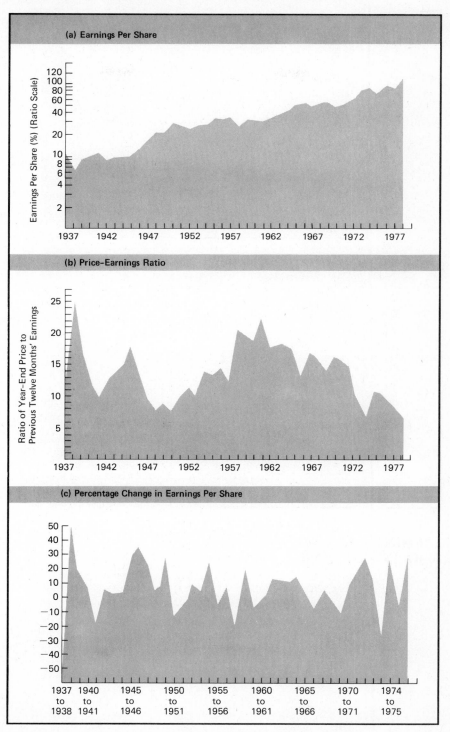

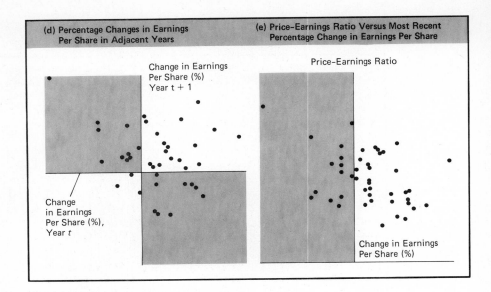

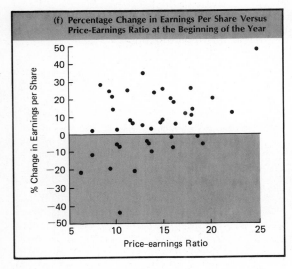

FIGURE 15-3 (*continued*) Percentage Changes in Earnings Per Share in Adjacent Years, Price-Earnings Ratio Versus Most Recent Percentage Change in Earnings Per Share, Percentage Change in Earnings Per Share Versus Price-Earnings Ratio at the Beginning of the Year

EARNINGS GROWTH
AND PRICE-EARNINGS RATIOS

The market seems to anticipate negative correlation in year-to-year earnings growth rates. Figure 15-3(e), which plots year-end price-earnings ratios against the year's percentage earnings change, shows that price-earnings ratios tend to be lower following a major increase in earnings than following a major decrease—behavior consistent with (1) a positive relationship between price-earnings ratios and expected near-term growth and (2) a negative relationship between recent growth and expected near-term growth. This implies that the price-earnings ratio can be used as a partial predictor of earnings growth. Figure 15-3(f) shows the relationship between the price-earnings ratio at the beginning of the year and the growth in earnings during that year (relative to the prior year's earnings). The relationship is slightly positive, but as the substantial scatter of the points shows, differences in price-earnings ratios reflect much more than differences in anticipations about the coming year's earnings.

A similar relationship is found when individual stocks are considered: earnings growth during a year is positively related to the price-earnings ratio at the beginning of the year. Some of the differences in price-earnings ratios of individual stocks may thus be due to temporary differences in earnings. Reported earnings usually include both *permanent* components that are likely to be repeated in the future and *transitory* components not likely to be repeated. Since value depends on future prospects, changes in a stock's price (the numerator in the price-earnings ratio) will be correlated with permanent changes in its earnings (the denominator in the ratio) but not with transitory changes. Transitory changes in earnings will thus change the denominator but not the numerator, causing the price-earnings ratio to change in the opposite direction.

If this were the only relevant factor, differences in price-earnings ratios would themselves be transitory. But they are not. Figure 15-4 shows the behavior of the ratios for two groups of stocks over time: one includes stocks with high price-earnings ratios at the beginning of the period; the other includes stocks with low price-earnings ratios at the beginning of the period. As the figure shows, over time the price-earnings ratios tend to *revert to the mean* ratio for the market as a whole. The changes are substantial in the first two years, owing undoubtedly to the influence of transitory components of earnings. But differences persist for many years — indicating that there is more to the phenomenon.

Two explanations can be offered for persistent differences in price-earnings ratios among stocks. First, appropriate discount rates (expected returns) differ because of differences in nondiversifiable risk, yield, and so on. Second, there may be permanent differences between economic and reported earnings due to the use of different accounting methods. For example, if two firms have the same economic earnings, their stocks should sell for the same price. But if one uses straight-line depreciation for reporting purposes and the other uses accelerated depreciation, the former may report lower earnings;[3] if so, its stock will have a higher price-earnings ratio. There is evidence that the market sees through such differences in reported earnings.[4] Thus it is not surprising that the price-earnings ratios of stocks differ and that some of the differences are long-lasting.

---

[3] If both firms are growing, the difference can continue for many years.

[4] See William H. Beaver, *Financial Reporting: An Accounting Revolution* (forthcoming) for more information on this and many other aspects of earnings.

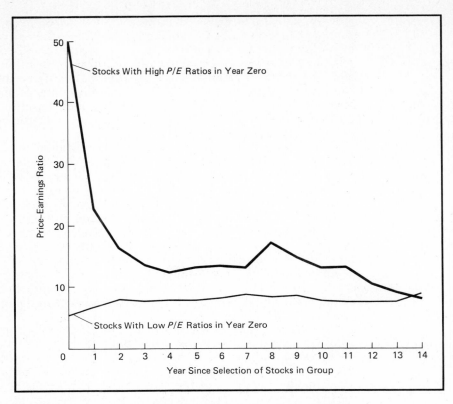

FIGURE 15-4 Price-Earnings Ratios Over Time for Two Groups of Stocks.

Source: William Beaver and Dale Morse, "What Determines Price-Earnings Ratios?" *Financial Analysts Journal,* July/August 1978.

RELATIVE GROWTH RATES OF FIRMS' EARNINGS

Since the average change in earnings for firms as a whole varies considerably from year to year, and in a rather unpredictable way, it is not surprising that the earnings of a given firm do so too. But the very idea of a "growth stock" suggests that growth in some firms' earnings will exceed the average growth of all firms' earnings in most years, while others' grow less than the average.

The results of a test of this hypothesis based on a study of 610 industrial company's earnings from 1950 through 1964 are shown in Table 15-2. In every year, each firm's earnings were compared with the previous year's and the percentage change computed; this was counted as "good" if it was in the top half of such figures for the year and "bad" otherwise. If some firms tend to consistently experience above- or below-average earnings growth, fairly long *runs* of consistently good years should occur for some stocks and fairly long runs of consistently bad years for others.

The first two columns of Table 15-2 indicate the actual number of runs of various lengths. The final column shows the number that would be expected if for every firm a fair coin had been flipped each year, with earnings classified as "good" if the coin came up heads and "bad" if it came up tails. The three columns are remarkably similar. Better-than-average earnings growth in the past does not appear to presage better-than-average growth in the future.

A study[5] using longer time periods for measuring growth reached generally similar conclusions. For each of 323 companies with positive earnings in each year from 1946 through 1965, average growth rates were computed for (1) the period from 1946 through 1955 and (2) the period from 1956 through 1965. Differences among firms' earnings growth rates in the first period accounted for less than 1% of the variation in the differences among their earnings growth rates in the second period. However, when adjustments were made for changes in economic activity and only firms with fairly steady earnings growth in the past considered, slightly more consistency was found: differences in past growth rates accounted for approximately 16% of the differences in future growth rates.

[5] John Lintner and Robert Glauber, "Higgledy Piggledy Growth in America," in James Lorie and Richard Brealey, ed., *Modern Developments in Investment Management* (New York: Praeger Publishers, Inc., 1972).

TABLE 15-2 Length and Number of Runs of Better-than-Average and Worse-than-Average Earnings Growth, 610 Firms, 1950–1964

Length of Run	Actual Number of Runs of Good Years	Actual Number of Runs of Bad Years	Number of Runs of Good or Bad Years Expected If the Odds Each Year Were 50-50, Regardless of Past Performance
1	1,152	1,102	1,068
2	562	590	534
3	266	300	267
4	114	120	133
5	55	63	67
6	24	20	33
7	23	12	17
8	5	6	8
9	3	3	4
10	6	0	2
11	2	0	1
12	1	0	1
13	0	0	0
14	0	1	0

Source: Reprinted from *An Introduction to Risk and Return from Common Stocks* by Richard Brealey by permission of The M.I.T. Press, Cambridge, Massachusetts. Copyright © 1969.

TABLE 15-3 The Proportion of the Variance of a Firm's Earnings Attributable to Economy-Wide and Industry Earnings Changes

| | PROPORTION ATTRIBUTABLE TO: | |
Industry	Economy-Wide Earnings Changes (%)	Additional Influence of Changes in Industry Earnings (%)
Aircraft	11	5
Autos	48	11
Beer	11	7
Cement	6	32
Chemicals	41	8
Cosmetics	5	6
Department stores	30	37
Drugs	14	7
Electricals	24	8
Food	10	10
Machinery	19	16
Nonferrous metals	26	25
Office machinery	14	6
Oil	13	49
Paper	27	28
Rubber	26	48
Steel	32	21
Supermarkets	6	33
Textiles and clothing	25	29
Tobacco	8	19
All firms	21	21

Source: Reprinted from *An Introduction to Risk and Return from Common Stocks* by Richard Brealey by permission of The M.I.T. Press, Cambridge, Massachusetts. Copyright © 1969.

COMOVEMENT OF FIRMS' EARNINGS

Past changes in security prices are of limited value for the prediction of future changes. And past changes in the overall level of the market are of limited help in the prediction of future market moves. Yet security price changes are related to *concurrent* market (and often industry and/or sector) changes, the strengths of the relationships differ among securities, and historic data can generally be utilized to help estimate the relative future strengths of the relationships for different securities. Since earnings measure changes in firms' accounting values, relationships among the earnings of different firms may well be similar to those among the changes in their market values.

Table 15-3 shows that this is the case, at least to some extent. Earnings reported by 217 corporations from 1948 through 1966 were compared first with the earnings for Standard and Poor's 425-stock index (which served as a surrogate for economy-wide earnings) and then with the average earnings of all firms in the same industry. The proportion of each firm's earnings variations that could be attributed to each of these factors was determined, and the results were averaged across all the firms in each industry. The results are shown in the table.

Some of the differences among industries may be statistical artifacts of the period analyzed, but some undoubtedly reflect continuing economic relationships—for example, the substantial extent to which the earnings of automobile manufacturers depend on the health of the economy and thus the earnings of all firms.

The final row of Table 15-3 shows the values obtained by averaging over all 217 corporations. Changes in economy-wide earnings accounted for 21% of the variation in the earnings of the typical firm, and changes in the earnings of firms in its industry accounted for another 21%. Anyone attempting to predict the earnings of a firm should undoubtedly (1) try to estimate the relationship between its earnings and those of the economy as a whole and/or the firms in its industry or sector, (2) make predictions of the latter, and then (3) use all these elements in the process of predicting the firm's future earnings.

ACCOUNTING BETAS

Security prices are related to expected future earnings; and the level of the market as a whole is related to expected future economy-wide earnings. When estimates of the future health of the economy change, the level of the market follows suit. And when estimates of the future level of a firm's earnings change, the price of its stock generally moves as well. Figure 15-5 shows these relationships diagrammatically. As expectations about the future change, causing changes in the price of a stock and the level of the market, we obtain information that can be used to estimate the stock's regular or *market beta*. Its magnitude will depend on the extent to which expectations of the firm's economic earnings are related to the expectations of economy-wide economic earnings—a relationship indicated in the figure as the firm's *economic earnings beta*. Clearly, market betas are closely related to such earnings betas.

FIGURE 15-5 Earnings, Prices, and Beta Values.

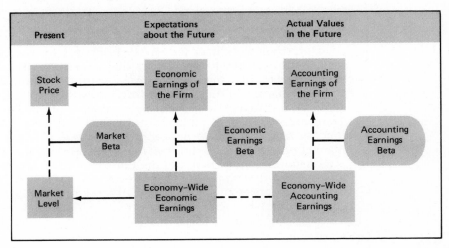

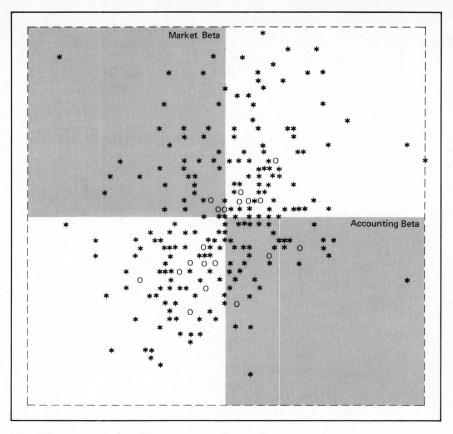

Note: "*" represents one firm, "°" represents more than one firm.

FIGURE 15-6 Accounting and Market Betas, 254 Firms, 1951–1969.

Source: William Beaver and James Manegold, "The Association between Market-determined and Accounting-determined Measures of Systematic Risk: Some Further Evidence," *Journal of Financial and Quantitative Analysis*, X, no. 2 (June 1975), 259.

Unfortunately, direct measures of changes in expected economic earnings are difficult to obtain. In their place analysts generally use changes in *actual* (instead of *expected*) *accounting* (instead of *economic*) earnings. Changes in such earnings can be used (along with book values of equity) to compute an *accounting earnings beta* (or, more simply, an *accounting beta*). While not likely to be as helpful as the directly relevant economic earnings betas, accounting betas should nevertheless shed some light on differences in firms' market betas.

Figure 15-6 shows that they do. Each point plots an accounting beta (horizontal axis) and market beta (vertical axis) for one of 254 firms, estimated using data from 1951 through 1969.[6] To compute the accounting

[6] William Beaver and James Manegold, "The Association between Market-determined and Accounting-determined Measures of Systematic Risk: Some Further Evidence," *Journal of Financial and Quantitative Analysis*, X, no. 2 (June 1975), 231–84.

betas, each earnings figure was used to compute an (accounting) return on equity by dividing the annual earnings by the beginning book value of assets.[7] Averaging such figures across all firms gave a comparable value for the "market" for each year. A firm's accounting beta over a period of years was then computed by comparing the annual values of its accounting return on equity to those of the market, using standard regression analysis. Market betas were computed in the usual manner, using (in effect) economic returns on equity.

While the two measures obviously differ for most firms, there is a positive relationship, as Figure 15-6 shows. When portfolios were analyzed, instead of individual stocks, the differences were considerably smaller.

ANALYSTS' ESTIMATES OF FUTURE EARNINGS

How well can analysts forecast earnings? And do their forecasts incorporate information other than that contained in past earnings? Table 15-4 provides some answers to these questions. Two sets of forecasts were examined for the earnings of 50 firms over the period from 1971 through 1975. The first set was obtained by applying sophisticated mechanical models[8] to the firms' previous earnings history. The second set was obtained from published earnings forecasts of security analysts.[9] The latter clearly outperformed the former. For example, 63.5% of the analysts' forecasts were within 25% of the actual earnings values, while only 54.5% of the forecasts made via mechanical means came as close. Analysts appear to base their forecasts on both past earnings and other information; and the latter appears to help.

[7] Beaver and Manegold (op. cit.) used several measures for their study. The values shown in Figure 15-6 were obtained using the ratio of net income before nonrecurring items to the book value of total assets.

[8] That is, Box-Jenkins techniques.

[9] That is, the forecasts published in the Value Line Investment Survey.

TABLE 15-4 Accuracy of Mechanical and Judgmental Earnings Forecasts

EARNINGS FORECAST ERROR AS A PERCENT OF ACTUAL EARNINGS	PERCENT OF FORECASTS WITH A SMALLER ERROR	
	Mechanical Model	Analysts' Forecasts
5%	15.0%	18.0%
10	26.5	32.0
25	54.5	63.5
50	81.0	86.5
75	87.5	90.5
100	89.5	92.0

Source: Lawrence D. Brown and Michael S. Rozeff, "The Superiority of Analyst Forecasts as Measures of Expectations: Evidence from Earnings," Journal of Finance, March 1978.

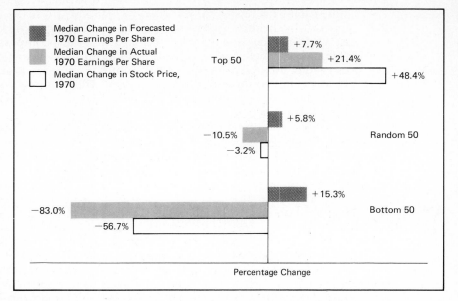

FIGURE 15-7 Earnings and Price Changes: Selected Stocks Listed on the New York Stock Exchange 1970.

Source: Victor Niederhaffer and Patrick J. Regan, "Earnings Changes, Analysts' Forecasts, and Stock Prices," *Financial Analysts Journal,* 28, no. 3 (May/June 1972), 67.

EARNINGS SURPRISES AND PRICE CHANGES

A number of studies have shown that stocks of companies reporting earnings differing substantially from consensus expectations experience substantial price changes. Figure 15-7 shows the median values for (1) forecasted change in earnings per share, (2) actual change in earnings per share, and (3) actual change in stock price during 1970 for three groups of stocks. The first group includes the 50 stocks listed on the New York Stock Exchange that experienced the greatest price increases during 1970, the second is made up of 50 stocks chosen randomly from the Exchange, while the third includes the 50 stocks that experienced the greatest price declines during 1970. Analysts' predictions[10] hardly suggested the differences that occurred. In fact, the median stock in the "bottom 50" was expected to increase earnings by more than that in the "top 50" (+ 15.3%, compared with +7.7%). Unfortunately, this prediction was disastrously wrong. In the bottom group the median firm's earnings declined 83.0%, while that of the top group increased 21.4%. And, as Figure 15-7 shows, prices very definitely followed suit. Unexpected changes in earnings do indeed affect prices.

But do earnings surprises affect prices before or after their announcement? In a completely efficient market, such information

[10] The predictions were taken from Standard and Poor's *Earnings Forecaster,* which reports estimates made by a number of investment research organizations.

would be reflected in prices as soon as it had been disseminated to a few major market participants. Afterward, only other (new) information would cause substantial price changes.

Two studies provide evidence on this issue. The first summarizes the performance of stocks of firms announcing greater-than-expected *annual* earnings. Each of 261 stocks was examined in each year from 1957 to 1965, at the time when the first estimate of annual earnings was published (typically, in February of the following year). The stock's price behavior during the preceding 12 months and succeeding 6 months then was examined and was adjusted to remove estimated changes due to market effects. Each case was classified as an announcement of either greater-than- or less-than-expected (or, in a minority of cases, equal-to-expected) earnings. All cases in which earnings were greater than expected were averaged to produce a composite picture of market-adjusted price changes for such instances; a similar procedure was applied to produce a composite picture for cases in which earnings were less than expected.

Figure 15-8 shows the results obtained when each year's expected earnings were assumed to equal the prior year's amount.[11] Prices of stocks with better-than-expected earnings did in fact rise prior to the announcement date (by 5.6%, after adjustment for market effects), while those with less-than-expected earnings fell (by roughly 11.3%, after adjustment for market effects). Such changes did not occur overnight when annual

[11] A more complex procedure for estimating expected earnings from historic data produced similar results. It should be noted, however, that analysts expectations, based on more extensive sources of information, may have differed and that as a result some "surprises" in both of the studies described in this section may have been misclassified.

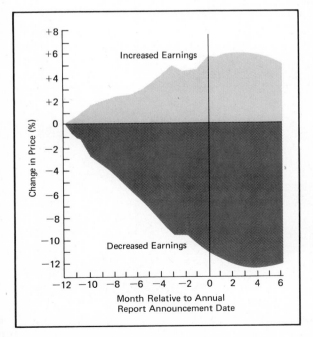

FIGURE 15-8 Relative Prices after Adjustment for Market Effects: Stocks with Increased Earnings versus Stocks with Decreased Annual Earnings.

Source: Ray Ball and Philip Brown, "An Empirical Evaluation of Accounting Income Numbers," *Journal of Accounting Research*, 6, no. 2 (Autumn 1968), 159–78.

earnings were announced, since previously published quarterly earnings provided substantial advance warning, leaving only a portion of the surprise until the end.

More relevant for the issue of market efficiency is the behavior of prices *after* the date of announcement. In neither case was there a dramatic change, after adjustment for market effects. Most of the information contained in annual earnings announcements appears to be reflected in prices before the announcement is more than a few days old.

A second study investigated the impact of better- or worse-than-expected *quarterly* earnings announcements. Prices and earnings for 96 firms were examined over the period from 1963 through 1968. As before, price changes were adjusted for estimated market effects and averaged to provide a composite picture. However, to obtain greater discrimination, only cases with *substantially* better- or worse-than-expected earnings were considered. Figure 15-9 shows some of the results.[12] The top curve plots the price behavior of the stocks of firms that announced quarterly earnings more than 40% greater than the corresponding amount four quarters earlier;[13] the bottom curve shows the results for firms that announced earnings 40% below the amount four quarters earlier, or worse.

Here, too, a certain amount of anticipation is apparent. Prices of the group with favorable results increased prior to the published announcement (by 6.0%, after adjustment for market effects), while those of the other group decreased (by 7.5%, after adjustment for market effects). But

[12] A more complex earnings expectations model was also studied, along with different classifications.
[13] This procedure was used to reduce possible distortion due to seasonal earnings patterns.

FIGURE 15-9 Relative Prices after Adjustment for Market Effects Stocks with Substantially Increased Quarterly Earnings versus Stocks with Substantially Decreased Quarterly Earnings.

Source: O. Maurice Joy, Robert H. Litzenberger, and Richard W. McEnally, "The Adjustment of Stock Prices to Announcements of Unanticipated Changes in Quarterly Earnings," *The Journal of Accounting Research*, Autumn 1977.

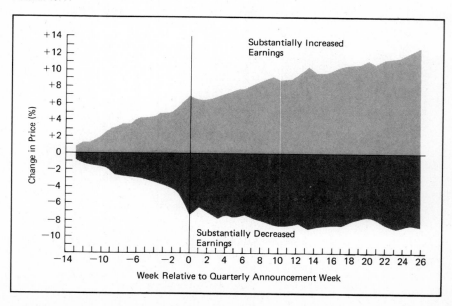

both changes began substantially before the week of the announcement. Official statements of quarterly earnings are apparently not the only source of information on a company's recent success or failure.

The movements of prices after the earnings announcements are more surprising. Those of the group with major earnings declines continued to fall but only slightly (by 1.3% over the next 26 weeks, after adjustment for market effects). On the other hand, those of the other group continued to rise (by 6.7% over the next 26 weeks, after adjustment for market effects).

If better-than-expected earnings announcements indicate attractive opportunities for stock purchases days or weeks after the announcement has been made, the market is not performing in a perfectly efficient manner. Some plausible reasons why this might occur can be given. Favorable news may be likely to be disseminated by those who deal with the public. Since this process is rather slow, an extended upward movement in prices might result. Conversely, bad news may be shared primarily within the community of professional investors, who may react more rapidly. However, if such reactions are predictable, professional investors should move more effectively to profit from good news. And when they do, such news, once public, will offer little opportunity for abnormal profit. The results are thus both puzzling and intriguing.

VALUE LINE RANKINGS

Further evidence on the usefulness of quarterly earnings surprises as an ingredient in stock selection is provided by the performance of stocks assigned different rankings for performance over the succeeding 12 months by the *Value Line Investment Survey*.[14] Each week, every one of approximately 1,700 stocks is assigned one of five ranks. By design the categories include the same number of stocks each week, as follows:

Rank	Number of Stocks
1 (highest)	100
2 (above average)	300
3 (average)	900
4 (below average)	300
5 (lowest)	100

Many factors go into the ranking procedure. Not surprisingly, exact details are not made public. However, the key elements[15] are:

1. The last year's earnings and average price relative to the comparable values for the previous ten years (all adjusted for changes in the prices and earnings of the market as a whole), and the stock's average price

[14] Published by Arnold Bernhard and Co., Inc., New York.
[15] For details see Arnold Bernhard, "Investing in Common Stocks with the Aid of the Value Line Rankings and other Criteria of Stock Value," Arnold Bernhard and Co., 1975.

over the preceding ten weeks relative to that of the preceding 52 weeks (also after adjustment for corresponding changes in the market as a whole). These factors are combined to determine a composite score, using an equation obtained empirically via cross-sectional analysis.

2. The stock's current price-earnings ratio relative to that of the market, compared with the average of the corresponding figures over the last five years.

3. "Earnings momentum": the most recent quarter's earnings are compared with the amount reported four quarters earlier; the stocks for which this ratio is within the top third of the values are assigned a high score, those within the middle third a medium score, and the remainder a low score.

4. "Earnings surprise": the most recent quarter's earnings are also compared with the amount estimated in advance by Value Line's security analysts. Five categories are used, as follows:

Deviation between Actual and Value Line's Estimated Quarterly Earnings
+30% or more (highest)
+15 to +29% (above average)
−14 to +14% (average)
−15 to −29% (below average)
−30% or worse (lowest)

A test[16] of the resulting rankings showed them to be of some value. Beginning in April, 1965, five portfolios were formed (on paper). The first included all stocks ranked "1" at the beginning of the month, in equal dollar values; the second included all stocks ranked "2," and so on. At the beginning of the next month each portfolio was altered as necessary to again include equal dollar values of all stocks with the appropriate ranks at the time. The procedure was continued until the end of 1970. Then each portfolio's performance was compared with that of the market (represented by the full set of stocks covered by the Survey). After adjustment for market sensitivity (risk exposure), the portfolio of top-ranked stocks "beat the market" by about 10% per year, while that of bottom-ranked stocks was beaten by the market by about 10% per year. Both figures were significantly different from zero in a statistical sense.

This does not provide a guaranteed formula for outstanding portfolio performance. No transactions costs were charged in the calculations, and turnover exceeded 130% per year. But the results do suggest that in choosing among stocks, Value Line rankings may prove useful.

One might conjecture that if Value Line rankings "work," it may be due primarily to the use of quarterly earnings (both "momentum"— which is a form of surprise—and the "surprise" factor itself). Even so, the persistence of such a phenomenon would be a sign of market inefficiency.

[16] Fischer Black, "Yes Virginia, There Is Hope: Tests of the Value Line Ranking System," *Financial Analysts Journal*, 29, no. 5 (September/October 1973), 10–14.

The Value Line Survey is available to everyone willing to pay the price (approximately $300 per year) and can be found in some libraries and brokerage offices. Its rankings are thus quite public. Of course, even if such information did help identify mispriced stocks in the past, an increasing awareness of the fact might diminish its usefulness for future investment decisions.

EARNINGS ESTIMATES AND STOCK SELECTION

One way to attempt to identify a mispriced security involves the estimation of all relevant data (e.g., future earnings and/or dividends, the relevant risk class and discount rate) and the insertion of such figures in a valuation equation to estimate the stock's intrinsic value. If a relevant equation is utilized, the resulting value will equal the stock's price if the analyst's estimates agree with the consensus of market opinion. If the analyst disagrees with this consensus, the two values will generally differ. If the difference of opinion concerns only one element, the direction of the implied divergence of price from intrinsic value is easy to predict, and it will be greater the greater the difference between the analyst's estimate and the market consensus.

As a practical matter, few analysts actually use detailed valuation procedures. Instead, they search for situations in which their opinion of the future differs from that of the market as a whole. Stocks likely to be most affected positively if and when the correctness of the analyst's opinion becomes obvious are recommended for purchase. Those likely to be most affected negatively are recommended for sale.

The test of any procedure for identifying potentially mispriced stocks is, of course, its record of performance. Figure 15-10 shows how

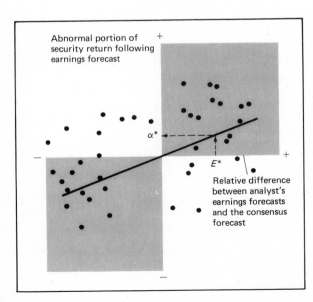

FIGURE 15-10 Comparing Abnormal Returns with the Difference between an Analyst's Earnings Forecasts and Those of the Consensus of Analysts.

this might be analyzed when an analyst concentrates on predicting earnings. Each prediction is represented by one point. The horizontal axis plots the difference between the analyst's estimate of the stock's future earnings and the consensus estimate at the time, with the difference expressed as a percent of, say, the firm's book value per share of stock. The vertical axis plots the abnormal portion of the stock's return over the relevant period after the earnings projection was made (for example: the difference between its return and that of the average stock in the same risk and yield class). If the analyst's estimates are worth considering, there should be some positive relationship between the two values; regression analysis can be used to estimate it and a line such as that shown in Figure 15-10 obtained. Henceforth, the analyst's predictions can be checked against the consensus, the result (e.g., E^*) located on the horizontal axis, and the associated expected abnormal return (e.g., α^*) estimated. This can be used directly by the portfolio manager, with no explicit use of a valuation model at any stage in the process.

Analysts do concentrate on the prediction of relatively near-term earnings and recommend stocks accordingly. This by no means implies that the principles of security valuation do not hold. As always, it is not the form but the substance that counts.

Problems

1. Do deviations from expected earnings represent a valid leading indicator of stock price changes? If so, what implications does this have for investment management?

2. Value Line's top-coded stocks appear to have "beaten the market" by about 10% per year. Should investors hold only stocks given such a code by Value Line? Why or why not?

3. Evidence shows that: (1) there is a statistically significant correlation between analysts' estimates of earnings changes and the subsequent actual changes and (2) there is also a significant statistical correlation between earnings changes and stock price changes. Does it then follow that (3) analysts' earnings forecasts must be useful in predicting price changes?

4. Should a security analyst buy stocks for which he or she forecasts large earnings increases and sell stocks for which he or she forecasts small increases, no increases, or decreases? Why or why not?

5. Why might the price of a stock react only partially to an "earnings surprise" on the first day or two after the earnings announcement?

6. Assume that you want to manage portfolios by trading off risk and return with a computerized "optimizer" (e.g., a quadratic programming rou-

tine). You have estimates of risk and have access to a "security market plane" estimated by one organization and the "security rankings" estimated by Value Line. You are convinced that all these estimates are valuable.

    a. How could you use the security market plane and your risk estimates to obtain estimates of "normal" (efficient market) expected returns for stocks?

    b. How could you use the Value Line rankings (1, . . . , 5) to obtain estimates of expected returns that incorporate both normal and "abnormal" elements?

    c. In what sense would your answer to (b) reflect your belief about the "predictive accuracy" of the Value Line rankings?

    d. When you use your estimates of expected returns and risks with the computer program, a set of suggested holdings will be produced. How will your answer to (b) affect the outcome?

7. Why might a steady trend in a firm's reported earnings from year to year suggest that the figures do not represent the firm's *economic* earnings?

8. If reported earnings are intended to simply provide a "source of information" about the value of a firm, may there not be many alternative procedures of equal use to investors? How might you evaluate a procedure's value in this role after many years of use?

9. The price per share of a firm's stock is less than its book value. Does this indicate that those who now hold the firm's shares have lost money in the past? Does it indicate that they are likely to lose money in the future? Does it indicate that the firm should not undertake any further capital investment?

10. Analysts often evaluate companies on the basis of their "return on equity"—the ratio of reported earnings to book value. What potential problems are involved in this procedure?

Warrants, Options, and Convertible Securities

16

INTRODUCTION

Option contracts are hardly new. In biblical times, Jacob bought an option to marry Rachel from her father Laban for seven years' labor.[1] But, since provisions against fraud were not enforced by regulatory authorities, Laban was able to switch daughters at the time of delivery, and Jacob found himself married to Leah, the elder daughter. Undeterred, he agreed to work another seven years to obtain Rachel as well. The three did not live happily ever after, but that is another story.

Webster's New Collegiate Dictionary defines an *option* in the financial sense as "a contract conveying a right to buy or sell designated securities or commodities at a specified price during a stipulated period."[2] More precisely, it is an agreement between two parties in which one grants the other the *right*, but not the *obligation*, to buy an asset from or sell it to him or her under stated conditions. The party retaining the option (i.e., having a choice to make) is usually termed the *option buyer*, since he or she must pay for the privilege involved. The party with no subsequent choice is termed the *option seller* or in some cases the *writer* or *maker* of the option.

TYPES OF OPTION CONTRACTS

The variety of contracts containing an option feature is bewildering. Even within the domain of publicly traded securities many types can be found. Traditionally, only certain instruments are termed options per se; the others, though similar in nature, are designated in other ways.

Call Options

The most prominent type is the *call option*. It gives the buyer the right to "call away" a specified number of shares of a given *underlying security*

---

[1] For further details, see the book of *Genesis*, Ch. 29. This slightly forced analogy with modern options comes from Julie Connelly, "How Institutions are Playing the Options Game," *Institutional Investor*, VIII, no. 2 (February 1974), 45–49, 109–10.

[2] By permission. From *Webster's New Collegiate Dictionary* © 1980 by G. & C. Merriam Co., Publishers of the Merriam-Webster Dictionaries.

from the option seller (writer) at a specified price, up to some indicated date. A *European* call option allows the security to be called away only on the specified date. An *American* call option allows it to be called away at any time up to and including the specified date. If and when the security is called away, the option is said to have been *exercised*. The final date on which exercise is allowed is termed the *expiration date*. The price at which the option can be exercised is termed the *exercise price* or, since it is in theory "struck" when the buyer and seller negotiate the terms of the option, the *striking price*.

Call options, usually termed just *calls*, are traded on exchanges in the United States. Each exchange facilitates transactions in calls for a given list of stocks for specific expiration dates and exercise prices.

Exchange-traded (or *listed*) options are considerably more important than the *over-the-counter* (*OTC*) or negotiated options created through the auspices of brokers and dealers. Prior to 1973, put and call dealers and brokers brought would-be-buyers and sellers together, arranged terms, helped with the paperwork, and charged the substantial fees required for the work involved. There was little standardization, low volume, and virtually no *secondary market*. A buyer wishing to close out a position prior to expiration could exercise an option, but it was usually too expensive to try to find another buyer. A seller would usually wait until the expiration date or the day the buyer chose to exercise an option, rather than incur the expense involved in finding someone to take over the obligation.

The advent of listed options changed this. Existing options can now be bought or sold on the exchanges as easily as new ones, and either a buyer or a seller can close out a position at any time.

The buyer of a call option must of course pay the seller for the privilege involved. The amount paid is called the premium, although "option price" is a more appropriate term.

The *Options Clearing Corporation* greatly facilitates trading in listed options, since such options exist only in the storage of a series of computers located at the Corporation and in the offices of its member firms. Each position in each option contract is recorded. The mechanics for keeping track of all of them are rather complex, but the principles are simple enough. As soon as a buyer and a seller decide to trade a particular option contract and the former pays the latter the agreed-upon premium, the Clearing Corporation steps in, becoming the effective seller to the buyer and the effective buyer from the seller: all direct links between original buyer and seller are severed. If a buyer chooses to exercise an option, the Clearing Corporation will randomly choose a seller who has not closed his or her position in it and *assign* the exercise notice accordingly. The Corporation also *guarantees* delivery of stock if the seller defaults.

The mechanism of a Clearing Corporation makes it possible for a buyer to "sell out" a position and a seller to "buy in" a position at any time. In effect, when offsetting positions in a specific contract are found in the same account, a computer simply wipes out both entries. Thus if an investor buys an "October 50 on Telephone" on Monday and sells another on Tuesday, his or her net position will be zero, and both records can be removed. The second trade is a *closing sale*, since it serves to close out the position created by the first trade. Closing sales transactions thus allow buyers to sell options rather than exercise them. A similar procedure allows a seller to pay to be relieved of the obligation to deliver stock on call. An investor who sells an October 50 on Telephone on Tuesday can buy one on Wednesday. The latter is a *closing purchase* and serves to close out the position entirely.[3]

Call options may be *protected* against stock splits, stock dividends, and even cash dividends on the underlying stock. Since any of these events will cause the stock's price to fall below what it otherwise would have been, they work to the disadvantage of the holder (buyer) of a call option. Virtually all option contracts specify that the exercise price and number of shares will be adjusted to account for splits and stock dividends on the underlying stock. For example, if a firm declares a 50% stock dividend, an outstanding option would be adjusted to cover one-and-a-half as many shares at two-thirds of the original exercise price per share. Over-the-counter options contain provisions for reducing the exercise price by the amounts of any cash dividends paid on the underlying stock, but such protection is not included in listed option contracts, except in the unusual case in which a dividend is formally designated a return of capital.

Put Options

A *put* is an option to sell an underlying stock to the option seller at a specified price, up to a given expiration date. As with calls, there are both American and European puts. The former provide the buyer the option of putting the stock at any time before the expiration date; the latter can be exercised only on one date.

In the United States puts are traded in the over-the-counter market and on exchanges.

The exercise price and the number of shares in a put contract are automatically adjusted to account for splits and stock dividends on the underlying stock. Over-the-counter puts also provide for reductions in exercise price equal to the amounts of any cash dividends paid on the underlying stock.

OPTION TRADING

Exchanges open trading in a new set of options periodically. When established, each option has roughly nine months remaining before expiration with a standardized exercise price equal to the price of the underlying stock, rounded, for example, to the nearest multiple of $5. Subsequently, as the stock price varies, new options may be declared eligible for trading. Once on the list, an option remains until expiration. Options generally expire on the Saturday after the third Friday of the specified month.

In 1980 options were traded on the Chicago Board Options Exchange and the American, Pacific, Philadelphia and Midwest Exchanges.

---

[3] A more extensive discussion of this clearing process, in the context of the commodity futures market, where it originated, can be found in Chapter 17.

Listed Options Quotations

Friday, December 21, 1979

Closing prices of all options. Sales unit usually is 100 shares. Security description includes exercise price. Stock close is New York or American exchange final price. p-Put option. o-Old shares.

Chicago Board

Option	&	price	– Feb – Vol.	Last	– May – Vol.	Last	– Aug – Vol.	Last	N.Y. Close
H Inns		. 20	215	¾	96	1⅝	47	2⅜	17⅞
H Inns		..25	70	1-16	152	7-16	b	b	17⅞
Honwll		..60	6	23¼	b	b	b	b	82⅞
Honwll	p	..60	140	1-16	b	b	b	b	82⅞
Honwll		. 70	517	13⅝	332	15½	1	17	82⅞
Honwll	p	70	607	½	53	1½	53	2⅜	82⅞
Honwll		..80	385	6⅜	124	8⅞	a	a	82⅞
Honwll	p	80	1413	2⅞	131	4⅜	1	5⅛	82⅞
Honwll		..90	585	1 13-16	99	3⅞	a	a	82⅞
Honwll	p	. 90	254	8½	58	9⅝	a	a	82⅞
In Flv		..20	10	1½	10	2¾	a	a	21
In Flv		..25	1	⅛	2	11-16	2	15-16	21
J Manv		25	77	¾	21	1½	33	2 1-16	24⅛
J Manv		30	40	1-16	a	a	a	a	24⅛
MGIC		...30	18	2 9-16	a	a	a	a	29¼
MGIC		...40	3	5-16	a	a	b	b	29¼
Mobil		.. 40	198	18⅛	108	19¼	b	b	57¼
Mobil		...45	238	13½	35	14¾	2	16⅝	57¼
Mobil		...50	2626	9⅜	108	11⅜	14	13	57¼
Mobil		...55	2756	6	349	8⅜	274	10	57¼
Mobil		...60	2990	3⅜	1008	6	326	7¼	57¼
N Semi		20	8	14½	b	b	b	b	33⅝
N Semi		.25	481	9¼	22	10⅝	9	11⅞	33⅝
N Semi		.30	740	5	111	7	20	8¾	33⅝
N Semi		.35	1297	2⅜	113	4¼	33	5¾	33⅝
Occi		 15	1	11½	b	b	b	b	26
Occi		... 20	420	6⅜	32	7½	b	b	26
Occi		... 25	562	2 13-16	183	4⅛	145	5	26
Occi		... 30	614	1	389	2⅛	296	3⅛	26
Raythn		. 40	230	26⅞	b	b	b	b	66¾
Raythn		. 45	230	22	b	b	b	b	66¾
Raythn		50	330	16½	160	17⅝	10	18¾	66¾
Raythn		. 60	78	7⅛	a	a	a	a	66¾
Raythn		. 70	57	1¾	13	3⅜	a	a	66¾
Rynlds		. 35	137	1	9	2⅛	6	2¾	34
Slumb		.. 60	3	32⅝	b	b	b	b	92⅜
Slumb		.. 70	69	23	a	a	b	b	92⅜
Slumb		.. 80	41	15⅛	a	a	2	20½	92⅜
Slumb		..90	55	7⅜	57	11¾	13	14⅜	92⅜
Slumb		100	354	2⅞	27	6⅜	42	9⅛	92⅜
Skylin		.. 10	30	2⅛	2	2½	a	a	11¾
Skylin		..15	88	¼	33	9-16	28	1	11¾
Southn		..10	a	a	1	2	2	2 1-16	11⅜
Southn		..15	a	a	16	⅛	38	¼	11⅜
St Ind		..70	67	10¼	7	12	5	14	78⅝
St Ind		..80	110	3¼	11	6½	2	8¼	78⅝
St Ind		..90	214	⅝	65	2¾	5	4	78⅝
Tx Glf		..25	7	9½	a	a	a	a	34¼
Tx Glf		..30	28	4¾	10	6⅝	a	a	34¼
Tx Glf		..35	45	2¼	16	3½	6	4⅝	34¼
U A L		..20	38	3½	a	a	a	a	22⅝
U A L		..25	103	⅞	69	1 15-16	4	2¾	22⅝
U A L		..30	31	⅛	16	⅝	b	b	22⅝
U Tech		. 35	30	9½	a	a	a	a	44
U Tech		.40	173	4½	39	6	30	6⅝	44
U Tech		.45	295	1 9-16	20	2 15-16	18	4	44
J Walt		..30	5	2⅛	a	a	a	a	30¾
J Walt		..35	a	a	3	1	a	a	30¾
Willms		..15	102	16½	b	b	b	b	31⅛
Willms		. 20	129	11¼	4	11¾	36	12	31⅛
Willms		. 25	2209	6½	501	7½	30	8	31⅛
Willms		. 30	2231	3¼	654	4½	194	5⅜	31⅛
Total volume			115,857			Open	interest		2,488,951

* a = not traded; b = unavailable

FIGURE 16-1 Price and Volume Quotations for Listed Options.

Source: Reprinted with permission of *The Wall Street Journal,* © Dow Jones and Company, Inc. (December 24, 1979). All Rights reserved.

Prior to any adjustment for stock splits, etc., options are traded in contracts, each of which covers 100 shares of stock. Figure 16-1 shows an example of a report on a day's trades in one set of such contracts. Puts are indicated with the letter "p"; all other entries refer to calls. Thus during the day, 517 contracts traded in Honeywell 70 calls of February. Each contract entitled the holder to call away 100 shares of Honeywell at $70 per share any time up to and including the third Friday of February. The last trade of the day was made at a price of $13\frac{5}{8}$ per one-share option, or $1,362.50 per contract. The price at which Honeywell last traded during the day on the New York Stock Exchange is also shown—in this case, it was $82\frac{7}{8}$ per share.

Some options are not traded during a day—these are indicated by the letter "a" in Figure 16-1. Others, though included because of the format of the report, have not been introduced and are thus unavailable for trading; they are indicated by the letter "b."

At the bottom of the listings for an exchange are shown the total volume (number of contracts traded) and open interest (number of contracts purchased but neither liquidated in the secondary market, expired, nor exercised).

Trading in options is far from continuous. In the financial press it is not unusual to find prices for various options that appear to be "out of line" with one another or with the price of the underlying stock. It is well to remember that each listed price is that of the last trade of the day, and that the trades may have taken place at different times. Apparent price disparities may simply reflect trades that occurred before and after major news, rather than concurrent values at which obviously profitable trades could have been made.

Margin

The buyer of an option desires some assurance that the seller can deliver as required if the option is exercised. In the case of a call, stock is to be delivered in return for the exercise price. In the case of a put, money is to be delivered, in return for stock. In either case, the net cost to the option seller will be the absolute difference between the exercise price and the stock's market value at the time of exercise. For listed options, the Clearing Corporation guarantees the buyer that this liability will be met. For over-the-counter options, a similar guarantee is provided by a brokerage firm via *endorsement* of the option contract. In each case the seller is also required to provide some sort of *margin* or backing to guarantee fulfillment of his or her obligation.

More Complicated Options

Listed option contracts follow standard forms and are relatively straightforward. However, negotiated options are subject to few restrictions, and buyers and sellers can and do agree on all sorts of forms. Race tracks offer bettors exotic combinations via the "daily double" and "exacta" races. Option brokers and dealers have strips, straps, straddles, and even more exotic types of options.

A *straddle* is a package involving one put and one call, on the same stock, at the same striking (exercise) price, and with the same expiration date. A *strip* is similar, but in this case two puts are combined with one call. A *strap* combines two calls and one put.

Commodity Options

Options to buy all sorts of commodities are used in ordinary business practice. For example, it is sometimes possible to rent a house with an option to buy it under certain conditions. Previous sections discussed put and call options written on an underlying security; similar options are written on other items, most notably agricultural commodities.

In the United States the sale of commodity options on domestic crops has generally been disallowed. In the 1970s, several firms offered options on other, unregulated commodities but failed to price them correctly or to back them adequately, resulting in default and in some cases jail terms for the promoters. With any option, some guarantee is required that the seller can meet his or her obligation. Subject to this requirement, commodity options are as viable as security options; nothing inherently disreputable is involved.

Executive Compensation Options

Many corporations give their executives options to purchase stock as an incentive device or to help the executive better manage tax liabilities. Such options typically do not expire while the individual remains with the firm, but they cannot be freely traded. Formally, the executive is the buyer and the corporation the seller; the premium is usually paid in hard work, increased devotion to the firm, and/or a lower salary.

Bond Call Provisions

As discussed in Chapter 11, many firms issue bonds with call provisions. This amounts to the sale of a straight bond and the concurrent purchase by the corporation of a call option sold by the purchaser of the bond. The premium is paid by the corporation in the form of a lower price for the bond than for one lacking the call provision. The seller of the call is the bond purchaser.

Bond call provisions usually can be exercised only after some specified date (e.g., five years after issue) and prior to another (the bonds' maturity date). Moreover, the exercise price may be different for different exercise dates. The implicit call option is thus both longer-lived and more complex than those usually traded on either the over-the-counter or the listed options markets.

Warrants

A *stock purchase warrant* or, more simply, a *warrant* is a call option issued by the firm whose stock serves as the underlying security. There are some exceptions: for example, occasionally a firm will issue warrants for some other security that it owns (e.g., that of a subsidiary).

At the time of issue, a warrant usually has a longer time to expiration (e.g., five or more years) than a typical call option. Some *perpetual warrants*, with no expiration date, have also been issued.

Most warrants are protected against stock splits and stock dividends, but few provide protection against cash dividends. Exercise prices may be fixed, or the amount may be programmed to change during the life of the warrant, usually increasing in steps. The initial exercise price is typically set to exceed the price of the underlying security at the time the warrant is issued, often by a substantial amount.

Generally, warrants may be exercised before expiration—i.e., they are American call options—but some require an initial waiting period.

At time of issue, one warrant typically entitles the holder to purchase one share of stock for the appropriate exercise price. However, adjustments for stock splits, etc. can alter the ratio, leading to many cases in which one warrant can be used to purchase more or less than one share of stock.

Warrants are often issued along with other securities to "sweeten" an offering. For example, a bond with warrants attached may be sold as a package. In some cases the warrants are *nondetachable*, except upon exercise or possibly the maturity of the bond. In other cases the warrants are *detachable* and may be traded separately.

Warrants may be distributed to stockholders in lieu of a stock or cash dividend or sold directly as a new security issue.

Terms associated with a warrant are contained in a *warrant agreement*, which serves the same function as an indenture for a bond issue. The scope of the warrant holder's protection is defined (for example, the treatment of warrants in the event of merger, reorganization, etc.), along with any relevant restrictions on corporate behavior.

Some warrants issued with bonds have an additional attribute. Although they may be detached and exercised in the normal way, with cash, an alternative is provided. Bonds from the initial issue may be used in lieu of cash to pay the exercise price, and the bonds will be valued *at par* for this purpose. This tends to prop up the price of such a *usable bond* and to maintain a closer relationship between the two securities than in the more common case in which detachable warrants must be exercised with cash.

One difference between warrants and options is the limitation on the amount of the former outstanding. A specific number of warrants of a particular type will be issued; the total cannot easily be increased and typically will be reduced as the warrants are exercised. An option can be created whenever two parties wish to create one: the number outstanding is thus not fixed. Exercise of an option on its stock has no more effect on a corporation than a transaction in the stock on the secondary market. But exercise of a warrant does. It leaves the corporation with more cash, fewer warrants outstanding, and more stock outstanding. Old stockholders find themselves with a smaller proportion of a larger firm.

Warrants are traded on major stock exchanges and on the over-the-counter market. Quotations for those with active markets are provided in the financial press in the sections devoted primarily to stocks.

Rights   *Subscription warrants* are issued to give stockholders their *preemptive right* to subscribe to a new issue before the general public. Each share of stock receives a *right*. A stated number of rights plus a specified subscription price are required to obtain one new share. To insure sale of the new stock, the subscription price is usually set below reasonable expectations of its market value. This does not mean that new subscribers get a bargain, since they must pay old stockholders for the required rights, which become valuable as a result.

Rights are generally short-lived (from two to ten weeks) and may be freely traded prior to exercise. Up to a specified date, old shares of the stock trade *cum rights*—the buyer is entitled to receive the rights when issued. Afterward, the stock trades *ex rights*, at a correspondingly lower price. Rights for popular issues of stock are sometimes traded on exchanges; others are available in the over-the-counter market. Often trading begins prior to actual availability, with the rights sold for delivery on a *when-issued* basis.

A right is, in effect, a warrant, although one with a rather short time before expiration. It also differs with regard to exercise price, which is typically set above the current stock price for a warrant and below it for a right. Because of their short lives, rights need not be protected against stock splits and dividends. Otherwise, they have all the attributes of a warrant and should be valued accordingly.

Convertible Securities

A particularly popular financial instrument is a security that can be converted into a different security of the same firm under stated conditions. The typical case involves a bond or preferred stock convertible into shares of the firm's common stock, with a stated number of shares received for each bond. Usually no cash is involved: the old security is simply traded in, and the appropriate number of new securities issued in return. *Convertible preferred stocks* are issued from time to time, but tax effects make them, like other preferred stocks, attractive primarily for corporate investment. For other investors many issues of *convertible bonds* are available.

If a $1,000 par bond can be converted into 20 shares of common stock, the *conversion ratio* is 20.0. Alternatively, the *conversion price* may be said to be $50 ($1,000/20), since $50 of the bond's *par* value must be given up to obtain one common share. Neither the conversion ratio nor the conversion price is affected by changes in a bond's market value.

Conversion ratios are typically set so that conversion will not prove attractive unless and until the stock price increases substantially from its value at the time the convertible security was first issued. This is similar to the general practice used in setting exercise prices for warrants.

Convertible securities of great complexity can be found. Some may be converted only after an initial waiting period. Some may be converted up to the bond's maturity date, others only for a stated, shorter period. Some have different conversion ratios for different years. A few can be converted into packages of two or more different securities; others require the additional payment of cash upon conversion, etc.

Convertible bonds are usually protected against stock splits and stock dividends via adjustment in the conversion ratio. For example, a bond with an initial conversion ratio of 20.0 could be adjusted to have a ratio of 22.0 following a 10% stock dividend. Protection against cash dividends is not generally provided, but some indentures require that the holders of convertible bonds be notified prior to payment of cash dividends so they may convert before the resultant fall in the stock's price, if desired.

Convertible securities often contain a call provision, which may be used by the corporation to *force conversion* when the stock price is sufficiently high to make the value of the stock obtained on conversion exceed the call price of the bond. Corporations can also encourage conversion by providing stockholders with large cash dividends, valuable subscription rights, etc.

Figure 16-2 shows a portion of a convertible bond report. Information on the prices and current yields of both bonds and their underlying stocks is given along with the quality ratings assigned to the bonds by either Moody's or Standard and Poor's. The conversion ratio for each bond is shown, along with an associated value and premium. The *conversion value*, obtained by multiplying the conversion ratio by the stock's current price, is the value that would be obtained by conversion; it is the bond's current "value as stock." The *conversion premium* is the amount by which the bond's current price exceeds its conversion value, expressed as a percent of the latter. Also shown is the *investment value*: an estimate, based on its maturity, coupon and rating, of the amount for which the bond might sell if it were not convertible. This is the convertible's estimated "value as a bond." The final figure, termed *price risk*, is the difference between the current price of the bond and its investment value, expressed as a percent of the former.

A convertible bond is, for practical purposes, a bond with nondetachable warrants plus the restriction that *only* the bond is usable (at par) to pay the exercise price. If the bond were not callable, the value of this package of one bond and several *latent warrants* would equal the value of a straight noncallable bond (i.e., the estimated investment value) plus that of the warrants. However, most convertible bonds are callable and thus involve a double option: the holder has an option to convert the bond to stock, and the issuing corporation has an option to buy the bond (typically, only after a stated number of years from issuance). To further complicate the situation, the value of a risky bond is greater, the smaller the risk of default—and, other things equal, the greater a corporation's stock price, the lower the risk that it will default on outstanding bonds.

When a convertible bond is exchanged for common stock, the firm's earnings per share typically will change. Interest costs will fall, increasing total earnings, but the larger amount must be divided among more shares of stock. Most corporations are now required to provide estimates of the value of earnings per share if all securities convertible into common stock were converted. Table 16-1 provides an example. Convertible bonds with a par value of $500,000 are outstanding, with an annual interest cost of $50,000. Each bond is convertible into twenty shares of stock; if all were converted, interest payments would fall by $50,000 and the number of

FIGURE 16–2 Portion of a Convertible Bond Report

Description	RECENT PRICES ($)		CURRENT YIELD (%)		CONVERSION		Premium (%)	Quality Rating	Investment Value-Est. ($)	Price Risk (%)
	Bond	Common	Bond	Common	Ratio	Value ($)				
ARA Services $4\frac{5}{8}$-96	75.00	52.25	6.2	2.0	9.867	51.56	45	BBB	51	32
Allied Stores $4\frac{1}{2}$-92	105.50	46.50	4.3	3.7	22.470	104.49	1	BA	51	51
Aluminum Co. of Amer. $5\frac{1}{4}$-91	105.00	52.63	5.0	2.5	17.857	93.97	12	BAA	61	41
Amer. Airlines $4\frac{1}{4}$-92	49.25	13.00	8.6	0.0	22.599	29.38	68	BB	39	20
Amer. Hoist & Der. $5\frac{1}{2}$-93	82.00	15.50	6.7	5.2	50.250	77.89	5	BA	53	35
Amfac $5\frac{1}{4}$-94	64.00	16.50	8.2	6.1	22.899	37.78	69	BB	40	37
Ashland Oil $4\frac{3}{4}$-93	73.75	29.13	6.4	5.8	20.000	58.25	27	BAA	60	18
Baxter Labs $4\frac{3}{8}$-91	108.00	34.75	4.1	0.6	26.316	91.45	18	BAA	54	50
Becton Dickinson 5-89	85.00	35.50	5.9	1.4	15.408	54.70	55	BAA	61	28
Burlington Inds. 5-91	82.00	25.50	6.1	6.3	25.641	65.38	25	BAA	61	25
Burlington Northern $5\frac{1}{4}$-92	91.25	43.38	5.8	0.7	18.182	78.86	16	BAA	63	30
Carrier Corp. $5\frac{5}{8}$-89	81.00	17.13	6.3	3.0	35.714	61.16	32	BAA	68	16
Caterpillar Trac. $5\frac{1}{2}$-2000	125.00	88.75	4.4	2.5	13.201	117.16	7	A	65	48
Chase Manhattan $4\frac{7}{8}$-93	64.63	27.38	7.5	8.0	18.182	49.77	30	NR	63	2
Chemical New York $5\frac{1}{2}$-96	68.00	37.25	8.1	7.7	13.652	50.85	34	AA	67	1
Citicorp $5\frac{3}{4}$-2000	98.50	33.13	5.8	2.9	24.390	80.79	22	NR	67	31
Com. Gen. Mtg. 6-96	64.50	15.75	9.3	10.2	30.769	48.46	33	NR	62	3
Crocker Natl. $5\frac{3}{4}$-96	75.00	22.88	7.7	7.3	22.727	51.99	44	NR	65	13

Dart Inds. $4\frac{1}{4}$-97	78.38	55.00	5.4	2.6	10.750	59.13	33	BAA	50	36
Dayco Corp. 6-94	73.50	15.25	8.2	3.3	35.000	53.38	38	B	44	40
Deere, John $5\frac{1}{2}$-2001	112.00	67.63	4.9	2.8	15.267	103.24	8	A	65	41
Eastern Air Lines $4\frac{3}{4}$-93	50.00	8.88	9.5	0.0	29.412	26.10	92	B	37	26
Engelhard Minerals $5\frac{1}{4}$-97	119.38	34.88	4.4	2.9	34.000	118.58	1	BBB	55	53
FMC Corp. $4\frac{1}{4}$-92	68.00	23.50	6.3	4.3	24.096	56.63	20	BAA	55	19
Federal Natl. Mtg. $4\frac{3}{8}$-96	71.00	13.88	6.2	6.3	50.955	70.70	0	NR	59	16
Fisher Foods $6\frac{1}{2}$-94	70.00	9.13	9.3	4.4	36.910	33.68	108	BA	59	15
Ford Motor Credit $4\frac{1}{2}$-96	75.00	54.88	6.0	4.4	12.800	70.24	7	BBB	55	26
Fruehauf Corp. $5\frac{1}{2}$-94	69.00	26.88	8.0	6.7	21.622	58.11	19	BA	53	23
Genl. Amer. Trans. $5\frac{3}{4}$-99	71.50	27.63	8.0	6.5	16.670	46.05	55	BAA	61	14
General Tel. & Elec. 5-92	67.50	25.38	7.4	7.1	21.697	55.06	23	BA	50	25
Georgia Pacific $5\frac{1}{4}$-96	111.25	52.25	4.7	1.5	20.760	108.47	3	BAA	54	51
Grace, WR $6\frac{1}{2}$-96	91.00	25.63	7.1	6.6	33.755	86.50	5	BA	57	37
Greyhound Corp. $6\frac{1}{2}$-90	89.13	15.25	7.3	6.8	54.420	82.99	7	BAA	63	29
Gulf & Western $5\frac{1}{2}$-93	101.00	24.63	5.4	2.4	39.050	96.16	5	B	45	55
Hercules $6\frac{1}{2}$-99	109.25	33.00	5.9	2.4	28.570	94.28	16	BAA	71	35
Heublein Inc. $4\frac{1}{2}$-97	86.00	49.88	5.2	2.4	14.388	71.76	20	BBB	43	50
Hilton Hotels $5\frac{1}{2}$-95	76.50	17.75	7.2	3.9	32.787	58.20	31	BB	52	32
Intl. Minerals & Chem. 4-91	90.13	34.88	4.4	6.9	26.330	91.83	−2	BAA	39	56
Intl. Paper $4\frac{1}{4}$-96	62.50	12.25	6.8	1.0	26.320	32.34	94	BAA	53	15
Intl. Tel. & Tel. $8\frac{5}{8}$-2000	112.00	26.00	7.7	6.2	39.410	102.47	9	BAA	82	26

Source: Merrill Lynch, Pierce, Fenner and Smith, Inc., *Convertible Bonds,* June 1976.

TABLE 16-1 The Calculation of Fully Diluted Earnings Per Share

	Item	Earnings as Reported ($)	Earnings Assuming Conversion ($)
	Earnings before interest and taxes	1,000,000	1,000,000
(less)	Interest payments	100,000	50,000
(equals)	Earnings before taxes	900,000	950,000
(less)	Tax (at 50%)	450,000	475,000
(equals)	Earnings after taxes	450,000	475,000
(divided by)	Number of common shares	100,000	110,000
(equals)	Earnings per share	4.50	4.32

shares would increase by 10,000. Earnings per share would fall from $4.50 to $4.32, as indicated in the table. The latter figure, known as the *fully diluted earnings per share*, can be found in the annual reports of firms with outstanding convertible securities. When warrants with an exercise price below the current market value of the stock are outstanding, earnings may also be adjusted by assuming the exercise of all warrants and the use of the proceeds to buy back some of the additional shares issued.

The calculation of fully diluted earnings provides recognition of the value of outstanding call options that the stockholders of a firm have issued to the holders of convertible securities. While the desirability of this particular method for reflecting the associated liability may be debated, the need to consider it is not subject to question.

Dual Funds

An interesting type of call option is that represented by the capital shares of *dual-purpose funds*. The idea is quite simple. For example, a fund is formed with a capitalization of $100 million. Of this, $50 million is provided by purchasers of *income shares* at, say, $10 each, and the other $50 million by purchasers of *capital shares*, also at $10 each. The proceeds are used to purchase a diversified portfolio of securities. Holders of income shares are entitled to all income produced by the portfolio, plus an amount equal to their investment ($10) at the end of, say, the tenth year. If total income falls below a stated minimum, the shortfall is added to the amount owed income shareholders at the end of the period. Holders of the capital shares receive nothing for ten years but are entitled to whatever is left over after the income shareholders have been paid off.

A capital share in such a fund is an option, although in practice a rather complex one. The capital shareholders have the option to buy the firm—i.e., its managed investment portfolio—from the income shareholders for an exercise price equal to the required income share payments. The income shareholders have, in effect, issued call options, using the premiums received (i.e., the money paid by the capital shareholders) plus their own money to buy securities and pay management. If the value of the portfolio does not decline too much, it will be called away from them for the exercise price (specifically, in the tenth year for the final payment of $50 million plus any income-share dividends in arrears).

Equity as an Option

Dual-fund capital shares are not unlike the common stock of any levered corporation. If payments are made on schedule to creditors, stockholders can keep a corporation's assets. Otherwise, the assets are forfeited. Economically, if not legally, shareholders hold a call option on the firm, an option sold initially by the creditors. The exercise price is the set of payments promised the creditors, and the expiration date is the maturity date of the debt. The creditors have, in a sense, invested their money plus the premium received from the stockholders (i.e., the proceeds from stock issue plus retained earnings) in the firm's assets. In the event of bankruptcy, the creditors retain the assets (minus payments to lawyers). Otherwise, they receive the promised payments (i.e., the exercise price) and have the assets called away from them.

Bankruptcy can be viewed as a decision by stockholders not to exercise their call option, on the grounds that the firm is worth less than the exercise price (required payments to the creditors). The ability to declare bankruptcy, which derives in turn from the limited liability of corporate stock ownership, thus gives common shares the attributes of call options.

The importance of the "option attribute" of a stock will depend on the extent to which a firm is levered and the probability of bankruptcy. Firms with substantial leverage typically have many kinds of debt with different maturities, payment schedules, associated restrictions, etc. The option implicit in common stock is thus likely to be exceedingly complex. However, the fact that many common stocks are themselves options underlines the importance of understanding the basic principles of option valuation.

TAXATION OF OPTION PROFITS AND LOSSES

There is nothing simple about United States income tax regulations, and the treatment of profits and losses from option transactions is no exception. Complicated cases require legal opinion, but the general approach is reasonably easy to understand.

When a call option is exercised, the buyer is considered to have bought stock for a total cost equal to the exercise price plus the premium paid for the option itself plus any commissions or other costs involved in the option purchase and its exercise. The seller of a call option that is exercised is considered to have sold the stock for a total value equal to the exercise price plus the premium received for the option, minus any commissions or other costs involved in the sale of the option and its exercise. The period between the initial sale of the option and its exercise is irrelevant for tax purposes; all profits and losses are attributed to the holding of the security itself, which begins on the exercise date for the option buyer and ends on that date for the option seller. Exercise of a put option is treated in an analogous manner.

If an investor purchases an option, then sells it, the difference between the prices is considered a *capital* gain or loss, short- or long-term, depending on the holding period.

Treatment of the results obtained by an option seller (writer) who closes out a position is not similar. The difference between the sale price initially received and the price paid for the subsequent closing purchase is always considered a *short-term capital* gain or loss.[4]

When a call expires unexercised, the buyer's loss is a *capital* loss, short- or long-term, depending on the length of the period from purchase to expiration. However, the seller's gain is always considered a *short-term capital* gain.

These and other rules give rise to a number of strategies that take tax consequences into account. For example, in the event of exercise, the results from an option transaction are incorporated into a stock purchase or sale for both the buyer and the seller, producing capital gains and losses for tax purposes. Moreover, timing of an exercise or closing transaction may make the difference between a short- and a long-term gain or loss. The decision on whether or not to close a position and, if so, whether to do it via exercise or a transaction in the secondary market thus requires analysis of tax aspects as well as the basic economics of the situation.

Taxes may affect option prices, explaining otherwise anomalous differences between actual prices and those expected in a tax-free environment. Before purchasing or selling any option, an investor should consider the possibility that its current price makes such a transaction better suited for those with a different relationship with the tax collector.

[4] Unless the option is written in the ordinary course of the taxpayer's business, in which case the result is treated as an ordinary gain or loss.

FIGURE 16-3 Values of Options at Expiration.

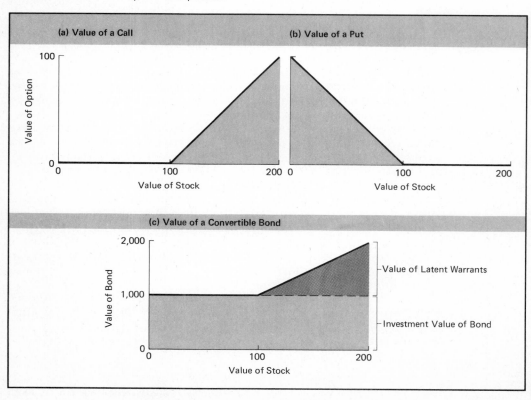

VALUE OF AN OPTION AT EXPIRATION

The value of an option is related to that of its underlying security, but the relationship is not strictly linear. This is particularly obvious just prior to expiration (which we will call "at expiration" to save verbiage). Figure 16-3(a) relates the expiration value of a call option with an exercise price of $100 to the price of the underlying stock. If the stock price is below $100, the option will expire worthless. If it is above $100, the option can be exercised for $100 to obtain a security with a greater value; the net gain will equal the difference between the security's actual price and the exercise price. Of course, there is no need to actually exercise the option. Instead, the option seller can simply pay the buyer the difference between the security price and the exercise price, avoiding the bother of exercise for both parties. This is commonly done for listed options, although a minority of investors choose to exercise their options, possibly for tax purposes.

Figure 16-3(b) shows the value of a put option with an exercise price of $100 at expiration. The holder of such an option will find it profitable to exercise it if the stock price is below the exercise price. In such a situation, the security can be sold for the difference between the two amounts. As with a call option, neither party need actually deal in the stock. The seller of *any* option worth exercising at expiration can simply buy off the associated obligation by paying the holder of the option the difference between the stock price and the exercise price.

Figure 16-3(c) shows the value at expiration of a noncallable convertible bond with a conversion ratio of 10.0, on the assumptions that the bond matures when its latent warrants expire and that its investment value at the time is $1,000. If the stock price is below the effective exercise price of $100 (=$1,000/10) at the time, it will not pay to convert; the bond should be allowed to mature and its par value received. But if the stock price exceeds the exercise price, conversion will be profitable. For example, if the stock price is $110, conversion will give ten shares worth $110 each, for a total value of $1,100, as shown in the figure. Comparison of Figures 16-3(a) and 16-3(c) highlights the fact that a noncallable convertible bond is equivalent to a straight bond (which would be represented in this type of diagram by a flat line at $1,000) plus a call option.

PROFITS AND LOSSES FROM POSITIONS HELD UNTIL EXPIRATION

Figure 16-3 showed the values of various options at expiration. To determine profits and losses we must also take premiums into account.[5]

Figure 16-4 shows the profits and losses associated with a number of

---

[5] For comparability, the actual premium paid when an option is purchased can be converted to an equivalent value at time of expiration, using an appropriate rate of interest: if the premium (i.e., the price of the option) is p, an equivalent value at the time of expiration is $p(1 + r)^t$, where r is an appropriate rate of interest and t is the time between purchase and expiration.

strategies. Each involves a purchase and/or a sale at an initial time when the stock under study sells for $100, plus one or more closing transactions at a subsequent time just prior to the expiration of all the options being considered. Outcomes are shown for investors choosing the two sides of each of six positions. Since the profit obtained by a buyer is the seller's loss, and vice versa, each diagram in the figure has a corresponding mirror image.

Figures 16-4(a) and (c) include the value of the initial premium along with the amounts shown in Figures 16-3(a) and (b). Figures 16-4(b) and (d) show the results obtained by the other party in each case. Figure 16-4(e) is obtained by adding the amounts shown in Figures 16-4(a) and (c) to obtain the net profit or loss from buying a straddle. Figure 16-4(f) is the mirror image of Figure 16-4(e), and also shows the sum of the amounts given by Figures 16-4(b) and (c).

Figure 16-4(g) shows the profit or loss made by an investor who avoids options entirely, but buys a share of the stock (at $100) when others purchase or sell options, and sells the stock when the options expire. If no dividends are paid in the interim, the relationship is that shown by the dashed line. Otherwise the dividends received[6] must be taken into account, giving a relationship like that shown by the solid line. Figure 16-4(h) shows the outcomes obtained by an investor who sells stock at the initial date, then buys it back at the terminal date. The initial sale might involve stock previously held, or it could be a "short sale" of stock borrowed for the interim.

Figure 16-4(i) plots the results obtained by an investor who buys one share of stock and simultaneously writes (sells) a call on it. The person involved is said to have written a *fully covered option*, since it is guaranteed by the holding of the required amount of stock. In contrast, the writer whose situation is depicted in Figure 16-4(b) must rely on cash or other assets to make good the associated obligation. An option seller who does not hold the underlying stock is said to have written a *naked option*.

Figure 16-4(j) shows the results obtained by an investor who sells one share of stock and simultaneously buys a call option. While the investor in Figure 16-4(i) faces limited gains and potentially larger losses, the investor in Figure 16-4(j) faces limited losses and potentially larger gains.

Figure 16-4(k) portrays the situation faced by an investor who buys one-half a share of the stock and sells one call (i.e., writes a *partially covered* option). A substantial price move in either direction can cause a loss. A large price increase will result in a call: additional stock will have to be obtained and given up at a loss. On the other hand, a large price decrease will cause a loss on the investor's stock holding. Figure 16-4(l) shows the results obtained by an investor who takes the opposite position, selling one-half a share of the stock and buying one call.

Comparison of the diagrams in Figure 16-4 suggests that similar results can be obtained via alternative strategies. Figures 16-4(f) and (k) are similar, as are (l) and (e), (j) and (c), and (i) and (b). Neither the pre-

---

[6] Expressed as an equivalent value at the terminal date.

FIGURE 16-4 Profits and Loss from Various Strategies.

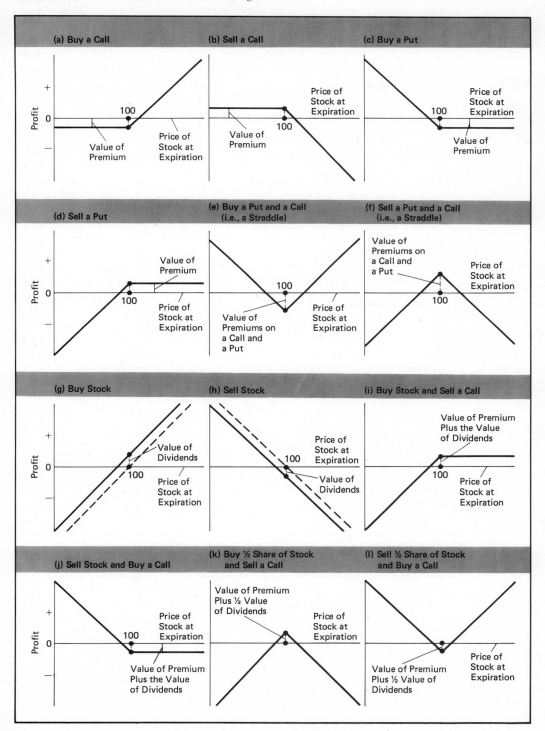

miums involved nor the initial investments required need be equal in every case. Nonetheless, the similarity of the results obtained with different "packages" of securities dictates that the total market values of the packages be similar as well.

OPTION VALUATION

Expressing Values as Percentages of the Exercise Price

Figures 16-3 and 16-4 plotted option values and profits and losses from option positions for various levels of the price of the underlying stock. All values were expressed in dollars, on the assumption that options were written with an exercise price of $100. To avoid circumlocution we will continue to discuss cases with this characteristic. However, the results are quite general. The horizontal axes in such diagrams can be interpreted as plotting the stock price expressed as a *percent* of the actual exercise price. Similarly, the vertical axes can be interpreted as plotting option values and/or position profits and losses expressed as percentages of the option exercise price. Thus a reference to a stock price of $92 can be interpreted as a price equal to 92.0% of the exercise price, and a reference to an option value of $2.50 as an amount equal to 2.5% of the exercise price. If the actual exercise price of an option were $40, the corresponding values would then be $36.80 (= .92 × $40) and $1 (= .025 × $40), respectively.

Limits on the Value of a Call Option

Throughout, this book has emphasized the importance of comparing securities or combinations thereof with others of similar characteristics. Nowhere is this more important than in the valuation of options. In this section comparisons will be used to determine *limits* on the value of a call option. The following sections will use additional comparisons to develop specific estimates of option values within these limits.

Consider three investments. One is a call option, not protected against cash dividends, with an exercise price (E) of $100; the second is the stock on which the option is written; and the third is a riskless investment. For simplicity, assume that funds can be invested in a bank at any time during the life of the option at a fixed rate of r per period.

What is the *most* one should pay for an option of this type? Since a call can be converted to a share of stock only upon payment of the exercise price, it clearly is less desirable than a share of the stock itself and should never sell at a higher price. This provides an upper limit on its value:

$$P_o \leq P_s \qquad (16\text{-}1a)$$

where:

P_o = the current price of the call option
P_s = the current price of the underlying stock

What is the *least* one should pay for such an option? Consider the following package:

---

one option, current price $= P_o$

plus a bank account, current value $= PV(E) + PV(d)$

---

where:

$PV(E)$ = the present value of the option's exercise price ($100) if the latter were paid at expiration

$PV(d)$ = the present value of all dividends to be paid on the stock (more precisely, for which the stock will go ex-dividend) prior to the option's expiration. For simplicity, all dividends and ex-dividend dates are assumed to be known with certainty.

Compare this package with one share of the stock itself. The bank account can be used to provide payments equal to the dividends received from the stock. At the expiration of the option, the account can also be used to exercise the option *if desired*, providing a share at that time. This will deplete the account but require no further investment. Thus the package can duplicate the benefits provided by a share of the stock. Moreover, in the event that exercise proves undesirable, the package will be better than the stock: if the stock price is less than the exercise price at expiration, a share can be purchased on the open market, leaving money in the bank account. Clearly, the package is as good as or better than a share of the stock and should sell for as much or more:

$$P_o + PV(E) + PV(d) \geq P_s$$

Rearranging:

$$P_o \geq P_s - PV(E) - PV(d) \tag{16-1b}$$

While this argument has considered exercise only at expiration, and thus applies most directly to a European option, an American option will always be at least as valuable, for it provides all the same options and more besides. Thus it is worth at least as much, and formula (16-1b) holds, *a fortiori*, for an American option.

Since a holder is never forced to exercise an option, it cannot be so unattractive that people must be paid to take it. This provides a third limit—the price of an option can never be negative:

$$P_o \geq 0 \tag{16-1c}$$

Formulas 16-1(a), (b), and (c) provide bounds on the value of a call option. If the price were to move outside these limits, there would be opportunities for profit via arbitrage. While transactions costs and taxes might make it unprofitable for some investors to take advantage of such situations, a substantial departure would certainly lead others to attempt to profit thereby, setting in motion forces that would quickly bring the option price back within bounds.

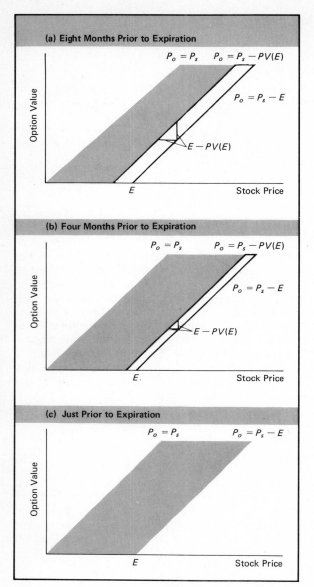

(a) Eight Months Prior to Expiration

$P_o = P_s$ $P_o = P_s - PV(E)$

$P_o = P_s - E$

$E - PV(E)$

Option Value

E Stock Price

(b) Four Months Prior to Expiration

$P_o = P_s$ $P_o = P_s - PV(E)$

$P_o = P_s - E$

$E - PV(E)$

Option Value

E Stock Price

(c) Just Prior to Expiration

$P_o = P_s$ $P_o = P_s - E$

Option Value

E Stock Price

FIGURE 16-5 Limits on the Value of a Call Option.

Figure 16-5 shows the way in which the limits on a call option's price change as expiration nears. For simplicity it has been assumed that the underlying stock is not expected to pay any dividends in the interim. Note that the region gets larger as expiration approaches and the present value of the exercise price rises. The exact relationship at expiration lies along the lower edge of the area, as shown in Figure 16-5(c). Earlier, this is not generally the case. To determine the likely location at some time prior to expiration requires more detailed comparisons, to which we now turn.

Valuation of a Call Option on a Stock with Simple Price Changes

To make concrete some further principles of option valuation it will prove helpful to deal with a rather simple kind of stock. Figure 16-6(a) shows the general nature of its behavior. In any given period its price will either jump up to some higher value $(P^+_{s,t+1})$ or down to some lower value $(P^-_{s,t+1})$. Looking forward from time t to time $t + 1$, there are thus two possible states of the world—up $(+)$ and down $(-)$. Associated with each state is a known stock price; the probabilities of the two states $(p^+$ and $p^-)$ have also been estimated.

For every time and stock value there will be some corresponding value for a call option on the stock. These amounts are also indicated in Figure 16-6(a).

The final item in Figure 16-6(a) represents the results obtained by investing some amount of money, X, in the bank. It will grow to $(1 + r)$ times its initial value by the end of the period, and this return is certain.

All assumptions used previously will be retained. The option under study has an exercise price of $100, the stock pays no dividends prior to expiration, and the riskless rate of interest is fixed at r per period.

Figure 16-6(b) shows specific numeric values that will be used henceforth. The stock price is assumed to have a 60% chance of increasing 5% each period and a 40% chance of decreasing 5%; its expected return thus equals $(.6 \times +5) + (.4 \times -5)$, or 1% per period. The riskless interest rate is half this, .5% per period (i.e., $r = .005$).

Figure 16-6(c) fills in some more values. It covers the situation when the stock price is $100 one period prior to expiration. The time of expiration is denoted e, one period prior to expiration, $e - 1$, two periods prior, $e - 2$, etc.

There is a good reason for starting with the period prior to expiration. At expiration, the option value associated with every possible stock price is known: it is $(P_{s,e} - E)$ or zero, whichever is larger. In the situation shown in Figure 16-6(c), the end-of-period option value will be either $5 or $0.

What does this imply for the price of the option at the beginning of the period—i.e., how was the box for $P_{o,e-1}$ in Figure 16-6(c) filled in? Not surprisingly, by analogy, as we will see.

Figure 16-6(d) plots the end-of-period values for the stock and the option. Since there are only two possibilities, all (two) of the points lie on a straight line. The securities' returns are perfectly positively correlated. Whenever this is the case, it is possible to *hedge* one against the other and eliminate all risk.

The difference between the stock prices in the two states is $10; the difference between the option prices is $5. It is possible to hold stock and write a call option, and to arrange the proportions so that the differences in payoffs in the two positions are exactly equal. The investor's end-of-period net worth will then be the same in either event. In this case, the appropriate *hedge ratio* is .5; for every option written (sold), one-half a share of stock should be purchased. More generally, the appropriate hedge ratio, denoted h in Figure 16-6, is simply the difference between

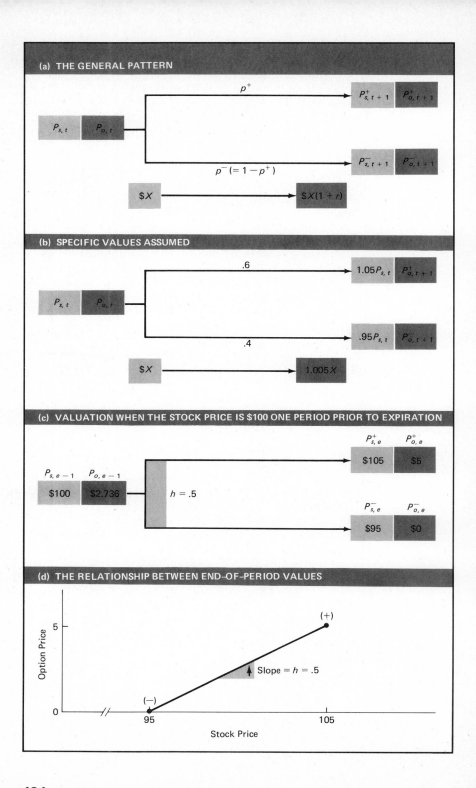

(e) BALANCE SHEETS FOR A HEDGED POSITION

Time: $e - 1$		Time: e			
		State: +		State: −	
½ Share of Stock: $50	1 Option: $P_{o,e-1}$ Net Worth: $50 - P_{o,e-1}$	½ Share of Stock: $52.50	1 Option: $5 Net Worth: $47.50	½ Share of Stock: $47.50	1 Option: $0 Net Worth: $47.50

(f) BALANCE SHEETS FOR A HEDGED POSITION WHEN THE OPTION IS CORRECTLY PRICED

Time: $e - 1$		Time: e			
		State: +		State: −	
½ Share of Stock: $50	1 Option: $2.736 Net Worth: $47.264	½ Share of Stock: $52.50	1 Option: $5 Net Worth: $47.50	½ Share of Stock: $47.50	1 Option: $0 Net Worth: $47.50

$$\text{Return} = \frac{47.50 - 47.264}{47.264} = .005 = .5\%$$

(g) BALANCE SHEETS FOR A HEDGED POSITION WHEN THE OPTION IS OVERPRICED

Time: $e - 1$		Time: e			
		State: +		State: −	
½ Share of Stock: $50	1 Option: $2.80 Net Worth: $47.20	½ Share of Stock: $52.50	1 Option: $5 Net Worth: $47.50	½ Share of Stock: $47.50	1 Option: $0 Net Worth: $47.50

$$\text{Return} = \frac{47.50 - 47.20}{47.20} = .006 = .6\%$$

(h) BALANCE SHEETS FOR A REVERSE HEDGE WHEN THE OPTION IS UNDERPRICED

Time: $e - 1$		Time: e			
		State: +		State: −	
1 Option: $2.60 Bank Account: $50	½ Share of Stock: $50 Net Worth: $2.60	1 Option: $5 Bank Account: $50.25	½ Share of Stock: $52.50 Net Worth: $2.75	1 Option: $0 Bank Account: $50.25	½ Share of Stock: $47.50 Net Worth: $2.75

$$\text{Return} = \frac{2.75 - 2.60}{2.60} = .058 = 5.8\%$$

FIGURE 16-6 Stock and Option Prices
(a)–(d) at left; (e)–(h) above.

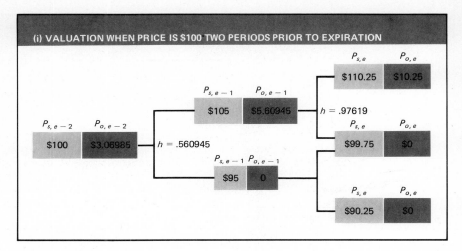

$P_{s,e-2}$ $P_{o,e-2}$

$100 $3.06985

$P_{s,e-1}$ $P_{o,e-1}$

$105 $5.60945

$P_{s,e-1}$ $P_{o,e-1}$

$95 0

$h = .560945$

$h = .97619$

$P_{s,e}$ $P_{o,e}$

$110.25 $10.25

$P_{s,e}$ $P_{o,e}$

$99.75 $0

$P_{s,e}$ $P_{o,e}$

$90.25 $0

FIGURE 16-6 (Continued)

the end-of-period option values, divided by the difference between the end-of-period stock values:

$$h = \frac{P^+_{o,t+1} - P^-_{o,t+1}}{P^+_{s,t+1} - P^-_{s,t+1}} \tag{16-2}$$

Figure 16-6(e) shows how this can be employed. An investor buys half a share of stock and sells one call option. The initial investment required is $50 minus the (yet-to-be-determined) price received for writing the option. The value of the "portfolio" at the end of the period will be $47.50, *no matter which state occurs.* The investor has set up a *riskless hedge* by using the appropriate hedge ratio indicated by formula (16-2).

Now for the analogy. The rate of interest on a riskless investment is .5% per period. The option should be priced so that a riskless strategy utilizing it also returns .5% per period. Since the ending value will be $47.50, the required option value is that which satisfies:

$$(50 - P_{o,e-1})1.005 = \$47.50$$

The solution is:

$$P_{o,e-1} = \$2.736$$

Figure 16-6(f) shows that the hedging strategy will in fact give a certain return equal to the riskless rate if the option price equals $2.736. Figure 16-6(g) shows that if the option were overpriced, at $2.80, the hedging strategy could give a certain return greater than the riskless rate. Such a situation would attract attention, bringing out would-be option sellers whose activities would shortly drive the price back down.

What if the option were underpriced, say at $2.60? Then clever investors could *reverse hedge*, buying options and selling stock. Figure 16-6(h) shows a case in which the stock is sold short and the proceeds placed in an interest-earning bank account.[7] A certain 5.8% per period is returned on invested funds. Such a situation would attract would-be option buyers, driving the price back up.

Figure 16-6(f) thus portrays the likely situation, and we have an option pricing formula. The option price at time t must satisfy:

$$(hP_{s,t} - P_{o,t})(1 + r) = \begin{cases} [hP^+_{s,t+1} - P^+_{o,t+1}] \\ [hP^-_{s,t+1} - P^-_{o,t+1}] \end{cases} \qquad (16\text{-}3)$$

where h is the hedge ratio required to give a riskless return. The first parenthesized expression on the left represents the funds invested at the beginning of the period. The brackets on the right indicate that either of the two included expressions can be used, for they are both equal to the certain end-of-period value. The formula simply requires the option to be priced so that a portfolio hedged to remove all risk will return the riskless rate on the funds invested.

Having established the principles summarized in formulas (16-2) and (16-3), it is possible to determine the option value for any time and stock price. Figure 16-6(i) does this for the case in which the stock price is $100 two periods prior to expiration. The option price boxes are filled in from right to left. Option values at expiration are simply $(P_s - 100)$ or zero, whichever is larger. This takes care of the option values at time e. Turning to time $e - 1$, note that if a situation will lead to a worthless option no matter what, the option is already worthless. Thus if the stock price is $95 one period prior to expiration, the option will definitely expire worthless, and the option value is zero. This takes care of another box. Turning to the situation in which the stock price is $105 one period prior to expiration, formula (16-2) is used to determine the hedge ratio (.97619) and then formula (16-3) applied to determine the option price ($5.60945). To find the remaining hedge ratio (.560945) and option price ($3.06985), we again apply formulas (16-2) and (16-3), using the relevant stock values ($105 and $95) and the previously computed associated option values ($5.60945 and $0).

Figure 16-7 shows some values obtained with this kind of *recursive* calculation. Each curve plots option values associated with various stock prices at a specific time prior to expiration.

One characteristic of the curves in Figure 16-7 is quite general:

If two call options are otherwise identical but one has a longer time remaining before expiration, the latter will be worth at least as much as the former and generally will be worth more.

This is obviously true of American call options, for the one with a longer time to expiration can be used to do anything possible with the other, and more besides. Except in pathological cases caused by large dividend payments, the statement also applies to European call options.

---

[7] This is generally not possible in practice, lowering or eliminating the profit from such a hedge and raising the possibility that the option could sell at any price within a band limited by the prices at which hedging or reverse hedging would become profitable.

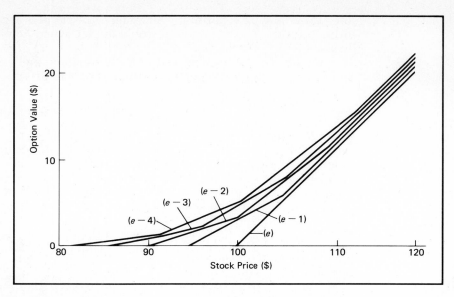

FIGURE 16-7 Option Values at Various Times Prior to Expiration (based on the numeric example in Figure 16-6).

The Black-Scholes Call Option Valuation Formula

In a world not bothered by taxes and transactions costs, one could adjust hedge positions almost constantly. The effective length of a "period" would thus be very small. And the smaller the length of each period, the closer the value of a call option calculated in the manner described in the previous section would be to that given by an option valuation formula developed by Black and Scholes.[8] It is widely used by those who deal with options professionally (and occasionally by amateurs) to search for situations in which price appears to differ from value. The formula is:

$$P_o = P_s N(d_1) - \frac{E}{e^{rt}} N(d_2) \qquad (16\text{-}4a)$$

where:

$$d_1 = \frac{\ln (P_s/E) + (r + \frac{1}{2}\sigma^2)t}{\sigma\sqrt{t}} \qquad (16\text{-}4b)$$

$$d_2 = \frac{\ln (P_s/E) + (r - \frac{1}{2}\sigma^2)t}{\sigma\sqrt{t}} \qquad (16\text{-}4c)$$

[8] Fischer Black and Myron Scholes, "The Pricing of Options and Corporate Liabilities," *Journal of Political Economy*, 81, no. 3 (May/June 1973), 637–54. © 1973 by the University of Chicago. All Rights Reserved. For a discussion of the conditions under which the process described in the previous section converges to the Black-Scholes formula, see John C. Cox, Stephen A. Ross, and Mark Rubenstein, "Options Pricing: A Simplified Approach," *Journal of Financial Economics*, September 1979.

and where:

$$P_o = \text{the current value of the option}$$
$$P_s = \text{the current price of the stock}$$
$$E = \text{the exercise price of the option}$$
$$e = 2.71828$$
$$t = \text{the time remaining before expiration (in years)}$$
$$r = \text{the continuously compounded riskless rate of interest}$$
$$\sigma = \text{the standard deviation of the continuously compounded annual rate of return on the stock}[9]$$
$$\ln{(P_s/E)} = \text{the natural logarithm of } (P_s/E)$$
$$N(d) = \text{the probability that a deviation less than } d \text{ will occur in a normal distribution with a mean of zero and a standard deviation of one}$$

The Black-Scholes option valuation formula can be applied directly to value a call option on a stock that pays no dividends prior to expiration. Modifications designed to account for dividends will be discussed later. First, however, the general use of the formula will be illustrated.

Using the Black-Scholes Formula

Table 16-2 provides values of $N(d)$ for various levels of d.[10] This and a table of logarithms suffice for the calculations required by the option valuation formula. For example, consider the following values:

$$P_s = \$36$$

$$E = \$40$$

$$t = .25 \text{ (i.e., one-fourth of a year, or three months)}$$

$$r = .05 \text{ (i.e., 5\% per year, continuously compounded)}$$

$$\sigma = .50 \text{ (i.e., the standard deviation of the continuously compounded annual return is 50\%)}$$

Formulas (16-4b) and (16-4c) give the values of d_1 and d_2:

$$d_1 = \frac{\ln(36/40) + [.05 + \frac{1}{2}(.50^2)].25}{.50\sqrt{.25}} \approx -.25$$

$$d_2 = \frac{\ln(36/40) + [.05 - \frac{1}{2}(.50^2)].25}{.50\sqrt{.25}} \approx -.50$$

Table 16-2 can be used to find the corresponding values of $N(d_1)$ and $N(d_2)$:

[9] The Black-Scholes formula assumes that σ is constant throughout the life of the option. Formulas based on other assumptions have also been derived. For examples see John Cox and Stephen Ross, "The Valuation of Options for Alternative Stochastic Processes," *Journal of Financial Economics*, no. 3, 1976.

[10] Table 16-2 is an abbreviated version of a standard cumulative normal distribution table. More detailed versions can be found in most statistics textbooks.

$$N(d_1) = N(-.25) = .4013$$

$$N(d_2) = N(-.50) = .3085$$

Thus:

$$P_o = (36 \times .4013) - \left(\frac{40}{e^{.05 \times .25}} \times .3085 \right) \approx \$2.26$$

Only a hand calculator is needed to estimate the value of an option using the Black-Scholes formula. In fact, for some programmable hand calculators, magnetic strips or plug-in modules precoded with the formula are available; with them, the entire job is done automatically as soon as the key values are input.

TABLE 16-2 Values of $N(d)$ for Selected Values of d

d	$N(d)$	d	$N(d)$	d	$N(d)$
		−1.00	.1587	1.00	.8413
−2.95	.0016	−.95	.1711	1.05	.8531
−2.90	.0019	−.90	.1841	1.10	.8643
−2.85	.0022	−.85	.1977	1.15	.8749
−2.80	.0026	−.80	.2119	1.20	.8849
−2.75	.0030	−.75	.2266	1.25	.8944
−2.70	.0035	−.70	.2420	1.30	.9032
−2.65	.0040	−.65	.2578	1.35	.9115
−2.60	.0047	−.60	.2743	1.40	.9192
−2.55	.0054	−.55	.2912	1.45	.9265
−2.50	.0062	−.50	.3085	1.50	.9332
−2.45	.0071	−.45	.3264	1.55	.9394
−2.40	.0082	−.40	.3446	1.60	.9452
−2.35	.0094	−.35	.3632	1.65	.9505
−2.30	.0107	−.30	.3821	1.70	.9554
−2.25	.0122	−.25	.4013	1.75	.9599
−2.20	.0139	−.20	.4207	1.80	.9641
−2.15	.0158	−.15	.4404	1.85	.9678
−2.10	.0179	−.10	.4602	1.90	.9713
−2.05	.0202	−.05	.4801	1.95	.9744
−2.00	.0228	.00	.5000	2.00	.9773
−1.95	.0256	.05	.5199	2.05	.9798
−1.90	.0287	.10	.5398	2.10	.9821
−1.85	.0322	.15	.5596	2.15	.9842
−1.80	.0359	.20	.5793	2.20	.9861
−1.75	.0401	.25	.5987	2.25	.9878
−1.70	.0446	.30	.6179	2.30	.9893
−1.65	.0495	.35	.6368	2.35	.9906
−1.60	.0548	.40	.6554	2.40	.9918
−1.55	.0606	.45	.6736	2.45	.9929
−1.50	.0668	.50	.6915	2.50	.9938
−1.45	.0735	.55	.7088	2.55	.9946
−1.40	.0808	.60	.7257	2.60	.9953
−1.35	.0885	.65	.7422	2.65	.9960
−1.30	.0968	.70	.7580	2.70	.9965
−1.25	.1057	.75	.7734	2.75	.9970
−1.20	.1151	.80	.7881	2.80	.9974
−1.15	.1251	.85	.8023	2.85	.9978
−1.10	.1357	.90	.8159	2.90	.9981
−1.05	.1469	.95	.8289	2.95	.9984

Figure 16-8 provides an alternative method for valuing call options that expire in a year or less. Figure 16-8(a) is an option and warrant valuation *nomogram*; Figure 16-8(b) illustrates its use with the previous example—that of an option with three months to expiration and an exercise price of $40, written on a stock with an estimated standard deviation of annual return of 50% currently selling for $36. As before, the relevant rate of interest is assumed to be 5% per year.

To value the option, a box is constructed. The position of the left side is determined by the time to expiration (labeled "maturity" in the nomogram). The top of the left side is determined by the estimated standard deviation of the stock's annual return, and the bottom by the interest rate (interpolation is used if a desired value is not plotted). The position of the right side of the box is determined by the ratio of the current stock price to the exercise price (here, $36/$40, or 90%). The box is then closed and the option value estimated, based on the location of the upper right-hand corner. In this case the nomogram indicates that the option value is somewhat more than 5% of the exercise price, or $2 (.05 × $40).

Figure 16-8 shows that, other things equal, a call option is generally *more* valuable:

the *higher* the current stock price relative to the exercise price
the *longer* the time remaining before expiration
the *higher* the riskless rate of interest, and
the *greater* the risk of the underlying stock

Only the last of these factors requires estimation but, as the nomogram shows, it is of crucial importance.

Estimating Stock Risk

Since the risk of the underlying stock greatly influences the value of an option, it is important to give it due consideration. Note that for *option valuation* the *total risk* of a stock is relevant, since a "portfolio" involving another security (the option) highly correlated with it is being analyzed. On the other hand, for *security valuation* only *market-related risk* is relevant. Option valuation fixes the value of an option *relative* to that of its underlying security. Security valuation is required to fix the value of both the security and options written on it.

To estimate the total risk of a security, historic data can be analyzed, subjective estimates of various future possibilities made, or the two combined. For any estimate of future uncertainty, historic data are more likely to prove helpful than definitive. And since recent history may prove more helpful then ancient history, some analysts study daily price changes over the most recent six to twelve months, sometimes giving more weight to later days than to earlier ones. Others take into account the price histories of related stocks and the possibility that a stock whose price has recently decreased may be more risky in the future than it was in the past. Still others make explicit subjective estimates of the future, taking into account changes in uncertainty concerning the economy in general, specific industries, sectors, and/or stocks. In some cases an ana-

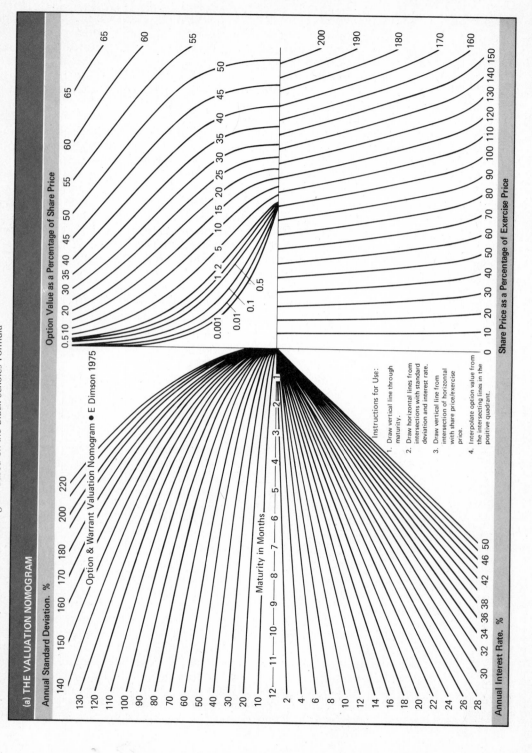

(a) THE VALUATION NOMOGRAM

Option & Warrant Valuation Nomogram ● E Dimson 1975

Instructions for Use:

1. Draw vertical line through maturity.

2. Draw horizontal lines from intersections with standard deviation and interest rate.

3. Draw vertical line from intersection of horizontal with share price/exercise price.

4. Interpolate option value from the intersecting lines in the positive quadrant.

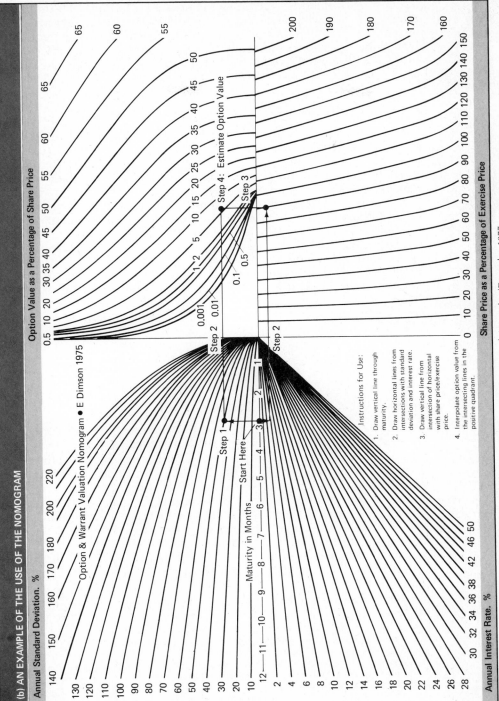

Option & Warrant Valuation Nomogram ● E Dimson 1975

Instructions for Use:

1. Draw vertical line through maturity.
2. Draw horizontal lines from intersections with standard deviation and interest rate.
3. Draw vertical line from intersection of horizontal with share price/exercise price.
4. Interpolate option value from the intersecting lines in the positive quadrant.

Source: Material from E. Dimson "Option Valuation Nomograms" *Financial Analysts Journal*, November/December 1977.

lyst's estimate of a stock's risk over the next three months may differ from that for the following three months, leading to the use of different tables for options on the same stock, but with different times to expiration.

Some beta services indicate the total variability of stock prices over a historic period,[11] and certain specialized option services also include related measures.[12]

Estimating the Market Consensus of a Stock's Risk

One way to estimate a stock's total risk is to let "the market" do it. Given the observable characteristics of a stock and an option on the stock, and given an estimate of the stock's risk, one can find the appropriate value for the option. If investors value options in accordance with their own estimates of stock risk, the procedure can be reversed to obtain a market consensus opinion of that risk. For example, assume that the riskless interest rate is 6%, and that a six-month option with an exercise price of $40 sells for $4 when the price of the underlying stock is $36. Relative to the exercise price, the stock price is 90% (36/40 = .90) and the option price is 10% (4/40 = .10). The nomogram (Figure 16-8) can be used to estimate the implicit standard deviation: the right-hand side of the box is constructed first, then the lower left-hand corner; completion gives the upper left-hand corner and the estimated standard deviation. In this case the current situation is consistent with an estimated annual standard deviation of .40 for the underlying stock over the next six months.

This procedure can be used to estimate a stock's risk over any given horizon by averaging values obtained from options with different exercise prices.

The CBOE Call Option Index

Once the risk of a stock has been inferred from the prices of options written on it, one can readily use the result to determine the appropriate price of a six-month call option with an exercise price equal to the stock's current market price using the Black-Scholes formula. The option price can then be expressed as a percentage of the stock price for comparison purposes. By averaging several such values, for each of a number of stocks, a "typical" premium for such an option can be determined.

The Chicago Board Options Exchange employs a procedure that, although different in form,[13] provides results similar to those that would be obtained if this were done for all the stocks on which options are written on the CBOE. Figure 16-9 shows the level of the resulting "call option index" since early 1976. While expressed as a percentage premium for the typical six-month call option with exercise price equal to the current stock price, it also provides information about *uncertainty*, since the

[11] The "beta book" published by Merrill Lynch, Pierce, Fenner and Smith includes statistics from which the desired figures can be estimated.

[12] The *Value Line Options and Convertibles*, published weekly by Arnold Bernhard and Co., Inc. (New York), gives a figure for each stock's relative volatility: "the overall risk of the common stock expressed as a percentage of the risk of the typical common stock."

[13] For details, see *The CBOE Call Option Index*, Chicago Board Options Exchange, 1980.

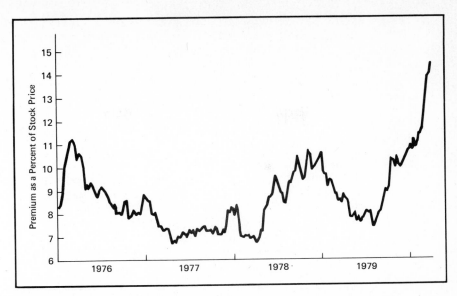

FIGURE 16-9 CBOE Call Option Index January 8, 1976 Through March 27, 1980.

Source: Chicago Board Options Exchange, *Annual Report,* 1980.

values of such options depend heavily on investors' estimates of the risks of the underlying securities. Other things equal,[14] the greater such uncertainty, the higher will be the level of the index.

Hedge Ratios

Figure 16-10 plots the values of a call option with an exercise price of $100 when nine months remain before expiration. An interest rate of 5% and annual stock price standard deviation of .50 are assumed. The figure also shows the values of such an option eight months before expiration and at expiration.

The *slope* of the option value curve at any point represents the expected change in option price per dollar change in the stock price. This amount is the *hedge ratio* that will neutralize the effects of small stock price changes on an investor's portfolio in a manner similar to that of the simple case shown in Figure 16-6. In general:

An option's *hedge ratio* is the estimated change in the price of the option associated with a $1 change in the price of the underlying security.

The Black-Scholes formula provides a direct estimate of the hedge ratio: it equals $N(d_1)$ in formula (16-4).

An option's hedge ratio never exceeds 1.0 and is usually less than one. Thus a $1 change in the stock price will typically move an option's price by less than $1. However, the price of the option will generally

---

[14] That is, interest rates.

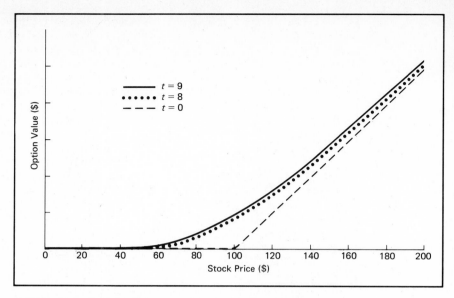

FIGURE 16-10 Option Values at Various Times Prior to Expiration.

change by a greater *percentage* than will that of the stock. It is this relationship that leads people to say that options offer *high leverage*.

If a stock is hedged against an option, or vice versa, with the relative proportions equal to the appropriate hedge ratio, the effect on the investor's net worth of a change in the price of the stock will be roughly the same, whether the price goes up or down. Moreover, a small change in stock price will have little effect on net worth. Stock price risk is not eliminated; to do this the hedge ratio would have to be adjusted continuously as the stock price changed. But the risk is reduced.

Adjustment of the Black-Scholes Formula for Dividends

Thus far the issue of dividend payments on the underlying stock during the life of an option has been avoided. Other things equal, the greater the dividends to be paid during the life of a call option, the smaller its value. Moreover, it may pay to exercise an American call option just prior to an ex-dividend date. This possibility will be considered shortly. First we describe a way to deal with dividends on the assumptions that they can be predicted with certainty and that the option will not be exercised prior to expiration.

The procedure is straightforward. One simply assumes that all relevant dividends have already been announced and that the stock has already gone ex-dividend for all of them. The current stock price is reduced by an amount equal to the expected dividends (or their present value), and the option valuation formula or tables are used with this "dividend-adjusted" price instead of the actual value.

In the absence of dividends an American call option would be worth at least as much "alive" (not exercised) as "dead" (exercised), up to its expiration date. When dividends are involved, however, the situation may be different. This is shown in Figure 16-11. The option's value if exercised immediately lies along the border OEZ. If allowed to live, the option's value will lie along a higher curve such as that shown in the figure. Imagine that the stock is currently priced at P_s and is about to go ex-dividend for the last time prior to the option's expiration. Afterward, it can be expected to sell for a lower price, P_s'. The Black-Scholes formula can be used to find the option's value if it remains "alive." In Figure 16-11 it is P_o^a. If instead the option is exercised while the stock price is still P_s, a value of P_o^d will be obtained. If this is greater, the option should be exercised early; if not, it should not.

To take this possibility into account when computing the value of an option at an earlier date, two estimates can be made. The first assumes holding until expiration and subtracts the present value of all dividends from the current stock price before applying the usual procedure. The second assumes holding until just before the final ex-dividend date and subtracts the present value of all dividends but the last from the current stock price before applying the procedure. The current value of the option can be assumed to equal the larger of these two values. While not exact,[15] this procedure is probably sufficient for many listed options.

[15] For an exact method, see Richard Roll, "An Analytic Valuation Formula for Unprotected American Call Options on Stocks with Known Dividends," *Journal of Financial Economics*, vol. 5 (1977). For a practical method that can come as close as desired to the exact value, see Cox, Ross, and Rubenstein, *op. cit.*

FIGURE 16-11 Option Values Before and After an Ex-Dividend Date.

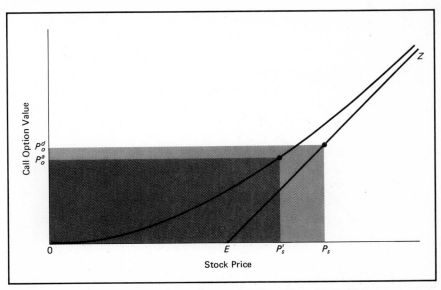

The Valuation of Put Options

If similar results can be obtained in different ways, then unless certain relationships hold among prices of related instruments there will be possibilities for arbitrage. When such opportunities arise, investors will rapidly take advantage of them, causing prices to return quickly to more appropriate values.

An example is provided by European puts and calls. Assume that a call with an exercise price of E sells for P_c and that a put on the same stock with the same exercise price and expiration date sells for P_p. Assume also that it is possible to obtain a loan of $PV(E)$ dollars today in return for a promise to pay back E dollars on the day that the options expire. Finally, assume that the stock in question is not expected to pay any dividends prior to the options' expiration date.

Figure 16-12(a) shows the position on the day of expiration of an investor who buys a share of the stock, borrows $PV(E)$ dollars today, and then sells the stock and pays back the loan on the options' expiration date.

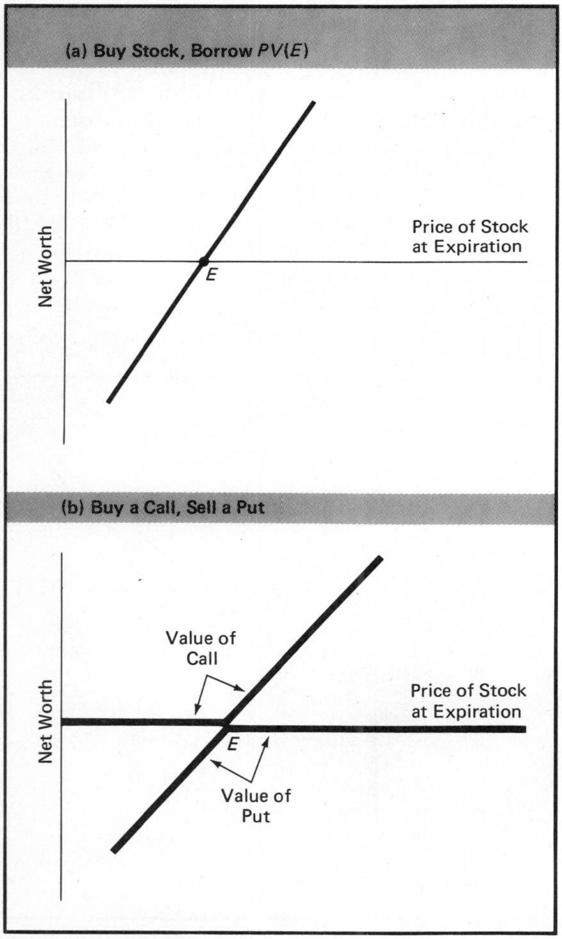

FIGURE 16-12 The Put-Call Parity Theorem.

(a) Buy Stock, Borrow $PV(E)$

Net Worth

Price of Stock at Expiration

E

(b) Buy a Call, Sell a Put

Net Worth

Value of Call

Price of Stock at Expiration

E

Value of Put

Figure 16-12(b) shows the position of an investor who buys the call and sells the put. The pictures are exactly the same, thus the two strategies should have the same cost. If P_s is the current price of the stock, the net outlay required for the first strategy is:

$$P_s - PV(E)$$

while that required for the second strategy is:

$$P_c - P_p$$

And the prices should be such that:

$$P_c - P_p = P_s - PV(E) \tag{16-5}$$

This is the *put-call parity theorem*. Given the prices of any two of these securities, the "appropriate" price of the third can be found using formula (16-5).

Since the Black-Scholes formula provides an estimate of the appropriate value for a European call option, the appropriate value of a European put can be determined using the formula and formula (16-5):

$$P_p = P_c - P_s + PV(E) \tag{16-6}$$

where:

P_c = the value of a European call, using the Black-Scholes formula

P_p = the appropriate value of a European put.

While formula (16-6) applies to European options on stocks that will not pay dividends prior to the options' expiration, simple modifications can give reasonable approximations for the values of options on stocks paying dividends.[16] A more serious problem arises when American options are to be valued. To obtain exact values for the appropriate price for an American put option, extensive computer calculations may be required.[17] However, some of the errors involved in applying (16-6) are offsetting, so this formula provides a reasonable starting point for evaluating the current price of an American put option.[18]

OPTION TERMINOLOGY

Those who deal in listed options have invented a number of new terms to spice up conversations that would otherwise be devoted almost wholly to numbers. Figure 16-13 shows some of them, using a call option for illus-

---

[16] If the dividends are known with certainty, an amount—$PV(D)$—equal to the present value of the dividends to be paid to holders of record prior to expiration can be borrowed as part of the first strategy, with the loan repaid with the dividends received. The right-hand side of (16-5) would thus be: $P_s - PV(E) - PV(D)$, and (16-6) would become:

$$P_p = P_c - P_s + PV(E) + PV(D)$$

[17] For alternative procedures see Michael J. Brennan and Eduardo S. Schwartz, "The Valuation of American Put Options," *Journal of Finance*, May 1977, and Cox, Rubenstein, and Ross, *op. cit.*

[18] For further discussion of this point, see John C. Cox and Mark Rubenstein, *Options Markets* (forthcoming).

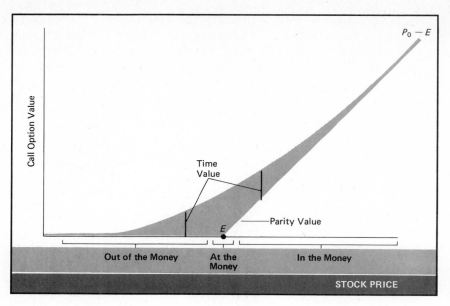

FIGURE 16-13 Option Terminology.

tration. Options with exercise prices near the current stock price are said to be *at the money*. Those with exercise prices well above the current stock price are *out of the money*, while those with exercise prices well below the current stock price are *in the money*. Occasionally finer gradations are invoked, and one hears of "near-the-money," "deep-in-the-money," "far-out-of-the-money," etc.

The amount an option would command if it were exercised immediately is termed its *parity value*. The excess of its price over this amount is the option's *time value*, which is due to its attributes and the time remaining before expiration. As illustrated in Figure 16-13, the time value of an option near the money is larger than that of one that is far out of the money or far in the money.

OPTION SPREADS

If one can find overpriced options and underpriced options on the same stock, why not try to profit from the redress of this presumably transitory imbalance and avoid the stock itself entirely? Such is the reasoning behind the creation of an *option spread*.

A *money or price spread* involves the purchase of one call option and the sale of another written on the same stock with the same expiration date but with a different exercise price. A *time or calendar spread* involves the purchase and sale of call options on the same stock with the same exercise price but with different times to expiration. In a *butterfly spread*, one call option is bought and two sold—one on either side (in time or money), or vice versa.

To reduce the exposure of a spread to movement in the price of the underlying stock, the hedge ratios of the options can be utilized. Consider a stock currently selling for $40, with an annual standard deviation of .50. Two nine-month call options on it are available: one with an exercise price of $50, the other with an exercise price of $40. Formula (16-4) indicates that the first should sell for $3.40 and the second for $7.49. It also gives the hedge ratios: .42 for the "out-of-the-money" option and .62 for the "at-the-money" option.

Assume that the actual option prices are not $3.40 and $7.49 but $4 and $7, respectively. An investor attempting to profit from this apparent aberration would want to buy the underpriced option and sell the overpriced one. However, equal amounts of the two options would leave the portfolio highly exposed to stock price movements, since a one-dollar change in stock price may be expected to change the out-of-the-money option's price by $.42 and the other option's price by $.62. The solution is to utilize only .68 (= .42/.62) times as many of the latter options as the former.

VALUING CONVERTIBLE BONDS

Valuation of a noncallable convertible bond is difficult enough. Valuation of a callable convertible is even worse. And most convertible bonds are callable. No simple formula is available for the purpose.[19] But the relevant relationships can be indicated; they are illustrated in Figure 16-14.

[19] For a discussion of numerical procedures that can be used, see M.J. Brennan and E.S. Schwartz, "Convertible Bonds: Valuation and Optimal Strategies for Call and Conversion," *Journal of Finance*, December 1977.

FIGURE 16-14 Components of Value for a Convertible Bond.

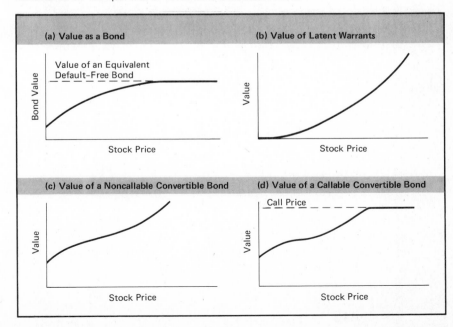

Figure 16-14(a) shows, for various prices of the corporation's stock, the value such a security would have were it a nonconvertible, noncallable (but risky) bond. The greater the value of the corporation's stock, the smaller the risk of default and the closer the convertible's "value as a bond" comes to that of an otherwise equivalent default-free noncallable, nonconvertible bond.

Figure 16-14(b) shows a likely pattern for the value of the latent warrants implicit in the conversion privilege. Were the bond not callable, the sum of the values shown in Figures 16-14(a) and (b) would equal the total value of the bond, giving a pattern such as that shown in Figure 16-14(c). But the presence of a call provision restricts a bond's value: once the deferral period has passed, the price is not likely to rise significantly above the call price (if it did, the corporation would undoubtedly call the bond). The overall relationship is thus likely to be more like that shown in Figure 16-14(d).

Almost all options and securities with option characteristics are difficult to value. This undoubtedly accounts for much of their fascination. When the value of a security is especially difficult to estimate with precision, an investor may hope that mispricing will occur and that he or she will be able to detect it and profit thereby. However, such a profit is likely to be someone else's loss. In a relatively efficient market, one is not likely to be able to make this kind of gain repeatedly.

Problems

1. The Jay Gould Corporation has an issue of 5% convertible debentures outstanding which will mature in ten years. The present conversion price is $40; the call price is 110. Nonconvertible bonds of similar quality are selling to yield 5%. Dividends on the common stock of Jay Gould are $2 per share.
   a. If the common stock sells at 30, what will be the minimum price of the bond?
   b. If the bond is quoted at 120 (bond points), what can be said about the price of the common stock?
   c. Assume that when the common stock sells at 60, the bond sells at 170.
      (1) What is the conversion premium?
      (2) If the bonds are called, with the common at 60, what will be the price of the bond on the day after the call is announced?
      (3) Will the call be likely to force conversion? Explain your answer fully.
2. Russell Sage has only a few hours left to decide whether to exercise his call option on Levi Strauss. Levi is currently selling at $60, and the call

option in question has an exercise price of $54. Russell originally purchased the call six months ago for $400.

    a. For what range of stock price on LVI should Russell exercise the call on the last day of the call life?

    b. For what range of stock price on LVI would Russell realize a net loss (including the original market price of the call)?

    c. If Russell had purchased a put instead of a call, how would you answer parts a through c?

3. Warrants issued by the Dutch East India Corporation allow the holder to buy six shares of Dutch East India common for each warrant held. The stock sells for $25 per share and the exercise price is $20. The warrants are selling for $40. What premium over the conversion value are investors paying for this warrant?

4. Given the information below, calculate the three-month call option price that is consistent with the Black-Scholes model.

$$P_S = \$47, \ E = \$45, \ r = .05, \ \sigma = .40$$

5. If the risk of a stock increases, what is likely to happen to the prices of call options on the stock? To the prices of put options? Why?

6. Some assert that if one writes call options on stocks held in a portfolio it is possible to increase return *and* reduce risk. Do you agree with both assertions, one, or neither? Why?

7. If the average premium on call options has recently declined, does this indicate that such options are better buys than they were previously? Why or why not?

8. On Thursday, February 7, 1980, three call options on Monsanto stock, all expiring in July 1980, sold for the following prices:

Exercise price	Option price
$50	7\frac{1}{2}$
60	3
70	1$\frac{1}{2}$

Consider a "butterfly spread" with the following positions:

> *buy* 1 call at $50
> sell (write) 2 calls at $60
> buy 1 call at $70

What would be the values at expiration of such a spread for various prices of Monsanto at the time? What investment would be required to establish the spread? Given information about the prices of the $50 and $70 options, what could you predict about the price of the $60 option?

9. A six-month call option with an exercise price of $40 is selling for $5. The current price of the stock is $41.25. According to the Black-Scholes formula, if the price of the stock changes by $1, the price of the option will change by $.65.

a. What *percentage* change in the option price is likely to accompany a 1 *percent* change in the stock price?

b. If the stock's beta is 1.10, what is the beta of the option?

c. If securities are currently priced so that zero-beta stocks have an expected return of 8% and stocks with a beta of 1.0 have an expected return of 15%, what should be the expected return on the option?

d. Let P_o be the price of a call option, h its hedge ratio, P_s the price of the stock, and β_s the beta of the stock. Write a formula relating β_o, the beta of the option, to P_o, h, P_s, and β_s.

10. In early February 1980 a September call at $55 on Corning Glass Works sold for $4.375 and a September put at $55 sold for $6. At the time Treasury bills coming due in September were priced to give an annual yield of 12.6% and Corning stock was selling for $53.

a. What value would formula (16-6) suggest was appropriate for the Corning put?

b. Corning was expected to make three dividend payments between February and September. Could that account for the discrepancy between your answer to (a) and the actual price of the put? Why?

c. If Corning stock were to fall to a very low value before September, might it pay the owner of the put to exercise it? Why?

Futures Contracts

17

INTRODUCTION

There is nothing unusual about contracts made in advance of delivery. Whenever something is ordered instead of purchased on the spot, a *forward* or *future* contract is involved. The price is decided at the time the order is placed, but cash is exchanged for merchandise later. For some items the lag may be a few days; for others, such as houses, several months. In either case the buyer may be requested to earmark some money to guarantee fulfillment of the obligation. This need not equal the full value of the purchase, only enough to cover the seller's loss in the event that another buyer must be found.

Commodity futures provide a standardized means for engaging in such transactions for agricultural and other commodities. One person may want to deliver wheat nine months hence but not know anyone who wishes to receive it, while someone else may want wheat for delivery at that time and not know a seller. An exchange that establishes a standard futures contract for a specified amount and type of wheat makes it possible for such traders to execute their transaction on the floor of the exchange without personal contact. For example, a contract might specify that the seller will deliver 5,000 bushels of a particular grade of wheat to the buyer nine months hence. The exchange of cash for wheat will occur on the delivery date, but each party is required to provide some sort of guarantee that his or her obligation can be met. The amount does not have to equal the full value involved, only the likely loss to the other party in the event that a new partner must be found.

This chapter deals primarily with commodity futures traded on exchanges. However, markets for forward currency exchange and futures markets for financial instruments are also described, since they are similar in form and function.

THE COMMODITY FUTURES CONTRACT

The essence of a futures contract is standardization. For example, the Chicago Board of Trade specifies the following requirements for its July wheat contract:

1. The seller agrees to deliver 5,000 bushels of either:
   —No. 1 northern spring wheat
   —No. 2 hard winter wheat
   —No. 2 dark hard winter wheat
   —No. 2 soft red wheat
   —No. 2 yellow hard winter wheat, or
   —No. 2 dark northern spring wheat
   at the agreed-upon price. Alternatively, a number of other grades can be delivered at specified premiums or discounts from the agreed-upon price. In any case the seller is allowed to decide which grade shall be delivered.
2. The grain will be delivered in a regular warehouse in the Chicago area or, at the end of the delivery period, in a railroad car in the Chicago area or, at a discount from the agreed-upon price, in Toledo.
3. Delivery will take place during the month of July, with the seller allowed to decide the actual date.
4. Upon delivery of the warehouse receipt from the seller to the buyer, the latter will pay the former the agreed-upon price in cash.

A commodity exchange sets all the terms of a futures contract but the price, then authorizes trading in it. Buyers and sellers or their agents meet on the floor of the exchange, usually in a "pit" provided for the purpose, and try to agree on a trade. If they succeed, one or more contracts will be created, with all the standard terms plus an additional, individual, one—the price involved.

Legally, the seller of a wheat futures contract is obligated to deliver wheat and the buyer to accept delivery. However, as we will see, few contracts are held open until the specified delivery date. The spectre of a hapless buyer's front lawn covered with unwanted wheat is part of the folklore of the futures market, not the reality.

Prices are normally stated on a per-unit basis. Thus if a buyer and seller agree to a price of $4.40 per bushel for a contract of 5,000 bushels of wheat, the amount of money involved is $22,000.

Figure 17-1 shows a set of quotations giving the prices at which major futures contracts were traded on one day and the total volume of sales for each type of contract. Such listings, published daily in the financial press, indicate the active futures markets, the number of units per contract, and the terms on which prices are stated. Details of contracts made during the day are given for each type of contract. The *open* price is that at which the first transaction was made; the *high* and *low* represent the highest and lowest prices during the day, and the *settlement* is a representative price within the range of the market at the end of the day. In many cases a range of closing prices is given; this indicates the range within which prices were agreed upon during the time designated as the "closing period" by the exchange in question. After the change (or changes) from the previous day's settlement price, the highest and lowest prices recorded during the lifetime of the contract involved are indicated. Also shown is the *open interest* (the number of outstanding contracts) on the previous day. For each commodity summary figures are given for the

Open High Low Settle Change | Lifetime High Low | Open Interest

—LIVESTOCK & MEAT—

CATTLE—FEEDER (CME)—42,000 lbs.; cents per lb.

CATTLE—LIVE (CME)—40,000 lbs.; cents per lb.

HOGS (CME)—30,000 lbs.; cents per lb.

PORK BELLIES (CME)—38,000 lbs.; cents per lb.

—FOOD & FIBER—

COCOA (CSC)—30,000 lbs.; cents per lb.

—METALS—

COPPER (CMX)—25,000 lbs.; cents per lb.

COFFEE (CSC)—37,500 lbs.; cents per lb.

COTTON (CTN)—50,000 lbs.; cents per lb.

ORANGE JUICE (CTN)—15,000 lbs.; cents per lb.

SUGAR—WORLD (CSC)—112,000 lbs.; cents per lb.

—GRAINS AND OILSEEDS—

CORN (CBT)—5,000 bu.; cents per bu.

OATS (CBT)—5,000 bu.; cents per bu.

SOYBEANS (CBT)—5,000 bu.; cents per bu.

SOYBEAN MEAL (CBT)—100 tons; $ per ton.

SOYBEAN OIL (CBT)—60,000 lbs.; cents per lb.

WHEAT (CBT)—5,000 bu.; cents per bu.

WHEAT (KC)—5,000 bu.; cents per bu.

WHEAT (MPLS)—5,000 bu.; cents per bu.

FLAXSEED (WPG)—20 metric tons; Can$ per ton

WHEAT (WPG)—20 metric tons; Can$ per ton

BARLEY (WPG)—20 metric tons; Can$ per ton

RAPESEED (WPG)—20 metric tons; Can$ per ton

FIGURE 17-1 Futures Prices Quotations

ACE — Amex Commodities Exchange, New York; CBT—Chicago Board of Trade; CME—Chicago Mercantile Exchange; CMX—Commodity Exchange, New York; CSC—Coffee, Sugar & Cocoa Exchange, New York; CTN—New York Cotton Exchange; IMM — International Monetary Market at CME, Chicago; KC — Kansas City Board of Trade; MPLS—Minneapolis Grain Exchange; NYM—New York Mercantile Exchange; WPG—Winnipeg Commodity Exchange

total volume (number of contracts) traded on the day in question and on the previous trading day as well as the total open interest in such contracts and change in open interest over the previous day.

Several contracts are usually available for trading in a specific commodity on a single exchange. They differ only with respect to delivery month. Thus Figure 17-1 shows that at the end of December 1979 the Chicago Board of Trade offered contracts in wheat for delivery in July 1980, September 1980, December 1980, and March 1981.

THE CLEARING HOUSE

Every American commodity exchange has an associated clearing house, which becomes the "seller's buyer" and the "buyer's seller" as soon as the transaction is concluded. The procedure is similar to that used for options. This is not surprising, since the first market in listed options was set up by people associated with the Chicago Board of Trade. The essential procedures were given in Chapter 16; a detailed description in the context of commodity futures follows.

Figure 17-2 shows how the clearing house operates in this market. When trading in July wheat is first allowed, A agrees to buy 5,000 bushels (one contract) from B at $4.40 per bushel, as shown in Figure 17-2(a). The clearing house immediately steps in and breaks the transactions apart, as shown in Figure 17-2(b). Now it is the obligation of the clearing house to deliver the wheat to A and to accept delivery from B. There is now an *open interest* of 5,000 bushels in July wheat, since a contract exists to deliver that much and, of course, to buy it.

At some later time, but well before July, A finds that C will buy July wheat for $4.50 per bushel. This represents a chance for a sure profit of $.10 per bushel, since A has already arranged to buy wheat in July for $4.40 per bushel, and could simply wait until July, accept delivery, then turn around and sell the wheat to C for $4.50. As shown in Figure 17-2(c), A makes a *reversing trade* with C, although C neither knows nor cares about A's reasons. Again, the clearing house steps in, as shown in Figure 17-2(d).

Now the benefits of a clearing house, with its ability to break traders apart and depersonalize agreements, become apparent. Figure 17-2(e) shows the current positions of all parties. A's situation can clearly be simplified. Figure 17-2(f) shows how it is done. Nominally, A is obligated to deliver 5,000 bushels of wheat to the clearing house in July, which is in turn obligated to deliver it back to A. In addition, A must deliver $4.40 per bushel, or $22,000, to the clearing house, which must in turn deliver $4.50 per bushel, or $22,500, to A. To save expense, the clearing house can just deliver $.10 per bushel, or $500, to A in July and forget the wheat entirely. In fact, the clearing house will deliver the money immediately, just to clear the accounts.

Figure 17-2(g) shows the situation after A is dispatched, profit in hand. If no further trades took place, in July B would deliver wheat to the clearing house, which would deliver it to C (in fact, the clearing house would *assign* the delivery of B's wheat to C). C would pay the clearing

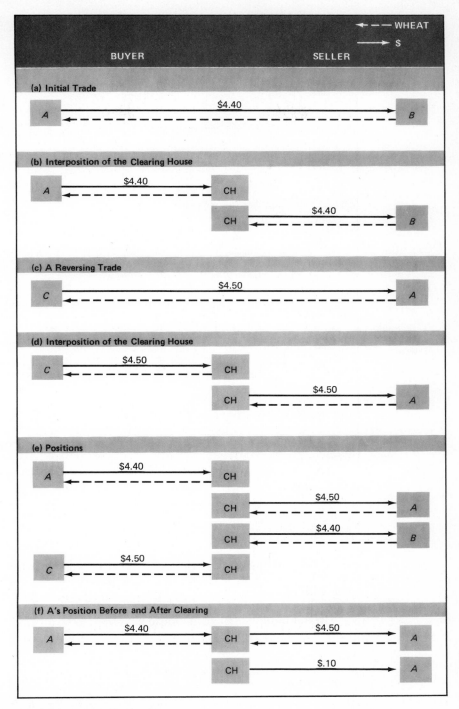

FIGURE 17-2 The Clearing Process.

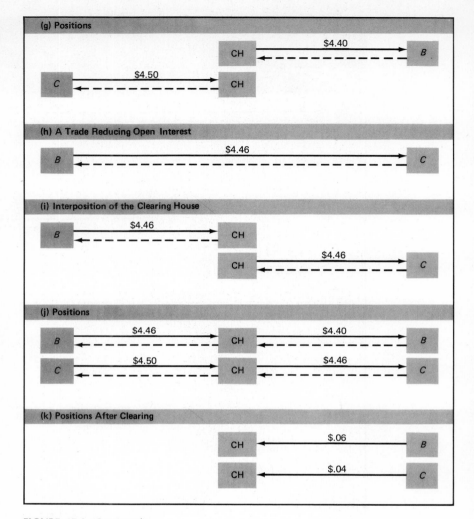

FIGURE 17-2 (Continued).

house $4.50 per bushel ($22,500) and the clearing house would pay B $4.40 per bushel ($22,000), keeping the difference. Although B and C did not trade with one another initially, they can be paired by the clearing house in this manner, if desired.

In this case, the clearing house pays $500 to A, an amount just equal to that due from the others (B and C).[1]

[1] The situation is in fact more complex than indicated here. Only brokers belong to a clearing house, and their accounts are settled by the clearing house at the end of every day. In effect, a futures contract is a forward contract that is settled every day and replaced with a new contract, with both the old contract's settlement price and the new contract's delivery price equal to the day's settlement price. This daily settlement process insures that the clearing house is even at the end of each day. In effect, each brokerage firm acts in a similar way and thus serves as a clearing house for its own clients.

What if B and C also want to avoid delivery of actual wheat? Imagine that they trade with each other at a price of $4.46, as shown in Figure 17-2(h). The clearing house comes in again, as shown in Figure 17-2(i), giving the net positions shown in Figure 17-2(j). The positions are then closed out, resulting in a payment of $.06 per bushel ($300) to the clearing house by B and $.04 per bushel ($200) by C. Open interest is reduced by 5,000 bushels and the clearing house is again even (as it always is, eventually).

These rather complex arrangements make it possible for commodity futures traders to think in very simple terms. In the example, A bought a contract of July wheat at $4.40 and later sold it for $4.50, making a profit of $.10 per bushel, or $500, which was *realized* as soon as the *reverse transaction* was completed. B sold a contract of July wheat for $4.40 and later bought it back for $4.46, suffering a loss of $.06 per bushel, or $300, which was realized as soon as the reverse transaction was completed. And C bought a contract at $4.50 and had to sell it for $4.46, realizing a loss of $.04 per bushel, or $200, when the reverse transaction was completed.

FUTURES CONTRACTS VERSUS CALL OPTIONS

People occasionally make the mistake of considering a futures contract an option. It is not. While the seller is allowed some alternatives concerning the delivery date and grade, both parties are obligated to complete the transaction, either by a reversing trade or actual delivery.

Figure 17-3 contrasts the situations faced by (a) the buyer and seller of a call option and (b) the buyer and seller of a commodity futures contract. In each case, positions are held until the last possible moment—the expiration date for the option, and the delivery month for the futures contract.

As shown in Figure 17-3(a), no matter what the price of the underlying stock, at expiration an option buyer cannot lose and an option seller cannot gain. Option buyers compensate sellers for putting themselves in

FIGURE 17-3 Values of Positions.

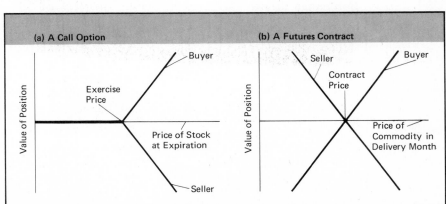

this position by paying them a premium when the agreement is first concluded. The exercise price is set more or less arbitrarily, and the premium negotiated. In a broader sense, the *premium* is the equilibrating factor, bringing quantity demanded and quantity supplied together in the options market.

The situation is quite different with a futures contract. As shown in Figure 17-3(b), the buyer may gain or lose, depending on the commodity price in the delivery month, and so may the seller. The higher the original contract price, the greater the likelihood that the buyer will lose and the seller will gain. The lower the original contract price, the greater the likelihood that the seller will lose and the buyer will gain. If the contract price were set arbitrarily, some sort of payment from one party to the other would undoubtedly be required to obtain agreement. However, this is not done. Instead, the contract price is negotiated in the attempt to find a value that will lead both parties to consider the resulting prospects worth their while.

In the futures market, the *contract price* is the equilibrating factor, bringing together the quantity demanded and the quantity supplied. No money is paid by either party to the other.

MARGINS

Strictly speaking, the purchase or sale or a commodity futures contract is not an investment. The buyer of July wheat does not own wheat, only the obligation to exchange a specified amount of money for wheat in July. Similarly, the seller is obligated solely to deliver wheat in July at that price. The only money involved before July is that needed to meet *margin* requirements, security deposits intended to guarantee that people with positions in commodity futures will in fact be able to fulfill their obligations.

To see how this works consider a speculator who buys a contract of July wheat at $4.40 per bushel. He or she now has a *long position* and is said to be *long* 5,000 bushels of July wheat. Initially, the value of the position equals its cost and there are no unrealized gains or losses involved. Net worth is neither smaller nor larger than it was before the purchase.

Now assume that some time has passed and July wheat contracts are selling at $4.50. If the speculator closed out the long position by selling July wheat, he or she would realize a profit of $.10 per bushel, or $500 (less commissions). The long position thus represents an *unrealized gain* of $500, and the speculator's net worth is larger by that amount than it would have been had the position not been taken. Conversely, a fall in the price would generate an *unrealized loss*.

An open position created by the *sale* of a commodity future is termed a *short position*, and the account holder is said to be *short* the contract. A rise in the price of a short position creates an unrealized loss; a fall, an unrealized gain.

Calculations of unrealized gains and losses are made routinely by brokerage firms handling customers' *commodity accounts*. Each account of this type must be kept separately from other, noncommodity accounts.

A commodity account can include cash, interest-earning default-free assets (e.g., Treasury bills), and open commodity positions. The key figure is the net *equity* in the account, defined as follows:

equity = cash and/or cash-equivalents (e.g., U.S. Treasury bills)
        plus unrealized gains on open positions
        less unrealized losses on open positions

If a position were to be closed out immediately, the account holder would have to pay an amount equal to the realized capital loss or would receive an amount equal to the realized capital gain. If all positions were to be closed out immediately, the account's cash and cash equivalents would equal the current equity, less any commissions involved.

Margin requirements are designed to insure that a commodity account has a sufficiently large equity, relative to the size of all open positions, to make the probability of reaching a negative equity position in a day or two very small.

Each exchange sets minimum margin requirements for its contracts; brokers often require additional amounts. Practice varies, but the *initial margin*, assessed when a position is first opened, is usually 5% to 10% of the value of the contract. If the equity in an account falls below this amount, the customer may be required to add cash to the account to increase the equity. The *maintenance margin*, below which equity is not allowed to fall without remedial action, is usually 75% to 80% as large as the initial margin. The initial margin and the maintenance margin are typically stated as fixed dollar amounts per contract. In general, the greater the value of a contract and the variability of its price, the larger will be the required margins.

When the equity in an account falls below the maintenance margin, the customer receives a *margin call*. If additional cash is not obtained, the broker may close out one or more positions to reduce the required margin until it conforms to the current value of the equity in the account. When the equity exceeds that required for margin, cash may be removed, in some cases up to the point at which the margin requirements are just met.

Some brokers require a minimum dollar value of equity in a commodity account. Some allow only cash to be used and pay no interest on it. Others allow the use of interest-earning cash equivalents (usually U.S. Treasury bills), at least for accounts with equity greater than a specified minimum.

If interest-earning securities can be posted to meet margin requirements, it is clear that no investment is involved in an open commodity position. The individual's funds are invested, but in Treasury bills. Open commodity positions can be regarded as bets that have yet to be settled. On the other hand, if only cash is allowed, the required margin may be considered the investment needed to support the open commodity positions. This will be small relative to the values of such positions, and even relative to the possible gains and losses from them. This has led many to argue that commodity futures are "highly levered" and extremely risky investments. Taking the margin required as an investment base, they certainly are, but there is no more need for an investor to maintain such high leverage than there is to purchase stocks using the maximum allowable amount of margin.

HISTORICAL RETURNS ON COMMODITY
FUTURES CONTRACTS

During the period from 1950 through 1976 a portfolio made up of unlevered positions in 23 different commodity futures contracts provided results similar to those that could have been obtained with a diversified portfolio of common stocks:[2]

	Average Return (% per year)	Standard Deviation of Return (% per year)
23 commodity futures	13.83	22.43
Standard and Poor's 500-stock index	13.05	18.95

Historically, commodity futures have been similar to common stocks in terms of risk, when evaluated on a comparable basis. They have also provided similar returns. Given a choice of one type of investment or the other, an investor might consider the two alternatives equally desirable. But either one would have been dominated by a combination of the two. During the period covered, the returns of these portfolios were *negatively* correlated, so the return on a diversified futures/stock portfolio would have varied considerably less.[3]

Not surprisingly, commodity futures have served as at least a partial hedge against inflation. During the 1950–76 period the returns on the portfolio of 23 commodity futures were positively correlated with changes in the consumer price index.[4] As a result, the variation in real returns was less than that of nominal returns. This contrasts with the results for common stocks, where the results were just the opposite:[5]

[2] Source: Zvi Bodie and Victor Rosansky, "Risk and Return in Commodity Futures," *Financial Analysts Journal* (forthcoming).

[3] The correlation coefficient was −.24; the standard deviations of return for portfolios with different proportions were:

Percent in Stock	Percent in Futures	Standard Deviation
0	100	22.43
20	80	17.43
40	60	13.77
60	40	12.68
80	20	14.74
100	0	18.95

Source: Bodie and Rosansky, *ibid.*

[4] The correlation coefficient was .58 (unfortunately the study did not differentiate between the effects of expected and unexpected inflation). Source: Bodie and Rosansky, *op. cit.*

[5] The correlation coefficient between stock returns and changes in the consumer price index was −.43. Source: Bodie and Rosansky, *op. cit.*

	STANDARD DEVIATION OF TOTAL RETURN (% PER YEAR)	
	Nominal Return	Real Return
23 commodity futures	22.43	19.44
Standard and Poor's 500-stock index	18.95	19.65

OPEN INTEREST

When trading is first allowed in a contract, there is no open interest; it grows as people begin to make transactions. At any time, open interest equals the amount of the commodity that those with short positions are currently obligated to deliver. It also equals the amount that those with long positions are obligated to accept and pay for.

Open interest figures are shown with commodity futures prices. For example, Figure 17-1 indicates that on December 20, 1979, a total of 24,963 contracts in March 1980 wheat were outstanding on the Chicago Board of Trade. Note the substantial differences in the open interest figures for the other wheat contracts on the Chicago Board of Trade on that day. This is quite typical. Figure 17-4 shows why. Open interest in the December 1978 wheat contract is shown for every month from January 1978 until the contract expired at the end of the delivery month (December 1978). From January until the end of September, more trades were generally made to open new positions than to close out old ones, and open interest continued to increase. As the delivery month came closer, reversing trades began to outnumber those intended to open new positions, and open interest began to decline. The amount remaining at the beginning of December was the maximum number of bushels of wheat that could have been delivered against futures contracts, but most of these contracts were also settled by reversing trades instead of delivery.

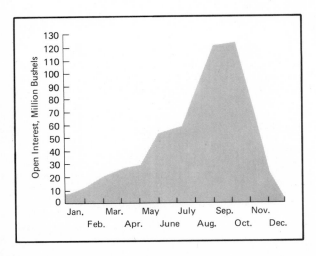

FIGURE 17-4 Open Interest December 1978 Chicago Board of Trade Wheat Contract: January 3, 1978 through December 28, 1978.

Relatively few positions in the futures market—less than 3% of the total[6]—end in actual delivery of the commodity involved, but the fact that delivery is a possibility makes a contract's value in the delivery month differ only slightly, if at all, from the price of the actual commodity. No more is needed, as an analogy from the insurance industry will illustrate.

Policies that insure against loss from fire or theft generally guarantee replacement with an equivalent item. In fact, settlement is often made in cash, which the insured party can use to purchase an equivalent item (or not, as desired). As long as the cash involved bears a close relationship to the value of the designated item, there is no need for actual "delivery." The commodities futures market, which provides a kind of insurance, can also function effectively with a few if any deliveries. The potential for delivery insures that in the final month the futures price will bear a close relationship to the commodity's spot price. Few buyers wish to have the specific commodity offered by the futures contract: most prefer to settle in cash and acquire the grade they want at the location they want.

PRICE LIMITS

It is said that a farmer, tired of violent fluctuations in temperature, had his thermometer altered so it could not move more than 5 degrees in either direction from the previous day's reading. The story is undoubtedly apocryphal, but it is instructive.

The U.S. Commodity Futures Trading Commission, which regulates trading on all U.S. commodity exchanges, places limits on the extent to which futures prices are allowed to vary from day to day. For example, if July wheat closed at $4.40 on the previous day, contracts at prices outside the range from $4.20 to $4.60 might be forbidden. If a major piece of news during the day led traders to consider $4.65 a reasonable value for the contract, they would have to: (1) trade privately, foregoing the advantages offered by the exchange, (2) trade on the exchange at the *limit price* of $4.60, or (3) wait until the next day, when prices from $4.60 to $4.80 would be allowed, based on the current day's closing price of $4.60 (a "limit move"), even though the latter price might simply represent an unfulfilled bid.

The placing of limits on price fluctuations derives from a feeling that traders may overreact to major news and should be "protected" from voluntarily entering into agreements under such conditions. However questionable the position, it is firmly held and of long standing.

TAXATION OF COMMODITY FUTURES PROFITS AND LOSSES

A *speculator* in a futures market is considered to have a *capital asset* for tax purposes, whether he or she is long or short. When the position is closed out, the resultant profit or loss is treated as a *capital* gain or loss. If

---

[6] Merrill Lynch, Pierce, Fenner and Smith, Inc., *Speculating on Inflation: Futures Trading in Interest Rates, Foreign Currencies and Precious Metals* (July 1979).

the holding period is less than six months, the gain or loss is *short-term*; otherwise it is *long-term* for tax purposes.[7]

Hedgers' positions in the futures market are considered part of their commercial activities. Profits and losses are thus treated as *ordinary* income or loss for tax purposes.

HEDGING

When two horse race enthusiasts bet with each other, the activity is termed *gambling*. This has an antisocial connotation, as it involves the creation of a new risk where there was none before. However, when the owner of one of the horses in a race makes a bet on one or more of the other horses, the situation is different (and generally illegal). The other party involved may be a gambler, but the owner is "hedging his bets" and can be termed a *hedger*. If the owner's horse wins, there will be good news and bad news: the good news is winning the prize money, the bad news is losing the bets. Conversely, if the horse loses, the prize money will be lost, but not all the bets. Astute betting may even allow the initial risk to be *completely hedged*, so the owner's income will be unaffected by the outcome of the race. In this case all the original risk has been *transferred* from the owner to the gambler. If the risk were only partially hedged, of course, there would only be a partial transfer.[8]

If two disinterested parties make a bet on whether or not your house will burn down, they are gambling—creating risk. But if you make a bet that it will burn down, you are hedging. This is usually done by purchasing fire insurance, and the "gambler" involved is an insurance company. The result is usually considered socially desirable. The insurance company, able to pool risks, is willing to take on a homeowner's risk at a price that he or she is willing to pay to reduce exposure to a single, uncertain event.

The same situation occurs in the futures market. Farmers, dealers, processors, and others heavily exposed to possible fluctuations in commodity prices are willing to pay others to take over some or all of the associated risk. Outsiders who act as the insurance companies are called *speculators*.

The view of a futures market as a place in which everyone "in the trade" completely hedges all risk by dealing with speculators who make themselves available to serve as bearers of such risk is both too simple and too idealistic. First, many people in the trade choose to bear some risk, either the risk due to general fluctuations in the price of a commodity or that due to fluctuations in the differences between the prices of different grades, the same grade in different locations, etc.: partial hedging is far more common than complete hedging.[9] Second, many hedgers trade

---

[7] This contrasts with the one-year cutoff for other capital assets.

[8] An owner who bets on his own horse, thereby increasing risk instead of transferring and reducing it, is said to have taken a "Texas hedge" (Merrill Lynch, Pierce, Fenner and Smith, Inc., *The Hedger's Handbook*, 1971).

[9] Indeed, an individual in the trade may choose to take a large hedged position with more risk than that of the original unhedged position.

with one another. Finally, speculators also trade with one another. Both gambling and insurance can be found in most commodity futures markets.

The usual characterization of a hedger is that of someone forced to hold a large inventory of a commodity that for some reason cannot be sold until a later date. To "fix the price" such a person can sell a corresponding futures contract. This is termed *short hedging*, since the hedger is long (owns) the actual commodity and *short* (has sold) a futures contract. As long as the value of the actual inventory moves in concert with the commodity futures price, this will provide a hedge: when the actual commodity is sold, the hedge can be "lifted" via a reversing trade. Any gain on the commodity will be offset by a comparable loss on the futures contract, while any loss on the commodity will be offset by a comparable gain on the futures contract.

The opposite situation can also occur. A manufacturer or dealer may have contracted for delivery of a commodity or a product that uses it as input at some later date. Purchase of the commodity at present may be undesirable due to space limitations, etc. To fix the price, a *long* position in an appropriate commodity futures contract can be opened; this is termed *long hedging*. Assuming that the futures price moves with that of the commodity, the implicit short position in the actual good can be offset by the position in the futures market. When the commodity is purchased, the hedge can be lifted via a reversing trade. Any gain on the commodity due to a fall in price prior to purchase will be offset by a loss on the commodity futures contract; any loss due to a rise in price prior to purchase will be offset by a gain on the futures contract.

In some cases a short hedger will literally deliver his or her commodity inventory to the buyer of a contract. In others a long hedger will actually take delivery. But such instances are rare, for they are likely to involve the "wrong" grade, place, or time.

BASIS

An investor with both long and short positions has, in effect, invested in the difference between them, since this is what determines his or her net worth. For a hedger with a position in the actual commodity and an opposite position of equal magnitude in a futures contract, the difference between the futures price and the price of the commodity for immediate delivery is crucial. The latter is termed the *cash*, or *spot*, price. The difference is the *basis:*

$$\text{basis} = \text{futures price} - \text{cash price}$$

A person with a long position in a commodity futures contract and a short position in the actual commodity, said to be *short of the basis*, will profit if the basis widens and lose if it narrows. One with a short position in a commodity futures contract and a long position in the actual commodity, said to be *long of the basis*, will suffer a loss if the basis widens and gain if it narrows.

Anyone who has "completely" hedged a commodity position has exchanged price risk for basis risk. Only uncertainty about the difference between the value of the specific commodity and that of the futures contract remains. The individual can thus be said to be *speculating on the basis*, i.e., differences in the prices of different grades, geographic locations, etc. Many dealers do this intentionally, for success requires knowledge of local conditions that affect price differences, not global conditions that affect price levels.

SPREADS

It is quite possible to take a long position in a futures contract and a short position in another contract in the same commodity, but with a different delivery date. The person who does this is speculating on changes in the difference between the prices of the two contracts, a difference that constitutes the "basis" for this particular hedge.

Others attempt to profit from temporary imbalances among the prices of futures contracts on different but related commodities. One popular combination involves a position in soybeans with offsetting positions in the items produced from them: soybean oil and soybean meal. Another involves a position in wheat with an offsetting position in corn, which serves as a substitute for wheat in many applications.

Like a hedger, a *spreader* reduces or eliminates the risk associated with general price moves, taking on instead the risk associated with changes in price *differences*. Superior knowledge and ability are required to attain a profit from such changes, and spreaders believe they have what is required to handle such a risk.

COMMODITY PRICES

Most commodity futures exchanges provide areas in which buyers and sellers can negotiate cash (or spot) sales. No attempt is made to standardize such agreements; everything, including grade, location, and delivery, is negotiable. For this reason there is no such thing as a standardized spot price. Instead, the nearest futures price is often used as a surrogate for one. In fact, deals in the spot market may even be made in terms of the price of the nearest futures contract—for example, two parties might agree to trade at 2 cents per bushel more than the relevant futures price. In essence, trades are conducted in terms of the basis.

The price of any commodity is determined by demand and supply. It is in the realm of supply that wheat differs from, say, automobiles. Wheat is a *seasonal* commodity, generally harvested in the United States from late May through September (although in other countries harvests occur at other times). Seasonality has important implications for price determination, and most of the discussion that follows will deal with the prices of seasonal commodities. However, many of the relationships also apply to commodities not characterized by seasonal production patterns.

Spot Prices in a World of Certainty

To understand commodity prices it is useful to consider first a world with no uncertainty. To further simplify matters, differences in grades and location will be ignored so the spot and futures markets can be assumed to deal in the same commodity, differing only in date of delivery.

Assume that all wheat is harvested instantly on June 1 every year, that the size of each year's harvest is known with certainty, and that the *carrying charges*—primarily interest, insurance, and storage—are also known.

Initially, assume that carrying costs are unaffected by the amount of wheat stored. This means that enough storage capacity for an entire harvest (or possibly more) is available at the same rental rate or opportunity cost. More realistic conditions will be considered shortly.

FIGURE 17-5 Inventories and Prices in a World of Certainty; Equal Crop Sizes.

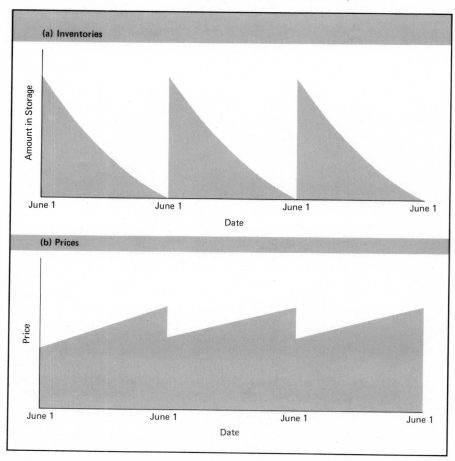

Assume further that carrying costs are not related to the price of the commodity. This is clearly incorrect for interest and insurance charges; however, the effect of a price change on total carrying costs is small for most commodities and can often be disregarded.

Under what conditions would anyone carry (store) an inventory of wheat from one day to the next in this kind of world? The answer depends on the magnitude of the projected price change:

1. If price is certain to rise by an amount less than carrying costs, no one will store a commodity.
2. If price is certain to rise by an amount greater than carrying costs, all available supplies will be stored, leaving nothing for consumption. But then the present price will increase, making storage less desirable. This will continue until someone is willing to sell the commodity rather than store it—e.g., when the price rise is no longer certain to be more than carrying costs.

Two implications are:

1. Under no conditions will price be certain to rise by an amount exceeding carrying costs.
2. If supplies are being stored (carried over to the future) in a world of certainty, price will increase by an amount equal to carrying costs.

Figures 17-5 through 17-8 build on these principles. Figure 17-5 shows the patterns of (a) inventory on hand, and (b) price in a world of certainty where every crop is the same size and demand conditions do not change from year to year. As soon as a new harvest is in, price begins to rise by the amount required to cover carrying costs. Inventory is reduced as wheat is used up—initially at a fast rate, then later at a slower rate as the price increases. Since the size of each crop is the same, and everything is known with certainty, the last grain of the old crop is used up at the end of May.

Figure 17-6 shows the situation when each year's crop is expected to be larger than its predecessor while demand conditions remain the same. No one would want to carry wheat over from a year of a small crop to one of a large crop. And it is impossible to carry any wheat backward in time from years of plenty to years of scarcity. Thus each crop is used up in its entirety. Prices follow a linear trend, increasing at a rate equal to carrying charges, but each year's trend begins at a lower point than the previous one.

Figures 17-7 and 17-8 show the situation when each year's crop is expected to be smaller than its predecessor while demand conditions remain unchanged. In such cases it may or may not pay to carry wheat forward from one crop year to the next. If it does pay, price will not fall when the new crop is harvested, as illustrated in Figure 17-7. If it does not pay to carry wheat from one crop year to the next, price will fall on June 1, but not back to the original level prevailing at the beginning of the previous crop year, as illustrated in Figure 17-8.

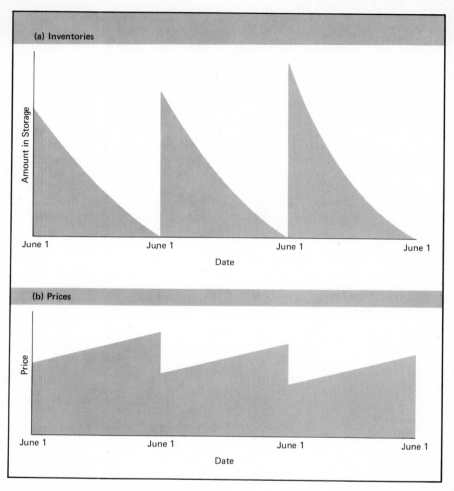

(a) Inventories

Amount in Storage

June 1 June 1 June 1 June 1

Date

(b) Prices

Price

June 1 June 1 June 1 June 1

Date

FIGURE 17-6 Inventories and Prices in a World of Certainty; Increasing Crop Sizes.

Figure 17-9 shows the situation when one of the previous assumptions is dropped. Here the harvest extends over some time, instead of appearing magically on June 1. Some wheat becomes available on May 1, with the harvest continuing until September 1. As harvesting begins, both old and new stocks are consumed, and inventory remains positive until the new wheat begins to arrive in quantity. For a few weeks the new crop is used up as it is harvested, and no inventory of any kind is held. Later, only part of the amount being harvested is used up, the remainder going into storage. Inventory builds to the peak of the season, from which it begins to decline until the next harvest. In Figure 17-9(a) each harvest is assumed to be the same, and demand conditions do not change from year to year. Under these conditions, price increases at a rate equal to carrying charges whenever inventory is held, as shown in Figure 17-9(b). During the period when no wheat is in storage, prices will depend on demand and supply conditions but will not increase at a rate exceeding carrying costs. Figure 17-9(b) shows a possible pattern.

Cases in which future harvests will be larger or smaller than previous ones can be analyzed similarly. The previous figures (17-6, 17-7, and 17-8) need only be altered to reflect the changed inventory situations with the corresponding price patterns having "wiggly" lines (that never increase by more than carrying charges) during periods of zero inventory. Commodi-

FIGURE 17-7 Inventories and Prices in a World of Certainty: Decreasing Crop Sizes with Carryover.

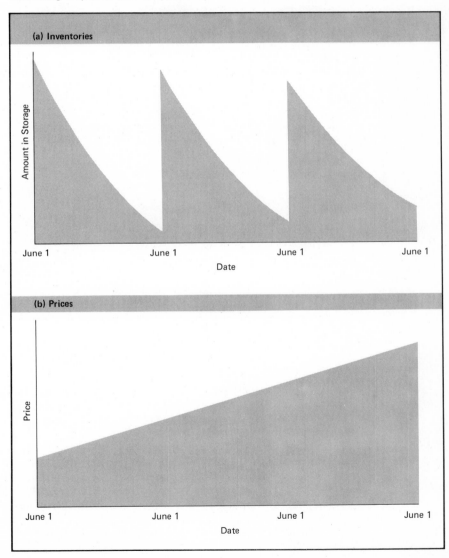

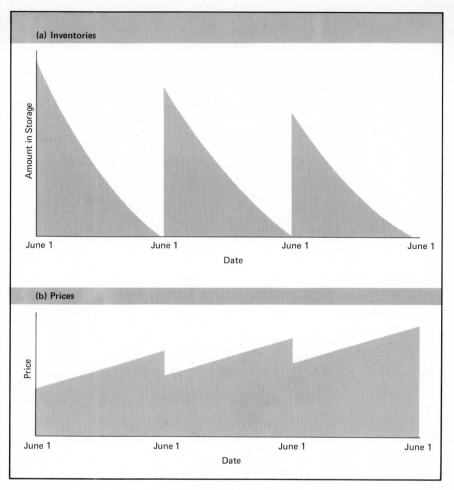

FIGURE 17-8 Inventories and Prices in a World of Certainty: Decreasing Crop Sizes and no Carryover.

ties not subject to seasonal production conditions can be considered instances of year-long harvests. Under certainty their prices would increase by an amount equal to carrying costs when inventories were being held and by less at other times.

Before leaving the comfort of a world of certainty, we should consider more realistic storage situations. Figure 17-10(a) shows the conditions assumed thus far: for any future price change greater than c all available supplies will be stored; for any smaller change nothing will be stored. Under such conditions only a price rise of c will induce people to store inventory; conversely, in this world of certainty, the existence of any inventory in storage indicates that price will rise at a rate equal to carrying costs (c).

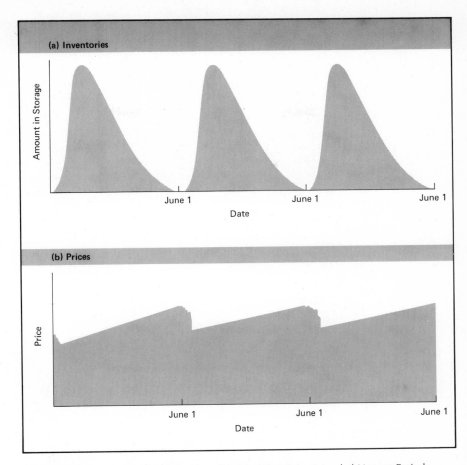

FIGURE 17-9 Inventories and Prices in a World of Certainty: Extended Harvest Periods.

FIGURE 17-10 Inventory versus Price Increase.

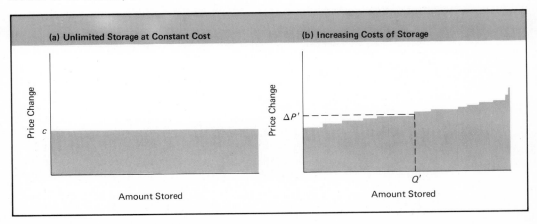

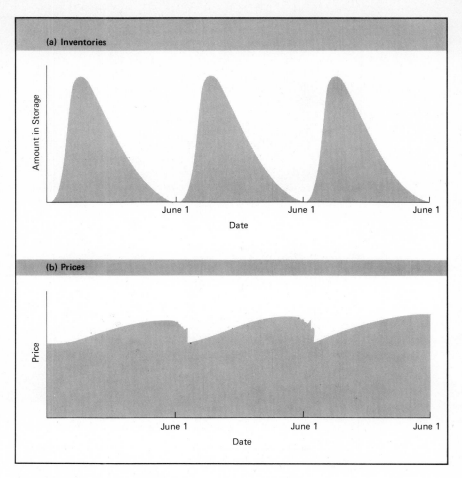

FIGURE 17-11 Inventories and Prices in a World of Certainty:
Increasing Costs of Storage.

Figure 17-10(b) shows a more realistic situation. There are many different types of storage, with different costs. When price is going to increase slightly, only the low-cost storage will be used, and the total inventory held (carried over) will be small. When price is going to increase substantially, low- and high-cost storage will be used, and a large inventory will be held. In Figure 17-10(b), given a projected price increase of $\Delta P'$, a total inventory of Q' will be held. Conversely, if Q' is currently being stored, people must expect prices to increase by $\Delta P'$.

Some of the effects of storage costs of this type are shown in Figure 17-11, which portrays the case of equal harvests and unchanging demand conditions, with wheat harvested in June, July, and August. When inventory is large, price increases at a rapid rate to cover the costs of marginal, high-cost storage. When inventory is small, price increases at a slower rate, since only low-cost storage need be used.

Futures Prices in a World of Certainty

If all spot prices could be predicted with certainty, there would be little reason to make a contract for future delivery; however, nothing would preclude people from doing so. If they did, each futures price would simply equal the (perfectly predictable) spot price on the relevant delivery date.

Figure 17-12(a) shows this relationship for the situation analyzed earlier. Three futures contracts are assumed to be traded at any time, offering delivery on the last day of March, July, and September, respectively. Each contract is traded during the 364 days prior to the specified delivery date. Since no uncertainty is involved, no margin need be posted by either party. With no investment and no uncertainty, it is hardly surprising that the price of a futures contract would not change during its life.

Note that during the life of any contract the spot price is sometimes above and sometimes below the futures price. Note also that at some times "distant" futures contracts sell for more than "near" ones, and at other times the situation is reversed. This is shown in Figures 17-12(b) and 17-12(c), which plot the prices of various contracts versus their remaining lives at two times of the year. In this case, if contracts were available for every possible delivery date, their prices would plot along the dashed curves, which reflect the (known) future pattern of spot rates.

FIGURE 17-12 Commodity Prices in a World of Certainty.

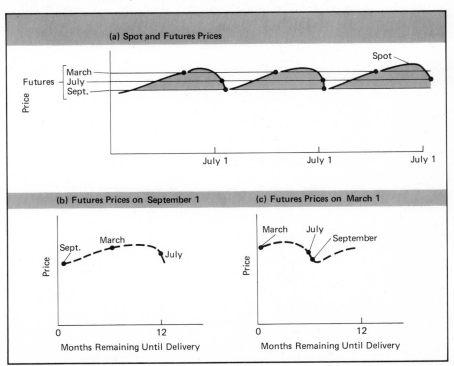

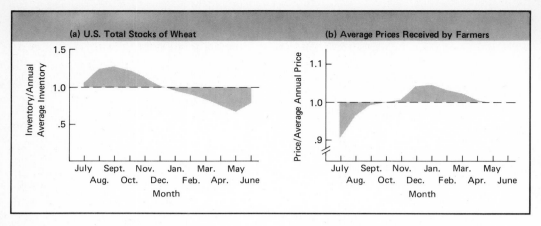

FIGURE 17-13 Average Inventories and Prices for Wheat in the United States, July 1964–June 1974.

Spot Prices

Figure 17-13 shows *actual* patterns of (a) inventories and (b) prices of wheat over a ten-year period. The diagrams were constructed by expressing the values for each month in a crop year as percentages of the average value for the year, then averaging the resulting figures over the ten crop years. This procedure is designed to reduce the "noise" due to unanticipated events and bring out underlying patterns.

Two differences from the earlier diagrams are evident. Prices declined, on average, from January through June—a much longer period than likely in a world of certainty. And substantial inventories (well over half the average level) were carried over from each crop year to the next.

FIGURE 17-14 The Supply of Storage.

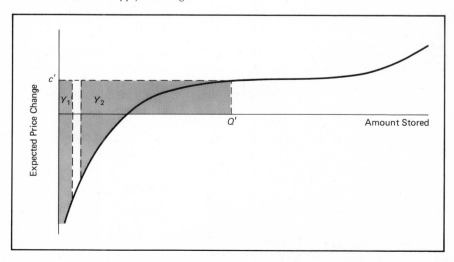

Such phenomena can be explained to some extent by government price support programs. But more is involved.

To explore the reasons, it is useful to consider the *supply of storage*. This slightly misleading term refers to the relationship between the *expected* increase in a commodity's price and the amount of inventory that people are willing to store.

Figure 17-14 shows a typical supply-of-storage curve. Part is familiar and can be explained in familiar ways. But part is rather surprising.

The most natural assumption about the supply of storage would hold that it reflects the cost of actually storing a commodity plus an appropriate expected return on the investment involved—the appropriate return depending, as usual, on the relevant risk of the position. Since investment in wheat is not qualitatively different from any other investment, the relevant aspect should be the risk that a position would add to a well-diversified (e.g., market) portfolio. While investment in any single commodity is risky, a "portfolio" of many commodities plus a number of bonds and stocks is less so. Figure 17-15 provides some relevant evidence.[10] It shows the beta values measured relative to Standard and Poor's 500-stock index for investments in 23 different commodities. Less than half are positive.

While the producer or user of a commodity may wish to hold it in inventory, the *risk* involved can be reduced or avoided by hedging in the futures market. Those who take on the risk can certainly hold diversified portfolios. If the beta value of a commodity futures contract relative to common stocks is negative, adding such a contract to an equity portfolio can reduce the investor's risk. If the beta value is zero, and the amount added is small, portfolio risk will not increase substantially. This suggests that only contracts with positive beta values should be priced to give expected returns well above the riskless rate of interest.

[10] The values in Figure 17-15 are based on changes in futures prices over quarterly holding periods. The high correlation between spot and futures prices make the latter adequate surrogates for the former for this purpose.

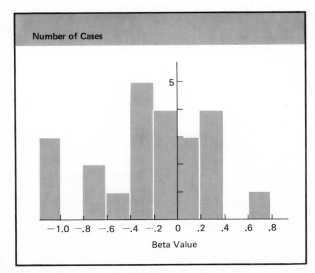

FIGURE 17-15 Beta Values Relative to Standard and Poor's 500-Stock Index: 23 Commodity Investments, 1950–1976.

Source: Zvi Bodie and Victor Rosansky, "Risk and Return in Commodity Futures," *Financial Analysts Journal* (forthcoming).

If only these factors were involved, the supply of storage would be identical to that shown in Figure 17-10(b), with the vertical axis simply reinterpreted as the *expected* change in the spot price. Such an explanation serves quite well for the portion of the curve in Figure 17-14 associated with stocks greater than Q', but not for the other part.

The behavior of the curve to the left of Q' is generally attributed to the existence of *convenience yield*. Thus, in Figure 17-14, someone is willing to hold inventory when the expected loss after paying storage and opportunity costs is y_1. Another is willing to do so when the expected loss is y_2. Given any expected price change below c' (the minimum storage and opportunity cost), only people with sufficiently large convenience yields will hold inventory. And the greater the expected loss, the smaller the amount held.

Figure 17-16 shows that this is no ivory-tower exercise. The horizontal axis plots the amount of wheat stored at the end of the month, expressed as a percentage of the average amount stored over the preceding 13 months. The vertical axis plots the *difference* between (1) an estimate of expected price change[11] over the forthcoming month and (2) the typical cost of storage, interest, and insurance (c' in Figure 17-14). When prices were expected to increase by enough to cover the cost of storage, insurance, and an expected return equal to the riskless rate, slightly above-average stocks were held. When prices were expected to increase by more than this, considerably above-average stocks were held. And when prices were expected to increase by less, or even to decrease, smaller-than-average stocks were held. Similar results have been obtained for other commodities and other time periods.

The concept of convenience yield is more a name for the sort of empirical relationship shown in Figure 17-16 than it is a well-understood aspect of commodity ownership. Divergent opinions may explain part of the phenomenon: when the consensus view expects a price decrease, some congenital optimists who expect a substantial increase might consider storage of the commodity a good investment and hold at least some stocks. Alternatively, the multiperiod nature of the situation may lead one to store a commodity even when prices are expected to change by less than carrying costs; put slightly differently, inventory is desirable because it gives an *option* to sell large amounts if prices go higher or to sell little if prices fall temporarily.[12]

Whatever the nature of convenience yield may be, it appears to be a fact of life. Note that in Figure 17-13 prices begin to decline shortly after inventories fall below their average level. While the prices shown are ex post averages, not ex ante expectations, it seems unlikely that people fail to expect price declines toward the end of the crop year. Yet they continue to hold inventory.

The supply-of-storage curve provides useful information for predicting price changes. The causal relationship runs from expected price change to the amount stored, but for predictive purposes the order can be reversed, with the size of current stocks on hand used to estimate ex-

---

[11] The estimates in Figure 17-16 are based on trend-line projections, adjusted for seasonal and other effects. Similar results were obtained using futures prices as estimates of expected future spot prices.

[12] This explanation of convenience yield is due to Paul Cootner.

pected price change and hence expected future spot price. As we will see, futures prices are closely linked to expected future spot prices, so this is an important exercise for those planning to speculate in commodity futures.

Since inventories are carried over from one season to the next, factors affecting prices in future years will affect the value of present stocks and hence the current spot price. Virtually any news concerning present or future demand or supply conditions will alter the current price of a commodity and also predictions of all future prices. Since real news is

FIGURE 17-16 The Supply of Storage for Wheat.

Source: Based on data for No. 2 hard winter wheat, 1924–1932, in Michael J. Brennan, "The Supply of Storage," *American Economic Review*, XLVIII, no. 1 (March 1958), 64.

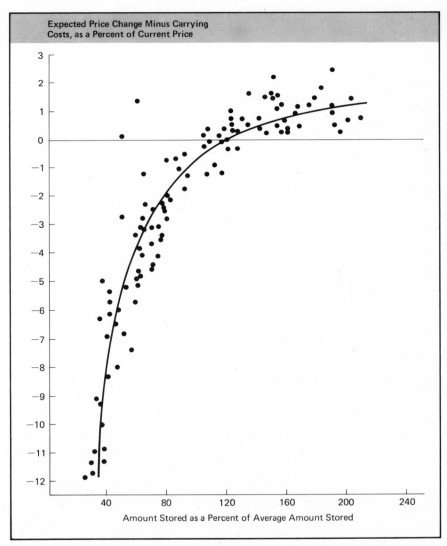

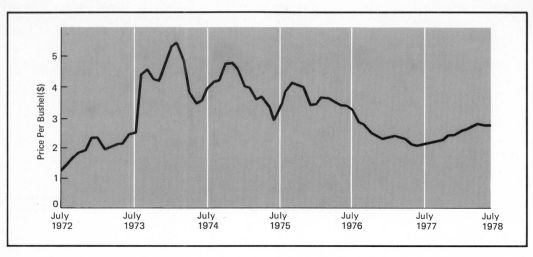

FIGURE 17-17 Wheat: Average Monthly Prices Received by Farmers, July 1972–June 1978.

Source: Chicago Board of Trade, *Statistical Annual,* 1978.

"new," such changes are likely to come at random times and affect prices by random amounts, either positively or negatively. This can be seen in Figure 17-17, which shows the average prices received by farmers for wheat in each month from July 1972 through June 1978. Some traces of the "normal" seasonal pattern can be seen, but new information frequently moved the entire pattern up or down. Uncertainty brings relatively random price changes; commodity prices are no exception to the general rule.

FUTURES PRICES

It is easier to say what futures prices will *not* be than what they *will* be. Assume, for example, that wheat currently sells for $4 per bushel, that the riskless rate of interest is .5% per month, and that storage costs 2.5 cents per bushel per month. What can be said about the current price for a 12-month futures contract? If it were, say, $4.60, a *certain* profit could be made in the following manner:

Now
borrow $4
use the loan to buy wheat at $4 per bushel
sell (short) a 12-month contract at $4.60 per bushel

12 Months from Now	
pay back loan for $4 × (1.005¹²)	= $4.25 per bushel
pay storage (12 months at $.025 per bushel)	= $ .30 per bushel
	$4.55 per bushel
deliver wheat to purchaser of futures contract; receive:	$4.60 per bushel
net profit:	$ .05 per bushel

Opportunities for a certain profit are rare indeed. In all likelihood the futures contract in question would sell for less than $4.55.

This can be stated more generally:

$$P_t^f \leq P^s(1 + r)^t + kt \qquad (17\text{-}1)$$

where:

P_t^f = the current price of a futures contract for delivery in t months

P^s = the current spot price

r = the riskless rate of interest per month

k = the cost of storage per month (insurance can be included in k or, if dependent on price, in r)

Similar reasoning can be used to place limits on the relationship between the prices of futures contracts for delivery in two different months:[13]

$$P_{t_2}^f \leq P_{t_1}^f(1 + r)^{(t_2 - t_1)} + k(t_2 - t_1) \qquad (17\text{-}2)$$

where

$P_{t_2}^f$ = the current price of a futures contract for delivery in t_2 months

$P_{t_1}^f$ = the current price of a futures contract for delivery in t_1 months (where $t_1 < t_2$)

If formula (17-2) did not hold, one could take a long position in the contract for delivery at time t_1 and a short position in the contract for delivery at time t_2. By taking delivery at t_1 for $P_{t_1}^f$, storing the commodity, then delivering at t_2 for $P_{t_2}^f$, a certain profit could be obtained. Since this is literally too good to be true, the relationship in formula (17-2) is almost never violated.

While this places limits on the relative values of various futures prices, it does not imply that they must move in lockstep with each other. Nonetheless, the linkages are very close, as shown in Figure 17-18, which plots the daily prices of three different futures contracts over a seven-month period. Each price is related to expectations of the future pattern of spot prices, although the contracts are tied to three different points on that pattern. When new information shifts the expected pattern upward, all three prices rise; when it shifts the expected pattern downward, all three prices fall. Unless the pattern of expected future spot prices is altered substantially, in addition to being shifted, prices of all futures contracts for a commodity are likely to change by roughly similar amounts.

Although lack of standardization makes it difficult to analyze the relationship between movements in futures prices and the current spot price for a commodity, the price of an expiring futures contract can be used as a surrogate for the spot price. Not surprisingly, spot and futures prices are also highly correlated, as Figure 17-18 suggests.

The interrelationship of spot and futures prices makes hedging both possible and effective. This is fortunate, since exposure to the fluctuations

[13] Formula (17-1) can be considered a special case of formula (17-2) with $t_1 = 0$.

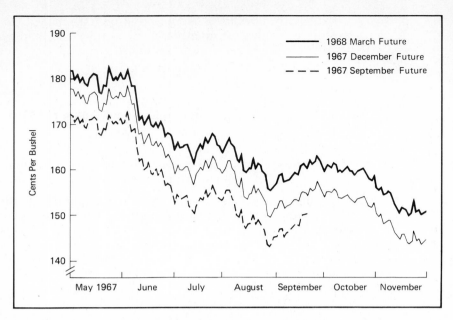

FIGURE 17-18 Daily Closing Prices, Three Futures Contracts for Wheat on the Chicago Board of Trade, May 1 to November 30, 1967.

of commodity prices may entail substantial risk, as Figures 17-17 and 17-18 amply indicate.

Futures Prices and Expected Spot Prices

It is good to know something about the way in which futures prices are related to each other, but a more important question remains: exactly how are futures prices related to expected spot prices?

The simplest answer is that given by the *expectations hypothesis*: the current price of a futures contract equals the market consensus expectation of the spot price on the delivery date. In symbols:

$$P^f = \exp(\tilde{P}^s)$$

where:

P^f = the current price of a futures contract
$\tilde{P}^s$ = the spot price at the delivery date of the futures contract
$\exp(\tilde{P}^s)$ = the current expectation of $\tilde{P}^s$

If this hypothesis is correct, a speculator can expect neither to win nor to lose from a position in the futures market, be it long or short. Neglecting margin requirements, a speculator who takes a long position at P^f must pay P^f at the delivery date for a commodity worth $\tilde{P}^s$ at the time. His or her profit (which is uncertain in advance) will be:

$$\tilde{P}^s - P^f \tag{17-3a}$$

while the expected profit will be:

$$\exp(\tilde{P}^s) - P^f \tag{17-3b}$$

which will equal zero if the expectations hypothesis holds.

A speculator with a short position will have to pay P^f for a commodity worth $\tilde{P}^s$ on the delivery date, giving a profit of:

$$P^f - \tilde{P}^s \tag{17-4a}$$

and an expected profit of:

$$P^f - \exp(\tilde{P}^s) \tag{17-4b}$$

which will also be zero if the expectations hypothesis holds.

Another way to look at the situation is to imagine a speculator who posts 100% margin—i.e., P^f—in the form of interest-earning assets. If a long futures position is initiated at time zero and closed out just prior to the delivery date at time t, the following results will be obtained:

at time zero:
invest P^f (as interest-earning margin)

at time t:
value of margin $= (1 + r)P^f$
proceeds from closing out the futures position $= (\tilde{P}^s - P^f)$

actual return

$$
\begin{aligned}
1 + \tilde{r}_a &= \frac{(1 + r)P^f + (\tilde{P}^s - P^f)}{P^f} \\
&= (1 + r) + \left(\frac{\tilde{P}^s - P^f}{P^f}\right)
\end{aligned}
\tag{17-5a}
$$

where:

$\tilde{r}_a =$ the actual holding-period return on the position from time zero to time t

If the spot price turns out to exceed the futures price, a speculator with such a position will obtain a return greater than that obtained from riskless assets. If the futures price equals the *expected* spot price, a speculator will *expect* to earn only the riskless rate.

The situation faced by a speculator with a short position can be approached in the same manner:

at time zero:
invest P^f (as interest-earning margin)

at time t:
value of margin $= (1 + r)P^f$
proceeds from closing out the futures position $= (P^f - \tilde{P}^s)$

actual return:

$$1 + \tilde{r}_a = \frac{(1 + r)P^f + (P^f - \tilde{P}^s)}{P^f}$$

$$= (1 + r) + \left(\frac{P^f - \tilde{P}^s}{P^f}\right) \qquad \text{(17-5b)}$$

In this case actual return will exceed the riskless rate if the spot price turns out to be below the futures price. If the futures price equals the *expected* spot price, a short speculator (like a long speculator) can *expect* to earn only the riskless rate of interest.

The expectations hypothesis is often defended on the grounds that speculators are indifferent to risk and are thus happy to accommodate hedgers without any compensation in the form of a risk premium. This seems unlikely. However, as we have seen, the impact of a commodity position on the risk of a diversified portfolio that includes equities may be very small. Diversified investors should thus be willing to take over some risk from hedgers with little if any compensation in the form of expected returns over and above the riskless interest rate. This is the strongest argument in favor of the expectations hypothesis.

Figure 17-19 shows the pattern of futures prices implied by the expectations hypothesis, when the expected spot price does not change during the life of the contract.

John Maynard Keynes,[14] no stranger to speculative markets, felt that the expectations hypothesis did not correctly explain futures prices. He argued that hedgers wish to transfer risk to speculators, and that, on net, hedgers will be short the commodity and speculators will have to be long. To entice speculators to take such risks (i.e., to provide desired insurance), he suggested, the expected return from a *long* position would have to exceed the riskless rate. As formula (17-5a) shows, this requires the futures price to be less than the expected spot price. Such a relationship, termed *normal backwardation*, implies that the price of any futures contract can be expected to *rise* during its life, as shown in Figure 17-19.[15]

A contrary hypothesis holds that, on net, there is long hedging. Speculators must be enticed to take on *short* positions and be rewarded for doing so via expected returns exceeding the riskless rate. As formula (17-5b) shows, this requires the futures price to exceed the expected spot price. Such a relationship, which might be termed *normal contango*, implies that the price of any futures contract can be expected to *fall* during its life, as shown in Figure 17-19.[16]

A fourth hypothesis is that portrayed by the dashed curve in Figure 17-19. This approach[17] reflects the fact that hedgers may wish to attract

[14] J. M. Keynes, *Treatise on Money*, 2 (London: Macmillan, 1930), 142–44. By permission of Macmillan London and Basingstoke, and the International Economic Association.

[15] If expected spot prices for different delivery dates are the same, normal backwardation also implies that prices of futures with early delivery dates will exceed those with later delivery dates. In fact, to describe the relationship, Keynes adapted the term "backwardation," which characterizes a situation in which futures prices are below spot prices.

[16] If expected spot prices for different delivery dates are the same, normal contango will result in lower prices for futures with early delivery dates than those with later delivery dates. The term is derived from "contango," which describes a situation in which futures prices are above spot prices.

[17] See Paul H. Cootner, "Speculation and Hedging," Stanford University, *Food Research Institute Studies*, Supplement, 1967.

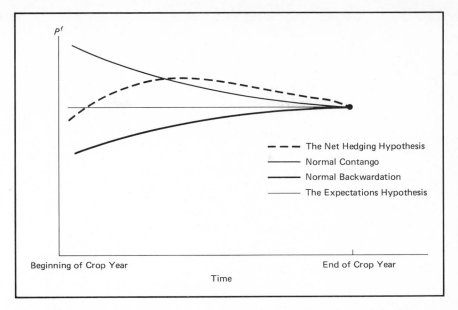

P^f

The Net Hedging Hypothesis
Normal Contango
Normal Backwardation
The Expectations Hypothesis

Beginning of Crop Year   End of Crop Year

Time

FIGURE 17-19 Price of a Futures Contract for Delivery at the End of the Crop Year When the Spot Price Expected at the Time of Delivery Does Not Change.

long speculators during the first part of a crop year when stocks are large, and short speculators during the latter part when stocks are small. If speculators have to be rewarded for bearing the risk involved, prices of futures contracts may be expected to rise when hedgers are short and speculators long, then fall when hedgers are long and speculators short. Another version holds that futures prices may be expected to rise when there is a large amount of net short hedging and fall when there is *either* a small amount of net short hedging *or* net long hedging.

The suggestion that hedgers may choose to be long on the futures market may seem surprising. At any time some people (e.g., farmers, grain elevator operators) with too much inventory for their comfort will wish to *short hedge*, while others (e.g., processors) with commitments in excess of inventories will wish to *long hedge*. When total stocks are large, the former may outnumber the latter, and there will be *net short hedging*, requiring speculators to make up the gap with long positions. As inventories fall, the balance may begin to shift, leading eventually to net long hedging, requiring speculators to make up the gap with short positions.

CURRENCY FUTURES

Anyone who has crossed a national border knows that there is an active market for foreign exchange, and that the rate at which one currency can be exchanged for another varies frequently. At any particular time, however, all such rates must be in conformance or else a riskless arbitrage situation would arise. For example, it is usually possible to exchange U.S. dollars for British pounds, then exchange the British pounds for French francs, and finally to exchange the French francs for dollars. If the three exchange rates were not in line, one might end up with more dollars at the end of this chain of transactions than at the beginning. Such an opportunity would attract large amounts of money, placing pressure on exchange rates and rapidly restoring balance. On the other hand, if a profit could be made by completing the circle in the opposite direction (dollars to francs to pounds to dollars), heavy pressure would soon move exchange rates accordingly, again restoring the balance.

Transactions costs and exchange restrictions limit the ability of arbitrageurs to exploit temporary imbalances among exchange rates. But the limits are still quite narrow.

The familiar market in foreign exchange, operated by banks, travel agents, etc., is in effect a *spot market*, since both the agreement on terms and the exchange of currencies occur at the same time. There are also markets for agreements involving future delivery of foreign exchange.

The largest such market is operated by banks and specialized brokers, maintaining close communications with each other throughout the world. Corporations, institutions, and some individuals deal in this market via large banks. Substantial amounts of money are involved, and every agreement is negotiated separately. Typical rates are quoted in the financial press.

This network of large institutions is generally termed the market for *forward exchange*, since standardized contracts are not used, and there is no organized secondary market.

The other market deals in futures contracts for foreign exchange. Procedures are similar to those used for commodity futures. For example, one of the *currency futures* contracts traded on the International Monetary Market of the Chicago Mercantile Exchange requires the seller to deliver 25,000 British pounds sterling to the buyer on a specified date for a number of U.S. dollars agreed upon in advance. Only the price of the transaction (expressed in dollars per British pound) is negotiated by the parties involved; all other terms are standard. Clearing procedures allow

FIGURE 17-20 Relationships Among Interest and Exchange Rates.

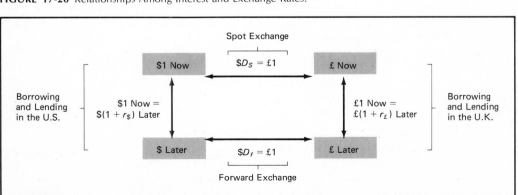

positions to be covered by reverse transactions, and few if any contracts result in the actual delivery of foreign currency. Price and volumes for such contracts are quoted with those for commodity futures in the financial press, as shown in Figure 17-1.

Markets for future foreign exchange, like markets for commodity futures, attract both hedgers and speculators. The former wish to reduce or possibly eliminate risk associated with planned future transfers of funds from one country to another. The latter hope to profit from a difference between the current rate for future exchange and the actual spot rates in the future. Contrary to popular opinion, many institutions take speculative positions in addition to engaging in hedging operations for themselves and their customers.

Interest-Rate Parity

Using U.S. dollars and British (U.K.) pounds, Figure 17-20 illustrates the relationship among (1) the spot exchange rate, (2) the interest rate in the U.S., (3) the interest rate in the U.K., and (4) the forward exchange rate. All four links are two-way. Thus it is possible to trade D_s dollars now for one pound now, or vice versa. It is also possible to contract now to trade D_f dollars for one pound "later." On the U.S. domestic market for loans a dollar now can be traded for $(1 + r_s)$ dollars later, or vice versa, while on the U.K. domestic market a pound now can be traded for $(1 + r_£)$ pounds later, or vice versa.

This circle of possible transactions allows one to trade any of the four items for any other in either of two ways—clockwise or counterclockwise—in Figure 17-20. For example, if one pound later is desired, with payment in dollars later, a contract can be made directly on the forward exchange or currency futures market to:

pay D_f dollars later and receive 1 pound later

Alternatively, the other three links can be used:

Now:
(1) borrow $D_s/(1 + r_£)$ dollars in the U.S.,
(2) exchange these dollars for $1/(1 + r_£)$ pounds, and
(3) lend these pounds in the U.K.
Later:
(1) receive the proceeds of the loan in the U.K.

$$= (1 + r_£) \left(\frac{1}{1 + r_£} \right) = 1 \text{ pound}$$

(2) pay off the loan in the U.S.

$$= (1 + r_s) \left(\frac{D_s}{1 + r_£} \right) \text{ dollars}$$

Since only other people's money is used in the initial period, the net effect is to:

pay $\left(\dfrac{1 + r_\$}{1 + r_\$} D_s\right)$ dollars later and receive 1 pound later

If markets are in balance, the two procedures should give the same results. Thus:

$$\left(\frac{1 + r_\$}{1 + r_\pounds}\right) D_s = D_f \tag{17-6a}$$

Rearranging and omitting a term of secondary importance:

$$\left(\frac{D_f - D_s}{D_s}\right) \approx r_\$ - r_\pounds \tag{17-6b}$$

This is known as the *interest-rate parity theorem*, which holds that the percentage difference between forward and spot exchange rates will equal the difference between interest rates in the two countries.

If interest-rate parity did not hold, and if there were no transactions costs, exchange restrictions, or transfer risk (i.e., possibility of future exchange restrictions), it would be possible to make money with no risk by running the circle in the appropriate direction. Of course, such ideal conditions are not found in the real world. Thus interest-rate parity only holds approximately.

During February 1980 *The Wall Street Journal* quoted the following rates for British pounds:

spot:	$2.3005
180-day futures:	$2.2737

Applying formula (17-6b):

$$\left(\frac{2.2737 - 2.3005}{2.3005}\right) = -.012 = r_\$ - r_\pounds$$

At the same time, rates for West German Deutschemarks were:

spot:	$.5749
180-day futures:	$.5935

Which implied:

$$r_\$ - r_{DM} = .032$$

To a major extent, differences in interest rates can be attributed to differences in expected rates of inflation. In 1980 the expected rate of inflation for the U.K. could well have exceeded that for the U.S. by 1.2% per 180 days, or 2.4% per year. And the expected rate of inflation in the U.S. could have exceeded that for West Germany by 3.2% per 180 days, or 6.4% per year. It is not surprising that at the time people expected exchange rates to move against the pound and in favor of the Deutschemark.

While arbitrage maintains a close relationship among exchange rates and interest rates, none is in any sense determined by the others. Instead, all are determined jointly by present and future levels of international trade, the demand and supply for loans, and estimates of future rates of inflation. Anyone who believes he or she has superior ability to predict such factors can attempt to profit by speculating, using either one of the markets for currency futures or the spot market plus the loan markets in the two countries. Transactions costs, margin and collateral requirements, etc. will determine the relative advantages of the various alternatives for any particular speculator or hedger.

FUTURES MARKETS FOR FINANCIAL INSTRUMENTS

Chapter 4 discussed the concept of the forward interest rate: the terms of a loan to be made at some future date and repaid subsequently, but with the rate of interest negotiated now. Forward loans can be made implicitly by issuing short-term instruments and using the proceeds to purchase longer-term instruments. But such procedures may be cumbersome. Instead, an explicit forward interest market may be utilized.

A good example is provided by the futures markets for three-month U.S. Treasury bills. As Figure 17-1 indicates, in December 1979 someone purchased a contract calling for delivery in December 1980 of $1,000,000 face value of three-month Treasury bills maturing in March of 1981 for a "price" of 90.83. More precisely, the seller of the contract was obligated to deliver the bills in December 1980 for an amount that would make the return, stated on a discount basis, equal to 9.17% per year. As shown in Chapter 11, the actual discount was thus:

$$\frac{90}{360} \times 9.17\% = 2.2925\%$$

and the purchaser agreed to pay $(1.0 - .022925) \times \$1,000,000$, or $977,075 in December 1980 for Treasury bills that would provide $1,000,000 in March 1981.

As with commodity futures, neither the buyer nor the seller of a contract must hold a position until the delivery date. Reversing trades can be made at any time, and relatively few contracts result in actual delivery.

As Figure 17-1 shows, in December 1979 the structure of three-month forward rates[18] was downward-sloping, with discounts ranging from 11.09% for March 1980 delivery to 9.15% for December 1981 delivery. If the expectations hypothesis characterizes this market, such rates can be considered unbiased estimates of future spot rates. If forward rates include a liquidity premium, forward rates will exceed expected future spot rates. In either event, it seems likely that at the time the consensus opinion of investors held that three-month rates could be expected to decline over the next two years.

---

[18] Strictly speaking, the rates in Figure 17-1 are *futures* rates, not *forward* rates. Since a futures contract is *marked to market* every day, with the parties required to put up cash for decreases in value and allowed to remove cash for increases in value, it differs from a pure forward contract. This difference often leads to disparities between futures rates and forward rates implicit in the prices of instruments of different maturities.

FIGURE 17-21 Characteristics of Active Futures Contracts for Financial Instruments, December 1979

FUTURES CONTRACTS ON TREASURY SECURITIES

	TREASURY BILLS				INTERMEDIATE-TERM TREASURY COUPON SECURITIES		TREASURY BONDS	
	ACE	COMEX	IMM	IMM	CBT	IMM	ACE	CBT
Deliverable items	$1 million par value of Treasury bills with 90, 91, or 92 days to maturity	$1 million par value of Treasury bills with 90, 91, or 92 days to maturity	$1 million par value of Treasury bills with 90, 91 or 92 days to maturity	$250,000 par value of Treasury bills due in 52 weeks	$100,000 par value of Treasury notes and noncallable bonds with 4 to 6 years to maturity	$100,000 par value of Treasury notes maturing between 3½ years and 4½ years	$100,000 par value of Treasury bonds with at least 20 years to maturity	$100,000 par value of Treasury bonds with at least 15 years to first call or to maturity
Initial margin* (per contract)	$800	$800	$1,500	$600	$900	$500	$2,000	$2,000†
Maintenance margin* (per contract)	$600	$600	$1,200	$400	$600	$300	$1,500	$1,600†
Daily limits‡	50 basis points	60 basis points	50 basis points	50 basis points	1 point (32/32)	¾ point (48/64)	1 point (32/32)§	2 points (64/32)
Delivery months (each year)	January, April, July, October	February, May, August, November	March, June, September, December	March, June, September, December	March, June, September, December	February, May, August, November	February, May, August, November	March, June, September, December
Total open interest (December 31, 1979)	106	913	36,495	435	715	265	207	90,676
Date trading began	June 26, 1979	October 2, 1979	January 6, 1976	September 11, 1978	June 25, 1979	July 10, 1979	November 14, 1979	August 22, 1977

FUTURES CONTRACTS ON NON-TREASURY SECURITIES

	GOVERNMENT NATIONAL MORTGAGE ASSOCIATION (MODIFIED PASS-THROUGH MORTGAGE-BACKED CERTIFICATES)				COMMERCIAL PAPER	
	CBT (old)	CBT (new)	ACE	COMEX	CBT (30-day)	CBT (90-day)
Deliverable items	Collateralized depository receipt covering $100,000 principal balance of GNMA certificates	$100,000 principal balance of GNMA certificates	$100,000 principal balance of GNMA certificates	$100,000 principal balance of GNMA certificates	$3 million face value of prime commercial paper rated A-1 by Standard & Poor's and P-1 by Moody's	$1 million face value of prime commercial paper rated A-1 by Standard & Poor's and P-1 by Moody's
Initial margin* (per contract)	$2,000	$2,000	$2,000	$1,500	$1,500	$1,500
Maintenance margin* (per contract)	$1,500	$1,500	$1,500	$1,125	$1,200	$1,200
Daily limits‡	1½ points (48/32)	1½ points (48/32)	¾ point (24/32)§	1 point (64/64)	50/100 point	50/100 point
Delivery months (each year)	March, June, September, December	March, June, September, December	February, May, August, November	January, April, July, October‖	March, June, September, December	March, June, September, December
Total open interest (December 31, 1979)	88,982	4,478	3,248	64	12	533
Date trading began	October 20, 1975	September 12, 1978	September 12, 1978	November 13, 1979	May 14, 1979	September 26, 1977

All specifications are as of year-end 1979.

* The speculative margin is shown where margins vary according to whether the contracts cover speculative, hedged, or spread positions.
† For all contracts but those which mature in current month. Then initial margin is increased to $2,500 and maintenance margin is raised to $2,000.
‡ Exchanges frequently have rules allowing expansion of daily limits once they have been in effect for a few days (margins may change also).
§ Limits in suspension as of the year-end.
‖ Principal trading months; rules allow trading for current plus two succeeding months.

Source: Marcelle Arak and Christopher J. McCurdy, "Interest Rate Futures," *Federal Reserve Bank of New York Quarterly Review,* Winter 1979–1980.

Figure 17-21 provides information on "interest-rate futures" contracts actively traded at the end of 1979. As indicated by the open interest figures, the major markets at the time were the three oldest: the International Monetary Market's three-month Treasury bill, and the Chicago Board of Trade's Treasury bond and Government National Mortgage Association pass-through contracts.

GNMA futures provide a convenient device for hedging by institutions active in the mortgage market. Mortgage bankers can short hedge to offset exposure to interest-rate fluctuations arising from the issuance of mortgages not yet assembled into a pool for subsequent resale. Savings and loan companies can long hedge to "lock in" current interest rates for funds they expect to receive in the near future. And speculators who believe they can predict interest rates more accurately than others can attempt to exploit such skills in this market.

As shown in Figure 17-1, prices for longer-term instruments are generally stated in terms of "points"—percentages of par value for representative instruments. A yield-to-maturity corresponding to the settlement price is also shown.

Given sufficient interest, almost anything can be the subject of futures trading. Where there is risk, there will be a demand for insurance. Futures markets accommodate this demand and facilitate speculation as well. In the future, as in the past, new markets will open and old ones will close as dictated by the interests of hedgers and speculators.

Problems

1. Do exchange-imposed price limits protect the futures trader from losses that would result in the absence of price limits?

2. Is a contango relationship consistent with the thesis that, on net, hedgers hold short positions?

3. With reference to futures trading, explain what long hedging is and give an example. Also give an example of short hedging. Cite the occupations of the hedgers in your examples.

4. What are some differences between a futures contract and a call option?

5. In early 1980, the spot and one-year forward rates for Swiss francs were $.6968 and .6700, respectively. What risk-free interest rate on Swiss francs would be consistent with the interest-rate-parity theorem if the one-year risk-free rate on U.S. dollars was 15% at the time?

6. Based on the information in Figure 17-1, what can be said about investors' opinions on December 21, 1979 concerning:
   a. The prospects for near-term inflation in West Germany relative to the prospects in the United States?

b. Interest rates on U.S. Treasury bonds in 1982?

c. Interest rates on GNMA pass-through certificates in 1982?

d. Interest rates on three-month U.S. Treasury bills at the end of 1981?

e. Changes in the price of orange juice between November 1980 and January 1981?

f. The trend in the price of gold over the next two years?

7. According to Figure 17-1, in December 1979 it was possible to buy a January 1980 contract in gold at the New York Commodity Exchange for $487.50 per ounce and sell an October 1981 contract for $614.80 on the same day. Would this have been profitable? Exactly what could you have done if you had taken these positions? Is the rate of interest at the time relevant in this context?

8. Assume you are convinced that the spread between long- and short-term interest rates is going to narrow within the next few months but do not know whether rates in general will be higher or lower than they are at present. Other investors disagree with your prediction: they expect the spread to remain constant. How could you profit from your superior predictive ability by using the markets for futures in financial instruments?

9. A publication used by farmers provides diagrams of the typical annual patterns of "cash prices" for a number of seasonal commodities. Should one expect that the price of a futures contract should follow the same pattern as the cash price of the commodity for which it is written? Why or why not? What kind of pattern might one expect a futures price to follow? Why?

10. In early 1980 a number of exchanges presented proposals for approval of futures contracts on stock market indices. For example, a contract might be written calling for delivery of one share of each of the 30 stocks in the Dow Jones Industrial Average. Assume that the DJIA is now 1,000 and that the price for delivery a year hence (stated on the same basis) is 1,300. If you could borrow money at an interest rate of 20%, what would you do? What if the price for delivery a year hence were 1,100 and you could buy one-year Treasury bills with a yield of 20%? Is a contract of this sort likely to provide good information on whether "people expect the stock market to go up or down" (as some have asserted)?

Investment Companies

18

INVESTMENT COMPANY FUNCTIONS

Investment companies are *financial intermediaries*. They obtain money and invest it in financial assets (e.g., stocks, bonds, commercial paper). The people who provide the money are given claims on the assets and the earnings from them. The process typically involves the *packaging* of a set of assets into a single combination. If only one type of claim is issued each claimant owns a proportionate share of the package of assets. However, some companies issue two or more types of claims. In effect, the assets originally packaged together are *repackaged*. A clear example is provided by a dual fund that divides a package of medium-risk assets into a set of relatively low-risk claims with regular payments (the income shares) and a set of relatively high-risk claims with deferred payments (the capital shares).

Investment companies can:

1. *administer* an account: prepare tax records, reinvest dividends, etc.
2. *diversify* a portfolio: hold many different securities
3. *tailor* a portfolio: select investments meeting a specified set of conditions (e.g., high yield, medium risk, etc.)
4. *control* a portfolio: insure that the specified set of conditions continues to be met
5. *select* securities that seem to be mispriced, in an attempt to "outperform"—i.e., achieve a higher return relative to risk than available elsewhere.

Economies of scale make it possible for a firm to perform the first four functions at a lower cost per dollar of investment than would be incurred by a small investor. Given a sufficiently large number of investors with similar objectives, the potential advantages to be gained from joint investment through an investment company may well outweigh any disadvantages.

The fifth function is subject to more dispute. Many investment company managers hope to identify areas of inefficiency in the market, exploit them, and share the resultant abnormal gains with investors by charging less for their services than they add in value. Unfortunately, they may instead fail to find abnormal situations while incurring additional costs in the form of increased management fees, transactions costs resulting from continuing turnover of the portfolio, and inadequate diversification.

Investment companies differ in many ways, and classification is difficult. We will follow common practice and restrict the term to apply to financial intermediaries that do not obtain money from "depositors." Thus savings and loan companies and banks will be excluded. However, the distinction is becoming increasingly a semantic and legal one, since some investment companies (the "money market funds") provide check-writing services.

MAJOR TYPES OF INVESTMENT COMPANIES

The United States Investment Company Act of 1940 classifies investment companies as follows:[1]

> unit investment trusts
> management companies
>> closed-end companies
>> open-end companies

Unit Investment Trusts

In the United Kingdom, a "unit trust" is an open-end investment company (described in a later section). In the United States the term is used in a more limited sense to refer to a *fixed* unit trust—i.e., a company with a portfolio that is, in essence, fixed for the life of the fund.

To form a unit trust, a *sponsor* (e.g., a large brokerage firm) purchases a specific set of securities, deposits them with a *trustee* (e.g., a bank or trust company), and receives in turn a number of shares representing proportional interest in those securities. These shares, known as *redeemable trust certificates*, are then sold to investors by the sponsor. All income received from the portfolio is paid out by the trustee to shareholders, as are any repayments of principal. Only in exceptional circumstances is the portfolio altered. There is no active management of a unit trust, only the custodial and administrative services provided by the trustee. Correspondingly, fees charged during the life of the trust are low (e.g., $1.50 per year per $1,000 of asset value).

Most U.S. unit trusts hold fixed-income securities and expire after the last one has been paid off (or, possibly, sold). Durations range from six months for unit trusts of "money market" instruments to over twenty years for trusts of "bond market" instruments. Some trusts include only federal government bonds, others only corporate bonds, others only municipal bonds, etc.

The sponsor of a unit trust will, of course, wish to be compensated for the effort and risk involved. This is accomplished by setting a selling

[1] Another classification covers certain companies that issue "face-amount certificates" promising specific payments. This type of company is rare and will not be discussed here.

price for the shares that exceeds the cost of the underlying assets. For example, a brokerage firm might purchase $10 million worth of bonds, place them in a unit trust, and issue 1 million shares. Each share might be offered for $10.35. If all were sold, the sponsoring organization could cover the cost of the portfolio and have $350,000 left for selling expenses and profit. Markups, or *load charges*, of this sort range from less than 1% for short-term trusts to 3.5% for long-term trusts.

Dealers in fixed-income securities generally quote both bid and ask (offer) prices. The bid price is the amount the dealer will pay for a security; the ask, or offer, price is the amount an investor must pay to purchase the security. Most unit trusts redeem shares at *net asset value* calculated on the basis of *bid* prices. First the value of the portfolio is determined, using dealers' bid quotations; then this amount is divided by the number of shares outstanding to obtain the net asset value per share. When a share is presented for redemption, the trustee simply sells one or more securities to raise the required cash.

Many fund sponsors make a market in the shares of the trusts they create. Shares are purchased at prices above the net asset value used by the fund for redemption. Typically the sponsor's price is determined by valuing the fund's securities using dealers' ask (offer) quotations. Shares acquired in this manner, and any left over from the initial offering, are offered for sale by the sponsor at a still higher price—usually the current purchase price plus a load charge equal to that in effect at the time the trust was created.

Management Companies

Unit trusts have no board of directors and no managers as such. Other investment companies have both. In theory, the board of directors, elected by shareholders, hires a firm—the "management company"—to manage the fund for a fee based at least in part of the total value of the fund. In practice, however, the management company is usually the business entity that started and promoted the fund. One management company may have contracts to manage a number of funds, each of which is a separate corporation with its own board of directors. Boards of directors of funds rarely fire management companies, and management companies sometimes sell the "right" to manage a fund to other firms. In form, directors choose managers; in substance, the reverse is often closer to the truth.

Annual management fees range from less than $\frac{1}{4}$ of 1% of the value of net assets to well over 1% of net assets. Fees are usually based on the market value of the fund's total assets, with the percentage sometimes declining as the value increases. This provides management a certain amount of incentive to perform well; the better the fund's performance, other things equal, the larger the value of its assets.

In addition to the fee paid by a fund to its management company, there are administrative and custodial expenses. These services are usually provided by the management company, but the costs are charged to the fund. Total annual expenses, including the management fee per se, average well below 1% of the value of all assets for large investment companies. Many funds require their management company to cover all costs over a specified amount, effectively limiting total expenses, typically to 1% to 2% of the net asset value.[2]

Funds may be managed by independent management companies, investment advisers, firms associated with brokers, or insurance companies.

Closed-End Funds

Unit trusts are *closed* in one direction—the number of shares outstanding cannot be increased. However, they are *open* in the other direction—the number can be reduced whenever someone decides to redeem shares.

Investment companies that do not stand ready to redeem shares continuously are termed *closed-end funds*. Most (but not all) have unlimited lives. Dividends and interest obtained from the portfolio are paid out to shareholders, as are realized capital gains, less realized capital losses. However, most funds allow (and encourage) the reinvestment of such payments. The fund keeps the money and sends the investor additional shares based on the net asset value per share, obtained by computing the market value of all assets, subtracting any liabilities, and dividing by the number of shares outstanding. For example, immediately after a dividend of $1 per share, if net asset value were $15 per share, the holder of 30 shares would be given the option of receiving either $30 ($= 30 \times \$1$) or 2 shares ($= \$30/\$15$). This feature allows a fund (and its management) to increase in size and makes it partially open-ended in one direction.

Closed-end funds are corporations whose assets are invested in other securities. Like other corporations, most such funds can issue new shares via stock offerings. However, this is done infrequently, not continuously, and the corporation's capital structure is "closed" most of the time.

Most closed-end funds can repurchase their own shares in the open market. Whenever market price falls well below net asset value, repurchase of shares will increase the fund's net asset value per share. For example, if net asset value per share were $20 and shares could be purchased for $16, the managers could sell $20 worth of securities from the fund's portfolio, buy back one of the fund's outstanding shares, and have $4 left over. If the $4 were burned, the net asset value of the remaining shares would still be $20; if it were added to the fund, the net asset value per share would increase.

Managers of closed-end funds rarely seize opportunities of this sort, perhaps because their fee is a function of the total value of assets managed. However, some do reinvest shareholders' dividends by purchasing shares in the open market when the price falls below net asset value.

In the 1930s, closed-end funds in the United States engaged in highly creative financing. Money was obtained via bank loans, and by issuing bonds, preferred stocks, and warrants, in addition to the sale of common stock. This made the valuation of the various claims on a fund an interesting exercise and provided otherwise unavailable investment

---

[2] Wiesenberger Investment Companies Service, *Investment Companies, 1979.* By permission from the *Wiesenberger Investment Companies Service*, 39th Annual Edition. Copyright © 1979, Warren, Gorham and Lamont Inc., 210 South Street, Boston, Mass. All rights reserved.

opportunities. Restrictions incorporated in the Investment Company Act of 1940 put a damper on such activities. Perhaps as importantly, investors' interest in managed funds using diverse forms of financing appears to have waned, and most closed-end funds now have few if any claims outstanding besides those of their common stock holders. Some preferred issues remain, and a few warrants. But only dual funds and a few similar institutions provide examples of this sort of repackaging of the prospects packaged together in a fund's portfolio.

Dual Funds

A *dual closed-end fund* has two important characteristics: when the fund is started, money is raised by issuing two quite different types of claims; and the fund's life as initially constituted is limited.

When formed, dual funds usually issue equal dollar amounts of *income* and *capital* shares. The holders of income shares receive all dividends and interest earnings from the fund's portfolio up to a specified *termination date*. At that time they also receive a stated *redemption* (par) value, or the value of the fund's portfolio, whichever is smaller. During each year of the fund's life, income shareholders are entitled to specified *minimum dividend payments*; any shortfalls are added to the redemption value to determine their total claim at termination.

Prior to the termination of a dual fund, capital shareholders receive little[3] or nothing. At termination, they are entitled to anything left over after the income shareholders have been paid off.

Termination usually is scheduled to occur between twelve and twenty years after the date on which a fund is formed. At termination the income shares must be paid off. In addition, the entire fund may be liquidated, and all shareholders paid off in cash; alternatively, the fund may be converted to a standard closed-end or open-end investment company, with only one class of shares outstanding.

Some dual funds' charters place restrictions on investment policies, but most managers enjoy wide latitude. This adds significantly to the uncertainty faced by the holder of either type of share. Any change in a fund's portfolio that does not alter its total market value should have little if any effect on the total value of all the claims on that portfolio. But if the portfolio's risk is increased, the risk of the income shares, which have *restricted* claims on the portfolio, will generally increase as well. This will tend to lower the value of the income shares and, since the total value of all shares will have changed little if at all, raise the value of the capital shares. Conversely, a decrease in the risk of the portfolio will generally benefit the income shareholders at the expense of the capital shareholders. Since neither type of shareholder knows for certain just what types of investments will be made by the managers in the future, uncertainty is increased. Possible benefits associated with holding either of the two types of shares may thus be partially or wholly offset.

There is nothing unique about dual funds in this regard. By changing the riskiness of a corporation's activities, management can alter the

---

[3] Tax considerations have led some companies to distribute limited amounts of realized capital gains prior to termination.

distribution of value between those with fixed claims (e.g., bondholders) and those with residual claims (e.g., stockholders). Bond indentures can guard against extreme abuses through restrictions on dividend payments, etc. More important, operating corporations are not often motivated to make major changes of this sort. The cost of converting from steel production to oil drilling to alter risk is too great to incur simply to reallocate value from bondholders to stockholders. But it is neither difficult nor very costly for an investment company to radically alter the risk of its portfolio.

Closed-End Fund Price Quotations

Shares of closed-end funds are traded through brokers at prices agreed upon by the parties involved. Some are listed on national exchanges and are fairly actively traded. Others change hands only rarely. There is no necessary relationship between the *price* of such a share and its net asset value. If a fund does not stand ready to redeem shares or to buy them in the open market at net asset value, there is no obvious floor under the price. And if new shares cannot be purchased from the fund at the net asset value, there is no obvious ceiling.

At the end of 1978 there were approximately 60 closed-end funds in the United States, managing portfolios worth approximately $6.1 billion.[4]

The net asset values of regular *closed-end fund shares*, based on security values computed using Friday's closing market prices, are published in the financial press. Figures 18-1(A) and 18-1(B) provide examples. Both the net asset value and the last price at which the fund's shares

[4] Wiesenberger Investment Companies Service, *Investment Companies*, 1979. By permission from the *Wiesenberger Investment Companies Service*, 39th Annual Edition. Copyright © 1979, Warren, Gorham and Lamont Inc., 210 South Street, Boston, Mass. All rights reserved.

FIGURE 18-1 Closed-end Fund Net Asset Value and Price Quotations. (a) Equity and Convertible Bond Funds; (b) Bond Funds.

Source: Reprinted with permission of *The Wall Street Journal*, © Dow Jones & Company, Inc. (a) December 24, 1979. (b) March 26, 1980. All Rights Reserved.

Publicly Traded Funds

Friday, December 21, 1979

Following is a weekly listing of unaudited net asset values of publicly traded investment fund shares, reported by the companies as of Friday's close. Also shown is the closing listed market price or a dealer-to-dealer asked price of each fund's shares, with the percentage of difference.

	N.A. Value	Stk Price	% Diff
Diversified Common Stock Funds			
AdmExp	z	z	z
BakerFen	80.31	53½	−33.4
GenAInv	18.31	15⅜	−16.0
Lehman	16.25	12¾	−21.5
Madison	22.92	18⅝	−18.7
NiagaraSh	18.57	15⅛	−18.5
OseasSec	5.22	4⅛	−21.0
Source	23.73	19⅜	−18.4
Tri-Contl	25.68	19½	−24.1
US&For	25.02	18⅞	−24.6
Specialized Equity and Convertible Funds			
aAmGnCv	26.48	20¼	−23½
bASA	46.49	35⅛	−24.5
BancrftCv	26.29	21¼	−20.3
Castle	24.40	19	−22.1
CentSec	10.14	7	−31.0
ChaseCvB	12.21	10⅝	−13.0
Claremont	19.26	14	−27.3
CLAS	z	z	z
CLAS Pfd	z	z	z
Cyprus	1.32	2¾	+08.0
aDrexelUt	18.27	18	− 1.5
Engex	8.06	5¾	−28.7
Japan	11.23	9¼	−17.6
Nautilus	16.02	13	−18.8
NewAmFd	28.33	21¾	−23.2
Pete&Res	z	z	z
RETIncC	3.61	3½	− 3.1
ValueLn	4.27	3⅛	−26.0

a-Ex-Dividend. b-As of Thursday's close. z-Not available.

(a)

Closed-End Bond Funds

Tuesday, March 25, 1980

Unaudited net asset values of closed-end bond fund shares, reported by the companies as of Friday, March 21, 1980. Also shown is the closing listed market price or a dealer-to-dealer asked price of each fund's shares, with percentage of difference.

	N.A. Value	Stk Price	% Diff
AmGenBD	17.71	15⅞	−10.4
BunkerHill	17.45	14⅞	−14.8
CircleInc	11.16	9⅝	−13.8
aCNAInc	9.62	9	− 6.5
bCurrentI	8.98	8¼	− 8.1
DrexelBd	15.50	13½	−12.9
Excelsior	15.52	13½	−13.0
bFdIncPP	8.29	7⅜	−11.0
FtDearInc	10.95	9⅞	− 9.8
Hatteras	14.02	12⅛	−13.5
INAInvS	15.62	13	−16.8
IndSqIs	14.75	13⅛	−11.0
Intercap	16.32	14⅜	−11.9
JHanInv	17.23	14	−18.7
JHanSec	12.77	11½	−10.0
MMIncInv	10.20	9¼	− 9.3
MntgSt	16.10	14½	− 9.9
MuOmahI	12.34	10⅝	−13.9
PacAmInc	11.87	9¾	−17.9
StPaulS	9.45	8⅜	−11.4
StateMSec	9.93	8½	−14.4
TransamI	17.08	15¾	− ⅞
USLIFE	8.66	7¾	−10.5

a-Ex-Dividend. b-Thursday's close.

(b)

Dual Purpose Funds

Friday, December 21, 1979

Following is a weekly listing of the unaudited net asset values of dual-purpose, closed-end investment funds' capital shares as reported by the companies as of Friday's close. Also shown is the closing listed market price or the dealer-to-dealer asked price of each fund's capital shares, with the percentage of difference.

	Cap. Shs. Price	N.A. Val Cap. Shs.	% Diff.
Gemini	26¼	31.12	−15.6
Hemisphere	2¾	1.09	+152.3
Income and Cap	7⅝	9.73	−21.6
Leverage	19⅝	23.75	−17.4
Putnam Duo Fund	11¼	13.34	−15.7
Scudder Duo-Vest	9¾	11.87	−17.9
Scudder D-V Exch	22	31.55	−30.3

Lipper Analytical Distributors.

FIGURE 18-2 Dual Fund Net Asset Value and Price Quotations.

traded on the day in question are shown (if no trade price is available, the last dealer's asked price is indicated). The final column indicates the associated percentage discount (if negative) or premium (if positive).

Figure 18-2 provides an example of a weekly listing of prices and net asset values of dual fund capital shares. The net asset value is computed by summing the market values of the securities in a fund's portfolio, then subtracting the redemption (par) value of its outstanding income shares. The final column shows the percentage difference between the price and net asset value, so computed. Since income shares rarely sell at par, the economic significance of this figure is subject to dispute.

Closed-end shares listed on exchanges or actively traded over the counter are included in daily summaries of stock prices and volumes. However, net asset values are published only once each week.

Open-End Funds

A management investment company that stands ready to redeem shares at or near net asset value at all times is termed an *open-end fund* or, more commonly, a *mutual fund*. All such companies are open in at least one direction, since outstanding shares may be redeemed at the shareholders' discretion. Most are also open in the other direction. The fund continuously offers new shares for a price at or near net asset value.

When old shares are redeemed, securities in a fund's portfolio may be sold to raise the needed cash. Conversely, when new shares are issued, the proceeds may be used to purchase new securities for the portfolio. When some shares are redeemed and others sold in a single day at the same net asset value, only the net amount paid out or received need be used for the sale or purchase of securities in the fund's portfolio. To avoid excessive brokerage fees, most funds maintain a small average cash balance to cushion some of the day-to-day fluctuations in these flows.

A few funds charge a redemption fee (e.g., 2% of net asset value), but the vast majority redeem shares for their full net asset value.

Mutual Funds

Friday, December 21, 1979
Price ranges for investment companies, as quoted by the National Association of Securities Dealers. NAV stands for net asset value per share; the offering includes net asset value plus maximum sales charge, if any.

	NAV	Offer NAV Price Chg.		NAV	Offer NAV Price Chg.
Acorn Fnd	25.66	N.L. − .04	Industl	4.91	N.L. − .02
ADV Fund	12.29	N.L. + .01	Income	8.23	N.L. − .05
Afuture Fd	16.03	N.L. − .11	**First Investors Fund:**		
AGE Fund	3.94	4.25 ...	Bond Ap	(z)	(z) ...
Alpha Fnd	14.10	N.L. − .06	Cash Mg	1.00	(z) ...
Am Birthrt	10.90	11.91 − .05	Discovr	7.84	8.57 ...
American Funds Group:			Growth	9.24	10.10 − .05
Am Bal	8.14	8.90 − .04	Income	(z)	(z) ...
Amcap F	11.56	12.63 − .02	Optn⁻ Fd	6.60	7.12 − .01
Am Mutl	10.79	11.79 − .05	Stock Fd	7.39	8.08 − .04
An Gwth	7.98	8.72 − .04	Tx Exmt	9.70	10.46 ...
Bnd FdA	12.72	13.90 ...	Fst VRate	1.00	N.L. ...
Cash Mt	1.00	N.L. ...	44 Wall St	17.85	N.L. − .16
Fund Inv	7.27	7.95 − .05	Fnd Grwth	4.46	4.87 − .01
Gth FdA	10.11	11.05 − .05	**Founders Group Funds:**		
Inc FdA	7.69	8.40 − .03	Growth	x6.18	N.L. − .31
I C A	8.42	9.20 − .06	Income	13.45	N.L. + .01
Nw Prsp	7.18	7.85 − .02	Mutual	8.20	8.96 − .06
Wash Mt	6.76	7.39 − .05	Special	x14.91	N.L. − .42
American General Group:			**Franklin Group:**		
A GnCBd	7.45	8.14 − .01	Brwn Fd	4.37	4.71 − .03
AG Entp	8.78	9.60 − .07	D N T C	10.77	11.61 − .01
High Yld	10.53	11.29 − .03	Growth	6.75	7.28 − .04
A G Mun	20.88	21.92 − .01	Income	1.94	2.09 ...
A G Res	⁻1.00	N.L. ...	Liqd Ast	1.00	N.L. ...
A GnVen	17.84	19.50 − .05	US GvSc	8.38	9.04 − .08
Comstk	10.31	11.27 − .02	Utilities	4.24	4.57 − .03
Eqty Gth	x8.92	9.75 − .34	Res Capt	6.71	7.23 + .12
Fd Amer	8.53	9.32 − .04	Res Eqty	4.76	5.13 − .02
Harbor	10.06	10.99 ...	Fundpack	5.36	5.44 ...
Pace Fd	20.97	22.92 − .05	**Funds Incp Group:**		
Prov Inc	3.66	3.95 ...	Cm IncS	8.71	N.L. − .01
Am Grwth	8.55	9.22 ...	Currt Int	1.00	N.L. ...
Am Heritg	2.53	N.L. + :16	Indus Tr	10.82	11.10 − .03
Am Ins Ind	4.87	5.32 − .03	Pilot Fd	9.89	N.L. − .03
Am Invest	9.08	N.L. − .12	GT Pac Fd	11.60	N.L. − .08
AmInv Inc	11.87	N.L. − .02	Gatewy Op	15.71	N.L. − .05
AmNat Gw	3.68	4.02 − .01	GE S&S Pr	29.64	N.L. − .17
Amway Mt	7.92	8.47 + .02	Genl Secur	11.12	N.L. − .14
Am Opt Eq	(z)	(z) ...	Grad CRsv	1.00	N.L. ...
Axe-Houghton:			Grth IndSh	27.04	N.L. + .07
Fund B	7.72	8.39 − .01	**Hamilton Group:**		
Income	4.31	4.68 ...	Fund	4.51	4.93 − .03
Stock Fd	7.20	7.87 − .03	Growth	8.94	9.77 − .07
BLC Gwth	14.38	15.72 − .04	Ihcome	7.26	N.L. ...
Babsn Inc	1.55	N.L. ...	Hartwll Gt	22.56	N.L. − .11
Babsn Inv	10.98	N.L. − .03	Hartwll Lv	15.14	N.L. − .13
Beacon Gr	10.18	N.L. ...	HiYld Sec	10.08	10.78 − .01
Beacon Hll	10.12	N.L. − .05	Holding Tr	1.00	N.L. ...
Berger Group Funds:			Horace Mn	17.44	18.85 − .13
100 Fund	10.52	N.L. ...	INA HiYld	10.34	11.09 ...
101 Fund	9.35	N.L. − .02	IndsFd Am	5.61	N.L. + .03
Bondsk Cp	6.04	6.60 − .07	Intcap HiY	14.47	15.31 + .01
Bos Found	9.46	10.34 − .02	Intercap	1.00	N.L. ...
Bull & Bear Group:			Int Investr	23.41	25.58 + .44
Capam	x9.23	N.L. − .14	Inv Guidan	12.22	N.L. − .05
Capitl Sh	9.70	N.L. − .05	Inv Indicat	1.26	(z) − .01
Golcnd	10.33	N.L. + .17	Inv Tr Bos	x10.60	11.43 − .14
Calvin Bullock Funds:			**Investors Group Funds:**		
Bullock	13.96	15.26 − .04	IDS Bnd	4.93	5.11 ...
Canadn	8.34	9.11 ...	IDS Cash	1.00	N.L. ...
Div Shrs	2.68	2.93 − .02	IDS Gth	8.45	9.19 ...
Income	11.72	12.81 − .03	IDS HYd	4.51	4.70 ...
Ntwide	9.01	9.85 − .04	IDS nwD	6.98	7.59 − .04
Cash Rsrv	1.00	N.L. ...	IDS Prog	3.88	4.22 − .02
Cap Presv	1.00	N.L. ...	IDS Tax	4.16	4.33 ...
Cent Capitl	1.00	N.L. ...	Mutual	9.00	9.78 − .02
Century Sh	11.97	12.91 − .03	Stock Fd	19.66	21.36 − .07
Chan HlYd	10.80	11.58 + .01	Selectv	7.92	8.52 ...
Charter Fd	16.64	18.19 − .05	Var Pay	7.80	8.48 − .03
Chase Group of Boston:			Inv Resrch	5.52	6.03 − ⁰
Fnd Bost	7.47	8.16 − .02	**I S I Group:**		
Front Cp	5.96	6.51 + .01	Growth	⁄⁻	
ShTr Bos	7.60	8.31 − .03	Income		
Special	8.67	9.48 + .01	T⁻⁻		
Chem Fnd	8.56	9.36 − .07			
Chepsd Dol	14.88	N.l	z-Quote not available. NL-No load. x-Ex-dividend. r-Ex-rights. d Ex-distribution. a-funds redemption price.		
Colonial Funds:					
Fund					
Gro⁻⁻⁻					

FIGURE 18-3 Mutual Fund Net Asset Value Quotations.

Some open-end companies, known as *no-load funds*, sell their shares at net asset value. Others, known as *load funds*, offer shares through brokers or other selling organizations, which add a percentage *load charge* to the net asset value. The percentage charged is usually smaller, the greater the amount invested. For example, a selling organization receiving $1,000 to be invested in a fund might retain $85, leaving $915 to be used to purchase the fund's shares at the current net asset value per share. This is usually called a load charge of 8.5%, but it is actually 9.3% (85/915 = .093) of the amount ultimately invested. Load charges of this magnitude are levied by many funds for small purchases.

The performance of no-load funds as a whole does not differ in any systematic way from that of load funds. This is not surprising. The load charge, which goes to the selling organization, represents the cost of education and persuasion. Mail-order firms often sell items for less than stores. Salespersons who work in stores and those who sell mutual funds provide service and require compensation. Buyers who consider such services worth less than they cost can and should avoid paying for them.

Shares of load funds may not be resold by dealers at prices below that based on the stated schedule of load charges. Such resale price maintenance seems relatively harmless, since there are a great many similar open-end funds and an adequate number of no-load funds for those who prefer self-education.

At the end of 1978 there were over 700 open-end investment companies with assets worth approximately $58.1 billion. Of these, 254 were no-load funds, which held about $22 billion worth of assets.[5]

Figure 18-3 shows a portion of the quotations for mutual funds provided for each trading day in the financial press. The net asset value, based on closing prices for the fund's securities on the day in question, is shown first. This is followed by the "offer" price—the net asset value plus the load charge applicable to the smallest possible purchase; for no-load funds this column contains the letters "NL". The final column indicates the difference (in dollars) between the day's net asset value per share and that computed at the close of the previous trading day.

RELATED INVESTMENT MEDIA

A number of investment-company-like institutions exist. This section describes some of the more important types.

Variable Annuities

In 1952 the College Retirement Equities Fund, which serves as an investment medium for the faculty and staff of a number of academic and non-profit institutions, pioneered the concept of a variable annuity. Since then a number of insurance companies have developed similar plans.

Two quite different aspects are involved in such a plan. During an *accumulation period* the investor in effect contributes money periodically

[5] *Ibid.*

(e.g., monthly) to an open-end mutual fund, withdrawing nothing. Typically some sort of life insurance (e.g., a policy guaranteed to pay an amount equal to the total dollar value contributed) is included. The premium for this insurance is deducted from each contribution, along with any load charge, and the remainder used to purchase shares (or "units") of the fund.

At the end of the accumulation phase (usually upon retirement), the investor will hold shares with some current market value. He or she might cash in the shares and spend the money in any desired way (although many plans do not allow this). Alternatively, the money might be used to purchase a *fixed annuity*. This is a contract in which an insurance company promises to pay a given amount each month to the purchaser, until the latter dies. If a *joint survivor option* is included, payments continue (perhaps at a reduced amount), until the purchaser's spouse dies.

For rate-setting, insurance companies utilize *mortality tables*, which indicate the probabilities, based on experience, that persons of various ages will die within a year. While no one can predict the day on which a specific individual will die, it is possible to determine with reasonable accuracy how many of a large number of people in a given age group will die in each future year. When a group of 65-year-olds is sold a set of annuities, the insurance company that sells the policies can estimate the amount of cash required in each future year to meet its resulting obligations. This can be converted into a *present value* in one of two ways. The simplest procedure is to find the cost of a portfolio of default-free bonds that will produce cash on the required dates. If the insurance company were to buy such bonds, it could completely hedge its bets; thus the annuities could be sold for this amount plus commissions, sales charges, etc.

In practice this is rarely done. Instead, the present value of the annuity obligation is computed by discounting the expected payments using some low rate of interest. The insurance company hopes to earn a higher return on its portfolio, but must make up the difference if there is a shortfall. *Reserves* are maintained to cover the latter possibility. If and when actual returns exceed the assumed interest rate, some of the excess may be paid the insurance company's stockholders and/or returned to policyholders. The use of a low interest rate, along with "dividends" to holders of annuities, benefits those who live longer and thus receive such dividends, at the expense of those who die early and miss them.

The cost of a fixed annuity is a function of the stated amount (e.g., dollars to be received per month), the mortality characteristics of the purchaser at the time the annuity is written (based primarily on age and sex), and the assumed interest rate. Other things equal, the higher the interest rate utilized, the lower will be the stated cost of a fixed annuity.

A *variable annuity* is similar in many respects to a fixed annuity. But there is one major difference: the amount received every month is not fixed, but varies, depending on the investment experience of a fund. Risk is borne by the annuitant; moreover, assets are usually invested in common stocks instead of bonds, so there is more risk to be borne.

The procedure is best described with an example. Assume that at retirement the present value of a fixed annuity of $1 per month for a particular individual will be $100 based on an assumed rate of interest of 4%. If the person's account is worth $50,000 at the time, a fixed annuity paying

$500 (=$50,000/$100) can be purchased. Alternatively the money can be used to buy units of a variable annuity. If the current value of an *annuity unit* is $5, a total of 100 (=$500/$5) units can be purchased. Henceforth, the amount paid each month will vary with the value of an annuity unit. If the unit value falls to $4.50, the monthly check will fall to $450; if the value of a unit rises to $5.50, the check will rise to $550, etc.

The value of an annuity unit is determined by the experience of an investment fund. The procedure is straightforward. The percentage change in the value of the fund—including dividends, interest received, capital gains and/or losses (realized or not), less any expenses—is computed. From this the interest rate assumed in the original annuity valuation is subtracted. The value of each annuity unit is then increased or decreased by the difference. In effect, the insurance company pays itself a dividend equal to the amount required to cover the interest the company assumed it would receive when the annuities were priced; and this dividend is paid no matter what the experience of the fund might have been. Thus the risk is shifted from the insurance company to the purchasers of the annuities.

As with fixed annuities, the lower the assumed interest rate, the greater the relative benefits received by those who live longer and the smaller the relative benefits received by those who die early. Correspondingly, those holding variable annuities based on lower interest rates can expect greater increases in monthly payments over time than can those holding similar annuities based on higher interest rates.

To implement a variable annuity, an insurance company must set up a *separate account*, which may be invested directly in a diversified portfolio or simply used to purchase shares in an open-end mutual fund—usually one run by the same company. The separate account typically backs both *accumulation units*, similar to the shares of an open-end fund that pays no dividends, and *annuity units*. The former are relevant to the investor during the accumulation phase; the latter during the payout phase, after retirement.

Variable annuities are often advertised as providing at least a partial hedge against unanticipated inflation during one's retirement years. They will serve this function only to the extent that stock returns are positively correlated with this component of inflation. As shown in Chapter 10, this has not been the case in recent years.

Common stocks appear to provide higher expected returns than do bonds or fixed annuities. But they also provide greater risk. Such statements remain true even when returns are measured in real terms. Thus the choice between a variable and a fixed annuity is similar to that involved in most investment decisions. To what extent is a person willing to take on added risk to get a higher expected return? Although professional advisers can help assess the magnitudes involved, the final decision must rest with the individual who will bear the risk.

Commingled Funds

Banks and insurance companies invest money for individuals and organizations. Banks manage personal trust funds; both banks and insurance companies manage employee retirement funds. Any such fund can be invested on an individual basis, with specific securities selected and held in a separate account. This is often done for large accounts, but to capture economies of scale, small accounts are often *commingled*, allowing joint participation in one or more large pools of securities.

The vehicle utilized in this process is the *commingled fund*. In form it is similar to an open-end mutual fund.[6] The securities in the fund are valued at least once every three months, and the total value divided by the current number of *units* to determine a *net asset value per unit*. On any valuation date, money from an account may be used to purchase units at this value. Alternatively, units purchased previously may be redeemed at the current unit value.

A bank or insurance company may offer several commingled funds. One fund may hold only short-term money market instruments; another, long-term bonds; yet another, common stocks. A commingled fund investing in mortgages may be offered, as may one investing in real property.[7] When a complete menu of this sort is available, money from a given trust or employee retirement account can be invested in two or more commingled funds and/or in individual securities, as desired by the beneficiaries and the account manager.

Real Estate Investment Funds

The real estate investment trust (REIT), although not classified as an investment company for legal purposes, is similar to a closed-end fund. Like an investment company, it can serve as a conduit for earnings on investments, passing them on to claimants and avoiding corporate taxation.

REITs must invest primarily in real estate or loans secured by real estate. They can obtain capital by issuing stock, bonds (convertible or not), and even warrants. They can also borrow from banks, issue mortgages on some or all of their property, and issue commercial paper.

Like managed investment companies, REITs "hire" a management firm for a fee—typically about 1% of the value of assets per year. Most trusts are affiliated with bankss, life insurance companies, or mortgage firms, which set them up and serve as their investment managers.

The stocks of many real estate investment trusts are listed on major exchanges. Price and volume quotations are listed with those of other stocks in the financial press.

There are two major types of REITs. *Mortgage trusts* invest primarily in mortgages and construction and development loans. The latter, which constitute the bulk of the assets of many trusts, are loans made to the builder or developer of a project, with the property serving as collateral. The loans, generally fairly short-term, are made on the premise that the property will be finished on time and sold for an amount sufficient to allow the developer to pay off the loan on time and in full. *Equity trusts* invest in real estate property directly; in effect, they serve as landlords. The property may be financed in part by issuing mortgages. A few firms,

---

[6] But not in legal status, since by law, banks are not allowed to manage and sell mutual funds (e.g., only trust funds and employee retirement accounts may invest in a bank's commingled fund).

[7] Real property commingled funds may be only partially open-ended; owing to the illiquidity of the assets, some sponsoring organizations reserve the right to limit the redemption of units, either temporarily or until sale of the underlying property.

termed *mixed* or *hybrid* trusts, are neither predominantly mortgage nor equity trusts, but combine the two modes.

Most REITs are highly levered. A typical trust might issue fixed claims worth 70% of its total assets. Any fall in the value of the property held by such a firm will generally cause a greater percentage change in the value of its common stock, as will an adverse shift in the relationship between the interest paid on its short-term debt and that earned on its assets.

In the recession of 1973–74 the construction industry was particularly hard hit. This caused a large number of defaults on construction and development loans and on some long-term mortgages. Many REITs were left with half-finished buildings. Moreover, short-term interest rates, at which REITs traditionally obtain substantial amounts of capital, climbed above mortgage interest rates. From October 25, 1973, to August 19, 1974, the Dow-Jones Industrial Average fell 27%; an index of the prices of shares in equity REITs fell more than 50%; and an index of the prices of shares in mortgage REITs fell over 70%?[8] Many trusts went bankrupt, including some associated with extremely well-known (and reputedly conservative) financial institutions.

The experience of the early 1970s undoubtedly diminished the enthusiasm of those who invested heavily in REITs (especially those who failed to appreciate the fact that leverage increases risk as well as expected return). However, the poor initial results should not cause the rejection of the concept. Such trusts provide a vehicle for the inclusion of important types of assets in a portfolio. Owing to their specialized investment policies and typically high leverage, only a portion of an individual's assets should of course be invested in such securities. Properly utilized, however, they should be desirable investment media.

INVESTMENT POLICIES

Different funds follow different investment policies. Some are designed as substitutes for an investor's entire portfolio; others expect their investors to hold other securities, and possibly shares in other funds. Some restrict their domain and/or selection methods severely; others give their managers wide latitude. Many engage in highly active management, with substantial portfolio changes designed to exploit hoped-for superior investment predictions; others are more passive, concentrating instead on tailoring a portfolio to serve the interests of a particular clientele.

While categorization is difficult, and many funds pursue mixed strategies, broad classes can be identified.

Money market funds hold short-term (typically less than one year) fixed-income instruments such as bank certificates of deposit, high-grade commercial paper, bankers' acceptances, U.S. Treasury bills, etc. These open-end funds make it possible for small investors to move in and out of the portion of the short-term market in which interest rates are not regulated. When ceilings on small deposits at banks and savings and loan asso-

[8] "Real Estate Investment Trusts: A Background Analysis and Recent Industry Developments, 1961–1974," Economic Staff Paper 75, No. 1, Office of Economic Research, U.S. Securities and Exchange Commission (1975).

ciations become restrictive, it behooves an investor to consider joining others in a money market fund, thereby participating in a large deposit at a higher interest rate. The fund manager will extract a fee for this service, of course—usually between ¼ of 1% and 1% of the average asset value per year. There are usually no load charges, and money may be added to or removed from an account at almost any time. Dividends are usually declared daily. Arrangements with a cooperating bank often make it possible to write a check on an account—the bank obtains the amount involved by redeeming "shares" in the fund when the check clears.

A few *money market unit trusts* have been formed. Federal Deposit Insurance protection is extended to the holders of shares in such a trust; thus a $60,000 investment in the shares of a trust holding equal amounts of certificates of deposit in six different banks would be considered equivalent to deposit accounts of $10,000 in each of the banks. Similar protection is not accorded to the investor in an open-end money market fund.

The major expense for the holder of shares in a money market unit trust is the initial load charge (sponsor's markup)—approximately ¾ of 1% for a one-year trust.

Bond funds invest in fixed-income securities. Some go farther, specifying that only particular types of instruments will be purchased. There are high-grade bond funds, medium-grade bond funds, corporate bond funds, government bond funds, municipal bond funds, convertible bond funds, etc. Some are organized as open-end companies, but there are many closed-end bond funds. A number of the latter are run by subsidiaries of banks and insurance companies.

As indicated earlier, the predominant type of unit trust in the United States is the *bond unit trust*. Some are based on government issues, others on corporate issues, and still others on specialized types. Municipal bond unit trusts, like open-end municipal bond funds, make it easier for those in high tax brackets to obtain diversification and, possibly, increased liquidity while taking advantage of the exemption of such securities from personal income taxation.

Bond unit trusts typically hold securities with different coupon payment schedules and pay roughly equal dividends every month.

A few open-end companies and some unit trusts are restricted to holdings of *preferred stocks*. Others include both bonds and preferred stocks in their portfolios.

Many open-end companies consider themselves managers for the bulk of the investment assets of their clients. Funds that hold both equity and fixed-income securities particularly fit this description. Wiesenberger Investment Companies Service's annual *Investment Companies* manual classifies such companies as belonging to one of two groups. *Income funds* wish to "provide as liberal a current income from investments as possible."[9] *Balanced funds* wish to "minimize investment risks so far as this is possible, without unduly sacrificing possibilities for long-term growth and current income."[10] Some funds hold relatively constant mixes

---

[9] Wiesenberger Investment Companies Service, *Investment Companies, 1979*. By permission from the *Wiesenberger Investment Companies Service*, 39th Annual Edition. Copyright © 1979, Warren, Gorham and Lamont Inc., 210 South Street, Boston, Mass. All rights reserved.
[10] *Ibid*.

of bonds, preferred stock, convertible bonds, and/or equities; others alter the proportions periodically in attempts to "time the market."

In the United States the most popular type of open-end investment company is the *diversified common stock fund*. Such a firm invests most of its assets in common stocks, although short-term money market instruments may be held to accommodate irregular cash flows and/or to engage in some market timing.

In 1979, Wiesenberger's manual classified the majority of diversified common stock funds as having one of three types of objectives: (1) maximum capital gain, (2) growth, (3) growth and income. Two factors appear to be involved in this classification: the relative importance of dividend income versus capital gains and the overall level of risk to be taken. The classifications "are arranged in descending order of emphasis on capital appreciation and, consequently, in ascending order of the importance placed on current income and relative price stability."[11] Since high-yield portfolios are generally less risky than those with low yields, relatively few major conflicts arise, although two rather different criteria are involved.

Borderline cases remain: "The difference between a Capital Gain Fund and a Growth Fund is a matter of degree, and in some cases little distinction may exist. Similarly, there is no sharp line of demarcation between a Growth Fund and a Growth-Income Fund."[12] Classification is difficult because the official statement of objectives in a fund's prospectus is usually fuzzy, to say the least.

The Investment Company Act of 1940 defines a *diversified investment company* as one that invests at least 75% of its funds in a diversified manner: within this portion of the portfolio, no single issuer's securities may account for more than 5% of the fund's assets nor more than 10% of the value of such securities outstanding. Funds not meeting this standard are classified as *nondiversified investment companies*. Some choose the latter classification simply to maintain flexibility. Others do so to *specialize* in certain types of securities.

A few specialized funds concentrate on the securities of firms in a particular *industry*; there are chemical funds, aerospace funds, electronic funds, gold funds, etc. Others deal in securities of a particular type; for example, there are funds that hold restricted (letter) stock, over-the-counter stock funds, etc.[13] Others provide a convenient means for holding the securities of firms in a particular *country*—for example, the Japan fund, various Canadian funds, etc. Specialized funds may be either open-end or closed-end.

Hedge funds finance their portfolios in part by issuing securities other than common stocks. Some actually hedge, taking short positions in stocks, options, etc. to reduce some of the risk arising from long positions. Others simply lever their portfolios by issuing debt. In common usage the term is often applied (misleadingly) to any "aggressively managed, high-risk mutual fund."[14]

[11] *Ibid.*

[12] *Ibid.*

[13] In addition, there are commodities futures funds, formed as limited partnerships and thus not legally investment companies.

[14] *Ibid.* In addition, there are many hedge funds organized as limited partnerships.

A few funds emphasize a *security selection method*. Thus the Fidelity Group's Contrafund seeks capital growth by following a "contrary opinion approach to investment. . . . Its management searches for growth opportunities among stocks with solid investment value that are priced attractively because they are currently out of favor in the market place."[15] The Dreyfus Third Century Fund selects investments ". . . in companies which, in the opinion of the Fund's Management, not only meet traditional investment standards but also show evidence in the conduct of their business, relative to other companies in the same industry, of contributing to the enhancement of the quality of life in America. . . ."[16]

Open-end *tax-free municipal bond funds* were first offered in 1976. *Municipal bond unit trusts* have been available longer. Some municipal bond investment companies hold issues from many states. Others specialize in the issues of governmental units in one state to provide a vehicle for residents of that state who wish to avoid paying state taxes on the income.

A relatively new idea is the *index fund*, which attempts to provide results similar or identical to those computed for a specified market index, such as Standard and Poor's 500-stock index. Since the agencies that compute such measures sometimes change the securities included, and since some indices (but not those computed by Standard and Poor's) by their very construction require changing portfolios, a certain amount of management may be required to insure that the returns from a fund do not diverge significantly from those of the desired index. Possible savings in commission and other expenses by holding proportions differing slightly from those in the index, and restrictions that may preclude holding certain stocks (e.g., those of firms with substantial probabilities of bankruptcy),[17] may also increase the need for management.

Interest in index funds is relatively recent, springing in part from accumulating evidence of market efficiency. A number of banks have established commingled index funds, and corporations and other organizations have set up index funds for their own employee retirement trust funds. The *First Index Investment Trust*, a no-load investment company, provides a vehicle for small investors who wish to obtain results similar to those of Standard and Poor's 500-stock index.

Table 18-1 provides an indication of the number of mutual funds of various types and the amount of assets under their control.

MUTUAL FUND ACCOUNTS

The United States Internal Revenue Code allows an investment company to avoid corporate income taxation. A unit trust, closed-end or open-end

---

[15] "Contrafund: Seeking Investment Growth Through the Discipline of Contrary Thinking," Fidelity Group. October 1975.

[16] The Dreyfus Third Century Fund, Inc., *Prospectus*, September 30, 1976.

[17] The exclusion of likely bankruptcy candidates is widely practiced by the managers of such funds, although in an efficient market the prices of such stocks would reflect their situation and the net effect of their omission would be a lowering of the overall suitability of the portfolio, taking both risk and return into account.

TABLE 18–1 Mutual Funds, Classified by Investment Policy (as of December 31, 1978)

Type of Fund	Number of Funds	Combined Assets ($ billions)
Common stock:		
Maximum capital gain	103	4.6
Growth	143	12.6
Growth and Income	80	13.2
Specialized	23	0.7
Balanced	25	3.8
Income	119	8.9
Bond and preferred stock	11	1.1
Money market	59	10.5
Tax-exempt municipal bond	37	2.6

Source: Wiesenberger Investment Companies Service, *Investment Companies, 1979.* By permission from the *Wiesenberger Investment Companies Service,* 39th Annual Edition. Copyright © 1979, Warren, Gorham and Lamont Inc., 210 South Street, Boston, Mass. All rights reserved.

fund can qualify as a *regulated investment company* by meeting certain standards concerning diversification[18] and paying out at least 90% of its net income, exclusive of capital gains, each year. Net realized capital gains may be distributed or retained. If the company chooses the latter course, it must pay a tax calculated at the maximum rate applied to capital gains for personal income taxes. Shareholders are then given credit for having paid tax at this rate on the gains on their shares.

Most mutual funds "pay out" both income (dividends and interest) and net realized capital gains. However, at a shareholder's option, payments may be made in shares rather than in cash. In either event, the shareholder must pay personal income tax on the dividends and capital gains distributions on his or her holdings.

While an investor can purchase shares in a fund and receive all distributions in cash, this is only one of many possible arrangements. Mutual funds offer plans of several types to satisfy investors' desires for different patterns of contributions and withdrawals over time.

Accumulation plans are designed for those who prefer to make no withdrawals over some period of time. The simplest procedure involves automatic reinvestment of all dividends and capital gains. As with other plans, this often results in positions involving fractional shares, but, since most accounts are maintained via computerized records, this poses no problem.

V*oluntary* accumulation plans allow an investor to add to an account as desired, subject only to some minimum amount that must be invested each time. Alternatively, a fixed dollar amount may be invested at periodic intervals—in some cases via automatic bank transfers.

Contractual accumulation plans call for a fixed amount to be contributed regularly (usually monthly) over a relatively long period (often

[18] At least 50% of the company's assets must be diversified: within this portion, no more than 5% of total assets can be invested in the securities of any one issuer. Moreover, no more than 25% of total assets may be invested in any one company.

five or more years). Sales charges may or may not be lower than those applicable to a voluntary plan. The investor is not legally bound to make all the payments, but since a large proportion of early contributions typically goes toward sales charges, commitment to a contractual plan should not be considered if cancellation is at all likely.

The Investment Company Amendments Act of 1970 placed limits on the load charges for contractual plans. The total amount may not exceed 9%, and no more than 50% of the first year's contribution may be allocated to sales charges (i.e., at least half must be invested in fund shares). Moreover, if a 50% "front-end" load charge is assessed in the first year, cancellation of the plan within 18 months entitles the investor to a refund reducing the effective charge to 15% of the amount paid in.

Accumulation of funds for retirement may also be accomplished via an *individual retirement account* or a *Keogh plan*. In 1980 individuals not covered under another retirement plan could contribute 15% of their compensation, up to a maximum of $1,500 ($1,750 if the individual's spouse did not work outside the home), to an individual retirement account, deducting the amount contributed from gross income when calculating their personal income tax. Alternatively, an employer not providing another retirement plan could contribute 15% of an employee's compensation to an individual retirement account, up to a maximum amount of $7,500 per year. Self-employed individuals could contribute 15% of their earned income, up to a maximum of $7,500, to a Keogh plan account, with such contributions also deductible from gross income for tax purposes. Either type of account is maintained by a *custodian*— usually a bank. Contributions and any cash received from investments are invested in accordance with the investor's desires. Funds may be withdrawn beginning at age $59\frac{1}{2}$ and withdrawals must begin by age $70\frac{1}{2}$.

All money taken out of a custodial account is taxable income,[19] but there is no additional tax on dividends and interest received during the accumulation period, and the investor is likely to be in a lower tax bracket after retirement. Thus the "tax shelter" aspect of such plans can be quite attractive.

Many institutions have made arrangements for custodial accounts with investment restricted to their offerings. There are, for example, savings and loan company plans, security broker's plans, and investment company plans. The latter often allow the investor to direct the custodian to switch money among separate investment companies under the same management.

It is increasingly common to find several investment companies operating as a *family of funds*. An investor may purchase shares in one or more of the funds under common management and also switch money from one to another. Sales charges are typically lower than those applicable to similar transactions involving funds managed by different companies; in some cases transfers within a family may be made without charge. In any event, a single account is usually maintained, with all contributions, withdrawals, and tax information included in one statement.

---

[19] With the exception of money contributed to a Keogh plan prior to 1974. Special averaging provisions for tax purposes may also be used in some cases.

Many mutual funds offer voluntary *withdrawal plans*. The investor instructs the fund to pay out either a fixed amount or a specified percentage of the account's value periodically (e.g., monthly). When payments exceed regular distributions, the number of shares is reduced; when payments are less than distributions, the number of shares is increased.

A few funds offer *insurance*. A contractual accumulation plan may include a provision that contributions will be completed if the investor dies or is disabled. The premium for such insurance is, in effect, added to the sales charge. Some funds offer insurance that makes up any difference between the ending value of an account and the total amount contributed over an accumulation period. For example, 6% of each year's contributions might be deducted to insure a ten-year contractual plan, with the remainder (less the normal load charge) plus all dividends and capital gains distributions received during the ten years invested in fund shares. At the end of the tenth year, if the value of the accumulated shares fell below the total amount paid in by the investor, the difference would be paid by the insurance company.

Even more exotic arrangements are offered by some funds. The convenience of centralized accounting and preparation of needed tax documents, coupled with arrangements conforming to individual's particular situations, allow mutual funds to effectively fill the role of an investment manager for small (and some not-so-small) investors.

MUTUAL FUND PERFORMANCE

The need to compute net asset values daily, and the public nature of such figures (and of the amounts distributed to shareholders), make open-end investment companies ideal candidates for studies of the performance of professionally managed investment funds. United States mutual funds have frequently been the subject of extensive (and sometimes unwelcome) study. Open-end funds in other countries have also been examined, as have U.S. closed-end funds.

Recently, data on professionally managed pension funds and bank commingled funds have become available. The performance of the managers of such funds appears to be similar to that of mutual fund managers: they do reasonably well tailoring portfolios to meet clients' objectives, but few seem to be able consistently to "beat the market." While the following sections deal only with U.S. investment companies, many of the results apply to other professionally managed funds, both in the United States and in other countries.[20]

[20] For evidence on funds outside the United States see, for example: James R. F. Guy, "The Effect of International Diversification on the Historical Performance of British Mutual Funds," University of California Graduate School of Business Administration (Berkeley Working Paper No. 36, July 1975); John G. McDonald, "French Mutual Fund Performance: Evaluation of Internationally Diversified Portfolios," *Journal of Finance*, XXVIII, no. 5 (December 1973), 1161–80; Juan A. Palacios, "The Stock Market in Spain: Tests of Efficiency and Capital Market Theory" (Ph.D. dissertation, Stanford University, June 1973); G. Pogue, B. Solnik, and A. Rousselin, "The Impact of International Diversification: A Study of the French Mutual Fund Industry," (MIT Working Paper 658–73, June 1973), and Michael A. Firth, "The Investment Performance of Unit Trusts in the Period 1965–75," *Journal of Money, Credit and Banking*, November 1977.

Risk Control

One of the functions that a mutual fund can perform for its investors is the maintenance of a particular risk posture. Formal statements of objectives provide some idea of a fund's intended posture, but typically the wording is (perhaps intentionally) vague. Nonetheless, there is a relationship between portfolio risk and stated objectives, as Figure 18-4 shows.

Monthly excess returns over the Treasury bill rate were calculated for 123 funds from 1960 through 1969. Then two ex post measures were calculated to estimate the average risk exposure of each fund during the period. The first, *beta*, was in this case defined as the sensitivity of the fund's return to changes in an unweighted index of all stocks listed on the New York Stock Exchange; it provides a measure of market risk. The second, the *standard deviation* of monthly excess returns, provides a measure of total risk.

Values of these statistical measures for all the funds with similar objectives, using classifications assigned by Wiesenberger at the beginning of the period, are summarized in Figure 18-4(a), which uses beta as a measure of risk, and Figure 18-4(b), which uses the standard deviation of excess returns. Each bar plots the range of values obtained; the mean values, included in the figure, are shown by squares. On average, funds that promised low risk provided it. However, some funds with conservative objectives took on more risk than others with less conservative objectives: the bars in Figure 18-4 overlap considerably.

Perhaps it is too much to expect a fund to state once and for all a specific risk target. Some managers like to change market exposure periodically in attempts at market timing. Others wish to avoid the possibility of stockholders' suits claiming that objectives were not met. In either

FIGURE 18-4 Risk versus Fund Objectives: 123 Mutual Funds, 1960–1969.

Source: John G. McDonald, "Objectives and Performance of Mutual Funds, 1960–1969," *Journal of Financial and Quantitative Analysis*, IX, no. 3 (June 1974), 316.

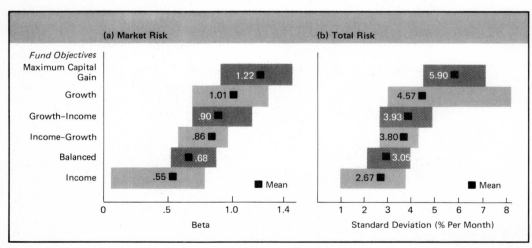

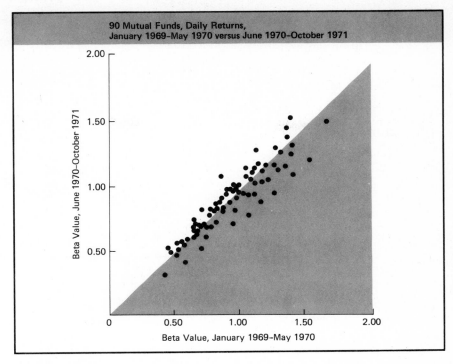

FIGURE 18-5 Past versus Future Beta Values: 90 Mutual Funds, Daily Returns, January 1969–May 1970 versus June 1970–October 1971.

Source: Gerald A. Pogue and Walter Conway, "On the Stability of Mutual Fund Beta Values" (unpublished working paper, MIT Sloan School of Management, June 1972.

case, past risk exposure may be a better guide to future risk exposure than the rather general statements found in a fund's prospectus.

Figure 18-5 shows that this is often the case. Each point plots the beta values for a fund in two different periods (based on daily returns). While the points do not plot neatly along a 45-degree line from the origin (which represents equal beta values in both periods), there is a clear relationship between "past beta" and "future beta." Most funds do control risk at least within limits.

Diversification

An important task for any investment manager is the provision of an appropriate degree of portfolio diversification. The correct amount depends on the proportion of client's funds managed and on the likelihood that superior abnormal returns can be obtained by sacrificing diversification. Since most mutual funds are intended to be a major component of a shareholder's portfolio, one would expect them to be well diversified. Figure 18-6 shows that many are. Quarterly excess returns from 1970 through 1974 were computed for 100 funds and compared with corresponding val-

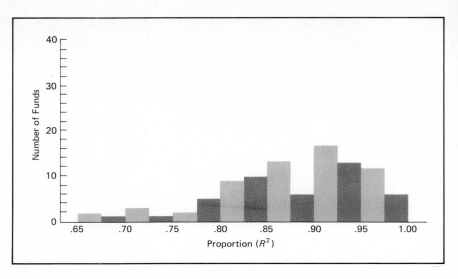

FIGURE 18-6 Proportion of Variation in Quarterly Returns Attributable to Market Fluctuations: 100 Mutual Funds, 1970–1974.

Source: Merrill Lynch, Pierce, Fenner, and Smith, Inc. *Investment Performance Analysis, Comparative Survey, 1970–1974.*

ues for Standard and Poor's 500-stock index. For each fund a value of *R-squared* was computed. This indicates the proportion of the variation in a fund's returns that can be attributed to variations in returns on the market (as represented by the index used). As the figure shows, approximately 90% of the quarter-by-quarter variation in a typical fund's return could be attributed to market swings during this period, but the values ranged from 66% to 98%.

Diversification is particularly important, for in an efficient market the only type of risk for which extra return can be expected is market risk. A fund with an R^2 value of .90 has chosen a portfolio with only 10% nonmarket—and thus potentially unrewarded—risk. One with an R^2 value of .70 has chosen a portfolio with 30% nonmarket—and thus potentially unrewarded—risk. If two funds have the same beta values, the one with the lower value of R^2 will have more risk; it may achieve a greater return only if its management, through skill or luck, selects an adequate number of underpriced securities. Other things equal, the less a fund's diversification, the less likely it is to be suitable for a major commitment of an investor's funds.

Returns

It is clearly inappropriate to compare returns of funds with substantially different risk exposure. However, as was shown in Figure 18-4, funds with similar objectives are at least roughly similar in terms of risk. Thus one would expect that in periods in which market returns exceed short-term interest rates, conservative funds should return less than those with more aggressive objectives.

Figure 18-7 shows that from 1960 to 1969 this was the case for the funds used to construct Figure 18-4. The mean excess return on the index used to represent the market was slightly over .5% per month (e.g., approximately 6% per year). The ranges of values for the mean monthly excess returns of the funds in each objective class are shown by the bars in Figure 18-7: the average value for each group is also indicated, and represented by a square. Although the relationship is far from perfect, the results are broadly consistent with expectations; in up markets, more aggressive funds tend to do better than less aggressive ones. In down markets, of course, the relationship tends to be reversed.

Risk-Adjusted Returns

To measure a fund's ability to "beat the market," one must compare its performance with that which could have been obtained in some simple or passive manner. Both risk and return should be considered, so a means must be found to incorporate both in a single number. Moreover, a measure of risk relevant for the investor in question should be chosen.

One relatively simple method uses the ratio of average excess return to a relevant measure of risk. For example, dividing the average monthly excess return by the standard deviation of the excess returns over the period from 1960 through 1969, the following "reward-to-variability ratios" were obtained for a large group of mutual funds:[21]

Average value for 123 funds:	.112
Average value for an index of all stocks listed on the New York Stock Exchange:	.133

[21] John G. McDonald, "Objectives and Performance of Mutual Funds, 1960–1969," *Journal of Financial and Quantitative Analysis*, IX, no. 3 (June 1974), 311–34.

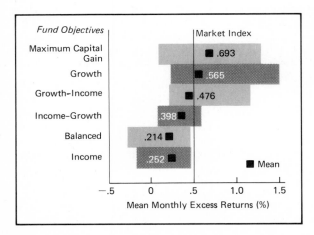

Fund Objectives

FIGURE 18-7 Average Excess Return versus Objectives: 123 Mutual Funds, 1960–1969.

Source: John G. McDonald, "Objectives and Performance of Mutual Funds, 1960–1969," *Journal of Financial and Quantitative Analysis*, IX, no. 3 (June 1974), 317.

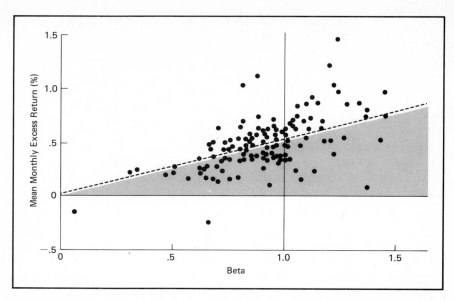

FIGURE 18-8 Average Excess Returns versus Beta Values: 123 Mutual Funds, 1960–1969.

Source: John G. McDonald, "Objectives and Performances of Mutual Funds, 1960–1969," *Journal of Financial and Quantitative Analysis*, IX, no. 3 (June 1974), 317.

After paying management fees, expenses, and brokerage charges, investors in the typical fund did worse in this sense than they could have done by investing in the market index (assuming that no expenses would have been incurred).

This comparison is, however, based on total risk, and some investors may be concerned primarily with market risk. A comparison based on the ratio of average excess return to the value of beta (representing only market risk) tells a different story:[22]

Average value for 123 funds:	.518
Average value for an index of all stocks listed on the New York Stock Exchange:	.510

Using this measure, the typical fund slightly outperformed the market during this period. The funds appeared to have picked securities with somewhat superior performance, but the gains were not large enough to offset the added nonmarket risk.

Figure 18-8 provides additional detail. Each point plots the average beta value and average monthly excess return for a fund over the 1960–1969 period. The dashed line connects the points representing an investment in Treasury bills (with both beta and mean excess return equal to zero) and an investment in the market index (with beta equal to 1.0). In

[22] *Ibid.*

a sense, funds plotting above the line can be said to have beaten the market, and those below it to have been beaten by the market. Moreover, the vertical distance from a fund's point to the line can be used as a measure of performance. This value, generally termed *alpha* or *average differential return*, indicates the average difference between the return on (1) the fund and (2) a combination of the market index and Treasury bills with a constant beta equal to the fund's average beta level. A fund can obtain a positive alpha value by market timing (moving to higher-than-average beta levels prior to market rises and to lower-than-average beta levels prior to market declines) and/or by security selection (purchasing securities that return more than others with the same beta levels).

FIGURE 18-9 Mutual Fund Performance: Alpha Values.

Source: (a) Norman E. Mains, "Risk, the Pricing of Capital Assets, and the Evaluation of Investment Portfolios: Comment," *Journal of Business*, July 1977 By permission of the University of Chicago Press © 1977. (b) United States Securities and Exchange Commission, *Institutional Investor Study Report*, March 10, 1971 (U.S. Government Printing Office), (c) Merrill Lynch, Pierce, Fenner and Smith, Inc., *Investment Performance Analysis, Comparative Survey, 1970–1974.*

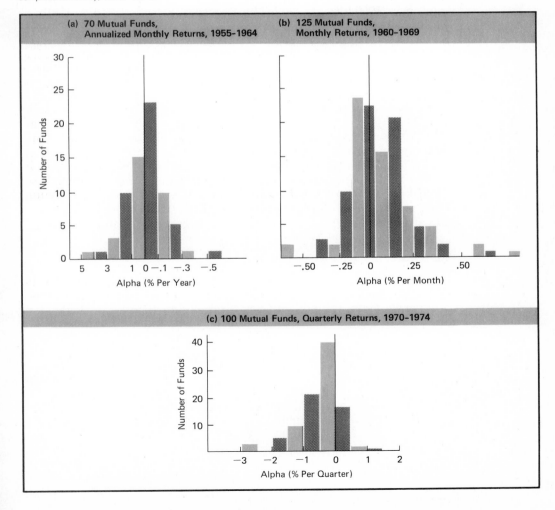

Alpha values consider only market risk and thus do not penalize funds for taking on nonmarket risk, although they do include any reward (in higher returns) such risk may entail. Thus they indicate only the *return* associated with active management, without assessing the risk taken to get that return. A detailed discussion of such aspects is included in Chapter 20. For present purposes it suffices to indicate that alpha values are commonly employed performance measures, and they provide useful insights concerning professional investment management in general and that of mutual funds in particular.

Figure 18-9(a), on page 523, shows the distribution of alpha values for 70 funds, based on annual returns from 1955 through 1964. The average value was −.09% per year (continuously compounded). Thus, net of expenses (other than load charges), the typical fund provided approximately the same return as a market-based, passive fund with a constant beta value equal to the fund's average beta value. Of the 70 funds, 40 outperformed the market index—i.e., had positive alpha values.

Different periods[23] give slightly different results. Figure 18-9(b) shows the distribution of alpha values based on monthly returns for 125 funds from 1960 through 1969. The average value was .05% per month, or about .6% per year. During this period the typical fund outperformed a passive fund of similar average risk by slightly more than ½ of 1% per year, and slightly over half (53%) of the funds outperformed the market (had positive alphas).

Figure 18-9(c) provides a third example. It shows results for 100 funds based on quarterly returns from 1970 through 1974. The average alpha value was −.5% per quarter, or approximately −2% per year, and only 20 of the funds outperformed the market (had positive alphas).

These results suggest that, net of expenses, the average mutual fund does not significantly outperform the market over any extended period. This is not too surprising. After all, the market's performance is itself an average of the performance of all investors. If, on average, mutual funds could beat the market, some other investors would have to be beaten. With substantial professional management in today's stock market it is difficult to conjure up the image of a likely group of victims.

Consistency of Performance

Despite the rather negative results described thus far, there remains the possibility that a few funds may consistently beat the market due to superior management. If funds with, say, a run of four superior years are identified, some will be included due to good luck, and others (potentially), due to skill. The former have a 50-50 chance of above-average performance in the next year; the latter, a better than 50-50 chance. The greater the number of consistently superior managers, the greater the proportion of such a group that will turn in an above-average performance in the fifth year.

Unfortunately, the record provides little support for the thesis that a significant number of mutual fund managers can consistently outperform

---

[23] And/or different statistical procedures.

a passive portfolio with equal market risk. The following results were obtained using a measure of annual differential returns for 115 funds from 1955 through 1964.[24]

Number of Consecutive Years Funds' Performance Exceeded That of a Passive Portfolio with Equal Market Risk	Proportion of Group with Performance Exceeding That of a Passive Portfolio with Equal Market Risk in the Subsequent Year (%)
1	50.4
2	52.0
3	53.4
4	55.8
5	46.4

If there are superior mutual fund managers, they either extract an amount equal to their superior returns in salaries or move from fund to fund often enough to make it difficult to verify their existence.

Expenses

Funds incur two kinds of expenses. Management fees and administrative expenses are direct and generally reported. Transactions costs are only partly measurable: brokers' commissions are reported, but bid-ask spreads and the price impacts of trading are usually not even estimated.

By adding back management and administrative expenses and explicit transactions costs one can obtain an estimate of a fund's performance net of only implicit transactions costs. Figure 18-10 shows the distribution of alpha values based on this measure of "gross" performance for

[24] Michael C. Jensen, "Risk, the Pricing of Capital Assets, and the Evaluation of Investment Portfolios," *The Journal of Business*, 42, no. 2 (April 1969), 167–247.

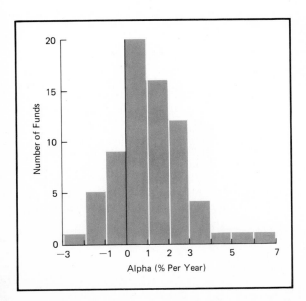

FIGURE 18-10 Mutual Fund Performance: Alpha Values Based on Gross Returns.

Source: Norman E. Mains, "Risk, the Pricing of Capital Assets, and the Evaluation of Investment Portfolios: Comment," *Journal of Business*, July 1977.

the funds covered in the analysis previously summarized in Figure 18-9(a). While alpha values *net* of all expenses averaged .09% per year, the values based on *gross* performance averaged 1.07% per year. Moreover, 50 of the 70 funds outperformed the market (had positive alpha values) based on this measure of performance.

A study by the United States Securities and Exchange Commission[25] attempted to estimate the impact of turnover and several other factors on performance. Alpha values were computed for 132 mutual funds using monthly returns from 1965 through 1969. Then these values were compared with various measures, including turnover, measured by the ratio of (1) the smaller of purchases or sales during a month divided by (2) the month-end asset value. Performance was not significantly related to *any* of the other factors. For example:

large funds did no better, other things equal, than small funds.
funds with load charges did no better, other things equal, than those with no load charges (and therefore, investors in such funds did worse, net of load charges, then those in funds with no load charges).
funds managed by firms with substantial assets under management did no better, other things equal, than others.

But, performance net of costs *was* related to turnover—negatively so. The analysis indicated that, on average, a 10% increase in the rate of turnover (e.g., from 50% per year to 60% per year) reduces net performance by .3 to .6% per year. This corresponds to transactions costs of 3% to 6% for the sale of a security and the subsequent purchase of another (e.g., 1.5% to 3% for the sale and 1.5% to 3% for the purchase), with no improvement in performance.

The results of this study suggest that, on average, portfolio revisions lower net performance (as measured by alpha values). Alterations in a fund's portfolio may be desirable to maintain a desired posture vis-á-vis risk and/or dividend yield. But changes intended to exploit supposed market inefficiencies will, for the average investment manager, prove undesirable net of all costs.

Market Timing

To achieve superior portfolio performance one must either select securities that outperform others of comparable risk or switch from risk class to risk class at appropriate times. The latter strategy is often called *market timing*. The idea is to hold high-beta securities prior to market rises and low-beta securities prior to market declines. An all-equity fund can change its beta level by switching among stocks with different beta values; a balanced fund can also alter its bond/stock mix.

Successful market timing will eventually be reflected in a positive alpha value based on long-term performance. Overall performance may also be separated into parts: for example, one part attributed to security

---

[25] United States Securities and Exchange Commission, *Institutional Investors Study Report* (March 10, 1971), U.S. Government Printing Office.

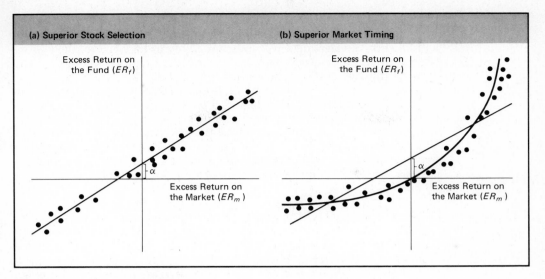

(a) Superior Stock Selection

Excess Return on
the Fund (ER_f)

α

Excess Return on
the Market (ER_m)

(b) Superior Market Timing

Excess Return on
the Fund (ER_f)

α

Excess Return on
the Market (ER_m)

FIGURE 18-11 Superior Fund Performance.

selection, and another to market timing. Details of such procedures are given in Chapter 20. For present purposes only an approach designed to test for evidence of superior market timing will be considered.

Figure 18-11 illustrates the procedure. The excess returns of two hypothetical funds are plotted (on the vertical axes) against those of a market index (on the horizontal axes). Straight lines fit via standard regression methods give positive alpha values in each case. But the causes differ. The fund shown in Figure 18-11(a) held securities with roughly the same beta value at all times but managed to find some that were underpriced. The fund shown in Figure 18-11(b) held securities with high beta values in periods in which the market return was high and securities with low beta values in periods in which the market return was low or negative.

To try to detect cases of market timing, one can fit a *curve* instead of a line to the points in diagrams of this type. The simplest way to do this uses multiple regression to estimate the parameters of a quadratic equation of the form:

$$ER_f = a + b(ER_m) + c(ER_m^2) \qquad (18\text{-}1)$$

where:

$$ER_f = \text{the excess return on the fund}$$
$$ER_m = \text{the excess return on the market index}$$
$$ER_m^2 = \text{the excess return on the market index, squared}$$
$$a, b, c = \text{values to be estimated by regression analysis}$$

The curve in Figure 18-11(b) plots such an equation. The value of c is positive, indicating that the curve becomes steeper as one moves to the right—i.e., that the fund successfully timed the market.

In a study[26] using this method to examine the performance of 57 mutual funds over the period from 1953 through 1962, only one was found with a record suggesting any significant ability to time the market. Moreover, even its curve was remarkably close to a straight line (i.e., the value of c was positive and statistically significant, but small).

Such results are not surprising. If many funds were consistently successful at market timing, they would show up in tests for superior overall performance, unless they were consistently engaging in inferior security selection and thus losing the fruits of their ability to predict the market. The latter situation seems highly improbable. More likely, investment managers find it as difficult to time the market as to select underpriced securities. Such is the lot of a participant in a highly efficient market.

CLOSED-END FUND PREMIUMS AND DISCOUNTS

Several studies[27] have shown that the performance of managers of diversified closed-end investment companies[28] in the United States is similar to that of open-end fund managers. When returns are measured by changes in *net asset values* (plus all distributions), closed-end funds appear to be neither better nor worse than open-end funds. Risk is controlled reasonably well, funds formed to provide diversification do so, and there is little evidence that managers can either select underpriced securities or time the market successfully. Performance gross of expenses is roughly equal to that of comparable passive portfolios and performance net of expenses somewhat lower.

But there is more to be said about closed-end funds. An investor can purchase an open-end fund's shares for their net asset value (plus any required load charge) and sell them later at the subsequent net asset value. Except for any load charges, the performance of the *management* of such a fund, based on net asset values, is equal to that of the *shareholders*. Not so with closed-end funds. Owners buy and sell shares at prices determined on the open (secondary) market. Shareholders' returns depend on these prices, which may or may not equal net asset values.

A closed-end fund's shares may sell for the current net asset value per share, for more (i.e., at a *premium*), or, most commonly, for less (i.e., at a *discount*).

---

[26] Jack L. Treynor and Kay Mazuy, "Can Mutual Funds Outguess the Market?" *Harvard Business Review*, 44, no. 4 (July–August 1966), 131–36. Copyright © 1966 by the President and Fellows of Harvard College. All Rights Reserved.

[27] See, for example: William F. Sharpe and Howard B. Sosin, "Closed-end Investment Companies in the United States: Risk and Return," *Proceedings, 1974 Meeting of the European Finance Association*, ed. B. Jacquillat (Amsterdam: North-Holland Publishing Co., 1975). Similar results apply to dual funds, as shown in Robert H. Litzenberger and Howard B. Sosin, "The Theory of Recapitalizations under Incomplete Capital Markets and the Evidence of Dual Purpose Funds," Graduate School of Business, Stanford University, Research Paper No. 264 (May 1975); Antonio Vives, "Analysis of Forecasting Ability of Closed-end Fund's Management," Carnegie-Mellon University, September 1975 (unpublished), and "Discounts and Premiums on Closed-end Funds: A Theoretical and Empirical Analysis," Carnegie-Mellon University, 1975 (unpublished).

[28] Companies that invest in specific industries or countries and/or in restricted (letter) stock are, of course, quite different. This section is concerned primarily with funds holding diversified portfolios, primarily of common stocks.

Figure 18-12 shows the *ratio* of (1) the market value of all outstanding claims (stock and any bonds, warrants, etc.) for a group of diversified closed-end funds to (2) the total value of the assets held by these funds at the end of each year from 1933 through 1978. With rare exceptions the ratio was less than 1.0: on average, the funds sold at discounts. Equally noticeable is the substantial variation from year to year.

The fact that the price of a closed-end fund differs from its net asset value, with the magnitude of the difference varying from time to time, introduces an added source of risk and potential return. By purchasing shares at a discount, an investor may be able to increase his or her return. Even if the discount remains constant, the effective dividend yield will be greater than that of an otherwise similar no-load open-end company. If the discount is substantial when the shares are purchased, it may subsequently narrow (i.e., the ratio will increase) and the return will be even greater. On the other hand, if the discount increases (i.e., the ratio falls), overall return may be less than that of an otherwise comparable open-end fund. This latter possibility makes closed-end fund shares riskier than those of similar open-end funds.

Some of the risk associated with varying discounts can be reduced by holding a *portfolio* of shares in several closed-end funds. Discounts on different funds move together, but not perfectly. For example, past data suggest that the standard deviation of the percentage change in the ratio of price to net asset value for a portfolio of 10 to 12 funds is likely to be approximately half that of a typical investment in the shares of a single fund.[29]

[29] Sharpe and Sosin, *op. cit.*

FIGURE 18-12 The Ratio of the Value of Claims to the Value of Assets for a Group of Diversified Closed End Funds, 1933–1978.

Source: 1933–1972: William F. Sharpe and Howard B. Sosin, "Closed-End Investment Companies in the United States; Risk and Return," *Proceedings, 1974 Meeting of the European Finance Association*, ed. B. Jacquillat (Amsterdam; North-Holland Publishing Co. 1975); 1973–1978: updated by the author using data for eight funds (Adams Express, Carriers and General, General American Investors, Lehman, Madison, Niagara, Tri-Continental, and U.S. and Foreign).

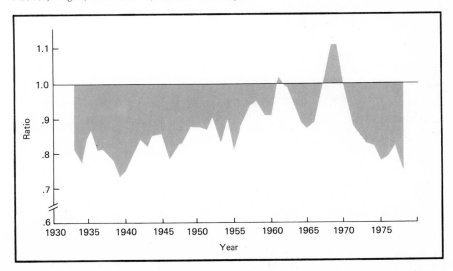

Explanation of the behavior of closed-end fund prices provides a challenge for the person who believes that capital markets are perfectly efficient. For one not firmly committed to such a view, the purchase of shares of closed-end companies at prices sufficiently below net asset values may provide an opportunity for superior performance.

Problems

1. Explain fully the differences between closed-end and open-end investment companies. Include a discussion of the determination of share purchase price and of the extent to which the number of shares outstanding may be varied for each of these two forms of investment companies.

2. Referring to Figure 18-3, what are the load charges for (a) the Acorn Fund and (b) the AGE fund? What percentage of *value* is the load charge for ICA (Investment Company of America)—a fund offered by the American Funds Group?

3. Referring to Figure 18-1(a), was any diversified common stock fund selling for a premium on the date in question? What was the discount on Tri-Continental? Did this offer an opportunity for riskless arbitrage? Why or why not?

4. Some have suggested that closed-end fund discounts do not follow a random walk but tend instead to be mean-reverting (i.e., a discount is more likely to move toward some sort of historic average than it is to move away from it). If this were true, how might you "play" a fund's discount to increase your expected return? What about the risk involved? If discounts do not behave in this manner and you could buy either a no-load open-end fund or a closed-end fund at a discount, which would you do? Why? Would your answer depend on the length of time you planned to keep your money invested?

5. Why should anyone pay management fees to those who operate a tax-exempt municipal bond fund when bonds of this type can be purchased directly?

6. Some have argued that the fact that the average mutual fund appears to provide average performance is more a test of arithmetic than of market efficiency. They point out that many funds appear in the right-hand portions of Figures 18-9(a), (b), and (c) because they outperformed comparable passive strategies. In what sense is "alpha" only a partial measure of performance for such funds? Even if alpha were a completely adequate measure of performance, is the fact that some funds achieve a positive alpha in a given period inconsistent with the efficient-market hypothesis? What evidence would be inconsistent with market efficiency? What does the record show?

7. Under what conditions might it make sense to invest all of one's money in a mutual fund specializing in stocks of companies in the energy sector? In a fund specializing in companies with above-average earnings growth? In a diversified common stock fund? In a balanced fund?

8. Could a money market fund ever provide its investors with a negative return (e.g., over a period as short as a day)? What would be a reasonable way for such a fund to compute its net asset value and dividend each day? What problems might arise if the value of each holding were computed by "amortizing" the value from its purchase price to the amount it is scheduled to pay at maturity?

9. Wiesenberger's *Investment Companies* provides data on the *expense ratio* (the total amount spent on management fees and administrative costs during a year divided by total asset value) for each of a number of open-end and closed-end investment companies. Does this cover all the costs borne by investors in such funds? What other costs may be relevant? How does an expense ratio differ from a load charge? Is the length of time one plans to keep one's money in a fund relevant for assessing the cost associated with an expense ratio? A load charge?

Financial Analysis

19

THE FINANCIAL ANALYST

In the broadest sense, financial analysis involves determining the values of financial assets, levels of risk and return, and the relationship between risk and return in financial markets. An alternative definition is more pragmatic: financial analysis is what financial analysts do.

The *Financial Analyst's Handbook*[1] defines the term *financial analyst* as synonymous with security analyst or investment analyst—"one who analyzes securities and makes recommendations thereon."[2] Such people may be called economists, market analysts, technical analysts, chartists, industry analysts, or security analysts. A broader interpretation (and the membership of the Financial Analysts Federation) includes those who manage portfolios and/or exercise general responsibility for the investment of funds.

Some restrict the term financial analyst to cover persons who provide inputs for the portfolio management process; those who manage portfolios and guide the overall investment of funds are described as *investment managers*. This chapter deals primarily with financial analysis in this narrower sense; the next, with investment management.

Professional Organizations

In the United States and Canada, those who belong to a local society of financial analysts automatically belong to the Financial Analysts Federation. Among other things, this entitles them to a subscription to the *Financial Analysts Journal*, a major source of information on basic research done by other analysts and members of the academic community. In 1980 there were about 14,500 members in the 51 societies of the Federation.

In 1962 the *Institute of Chartered Financial Analysts* was formed by the Financial Analysts Federation to award the professional designation of *Chartered Financial Analyst* (C.F.A.). Fourteen years later over 6,000 analysts had qualified. To become a C.F.A. one must have several years

---

[1] Sumner N. Levine, ed., *Financial Analyst's Handbook* (Homewood, Ill.: Dow Jones-Irwin, Inc., 1975).
[2] William C. Norby, "Overview of Financial Analysis," in *Financial Analyst's Handbook*, p. 3.

FIGURE 19-1 The C.F.A. Candidate Study Program—General Topic Outline

Ethical and Professional Standards, Securities Laws and Regulations

Securities Laws and Regulations:
—Nature and applicability of fiduciary standards
—Pertinent laws and regulations
—Organization and purpose of governing regulatory bodies

Professional Code and Standards:
—Code of Ethics
—Standards of Professional Conduct
—By-Laws, Article VIII, Sections 4, 5 and 6
—Rules of Procedure

Ethical Standards and Professional Obligations:
—Public

—Customers and clients
—Corporate management
—Employers
—Associates
—Other analysts
—Conflicts of interest
—Insider information
—Recommendations
—Compensation

Identification and Administration of Ethical Conduct:
—Nature and applicability of fiduciary standards
—The evolution of the Code and the Standards of Professional Conduct

—Intra-firm relationships
—Supervisory responsibilities
—The principles of a professional's code of ethics
—Competency and proper care
—The concept of self-regulation
—Changes in the public's perception of professional ethics
—Social obligations

Financial Accounting

Principles and Construction of Accounting Statements:
—Income statements
—Balance sheets
—Sources and uses of funds

Content and Usefulness of Accounting Reports to Regulatory Agencies

Financial Analysis of Accounting Statements:
—Adjustments for comparability

—Ratio analysis
—Adjustments for subsidiaries, affiliates and foreign operations
—Stock splits and dividends
—Rights, warrants and convertible securities
—Effect of price level changes

Areas of Judgment:
—Inventories
—Depreciation

—Tax treatment
—Intangibles
—Consolidation
—Acquisitions and mergers
—Deferred assets and liabilities
—Off balance sheet financing
—Pension plans

Current Accounting Principles and Practices:
—AICPA and FASB pronouncements
—Regulatory decisions

Application of Quantitative Techniques

Elementary Statistics:
—Averages and measures of dispersion

Mathematics of Finance:
—Compound growth
—Present value of stocks and bonds
—Performance measurement techniques

Probability Theory:
—Expected values
—Strategies

Hypothesis Testing:
—Sample testing and confidence limits
—Analysis of variance

Simple and Multiple Regression and Correlation

Matrix Algebra

Mathematical Programming in Portfolio Theory

Applications of Computer Systems to Financial Analysis

Economics

Markets and the Price System:
—Demand, supply, and elasticity
—Cost curves and market structures
—Production and resource allocation
—Capital, interest, and profits

Aggregate and Sectoral Analysis:
—National income accounts
—Output, employment, and income
—Long-term economic growth
—Input-output analysis

—Balance of payments and exchange rates

The Historical Record:
—History of 20th Century business cycles (emphasis on post-World War II era)
—Secular trends in the economy
—Monetarist interpretation of history
—Interrelationships of prices, output, profits, interest rates, monetary aggregates, and securities prices.

—Economic indicators and flow of funds
—Forecasting interest rates, corporate profits, and equity price indexes
—Applications to companies and industries

Economic Policies:
—Goals of economic policies
—Fiscal, monetary, and incomes policies
—Environmental, social, and regulatory issues

Monetary and International
Economics:
—Structure and operations of
the banking system
—Contemporary issues in
monetary theory

Forecasting Techniques:
—Methodology and model
building
—Econometric approach and
limitations

—Economic scarcity and
resource allocation
—International policy issues
—Implications for profits,
interest rates, and securities
prices

**Techniques of Analysis—
Fixed Income Securities**

Bond Instruments and Credit
Evaluation:
—Fixed income instruments:
taxable, tax exempt
corporate, government
conventional, mortgage-
backed, convertible
security, contractural
obligation
fixed coupon, floating
coupon, call protection
sinking fund, put, ex-
tensible, retractable,
fixed maturity

average life, half life of
amortizing, mortgage-
backed bonds
—Credit quality: bond ratings;
earning power tests; asset tests
Credit Markets: yield curve; yield
spread; investor expectations;
relative value; interest rate
forecasting
Mathematical Properties of Bonds:
—Yield and duration
—Bond swapping

Comparative Returns: Stocks vs.
Bonds
Bond Management, Policy,
Implementation:
—Utilization of the bond basics,
investor expectations and
client objectives to frame
bond policy in terms of
maturity, quality, diversification, coupon and unit
commitments

**Techniques of Analysis—
Equity Securities**

Sources of Information
Financial Instruments:
—Stocks, warrants, rights,
options
Industry Appraisal and Evaluation:
—Interindustry competition,
supply-demand, product
prices, costs and profits
—Security market evaluation of
profits, historical and
projected

Company Appraisal and
Evaluation:
—Sales volume, product prices,
product research, intraindustry
competition
—Ratio analysis-balance sheet
and income statement and
analysis of corporate profitability, liquidity, solvency,
operating and financial
leverage
—Management appraisal
—Earnings and dividend

evaluation and projection,
near- and long-term
—Valuation techniques—long-
and short-term:
discounted cash flow
earnings multiples,
absolute and relative
valuation models
growth stock valuation
—Risk analysis—quantitative
and qualitative
—Valuation analysis

**Objective of Analysis—
Portfolio Management**

Principles of Portfolio
Management:
—Definition of portfolio man-
agement, basic concepts—
return, risk, diversification,
portfolio efficiency
—Evolution of portfolio
management—traditional
and recent developments
—Fixed income management
Portfolio Objectives, Constraints
and Policies:
—Liquidity
—Return requirement
—Risk tolerance
—Time horizon

—Tax, regulatory and legal
considerations
—Unique circumstances,
needs and preferences
—Determination of portfolio
policies
Portfolio Construction:
—Financial asset characteristics
—Asset allocation
—Portfolio risk
—Portfolio return
—Implication of constraints
—Portfolio efficiency
—Portfolio optimization
—Issue selection
—Transaction and execution
considerations

Portfolio Performance:
—Measurement techniques
—Establishing criteria
—Evaluating portfolio results
Portfolio Timing and Revision:
—Capital market conditions
—Active and passive
management
—Methods of portfolio revision
—Equity and fixed income
portfolios
Organization of the Portfolio
Management Process:
—Relationship of client, security
analysts, traders

Source: The Institute of Chartered Financial Analysts, 1979–1980 Announcement of C.F.A. Programs
(Charlottesville, Va.), 1979.

of practical experience and pass three examinations. Figure 19-1, which shows the subjects covered, provides a good summary of the types of knowledge the successful financial analyst needs.

Societies of financial analysts have been formed elsewhere. Those of ten European countries constitute the European Federation of Financial Analysts Societies. There are also societies in Japan, Australia, Brazil, and other countries.

THE GOALS OF FINANCIAL ANALYSIS

Estimating Security Characteristics

Financial analysts may attempt to achieve either or both of two possible goals. The first goal is to determine the *characteristics* of a security, a group of securities, or the market as a whole. For example, an analyst may wish to estimate the yield of a security over the next year or so in order to determine its suitability for portfolios in which yield per se is relevant (owing to, say, tax or legal restrictions). Careful analysis of a company's dividend policy, likely future cash flows, etc. should lead to better estimates than can be obtained by simply dividing last year's dividends by the current stock price.

Another analyst may wish to estimate a security's future beta value and nonmarket risk, both of which are relevant for the management of any portfolio not simply invested in "the market."

In some cases it may be desirable to know more about the sources of a security's nonmarket risk. If a portfolio is being managed for a Texas oil man, one might want to minimize the sensitivity of its return to changes in oil prices. Careful analysis of a company's business, and perhaps the business of its customers and suppliers, is required to estimate sensitivities of this type.

Financial analysis is also needed to estimate the current risk-return trade-offs (e.g., a security market line, plane, or hyperplane) and the magnitude of the risk associated with the market portfolio.

Attempting to Identify Mispriced Securities

The second possible goal is to find *mispriced* securities. Naive versions assume that some securities are so overpriced that no one should hold them, and other securities so underpriced that everyone should hold them. Such situations are, of course, improbable. More sophisticated versions assume that some securities are sufficiently underpriced to make larger-than-normal holdings desirable, and others sufficiently overpriced to make smaller-than-normal holdings (including zero) desirable, where a "normal" holding is that which would be recommended were the stock priced correctly.

A search for a mispriced security is, in essence, a search for an area in which the financial analysts' estimates:

1. differ from the consensus estimates of the "market"

2. are generally closer to the actual values, and
3. will (preferably) eventually be reflected in security prices

Two rather different approaches may be taken in the search for mispriced securities. Valuation analysis attempts to determine the appropriate "intrinsic value" for a security, then compares this with the current price (which represents the consensus of market opinion). This may be done in great detail, using estimates of all major factors (e.g., the economy, industry sales, firm sales, capitalization ratios, growth rates, etc.). Alternatively, a short-cut method may be utilized—for example, an estimate of earnings may be multiplied by a "justified" or "normal" price/earnings ratio. A related method attempts to estimate the return expected from a security over a specified period, given its current price, then compares this with the "appropriate" return in the market for stocks with similar characteristics (e.g., risk, yield, etc.).

Another approach considers only one or two factors and compares estimates directly with the consensus estimates. For example, next year's earnings for each of a group of stocks may be estimated. If an analyst's estimate for a stock exceeds the consensus of other analysts' estimates, the stock may be considered attractive: he or she expects the actual earnings to provide a happy surprise for the market, which will bring a greater-than-normal year-end price and thus a greater-than-normal annual return. Conversely, when an analyst's estimate of earnings is below that of the market, a smaller-than-normal year-end price and thus annual return is expected.

At a more aggregate level, an analyst or investment organization may be more (or less) optimistic about the economy than the consensus of other investors. A more bullish (or less bearish) opinion could suggest that a larger-than-normal position in equities be taken; while a less bullish (or more bearish) opinion calls for a smaller-than-normal position.

Alternatively, an organization might agree with the market's views on the economy and the individual characteristics of specific securities but feel that others have misjudged the prospects for particular industries. In such cases larger-than-normal holdings may be taken in stocks representing industries with prospects that the market is thought to have underestimated, and smaller-than-normal holdings in stocks representing industries with prospects that the market is thought to have overestimated.

Beating the Market

Other examples could be given, but the difference between the two possible goals should be clear. Financial analysis may be used to *understand* the market or to try to *beat* it.

Many books and articles have been written that assertedly show how analysis can be used to beat the market. Unfortunately, no prescription that has been in print for long is likely to work without fail. Even if an approach has worked in the past, as more and more investors apply it, prices will be driven to levels at which it will not work in the future. Any system designed to beat the market, once known to more than a few people, carries the seeds of its own destruction.

There are two reasons for not including advice on guaranteed ways to "beat the market" in this book. First, to do so would make a successful system public and hence unsuccessful. Second, the author knows of no such system. Some apparent anomalies and possible inefficiencies have been described in previous chapters, and some systems proposed by others will be described in this chapter. But any book that purports to open the door to the certainty of abnormally high returns for those who follow its advice should be regarded with the greatest skepticism.

FINANCIAL ANALYSIS AND MARKET EFFICIENCY

The concept of an efficient market may appear to be firmly founded on a paradox. If financial analysts carefully analyze the prospects for the economy, various industries, and individual companies, security prices will efficiently reflect values. But if this is the case, why should anyone do financial analysis?

There are two responses to this question. First, people should engage in financial analysis only to the point at which the added benefits cover the added costs. Those who help create market efficiency must earn a living. Barring government support of such praiseworthy activity, one would expect that in a completely free market, prices would be close enough to value to make it worthwhile for only efficient analysts to search for mispriced securities. The market would thus be nearly, not perfectly, efficient. As discussed in Chapter 3, prior to 1975 brokerage firms, faced with cartel-fixed lower limits on commission rates, competed with each other by offering "free" financial analysis to clients. This may well have led to an unusually high level of market efficiency (and demand for financial analysts).

The other response to the question focuses on the less controversial goal of financial analysis. Even in a perfectly efficient market there is work to be done. Investors do differ in circumstances, portfolios should be *tailored* to accommodate such differences, and successful performance of this task generally requires estimation of the sources and magnitudes of risk and return.

NEEDED SKILLS

To understand and estimate the risk and return of the overall market, specific types of securities (e.g., bonds versus stocks), industries, sectors, and/or individual securities, one must understand financial markets and the principles of valuation. Much of the material required for such an understanding can be found in this book. But, as Figure 19-1 indicates, much more is required. Future prospects must be estimated (perhaps probabilistically) and interrelationships assessed. This requires the skills of the economist and an understanding of industrial organization. And to process relevant historical data, one should have some command of quantitative methods and understand the nuances of accounting.

The most effective financial analysts might well be described as *applied economists*. They spend relatively little time applying mechanical procedures to published data, preferring instead to concentrate on analyzing the underlying economics of firms and industries.

This chapter cannot provide all the material one needs to become a successful financial analyst. Books on accounting, economics, industrial organization, specific industries, and quantitative methods are required. Instead, we will discuss some techniques used by financial analysts, some of the pitfalls involved, and useful sources of investment information.

EVALUATING MARKET SYSTEMS

". . . switch from bonds to stocks after the growth rate of the money supply has risen for two months; switch from stocks to bonds after the growth rate of the money supply has been below its most recent peak for 15 months. Historically, such a policy would have produced over twice the return obtained by simply holding stocks."

". . . this simple formula predicted over 95% of the quarterly variation in Standard and Poor's 500-stock index over the period studied."

". . . A portfolio of the 25 stocks with the greatest historical relative strength would have outperformed a portfolio of the 25 stocks with the smallest relative strength in 8 months out of 12."

". . . This completely objective stock selection procedure, which can be performed without error by a high-speed computer, would have outperformed 80% of the professionally managed portfolios during the period in question."

Statements such as these have been made in the past and will be made in the future. All assert that a mechanical *system*, using only available historical data, can provide results superior to those obtained via sensible but passive portfolio management. Some simply provide predictions of the (stock) market; others prescribe a complete set of instructions for portfolio management. All present impressive statistics based on "as if" tests using data from some past period.

Advocates of such systems may well believe they have found the path to instant affluence. But their proofs often rest on shaky ground. When considering any system, it is imperative that one be certain that none of several sins has been committed.

Failure to Adjust for Risk

Any procedure that, *de facto*, selects high-beta stocks is likely to produce above-average returns in bull markets and below-average returns in bear markets. Over the long run it will generally produce above-average returns.

Properly adjusted for risk, systems that simply select high-beta (or low-beta) stocks are less likely to outperform sensible passive strategies. Many systems do little more than this, and their advocates often publicize only their average returns, with no consideration given to risk.

Failure to Consider Transactions Costs

Systems that rely on constant trading may possibly produce *gross* returns that exceed those of passive strategies of comparable risk. But this is not the ultimate test. Returns *net* of required transactions costs should be considered. Only trades that increase performance by more than their cost can be justified.

Failure to Consider Dividends

When the performance of a system is compared with that of some passive but sensible strategy, dividends (and interest payments) are often ignored. This may seriously bias the results. For example, a system may be advocated that, in effect, selects low-yield (high-growth) stocks. The prices of such stocks *should* increase at a faster rate than those of stocks in a broadly based index. When yields differ significantly, it is important to compare total returns.

Nonoperational Systems

To be useful, a system must not require information about the future.

Many systems require action after some series of values has reached a "peak" or "trough." But it is rarely obvious until well after a peak or trough has been reached that it was in fact a peak or trough.

A similar situation arises when an equation is *fit* to a body of data. For example, a system might posit a relationship between the money supply at time $t - 1$ and stock prices at time t. The general relationship might be:

$$SP_t = a + bM_{t-1} \tag{19-1}$$

where:

$$SP_t = \text{stock price index at time } t$$
$$M_{t-1} = \text{money supply at time } t - 1$$
$$a, b = \text{constants}$$

To make such a system operational, specific numeric values for a and b are needed. A "test" of such a system might involve fitting the equation to a body of data. The predictive ability of the equation would then be assessed. But the values for a and b found in this manner could not have been known in advance. A true test must use values that do not require advance knowledge of the results.

Spurious Fits

Given a set of data from a past period, it is not too difficult to find a system that would have worked at the time. For example, an equation with many constants can be fitted to stock data statistically; with the values thus obtained, the system would have worked well. Alternatively, simple systems can be tried, in turn, until one is found that would have worked well.

If one hundred irrelevant systems are tried with a set of data, one of them is likely to give results that are "statistically significant at the 1% level." This should not cause undue excitement. But what if the system in question were the first one tried? Its author might be forgiven for a certain amount of enthusiasm. However, subsequent experience would show that the success was in fact due to chance and not likely to be repeated.

A high correlation has been found between births in Sweden and the sighting of storks in the area. Similarly, stock prices in the United States have been shown to be correlated with sunspot activity and with women's skirt lengths. Few would associate causal relationships with such phenomena; coincidental correlations abound. Without solid reasons to believe that a relationship is due to underlying forces, it would be foolish to predict its continuation in the future.

Comparisons with Easily Beaten Systems

Often a predictive system is said to "explain" a large part of the variation in some stock index. Figure 19-2 shows the quarterly level of Standard and Poor's 500-stock index from 1960 through 1969 (the solid curve) and the levels predicted by a system based on historical values of the money supply (the dotted curve). The two sets of values are clearly quite similar.

Impressive? Not very. An extremely simple set of predictions, shown by the dashed curve in Figure 19-2, is even better. This procedure predicts that each quarter's index will equal that of the preceding quarter:

$$SP_t = SP_{t-1} \qquad (19\text{-}2)$$

FIGURE 19-2 Actual and Predicted Levels, Standard and Poor's 500-Stock Index, Second Quarter 1960 through Fourth Quarter 1969

Source: Kenneth E. Homa and Dwight M. Jaffee, "The Supply of Money and Common Stock Prices," *The Journal of Finance*, XXVI, no. 5 (December 1971), 1045–66.

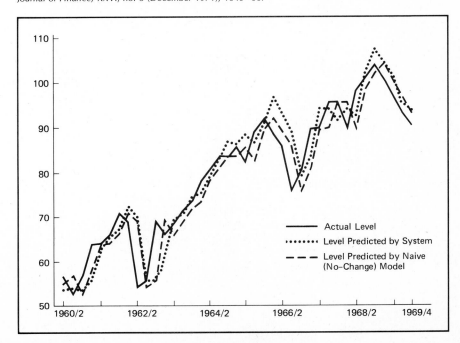

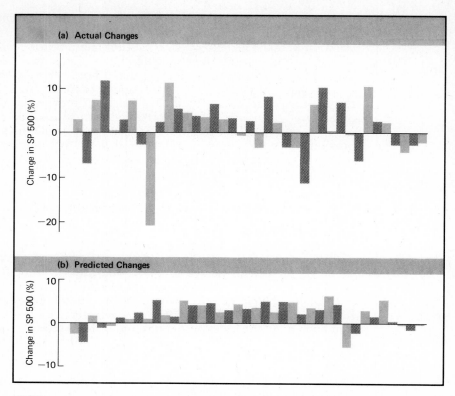

FIGURE 19-3 Actual and Predicted Quarterly Percentage Changes, Standard and Poor's 500-Stock Index. Second Quarter 1960 through Fourth Quarter 1969

Source: Kenneth E. Homa and Dwight M. Jaffee, "The Supply of Money and Common Stock Prices," *The Journal of Finance*, XXVI, no. 5 (December 1971), 1045–66.

Any system that is purported to be able to beat the market must predict *returns*, not price levels, since returns determine profits and losses. A good test is thus the extent to which predicted returns conform to actual returns. Figure 19-3 shows the price-change portion of return predicted by the system analyzed in Figure 19-2, along with the actual amount for each quarter. The relationship is tenuous, at best.

Ex Post Selection Bias

Many studies describe a stock selection procedure that outperformed standard stock market indices. Some of these avoid the sins considered thus far, but another factor may be involved. To facilitate computer processing, a standard set of data is usually employed. For example, an investigator might use a data tape prepared in 1981 with statistics relating to the period from 1971 through 1981. The stocks included on the tape were probably chosen because they existed and were important (i.e., had substantial market value) in 1981. Any system that could have selected stocks in 1971 that were certain to be alive, well, and important in 1981 should have done well.

Implicitly, studies of this type commit the sin described earlier—they require some information not available in advance. Their security selection is based in part on performance after (ex post) the selection date. Although the magnitude of this type of bias is hard to assess, its existence casts considerable doubt on the results of such studies.

Failure to Use Out-of-Sample Data

Can any evidence concerning a system's ability to beat the market be persuasive? Probably not to one who firmly believes in market efficiency. But an appropriate test can be undertaken.

The *search* for a system should be conducted using one set of data, and the *test* of its efficacy performed using an entirely different set of

FIGURE 19-4 Actual and Predicted Quarterly Percentage Changes, Standard and Poor's 500-Stock Index. Third Quarter 1970 through Second Quarter 1972

Source: James E. Pesando, "The Supply of Money and Common Stock Prices: Further Observations on the Econometric Evidence," *The Journal of Finance*, XXIX, no. 3 (June 1974), 909–22, Table 2.

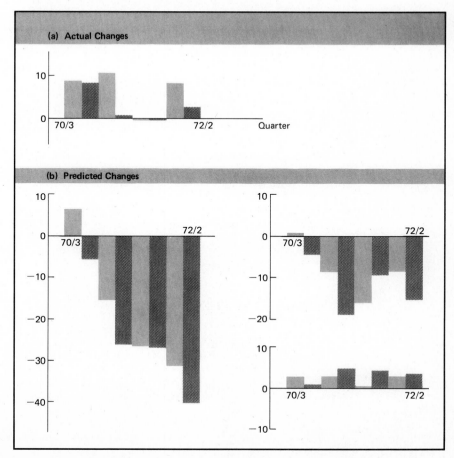

data. To be complete, such a test should involve the (simulated) management of a portfolio and be designed so that each investment decision is based solely on information available at the time the decision is made. Finally, the performance of the system should be measured in the way one would measure the performance of any investment manager—both risk and return should be taken into account, and the probability that results were due to chance rather than inherent superiority should be estimated.

Figure 19-4 shows how sobering such an exercise can be. Quarterly percentage changes in Standard and Poor's 500-stock index are shown, along with values forecast by three predictive systems, each of which fit *past* data extremely well. Presumably, the proponents of the systems had hoped for something better.

Reliance on Misleading Visual Comparisons

Occasionally the proponent of a system will produce a graph that plots both the levels of an indicator intended to predict future market moves and the levels of the market itself. Visual comparison of the two curves may suggest that the indicator has indeed predicted changes in the market. However, the eye cannot easily differentiate between a situation in which changes in a market "predictor" *follow* the market and one in which the changes *precede* the market. But the distinction is crucial, for only a situation of the latter type can bring superior investment performance.

FUNDAMENTAL VERSUS TECHNICAL ANALYSIS

One of the great divisions in the ranks of financial analysts is that between the fundamentalists and the technicians. The fundamentalist tends to look forward; the technician backward. The fundamentalist is concerned with future earnings and dividends, risk, and the appropriate rate at which to discount future prospects. The technician thinks little if at all about such things:

Technical analysis is the study of the internal stock exchange information as such. The word "technical" implies a study of the market itself and not of those external factors which are reflected in the market. . . . [A]ll the relevant factors, whatever they may be, can be reduced to the volume of the stock exchange transactions and the level of share prices; or more generally, to the sum of the statistical information produced by the market.[3]

The technician's emphasis on price is not entirely inconsistent with market efficiency:

The current market price is assumed to represent the total knowledge of the investment community about any given security at a particular moment; that price dis-

[3] Felix Rosenfeld, ed., *The Evaluation of Ordinary Shares*, a summary of the proceedings of the 8th Congress of the European Federation of Financial Analysts Societies (Paris: Dunod, 1975), 297.

counts all the good news and all the bad. The sum of the knowledge which has led to the determination of price is greater than that available to any individual investor or to any group of investors.[4]

In fact, technical analysis is often termed *demand and supply* analysis, since these are the forces that determine price.

The technician usually attempts to predict short-term price movements and thus makes recommendations concerning the *timing* of purchases and sales (of specific stocks or of stocks in general). It is sometimes said that fundamental analysis is designed to answer the question "What?" and technical analysis to answer the question "When?"

While much of the basis for technical analysis can be justified in the context of market efficiency, the key concept cannot:

. . . the methodology of technical analysis . . . rests upon the assumption that history tends to repeat itself in the stock exchange. If a certain pattern of activity has in the past produced certain results nine times out of ten, one can assume a strong likelihood of the same outcome whenever this pattern appears in the future. *It should be emphasized, however, that a large part of the methodology of technical analysis lacks a strictly logical explanation.*[5] (italics added)

Even this statement can be interpreted charitably. For example, the use of past data to estimate a future beta value is based on stock market data, assumes that history tends to repeat itself, and has some empirical validity, as shown in Chapter 13. But technicians go beyond this to assert that study of past patterns of price, volume, etc. can identify times when certain stocks, or stocks in general, are overpriced or underpriced:

Like a medical thermometer, (technical analysis) is a signalling device; sometimes a false indication is given when there is no cause for alarm, but when there is cause for alarm, the signal will almost invariably be flashed.[6]

Much of this book is concerned with the principles of fundamental analysis, for such analysis is essential if capital markets are to be efficient. Technical analysis is given less attention, for it rests on a *non sequitur*. If current prices reflect all that can be known about the future, including whatever can be deduced from the past behavior of prices, volumes, etc., it will be impossible to identify mispriced securities using technical analysis. Not surprisingly, there is little evidence showing the efficacy of technical methods. Many "proofs" have been offered, but most are based on studies in which at least one of the sins described earlier has been committed.

METHODS OF TECHNICAL ANALYSIS

Most (but not all) technical analysts rely on charts of prices and trading volumes. Virtually all employ colorful, and sometimes even mystical, ter-

[4] *Ibid.*, p. 297.
[5] *Ibid.*, pp. 297–98.
[6] Robin J. Russo, *Compare—A Technical Timing System* (New York: Dean Witter & Co. Inc., 1976).

minology. Thus a price rise on large volume may be termed an *accumulation*, in which stock is moving from "weak hands" to "strong hands." On the other hand, a price decline on large volume may be described as a *distribution*, in which stock is moving from "strong" hands to "weak" hands. When price rises, demand is said to be stronger than supply, and when price falls, supply is said to be stronger than demand. Large volume may be considered a sign of a sustainable move, while small volume indicates a transitory change. Periods in which price moves within a narrow band are *consolidation phases*; prices through which stocks move with difficulty are *resistance levels*, etc.

FIGURE 19-5 Chartists' Patterns

Source: Alan R. Shaw, "Technical Analysis," in Sumner N. Levine, ed., *Financial Analyst's Handbook* (Homewood, Ill.: Dow Jones–Irwin, Inc., 1975) I, 944–88.

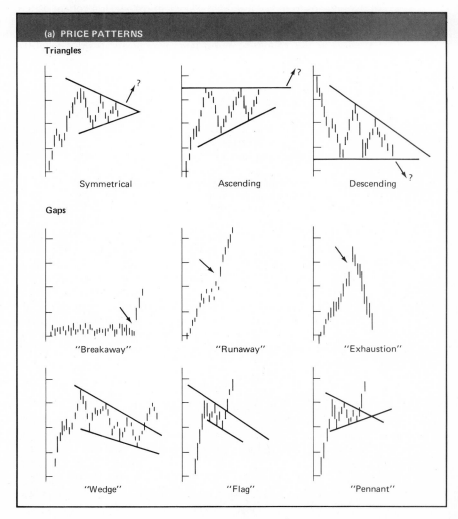

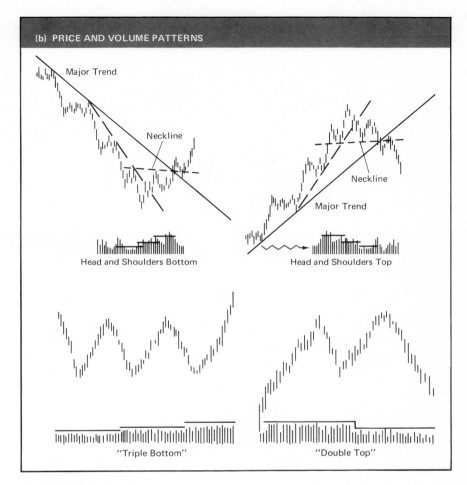

(b) PRICE AND VOLUME PATTERNS

Major Trend

Neckline

Head and Shoulders Bottom

Neckline

Major Trend

Head and Shoulders Top

"Triple Bottom"

"Double Top"

FIGURE 19-5 (Continued)

Such statements may sound profound, but they fail to pass the tests of simple logic. A price will change when the consensus estimate of value changes. Large volume associated with a price change reflects a substantial difference of opinion concerning the impact on value of new information. Small volume reflects less disagreement. If price or volume data could be used to predict future short-term price moves, investors would rush to exploit such information, moving prices rapidly enough to make the information useless.

Chartists (technicians who rely on chart formations) nonetheless believe that certain patterns carry great significance, although chartists often disagree on the significance of a pattern or even its existence on a particular chart. Figure 19-5 shows some of the more popular forms. Those in Figure 19-5(a) rely primarily on price activity, while those in Figure 19-5(b) require that price moves be "confirmed" by appropriate changes in trading volume.

Many chartists use "bar charts," such as those shown in Figure 19-5, which plot each day's price range as a vertical bar, along with the corresponding volume. Others use "line charts," which simply connect points representing daily closing prices. Still others believe that the future can be predicted only by analyzing "point and figure" charts.

Details of construction of point and figure charts vary, but the idea is to plot prices constituting a trend in a single column, moving to the next column only when the trend is reversed. For example, prices might be rounded to the nearest dollar and the chart begun by plotting a beginning rounded price. As long as the (rounded) price does not change, nothing is done. When a different price is recorded, it is plotted. As long as new prices continue in the same direction, they are plotted in the same column. When there is a reversal, a new column is started.

Point and figure enthusiasts find all sorts of patterns in their charts. Figure 19-6 presents some examples. As with all chartist techniques, the idea is to recognize a pattern early enough to profit from one's ability to foresee the future course of prices—a neat trick, if one can do it.

Many other approaches are used by technicians. Some construct *moving averages* to assess "intermediate" and "long-term" trends, which can then be compared with each other and/or with current prices. For example, prices over the previous 30 weeks may be averaged; if price is currently above this amount, it may be considered "too high." Alternatively, a long-term average may be compared with a short-term average. When the latter crosses the former, a "signal" is said to have been given; the action recommended will depend on whether the averages are rising or falling, the direction from which the short-term average crosses the long-term, etc.

Moving averages are widely used for speculation in commodity futures.[7] As indicated in Chapter 17, it may be desirable to detect the side of a market on which there is net hedging, since only by taking the other side might a speculator expect to be compensated for any risk borne. If prices do follow a seasonal pattern as hedging shifts from short to long, a moving-average strategy may help keep the speculator on the appropriate side of the market.

Another procedure used by technicians measures *relative strength*. For example, a stock price may be divided by an industry price index to indicate the stock's movement relative to its industry; an industry index may be divided by a market index; or a stock price may be divided by a market index.

Often the rate of change of a stock price or market index over some recent period is measured; this is typically termed *momentum*.

Some technical analysts focus on relationships among different indexes. For example, the venerable *Dow Theory* required that a pattern in the Dow Jones Industrial Average be "confirmed" by a required movement in the Dow Jones Railroad (now Transportation) Average before action be taken.

Some technicians compute a cumulative index of the difference between the number of issues advancing and the number declining each

---

[7] For an example, see Richard D. Donchian, "Donchian's 5- and 20-day Moving Averages," *Commodities*, III, no. 12 (December 1974), 10–16.

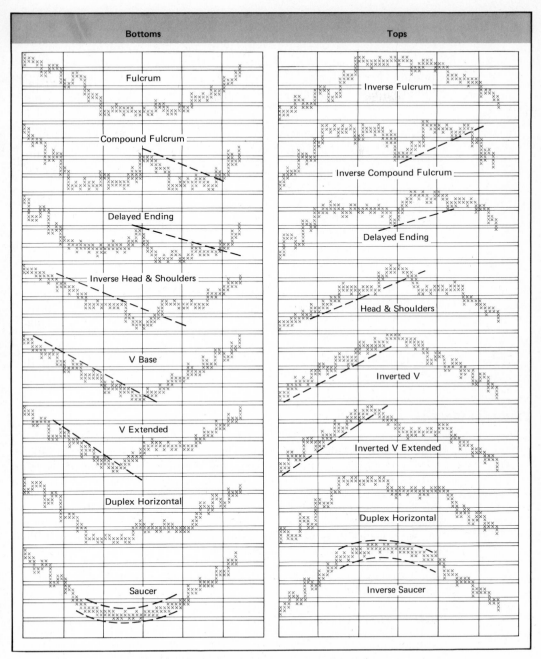

Bottoms — Tops

Fulcrum — Inverse Fulcrum

Compound Fulcrum — Inverse Compound Fulcrum

Delayed Ending — Delayed Ending

Inverse Head & Shoulders — Head & Shoulders

V Base — Inverted V

V Extended — Inverted V Extended

Duplex Horizontal — Duplex Horizontal

Saucer — Inverse Saucer

Courtesy: Morgan, Rogers, and Roberts. 150 Broadway, New York.

FIGURE 19-6 Point and Figure Chart Patterns

Source: Alan R. Shaw, "Technical Analysis," in Sumner N. Levine, ed., *Financial Analyst's Handbook* (Homewood, Ill.: Dow Jones–Irwin, Inc., 1975), I, 971.

day and compare this *advance-decline line* with the Dow Jones Industrial Average.

A whole host of technical procedures is based on the idea of *contrary opinion*. The idea is to determine what the losers are doing, then do the opposite. For example, one might see whether the "odd-lotters" (those who buy and sell in lots of less than 100 shares each) are buying or selling. If "the little investor is usually wrong," this is a certain way to be (usually) right. Fortunately for the little investor, and unfortunately for the contrary-opinion technician, the premise has not been established.

A different approach is taken by other technicians. Their idea is to identify the winners, then follow their example. Thus one might watch for situations in which specialists (market-makers) have large short positions in a stock (i.e., have borrowed and sold stock they do not own). This suggests that they think its price will go down, and "they must know something." Perhaps so, but by the time the specialists' positions are made public, it may be too late to share their profits.

Some technicians believe that large short positions are a bearish signal (since the short-sellers are pessimistic); others regard them as a bullish signal (since the short-sellers will eventually have to buy stock to return it to the lender). Neither hypothesis has been confirmed.

Many regard technicians as members of the lunatic fringe of the investment world. Descriptions of their activities are felt to be a suitable subject for anthropologists, but inappropriate in a book intended for the serious investor.

Fundamentalists far outnumber technicians, a situation that may be expected to continue in the future.

FUNDAMENTAL ANALYSIS

Fundamental analysts forecast future levels of the economy, industry sales and earnings, company sales and earnings, etc. Eventually such forecasts have to be converted to estimates of likely returns: those obtained from holding general types of securities (e.g., stocks versus bonds), the securities of firms in different industries, and/or the securities of specific firms. In some cases the conversion is made explicitly—for example, an estimate of next year's earnings may be multiplied by a projected price-earnings ratio to estimate price a year hence. In other cases the conversion is implicit—for example, stocks with projected earnings exceeding consensus estimates may be placed on an "approved" list.

Top-Down versus Bottom-Up Forecasting

A single individual analyzing investment prospects has no organizational problems. Consistent assumptions may be maintained with no need to explicitly structure the prediction process. Organizations in which two or more people divide the task of making predictions lack this advantage. Procedures are required to coordinate predictions, including any made outside the organization.

Some investment organizations follow a sequential approach. Forecasts are made first for the economy, next for industries, and finally for companies. The industry forecasts are *conditional* on the economic forecasts, and the company forecasts are conditional on both the industry and economic forecasts. Such *top-down* approaches may also provide estimates of the prospects for particular securities markets or segments thereof.

Other organizations begin with estimates of the prospects for companies and/or industries, then build to estimates of the prospects for the economy, securities markets, etc. Such *bottom-up* approaches may (implicitly) involve inconsistent assumptions. Top-down systems are less susceptible to this danger.

Probabilistic Forecasting

Explicit probabilistic forecasting often focuses on economic forecasts, since uncertainty at this level is of the greatest importance of the performance of diversified portfolios. A few alternative economic scenarios may be forecast and accompanying projections made of the prospects for industries, companies, and securities. Such an exercise provides an idea of the likely sensitivities of different securities to surprises concerning the economy. By assigning probabilities to the different scenarios, an idea of the market risks of various securities may also be obtained.

Probabilistic forecasting may also be used to estimate nonmarket risks. A specific economic or market environment is assumed and the likelihood of alternative outcomes for the firm or its securities assessed.

Econometric Models

An *econometric model* provides a means for estimating future levels of one or more *endogenous* variables, based on the assumed future levels of one or more *exogenous* variables. The model may be extremely complex (and regarded by many of its users as a mysterious "black box"), or it may be a simple formula computed with a desk calculator. In any event, it should reflect a happy marriage in which *economics* is used to suggest the forms of relevant relationships and *statistical procedures* are applied to historic data to estimate the quantitative magnitudes involved.

Econometric procedures are widely used to provide estimates of market, extramarket, and specific risks. In addition, many investment organizations utilize large-scale econometric models to translate predictions about such factors as the federal budget, expected consumer spending, and planned business investment into predictions of future levels of gross national product, rates of inflation, amounts of unemployment, etc. Several firms and nonprofit organizations maintain such models, selling outputs and/or the use of computer programs to investment organizations, corporate planners, public agencies, and others.

The producer of such a large-scale model usually provides several "standard" projections, based on judgments about exogenous variables; some also assign probabilities to alternative scenarios. Models are computerized, and users may substitute their assumptions (sometimes via a computer terminal in their own offices) to estimate the implications of different predictions. Such exercises also provide estimates of the sensitivities of various factors to key assumptions.

Large-scale econometric models of this type employ one or more equations and from several to several hundred quantitative estimates of important relationships. Estimates of the magnitudes of such relationships (*parameters*) obtained from historic data may or may not enable a model to work well in the future. When predictions turn out to be poor, it is sometimes said that there has been a *structural change* in underlying economic relationships. However, the true relationships may in fact be the same, the failure being due to the influence of factors omitted from the model. In any event, such a situation necessitates changes in the values of parameters and/or the basic form of the econometric model. Rare indeed is the user who does not "fine tune" (or completely overhaul) such a model from time to time as further experience is accumulated.

Input-Output Analysis

One firm's output may be another's input. The interdependence of firms and industries makes it difficult to do analysis in isolation. The use of different econometric models for various industries may thus yield forecasts inconsistent with *interindustry* relationships, even if each model is utilized in conjunction with a single large-scale model of the economy.

Input-output analysis can help in this regard. Interindustry relationships are considered explicitly to obtain consistent estimates of the sales of different industries, given projections of the levels of various aggregate variables.

Figure 19-7 illustrates the approach. In a basic table, such as that shown in Figure 19-7(a), many industries are included, along with several different types of nonindustry "final demand" (e.g., major classes of consumption, government spending, etc.). Each entry in the table estimates the dollar value of an industry's output required per dollar of the item in question (e.g., the output of another industry or type of final demand). In Figure 19-7(a) each dollar of the output of industry 1 is estimated to require 2 cents worth of steel as input. Similarly, 1 cent of each dollar of final demand type 1 is estimated to be spent on the output of the steel industry.

Coefficients in tables of the type shown in Figure 19-7(a) represent only the *direct* demands for the output of each industry. There are *indirect* demands as well. For example, a dollar of government spending may include 3 cents for the output of the automobile industry. But the automobile industry will require steel to produce that output; it will also require other items that use steel. Producers of those items will want products that use steel, and so on. Any change in government spending will thus have indirect as well as direct impacts on the steel industry.

Mathematical manipulation of a table such as the one shown in Figure 19-7(a) can provide a table of the type shown in Figure 19-7(b), which combines both the direct effects and all the indirect effects of a change in each type of final demand on the sales of every industry. In Figure 19-7(b) a change of one dollar in final demand of type 1 is estimated to lead even-

(a) DIRECT RELATIONSHIPS

Industries			Final Demands		
	1	2 . . .		1	2 . . .
1					
2					
Steel	.02			.01	

(Industries — Steel)

(b) DIRECT AND INDIRECT RELATIONSHIPS

Final Demands

	1	2 . . .
1		
2		
Steel	.015	

(Industries — Steel)

(c) ESTIMATED RELATIONSHIP FOR STEEL SALES

Sales for Steel Generated Using Input-Output Table

```
= .13995 Consumption of Autos and Parts
+ .05281 Consumption of Furniture
+ .03888 Consumption of Other Durables
+ .00758 Consumption of Clothing and Shoes
+ .01680 Consumption of Food and Beverages
+ .00984 Consumption of Gasoline
+ .01697 Consumption of Other Nondurables
+ .00663 Consumption of Household Operations
+ .02310 Consumption of Transportation Services
+ .00583 Consumption of Other Services
+ .14648 Investment in Producers Durable Equip.
+ .10187 Investment in Construction
+ .10679 Inventory Investment
+ .07208 Exports
− .06661 Imports
+ .04250 Federal Government Spending
+ .03867 State and Local Government Spending
```

FIGURE 19-7 Input-Output Analysis

Source: Data Resources, Inc., *Methodology of the DRI Industry Financial Service* (undated).

tually to a change of 1.5 cents in the sales of the steel industry. Figure 19-7(c) shows some actual values obtained in this manner (note that the coefficient relating steel sales to the level of imports is negative—other things equal, an increase in imports is expected to decrease steel sales).

The U.S. government prepares input/output tables every few years, as do other governments. Since such tables are based on ratios of past values (and are updated infrequently), projections using input-output analysis typically incorporate modifications. The judgments of experts may be used to adjust the coefficients in the basic input-output table. In addition, econometric models may be used to relate actual industry sales to both the values predicted using input-output analysis and various "adjusting" factors. Such procedures are needed because industries change both the relative quantities and the relative values of different inputs in response to changes in their relative prices.

Financial Statement Analysis

For some, the image of a typical investment analyst is that of a gnome, fully equipped with green eyeshade, poring over financial statements in some back room. This is rarely accurate, but security analysts do study such statements. Some try to dissect and rearrange them; others simply try to project them into the future.

A company's financial statements can be regarded as the output of a model of the firm—a model designed by management, the company's accountants, and (indirectly) the tax authorities. Different companies use different models and treat similar events in different ways. Examples (many of which were treated in Chapter 9) include: depreciation (straight-line or accelerated? short life or long?), the valuation of pension liabilities (which actuarial method? what assumed rate of interest?), inventory valuation (FIFO or LIFO?), the treatment of products leased to customers (as inventory with rental income, or immediate sales?), etc.

To fully understand a company, and to compare it with others that use different procedures, one must be a financial detective, looking for clues in footnotes and accompanying text. Those who take bottom-line figures (e.g., earnings) on faith may be more surprised by future developments than those who try to look behind the accounting veil.

The ultimate goal of the fundamental analysis of a corporation is, of course, to determine the values of the outstanding claims on its earnings. First, the firm's earnings must be projected, then the possible distributions of those earnings among the claimants must be considered and relevant probabilities assessed.

In practice, short-cut procedures are often used. Many analysts focus on reported accounting figures, even though such numbers may not adequately reflect true economic values. In addition, simple measures are often used to assess complex relationships. For example, some attempt to estimate the probability that short-term creditors will be paid in full and on time with the ratio of liquid assets to the amount of short-term debt; the probability that interest will be paid to bondholders with the ratio of earnings before interest charges to the amount of such charges; and the prospects for a firm's common stock with the ratio of earnings to the book value of equity.

The use of *ratios* for such purposes is widespread. Some ratios use items from the same statement (e.g., a particular balance sheet or income statement). Some use items from two different types of statements, others use items from two or more statements of the same type (e.g., this year's balance sheet and last year's balance sheet), and still others incorporate data on market values.

Ratios may be used in several ways. Some analysts apply absolute standards, on the grounds that a substandard ratio indicates a need for further analysis. Others compare a company's ratios to those of the "average" firm in the same industry to detect differences worthy of further consideration. Yet others analyze trends in a company's ratios over time, hoping thereby to better predict future changes.

One popular use of ratios is illustrated in Figure 19-8. If the future value of every ratio shown could be forecast, one could compute the implied forecast for the price of the firm's stock. The reciprocal of the turnover ratio equals the sum of the reciprocals of the four ratios to its right; every other value equals the product of the two items to its right. The problem with such an approach is the lack of a simple way to obtain independent estimates of such interrelated elements: for example, a stock's P/E ratio is typically related to the firm's current earnings and estimated future earnings growth.

Ratio analysis can be very sophisticated, but it can also be overly simplistic. Routine extrapolation of a present ratio (or its recent trend) may produce a poor estimate of its future value (for example, there is no reason for a firm to maintain a constant ratio of sales to inventory). Moreover, a series of simple projections may produce inconsistent estimates —e.g., predictions of balance sheet items that would not even balance.

FIGURE 19-8 The Use of Predicted Ratios to Compute Predicted Price

Source: Samuel S. Stewart, Jr., "Corporate Forecasting," in Sumner N. Levine, ed., *Financial Analyst's Handbook* (Homewood, Ill.: Dow Jones–Irwin, Inc., 1975), I, 912.

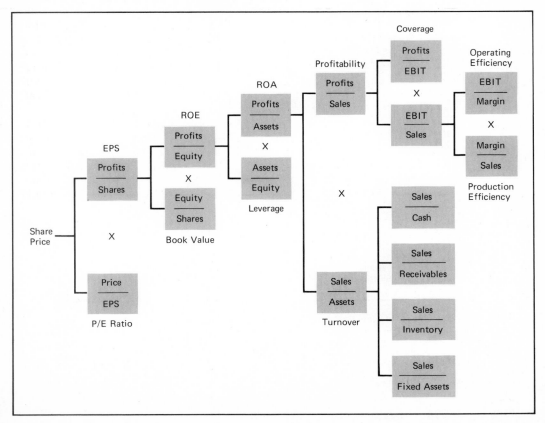

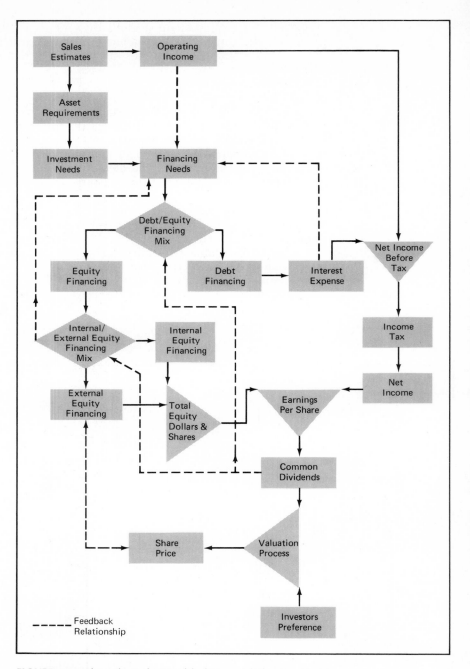

FIGURE 19-9 Flow Chart of a Simplified Financial Planning Model

Source: James M. Warren and John P. Shelton, "A Simultaneous Approach to Financial Planning," *The Journal of Finance*, XXVI, no. 5 (December 1971), 1126.

To project future financial statements, one should build a model (or models) of the relationships among the items on such statements and (usually) outside factors. Traditional ratio analysis does this, albeit crudely. Figure 19-9 illustrates a more detailed approach, which incorporates a submodel of the manner in which investors value shares and thus provides estimates of share prices as well as future earnings, dividends, etc.

In degree of complexity, many procedures lie between mere extrapolation of historical ratios and detailed models of financial relationships. Figure 19-10 provides an illustration. Profits in the chemical industry were assumed to depend on sales and capital, as follows:

$$P = S - c_f K - c_v S \qquad\qquad (19\text{-}3a)$$

where:

P = industry quarterly profits (measured by operating income before depreciation)

K = capital (measured by industry gross plant)

S = industry quarterly sales

c_f = fixed cost (dollars per quarter per dollar of invested capital)

c_v = variable cost (dollars per quarter per dollar of quarterly sales)

Rearranging the equation gives a relationship between two ratios:

$$\frac{P}{S} = (1 - c_v) - (c_f)\frac{K}{S} \qquad\qquad (19\text{-}3b)$$

FIGURE 19-10 Operating Profit Margin to Gross Plan/Sales Relationship for the Chemical Industry 1958–1970

Source: Baker Weeks and Co., Inc., *Investment Opportunities in the Chemical Industry*, April 5, 1971.

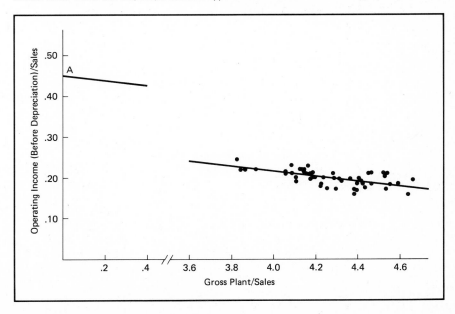

In Figure 19-10, values of P/S (vertical axis) and K/S (horizontal axis) are plotted, using quarterly data from 1958 through 1970 compiled by the Securities and Exchange Commission and the Federal Trade Commission. The regression line fit to the data intercepts the vertical axis at .45. Since this is an estimate of $(1 - c_v)$, the value of c_v appears to be approximately .55. This suggests that each additional dollar of sales adds 55 cents to costs and 45 cents to profits. The slope of the line (c_f) is .06, suggesting that each additional dollar of plant adds \$.06 per quarter to total costs.

Given these estimates, equation (19-3a) may be used to translate estimates of industry sales (S) and plant (K) into estimates of industry profits. A more detailed analysis could break sales (revenues) into indices of price per unit and number of units sold (e.g., sales = price times quantity). Explicit estimates of demand conditions (quantities sold at different prices) and supply conditions (quantities produced with various amounts of plant) could then be obtained and potentially more accurate projections made.

The advent of computerized data bases has made the analysis of accounting statements much easier. For example, Investment Management Sciences, Inc., as part of its "Financial Dynamics" service, routinely produces reports that include over 150 different values, most of them ratios or growth rates, for both individual firms and industries.

Financial statement analysis in general, and the use of ratios in particular, can help an analyst understand what a company is, where it may be going, the factors likely to affect it, and the sensitivity of its prospects to such factors. If other analysts are doing such analysis and doing it well, it will be difficult to find mispriced securities in this manner. But it should be possible to better identify firms likely to go bankrupt (as shown in Chapter 11), those with higher or lower beta values, those with greater or lesser exposure to various sources of nonmarket risk, etc. Increased understanding of such aspects may well provide ample reward for the effort entailed.

The Impact of Analysts' Recommendations on Stock Prices

When a security analyst decides that a stock is mispriced, he or she tells clients, at least some of whom act on the information. As they do so, the price of the security is likely to be affected. As news of the analyst's recommendation spreads, more investors will act on it, and the price will react even more. At some point the analyst's information will be "fully reflected" in the stock price.

If it is considered that a stock is underpriced and the analyst's clients then purchase it, the stock's price will tend to rise. Conversely, if a stock is considered overpriced and the analyst's clients then sell it, the stock's price will tend to decline. If the analyst's views were well-founded, no subsequent "counterreaction" should be expected. Otherwise, the price is likely to return to its prerecommendation level at some later stage.

An interesting example of the impact of analysts' recommendations is provided by the behavior of prices of stocks mentioned in *The Wall*

Street Journal's "Heard on the Street" column, which periodically summarizes recent stock recommendations.

An analyst's opinion is typically published in "Heard on the Street" some time after it was first given to clients. The analyst's view is thus "somewhat public" for several days before publication, but when the column appears the opinion becomes "very public," since it then reaches a substantially larger audience.

Figure 19-11(a) shows the reactions of security prices to publication in "Heard on the Street" of positive opinions about 597 stocks in 1970 and 1971. Figure 19-11(b) summarizes the reactions to negative opinions about 188 stocks during the same period. In each diagram the vertical axis plots the average cumulative "abnormal return"—that is, return adjusted

FIGURE 19-11 Effect on Stock Prices of Stock Recommendations in "Heard on the Street": 1970 and 1971

Source: Peter Lloyd Davies and Michael Canes, "Stock Prices and the Publication of Second-Hand Information," *Journal of Business,* 51, no. 1 (1978). By permission of the University of Chicago Press. © 1978.

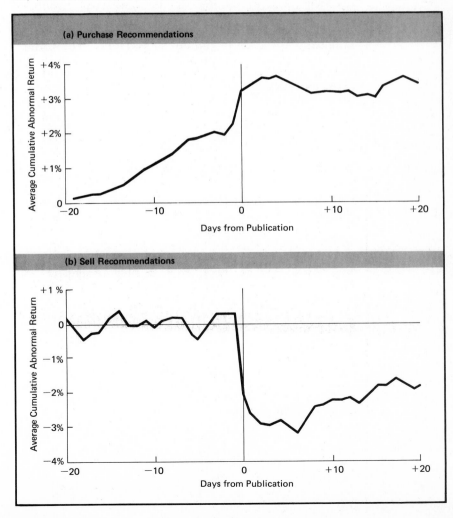

for normal reactions to overall market moves. The horizontal axes indicate trading days, relative to the date of publication of the recommendation. The cumulative abnormal returns are expressed relative to dates twenty trading days prior to publication.

As the figures indicate, on average the publication of such a recommendation does affect a security's price. After adjusting for market moves, on the date of publication the average stock recommended for purchase rose .923%, while the average stock recommended for sale fell 2.374%. After adjustments for changes in the overall market, of the 597 stocks recommended for purchase, 70% rose on the date of publication; of the 188 recommended for sale, 90% fell.

Both types of recommendation appear to contain information: twenty trading days after publication, prices were not significantly different (after adjustment for market moves) than they were at the end of the day they were published.

The upward moves in Figure 19-11(a) prior to day zero are consistent with impact of prior purchases by clients of the analysts. An alternative hypothesis would hold that analysts simply recommended purchase of stocks that had recently risen in price. Note, however, that Figure 19-10(b) is quite different: there is no distinct pattern prior to the date of publication of a sell recommendation. The analysts did not tend to recommend the sale of securities that had recently fallen in price. And on average any prior actions by their clients had little effect on price. This is consistent with the fact that to take advantage of a negative opinion one has to hold the stock initially and/or incur the extra costs associated with a short sale. Thus negative information known to relatively few investors may well impact stock prices more slowly than positive information.

SOURCES OF INVESTMENT INFORMATION

Virtually any information that affects the value of an investment can be considered "investment information." The serious financial analyst must thus be truly well informed. Even an analyst who specializes in one or two industries must cope with a staggering array of information sources.

Space precludes a detailed listing of industry-related publications here. An excellent bibliography of such sources, compiled by the New York Society of Security Analysts, can be found in the *Financial Analyst's Handbook*.[8] Periodical literature of interest to the investment analyst is indexed by industries, products, and companies in the *F&S Index of Corporations and Industries*.[9]

Figure 19-12 presents a selected bibliography of general sources, based on the holdings in the Jackson Library[10] of the Stanford University Graduate School of Business. Nothing can substitute for a careful perusal of these (and other) publications, and no attempt will be made here to describe each one. Instead, some of the more essential sources of information will be discussed.

[8] Levine, ed., *Financial Analyst's Handbook*, II, 883–926.
[9] Predicasts, Inc., 200 University Circle Research Center, 11001 Cedar Ave., Cleveland, Ohio 44106.
[10] Prepared by Martha Ashmon.

FIGURE 19-12 Selected Sources of Financial Information

I. GENERAL INFORMATION ON BUSINESS AND FINANCIAL DEVELOPMENTS

A.   Economic data handbooks:

1. Economic Statistics Bureau of Washington, D.C. *Handbook of Basic Economic Statistics.*
2. Financial Times. *International Business & Company Yearbook.*
3. Standard & Poor's *Statistical Service. Current Statistics.*
4. U.S. Bureau of the Census. *Statistical Abstracts of the U.S.*
5. *County & City Data Book.* Suppl. to *Statistical Abstracts of the U.S.*
6. *Pocket Data Book.*
7. U.S. Office of Business Economics. *Business Statistics.*

B.   Daily newspapers: (For locations see *periodical catalog*)

1. *American Banker.*
2. *Daily Commercial News.*
3. *Financial Times* (British).
4. *Journal of Commerce.*
5. *New York Times.*
6. *Wall Street Journal.*
7. *Washington Post.*

C.   Weekly newspapers:

1. *Barron's.*
2. *Commercial and Financial Chronicle* (twice weekly).
3. *Financial Post* (Canadian).
4. *Money Manager.*
5. *National Observer.*
6. *Market Chronicle.*
7. *Wall Street Transcript.*
8. *Weekly Bond Buyer.*

D.   Weekly periodicals:

1. *Business Week* (see especially "Finance" section).
2. *Financial World.*
3. *Investment Dealers' Digest.*
4. *Japan Stock Journal.*
5. *California Business.*
6. *Weekly Business Statistics.*
7. *San Francisco Business.*
8. *Newsweek* (especially "Business and Finance" section).
9. *Time* (especially "Business" or "Economy and Business" section).
10. *U.S. News and World Report.*
11. *United States Investor.*

E.   Biweekly periodicals:

1. *Chase Manhattan Bank. International Finance.*
2. *Forbes.*

F.   Monthly periodicals:

1. *Business Conditions Digest.*
2. *Conference Board Record.*
3. *Conference Board Statistical Bulletin.*
4. *Dun's.*
5. *Economic Indicators.*
6. Federal Reserve Bank Reviews: Monthly reviews are issued by all the Federal Reserve Banks.
7. *Federal Reserve Bulletin.*
8. *Federal Reserve Monthly Chart Book.*
9. *Finance.*
10. *Financial Executive.*
11. *Fortune.*
12. *Donoghue's Money Fund Report*
13. *Institutional Investor* (incorporates *Corporate Financing* and *Pensions*).
14. *Management Science.*
15. *Market Value Index.*
16. *Nation's Business.*
17. *OTC Review.*
18. *Stock Market Magazine.*
19. *Survey of Current Business.*
20. Bank letters: issued by various banks, e.g.: *Cleveland Trust Company; First National City Bank of New York; Morgan Guaranty; Chase Manhattan; Bank of America; Wells Fargo.*
21. *Venture Capital.*

Figure 19-12 (Continued)

G.   Bimonthly periodicals:

1. *Financial Analysts Journal.*
2. *Financial Planner.*
3. *Harvard Business Review.*
4. *Investment Strategy.*

H.   Quarterly periodicals:

1. *Journal of Business.*
2. *Journal of Finance* (five issues a year).
3. *Journal of Financial and Quantitative Analysis* (five issues a year).
4. *Journal of Money, Credit and Banking.*
5. *Mergers and Acquisitions.*
6. *Business Starts.*

I.   Annual economic reviews:

1. U.S. President. *Economic Report . . . together with the annual report of the Council of Economic Advisers.*
2. U.S. Bureau of Domestic Commerce. *U.S. Industrial Outlook.*
3. U.S. Congress. Economic Joint Committee. *The . . . Economic Report of the President; Hearings* (i.e., hearings held to consider the President's *Economic Report*).
4. U.S. Congress. Economic Joint Committee. *Joint Economic Report* (i.e., the Committee's report on their hearings on the President's *Economic Report*).
5. U.S. Office of Business Economics. *Business Statistics* (biennial; published as a supplement to the *Survey of Current Business*).

II.   INDUSTRY INFORMATION

A.   Business and financial journals and periodicals (see Section I above).
B.   Government publications and documents; see especially:

1. U.S. Census Bureau. *Census of Manufacturers' Census of Services Industries* (every four to five years).
2. _____. *Census of Retail Trade.*
3. _____. *Census of Wholesale Trade.*
4. _____. *Current Industrial Reports.*
5. U.S. Bureau of Domestic Commerce. *U.S. Industrial Outlook.*
6. U.S. Census Bureau. *Statistical Abstracts of the U.S.*
   U.S. Office of Business Economics. *Business Statistics.*
8. U.S. Mines Bureau. Minerals Year book.
9. U.S. Census Bureau. *Annual Survey of Manufacturers.*
10. *Survey of Current Business* (monthly periodical).
    Treasury Bulletin (monthly periodical).
    Annual reports of regulatory commissions such as the F.P.C., F.T.C., I.C.C., and the S.E.C.

C.   Reports of investment and business services:

1. Arnold Bernhard & Co.
   a. *Value Line Investment Survey.*
   b. *Value Line Options and Convertibles.*
2. Moody's
   a. *Manuals.*
   b. *Bond Survey* (weekly).
3. Howard & Company. *Going Public.*
4. Kidder, Peabody & Co., *Research Service.*
5. Smith Barney, Harris Uphan & Co. *Research Service.*
6. Standard and Poor's:
   a. *Investment Advisory Survey* (weekly).
   b. *Industry Surveys.*
   c. *Outlook.*
   d. Statistical Service. *Current Statistics.*
7. Wells Fargo Bank. *Security Market Plane Report.*

D. Special bibliographies (indexes to periodicals):

1. *Business Periodicals Index.*
2. *Public Affairs Information Service. Bulletin.*
3. *Wall Street Journal Index.*
4. *F & S Index of Corporations and Industries* (Domestic and International).
5. *Predicasts* (abstracts periodical articles that contain forecasts for various industries).
6. *F & S Index of Corporate Change.*
7. *Disclosure Journal* (indexes 10-K Reports, Annual Reports to Shareholders, Registration Statements).

E. Special reports of private agencies:

1. Audit Investment Research, Inc.
   a. *Audit's Realty Trust Review.*
   b. *Real Estate Disclosure Review.*
2. Creative Strategies Inc. *Industry Analysis Service.*
3. *Retail Automation Report.*
4. Stanford Research Institute. Long Range Planning Service. *Reports.*

F. Announcements of Mergers and Acquisitions (monthly publication of the Conference Board).

G. Reports and brochures of brokerage and banking firms:

1. *Wall Street Transcript* (weekly newspaper, most of whose contents are reprints of brokerage house reports).
2. *Merrill Lynch Review.*
3. M.A. Schapiro & Co.
4. Kidder Peabody & Co.
   a. *Economic Perspectives.*
   b. *Financial Perspectives.*
   c. *Money and Capital Markets.*
   d. *Portfolio Manager's Digest.*
   e. *Portfolio Strategy.*
   f. *Portfolio Managers Digest.*
5. *Bank of America*
   a. *Daily Quotation Sheets: U.S. Government Securities,* Federal Agencies. . .
   b. *Federally Guaranteed Tax Exempt Notes.*
   c. *Weekly Monetary Summary.*
6. Bankers Trust. *Credit and Capital Markets.*
7. Siegel Trading Company. *Weekly Market Letter.*
8. Smith Barney, Harris Upham & Co. *Analysts Roundtable.*
9. Thomson and McKinnon Auchincloss Kohlmeyer (location Table B-1).
   a. *Commodity Letter.*
   b. *Technical Analysis.*
10. Goldman, Sachs. *Risk, Return and Equity Valuation.*

H. Trade association publications (especially annual review numbers):

1. *Dow Jones Investor's Handbook.*
2. *Symbol Stock Guide,* GTE.
3. *Security Traders Handbook.*

I. Trade Journals (especially annual statistical numbers).

III. COMPANY INFORMATION

A. Corporation reports:

1. *Annual reports to shareholders.*
2. *10-K reports.*
3. *Prospectuses.*
4. *Registration statements.*
5. *Disclosure Journal* (indexes annual reports to shareholders, 10-K reports, registration statements).
6. Financial Stock Guide Service. *Directory of Obsolete Securities.*

Figure 19-12 (Continued)

B. **Financial and business journals (see Section II, above; the *F & S Index of Corporations and Industries* indexes most of these extensively by S.I.C. and by company name).**

C. **Publications of *brokerage and banking firms*.**

D. **Manuals:**

1. *Moody's Manuals (Industrials; Transportation; Public Utilities; Banks and Finance; Municipals and Governments; O.T.C. Industrials).*
2. *Over-the-Counter Securities Handbook.*
3. *Penny Stock Handbook.*
4. *Standard and Poor's Standard Corporation Descriptions.*
5. *Standard and Poor's Stock Reports* (American Stock Exchange; New York Stock Exchange; Over-the-Counter and Regional Exchanges).
6. *Walker's Manual of Far Western Securities* (Industrial & Financial).

E. **Publications of financial services:**

1. Moody's
   a. *Bond Record.*
   b. *Bond Survey.*
   c. Manuals (see Section III, above; note especially the semiweekly supplements and the blue sections in the center of annual volumes).
   d. *Dividend Record.*
   e. *Handbook of Common Stocks.*
   f. *Stock Survey.*
2. Standard and Poor's
   a. Analysts Handbook (annual, with monthly supplements).
   b. *Bond Guide.*
   c. *Called Bond Record.*
   d. *Commercial Paper Reports.*
   e. *Dividend Record.*
   f. *Earnings Forecaster.*
   g. *Fixed Income Investor.*
   h. *Industry Surveys.*
   i. *Outlook* (incorporates Investment Advisory Survey).
   j. *Standard Convertible Bond Reports.*
   k. *Standard Corporation Descriptions* (note especially the daily supplements).
   l. *Stock Guide* (also called the *Security Owner's Stock Guide*)
   m. Statistical Service. *Current Statistics.*
3. *Financial Dynamics* (see also its *Debt Analysis Supplement*).
4. *Vickers Guide to Insurance Company Portfolios* (Common Stocks).
5. _____. (Buying–Selling–Holdings of Common Stocks).
6. _____. (Buying–Selling–Holdings of Stocks & Bonds).
7. United Business Service. *United Business & Investment Report.*
8. Arnold Bernhard & Co.:
   a. Value Line *OTC Special Situation.*
   b. *Value Line Investment Survey.*
9. *R.H.M. Warrant and Stock Survey.*
10. John S. Herold, Inc. *Over-the-Counter Growth Stocks.*
11. Kalb, Voorhis & Co. *KV Convertible Fact Finder.*
12. *Quote* (American; New York; Over-the-Counter).

IV. SECURITIES MARKET INFORMATION: INVESTMENT ADVICE

A. **Bond and stock ratings:**

1. Moody's *Manuals* (Bonds).
2. Moody's *Bond Record.*
3. Standard and Poor's *Bond Guide.*
4. Call Bond Record.
5. *Value Line Investment Survey. Commercial Paper Rating Guide.*
6. *Value Line Options and Convertibles.*
7. *Value Line OTC Special Situation Service.*

B. Beta factors:

1. Merrill Lynch, Pierce, Fenner & Smith, Inc. *Security Risk Evaluation.*
2. Goldman, Sachs. *Risk, Return and Equity Valuation.*
3. *Wells Fargo Bank Security Market Plane Report.*
4. *Value Line Investment Survey.*

C. General market condition and outlook:

1. Moody's *Bond Survey.*
2. Moody's *Stock Survey.*
3. Standard and Poor's *Outlook.*
4. United Business Service. *United Business and Investment Report.*
5. Publications of brokerage and banking firms (see Section II).
6. Wells Fargo Bank. *Market Performance Report.*

D. Recommendation and appraisals of securities:

1. Wells Fargo Bank. *Security Report.*
2. Goldman, Sachs. *Risk, Return and Equity Valuation.*
3. Brokerage and banking house reports and brochures (see Section II).
4. Reports of financial reporting agencies and investment services, especially:
   a. Smith Barney, Harris Upham & Co. *Research Service.*
   b. Moody's *Bond Survey.*
   c. Moody's *Stock Survey.*
   d. Standard and Poor's *Outlook.*
   e. Standard and Poor's *Fixed Income Investor.*
   f. United Business Service. *United Business & Investment Report.*
   g. *Value Line Investment Survey.*
   h. Standard and Poor's *Investment Advisory Survey.*

V. SECURITY PRICE QUOTATIONS

A. Daily range and close:

1. *Commercial and Financial Chronicle* (Monday issue contains high and low, but not the close, for each day of the preceding week).
2. *New York Times.*
3. *San Francisco Chronicle.*
4. *Wall Street Journal.*
5. Standard & Poor's *Daily Stock Price Record.*

B. Weekly range and close:

1. *Barron's.*
2. *Financial Post* (Canadian).

C. Monthly range:

1. *Bank and Quotation Record.*
2. Standard and Poor's *Daily Stock Price Record.*

D. Annual range:

1. *Bank and Quotation Record* (January issue has range for preceding year; other issues have range for current year to date).
2. *Barron's* (first issue in January has range for preceding year; other issues have range for current year to date).

Figure 19-12 (Continued)

3. *Commercial and Financial Chronicle* (Monday issue).
4. Dow Jones *Investor's Handbook* (annual).
5. Standard and Poor's:
   a. *Standard Corporation Descriptions*.

b. *Standard Convertible Bond Reports*.
c. *Stock Reports* (A.S.E.; N.Y.S.E.; O-T-C and Regional Exchanges).
d. *Stock Guide*.
e. *Bond Guide*.

E.   **Other compendia of price quotations:**

1. *Daily Stock Price Record* (American Stock Exchange; New York Exchange; Over-the-Counter; each quarterly volume lists range for each stock for each day of the quarter).

2. *National Bond Summary; National Stock Summary* (list bid and asked prices on each O-T-C trade as reported to the National Quotation Bureau).

VI. SECURITY PRICE INDEXES AND AVERAGES

A.   **Daily and financial newspapers.**
B.   **Periodicals:**

1. *Barron's*.
2. *CPI Detailed Index*.
3. *Commercial and Financial Chronicle* (Monday issue).

4. *Federal Reserve Bulletin*.
5. *Survey of Current Business*.
6. *Producer Prices and Price Indexes* (formerly *Wholesale Prices Index*).

C.   **Special services:**

1. Standard and Poor's
   a. *Outlook*.
   b. Statistical Service. *Current Statistics*.
   c. *Daily Stock Price Index*.

2. Moody's
   a. *Manuals* (blue section).
   b. *Bond Survey*.
   c. *Stock Survey*.

D.   **Other compendia of price indexes and averages:**

1. *Dow Jones Averages 1885–1970* (averages for each day since the series began).
2. *Wall Street Journal Index* (pages at the back list the Dow Jones

averages for each day of the month covered in that volume of the index).
3. Fisher, L., and J.H. Lorie. *A Half Century of Returns on Stocks and Bonds*.

VII. DATA ON MONEY MARKETS

A.   *Weekly Bond Buyer*.
B.   **Salomon Brothers:**

1. *Analytical Record of Yields and Yield Spreads* (looseleaf).
2. *Comments on Credit* (weekly).
3. *Bond Market Roundup* (weekly).
4. *Annual Review of the Bond Market*.

5. *Preferred Stock Guide* (annual).
6. *Supply and Demand for Credit* (annual).

VIII. DATA ON MUTUAL FUNDS

Anyone planning to invest in anything but mutual funds should read *The Wall Street Journal*. It provides extensive statistical data, financial news, and even a bit of humor. An alternative is the financial section of *The New York Times*. Most other daily newspapers contain financial information, but much less than found in the *Journal* or the *Times*. A weekly publication with a wealth of statistical data is *Barron's*.

A useful source of daily price and volume figures for both stocks and mutual funds is Standard and Poor's *Daily Stock Price Record*. Each volume covers one calendar quarter, and all values for a given stock or fund are listed in a single column.

Dividend information, listed by stock, can be found in either *Moody's Dividend Record* or *Standard and Poor's Dividend Record*.

Historic beta values for stocks adjusted for mean reversion are shown in the *Value Line Investment Survey*. Merrill Lynch, Pierce, Fenner and Smith, Inc., publishes a *Security Risk Evaluation*, which includes adjusted and unadjusted beta values and associated statistics. Wells Fargo Bank's *Security Market Plane Report* service provides estimates of (beta-based) security risk classes, derived using both the analysis of historic data (including fundamental measures) and subjective judgments of analysts; an estimate of an ex ante security market plane is also included. Nomura provides a beta service for Japanese securities, the firm of Christian Jousset provides a service for French securities, and the London Business School provides a service for British Securities.

Many brokerage houses provide their major clients with the monthly *Stock Guide* and *Bond Guide* published by Standard and Poor's. Figures 19-13 and 19-14 illustrate the contents of these useful publications.

STANDARD & POOR'S CORPORATION

Title-Industry Code & Co. Finances (In Italics) / Individual Issue Statistics, Exchange	Ind / Interest Dates	Chgs. 1976 / S&P Quality Rating	Times Earn. 1977 / Eligible	Bond Form	Times Earn. 1978 / Legality (C t, M a, N H, N J, N Y)	Yr. End	Cash & Eqv (Million $) / Redemption Provisions: Refund Earliest/Other	Current Assets (Million $) / Call Price For S.F.	Current Liabs (Million $)	Date / Call Price Regular	L. Term Debt (Mil $) / Out-st'd'g (Mil $)	Debt % Prop / Underwriter Firm	Underwriter Year	Interim Times Earn. Period / Price Range 1960-77 High	1960-77 Low	Interim 1978 / Price Range 1978 High	Interim 1979 / 1978 Low	1979 High	1979 Low	Mo. End Price Sale(s) or Bid	Curr Yield	Yield to Mat.
Abbott Laboratories	***21a***	***4.28***	***4.73***		***5.77***	***Dc***	***66.7***	***766***	***502***	***9-79***	***214***	***48.3***		***9 Mo Sep***		***5.50***	***5.46***					
• SF Deb 6¼ s '93	Jj15	AA	X	R	- - ✓- -		....	100		102.30	13.9	G1	'68	103½	73⅛	92	86¼	89¼	79	A87	7.18	7.86
• SF Deb 7⅝ s '96	Ms	AA	X	R	- ✓✓- -		[1]103.56	100		+ 104.272	43.4	L5	'71	106	80	99	92½	93¾	92⅛	92⅛	8.28	8.53
• SF Deb 9.20s '99	aO15	AA	X	R	- ✓✓- -		[2]104.60	[2]100		+ 106.90	100	G2	'74	111½	99	105¾	99½	100	85	85½	10.76	11.01
Action Industries	***59***	***△3.27***	***△1.08***		***d△0.14***	***Je***	***3.65***	***29.7***	***8.12***	***9-79***	***20.0***	***172***		***3 Mo Sep***		***0.51***	***1.00***					
◆Sr SF Deb 11s '92	mS15	BB-	Y	R	- - - - -		[3]106¾	[4]100		+ 109.30	12.0	d1	'77	100	97⅝	99	78½	87½	74	74½	14.77	15.68
Aerojet-General	***2***	***Now General Tire & Rubber, see***																				
SF Deb 5¼ s '81	Mn	NR	X	CR	- - - - -		....	100		+ 100¼	[5]3.00	K2	'61	104	59	88¾	82¼	91	80	91	5.77	12.82
[6]***Aetna Business Credit***	***26e***	***1.27***	***1.30***		***1.26***	***Dc***	***58.2***			***9-79***	***264***			***9 Mo Sep***		***1.28***	***1.22***					
• Sr Notes 8¾ s '83	jJ15	A	X	R	- - - - -		....	....		[7]100	25.0	W2	'76	105	100	102	95½	98	86⅞	87¼	10.03	13.40
• Sr Sub Nts 9¾ s '86	jJ15	BBB	X	R	- - ✓- -		....	....		[8]100	20.0	W2	'76	107½	99⅜	105	99	100¾	83	s87⅝	11.13	12.58
Aetna Life & Casual	***35***	***N/A***	***32.60***		***20.44***	***Dc***					***592***			***9 Mo Sep***		***19.41***	***12.38***					
• Deb 8⅛ s 2007	aO15	AAA	X	R	- ✓- - -		....	[9]100		[10]104.58	250	M9	'77	101½	97⅝	97⅞	88	91	74	77	10.55	10.73
Airco, Inc	***14b***	***Subsid of BOC Int'l***																				
SF Deb 9⅜ s 2000	aO	A	X	R	- - ✓- -		[11]104.33	[12]100		+ 106.91	74.5	D4	'75	106½	98	106½	88	98¾	84	85	11.03	11.25
Akzona, Inc	***68b***	***1.40***	***1.46***		***2.20***	***Dc***	***11.2***	***369***	***146***	***9-79***	***224***	***58.8***		***9 Mo Sep***		***2.22***	***2.19***					
• SF Deb 7½ s '97	Fa15	BBB	X	R	- - - - -		[13]103¾	[14]100		+ 104⅞	60.0	M5	'72	100¼	75	84⅞	75	79⅞	76½	A79⅞	9.39	9.97
Alabama Bancorporation	***10a***	***1.31***	***1.32***		***1.29***	***Dc***					***60.4***			***9 Mo Sep***		***1.30***	***1.22***					
• Flt'g Rate Nts[15] 10.55s '99	mS	AA	X	R	✓- ✓- -		Z100	....		[16]100	25.6	F2	'74	104½	99	100½	98¾	102½	97½	98	10.77	....
• Notes 9½ s '84	jJ	AA	X	R	✓- ✓- -		....	....		[17]100	35.0	F2	'75	108⅝	100	106	99⅛	101¼	91½	92	10.33	11.84
[18]***Alabama Gas Corp***	***73b***	***△2.75***	***△2.59***		***△2.10***	***Sp***	***0.91***	***31.2***	***37.3***	***9-79***	***34.5***	***31.7***										
1st E 5⅛ s '84	fA	A	X	CR	✓- ✓✓✓		....	+ 100.33		+ 101.04	2.00	H2	'59	106	66	84⅜	79½	82⅛	77⅛	78¼	6.55	11.34
1st F 7¼ s '94	Fa	A	X	R	✓- ✓✓✓		....	100		105.55	8.50	W7	'69	101¾	70½	87⅝	79⅜	79⅞	70	70⅛	10.34	11.60
1st G 8¾ s '96	Jj	A	X	R	✓- ✓✓✓		....	100		+ 108.61	[19]14.4	W7	'71	108½	80¼	100½	90¼	90¾	78⅝	79	11.08	11.67
[20]***Alabama Power Co.***	***72a***	***1.71***	***2.70***		***1.56***	***Dc***	***99.5***	***335***	***629***	***9-79***	***1865***	***48.3***		***12 Mo Sep***		***1.72***	***1.46***					
1st 3¼ s '81	mS	BBB-	X	CR	✓- ✓- ✓		....	100		100	15.0	M9	'51	87⅜	58⅜	86¼	82	87	82	86⅛	3.77	12.79
1st 3⅜ s '82	Ao	BBB-	X	CR	✓- ✓- ✓		....	+ 100.41		+ 100.41	12.0	B9	'52	88⅜	59	83¾	80	84	80	83	4.07	12.28
1st 4⅛ s '83	Mn	BBB-	X	CR	✓- ✓- ✓		....	+ 100.46		+ 100.54	11.9	U3	'53	98	63⅛	82	77½	80⅝	76¾	79	5.22	11.95
• 1st 3⅛ s '84	Ms	BBB-	X	CR	✓- ✓- ✓		....	+ 100.35		+ 100.62	17.0	M9	'54	81½	56⅛	73⅛	70¼	75¼	69	71¾	4.36	11.93
1st 3½ s '85	Jd	BBB-	X	CR	✓- ✓- ✓		....	+ 100.71		+ 100.94	15.0	B9	'55	88½	54¼	72½	67⅜	70¼	65	67	5.22	11.95
1st 3½ s '86	Ms	BBB-	X	CR	✓- ✓- ✓		....	+ 100.93		+ 101.21	13.7	U3	'56	88	52½	70½	65	67⅝	61⅞	64	5.47	11.91
1st 4⅝ s '87	Mn	BBB-	X	CR	✓- ✓- ✓		....	+ 100.64		+ 101.48	14.5	M9	'57	104¼	57⅝	73¾	67⅝	69¾	63	64¾	7.14	11.98
• 1st 8⅝ s '87	aO	BBB-	X	R	✓- ✓- ✓		[21]103.62	[22]100		+ 106.32	75.0	B1	'77	99½	97⅞	99⅛	88⅛	94	76¼	s80½	10.71	12.64
1st 3⅞ s '88	Jj	BBB-	X	CR	✓- ✓- ✓		....	+ 100.18		+ 101.05	23.0	L5	'58	92¾	51⅜	67¾	62	64¼	57¼	59⅛	6.55	11.95
1st 4⅞ s '89	Mn	BBB-	X	CR	✓- ✓- ✓		....	+ 100.20		+ 101.64	20.0	M9	'59	107⅞	56½	71¼	65¼	66⅝	59	60	8.13	12.16
1st 5s '90	Ao	BBB-	X	CR	✓- ✓- ✓		....	+ 100.17		+ 101.84	6.96	B9	'60	105½	56⅜	70¾	64⅝	65¼	57¾	58⅜	8.57	12.23
1st 4½ s '91	Ms	BBB-	X	CR	✓- ✓- ✓		....	+ 100.93		+ 102.34	13.0	E1	'61	102	51⅝	65⅜	59¾	60¼	52⅞	53⅛	8.47	12.34
1st 4⅜ s '92	Jd	BBB-	X	CR	✓- ✓- ✓		....	100		+ 101.76	17.0	B9	'62	100½	49⅜	62⅝	57	57⅝	49⅝	49⅝	8.82	12.45
1st 4⅜ s '93	Mn	BBB-	X	CR	✓- ✓- ✓		....	+ 100.06		+ 102	16.0	L5	'63	100⅜	48½	61½	55⅝	56⅜	47¾	47¾	9.16	12.54
1st 4⅝ s '94	Mn	BBB-	X	CR	✓- ✓- ✓		....	+ 100.81		+ 102.83	29.0	F2	'64	102¼	49⅝	62½	56¼	57	47½	47½	9.74	12.65
1st 4⅞ s '95	mS	BBB-	X	CR	✓- ✓- ✓		....	+ 100.61		+ 102.91	40.0	B9	'65	102¾	50¾	63¼	56⅝	57⅜	47⅛	47⅛	10.34	12.75
1st 6¼ s '96	aO	BBB-	X	CR	✓- ✓- ✓		....	+ 101.05		+ 104.20	29.4	B9	'66	106½	61½	74⅛	66¾	67⅜	55⅛	55⅛	11.34	12.82
1st 6½ s '97	aO	BBB-	X	CR	✓- ✓- ✓		....	100		+ 103.82	28.0	L5	'67	100	63⅛	75½	68⅛	68¾	56	56	11.61	12.85
1st 7s '98	mN	BBB-	X	CR	✓- ✓- ✓		....	100		+ 104.35	25.0	L5	'68	100	67	79¼	71⅝	72⅜	58½	58½	11.97	12.92
1st 8⅝ s '99	mN	BBB-	X	CR	✓- ✓- ✓		....	+ 100.72		+ 106.18	35.0	M9	'69	108	78⅞	93¾	85	85¾	69¼	69¼	12.45	12.97
• 1st 9s 2000	mN	BBB-	X	R	✓- ✓- ✓		....	100		+ 106.21	44.9	H2	'70	111½	80	98¾	87	91	71	s71⅛	12.65	13.06
• 1st 8½ s 2001	jJ	BBB-	X	R	✓- ✓- ✓		....	+ 101		+ 106.88	85.0	F2	'71	108½	75	93	79⅛	84⅞	67¾	s67¾	12.55	12.98

Uniform Footnote Explanations—See Page 1. Other: [1]Fr 3-1-81. [2]Fr 10-15-84. [3]Fr 9-15-82. [4]Fr 9-15-83. [5]Call $0.8M 8-1-79. [6]Subsid of Aetna Life & Cas. [7]Fr 7-15-82. [8]Fr 7-15-83. [9]Fr 10-15-88. [10]Fr 10-15-87. [11]Fr 10-1-85. [12]Fr 10-1-86. [13]Fr 2-15-82. [14]Fr 2-14-83. [15]Int to 2-29-80,etc. [16]Fr 9-1-84:hldrs option,*100. [17]Fr 1-1-83. [18]Subsid & data of Alagasco. [19]Call $0.4M 2-15-78. [20]Subsid of Southern Co. [21]Fr 10-1-82. [22]Restricted to $0.75M yearly to 1982.

FIGURE 19-13 Standard and Poor's *Bond Guide*

8 AAR-Aff

STANDARD & POOR'S CORPORATION

INDEX	Ticker Symbol	STOCKS NAME OF ISSUE (Call Price of Pfd. Stocks)	Market	Com Rank. & Pfd. Rating	Par Val.	Inst. Hold Cos	Inst. Hold Shs. (000)	PRINCIPAL BUSINESS	PRICE RANGE 1960-78 High	1960-78 Low	1979 High	1979 Low	1980 High	1980 Low	Feb. Sales in 100s	February, 1980 Last Sale Or Bid High	Low	Last	% Div. Yield	P-E Ratio
1	AIR	AAR Corp	AS	B+	1	2	4	Mkts aviation parts/service	21⅜	2¾	12	7¾	15⅝	10⅞	943	14⅞	13⅜	14¾	2.7	10
2	AAV	AAV Co's	AS	B+	No	5	43	Vend sell'g: whlsler: food sv	22⅛	2⅞	5⅞	3¾	4¾	3⅞	210	4½	3⅞	3⅞	5.2	5
3	ABT	Abbott Laboratories	NY,B,C,M,Ph,P	A+	No	320	21754	Diversified health care prod	40	4 1/16	43⅜	29½	42½	36⅛	13213	40⅜	36⅛	37¼	2.7	13
4	ABITF	Abitibi-Price Inc	N,Mc,Tc,Vc	B+	No	67	2239	Canada's lgst forest prod co	16¾	1¾	20⅞	14⅛	20⅝	15¾	528	20⅝	19½	20⅝ B	7.8	4
5	ACIG	Academy Insur Gr	N	...	10¢	3	42	Accident,health,life insur	15	⅝	5⅝	1⅝	5⅞	4⅞	1900	5½	5	5⅛ B	...	18
6	ALAR	Acapulco Y LA Rest	N	NR	10¢	...	....	Mexican dining restaurants	4¾	2¼	6¾	3¼	5⅜	4⅞	91	5⅜	4⅞	4⅞ B	...	9
7	ACLE	Acceleration Corp	N	...	25¢	1	105	Insurance:credit life/disab	18⅛	5⅜	9	3¾	6¾	4¾	1101	6¾	4¾	5¼ B	...	5
8	ACRA	Accuray Corp	N	B—	1	4	89	Mfr,lease proc mgmt systems	44¼	2	5⅜	3½	8½	4⅞	5664	8½	6¾	7½ B	...	42
9	ACET	Aceto Chemical	N	B+	1¢	4	40	Chemical dstr & mfr	16⅞	¾	14¾	12⅞	14⅝	14¼	331	14⅝	14¼	14¼ B	s...	5
10	ACF	ACF Indus	NY,B,Ph,P	A	No	82	3040	Mfr & lease RR cars: auto eq	45⅝	5¼	39¾	29⅛	43¼	33⅝	3606	43¼	37	38½	5.8	7
11	ACK	Acklands Ltd	Tc,Vc	B	No	1	10	Auto & ind'l parts dstr	20½	4	17	14⅜	17	16¼	190	16¾	16¼	16½	3.6	6
12	ACMT	ACMAT Corp	N	B—	No	...	....	Interior systems contractors	29¼	¾	2⅞	1⅝	3⅝	2½	167	3⅝	3½	3⅝ B	...	10
13	AMT	Acme-Cleveland	NY	B+	1	28	1954	Mfr automatic mach tools	30⅞	7	27¾	17½	34¼	26	845	33⅞	26⅝	27	5.2	6
14	ALEC	Acme Electric	N	B+	1	...	....	Contr pwr sup: transform's	8¾	½	7⅜	4½	8⅜	6	408	8⅜	6½	7¼ B	s3.3	9
15	ACME	Acme General	N	B+	No	1	50	Door hardware systems	22¼	2¼	13¾	8	11¼	8¼	460	11¼	9	9½ B	6.3	5
16	ACL	Acme Precision Prod	AS	C	1	...	....	Zinc die castings-auto	11⅜	¾	2	1⅛	2¾	1⅛	292	2⅝	2	2	...	d
17	ACU	Acme United	AS	A—	2½	3	658	Shears,scissors:medic eq	17¼	2¼	17	10	15⅜	12½	116	13¾	12¾	13¼	2.6	12
18	ACX	Action Indus	AS	B—	10¢	...	....	Merchandising programs	31⅛	1½	4⅞	2⅝	4⅛	3⅛	227	3⅞	3⅛	3½	...	d
19	ATN	Acton Corp	AS,B,Ph	B	6⅔¢	...	....	Snack foods:CATV:tel eq	32½	¼	15⅝	7⅞	16⅜	11¾	1721	16⅜	13⅞	14⅜	2.1	9
20	ADAC	ADAC Laboratories	N	NR	No	9	166	Nuclear medicine comput sys	....	....	11¼	7½	12½	10	2004	12½	11	11¾ B	...	26
21	ADGE	Adage Inc	N	NR	1	...	....	Computer graphics term sys	33	½	10¼	4	15¾	9½	184	15¾	13¼	13¼ B	...	17
22	ADG	Adams Drug	NY	B+	9-10	3	823	Retail drug chain,East Coast	26¾	1⅜	4⅞	3¼	4	3⅝	319	4	3⅝	3⅝	1.1	5
23	ADX	Adams Express	NY,B,Ph	...	1	16	183	Closed-end investment co	22	7	13½	10¾	14½	12⅜	1620	13⅞	12⅜	12½	6.6	..
24	ALL	Adams-Millis	NY,Ph	B	No	5	158	Hosiery & yarn products	43⅝	1¾	6⅛	4¼	5¼	4⅛	400	5⅛	4½	4½	4.4	5
25	AE	Adams Res & Energy	AS	B	10¢	1	18	Oil dstr:transp:coal:o&g	6⅛	1½	12½	4⅝	15⅜	10¾	2139	15⅜	12½	12¾	...	16
26	AAR	Adams-Russell	AS	B+	50¢	1	3	Electronics mfg:CATV, TV	26½	⅜	20¼	7¼	23¾	17	927	23	20¼	21¼	0.6	18
27	ADSNB	Addison-Wesley Pub[62]	N	B+	No	4	116	Pub textbooks, prof, ref books	33⅛	3⅛	12½	8¾	12½	8¾	388	9¾	8¾	8¾ B	5.7	7
28	ADDC	Addmaster Corp	N	B—	10¢	...	....	Calculators,cash registers	19	½	1½	¾	1⅜	1⅛	448	1⅜	1¼	1⅜ B	...	12
29	AOI	Adobe Oil & Gas	AS	B+	30¢	11	453	Oil & gas: gasoline: coal	24⅞	3⅛	48½	16⅞	56	41	2028	56	47¼	50½	0.4	38
30	AROS	Advance Ross	N	B—	10¢	2	15	Elect.dstr,mfr:transp.prod	25	⅝	7¼	2⅛	6⅛	3½	2232	6⅛	5¼	5¾ B	...	44
31	AMD	Advanced Micro-Dev	NY	B	1¢	30	1763	Monolithic integ circuits	18⅞	⅝	38½	12⅛	46⅜	32⅛	4594	46⅜	41	42	...	16
32	ADVN	Advent Corp	N	C	10¢	1	.1	Speakers,tapes,video TVs	22	3½	5	2	3⅞	2⅛	2536	3⅞	2¾	2¾ B	...	d
33	ADLA	Adventure Lands Amer	N	NR	No	...	....	Theme park & motel, Iowa	3	1½	2⅝	1½	2	1½	157	1¾	1½	1¾ B	2.9	7
34	AO	Aegis Corp	AS,Ph	B	1¢	3	549	Rubber:shipyd:boats:o&g sv	11⅞	⅜	2¼	1⅛	2⅞	1⅝	10892	2⅝	2	2	...	12
35	AELNA	AEL Indus Cl A	N	B—	1	2	2	Gov't electronics, CATV sys	15¼	½	8¼	5⅛	11½	7⅛	3118	9⅞	8⅛	8¾ B	s...	16
36	AER	Aero-Flow Dynamics	AS	B+	1	1	8	Marine,ind'l distributor	18¾	1⅞	22½	12¾	27¾	21	157	27¾	24⅜	24⅜	2.1	6
37	AESM	Aero Systems	N	B—	2¢	1	136	Avionic sales & service	24½	1/16	3⅛	1¾	4	2⅞	10001	4	3⅜	3¾ B	...	47
38	ARN	Aeronca, Inc	AS,P	C	1	5	214	Aerospace comp:environ ctr	32	⅞	7	2⅛	8¼	4	2059	8¼	5⅛	5¼	...	d
39	ASON	Aerosonic Corp	N	B—	40¢	...	....	Make,overhaul aircraft instr	9⅛	1/16	12¼	4⅝	15⅛	12¼	833	15⅛	14⅝	15⅛ B	...	63
40	AEST	AES Technology Sys	N	NR	1¢	1	.1	Copying sys:slot mach mfr	6¾	¼	14½	5⅛	10	5¾	1653	10	7½	8¼ B	...	d
41	AET	Aetna Life & Casual	NY,B,C,M,Ph,P	...	No	271	24924	Multiline insurance business	30½	10⅛	36⅜	25⅝	36⅞	30¾	24570	36¼	30¾	31⅞	6.7	5
42	Pr	$2.00 cm Cv Pfd(45)vtg	NY	NR	No	...	....	R.E.,finance,motel subsids	67	25½	80	59	77	69	9	77	69	69	2.9	
43	AFAP	AFA Protective Sys	N	B+	1	...	....	Central station alarm sv	26¼	2¼	11¼	6	7¾	5½	21	7¾	5¾	7¾ B	5.7	8
44	AFBK	Affiliated Bkshrs Col	N	...	5	26	897	Bank holding co: Colorado	43¾	8¾	27¾	20½	26	24¼	985	26	24¼	24¼ B	5.8	5

Uniform Footnote Explanations—See Page 1. Other: [51]®$1.22,'79. [52]Incl subsid Pfd. [53]®$3.96,'78. [54]®$1.32,'78. [55]□$0.14,'77. [56]®$0.40,'79. [57]®$0.56,'79. [58]©$0.67,'80. [59]©$0.62,'79. [60]□$0.65,'79. [61]Fiscal Mar'79 & prior. [62]Cl'B' Stk. [63]®$0.99,'79. [64]△$0.09,'79. [65]Accum on Pfd. [66]△$0.04,'77. [67]□$1.09,'78. [68]F.C.& Pfd divds Times Earned.

FIGURE 19-14 Standard and Poor's *Stock Guide*

COMMON AND PREFERRED STOCKS

N D E X	Cash Divs Ea Yr Since	Pfd	Latest Payment $	Date	Ex Div	So Far 1980	Total Ind Rate	Paid 1979	Cash & Equiv	Curr Assets	Curr Liabs	Balance Sheet Date	Long Term Debt Mil-$	Pfd Shs 000	Com Shs 000	1975	1976	1977	1978	1979	Last 12 Mos	Period	1978	1979	N D E X
1	1973	Q	0.10	2-29-80	1-30	0.10	0.40	0.34	0.97	49.1	21.2	11-30-79	20.5	…	2117 My	0.05	0.87	0.85	0.96	*1.43	1.54	6 Mo Nov	0.66	0.77	1
2	1962	Q	0.05	1-24-80	12-21	0.05	0.20	0.20	2.06	12.2	6.25	11-30-79	5.65	…	1259 Fb	1.44	0.82	0.80	0.66		0.78	9 Mo Nov	0.46	0.58	2
3	1926	Q	0.25	2-15-80	1-14	0.25	1.00	0.96	66.7	485.	502.	9-30-79	214.	…	60318 Dc	1.29	1.63	1.98	2.48	P2.97	2.97				3
4	1949	g	0.40	2-1-80	12-21	0.40	1.60 †g	1.50	57.7	766.	184.	j12-31-79	269. 52p2314	683	18668 Dc	0.63	0.47	□1.83	□3.98	P△5.62	2.97				4
5			None Paid				Nil		8.04	370.	196.	9-30-79	9.55		4143 Dc	d2.23	d0.27	d0.23	△0.02		d5.29	9 Mo Sep	△0.07	△0.20	5
6			None Since Public				Nil		1.08	1.87	1.71	10-31-79	1.39	…	1969 Oc	0.29	0.25	△0.26	0.38	0.51	0.54	3 Mo Jan△	0.09	0.12	6
7		0.06		11-10-78	10-3		Nil			Equity per shr $3.19		9-30-79	8.00	.7	2099 Dc	△0.83	△1.21	△1.37	△0.61		1.08	12 Mo Sep	n/a	□1.08	7
8		0.06		12-20-74	12-4		Nil		2.47	Equity per shr $3.19	34.6	9-30-79	48.3		3434 Dc	△0.65	△0.83	0.04	*0.02		0.18	9 Mo Sep	*0.06	0.22	8
9		3%Stk		11-2-79	10-1		Stk	8½%Stk	1.02	37.9	16.7	12-31-79	7.06		992 Jc	2.10	2.14	2.24	2.45	2.64	2.73	9 Mo Sep	0.89		9
10	1951		0.56	3-14-80	2-25	0.56	2.24	†g1.50 2.20½	8.04	370.	196.	9-30-79	288.		8812 Dc	3.57	3.92	4.12	4.71	P5.44	5.44	6 Mo Dec	0.89	0.98	10
11	1973	gQ	0.15	5-31-80	5-8	g0.27	0.60	g0.48	6.93	154.	107.	j11-30-78	31.0	216	2520 Nv	△*2.50	△*1.10	△0.54	*△1.48	P2.62	2.62				11
12		0.02		5-15-72	4-25		Nil		0.21	6.40	3.35	9-30-79	1.81		1920 Dc	*0.01	*0.03	*0.05	*0.09		0.36	9 Mo Sep	*0.06	*△0.33	12
13	1936	Q	0.35	3-20-80	2-1	0.35	1.40	1.20	3.49	146.	50.3	12-31-79	54.3	*p4251	Sp	1.56	△0.65	*△1.22	2.96	4.38	4.49	6 Mo Dec	0.88	*0.99	13
14	1939	2%Stk		3-24-80	2-19	s0.057	0.24	0.228	0.06	16.0	4.37	12-31-79	3.21		2848 Jc	0.34	0.38	0.75	1.07	0.70	0.83	6 Mo Dec	0.32	0.44	14
15	1967	Q	0.15	1-18-80	12-28	0.15	0.60	0.60	1.61	17.0	6.10	10-28-79	1.50		1445 Oc	0.77	1.26	1.42	1.85	2.03	2.03				15
16		0.10		12-15-58	11-24		Nil		0.21	3.33	1.10	9-30-79			859	△0.30	0.47	0.20	d0.31	d0.31	d0.31	3 Mo Dec	d0.02	d0.02	16
17	1947	Q	0.08½	3-10-80	4-25	0.08½	0.34	0.31	0.40	16.9	2.59	9-30-79	6.75		1900 Dc	0.50	0.50	0.74	0.93	P1.12	1.12	6 Mo Dec	0.28	0.28	17
18		0.07		12-15-77	11-14		Nil		3.13	38.8	9.45	12-31-79	19.8		1693 Je	0.52	1.13	1.31	0.04	P1.16	d0.80	3 Mo Sep	0.94	1.22	18
19	1977	Q	0.07½	3-1-80	2-8	0.07½	0.30	0.272	3.13	38.9	36.7	12-31-79	32.1		2761 Dc	0.32	0.37	*0.94	*1.37		1.65	6 Mo Dec	*0.12	0.13	19
20			None Since Public				Nil		0.07	9.25	3.57	10-28-79	0.27	*2554 Sp		0.90	0.20	*0.46	*0.65	*△0.45	0.46	3 Mo Sep	*0.12	0.20	20
21	1973	Q	0.01	12-28-79	12-10	0.01	0.04	0.04	0.13	4.81	2.25	12-29-79	1.00		752 Mr	*0.33	0.59	*0.46	*0.60	…	0.80	3 Mo Dec	0.33	0.53	21
22		0.46		2-27-80	2-28	*0.46	0.82	*0.70	4.18	13.3	12-31-79	14.8		4063 Dc	0.59	0.68	0.71		0.66	9 Mo Sep	0.34	0.29	22
23	1936	Q	0.05	2-27-80	2-11	0.05	0.20	0.20	1.15	Net Asset Val $16.01	27.1	2-22-80		§1624 Dc		§13.17	§16.01	§14.51	§14.49	§16.14				23
24		0.10		8-15-78	7-10		Nil		2.69	4.18	22.0	11-30-79	33.3		2292 Dc	0.25	0.52	0.91	0.72	P0.82		9 Mo Sep			24
25	1977						Nil				28.8			* 40 p5409 Dc	0.44	0.33	0.43	0.57	P0.82	0.82				25
26	1977	S	0.06	11-27-79	11-5		0.12	0.02	n/a	10.0	4.63	12-31-79	10.5		1700 Sp	0.22	0.36	0.61	0.84	1.07	1.15	3 Mo Dec	0.21	0.29	26
27	1956	Q	0.12½	3-31-80	2-26	0.12½	0.50	0.50	2.35	41.9	14.2	11-30-79	12.1	†2464 Nv		1.74	1.14	1.34	*1.55	1.26	1.26	6 Mo Nov	0.04	0.01	27
28		0.04		7-12-72	6-23		Nil		0.39	5.66	1.14	11-30-79	60.7		1329 My	0.80	0.47	0.13	0.09	0.14	0.11	6 Mo Nov	0.80	1.06	28
29	1974		0.05	3-28-80	3-3	0.05	0.20		2.14	33.5	26.7	9-30-79	0.56	320	678 Dc	0.75	0.90	0.90	1.07		1.33	9 Mo Sep	0.80	1.06	29
30		h		11-27-64			Nil			17.3	9.46	9-30-79	1.23	31	3341 Dc	*0.08	*0.47	0.66	0.04		0.13	9 Mo Sep	0.05	0.12	30
31			None Since Public				Nil		2.83	73.4	50.7	12-30-79*	30.0		7149 Mr	0.24	0.73	0.79	.1.48	2.58		3 Mo Dec	1.01	2.11	31
32			None Since Public				Nil		0.05	15.1	10.1	12-31-79	1.00		2459 Mr	*0.06	*0.15	*0.51	d1.18	0.96	0.96	6 Mo Dec	△0.49	△0.28	32
33	1979		0.05		12-1-79 10-26		0.05		1.97	2.56	1.36	12-31-79	2.33		3891 Mr	0.05	0.01	*0.12	*0.18		0.17	9 Mo Dec	*0.26	0.12	33
34			None Paid				Nil		1.66	46.8	17.4	9-30-79	20.0		10870 Dc	0.17	0.22	0.31	0.31	0.17	0.17	9 Mo Sep	0.26	0.25	34
35		5%Stk		8-24-79	7-23		Stk	5%Stk	0.19	26.9	14.4	11-30-79			†1873 Fb	*0.08	*0.48	*0.95	0.31	0.54		40 Wk Nov	0.77	0.25	35
36	1958		0.12½	12-21-79	12-5		0.50	0.50	4.55	27.2	1.18	9-30-79	1.67		626 Dc	1.74	2.58	3.09	P△3.75	3.75		9 Mo Nov		3.75	36
37		5%Stk		3-31-76	3-15		Nil		1.10	8.54	3.49	11-30-79	1.55		5051 Fb	0.04	d5.01	0.06	*0.17	0.08		6 Mo Nov		△0.12	37
38		0.10		12-30-70	12-9		Nil		1.07	20.7	1.03	10-31-79	13.2	30 p2762	Dc	0.14	0.10*	*0.26	*0.27		d1.53	6 Mo Sep	△0.13	□1.67	38
39		0.01½		2-25-77	2-24		Nil		0.02	5.61	1.03	6-30-79	0.80		1807 Ja	0.17	0.10*	0.05	0.14		0.24	6 Mo Oct	0.11	0.21	39
40			None Since Public				Nil		0.38	3.58	4.81		1.30		4602 Dc	d0.14	0.06	0.04	0.04	d0.29	d0.20	6 Mo Dec	d0.03	*0.06	40
41	1934	Q	0.53	5-15-80	3-14	0.98	2.12	1.716		Conv into 2.25 shrs common		12-31-79	511.	32	80622 Dc	△1.27	△2.61	△5.17	*6.39	P△6.93	6.93				41
42	1969	Q	0.50	4-15-80	3-14	1.00	2.00	2.00							P△6.93		*20.35	9 Mo Sep		0.55	42
43	1889	Q	0.11½	2-14-79	11-15		0.44	0.44	0.38	1.55	1.27	9-30-79	28.9	33	404 Dc	0.72	0.57	0.76	0.81		0.97			0.71	43
44	1934	Q	0.35	3-20-80	2-24	0.35	1.37	1.37	Book Value $31.24			12-31-79			2880 Dc	△2.20	△2.54	△3.32	△4.40	P△4.75	4.75	9 Mo Sep		0.55	44

◆ Stock Splits & Divs By Line Reference Index ¹10%,'78. ⁵5-for-4,'78,'80. ²2-for-1,'75,'78. ³3-for-1,'78. ¹⁰³-for-2,'76, ¹⁰10%,'78. ²2-for-1,'77,'79. Adj to 5%,'80. ¹³3-for-2,'75. ⁶6-for-5,'77. Adj to 3% Oct,'79. ¹⁰³-for-2,'76, ²²2-for-1,'80. ⁴4-for-3,'78. ⁸Adj to 5%,'77. ¹⁰10%,'78,'79. ²⁹7-for-5,'79. ²²2-for-1,'78,'79. ³³Adj to 5%,'76. ⁴⁴2-for-1,'78. To split 2-for-1,'ex Apr 1. ⁸²2-for-1,'79. ¹³3-for-2,'79.

FIGURE 19-14 (Continued)

The most comprehensive source of information about mutual funds in general, and the characteristics of individual funds, is Wiesenberger Investment Service's *Investment Companies* (annual). The standard source of information on virtually any important security is the most recent annual *Moody's Manual* (Industrials, Transportation, Public Utilities, Banks and Finance, Municipal and Government, or O-T-C Industrials).

Historic data and analyses for 1,700 stocks and most major industries can be found in the *Value Line Investment Survey*. The *Value Line Options and Convertibles* covers both convertible bonds and options. Both publications offer Value Line's estimates of the relative attractiveness of the investments at current prices.

Current forecasts of company earnings are published in Standard and Poor's weekly *Earnings Forecaster*.

Publications of major security analysts' societies are: the *Financial Analysts Journal* (U.S.), *Analyse Financiére* (France), and *The Investment Analyst* (United Kingdom). Academic journals that emphasize aspects of investments are: the *Journal of Business*, the *Journal of Finance*, the *Journal of Financial and Quantitative Analysis*, and the *Journal of Financial Economics*.

Anyone interested in the management of money for institutional or corporate investors (especially pension funds) should read the *Institutional Investor* (monthly), which manages to be both engaging and informative. An offspring, the *Journal of Portfolio Management*, publishes the views of both practitioners and academicians. A biweekly periodical widely read by institutional investors and money managers is *Pensions and Investments*.

While a company's annual report provides useful information, the annual business and financial report (10-K) required to be filed with the Securities and Exchange Commission usually includes more details. A similar report, the N-1R, is filed by management investment companies.

MARKET INDICES

What did the market do yesterday? How much would an unmanaged portfolio have returned last year? Such questions are often answered by examining the performance of a *market index*. Many are available. Some correspond to explicit portfolio strategies; others do not. Some are comprehensive; others merely representative. Indices differ in the securities included, the weights assigned to individual securities, and the computational procedures employed.

Most widely followed is the *Dow Jones Industrial Average*, computed by simply summing the prices of 30 large-value stocks (American Telephone and Telegraph and 29 industrials), then dividing the total by a constant (the "divisor"). The performance of the index thus corresponds to that of a portfolio in which the relative value of each holding is proportional to the price of the stock relative to that of the full set of 30 stocks. When one of the stocks splits, extra shares are assumed to be sold and the proceeds invested in equal numbers of shares of all 30 stocks (formally, this is accomplished by adjusting the divisor). Small stock dividends are ignored, making the index slightly biased downward.

Similar procedures are used to compute two other Dow Jones Averages: one uses 20 transportation stocks, the other, 15 utility stocks.

Levels of the Dow Jones Averages are reported in virtually every newspaper. Historical data and quarterly dividends and earnings figures are published from time to time in *Barron's*.

A more representative measure, used by most institutional investors, is Standard and Poor's Composite 500-Stock Index, a market-value-weighted average of 500 stocks, described in detail in Chapter 7.

The S&P 500 corresponds to a portfolio in which the relative value of each holding is proportional to the value of all the company's shares relative to the total value of all companies' shares. Except on occasions when the stocks used to compute the index are changed, the only rebalancing required to maintain an equivalent portfolio is that needed to accommodate new issues of stock, tender offers, etc. Reinvestment of dividends can, of course, cause problems, owing to the absence of fractional shares, but the S&P 500, like any market-value-weighted index, corresponds to a low-cost unmanaged portfolio strategy.

Market-value-weighted indices are *macroconsistent*: every investor could hold a portfolio invested in the same manner, and everything would add up. This is not true for indices such as the Dow Jones Averages (since there are different numbers of shares of various corporations' stocks) or equal-dollar-weighted indices (since there are different numbers of dollars invested in various corporations). Market-value-weighted indices represent the average *dollar* (or franc, pound, etc.) invested in the stocks included. They thus conform to a portion of the overall *market portfolio*.

In addition to its composite 500-Stock Index, Standard and Poor's also computes market-value-weighted industry indices. Indices for the 400 industrials, 20 transportation, 40 public utility, and 40 financial stocks used to make up the composite index are also prepared. Values for all indices, along with quarterly data on dividends, earnings, and sales, may be found in Standard and Poor's *Analysts' Handbook* (annual) and *Analysts' Handbook Supplement* (monthly).

As indicated in Chapter 7, more comprehensive market-value weighted indices for U.S. stocks are also computed. The New York Stock Exchange publishes a composite index of all stocks listed on that exchange, as well as four subindices (industrials, utilities, transportation, and finance). The American Stock Exchange computes an index of its stocks. The National Association of Securities Dealers, using its automated quotation service (NASDAQ), computes indices based on the market value of more than 2,000 over-the-counter stocks (industrial, bank, insurance, other finance, transportation, utilities, and a composite index). And Wilshire Associates computes the *Wilshire 5000 equity index*, which indicates the total market value of all stocks listed on the New York and American Stock Exchanges plus those "actively traded over-the-counter." Levels of all these indices are published weekly in *Barron's*, but dividend values are not included, limiting their usefulness for many applications.

Capital International Perspective publishes market-value-weighted indices using various combinations of 1,100 stocks from 18 different countries. An overall *World Index* is provided along with 18 national and 32 international industry indices. The 1,100 stocks account for approximately 60% of the aggregate market value of all stocks listed on the national exchanges of the countries represented. Month-end values, adjusted for changes in foreign exchange rates, are used to compute returns in U.S. dollars and in other currencies.

The *Dow Jones 20-Bond Index* is computed by averaging the prices of ten utility and ten industrial bonds.[11] More satisfactory are the *Salomon Brothers Corporate Bond Total Rate of Return Indices*.

All the indices discussed thus far can be computed by taking an *arithmetic* average (weighted or unweighted, depending on the index) of the percentage changes in the prices of the included securities. Thus each corresponds to a feasible portfolio strategy. One popular set of indices is not constructed in this manner. Each of four *Value Line Averages* (industrials, rails, utilities, and composite) is computed daily by multiplying the previous day's index by the *geometric mean* of the daily price relatives (today's price divided by yesterday's) of the relevant stocks in the Value Line Investment Survey. Each day's performance is therefore worse than that which would have been obtained using an arithmetic average of the same values. But an arithmetic average corresponds to the performance that would be achieved by a portfolio rebalanced daily to have equal dollar values of each of the included stocks. Thus the Value Line Averages are downward biased and correspond to no achievable portfolio policy.

Market indices play an important role in portfolio management and the measurement of investment performance—aspects of investment management, covered in the next chapter.

[11] Prior to 1976 a 40-bond index was computed, using 20 railroad bonds in addition to the industrial and utility issues.

Problems

1. Explain the reasoning behind the sentence "Any system designed to beat the market, once known to more than a few people, carries the seeds of its own destruction."
2. A phrase one often hears is "Buy low, sell high." Why is the system suggested by this phrase not operational?
3. Explain why the Dow Jones Industrial Index is not macroconsistent.

4. A brochure describes "a computerized system based on extensive analysis of the last 40 years of stock price movements." The firm selling the service says that it can provide "solid statistical evidence" that the system picks stocks that return 35% per year. Would you pay for its recommendations? Why or why not?

5. Compare picking stocks that will "beat the market" with (a) predicting rainfall, and (b) detecting the locations of enemy submarines. Would you expect methods developed for predicting rainfall to work well for picking mispriced stocks? What about methods designed to detect the locations of enemy submarines?

6. Is the evidence in Figure 19-11 consistent with market efficiency? If your sole source of security analysis were the "Heard on the Street" column, would your investment decisions be affected by it? If so, how would you use the information?

7. Assume that a detailed study of recent market history has shown that a change in the ratio of (1) a specialist's short position in a stock to (2) the amount held by mutual funds west of the Mississippi River is followed by a change in the price of the stock in the opposite direction. Does this prove that the ratio is a useful indicator for stock selection?

8. Would an input-output table prepared when crude oil cost $3 per barrel be especially helpful if crude oil now costs $30 per barrel?

9. It is commonly asserted that the Value Line Stock Index is more representative of the stock market than Standard and Poor's 500-stock index. What is an appropriate definition of "representative" in this context? How do the two indices differ? Which of the differences make the Value Line Index more representative? Which make the Standard and Poor's index more representative?

10. A company's return on assets is defined as the ratio of profits to assets. This can, in turn, be considered the product of two ratios:

$$\underset{\text{(ROA)}}{\frac{\text{profits}}{\text{assets}}} = \underset{\text{(profitability)}}{\frac{\text{profits}}{\text{sales}}} \times \underset{\text{(turnover)}}{\frac{\text{sales}}{\text{assets}}}$$

If you know with certainty what a firm's profitability and turnover will be, can you predict its return on assets? If you only have estimates of *expected* turnover and *expected* profitability and measures of the likely deviations of the two from these estimates (i.e., the standard deviation of profitability and the standard deviation of turnover), what can you say about the return on assets?

Investment
Management

20

INTRODUCTION

Investment management is the process by which money is managed. It may be active or passive, use explicit or implicit procedures, accord with the assumptions of market efficiency or not, be controlled or uncontrolled. The trend is toward more explicit, less active, more highly controlled operations consistent with the notion that capital markets are efficient, or nearly so. However, approaches vary, and many different investment "styles" can be found.

TRADITIONAL INVESTMENT MANAGEMENT ORGANIZATIONS

Few like to be called "traditional." However, many investment management organizations follow procedures little changed from those popular decades ago and thus deserve the title. Figure 20-1 shows the major characteristics of a typical organization of this type.

Projections concerning the economy, security and money markets, etc. are made (often qualitatively) by *economists*, *technicians*, and/or other market experts within or outside the organization. The projected environment is communicated via briefings, reports, etc.—usually in a rather implicit and qualitative manner—to the organization's *security analysts*. Each analyst is responsible for a group of securities, often those in one or more industries (in some organizations, analysts are called *industry specialists*). Often a group of analysts reports to a senior analyst responsible for a sector of the economy or market.

The analysts, often drawing heavily on reports of others (e.g., "street analysts" in brokerage houses), make predictions concerning securities for which they are responsible. In a sense, such predictions are conditional on the assumed economic and market environments, although the relationship is loose, at best.

Analysts' predictions seldom specify either an expected amount of return (either total return or return relative to that of securities of equal risk) or the time over which predicted performance will take place. In-

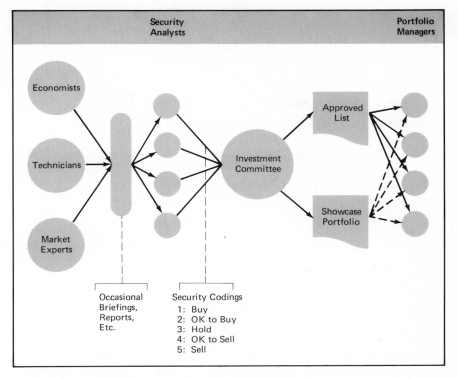

FIGURE 20-1 A Traditional Investment Management Organization

stead, an analyst's feelings about a security are summarized by assigning it one of five codes, as indicated in Figure 20-1 (some organizations reverse the numbers, so that 5 represents a buy recommendation, and 1 a sell recommendation; and some Europeans favor +, 0+, 0, 0−, and −).

Security codings constitute the information formally transmitted to the *investment committee*, which typically includes the senior management of the organization. In addition, analysts occasionally brief the investment committee on their feelings about various securities.

The investment committee's major formal output is the *approved* or *authorized list*, which includes the securities deemed worthy of accumulation in portfolios. The rules of the organization typically specify that any security on the list may be bought, while those not on the list should be either held or sold, barring special circumstances.

The presence or absence of a security on the approved list constitutes the major information transmitted explicitly from the investment committee to *portfolio managers* (including, in banks, trust officers). In some organizations senior management supervises a "showcase portfolio" (e.g., a bank's major commingled equity fund), the composition of which indicates to portfolio managers the relative intensity of management's feelings regarding different securities.

In many ways this description is a caricature of an investment organization—even one run along traditional lines.[1] But many of these attributes can be observed in practice. Traditional organizations are likely to deal with uncertainty only obliquely, utilize inconsistent estimates, and fail to fully take into account the high degree of efficiency of modern capital markets.

PORTFOLIO MANAGEMENT FUNCTIONS

Figures 20-2(a), (b), and (c) show the key ingredients required for each of the three major tasks associated with modern investment management. The three functions are:

1. *Portfolio analysis*—the determination of a portfolio's risk, expected return, and suitability for the client in question
2. *Portfolio revision*—the selection of a set of security purchases and/or sales
3. *Performance measurement and attribution*—the determination of the actual performance of a portfolio and the reasons for that performance

The three functions are designed to answer three questions: what *is* the portfolio, what *should* it be, and how *has* it done? The remainder of this chapter deals with the first two functions; the next chapter deals with the third.

Ingredients for Portfolio Analysis and Revision

To estimate a portfolio's risk and expected return one must have estimates of the expected returns of individual securities and their risks (including explicit or implicit estimates of covariances or correlations among security returns). To determine the suitability of a portfolio for a specific client (an individual, institution, or group of individuals) one must know the relevant attributes of the client—for example, tax status and risk aversion. To determine an appropriate set of revisions, one must also take transactions costs into account.

Selecting a "Normal" Bond/Stock Mix

One of the key attributes that differentiates clients from one another concerns attitudes toward risk vis-à-vis expected return. The smaller a client's *risk aversion*, or, equivalently, the greater his or her *risk tolerance*, the greater should be the risk and return of the overall portfolio.

Determining the extent to which a client is willing to accept greater risk in order to get greater expected return is not a simple task. In practice it is often done indirectly. The likely implications of investment in alter-

---

[1] For example, economists and technicians may report to the investment committee, which may act on their advice as well as communicate it (possibly altered) to the security analysts.

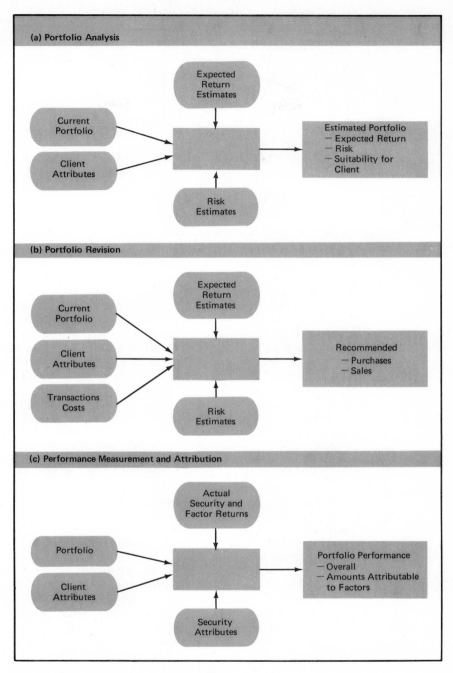

FIGURE 20-2 Three Portfolio Management Functions
    (a) Portfolio Analysis
    (b) Portfolio Revision
    (c) Performance Measurement and Attribution

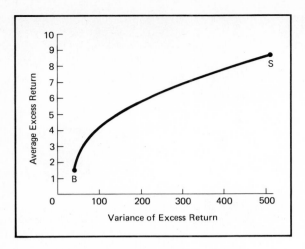

FIGURE 20-3 Average Excess Return and Variance of Excess Return for Different Bond/Stock Mixes, 1926–1978

Source: Based on data in Roger G. Ibbotson and Rex A. Sinquefield, *Stocks, Bonds, Bills and Inflation: Historical Returns (1926–1978)*, Financial Analysts' Research Foundation, 1979.

native *bond/stock mixes* are presented to the client, who then chooses a preferred mix. This provides guidance concerning the "normal" ("strategic," "target") mix of such assets. It also provides information about the client's risk tolerance—information that can be used to make "tactical" changes in holdings when opportunities are "abnormal."

The starting point is a set of estimates of the risks and expected returns for different bond/stock mixes. Figure 20-3 provides an example based on historic excess return (i.e., return minus the Treasury bill rate) from 1926 through 1978. The vertical axis plots the average excess return and the horizontal axis the *variance* of excess return. Point *B* represents investment in long-term corporate bonds, point *S* investment in common stocks, and intermediate points combinations of the two. In practice historic experience, judgment, or a combination of the two may be used to estimate the risks and returns of bond/stock mixes. In any event, given a range of opportunities, an investor should choose the combination of risk and return that best suits his or her objectives, circumstances, etc. When the choice is made on behalf of others (e.g., by a trustee for one or more beneficiaries), the task is much more difficult, but a decision is still required.

Investment managers and advisory organizations have developed various procedures for helping clients understand the trade-off between risk and return so they can make reasonable decisions in this regard. Figures 20-4, 20-5, and 20-6 illustrate some of these methods.

Figure 20-4 is taken from a study done[2] for a small college. At the time an amount equal to 6% of the market value of the college's endowment fund was being spent. The study assumed that in future years the amount spent would be the same *in real dollars*. Given this, what might be the *real* value of the fund at the end of 5, 10 or 15 years, and how might this be affected by the bond/stock mix?

To answer the question, historic *real* returns from representative

---

[2] By the author.

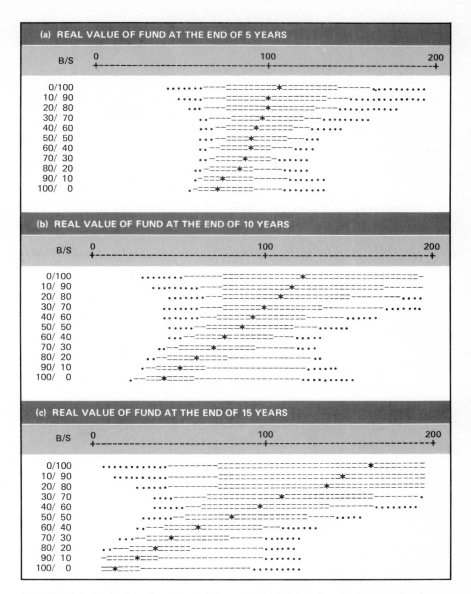

FIGURE 20-4 Effect of the Bond/Stock Mix on the Real Value of an Endowment Fund

portfolios of bonds and stocks were used. For example, to construct the bar graph at the top of Figure 20-4(a) a mix of 0% in bonds and 100% in stocks was assumed. The value of the fund was assumed to equal 100 at the beginning of 1926, and year-by-year results were computed for the period from 1926 through 1930, using the assumed spending rule and the actual real returns in each year. The real value of the fund at the end of 1930 was then determined. The procedure was repeated using returns from 1927 through 1931, 1928 through 1932, etc. The bar graph summarizes the frequency distribution of the end-of-period real values produced in this way, as follows:

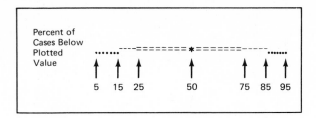

Figure 20-5 is taken from a study designed for a pension fund. Here the focus was on the probabilities that the ending asset value might be 10%, 20%, or 30% below the amount that would be obtained if returns equaled the rate projected by the fund's consulting actuary (6% per year). The figure plots such probabilities for various bond/stock mixes. In this study, actual returns on indices of bonds and stocks were used in a manner similar to that employed in the endowment study.

Figure 20-6 shows some of the results from a more detailed study of a pension plan. This analysis took into account the fact that the amount

FIGURE 20-5 The Effect of the Bond/Stock Mix on the Internal Rate of Return of a Pension Fund

Source: Peter O. Dietz and H. Russell Gogler, "The Debt/Equity Dilemma," Frank Russell Co., Inc., Capital Placement Division, 1975.

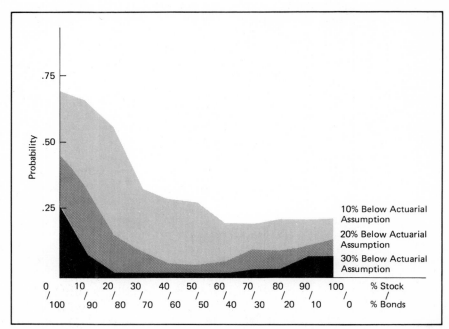

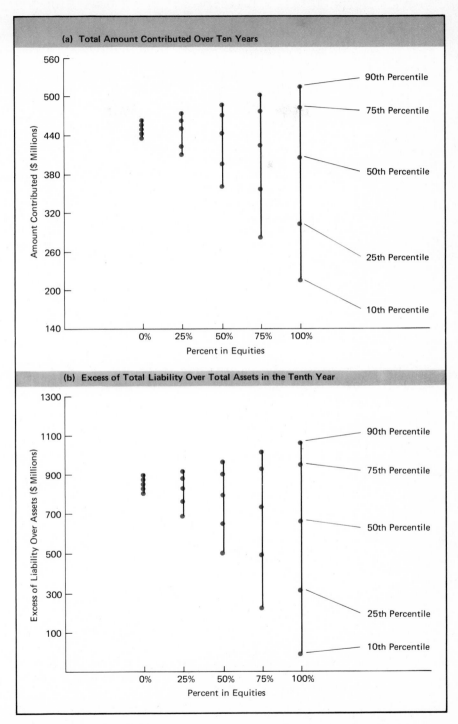

FIGURE 20-6 Effect of the Bond/Stock Mix on a Pension Fund's Cost and Value

Source: Frank C. McLaughlin, "Using Simulation to Chart the Way," *Pension World*, September 1975 (based on a study performed by Willshire Associates, Inc.).

contributed by a corporation to its pension fund each year usually depends on the performance of the fund's investments. Under such circumstances, two aspects are uncertain: the contributions in each year, and the value of the fund at the end of any given number of years. Figure 20-6(a) shows the estimated distribution of the total amount contributed over ten years, and Figure 20-6(b) the estimated distribution of the difference between the plan's obligations and the value of the assets in the fund in the tenth year. Not shown is the relationship between the two aspects—i.e., the extent to which good outcomes in one figure are associated with bad (or good) outcomes in the other figure.

This study differed from the previous ones in another way. Instead of year-by-year returns, *Monte Carlo simulation* was employed. Expected returns and standard deviations of return were specified for each of the investment media, along with the correlations among their returns. Then many cases were analyzed, with returns drawn randomly from such distributions for each one. The diagrams summarize the results from all the cases. This is a more versatile procedure and makes it easy to assume that the future will be different from the past.

Estimating Client Risk Tolerance

After a client has selected a normal bond/stock mix, what can be said about his or her risk tolerance? One would, of course, like to identify all the indifference curves that represent a client's attitude toward risk and return. However, in practice a more modest goal is usually adopted—to obtain a reasonable representation of the shape of such curves in the likely region of risk and return within which the client's optimal choices should fall.

The points in Figure 20-7 plot the alternative mixes presented to a client in a diagram with expected return on the vertical axis and variance on the horizontal axis. Curve BCS shows the risk-return characteristics of all possible bond/stock mixes and point C identifies the attributes of the mix chosen by the client.

If all the possible mixes had been presented to the client and point C had been chosen, we could infer that the slope of the client's indifference curve that goes through point C is precisely equal to that of curve BCS at

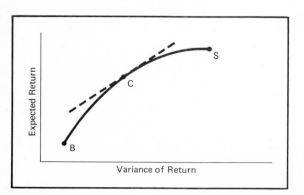

FIGURE 20-7 Inferring Client Risk Tolerance

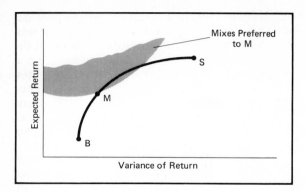

FIGURE 20-8 A Nonoptimal Mix

this point. This follows from the nature of indifference curves. If the curve through point C cut curve BCS, other points on the curve would have been preferred to C, as shown in Figure 20-8 for point M.

In principle the choice of a bond/stock mix provides only information about the slope of an indifference curve at one point. To go beyond this one must make an assumption about the general shape of client indifference curves. An assumption commonly made is that of *constant risk tolerance* over a range of alternatives in the neighborhood of the point originally chosen.

Figure 20-9(a) and (b) show the nature of the assumption. As indicated in Figure 20-9(a), indifference curves in a diagram with *variance* on the horizontal axis are assumed to be linear and parallel over the range in question. Figure 20-9(b) plots the same curves in a more familiar

FIGURE 20-9 Constant Risk Tolerance

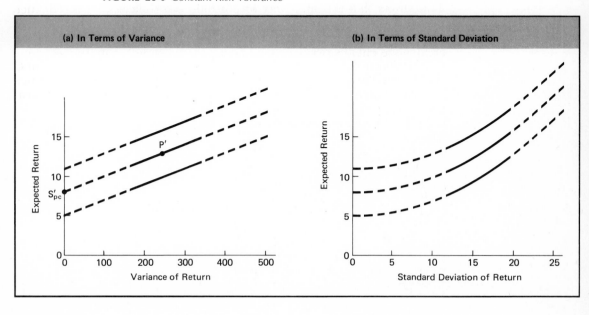

diagram—one with *standard deviation* on the horizontal axis. As shown, the curves have the conventional shape—they indicate that the investor requires more return to compensate for an additional unit of standard deviation as the risk of the portfolio increases.

The equation of a given indifference curve of this type can be written as:

$$E_p = S_{pc} + \lambda_c V_p \qquad (20\text{-}1)$$

where:

E_p = the expected return of the portfolio
V_p = the variance of return of the portfolio
λ_c = the client's *risk aversion*
S_{pc} = the vertical intercept if the indifference curve (line) in Figure 20-9(a) is extended to the vertical axis

If the indifference curve in Figure 20-9(a) were linear throughout, S_{pc} would be the portfolio's *certainty equivalent return*. Thus in Figure 20-9(a) portfolio P' is as desirable for this particular client as a portfolio with an expected return of S'_{pc} and no risk—i.e., one providing S'_{pc} with certainty.

Since there is no reason to assume that indifference curves have the same form all the way to the range of zero risk, it is preferable to interpret S_{pc} as simply an indicator of the height of an indifference curve. The term *suitability* has been used for this purpose. Rewriting (20-1):

$$S_{pc} \quad = \quad E_p \quad - \quad \lambda_c V_p \qquad (20\text{-}2)$$

$$\underset{\text{suitability}}{\phantom{S_{pc}}} \qquad \underset{\substack{\text{expected} \\ \text{return}}}{} \qquad \underset{\substack{\text{risk} \\ \text{penalty}}}{}$$

This shows that the suitability of portfolio p for client c is, in effect, a *risk-adjusted return*. From the expected return we subtract a *risk penalty* that depends on the client's risk aversion and the portfolio's risk. The greater the client's risk aversion and/or the portfolio's risk, the less suitable the portfolio.

A client's *risk aversion* (λ_c) indicates the *added expected return he or she requires as compensation for taking on one more unit of variance*. A related concept is *risk tolerance* (T_c), which indicates the *added variance he or she is willing to accept in order to get an added unit of expected return*.[3] Thus:

$$\lambda_c = \frac{1}{T_c}$$

and:

$$S_{pc} = E_p - \frac{V_p}{T_c}$$

---

[3] The terms *risk aversion* and *risk tolerance* are used here in a context in which expected return and variance indicate all the relevant aspects of uncertainty. For broader definitions, see J. Pratt, "Risk Aversion in the Small and the Large," *Econometrica*, January–April 1964.

To illustrate, consider two portfolios with the following risks and returns:

		RISK	
Portfolio	Expected Return	Standard Deviation	Variance
A	14%	20%	400 (%²)
B	19	30	900

And consider three clients, with the following attitudes toward risk:

	ATTITUDE TOWARD RISK	
Client	Risk Tolerance	Risk Aversion
1	80	1/80 = .0125
2	100	1/100 = .0100
3	120	1/120 = .00833

In this case the lower-risk portfolio (A) is more suitable for client 1 with the least risk tolerance:

$$S_{A1} = 14 - 400/80 = 14 - 5 = 9.00$$

$$S_{B1} = 19 - 900/80 = 19 - 11.25 = 7.75$$

while the higher-risk portfolio (B) is more suitable for client 3 with the greatest tolerance for risk:

$$S_{A3} = 14 - 400/120 = 14 - 3.33 = 10.67$$

$$S_{B3} = 19 - 900/120 = 19 - 7.5 = 11.5$$

For client 2 with an intermediate level of risk tolerance, the two portfolios are equally suitable:

$$S_{A2} = 14 - 400/100 = 14 - 4 = 10.0$$

$$S_{B2} = 19 - 900/100 = 19 - 9 = 10.0$$

To take taxes into account all the analysis should be done on an *after-tax* basis, using the relevant tax rates paid by the investor on dividends and capital gains. Since most investment decisions involve small changes, the relevant rates are usually the *marginal* tax rates on income and gains.

PASSIVE VERSUS ACTIVE MANAGEMENT

Within the investment industry the distinction is made between those who manage portfolios *passively*—holding securities for relatively long periods with small and infrequent changes—and those who take an *active* stance. Passive managers generally act as if the security markets were *efficient*. Put somewhat differently, their decisions are consistent with the acceptance of *consensus* estimates of risk and return. The portfolios may be surrogates for the market portfolio or they may be *tailored* to suit clients with attributes that differ from those of the average investor. But passive portfolio managers do not try to "beat the market."

Active managers believe that from time to time there are mispriced securities or groups of securities. They do not act as if they believed that security markets were efficient. Put somewhat differently, their estimates of risk and/or return differ from the consensus opinions. Of course, if some are more bullish than average about a security, others must be more bearish. The former will hold "more-than-normal" proportions of the security while the latter will hold "less-than-normal" proportions.

It is useful to think of a portfolio as composed of three components: (1) a market portfolio, (2) deviations designed to tailor holdings to reflect client attributes, and (3) deviations designed to take advantage of security mispricing. For example, a portfolio might break down as follows:

	Percent in Market	Percent in Tailored Portfolio	Percent in Actual Portfolio
Exxon	3.5	4.5	7.0
Schlumberger	1.1	.5	.2
.	.	.	.
.	.	.	.
.	.	.	.

The first column indicates the percentage in a broadly representative market portfolio—the holding that might be best for an average client in a perfectly efficient market. The second column shows the proportion that would be optimal for a tax-exempt investor in such a market. The third column shows the actual holdings in an actively managed portfolio for a tax-exempt client. The active holdings are represented by the differences between the last two columns:

	Active Position
Exxon	+2.5
Schlumberger	−.3
.	.
.	.
.	.

Such deviations arise because active managers disagree about risks and returns. And deviations in holdings represent *bets* such managers place against one another.

THE PARABLE OF THE MONEY MANAGERS

When thinking about active management, it is useful to ponder the following parable.[4]

Some years ago, in a land called Indicia, revolution led to the overthrow of a socialist regime and the restoration of a system of private property. Former government enterprises were re-formed as corporations, which then issued stocks and bonds. These securities were given to a central agency, which offered them for sale to individuals, pension funds, and the like (all armed with newly printed money).

Almost immediately a group of *money managers* came forth to assist these investors. Recalling the words of a venerated elder, uttered before the previous revolution ("Invest in Corporate Indicia"), they invited clients to give them money, with which they would buy a cross section of all the newly issued securities. Investors considered this a reasonable idea, and soon everyone held a piece of Corporate Indicia.

Before long the money managers became bored, because there was little for them to do. Soon they fell into the habit of gathering at a beachfront casino, where they passed the time playing roulette, craps, and similar games, for low stakes, with their own money.

After a while, the owner of the casino suggested a new idea. He would furnish an impressive set of rooms which would be designated the *Money Managers' Club*. There the members could place bets with one another about the fortunes of various corporations, industries, the level of the Gross National Product, foreign trade, etc. To make the betting more exciting, the casino owner suggested that the managers use their clients' money for this purpose.

The offer was immediately accepted, and soon the money managers were betting eagerly with one another. At the end of each week, some found that they had won money for their clients, while others found that they had lost. But the losses always exceeded the gains, for a certain amount was deducted from each bet to cover the costs of the elegant surroundings in which the gambling took place.

Before long a group of professors from Indicia U. suggested that investors were not well served by the activities being conducted at the Money Managers' Club. "Why pay people to gamble with your money? Why not just hold your piece of Corporate Indicia?" they said.

This argument seemed sensible to some of the investors, and they raised the issue with their money managers. A few capitulated, announcing that they would henceforth stay away from the casino and use their clients' money only to buy proportionate shares of all the stocks and bonds issued by corporations.

The converts, who became known as managers of *Indicia funds,* were initially shunned by those who continued to frequent the Money Managers' Club, but in time, grudging acceptance replaced outright hostility. The wave of puritan reform some had predicted failed to materialize, and gambling remained legal. Many managers continued to make their daily pilgrimage to the casino. But they exercised more restraint than before, placed smaller bets, and generally behaved in a manner consonant with their responsibilities. Even the members of the lawyers' club found it difficult to object to the small amount of gambling that still went on.

And everyone but the casino owner lived happily ever after.

---

[4] William F. Sharpe, "The Parable of the Money Managers," *Financial Analysts Journal*, 32, no. 4 (July/August 1976), 4.

While it lacks subtlety, this parable does say something about investment management. Most portfolios differ from the market portfolio: i.e., the relative amounts invested in various securities do not equal the relative amounts available to be held. Some of the differences reflect a need to tailor a portfolio to the special circumstances of a client. But many differences reflect feelings that a security, industry, or sector of the market is under- or overpriced. Specific opinions of this sort will not be universal, of course. If one portfolio includes a less-than-normal share of a security, some other (or others) must include a more-than-normal share, and these departures, based on feelings that securities are mispriced, must reflect differences of opinion.

As indicated earlier, an active portfolio can be thought of as a passive tailored portfolio plus a series of side bets. Such bets cost money (transactions costs) and add risk to a portfolio. On average they cannot bring rewards, for one bettor's gain must be another's loss.

Should a manager "place bets"? Only if he or she can make significantly better forecasts than the other bettors. The best policy for an average (or below-average) forecaster involves the creation of a passive tailored fund with positions consistent with client attributes and the efficient pricing of securities.

MAJOR INVESTMENT STYLES

There are many different ways to invest money, and few money managers adopt strategies that are either simple or extreme. Nonetheless, a few cases can be used to characterize the major approaches. The key styles are:

> *Passive*
> *Active:*
> Market timing
> Security selection
> Market timing and security selection

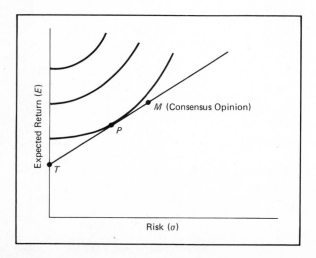

FIGURE 20-10 Passive Investment Management

To illustrate the key differences, we will consider a world in which only risk and return matter and clients differ only in risk tolerance (e.g., there are no tax effects). Moreover, we will assume that investors can borrow or lend at a single risk-free (Treasury bill) interest rate. If all investors agreed about security risks and expected returns, this would be the world of the original capital-asset pricing model, and all efficient strategies would involve mixtures of the market portfolio and (possibly) borrowing or lending. In a world in which investors disagree about risk and return, such strategies will be considered desirable by those who adopt consensus estimates of risk and return but not by those who hold different beliefs.

Passive Management

A passive manager adopts consensus estimates of risk and return. In the situation being considered here, such a manager would only have to choose the appropriate mixture of the market portfolio and Treasury bills. The best combination would, of course, depend on the client's risk tolerance.

Figure 20-10 provides an illustration. Point T plots the return offered by Treasury bills, and point M the risk and expected return of the market portfolio, using consensus estimates. Combinations of the two investments plot along line TM. The client's attitude toward risk and return is shown by the set of indifference curves, and the optimal position (P) lies at the point where an indifference curve is tangent to line TM. In this case the best mix uses both Treasury bills and the market portfolio. In other situations only one might be chosen, or the market portfolio might be levered up via borrowing.

When management is passive, the overall mix is altered only when (1) the client's preferences change and/or (2) the consensus opinion about the risk and return of the market portfolio changes. The manager must continue to assess the latter and keep in touch with the client concerning the former. But no additional activity is required.

The Supply of Risk-Bearing

Every investment manager should have as accurate a view as possible concerning the current consensus opinion of the risk and return associated with investment in the market as a whole. For the active manager this is an important input; for the passive manager it is all-important.

When estimates of overall economic uncertainty increase, security prices will usually adjust so that the risk and expected return of the market portfolio both increase. But what about the return per unit of risk?

Figure 20-11 shows a likely situation. In Figure 20-11(a) the market's prospects are initially those shown by point M. Given this alternative, plus the ability to borrow and lend at the interest rate shown by point T, investors collectively choose to hold all available risky securities.

Now, imagine that some unforeseen event causes investors' opinions about market risk and return to change, so that the market portfolio plots at point M'. Since the excess return per unit of risk is un-

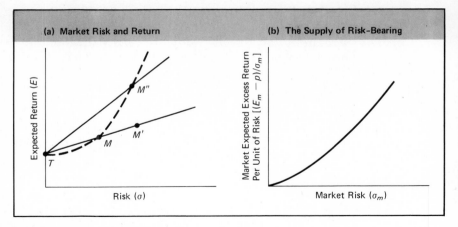

FIGURE 20-11 Changes in Market Risk and Return

changed, everyone will want the same amount of risk and return as before. But this will require the sale of some of everyone's now more risky securities. This cannot be done (who will buy?). Instead, the prices of risky securities will fall, increasing their expected returns.[5] Eventually the market portfolio will plot at a point such as M'' on a line with a higher slope (excess return per unit of risk).

The dashed line in Figure 20-11(a) shows the points at which the market portfolio is likely to plot as the assessment of risk changes, given investors' attitudes toward risk. Of course, changes in the society's average attitude toward risk and return can alter the relationship in any direction, but such variations are likely to be small and less frequent than changes in estimates of economic uncertainty.

Figure 20-11(b) summarizes the situation in a slightly different manner. It shows the premium per unit of risk (vertical axis) required to induce investors to accept various amounts of risk (horizontal axis). As shown, this *supply of risk-bearing curve* is upward-sloping.

Both the dashed line in Figure 20-11(a) and the curve in Figure 20-11(b) show that a change in the risk of the market portfolio is likely to be accompanied by a more-than-proportionate change in its expected excess return. This may explain the substantial changes in the slope of the estimated security risk line (as shown in Figure 14-1 in Chapter 14). Such changes can usually be explained by variations in uncertainty concerning the economy, but changes in the expected excess return appear to be more extreme than changes in uncertainty. As this discussion indicates, they should be.

Market Timing

Passive portfolio managers estimate the consensus opinion of market risk and return and accept it as correct. Market timers also estimate the con-

---

[5] And generally changing risk per dollar of price as well.

sensus opinion but reserve the right to consider it incorrect. When selecting a mix of Treasury bills and the market portfolio, a market timer will use his or her own opinion and thus may choose a different combination than would be recommended to the same client by a passive manager.

This is illustrated in Figure 20-12. Point M plots the consensus opinion concerning the market's prospects and point M^* the manager's opinion. Given the latter, the optimal mix with Treasury bills for the client in question is that which plots at point P^* (in this case, a 50-50 combination of the two ingredients).

If the manager is correct, all is well. But what if the consensus opinion is right? Then the appropriate mixture is that shown by point P (here, one with 30% stocks and 70% Treasury bills). The manager has made two mistakes. First, the mixture is inappropriate. Second, both the client and the manager are misinformed about the true prospects—here, they believe that the selected mix plots at point P^* when in fact it plots at point P'. This error might cause the client to make incorrect decisions in other domains (e.g., business, marriage, etc.). Of course, errors of the same type can arise when a passive manager misestimates the consensus opinion of the market, but they are likely to be less severe.

A market timer will generally alter a portfolio (i.e., the mix of risky and riskless securities) when his or her opinion about market prospects changes, even if there is no change in the consensus opinion or the client's attitude toward risk and return. The amount of the change will depend on the client's preferences; but the fact that such changes occur frequently and may be large makes market timing an *active* management style.

FIGURE 20-12 Market Timing

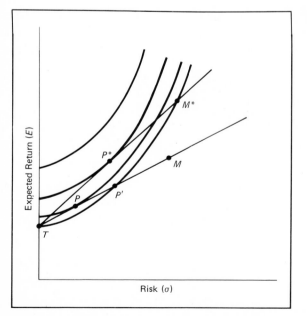

Formula Timing

Mechanical methods are sometimes employed in an attempt to "beat the market" through timing. Some sort of formula is used to alter exposure to the market from time to time, in the hope of thereby taking advantage of market cycles. For example, one might periodically switch between stocks and Treasury bills to maintain a *constant dollar* value of stocks. Or one might adjust holdings periodically to maintain a *constant ratio* of stocks to Treasury bills, based on market values (i.e., sell stocks after the market rises, and buy stocks after the market falls). Or one might fit a trend line to some market index and alter the ratio of stocks to bonds, based on the relationship of the index to its trend line (this is called a *variable ratio* plan).

All these procedures are motivated by the assumption that recent moves in the stock market (either absolutely, or relative to a trend of some sort) are more likely to be reversed than continued. Neither economic logic nor empirical evidence supports this view. Formula timing alters holdings in ways that are likely to be both costly and inappropriate, given a client's circumstances and attitude toward risk.

Dollar Averaging

A related concept is that of *dollar averaging*. The idea is to invest a constant dollar amount at regular intervals. For example, one might buy a thousand dollars' worth of American Telephone and Telegraph stock each month. The higher the price, the smaller the number of shares purchased; and the lower the price, the larger the number of shares. When the price changes, a dollar averager gets both good news and bad news (one based on the change in the value of previous holdings, the other based on the price at which new holdings can be purchased). For an investor buying a portfolio of stocks a similar relationship would hold between the average level of "the market" and the average cost of his or her "shares" in the market.

It is a mathematical certainty that the average cost of shares purchased via dollar averaging will be less than the average price of such shares (unless the price never changes). More shares are purchased at low prices and thus the average cost, which is a weighted average using shares purchased as weights, will be less than the average price, which is an unweighted average.[6] Moreover, the difference between the two values will generally be greater, the greater the variation in price from period to period.

While this is interesting mathematically, it has no obvious economic significance. Two questions are relevant, however: (1) is dollar averaging better than some alternative? and (2) is variance in stock price actually good for one who is dollar averaging?

The first question can be answered only if another question is asked: if one did not invest $1,000 per month in stocks, what would happen to

---

[6] The average cost will equal the *harmonic mean* of the prices (i.e., the reciprocal of the average of the reciprocals of the prices).

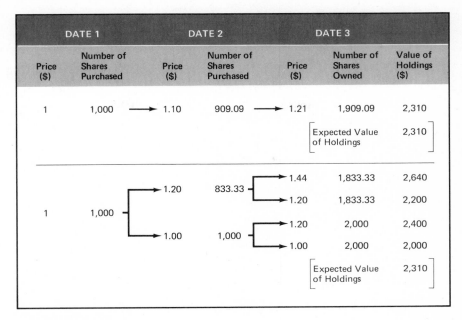

DATE 1		DATE 2		DATE 3		
Price ($)	Number of Shares Purchased	Price ($)	Number of Shares Purchased	Price ($)	Number of Shares Owned	Value of Holdings ($)
1	1,000 →	1.10	909.09 →	1.21	1,909.09	2,310
					Expected Value of Holdings	2,310
				1.44	1,833.33	2,640
		1.20	833.33	1.20	1,833.33	2,200
1	1,000			1.20	2,000	2,400
		1.00	1,000	1.00	2,000	2,000
					Expected Value of Holdings	2,310

FIGURE 20-13 Dollar Averaging

the money? For example, it could be used to buy Treasury bills until $12,000 (plus interest) was accumulated at year-end, the total then being invested in stocks. This would involve a different relative exposure to the market every month, with the differences more or less unrelated to the client's circumstances or attitude toward risk. Unless savings in transactions costs made possible by large stock purchases are significant, this is not likely to be as good an idea as dollar averaging.

The second question can be answered relatively easily, if the issue is posed carefully. Figure 20-13 shows two possible investments. The first earns 10% in each of two periods with certainty: its price goes from $1 per share to $1.10, and then to $1.21. The second investment is equally likely to earn either 20% or 0% each period. At each of the first two dates an investor buys $1,000 worth of shares. The ending values of the resulting holdings are shown in the figure. If the certain investment is chosen, a final value of $2,310 is obtained. If the other investment is selected, the outcome is uncertain. Its expected value is $2,310, but the actual value can be more or less.

The risky investment in Figure 20-13 is equivalent to buying the riskless investment and then betting each year's return (10%) on the flip of a fair coin to get double (20%) or nothing (0%). Adding risk without increasing expected return increases the uncertainty surrounding ending value without increasing the expected ending value, even for one who is dollar averaging. There is nothing inherently wrong with dollar averaging, but it has no magical properties. Dollar averaging certainly does not change uncertainty per se from a vice to a virtue.

SECURITY SELECTION

A third major investment style concentrates on *security selection*. The consensus opinion of prospects for the market as a whole is accepted as correct, but the prices of individual securities are questioned. On average, security prices are assumed to equal intrinsic values, but the selector believes that he or she can identify at least a few securities that are overpriced and others that are underpriced. Typically the manager estimates the expected return of an overpriced security to be less than the consensus estimate and the expected return of an underpriced security to be more than the consensus estimate. In some cases risk estimates that differ from consensus values are also employed. In any event the net result will be a decision to hold overpriced securities in less-than-normal (tailored passive portfolio) proportions and to hold underpriced securities in more-than-normal (tailored passive portfolio) proportions.

Adding bets to a market portfolio will add nonmarket risk as holdings are moved away from market proportions. If, on net, the bets are good, expected return will also increase.

Figure 20-14 illustrates this. As before, points *M* and *T* indicate the prospects of the market portfolio and Treasury bills, respectively. Passive strategies can be used to obtain any point on line 1. In this case, however, the manager has selected a set of bets that, when combined with the market portfolio, will give point (*M* + *B*). By combining this risky portfolio with Treasury bills, points along line 2 can be obtained—a clear improvement.

FIGURE 20-14 Security Selection: Optimal Use of Good Bets

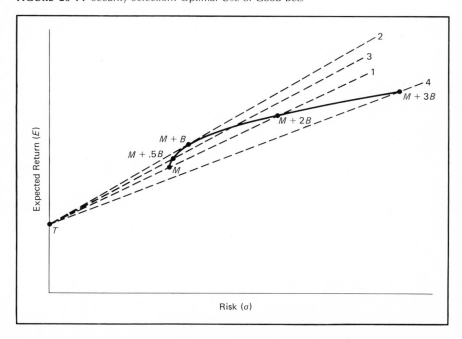

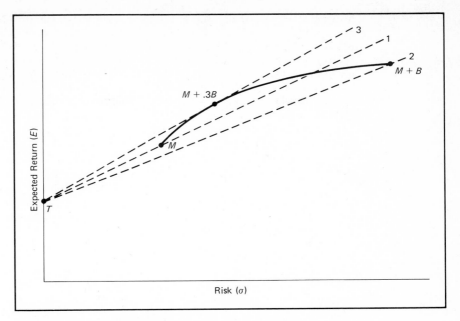

FIGURE 20-15 Security Selection: Suboptimal Use of Good Bets

Since the bets shown in Figure 20-14 are good, why not increase them? This will increase expected return, but it will also increase risk. Moreover, expected return will increase at a slower rate than risk. This is shown by the solid curve, which plots combinations of the market port-folio and the chosen set of bets, varying the size of the bets. For example, if the amount bet is doubled, point $(M + 2B)$ will be obtained; when mixed with Treasury bills, this gives points along line 1—no better than those available via passive management. If the bets are tripled, things will be even worse—line 4 lies below line 1. On the other hand, if the bets are halved, point $(M + .5B)$ will be obtained; this can be combined with Treasury bills to give points on line 3—worse than line 2, but better than line 1.

Figure 20-14 is typical of the situation when a series of good bets is being considered: the curve increases at a decreasing rate, with risk changing more rapidly than expected return.[7]

In the case shown in Figure 20-14 the manager has chosen the right amount to bet. This can be seen graphically—point $(M + B)$ lies on the ray from point T tangent to the curve. If either less or more is bet, a poorer set of combinations will be obtained when the risky portfolio is mixed with Treasury bills.

Figure 20-15 shows a very different situation. Here the manager has selected a good set of bets—properly used, they can improve perform-

---

[7] This is generally the case when risky assets (such as M and B) with less-than-perfectly positively corre-lated returns are combined. For details, see W.F. Sharpe, *Portfolio Theory and Capital Markets* (New York: McGraw-Hill Book Company, 1970).

ance. But excessive zeal has led the manager to bet too much, actually decreasing likely performance. Combinations of Treasury bills and the selected portfolio (M + B) lie on line 2—below line 1, available via passive management. But a portfolio in which bets are reduced to 30% of the amounts selected by the manager will do much better, allowing points along line 3.

This idea can be generalized. The optimal portfolio can be characterized as (M + wB), where w is the proportion of the manager's desired bets that will provide the best risk-return combination. When borrowing and lending are available, the best combination is the one that maximizes the expected excess return per unit of risk (i.e., the slope of the line from point T). In Figure 20-15 the optimal value of w is .30.[8]

Figure 20-15 showed a situation in which superior security analysis was misused, leading to a portfolio that was actually inferior to an "index fund." However, there is hope: in such a case smaller bets can produce a portfolio superior to the market.

Figure 20-16 shows a more gloomy situation. Here the bets are neither good nor bad. Security analysis is average. The recommended bets add nonmarket risk but do not change either the portfolio's beta value or its expected return. The curve of the previous figure becomes a horizontal line, and potential performance is lowered (from line 1 to line 2) if the manager's choice of bets is adopted. The situation will not be as bad if the bets are reduced. But the best value of w is zero!

[8] More generally, the best combination is the one that provides the most suitable risk-return combination for the client, taking all possible investment alternatives into account.

FIGURE 20-16 Security Selection: Average Bets

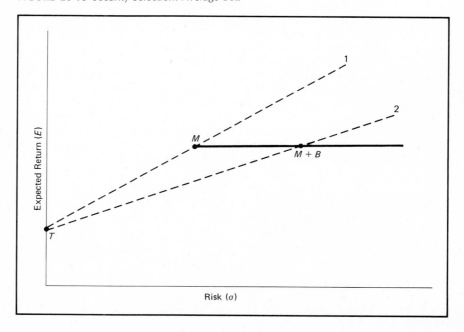

Security selectors are generally very active portfolio managers, for they will consider a change in holdings whenever they believe that the relative amounts by which different securities are mispriced have changed.

Tables comparing proportionate holdings of various securities in a portfolio with the proportions in an alternative passive portfolio are used by many investment management organizations for internal reporting and, increasingly, for external reporting to clients. Total holdings may be compared with a comprehensive index, or holdings in different sectors compared with market proportions, and holdings within each sector also compared with market proportions. In either case the goal is to show how the organization has placed its bets for a customer for whom the index is an appropriate passive portfolio. The former approach does this on a security-by-security basis, while the latter separates overall bets placed on sectors from those placed on specific securities within each sector.

Figure 20-17 shows an example of the process in reverse. In this case the organization characterizes its feelings about mispricing in terms of instructions to "underweight" or "overweight" the normal industry proportions in Standard and Poor's 500-stock index.

MARKET TIMING AND SECURITY SELECTION

Most managers combine styles, engaging in both market timing and security selection. Consensus estimates for both market and security prospects are considered, but not always adopted. Gains can be made via market timing, security selection, or both. On the other hand, erroneous forecasts on either front can reduce performance.

No new principles are required to guide the manager who engages in both security selection and market timing. The diagrams and computations used for security selection apply with only one modification: the manager's estimates of market risk and return are employed instead of consensus estimates. The portfolio of bets will be the same, but the mixture with the market (ω) will be different, as will the mix with Treasury bills considered appropriate for any given client.

This type of manager is likely to be especially active. Whenever he or she has a change of heart concerning either the market or individual securities, a change in holdings will be considered, even when the client's attitudes and the consensus opinions concerning security prospects remain the same.

Adjusting Predictions

Many organizations use security analysis to estimate expected returns, leaving the estimation of security nonmarket risk to computer departments instructed to assume that the future will be more or less like the past. Such estimates of risk may be wrong, but they are as likely to err in one direction as another.

This is not likely to be the case for the estimates of expected returns.

INDUSTRY AND STOCK RECOMMENDATIONS

INDUSTRY	S&P 500 WEIGHTING %	STRATEGY MT	STRATEGY LT	TECH- NICAL	ANALYST FUNDAMENTAL SELECTIONS ABOVE AVERAGE ATTRACTION— MARKET VALUE ($ MILLIONS) Over 250	Under 250	BELOW AVERAGE ATTRACTION
Aerospace	2.2	+	+	AA	Boeing General Dynamics McDonnell Douglas		
Appliance—TV	.2	−	=	BA	Corning Glass RCA	Scott & Fetzer	Zenith Radio
Autos	2.7	=	+	BA			
Auto Equipment	.8	+	+	A	Genuine Parts TRW	Echlin Mfg.	
Banks: Money Center	2.3	−	−	A	Bankers Trust Chase Manhattan Continental Ill. Morgan, J.P.		
Regional		−	−	A	First Bank System First City Bancorp. of Texas Mellon Natl. Seafirst U.S. Bancorp. Valley Natl. (Ariz.)	Rainier Bancorp. Pittsburgh Natl.	First Pennsylvania
Beverages: Brewers	.3	−	−	BA			
Distillers	.6	−	−	AA			Adolph Coors

Industry		Strategy	Medium Term	Technical	Companies
Soft Drinks	.9	+	+	BA	Heublein; Coca-Cola, PepsiCo
Broadcasting	.5	=	+	A	Capital Cities, Taft Broadcasting; John Blair, Viacom
Building	.6	−	+	A	
Chemicals	3.5	−	−	A	Dow, DuPont, Economic Labs., Ethyl; Betz Labs.
Coal	.2	+	+	AA	
Conglomerates	2.0	+	+	AA	Fuqua, Int'l Tel. & Tel., Litton Ind., Rockwell Int'l, United Technologies; Hexcel, Lear Siegler, Whittaker; Pittston
Containers	.5	−	−	A	
Cosmetics and Toiletries	.7	+	+	BA	

EXPLANATION OF TERMS:

N.R.: No Rating

Strategy—Medium Term (Time frame 3 months):
+ Overweight relative to market.
− Underweight relative to market.
= In line relative to market.

Technical (Time frame 3 months):
AA—Above Average—Strongest relative performers, appear to warrant above-average representation in portfolios on a technical basis.
A—Average—Likely to perform in line with the market and appear to warrant representation for diversification on a technical basis.
BA—Below Average—Likely to underperform market and appear to warrant below-average representation on a technical basis.

Fundamental (Time frame 0–12 months):
Above Average:　QRQ Rating Buy or OK to Buy.
Below Average:　QRQ Rating OK to Sell or Sell.

Strategy—Long Term (Time frame more than 6 months):
+ Overweight relative to market.
− Underweight relative to market.
= In line relative to market.

Source: Merrill Lynch, Pierce, Fenner and Smith, Inc., *Monthly Research Review*, February 1980.

Any given analyst may be optimistic or pessimistic and likely to exaggerate or understate. Moreover, an entire organization may have similar attributes. The appropriate value to use for a security is not necessarily the estimated value of its expected return but, rather, the expected return when such an estimate is given.

Typically the focus is on the *difference* between an organization's estimate of expected return and the consensus (efficient market) estimate. This difference, which may be estimated in a number of ways (e.g., by deviations from a security market line, plane, or hyperplane) can be termed a *predicted alpha*. To obtain an unbiased estimate of expected return one needs to add to the consensus value the best estimate of actual alpha when this sort of prediction is made. Historic data may be used to determine the average ex post alpha obtained when a similar value of alpha was predicted. This is similar to the procedure that was described in Chapter 15 and illustrated in Figure 15-10.

The idea can be extended. Given one or more types of prediction (e.g., unanticipated earnings changes, security codings, etc.), ex post alphas can be examined to find the typical relationship between predictions and outcomes. This relationship can then be used with current predictions to estimate expected alphas, which can then be added to consensus expected returns to obtain the best estimates of overall expected returns.

The principle applies as well to estimates used for market timing. The appropriate values for market return (E_M) and risk (σ_M^2) are those which summarize the likely distribution of market returns, given the current estimate. For example, assume that an organization simply predicts each year's market as being "bullish" or "bearish." To know how to act, given such a prediction, one would like a century or two of data on such predictions, made by the same people, using the same procedures. If this information were available, all the market returns in years predicted to be bullish could be analyzed and a mean and standard deviation obtained. These values could be used to estimate market prospects when the organization feels bullish. Similarly, the mean and standard deviation of market returns in years previously predicted to be bearish could be used when the organization feels bearish.

It may be possible to obtain a record for calibrating security analysis, since predictions for many securities can be made at any time. But a comparable record for market analysis is out of the question, since there is only one market to predict.

Lacking a definitive record with which to assess predictive accuracy, it behooves any analyst to be humble about his or her ability to detect errors in the consensus opinion regarding either the market as a whole, groups of securities, or specific securities. Overestimation of predictive ability leads to less-than-optimal performance and can lead to performance that is worse than that obtained via passive strategies. Underestimation also leads to less-than-optimal performance but better than passive performance. If predictors lack adequate humility, their enthusiasm can be tempered by directives from above reducing the size of the bets on individual securities and/or the amount of turnover allowed for the portfolio.

TRANSACTIONS COSTS

Thus far the unpleasant subject of *transactions costs* has been avoided. Simply put, even if a security's price is unchanged, the net proceeds available from its sale will be less than the total cost of acquiring it. At any time the best available price at which someone will buy a security (the *bid* price) is likely to be less than the best available price at which it can be purchased (the *asked* price). Moreover, any agents involved in the transaction (brokers, etc.) will require compensation (commissions), and there may be taxes to pay as well.

It is difficult to characterize the magnitude of such transactions costs, but the difference between sale proceeds and purchase cost is likely to exceed 1% for all but a few frequently traded securities and can range as high as 5% to 10% in less active markets.

The existence of transactions costs greatly complicates the life of any investment manager, and the more active the manager, the greater the complications. The hoped-for advantage of any move must be weighed against the cost of making it. Moreover, it is difficult to know how much of the cost to consider. Any move away from a long-term norm (in terms of risky versus riskless assets or the relative proportions of individual risky securities) is likely to be temporary and should be charged the cost of both getting there and getting back. In general, the desirability of the move will depend on the length of time the position is likely to be maintained as well as the advantage it is expected to give per unit of time while maintained.

PORTFOLIO REVISION

Figure 20-2(b) summarized the key ingredients required for rational portfolio revision decisions. Simply put:

The goal is to improve the suitability of a portfolio, net of an appropriate portion of the required transactions costs.

In practice sophisticated procedures (such as quadratic programming) and computer processing are required if this is to be accomplished efficiently. However, improvements in procedures and dramatic decreases in the cost of computers have made such approaches economically feasible for use by many investment managers.

The "bottom line" number to be maximized is *suitability net of transactions costs*:

$$NS_{pc} = E_p - \frac{1}{T_c} V_p - C_p \qquad (20\text{-}3)$$

where:

E_p = the expected return of the portfolio

V_p = the variance of return of the portfolio

C_p = the appropriate portion of the transactions costs incurred in the revision of the portfolio

T_c = the client's risk tolerance

NS_{pc} = the net suitability of the portfolio for the client

Key to the approach is the concept of *marginal net suitability*:

The marginal net suitability of security i (MNS_{ip}) is the change in the net suitability of portfolio p per unit change in the holding of security i if a small amount of security i is purchased or sold.

For example, assume a $1,000 portfolio has a net suitability of 10%. If $1 worth of security i with a net marginal suitability of 8.0% is sold and the proceeds used to buy $1 worth of security j with a net marginal suitability of 12.0%, the resulting portfolio's net suitability will be greater:

$$\begin{aligned}
\$1,000 \times 10.0\% &= 10,000 \\
-\$1 \times 8.0\% &= \underline{-8} \\
+\$1 \times 12.0\% &= \underline{+12} \\
& \ \ 10,004
\end{aligned}$$

$$NS_{pc} = \frac{10,004}{\$1,000} = 10.004\%$$

In general:

If one security has a higher marginal net suitability than another, a *swap* in which the former is purchased and the latter sold can increase the portfolio's net marginal suitability.

Figure 20-18 shows the typical relationship between the improvement and the *size* of the swap. If feasible, S' dollars worth of the two securities should be swapped in this case. If not (e.g., if this would require a disallowed short sale of the security being sold), the largest feasible swap should be made.

It is a relatively simple matter to compute the net marginal suitability of every security in a portfolio.[9] Having done this, the best swap can

---

[9] Formally, net marginal suitability is the derivative of NS_{pc} with respect to X_i:

$$MNS_{ip} = \frac{\partial NS_{pc}}{\partial X_i}$$

where:

X_i is the proportion of portfolio p invested in security i From (20-3):

$$MNS_{ip} = \frac{\partial E_p}{\partial X_i} - \frac{1}{T_c} \frac{\partial V_p}{\partial X_i} - \frac{\partial C_p}{\partial X_i}$$

$$= E_i - \frac{1}{T_c} \frac{\partial V_p}{\partial X_i} - c_i$$

where:

c_i is the change in the appropriate amount of transactions cost associated with a change in X_i
The definition of variance implies that:

$$\frac{\partial V_p}{\partial X_i} = 2C_{ip}$$

where:

C_{ip} = the covariance of security i's return with that of portfolio p
Thus:

$$MNS_{ip} = E_i - \frac{2}{T_c} C_{ip} - c_i$$

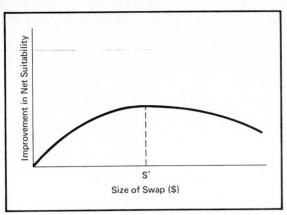

Improvement in Net Suitability

Size of Swap ($)

S'

FIGURE 20-18 (left)   Portfolio   Improvement versus Swap Size

FIGURE 20-19 (below) An Algorithm for Portfolio Revision

Source: Based on William F. Sharpe, ''An Algorithm for Portfolio Improvement,'' *Management Science* (forthcoming).

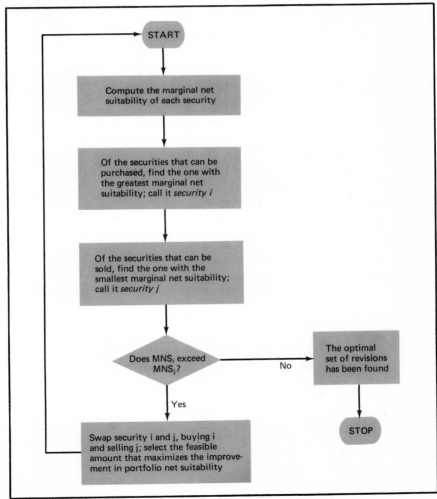

START

Compute the marginal net suitability of each security

Of the securities that can be purchased, find the one with the greatest marginal net suitability; call it *security i*

Of the securities that can be sold, find the one with the smallest marginal net suitability; call it *security j*

Does MNSᵢ exceed MNSⱼ?

No

The optimal set of revisions has been found

STOP

Yes

Swap security i and j, buying i and selling j; select the feasible amount that maximizes the improvement in portfolio net suitability

be found and the optimal swap size calculated. This will give a revised portfolio. Then the marginal net suitabilities can be recalculated and the procedure repeated. It is easy to know when to stop:

The optimal set of revisions have been found when the largest marginal net suitability of the securities that can be purchased is not greater than the smallest net marginal suitability of the securities that can be sold.

Figure 20-19 (page 605) provides a flow diagram of the *algorithm* (procedure). Figure 20-20 shows how portfolio net suitability typically increases as swaps are made.

Portfolio optimizers, such as this, designed to improve portfolio holdings are being used increasingly by professional investment managers.

MANAGER-CLIENT RELATIONS

The larger the amount of money managed, the more communication there is likely to be between investment manager and client. Not surprisingly, corporate, union, and government officials responsible for pension funds spend a great deal of time with those who manage their money. Such officials also concern themselves with a number of prior questions: who should manage the money, how should it be managed, and how should the managers be instructed and constrained?

Many of the aspects of manager-client relations can be characterized as responses to a difference of opinion concerning managers' abilities to make good bets.

For example, assume that a client thinks that a manager is betting too much. In the terms used earlier, the manager is choosing a portfolio of $(M + B)$, while the client prefers to have, say, $(M + .5B)$. One way to accomplish this is to invest half the funds in a passive (or "core") fund (M) and to give the other half to the manager. If the latter doesn't compensate for the change, the total portfolio will be invested in $(M + .5B)$.

A related situation occurs when a client is considering two managers who appear to have good ideas but exaggerated opinions concerning their

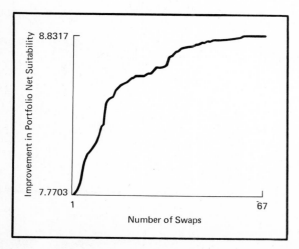

FIGURE 20-20 Portfolio Improvement versus Number of Swaps

Source: Canavest House Limited.

abilities. The first manager invests funds in $(M + B_1)$; the second, in $(M + B_2)$. By splitting the fund between the two, one can obtain $(M + .5B_1 + .5B_2)$ as long as the managers don't compensate for the change by increasing their bets.

This type of *split-funding* is used by most pension funds. Two reasons are given. First, it allows the employment of managers with different skills and/or different styles. More important: the impact of erroneous bets can be reduced by diversifying across different bettors. As more investment managers are used, the overall portfolio is likely to appear more like the market portfolio.

Split-funding reduces the money placed with one bettor, lowering both the risk and the possible return associated with betting. It is also likely to increase transactions costs. Moreover, substantial coordination is required to insure overall risk control, etc.

Extensive use of split-funding can give results similar to those obtained with an explicit passive fund, but at considerably greater cost, owing to the expenses associated with transactions and management fees.

Whether or not split-funding is used, a client who feels that a manager is betting too much would, if possible, like to simply reduce the size of the bets. For example, one might ask a manager to diverge only half as much as he or she normally would from passive proportions of individual securities, and to change the bond/stock mix for purposes of market timing only half the normal amount. But since there is no simple way to determine the normal response, compliance is difficult to monitor. Instead, a relatively inefficient approach is employed: limits are placed on the bond/stock mix, the holdings in any single security, the proportion invested in any single industry, the estimated degree of diversification of the portfolio, etc.

Institutional investors (pension funds, endowment funds, etc.) typically use more than one investment manager and provide each with a set of *objectives* (*target* or *normal* positions) and a set of *constraints* on allowed divergences from such normal positions. Individual investors who employ investment managers tend to give such instructions implicitly, if at all. This may reflect less sophistication, a less formal relationship with the manager, or the fact that the management fee for a small account is not large enough to cover the cost of dealing with a series of objectives and constraints.

Problems

1. In a world with no transactions costs what could you say about the marginal suitabilities of all the securities in an optimal portfolio if no legal or practical upper or lower limit were imposed on any holding?

2. A mutual fund manager is assessing the fund's portfolio. He estimates transactions costs to be 1% for a "round trip"—i.e., the purchase of one security and the sale of another. Legal restrictions require that no more than 5% of the portfolio be invested in any one security; short sales are also precluded by law. The current holdings and marginal suitabilities (before transactions costs) of five securities are:

	Percent Invested	Marginal Suitability
GM	5.0	12.3%
ATT	3.0	9.1
HON	2.1	9.5
IBM	4.0	9.8
XRX	0	5.2

Can you find a swap using these five stocks that would improve the portfolio? Why or why not?

3. Should an "overpriced" stock definitely be excluded from one's portfolio? Why or why not?

4. "When it comes right down to it, portfolio analysis involves only risk, return, client attributes, and transactions costs." How does the notion of *market efficiency* fit into this scheme?

5. An investment advisory firm has estimated the prospects for bonds and stocks as follows:

Expected returns:
Bonds   10%
Stocks   18%
Standard deviations:
Bonds   5%
Stocks   22%
Correlation coefficient, bonds and stocks: .5

Using these estimates, the firm has run a number of simulations, tracing out the implications of different bond/stock mixes for a client's future financial situation. After much thought the client has indicated that of the mixes considered, he would prefer a combination with 60% invested in stocks and 40% in bonds. What can you say about his *risk aversion* and *risk tolerance*? [*Hint:* Write an equation for the suitability of a 60/40 mix, using λ as the client's risk aversion. Then do the same for a 61/39 mix. Finally, find the value of λ that makes the two amounts the same. Why is this an adequate measure of the client's risk aversion? What is the corresponding measure of his risk tolerance? Over what range are these values likely to represent his feelings?]

6. Jay Gould began a dollar-cost-averaging program on January 2, 1980. He had decided to invest $210 bimonthly in the stocks of each of three companies ($630 total, purchase once every two months). The actual number of shares purchased depended upon their respective prices at the times of the transactions. On January 1, 1981, Mr. Gould sold all his securities. Prices for the stocks at the time Mr. Gould purchased and sold them were:

	Erie Railroad	New York World	Western Union
Jan. 2, 1980	$ 2	$35	$ 5
March 2	3	21	10
May 2	5	15	21
July 2	6	14	35
Sept. 2	7	10	21
Nov. 2	10	7	10
Jan. 2, 1981	14	5	5

    a.   Determine the average cost of shares for each of the three stocks.

    b.   Are the average costs you calculated in part (a) less than the average market prices of the stocks? Base your calculations upon market prices at the six times that stocks were purchased.

    c.   When adopting a dollar-cost-averaging approach to investing, can you be certain of any of the following?

       (1) A rate of return greater than the yield of U.S. government bonds.

       (2) A positive rate of return.

       (3) An average share cost that is less than the average price over the period of the cost-averaging program.

7.   The shorter the period during which a security is likely to be held, the shorter should be the period over which the transactions costs associated with its purchase should be amortized. Yet if a high proportion of transactions costs are "charged" for portfolio revision, the amount turned over will tend to be small. And the smaller the turnover, the longer the period over which the typical stock will be held. How might one achieve a consistent approach toward the amortization of transactions costs?

8.   What problems are involved in helping an individual investor select a "normal" bond/stock mix? What about the officers in charge of a corporation's pension fund? What should be the objective of such officers? If the corporation will definitely meet the required pension payments, aside from possible tax effects does the investment strategy of the fund matter? If so, for whom does it matter?

9.   Is it possible for more than half the managers of institutional portfolios to "beat" Standard and Poor's 500-stock index in a given year? If so, does this contradict the assertion that the "average dollar invested" cannot "beat the market"? Why or why not?

10.   If there were no transactions costs, would the average dollar under active management provide inferior performance to the average dollar passively managed over one month? What about the prospects (in terms of expected return and risk) of these two approaches over the next twelve months? Explain.

Performance Measurement and Attribution

21

INTRODUCTION

In one sense the measurement of investment performance is the last stage of the investment management process; in another sense it is simply part of a continuing operation.

An investor who pays someone to actively manage a portfolio, in the hope of achieving superior performance, has every right to insist on knowing what sort of performance is actually obtained. Such information can be used to alter the constraints placed on a manager, the objectives stated for the account, or the amount of money allocated to the manager. Perhaps more important: by measuring performance in specified ways, a client can forcefully communicate his or her interests to an investment manager and, in all likelihood, affect the way in which a portfolio is managed. Moreover, an investment manager, by measuring and diagnosing his or her own performance, can help isolate sources of strength or weakness.

Unfortunately, it is very difficult to separate performance due to skill from that due to luck. In this context, as in any other, a change should be made only when there is adequate reason to expect the advantages to outweigh the costs. Switching from one manager to another on the basis of minor differences in short-term performance will certainly incur transactions costs (as the new manager replaces old holdings with new ones that conform to his or her "style"), but there may or may not be any improvement in future performance. Differences in managers' past performance should be treated as interesting data, suggesting areas for more detailed examination and discussion. But drastic changes in management based solely on recent history should usually be avoided.

Superior past performance may well have been due to good luck; if so, it should not be expected to continue in the future. Inferior past performance may have been due to bad luck, but it may also have resulted from excessive turnover, management fees or other costs, or from unreasonably high nonmarket risk (lack of diversification). If so, more detailed diagnostic performance measurement may identify areas in which changes can improve performance. Only if a manager is reluctant to make such changes may it make sense to take one's money elsewhere.

Many investment management organizations measure the performance of individual employees and departments for internal purposes. The effectiveness of a trading department may be measured by comparing the prices at which securities are bought and sold with the highest and lowest prices recorded during the day. The usefulness of security analysts' codings may be measured by computing the performance of recommended securities relative to the performance of similar securities and comparing the average results for securities coded "1" with the results for those coded "2," etc. An investment committee's effectiveness may be measured by comparing the performance of a portfolio composed of all stocks on the approved list with one composed of all stocks recommended by security analysts but rejected by the committee. And so on.

The most widely publicized type of measurement is that used for external reporting to clients. Such *bottom-line* measurement is concerned primarily with the results obtained by the organization as a whole, with little concern for the manner in which the results were produced. Some investment managers routinely measure their own performance in this way; some sophisticated investors (e.g., corporate pension fund officials) measure their funds' performance; and a number of third parties provide measurement services for both investors and investment managers.

Making Relevant Comparisons

The essential idea behind performance measurement is to compare the returns obtained through active management with those of one or more appropriate alternatives. In some cases the focus is on the returns from "similar" actively managed funds; in others, a "similar" naive or passive strategy is considered.

With either approach it is important to choose relevant alternatives. The *comparison portfolio* should be *feasible* and should represent an alternative that would have been employed if the portfolio being measured had not been held. Moreover, dimensions of performance relevant for the decision being considered should be chosen. *Return* is a key aspect of performance, of course, but some way must be found to account for difference in funds' exposures to *risk*. A single measure that takes both elements into account may be employed; if so, almost any type of fund may be used for purposes of comparison. Alternatively, the comparison may be restricted to funds with similar exposure to risk, and their returns compared directly.

It is important to choose the most relevant type of risk. If the ultimate beneficiary of a fund has many other assets (including human capital), market risk may be the most relevant. On the other hand, if the fund provides its beneficiaries' sole support, all types of risk are relevant. Performance measurement may be based on one of these two extremes: taking either market risk or total risk into account. Or measures based on both types of risk may be calculated, leaving to the client the task of choosing the more relevant one (or using both measures to implicitly take both market and nonmarket risk into account).

Measures of Return

Most performance measurement covers a period of at least five years, broken into a number of subperiods—usually calendar quarters. This provides a fairly adequate sample size for statistical evaluation while avoiding the examination of ancient history.

Two measures of return are utilized in such analyses: total return and excess return (the fund's return during a quarter minus the return on a 90-day Treasury bill over the same period). Such figures may be averaged or cumulated to obtain annual or five-year measures of return.

Often a fund receives or distributes cash one or more times during a quarter. If possible, calculations are made as if unit (net asset) values had been determined each time a cash flow occurred, with units (shares) purchased or sold as needed at the time. The return on one unit for the quarter can then be calculated directly. This is often termed the fund's *time-weighted return*; it measures the manager's performance, without extraneous influences due to the timing of cash flows not under his or her control.

If the data needed to compute a time-weighted return (the market values of the fund prior to every cash flow) are not available, an internal rate of return (sometimes termed a *dollar-weighted return*) may be used to compute the return for a quarter.

Figure 21-1 shows a comparison between an equity fund's return each year and the returns of a group of managed equity funds.

FIGURE 21-1 Comparing Funds' Rates of Return

Source: A. G. Becker Incorporated *Funds Evaluation Service.*

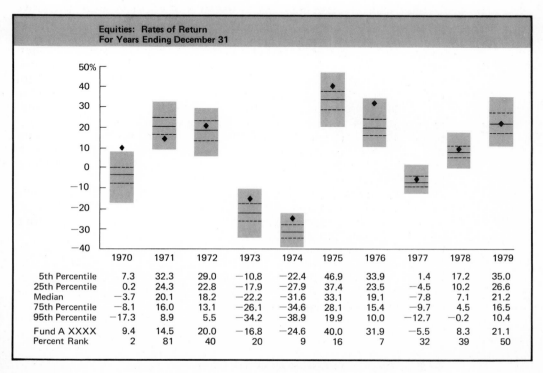

Equities: Rates of Return
For Years Ending December 31

	1970	1971	1972	1973	1974	1975	1976	1977	1978	1979
5th Percentile	7.3	32.3	29.0	−10.8	−22.4	46.9	33.9	1.4	17.2	35.0
25th Percentile	0.2	24.3	22.8	−17.9	−27.9	37.4	23.5	−4.5	10.2	26.6
Median	−3.7	20.1	18.2	−22.2	−31.6	19.1	19.1	−7.8	7.1	21.2
75th Percentile	−8.1	16.0	13.1	−26.1	−34.6	28.1	15.4	−9.7	4.5	16.5
95th Percentile	−17.3	8.9	5.5	−34.2	−38.9	19.9	10.0	−12.7	−0.2	10.4
Fund A XXXX	9.4	14.5	20.0	−16.8	−24.6	40.0	31.9	−5.5	8.3	21.1
Percent Rank	2	81	40	20	9	16	7	32	39	50

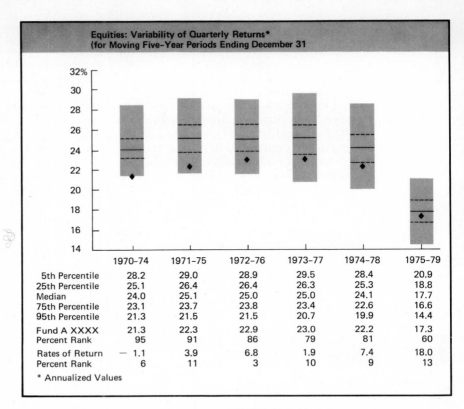

Equities: Variability of Quarterly Returns*
(for Moving Five-Year Periods Ending December 31

	1970-74	1971-75	1972-76	1973-77	1974-78	1975-79
5th Percentile	28.2	29.0	28.9	29.5	28.4	20.9
25th Percentile	25.1	26.4	26.4	26.3	25.3	18.8
Median	24.0	25.1	25.0	25.0	24.1	17.7
75th Percentile	23.1	23.7	23.8	23.4	22.6	16.6
95th Percentile	21.3	21.5	21.5	20.7	19.9	14.4
Fund A XXXX	21.3	22.3	22.9	23.0	22.2	17.3
Percent Rank	95	91	86	79	81	60
Rates of Return	− 1.1	3.9	6.8	1.9	7.4	18.0
Percent Rank	6	11	3	10	9	13

* Annualized Values

FIGURE 21-2 (above)
Comparing Funds' Variabilities

Source: A. G. Becker Incorporated *Funds Evaluation Service*.

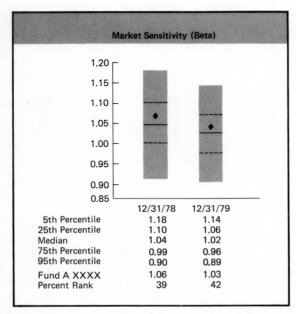

Market Sensitivity (Beta)

	12/31/78	12/31/79
5th Percentile	1.18	1.14
25th Percentile	1.10	1.06
Median	1.04	1.02
75th Percentile	0.99	0.96
95th Percentile	0.90	0.89
Fund A XXXX	1.06	1.03
Percent Rank	39	42

FIGURE 21-3 (left)
Comparing Funds' Beta Values

Source: A. G. Becker Incorporated *Funds Evaluation Service*.

Measures of Risk Exposure

Two measures of ex post performance are typically used as surrogates for ex ante risk exposure.

The standard deviation of quarterly returns (or excess returns) can serve as an estimate of a fund's average exposure to total risk over the period covered.

Figure 21-2 compares the variability of the equity portion of a fund with the variabilities of the equity portfolios of a group of funds.

The returns or excess returns of a fund may also be regressed on those of a market measure, such as Standard and Poor's 500-stock index, to determine the fund's *average beta* level during the period covered. Figure 21-3 compares such estimates for the equity portion of a fund with those of the equity portions of a sample of funds of similar size.

Ex Post Characteristic Lines

Figure 21-4 shows an ex post characteristic line fitted with standard linear regression techniques using the excess returns from an equity portfolio and a stock market index over twenty quarters. Three measures of performance are reported.

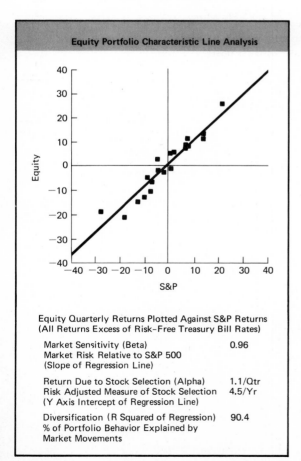

FIGURE 21-4 An Ex Post Characteristic Line

Source: Merrill Lynch, Pierce, Fenner and Smith, Inc., *Investment Performance Analysis.*

Equity Portfolio Characteristic Line Analysis

Equity Quarterly Returns Plotted Against S&P Returns
(All Returns Excess of Risk–Free Treasury Bill Rates)

Market Sensitivity (Beta)	0.96
Market Risk Relative to S&P 500	
(Slope of Regression Line)	
Return Due to Stock Selection (Alpha)	1.1/Qtr
Risk Adjusted Measure of Stock Selection	4.5/Yr
(Y Axis Intercept of Regression Line)	
Diversification (R Squared of Regression)	90.4
% of Portfolio Behavior Explained by	
Market Movements	

Market sensitivity is the fund's average beta level over the period. In this case the fund's equities were slightly defensive—the average beta value was .96.

The *alpha value* is the vertical intercept—i.e., the ex post value of alpha. The value was slightly positive—approximately 1.1% per quarter or 4.5% per year (the latter is not exactly four times the former, owing to rounding).

The third measure is 100 times the value of *R-squared*. In this case, 90.4% of the variance in the fund's excess returns could be attributed to variation in the excess returns on Standard and Poor's 500-stock index.

Differential Returns

It is relatively simple to compare a fund's returns, quarter by quarter, with those of a relevant comparison portfolio (e.g., a passive portfolio with similar risk exposure). Figure 21-5 shows an example. First, the fund's average beta value was determined from an ex post characteristic line (the one shown in Figure 21-4). Then the fund's total return in each period was compared with that of a fund invested only in Standard and Poor's 500-stock index and Treasury bills, with proportions of the two chosen to provide a constant beta value equal to the average value obtained by the fund.

Differential returns are generally computed by comparing a fund's returns with those of a comparison portfolio of similar risk. The usual procedure, illustrated in Figure 21-5, is based on market risk. But if desired, a mix with the same *total* risk can be employed. If a fund represents only a small part of its beneficiaries' assets, comparison with a portfolio of equal beta risk is more appropriate; but if it is the major asset for its beneficiaries, comparison with a fund of equal total risk is preferable.

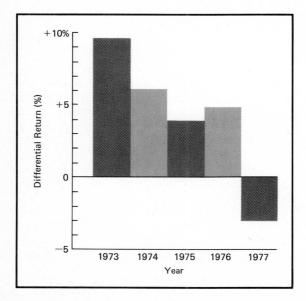

FIGURE 21-5 Differential Returns

Source: Merrill Lynch, Pierce, Fenner and Smith, Inc., *Investment Performance Analysis.*

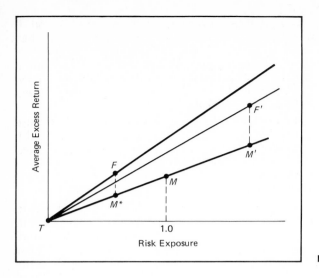

FIGURE 21-6 Reward-to-Risk Exposure Ratios

Ex Post Alpha Values

When comparison with an equal-beta portfolio of Treasury bills and a stock index is employed, the average differential return equals the fund's ex post alpha value—i.e., the vertical intercept obtained when an ex post characteristic line is fit using excess returns. Thus a fund's ex post alpha value can be interpreted as the average difference between its return and that of a passive strategy of equal (and constant) market risk.

If an equal-total-risk combination of Treasury bills and a security index is used as a comparison portfolio, a different average differential return will be obtained. This measure (which can be designated *alpha-prime*) indicates the average difference between a fund's return and that of a passive strategy of equal (and constant) total risk.

Ratios of Reward-to-Risk Exposure

In Chapter 18 the performance of a group of mutual funds was summarized in terms of the *reward* (mean monthly excess return) per unit of *risk* exposure (either the value of beta, representing market risk, or the standard deviation of monthly excess returns, representing total risk). Such measures have obvious intuitive appeal. They can also be justified on more formal grounds.

Figure 21-6 plots the average excess return (vertical axis) and risk (horizontal axis) for a fund (point F), a market index (point M), and Treasury bills (point T). Line TM shows the results that could have been obtained by combining Treasury bills and the market index, while line TF shows the results that could have been obtained by combining Treasury bills with investment in fund F. In each case, borrowing at the Treasury bill rate is assumed to be feasible. The measure of risk exposure could be either relative variability (for total risk) or a beta value (for market risk). In either case, the market index has a risk exposure of 1.0.

As shown in Figure 21-6, fund F can be said to have outperformed the market, in the sense that for any desired risk exposure an investor could have done better with a combination of Treasury bills and the fund than with a combination of Treasury bills and the market index. Graphically: line TF is steeper than line TM. But the slopes of these lines *are* the reward-to-risk ratios. Putting it in reverse: any risky investment's reward-to-risk ratio can be considered the slope of the line showing the results that could have been obtained by combining it with borrowing or lending.

The relationship between a fund's reward-to-risk ratio and its alpha value is also illustrated in Figure 21-6. Point M^* shows the results that could have been obtained via a passive strategy with the same risk exposure as the fund. The distance FM^* is the difference in the average returns of funds F and M^* or, equivalently, the average difference in their returns. But the latter *is* the fund's alpha value (if the horizontal axis plots market risk) or alpha-prime value (if it plots total risk).

Figure 21-6 also shows that alpha values may prove misleading when two funds are compared. The performance of fund F' was inferior to that of fund F, as the slopes of lines TF and TF' and the reward-to-risk ratios indicate. But fund F' has a larger alpha value (distance $F'M'$) than fund F (distance FM^*). Clearly, the alpha values of funds with significantly different exposures to risk may not be directly comparable.

Relative and Absolute Measures

In any comparison it is important to use a relevant alternative. If a comparison portfolio with positive amounts of both Treasury bills and stocks is used, some would argue that the contest has been arranged so that a fund can easily win, since Treasury bills provide excessively low returns to compensate for their high degree of liquidity. On the other hand, a comparison portfolio with negative amounts of Treasury bills assumes that it is possible to lever up stock holdings by borrowing at the Treasury bill rate; some would argue that realistic alternatives in this range of risk are less attractive, and that in this case the contest has been arranged so that it is very difficult for a fund to win. *Absolute* values of differential returns are thus said to discriminate in favor of conservative funds and against aggressive ones.

One way to meet such criticism is to compare the *relative* values of performance measures for funds of similar risk. Figure 21-7 provides both absolute and relative comparisons. Each point represents the beta value of a fund (horizontal axis) and its actual return in 1979 (vertical axis). Mutual funds, bank commingled equity funds, and market indices are included. The line plots results that could have been obtained by combining Standard and Poor's 500-stock index with Treasury bills. The vertical distance from a fund's point to the line indicates its differential return in 1979. This may be compared visually with the differential returns for other funds. Alternatively, the line may be ignored, and a fund's return compared directly with the returns of other funds in the same risk class (i.e., those plotting above and below its point).

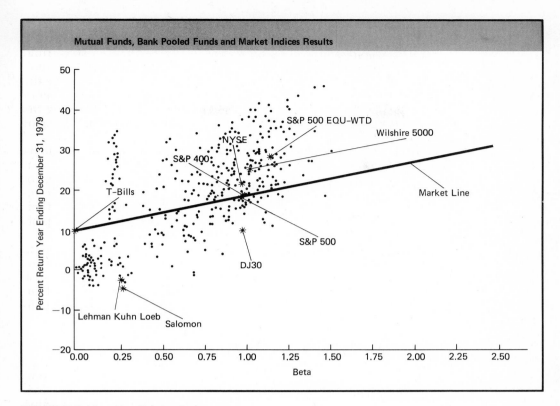

FIGURE 21-7 Measuring Relative Performance

Source: Wilshire Associates.

Performance Attribution

Bottom-line performance measurement concentrates on the question of *how* a portfolio did. Performance *attribution* attempts to determine *why* it did what it did.

Figure 20-2(c) indicated the major ingredients. In addition to security returns, *factor returns* are utilized. The idea is fairly simple. In any given period high-beta stocks may do better than low-beta stocks (even if the market has gone down). For example, each point in a graph such as that shown in Figure 21-7 could plot the actual return on a stock over a period and the value of its beta *attribute* at the beginning of the period. A regression line could then be fitted to the data and the information represented as follows:

$$R_{it} = Z_t + \beta_{it} F_{\beta t} + \epsilon_{it} \qquad (21\text{-}1)$$

where:

R_{it} = the return on security i in period t

$$\beta_{it} = \text{the beta attribute for stock } i \text{ at the beginning of period } t$$

$$Z_t, F_{\beta t} = \text{the intercept and slope of the } ex\ post\ (actual)\ security$$
$$market\ line \text{ in period } t$$

$$\epsilon_{it} = \text{security } i\text{'s } nonfactor\ (residual)\ return \text{ in period } t$$

The value of Z_t can be considered the return on a zero-beta security in period t, while $F_{\beta t}$, the *value of the beta factor in period* t, indicates the typical difference between the return of a security with a beta of, say, 1.5 and one with a beta of .5.

In this case the return on the security could be *attributed to* three factors:

$$Z_t = \text{a return common to all securities}$$

$$\beta_{it} F_{\beta t} = \text{the return attributed to (1) the security's beta attribute and}$$
$$\text{(2) the actual performance of the beta factor}$$

$$\epsilon_{it} = \text{the nonfactor performance of security } i$$

Precisely the same sort of attribution can be made for the return of a portfolio:

$$R_{pt} = Z_t + \beta_{pt} F_{\beta t} + \epsilon_{pt}$$

where:

$$R_{pt} = \text{the return on portfolio } p \text{ in period } t$$

$$\beta_{pt} = \text{the beta attribute of the portfolio at the beginning of period } t$$

$$\epsilon_{pt} = \text{the portfolio's nonfactor return in period } t$$

This kind of procedure has been applied to many factors that affect groups of stocks, such as yield, size, industry membership, etc. In essence an *ex post (actual) security market hyperplane* is fitted by regression analysis using data on security returns and attribute values. From such a regression one can obtain, for example, a *yield factor* indicating the difference

FIGURE 21-8 Performance Attribution

FACTOR	EXPOSURE TO FACTOR			FACTOR CONTRIBUTION TO RETURN AFTER TAX			CONTRIBUTION TO DIFFERENCE IN EQUITY RETURN AFTER TAX
	Brown	Comp	Brown − Comp	Brown	Comp	Brown − Comp	
Beta factor	1.02	1.00	.02	−.87	−.87	.00	−.02
Yield factor	4.43	4.76	−.33	−.22	−.22	.00	.07
Capitalization factor	3.37	3.50	−.13	.52	.52	.00	−.07
Industry selection	1.00	1.00	.00	−.16	−.01	−.15	−.15
Security selection	1.00	1.00	.00	.07	−.03	.10	.10
						Difference in equity return:	−.07

Source: Canavest House Limited.

in returns between two stocks differing only in predicted yield, a *steel factor* indicating the performance attributed solely to membership in the steel industry, etc.

With such results a portfolio return can be broken into portions due to common factor exposure (e.g., yield, beta), industry exposure (e.g., proportions invested in various industries), and security exposure (e.g., proportions invested in various securities). Moreover, two portfolios can be compared and the difference in their returns attributed to differences in beta, yield, average size of the stocks (capitalization), industry holdings, security holdings, etc.

Figure 21-8 provides an example of this type of comparison. In this case (representing a month's performance) the portfolio (Brown) underperformed the comparison portfolio (Comp—Standard and Poor's 500-stock index) by 15 basis points in terms of industry selection but outperformed it by 10 basis points in terms of stock selection.

Estimating the Significance of Past Performance

Most performance measurement concentrates on historic values. But what are the values likely to be in the future? Putting it another way: To what extent was the historic value due to luck (good or bad) and to what extent was it due to skill or the lack thereof?

The issue can be illustrated by considering the "bottom-line" alpha measure of fund performance. How much attention should one pay to *ex post* alpha—the average differential return?

Examination of the pattern of differential returns can provide some help in this regard. If a fund provided a differential return of exactly $+1\%$ every quarter, one might reasonably assume that such performance might continue in the future. But if the differential returns had ranged from -9% to $+10\%$, even though the average value might have been $+1\%$, one might reasonably assume that future performance would be virtually as likely to be positive as negative.

Some performance measurement services use the variability of differential returns to compute a statistical measure, the *standard error of alpha*, to be used in this connection. For example, the value of alpha might be $+1.0\%$ per quarter and its standard error $.8\%$ per quarter. Roughly, this means that the chances are (a) two out of three that the fund's "true" alpha value (ex ante expected differential return) lies within the range from $+.2$ $(=1.0 - .8)$ to $+1.8$ $(1.0 + .8)$ and (b) 95 out of 100 that it lies within the range from $-.6$ $(=1.0 - 2 \times .8)$ to $+2.6\%$ $(=1.0 + 2 \times .8)$. The latter range includes the possibility that the value is really zero; thus a *classical* statistician would say that "at the 95% confidence level" the hypothesis that the manager has no skill cannot be rejected. A *Bayesian* statistician would say that the sample of 20 quarters of data should lead to a revision of one's assessment: from a *prior* expectation, e.g., that the fund's true alpha value is zero, to a *posterior* expectation that it is larger. The extent of the revision will depend on the historic alpha value and its standard error, and the conviction with which one holds the belief that few funds can really outperform the market. The appropriate estimate of expected future results should, in this view, lie between the prior estimate and the historic performance measure; and it should be closer to the latter, the smaller its standard error.

In pragmatic terms: superior performance *on average* is interesting, but *consistently* superior performance is very interesting indeed.

Measuring the Performance of Fixed-Income Investments

Analysis of the performance of the nonequity portion of a fund may be limited to a quarter-by-quarter comparison of the total returns from such investments with those of an index representing a particular class of bonds; Figure 21-9 is typical.

Figure 21-10 illustrates a different approach. Here return is related to *duration*, with the return on the fund ("Manager A") compared with the returns of bond portfolios with similar durations.

Assessing Market Timing

As discussed in Chapter 18, the results of attempts to time the market may be investigated by seeing if the relationship between a fund's excess returns and those of a market portfolio follow a curve instead of a line. There is another way: A portfolio's posture vis-à-vis the market at the

FIGURE 21-9 Comparing the Performance of Fixed-Income Investments

Source: Merrill Lynch, Pierce, Fenner and Smith, Inc., *Investment Performance Analysis.*

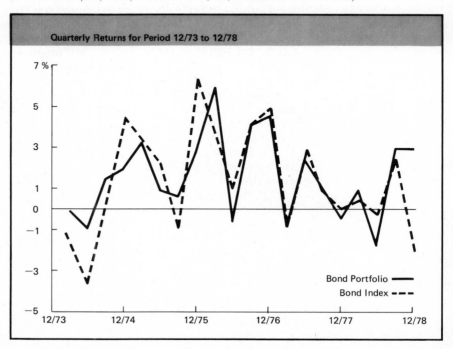

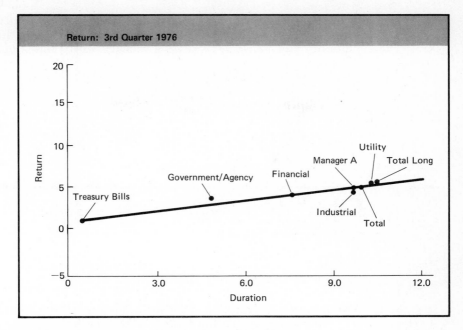

FIGURE 21-10 Return versus Duration for Bond Portfolios

Source: Wayne H. Wagner and Dennis A. Tito, "Definitive New Measures of Bond Performance and Risk," *Pension World,* May 1977.

beginning of each quarter can be compared with the market's subsequent performance.

Two basically different methods can be used to "time the market." The beta value of the equity portion of the fund can be changed, or the mix of fixed-income and equity investments can be altered.

Some of the variation in the estimated beta values of an equity portfolio will be automatic, due to changes in the relative values of different stocks; and some will be spurious, due to the use of historic instead of ex ante beta values.[1] Similarly, the relative values of the fixed-income and equity portions of a fund will change from time to time even if the fund's manager follows a strict "buy and hold" policy.

To analyze the effects of attempts to time the market, one needs to estimate "normal" positions (bond/stock mixes, equity beta levels) that would have been experienced had market timing not been tried. Deviations from such positions can be compared directly with the performance of the market. Alternatively, the results that would have been obtained by following the nontiming policy with investment in passive bond and stock portfolios can be compared with those that would have been obtained by following the timing policy with investment in such portfolios. Dif-

---

[1] For example, after the market rises or falls, if the same historic betas are used, the value-weighted average beta of existing stocks will generally change; since the true average beta value should always equal 1.0, changes of this sort must be spurious.

ferences in the returns provide estimates of the *gross* amounts that market timing added to (or subtracted from) performance. To estimate the *net* amounts, the transactions costs associated with each strategy must be considered.

Much more could be said about performance measurement. It suffices to indicate that, although some investment managers may not like it, performance measurement appears to be here to stay.

Problems

1. Why is the reward-to-variability ratio measure of performance more appropriate than the alpha measure if the fund being assessed represents its beneficiary's entire investment portfolio?

2. Does a fund's *ex post alpha* [the vertical intercept of a characteristic line fitted to points representing the fund's excess returns (on the vertical axis) versus those of a market index (on the horizontal axis)] measure gains and losses due to *security selection*, *market timing*, or both?

3. The performance of the commingled fund of a local bank over a ten-year period compared with that of Standard and Poor's 500-stock index was as follows:

	Fund	SP500
Average quarterly excess return	.6%	.5%
Standard deviation of quarterly excess returns	9.9%	6.6%
Beta	1.1	1.0

The William Mathews Trust Fund, which is the sole support of an elderly widow, was invested partly in Treasury bills (about 70% of the total), with the remainder in this fund. The bank has started a new fund, intended to match the SP500 index. Based solely on past performance, would it be desirable to use the new fund for this trust instead of the original commingled fund?

4. A major brokerage firm provides a performance measurement service in which the "bottom line" measure of a fund's performance is alpha—the intercept in a regression equation of the form:

$$R_f - p = \alpha + \beta(R_s - p) + \epsilon$$

where: R_f = the return on the fund
p = the return on a U.S. Treasury bill

R_s = the return on Standard and Poor's 500-stock index

α = alpha, a constant fitted by regression analysis

β = beta, a constant fitted by regression analysis

ϵ = a random error term

Provide an interpretation of "alpha" in terms of the difference between the return on the portfolio and that of some other investment strategy. Exactly what does this alternative strategy involve? Under what conditions is alpha a sufficient measure of performance? Under what conditions is it not?

5. A mutual fund changed its beta value from year to year in an attempt to "time the market." The accompanying table shows the values of the fund's beta in each of ten years, along with the return on the fund, the return on Standard and Poor's 500-stock index, and the return on Treasury bills.

Year	Fund Beta	Return on Fund	Return on SP500	Return on Treasury Bills
1969	.90	− 2.99%	− 8.50%	6.58%
1970	.95	.63	4.01	6.53
1971	.95	22.01	14.31	4.39
1972	1.00	24.08	18.98	3.84
1973	1.00	−22.46	−14.66	6.93
1974	.90	−25.12	−26.47	8.00
1975	.80	29.72	37.20	5.80
1976	.75	22.15	23.84	5.08
1977	.80	.48	−7.18	5.12
1978	.85	6.85	6.56	7.18

Assume that the beta value shown for each year was the fund's true beta during the entire year.

a. What was the fund's average beta over the ten-year period?

b. Compute the year-by-year returns for a fund made up of Treasury bills and the SP500 in the proportions required to have a constant beta value equal to the value found in (a).

c. Compute the year-by-year returns for a fund made up of Treasury bills and the SP500 in the proportions required to have a beta value equal to that of the fund *in each year*.

d. Compute the year-by-year amounts of the fund's returns attributable to *market timing*. Does the fund's record suggest an ability to time the market?

e. Compute the year-by-year amounts of the fund's returns attributable to *security selection*. Does the fund's record suggest an ability to select securities?

f. Compute the average *total* return and standard deviation of *total* return for (1) the fund, (2) the SP500, (3) the "policy fund" considered in (c), and (4) the "timing only" fund considered in (d). Which fund would have been best for an investor who had a risk tolerance of 100? Why?

Extended
Diversification

22

INTRODUCTION

One of the major themes of modern portfolio theory concerns the merits of *diversification:* in an efficient capital market sensible investment strategies will include holdings of many different assets. Previous chapters have considered traditional securities such as stocks and bonds and some less traditional ones, such as commodity and financial futures and options; owner-occupied real estate also has been discussed. It remains to deal with diversification extending beyond the borders of one's own country and with the holding of tangible assets. After completing these tasks, we turn briefly to a less lofty subject: sports and horse race betting. As indicated in Chapter 20, active investment management can be considered a form of betting. It is instructive to contrast this rather subtle form of wagering handled by security brokers and dealers with the more explicit form handled by race tracks and legal and illegal "bookmakers."

INTERNATIONAL DIVERSIFICATION

If the world were under one political jurisdiction, with one currency and complete freedom of trade among areas, one might think of "the market portfolio" as including all capital assets in the world, each in proportion to its market value. Limiting one's investments to securities representing firms domiciled in one area would, in such a situation, generally decrease return per unit of risk. Few advocate that Californians own only shares of firms with headquarters located in California. And in a world without political boundaries, few would advocate that, say, Americans own only shares of American firms.

But there are political boundaries, different currencies, and restrictions on trade and currency exchange. Such unpleasantries diminish, but do not destroy, the advantages to be gained from international diversification.

The World Market Portfolio

Table 22-1 provides two estimates of the relative proportions in the world market portfolio. Table 22-1(a) is based on the values of shares (common stocks) of 1,100 companies in the United States, Canada, Europe, Aus-

TABLE 22-1 Estimated Composition of the World Market Portfolio

(a) BASED ON SHARE VALUES FROM SELECTED COUNTRIES, DECEMBER 31, 1979

Area		Percent of Total
United States		52.3
Canada		5.3
Europe:		22.1
United Kingdom	7.7	
Germany	4.4	
France	3.0	
Switzerland	2.4	
Netherlands	1.3	
Belgium/Luxembourg	.7	
Italy	.7	
Spain	.7	
Sweden	.6	
Denmark	.2	
Norway	.2	
Austria	.1	
Far East:		16.9
Japan	14.9	
Hong Kong	1.3	
Singapore	.7	
Australia		2.1
South African Gold Mines		1.2

(b) BASED ON GROSS DOMESTIC PRODUCTS OF ALL MARKET ECONOMIES, 1977

Area		Percent of Total
United States		30.5
Canada		3.2
Europe:		32.5
Germany	8.4	
France	6.2	
United Kingdom	4.0	
Italy	3.2	
Spain	1.9	
Netherlands	1.7	
Sweden	1.3	
Belgium	1.3	
Switzerland	1.0	
Austria	.8	
Denmark	.7	
Norway	.6	
Other countries	1.4	
East and Southeast Asia (excluding Japan)		5.0
Japan		11.2
Oceania (except Australia)		.3
Australia		1.6
South Africa		.6
Africa (excluding South Africa)		3.8
Caribbean and Latin America		7.0
Middle East		4.4

Source: (a) *Capital International Perspective*, First quarter, 1980 (Geneva, Switzerland: Capital International). (b) *Yearbook of National Accounts Statistics, 1978*, II, 3–9. © United Nations, 1978. Reproduced by permission.

tralia, the Far East, and South Africa. Table 22-1(b) is based on the gross domestic products of all market economies, on the grounds that a country's annual product represents the income from its capital stock. Of course, only a portion of a country's capital is available for purchase by domestic investors (e.g., human capital is not), and less still can be purchased freely by foreign investors. Since Table 22-1(a) is based only on traded equity securities (and excludes many countries), while Table 22-1(b) includes many nonmarketable assets, neither provides the final answer. Together, however, they give an idea of the likely range of the relevant values.

International Investment Risks

Investment abroad brings all the risks associated with investment at home, plus at least two more. First, there is *exchange risk*. The return in U.S. dollars from a French security depends on both the security's return in francs and the rate at which francs can be exchanged for dollars in the future, and this latter rate is generally subject to at least some uncertainty. Second, there is *political risk*. Governments may restrict, tax, or completely prohibit the exchange of one currency for another. Since such policies change from time to time, the ability to repatriate one's foreign investments may be subject to some uncertainty. There may even be a possibility of complete expropriation, making political risk very large.

These two types of risk are generally related. For example, the exchange rate between two currencies may be fixed by mutual agreement, central bank stabilization actions, etc. But no price can be set at a level at which demand and supply are out of balance without some sort of rationing being invoked. When a currency becomes seriously undervalued, conversion to "hard" currencies is likely to be difficult (and in some cases, illegal). Eventually the "fixed" rate is likely to be altered; i.e., the currency is "devalued."

Sensible public policy involves "floating" exchange rates determined by market forces. Such rates make variations in the terms of trade more visible and may appear to add to uncertainty; in fact, however, they serve to focus existing uncertainty in an arena where it can be borne most efficiently.

To an extent, exchange risk can be reduced by hedging in the market for forward exchange. In the case of default-free fixed-income investment it may be possible to completely eliminate such risk in this way. For example, a one-year discount bond paying 1,000 British pounds might be purchased and a forward contract made to deliver £1,000 a year hence in return for, say $2,100. If the current (spot) exchange rate were $2.20 per pound, and the bond cost £850, the return in dollars would be 12.3%:

current cost: £850 × $2.20 per £ = $1,870
                   (spot rate)

proceeds: £1,000 × $2.10 per £ = $2,100
                     (forward rate)

return in dollars: $\dfrac{2,100 - 1,870}{1,870} = .123$

Except for political risk, this is a certain return. The exchange risk has been completely removed by hedging.

Unfortunately it is not possible to completely hedge the exchange risk associated with risky investments. Forward contracts can be made to cover *expected* cash flows, but if the *actual* cash flows are larger or smaller than expected, some currency may have to be exchanged at the spot rate prevailing at the time. Since future spot rates usually cannot be predicted with complete certainty, this will affect overall risk. The precise nature of the relationship will depend, however, on the correlation between the foreign exchange rate and investment return.

The importance of exchange and political risks can easily be exaggerated. Exchange rates may be negatively correlated with investment returns and may even reduce total risk. For example, inflation in the United Kingdom might raise the return in pounds on British stocks and decrease the number of dollars into which a pound could be converted. If so, the dollar return on such an investment might conform more to a real return and be subject to less uncertainty than the pound return. Moreover, most calculations assume that investors purchase only domestic goods and services and thus convert all proceeds from foreign investments into their own currency before engaging in any spending for consumption purposes. But most people buy foreign goods and many buy foreign services as well (e.g., as tourists). The cheaper another country's currency relative to one's own, the more attractive purchases of its goods and services will be. Other things equal, it may make sense to invest more in countries whose products and scenery one admires, for the effective exchange and political risks are likely to be smaller there than elsewhere.[1]

Some argue that investment abroad involves yet a third type of risk. If capital markets in foreign countries are inefficient, investors located there may well enjoy a comparative advantage in identifying mispriced securities. Any disadvantage of this sort can be ameliorated, however, by random investment selection or by employing an index approach—i.e., purchasing many securities in proportion to market values. If some securities obtained in this manner are overvalued, others will be undervalued. Institutionalized index funds for foreign investment make this approach eminently feasible.

International Investment Advantages

If all economies were tied together completely, stock markets in different countries would move together, and little advantage could be gained through international diversification. But this is not the case. Table 22-2 shows the proportion of the variance in the monthly percentage changes of various national stock indices explained by changes in a market-value weighted world stock index. The percentage for the United States is large, owing primarily to the dominance of the U.S. in the world index. Canada follows, since its economy is tied closely to that of the United States. Stock markets in the Netherlands, Belgium, Switzerland, and Germany

---

[1] As indicated in previous chapters, it is also desirable to tie one's investment portfolio to consumption preferences when constructing portfolios of domestic securities.

TABLE 22-2 Percent of the Variance of National Stock Indexes Explained by a World Stock Index: January 1959 to October 1973

Country	Percent Explained
Australia	11.1
Austria	4.5
Belgium	26.2
Canada	66.7
Denmark	.8
France	9.6
Germany	22.3
Italy	6.2
Japan	7.9
Netherlands	45.4
Norway	2.0
Spain	.4
Sweden	13.1
Switzerland	29.5
United Kingdom	16.9
United States	88.0
average:	21.9

Source: Donald R. Lessard, "World, Country and Industry Relationships in Equity Returns: Implications for Risk Reduction Through Diversification," *Financial Analysts Journal*, 32, no. 1 (January–February 1976), 33.

come next, owing no doubt to the positions of these countries in international trade.

The striking feature of Table 22-2 is, however, the fact that the figures are so small. Each of the national indices represents a well-diversified domestic equity portfolio. Yet in the average case only 22% of the risk of such a portfolio is nondiversifiable; the other 78% is nonworld-market risk and can thus be avoided through international diversification.

While exchange and political risk reduce the attractiveness of international diversification, Table 22-2 shows that the advantages are nonetheless likely to be very great. Other things equal, the smaller a figure in the table, the greater the potential gain. If security prices were determined primarily by the actions of international investors, expected returns would be related only to contributions to the risk of an internationally diversified world market portfolio. For an all-domestic portfolio, the expected return per unit of *total* risk would be smaller, the smaller the ratio of the portfolio's world market risk to its total risk. The historical values of such ratios, shown in Table 22-2, suggest that under these conditions a policy of buying only domestic stocks might be acceptable for a resident of the United States but would be very ill-advised for a citizen of, say, Spain or Denmark.

Since added risks may be associated with foreign investing, and since markets are segmented to some extent, it may make sense for an investor to hold a more-than-proportionate share of domestic securities vis-à-vis the world market portfolio. Nonetheless, even when these risks are taken into account, international diversification is still likely to give higher returns per unit of risk than an all-domestic portfolio, even for an investor in the United States.

Models of International Security Returns

Relationships among security returns are difficult to determine in a domestic context and even harder to analyze in an international setting. But the possibility of holding an international portfolio requires that such a setting be considered.

Figure 22-1 shows a simple structure that models some relationships of this type. Each country's market is assumed to be sensitive to a change in the world market, with the sensitivities measured by "country-world" beta values. The world market factor is risky, and each country market factor has two types of risk—one due to the world factor and another specific to the country. A security's return is sensitive to changes in its own country's market factor and, through it, indirectly to the world market factor. The degree to which a stock moves with its country market factor is indicated by a "stock-country" beta value, and the sensitivity of a stock to the world market factor is obtained by multiplying the two relevant beta values:

$$\beta_{sw} = \beta_{sc} \times \beta_{cw}$$

where:

β_{sw} = percentage change in the return on stock s per unit of percentage change in the world market factor

β_{sc} = percentage change in the return on stock s per unit of percentage change in the country market factor of country c

β_{cw} = percentage change in the country market factor of country c per unit of percentage change in the world market factor

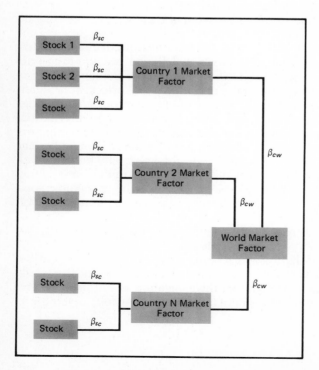

FIGURE 22-1 A Simple Model of International Security Returns

If international capital markets were completely integrated, each security's expected return would be proportional to the value of its stock-world beta (β_{sw}), and, in this model, the expected returns for all securities in any given country would be proportional to their stock-country beta values (β_{sc}'s) — a relationship that would hold even in a world of completely segmented domestic capital markets.

The model in Figure 22-1 is overly simplistic, however, and fails to account for a number of phenomena. For example, the returns of many *multinational firms* are affected by the economic fortunes of several countries. This can be modeled by tying the security of such a firm to several country factors. More simply, its return can be related directly to the world market factor and to its own country factor (which is also related to the world market factor). This approach captures at least some of the behavior of many securities, especially those with a high proportion of foreign sales.[2] It also suggests that to an extent, a portfolio may be diversified internationally by holding larger-than-proportionate shares of multinational companies in a nominally all-domestic portfolio. However, empirical evidence suggests that multinational firms provide less diversification than might be expected, given the international scope of their operations.[3]

Also missing in Figure 22-1 are *industry effects*. One could focus exclusively on such effects by replacing country market factors with international industry factors. However, such a drastic step would not be desirable—the average security's return tends to be more closely related to prospects for its domestic economy than to prospects for its world-wide industry.[4]

Figure 22-2 portrays part of a more general structure that can be used to model both industry and country effects. The main table represents a series of country-industry factors. For example, one box might stand for the U.S. steel industry, another for the Japanese shipping industry, etc. The entries at the bottom of the figure represent multinational industry factors, while those along the right-hand side represent multi-industry country factors. A security's return can be related to any or all of the factors represented in the figure via sensitivity (beta) coefficients. The particular factors chosen, and the relevant beta values, would depend primarily on the nature of the firm's business. In addition, estimates would have to be made of the interrelationships among the factors in the main part of the figure, the weightings to be used to obtain the aggregate factors at the bottom and along the right-hand side, and the magnitudes of the relevant components of risk and return.

The special characteristics of international investment make even the passive management of an internationally diversified portfolio a diffi-

[2] See Bruno H. Solnik, "The International Pricing of Risk: An Empirical Investigation of the World Capital Market Structure," *Journal of Finance*, XXIX, no. 2 (May 1974), 365–78, and Tamir Agmon and Donald Lessard, "The Multinational Firm as Vehicle for International Diversification: Implications for Capital Importing Countries," Massachusetts Institute of Technology Working Paper 847–76, April 1976.
[3] See Bertrand Jacquillat and Bruno Solnik, "La Valorisation des Enterprises Multi-nationales sur les Marchés Boursiers," *Analyse Financière* 4ᵉ Trimestre, 1976.
[4] Donald R. Lessard, "World, Country and Industry Relationships in Equity Returns: Implications for Risk Reduction Through International Diversification." *Financial Analysis Journal*, 32, no. 1 (January–February 1976), 32–38.

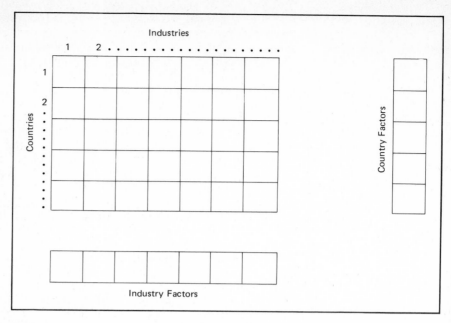

FIGURE 22-2 A Portion of a Detailed Model of International Security Returns

cult task. Active management is more arduous yet, as this discussion illustrates. But the potential advantages of international diversification are too great to be ignored. In investment, as in other spheres, parochialism is no virtue.

TANGIBLE ASSETS

In the 1970s marketable securities such as stocks and bonds provided returns that were relatively disappointing, especially in real terms. As shown in Chapter 10, neither bonds nor stocks have served as hedges against unanticipated inflation in recent years. Overall, *tangible assets* have been better hedges against inflation, although differences in relative price changes prevent any given asset from serving as a perfect hedge against changes in the cost of purchasing other assets. As shown in Chapter 10, owner-occupied real estate has been especially attractive in recent years. And, as shown in Chapter 17, commodity futures have proved to be desirable as well.

Not surprisingly, disenchantment with returns on marketable securities has led investors to reexamine a host of tangible assets. Partly as a result of the resultant increase in demand, prices of such items have risen substantially. Table 22-3 shows geometric mean returns over the period from 1968 through mid-1979 for several assets of this type, along with comparable values for the consumer price index and bond and stock returns.

TABLE 22-3 Returns on Tangible Assets, 1968 through mid-1979

Asset	Geometric Mean Return Per Year
Gold	19.4%
Chinese ceramics	19.1
Stamps	18.9
Rare books	15.7
Silver	13.4
Coins	12.7
Old masters	12.5
Diamonds	11.8
Consumer price index	6.5
Bonds	5.8
Stocks	3.1

Source: Salomon Brothers, *Portfolio Planning,* June 22, 1979.

Some of the figures in Table 22-3 are almost dazzling. However, the subsequent experience of gold provides a dash of reality. At the end of March 1980 a futures contract for delivery of gold in April 1980 was selling for $509 per ounce. In the previous two years it had sold for prices as low as $212 per ounce and as high as $895 per ounce. A loss of over 30% in a few months was presumably not what those who bought gold at $895 were expecting.

Many tangible assets provide income in the form of consumption. One can admire a Rembrandt, sit on a Chippendale, play a Stradivarius, and drive a Morgan. Value received in this manner is not subject to income taxation and is thus likely to be especially attractive for those in high tax brackets. However, the value of such consumption depends strongly on one's preferences. If markets are efficient, tangible assets will be priced so those who enjoy them most will find it desirable to hold greater-than-market-value proportions, while those who enjoy them least will find it desirable to hold less-than-market-value proportions (and, in many cases, none at all).

Institutional funds and investment pools have been organized to hold paintings, stamps, coins and other assets. Such arrangements are subject to serious question if they involve locking such objects in vaults where they cannot be seen by those who derive pleasure from this sort of consumption. On the other hand, if the items are rented to others, the only loss may be that associated with the transfer of a portion of the consumption value to the government in the form of a tax on income.

For any investment, risk is only part of the story: correlations of an asset's total return with the returns on other assets are also relevant. Historically, gold price changes have been slightly negatively correlated with stock returns.[5] This makes gold especially desirable as a means for diversifying a portfolio. It also suggests that unless the market is highly inefficient, the expected return on gold should be quite low. For tangible assets with comparable properties, similar expectations are in order.

[5] See John G. McDonald and Bruno H. Solnik, "Gold Mining Stocks: An Economic Analysis, 1968–1974," Stanford University Graduate School of Business Research Paper No. 200 (April 1974).

SPORTS BETTING

Throughout the world large amounts of money are wagered on the outcomes of sporting events. In the United States betting on horse races is conducted legally at race tracks in many states and via legal off-track betting establishments in some states. In addition, illegal "bookmakers" in every state accept bets on horse races. Bets on other events—most notably professional football games—are made legally in Nevada and illegally with bookmakers almost everywhere.

Spread Betting

A security dealer typically wishes to operate with a small average inventory and thus little exposure to loss through price fluctuations. To do this he or she usually sets a bid price and an ask price that will bring roughly equal orders for purchases and sales in, say, a week's time. The bid/ask spread represents the dealer's profit margin and the trader's transactions costs.

In sports betting the bookmaker acts as dealer and wishes to have relatively little "inventory" (exposure to loss). Two major methods are employed to achieve this: *spread betting* and *odds betting*. The former is used for bets on games such as football and basketball and the latter for bets on contests such as horse races and presidential elections.

A professional football example will illustrate spread betting. The San Francisco 49'ers are scheduled to play the Seattle Seahawks. It is widely felt that the Seahawks are likely to win. Thus the bookmaker establishes a *spread*. For example, if the Seahawks are "favored by 7 points," the final score will, in effect, be modified by subtracting 7 points from the Seahawks' score, then paying those who bet on the "winner" using that adjusted score. People who bet on Seattle bet that the team will "beat the spread"; those who bet on San Francisco bet that Seattle will not beat the spread.

The point spread serves as an equilibrating mechanism. Other things equal, the greater the spread, the smaller will be the amount bet on Seattle and the larger the amount bet on San Francisco. At some level the "books will be balanced." Given local prejudices, this may be accomplished by Seattle bookmakers "laying off" excess money bet on the Seahawks with San Francisco bookmakers who have excess money bet on the 49'ers.

How does the bookmaker make a living? With a range that corresponds to the security dealer's bid/ask spread. Typically, the bettor puts up $11 for a $10 bet; in other words, a winner will receive $10 (plus his or her initial bet, if paid in advance) while a loser is out $11. If the books are balanced, the bookmaker will pay out $10 for every $11 taken in.[6]

While bookmakers generally set point spreads to balance their books, in an efficient market such spreads would provide good estimates of the expected differences in points scored (and by and large the evidence is consistent with market efficiency).

---

[6] Unless the ending score equals the spread, in which case the general procedure is to return all the money bet.

Odds Betting

A goal of many "dealers" in bets is to be reasonably certain that after the contest is over, less will be paid out than is taken in. To do this, terms must be set so that bets on underdogs are attractive. Spreads are one way; *odds* are another.

An example from horse racing will illustrate the procedure. Assume that Doonesbury is favored to win the sixth race at Golden Gate Fields, while the other seven horses are considered inferior but of roughly equal speed. If the payoff per dollar bet were the same for all eight horses, most of the bets would be placed on the favorite. To spread the betting over the contenders, a larger amount must be paid per dollar bet if a long-shot wins.

Assume that the odds are set at 7 to 1 for each of the seven slow horses. This means that if $1 is bet on one of them, and the horse wins, the bettor will receive his or her $1 back plus $7 more.[7] Assume also that the odds on Doonesbury are set at 5-to-3, so that every $3 bet on the favorite will return $8 (the original $3 plus $5) if the horse wins. Now imagine that the amounts bet, given these odds, are as shown in Table 22-4. The total *pool* (amount bet) is $1,000, but no matter which horse wins the race, only $800 will be paid out, leaving $200 (or 20% of "the handle") for the track, the government, and/or the bookmaker.

The figures in Table 22-4 may seem contrived, but they represent the kind of situation achieved automatically by *pari-mutuel betting*. In this form of wagering (used at most horse race tracks) the actual payoff odds for a horse are determined *after all betting has finished* by subtracting the total take (typically about 20%) from the amount bet, then dividing this amount by the amount bet on that horse.[8] Thus the "dealer" is always assured of a fixed percentage in "transactions costs."

Betting on horses, like betting on stocks, is a negative-sum game: owing to transactions costs, the amount paid out is less than the amount

---

[7] Such odds are sometimes termed 8-*for*-1.

[8] This applies only to bets that a horse will win the race. More complex procedures are used for *place* (second or better) and *show* (third or better) bets. In addition, the actual payoff is usually rounded down to the nearest multiple of, say, 10 cents per $2 bet.

TABLE 22-4 Odds, Amounts Bet, and Payouts for a Horse Race

Horse	Amount Bet	Odds	Amount Paid Out If Horse Wins
#1 (favorite)	$ 300	5-to-3	$800
2	100	7-to-1	800
3	100	7-to-1	800
4	100	7-to-1	800
5	100	7-to-1	800
6	100	7-to-1	800
7	100	7-to-1	800
8	100	7-to-1	800
Total amount = $1,000 bet			

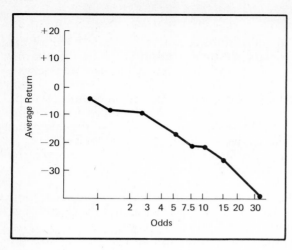

FIGURE 22-3 Average Return versus Odds in Horse Race Betting

Source: Wayne W. Snyder, "Horse Racing: Testing the Efficient Markets Model," *Journal of Finance,* September 1978.

paid in. The expected return on the average bet will therefore be negative. Since it is difficult to justify most such activity on the basis of hedging, bettors either (1) erroneously believe that they are all superior predictors, (2) are willing to pay in this manner for entertainment and/or (3) prefer risk. Undoubtedly all three aspects play a role. One attribute that makes betting entertaining is the suspension of one's usual mind set and the taking of risks with relatively small amounts of money. In such an environment and with limited exposure, even a conservative investor may take pleasure in acting like a riverboat gambler.

Evidence consistent with risk preference of this sort has been found in many analyses of the expected returns from bets on horses with different probabilities of winning races. Figure 22-3 summarizes a number of such studies. The horizontal axis indicates closing odds (on a logarithmic scale)—favorites plot at the left end of the scale and extreme long-shots at the right end. The vertical axis indicates average returns. All are negative, but the returns on favorites are considerably better than those on long-shots. "Investors" at the track are apparently willing to give up some expected return to get more risk—in this domain they appear to prefer risk.[9]

The Efficiency of Horse Race Betting

Investors in stocks can avail themselves of the results of financial analysis, both fundamental and technical. However, the high degree of efficiency of the stock market diminishes the value of such information for a single investor, since much of it is already reflected in security prices.

A similar situation prevails in the market for horse race betting. Fundamental analyses of the abilities of horses and trainers, the effects

---

[9] However, there is some evidence that a high-risk bet made up by "parlaying" bets on favorites (i.e., betting all winnings for horse one on horse two, betting all winnings on horse two on horse three, etc.) may offer higher expected returns than an equally risky single bet on a long-shot. For discussion of this point, see Richard N. Rosett, "Gambling and Rationality," *Journal of Political Economy,* December 1965. By permission of the University of Chicago Press, © 1979.

of weather, etc. abound, as do technical analyses of trends, reversals, and other changes in "form." If the market is efficient, reasonably public information provided by such analysts ("handicappers") will be reflected in prices ("closing odds").

A succinct statement of this hypothesis is the following:

Prob.(win | track odds) = Prob. (win | track odds and

publicly held information)

In words: the probability that a horse will win, given the information in the track odds, is the same as the probability given the odds *and* other public information. Put somewhat differently, widely reported handicapping information does not *add* to the information incorporated in the track odds (but it well may have influenced the odds).

In one test[10] the hypothesis was found to be roughly consistent with data for bets placed at Belmont track in New York State. The odds at the track appeared to incorporate the information contained in published "picks" by fourteen handicappers. However, this did not seem to be the case in the less "professional" (and higher-transaction-cost) off-track betting market—a fact that may give some solace to those who invest in small and little-followed stocks.

It is appropriate that we end this chapter and the book on this note. For the positive economist the highly efficient nature of security and betting markets is heart-warming, for it shows once more the efficacy of competition. For the investor or bettor it provides a challenge, to say the very least.

[10] Stephen Figlewski, "Subjective Information and Market Efficiency in a Betting Market," *Journal of Political Economy*, 87, no. 1, February 1979. By permission of the University of Chicago Press, © 1979.

Problems

1. What types of political risk are relevant only for a foreign investor? What types are relevant for both foreign and domestic investors? To what extent and in what manner would you expect each of these two types of risk to be taken into account in the current prices of securities?
2. How might a U.S. citizen or company use currency futures to partially hedge against exchange-rate risk?
3. When compared to a fixed-exchange-rate system, does a floating system present more, less, or equal exchange-rate risk to the multinational investor?
4. When a U.S. citizen is attempting to estimate the expected return and

variance of return for a foreign security, what factors, in addition to those recognized in domestic security analysis, should be considered?

5. Is low correlation between the percentage changes of market indices of two countries a sufficient condition to ensure that a portfolio containing securities of both countries dominates a portfolio containing only domestic securities?

6. Assume that the model in Figure 22-1 captures all the aspects of the risks of securities world-wide. If capital markets were completely integrated internationally, with a single currency, would the expected returns on the securities in a single country be related to their beta values relative to that country's stock market factor? If so, what would determine the nature of this relationship? What if each country's capital market were completely isolated from that of every other country?

7. Should gold bullion be considered part of the "market portfolio"? If the beta of gold relative to the stock market is negative, does this imply that its beta relative to the market portfolio is also negative? If the beta of gold relative to the market portfolio is negative, what should be its expected return?

8. One sometimes finds a variation of the following statement in a newspaper: "The bookmakers took a terrible beating this week, since 80% of the underdogs beat the point spread." Does this seem likely? Why or why not?

9. According to Figure 22-3 the returns on horses with odds of 1-to-1 appear to have averaged -8%, while those on horses with odds of 3-to-1 appears to have averaged -12%. The diagram below illustrates these situations:

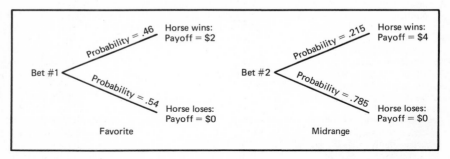

a. Show a comparable diagram for a bet of $1 on one favorite, with all the winnings (if any) bet on another favorite with the same odds and expected return. Would this *parlay* be better than a single bet of $1 on a midrange horse? Why or why not?

b. The returns for horses with odds of 7-to-1 appear to have averaged about -20%. What is the probability that such a "long-shot" will win a race? How does a bet on such a horse compare with a parlay of three favorites?

10. Does the fact that some handicappers' picks do not add to the information in track odds mean that they can't pick winners? Does it mean that their work is of no value? What aspects of security markets are comparable? In what way?

Index

653